PREFACE

Southeastern Pennsylvania, during our colonial period was the prolific hive from which the swarms of Swiss and German settlers of America almost exclusively came, who, during the latter years of that period and during the first several decades of our national existence, migrated westward and planted the seed of the Teutonic element of our population in the middle west, the southwest, the northwest and the far west, and whose descendants in our later decades have sprung from them by millions and have largely moulded the character of that vast empire, down to this day.

The valleys of the Susquehanna and Schuylkill Rivers being thus, the mother-land of so powerful and populous an influence, in our state and national existence, it was deemed by the compiler a matter of sufficient importance, to gather up the historical events in chronological order, leading up to the German-Swiss settlement here, from the time of remote ages. It was also thought equally important to set out in like chronological form, the first six decades or more of the growth and development of those same peoples here after their initial settlement about the beginning of the eighteenth century and to show their wonderful growth in power, in numbers, and their vigor in pushing the frontier line of our wealth and settlement westward.

These Annals record the outlines of a history of religious fervor and of tenacity of noble purpose stretching across a thousand years, as glorious as anything else that ever happened in the history of the world. As early as the year 900, strong men began to stand out as champions of religious liberty and the simple Gospel, against the great Romish Church, the only Christian Church of note then on the earth. They held fast to the faith, through fire and against sword. About the year 1150, Peter Waldo renounced the Romish Church and led the Evangelical Christians; and by hundreds of thousands they adhered to him. They held the faith nearly four hundred years more and went like lambs to slaughter. Then came the Reformation. Luther, Zwingli, Calvin, and Menno Simon, led the movement in the heart of Europe.

Menno held to the Waldenseon beliefs (and especially to the doctrine of non-resistance) and his followers became the prey of the militant faiths both Romish and Reformed. But neither fire, nor sword, nor drowning, nor prison, nor the galleys could turn them from their conviction; and while Zurich and Berne and other cities exterminated, imprisoned and deported them, they multiplied; and they were found by thousands everywhere. They obtained governmental favor in Holland by the year 1575 and thus they beheld that golden glow in the west and gravitated there at the close of nearly 200 years of suffering, holding on to their faith in all its simple purity.

Then they learned of America and in the next half century not less than fifty thousand embarked to reach the glorious land of Penn. Nearly twenty thousand who thus embarked died at sea; the remainder reached their happy goal.

They filled the valleys of Susquehanna and Schuylkill and of all their tributaries. Before the Revolution they flocked down the Shenandoah. They soon crossed the Alleghenies and filled the Cumberland. They multiplied and drifted into the Ohio Valley and by the beginning of the nineteenth century they settled in lower Canada. They opened up the Indiana and Illinois region, the Kansas section, the Dakotas and the Northwest. Their descending generations in all the vast empire of middle-western and far-western America as well as in eastern America, are sons and citizens of power and wealth and influence in the forces that are moving and making our great nation. Results such as these, make worthy of preservation, the origin and early struggles and gradual steps—the long, the arduous and ever conquering march—to such a goal.

H. FRANK ESHLEMAN.

Historic Background *and* Annals *of the* SWISS *and* GERMAN PIONEER SETTLERS

of Southeastern Pennsylvania

and of
Their Remote Ancestors, from the Middle of the
Dark Ages, Down to the Time of the
Revolutionary War

AN AUTHENTIC HISTORY, FROM ORIGINAL SOURCES, OF THEIR SUFFERING DURING SEVERAL CENTURIES BEFORE AND ESPECIALLY DURING THE TWO CENTURIES FOLLOWING THE PROTESTANT REFORMATION, AND OF THEIR SLOW MIGRATION, MOVED BY THOSE CAUSES, DURING THE LAST MENTIONED TWO HUNDRED YEARS, WESTWARD IN QUEST OF RELIGIOUS FREEDOM AND THEIR HAPPY RELIEF IN THE SUSQUEHANNA AND SCHUYLKILL VALLEYS IN THE NEW WORLD; WITH PARTICULAR REFERENCE TO THE GERMAN-SWISS MENNONITES OR ANABAPTISTS, THE AMISH AND OTHER NON-RESISTANT SECTS

H. Frank Eshleman, B. E., M. E., L.L. B.

Member of the Lancaster Bar; Member of the Lancaster County Historical Society; Member of the Historical Society of Pennsylvania at Philadelphia; and Member of the Pennsylvania History Club of Philadelphia

HERITAGE BOOKS
2008

HERITAGE BOOKS
AN IMPRINT OF HERITAGE BOOKS, INC.

Books, CDs, and more—Worldwide

For our listing of thousands of titles see our website
at
www.HeritageBooks.com

A Facsimile Reprint
Published 2008 by
HERITAGE BOOKS, INC.
Publishing Division
100 Railroad Ave. #104
Westminster, Maryland 21157

Copyright © 1917 H. Frank Eshleman
Lancaster, Pennsylvania

— Publisher's Notice —
In reprints such as this, it is often not possible to remove blemishes from the original. We feel the contents of this book warrant its reissue despite these blemishes and hope you will agree and read it with pleasure.

International Standard Book Numbers
Paperbound: 978-0-7884-1012-3
Clothbound: 978-0-7884-7205-3

ANNALS OF THE PIONEER SWISS AND PALATINE MENNONITES OF LANCASTER COUNTY, AND OTHER EARLY GERMANS OF EASTERN PENNSYLVANIA

Introduction and Background.

It is the purpose of the narration which shall follow to set out in an easy and attractive style, some of the leading events in the life of the early Swiss and Palatine Mennonites and other Germans of eastern Pennsylvania, and particularly of Lancaster County. This is a subject upon which much is known traditionally but not very much, accurately and authoritatively.

It is believed that the noble life and struggles of these pioneers who were the very backbone of early industrial Lancaster County and of other eastern Pennsylvania sections, should be publicly and familiarly known. And we feel that if they are truly known, a character will be shown to the public in every way the equal of that of the Puritans down east, upon whose early noble acts and life all generations of America have been taught to look with awe and reverence, as if all the good that was ever done for America in primitive days was done by those godly New Englanders. This, of course, is not the fact. It may be very truthfully said that the pioneer Swiss, and Germans and kindred nationalities who originally settled certain large portions of eastern Pennsylvania, have done as much for America and have lived as nobly, and have upheld the pure religion and gospel, of our nation as faithfully as the "witch-burning" Puritans ever did.

These Swiss and Germans of whom I shall write labored under many problems and difficulties, which our people of today will find it hard to believe. They were foreigners and held in disfavor for a time by the English government of this province, though Penn gave them a special invitation to come and settle here. They were looked upon with jealousy by other people settled among them because, these Swiss and Germans, early in the country districts at least, began making money and progress by their thrift, etc.

It is not our purpose to give a complete history of these peoples; but rather only a series of "Annals" depicting the most striking events of their life and progress here.

In order to understand fully the life, feeling and ideals of these peoples it will be necessary to go back many hundred years and supply the European historical background, and trace up the long train of religious causes which brought them to Pennsylvania. This foundation or early history of their troubles, etc., will be necessarily quite lengthy and go back to the time of Caesar. But inasmuch as familiar Lancaster County and other eastern Pennsylvania names will continually appear in it, we hope that it will not become tiresome.

The European Background — The Causes Which Forced the Swiss Into Pennsylvania.

Switzerland has passed through centuries of bloodshed, civil convulsion, war and religious persecution. Before Christ, Caesar fought the Helvetian War, partly on its soil. The objects were conquest and empire. The Romans held it four centuries; then the Allemani, in the German invasion, took possession; and in turn the Franks overthrew the Allemani, and the Burgundians. The Franks started a new civilization under Christianity, (Lippincott Gaz.). Persecutions against the Christians first reached Northern Italy and the borders of Switzerland and Germany about the year 600 A. D. Up to this time the fiercest persecution in other parts of Europe was that by the heathen Longabards upon the Christians for their refusal to honor idols, (Martyrs' Mirror, Elkart Edition of 1886, p. 210). But the Roman Church now began the same, and punished Bishop Adrian in 606 as a criminal for refusing to baptize infants, (Do.). About 850 there was a butchery of non-conformant Christians by the Franks, (Do., p. 233). At the opening of the 10th century persecutions were still raging in different parts of Europe on the question of baptism, of which the learned Giselbert writes, (Do., p. 245). But most of the religious persecutions during this century were those inflicted by Pagans upon Christians generally, all along the Mediterranean coast, (Do.). In 926 King Worm of Denmark persecuted the non-resisting Christians in and surrounding Denmark, (Do., p. 246). By 950 the current which the Danish King started reached Slavonia, whose ungodly tyrant King persecuted defenseless Christians there; and by the end of the century religious war was in progress by the Vandals, against the non-combatant Christians of Hamburg, Brandenburg and other parts of Germany. And, indeed, in Altenburg, Switzerland, he directed his fury against all Christians, but chiefly against Romanists. Then in 991 the Pagan Danish hordes again poured into Germany and vexed the Christians during 40 years there, (Do., p. 249).

In the 11th century the question of infant baptism and transubstantiation gave rise to furious persecution by the main Christian Church upon the separatists who refused to adhere to either of those doctrines. Many of these separatists were convicted of heresy and executed, (Do., p. 255). The Berengarians of Netherlands and Germany suffered in this persecution, (Do., p. 260). By the middle of this century the Holy Roman (German) Empire controlled Switzerland, (Lippincott).

1009—Earliest Authentic Appearance of the Herrs.

In the year 1009 we find the first trace in Switzerland, of any name common among us today in Lancaster county and Eastern Pennsylvania. It is one of the two most prominent and numerous names of the county—Herr. Miller is the other. The county directory shows us indeed that there are nearly twice as many Millers as Herrs in the county today.

In the year just stated the Herrs appear in Northern Switzerland, in the person of the Swabish Knight Hugo, the Herr or Lord of Bilried, (Vien in Herr Genealogy, p. 1). The race anciently lived in Swabia says the same author. Swabia was one of the districts into which Maximilian II divided ancient Germany, then including Switzerland. Prof. Rhoddy tells us that Swabia included nearly the whole of Northern Switzerland, and a large tract of Germany east of the Rhine, at one time called Alemania. Therefore the foundation of Lancaster county, was not only Swiss in 1710; but the pioneers in 1710 were descendants of a Swiss stock during a prior period of over seven hundred years.

1050—The Great Eby or Eaby Family Moved to Switzerland.

We will not vouch for the truth of the statement announced in the title to this paragraph. Ezra E. Eby late of Berlin, Ontario, author of the "Eby Family" states that the Ebys lived in Italy known as the Ebees and were heathen until the Waldenses in the 12th century or later brought them into Christianity. The Ebys were supposed to have come into Switzerland during the 11th century.

1050—The Reformed Spirit in the Roman Church.

Müller, page 57, recites a letter from the Papal legate Peter Damian to Adelaide Susa showing that the Reformed Spirit existed in the Church of Rome from 1050 at least. And it is added that the old Evangelical congregations to whom the Waldenses belonged existed from time immemorial. The diocese where the Waldenses lived maintained its independence of the Church of Rome until the 12th century says Müller. And as early as this time began the marriage and expulsion of priests. In this resistence against Rome Bishop Claudius of Turrene distinguished himself earlier than all others from 815 to 835—a true reformer says Müller, (Ernst Müller's Geschichte der Bernischen Taüfer, p. 57).

1160—Origin of the Waldenses.

In the middle of the 12th century at Utrecht and other places they were burning the Berengarians alive, (Do. M. Mirror, p. 281). About 1159 those who opposed the doctrines of the Holy Church which we have mentioned, began to have strong and able suporters in deposed Roman bishops and others. One of these was Peter Waldo of Lyons, who separated in 1160, (Do., p. 265). His adherents were first numerous in the province of Albi, (Do., p. 266). They were called Lyonites, Albigenes and finally nearly all Waldenses. They spread into every province and were objects of persecution during four centuries and more. The Roman Church began to call them Anabaptists, (Do., p. 267); and by that name their descendants in faith were called down to 1710 at least, as we shall show later. Their doctrine was essentially the same as that of the pioneers who in 1710 first settled Lancaster county. Their creed contained the following principles among others—opposition to infant baptism —to transubstantiation—to war—to participation in government—to oaths, etc., (Do., pp. 265-277). They early reached Northern Italy and the border of Switzerland, (Do., p. 279).

1150 to 1200—Troubles of Non-Resistants In Latter Half of the 12th Century.

In 1161, in the eighth year of Henry II, about 30 German men and women sailed over to England to escape Papal tortures. They were Berengarians or Lyonites and separated because of their views on infant baptism, etc. They were illiterate and led by a German of some learning called Gerard. They were apprehended in England. (M. Mirror, p. 283). Abram Millinus shows that their doctrine was similar to the Mennonite tenets of faith. They were scourged and banished and allowed to freeze to death. In 1163 six Waldenses were discovered in a barn near Cologne, in Prussia and were burned to death, (Do., p. 284).

Ernst Müller tells us (p. 64) that the Abbe of Steinfelden named Evervin wrote in 1164 to the Holy Bernard that an untold number are everywhere prepared to oppose priests and monks in their midst, and that this heresy has grown secretly ever since the time of the martyrs.

In 1191 the City Basle, Switzerland, was founded. It has today a population of 70,000 and was the scene of a like persecution and refuge.

During all this time the Waldesean doctrine was spreading rapidly. And by 1199 one of their enemies said a thousand cities were filled with them. They filled Southwestern Europe, England, Germany, Hungary and Northern Italy, (Do., p. 279), Jacob Mehring says these people who did not believe in infant baptism, transubstantiation, force, war or political affairs were contemptuously called Anabaptists, Waldenses, Berengarians, Mennonites, etc., by the papists, Lutherans and Calvanists (Do., p. 267). As far as the German, Swiss and Dutch are concerned the 12th century closed with the expulsion of many of these Waldesean Christians from Metz and the burning of their books, which books they had translated from the Latin into their native language.

1201 to 1300—The Thirteenth Century Religious Struggles

As far as religious persecution in this century affects the Dutch, Germans and Swiss we may notice that persecution about 1212 began to rage in Holland, (Do. p. 298); and at that time 108 Waldenses were burned to death in Strasburg, Germany; 39 at Bingen and 18 at Metz, (Do.). In 1214 Conrad of Marpurg was appointed by Pope Innocent III, the grand inquisitor of Germany to exterminate all who had strayed from the Roman faith. In 19 years he killed hundreds. He gave them red hot irons to hold and destroyed all who were burnt by it as heretics. They were burned to death. Another test was that of cold water, the accused being thrown into a canal and if they sank in it they were heretics, but if they floated they were not.

By 1203 these Waldenses or Anabaptists had the Holy Scriptures translated into their own language, (Müller, p. 59); and they did not practice any other doctrine. The parts of the Bible most carefully followed by them were the commandments and the sermon on the Mount.

Müller tells us that in 1212 in and about Strasburg, Germany there were more than 500 of these Waldenses (the parent faith of the Mennonites) and that they were made up of Swiss, Italians, Germans and Bohemians; and that in the early part of this century they had spread far and wide, (p. 64.) And about 1215, there were 80 more of them burned at Strasburg and more in other parts of Germany, (M. Mirror, pp. 300 and 304). And in 1231 throughout Germany many more of these Anabaptists — Waldenses suffered martyrdom, (Do., p. 306). By 1250 there was scarcely a land where the Waldensean sect had not found its way; and everywhere, where they existed they were known by their plain dress, moral life, their temperate living and their refusal to take part in government and oaths, (says Müller, p. 58).

In the year 1277 in Berne, (Müller, p. 64) the opponents of the Catholics from Schwarzenburg through the Bishop of Lousanne in Switzerland were brought before the Dominican Humbert and the inquisition plied against them; whereupon many of them were burned.

This shows how the Anabaptists—Waldenseans, as they were called, (the parent Church of the Mennonites) grew through the 13th century and how they were persecuted and tortured throughout that century in Germany, Switzerland and elsewhere.

Bracht says that about 1305, the light of the evangelical doctrine began to arise on the Alps, through a pious man and his wife who had accepted the Waldensean faith. Many followed his teaching but in 1308 he and his wife were torn limb from limb and 140 of his followers burnt alive (M. Mirror, p. 317). Throughout Austria also the persecution raged.

In 1315 a Waldensean teacher called Lölhard at his trial in Austria said he could find 80,000 persons who believed in his religion (Do., 318).

In 1330 we find that a man named Eckart or Eckert (who formerly had been a Dominican monk and had left the papists, because he became a non-resistant and opposed the doctrine of infant baptism and transubstatiation) was publicly burned in Germany for those reasons and because he embraced the whole doctrine of the Waldenses; and also many more were likewise tortured for similar doctrines in Bohemia and Poland, (Do., p. 319). This Eckert may have been an ancestral connection of the widely known Eckert family of Lancaster county.

In the year 1340 among the Martyrs, appears a name, now well known in Lancaster county,—Hager. This year Conrad Hager was martyred for having taught for 24 years the Waldensean faith. Many had followed his teaching, (Do.).

Ten years later John de Landuno of Ghent, a highly learned man broke away from the reigning church and embraced Anabaptism and was tortured, (Do.). "Landuno" may have been the Dutch form of "Landis".

Now about this time (1350) says Cassel, p. 378 the Keiser of Bavaria interposed and compelled the principal papal church in his dominions to cease its persecution upon the defenseless separatists.

In 1360 the name John de Rupe (Scissa) appears among the Martyrs. Three years later he was burned at Avignon, (Martyr's Mirror).

In 1374 a separatist named Löffler from Bremgarden was burnt on account of his belief in opposition to the established church—for being a free spirit says Müller, (page 64).

During the last decade of this century the torch of persecution was flaming against the Anabaptists—the Waldensean lambs—called hereitcs by the church of Rome, in Germany and Switzerland particularly.

From the year 1382 to the year 1393 Müller tells us (p. 64) that by order of Pope Clement VII the Minorite Franz Borell burned about a hundred of these Waldenses, or antecedents of the Mennonites round about Lake Geneva in Switzerland on account of their religion, the papal church declaring them heretics worthy of death.

In 1390 not less than 36 persons called Waldenses were burnt for their faith at Bingen on the Rhine, Germany. These martyrs were all citizens of Mentz, (M. Mirror, p. 320). Almost the same time on the borders of the Baltic sea 400 were destroyed.

Ernst Müller also tells us that in the old books the doctrines of the Waldenses are set out, as those doctrines were in the 12th century, and there can be no doubt that these Anabaptists that the church of Rome called heretics in the 14th century are the same in religious principle as the early Waldenses. He says those persecuted at Bern and Freyburg (Switzerland) had exactly the same religious belief of those who were tortured in 1398.

Thus we show that during the 14th century the persecutions against the separatists were very largely carried on in the heart of Europe to which places it spread northward from Rome. It crossed the Alps into Germany, Switzerland and Austria. Those who most fiercely felt its fire were, as in the previous century, the non-resistants or Anabaptists as they were called, the successors in faith of the old Waldenses, and the antecedents of the Mennonites.

Persecution of the Non-Resistant Christians in the Fifteenth Century

The Beghienen in 1403 through the Dominican, Maulberger of Basel were the instigators of the expulsion of defenseless Christians from Berne, but they staid in Switzerland until the reformation, (Müller, 65).

It was contended that John Wickliffe embraced a part of the Waldensean doctrine and that John Huss became a disciple and believer in the Wickliffe teachings (M. Mirror, pp. 323-24). In 1415 John Huss having examined and studied Wickliffe's book against the papal tenets and especially against war, oaths and infant baptism accepted nearly all of these Wickliffe teachings or principles, (Do.).

John Huss gained many of the Waldenses in Bohemia, when he began to preach. For want of a leader they had greatly diminished in the last 30 years; but he revived trem. Both Huss and Jerome were burned on the shores of Lake Constance, part of the Northeastern boundary of Switzerland, by the Roman Church. Then the Hussites began a war on the German electors and after the war having largely given up the mild Waldesean faith went back to the Church of Rome again. But they turned again from them and became the Grubenheimers or cave-dwellers.

In the Freyburg district (Switzerland) in 1429 Haris Michel of Wallace and Anna Grause from Erlaugh were burned, and the following year Peter Seager too, (Müller, p. 64).

Through imprisonment and torture during the early part of this century the congregations of Waldenses of Freyburg were entirely destroyed. Through this destruction it was found out that Swartzenberg was full of Waldenses too; and that the Freyburg brethren had communication with Zolathurn in Switzerland and in Germany and Bohemia, (Müller, p. 64).

In the year 1430 several Waldensean teachers from Germany came to Freyburg and settled there to counsel and strengthen the congregations, (Do., p. 65).

The benevolent converts of Begharden and Beghinen, says a papal authority were nurseries of Waldensean heretics and were polluted with Waldensean proceedings. The Zurich officer or chief police Felix Hammerlin wrote in 1440 a pamphlet opposing these "heretics" as he called them, and in it he tells of the great growth and spread of them up to that time. He says every year they came from Bohemia and preached in Switzerland and Germany, which induced a great number of people to accept their belief, in the cities of Bern, Zolathurn and many Swiss villages, (Müller, p. 65). About this time there were persecutions in Basle, Switzerland, and the so-called "heretics" burned, (M. Mirror, p. 335).

In the course of this narration of the sufferings of our early Swiss and German non-resistant ancestors, we now meet a name very familiar and very famous in our country,—the name Herr. Mr. Jacob Schnebell of Obfelden, Switzerland, a historian of note there informs me that in 1440 Hansley Herr was one of the brave garrison of Greifensee, Canton of Zurich, of 60 men, in the "Old Zurich War," who under Wildhans von Breitenlandenburg, defended the castle; and after the fall of the Castle was beheaded, May 27, 1444. Hansley

Herr was from Hagnau, Switzerland, near Uster. Thus while the Herrs are now non-resistant, some of them, at least, did not become Anabaptists or Waldenseans before 1450. But later they did largely become Waldenseans and eventually Mennonites; and a tradition in their own family is to the effect that, the broken spears which are a part of their coat of arms indicate that they denounced Knighthood and war and became non-resistant Christians.

Mr. Schnebeli wrote me also that the names of Christian and Hans Herr (now so familiar in our County) were found in 1450 in the Canton of Glarus, Switzerland; and that an early branch of the Herr family was settled in the upper part of the Canton of Zurich (Southeast) called Zuricher Oberland in very early times. The Tchudi and other familiar Lancaster county families came from Glarus.

In 1453 says the author of the "Eby Family" the whole valley of the Luzerne in Switzerland was put under an edict against the Waldenses by the Church of Rome.

Persecutions of the Non-Resistant Christians in the Fifteenth Century.

The next prominent persecution recorded by history against the non-resisting Waldenses is that which occurred in 1457 at Eichstadt, in Germany, (M. Mirror, p. 335).

In a convention in Sholka in 1467 the leader of the Bohemian brethren in the presence of the German Waldenses was consecrated through a Roman Waldensean priest, from the first church, (Müller, p. 65).

Showing that the doctrine of the Waldenses in every country where they existed was the same at all times as that which early in the 16th century they handed down to the Mennonites, I relate that infant baptism was rejected by the brethren of Bohemia and Moravia. (Thus also the early Moravians believed in the same faith.) They did not pay their preachers a salary but depended on hospitality. Their apostles or traveling preachers went throughout all the countries to Moscow, Asia Minor and Egypt. Their Bohemian teachers came on to Switzerland in 1474, (See Müller, p. 56). Bohemia as we all know is part of the Austria Hungarian Monarchy and lies northeast of Switzerland, being separated from it by the province of Bavaria, part of the German Empire. Thus in our Mennonite researches it is interesting to notice that not only from Italy on the south but from Bohemia on the east, the Waldensean faith came into Switzerland—one of the ancient homes of the Mennonites. In Bohemia too during this century the persecutions raged. The Spanish inquisition plied its fearful and horrible butcheries at this time, (M. Mirror, p. 336). In Germany also there were tortures and John of Wesel who was teaching the Waldensean faith at Worms was burned, (Do.).

The Waldenses who lived in the Catholic Bishopic of Basil where they began to be numerous about 1487 were one of the most zealous congregations in all Switzerland, and the authorities of the papal church were at their wits' end to know how to suppress them. As we shall show later the authorities of Basil and Berne in the 16th century held a convention to devise some plan to get rid of as they called them "these unchristian and damned heretics". (Müller, p. 235).

In 1487 came Pope Innocent's measures to exterminate the Waldenseans says the author of the "Eby Family", (Eby). This bill of the Pope was dated April 25 and in it he asked the whole confederation or league of Papal churches to help wipe the Waldenseans from the earth; and he also sent his legates and other military officers under Albrecht of Capitaneis to Wallace for this purpose, (Müller, p. 65).

In 1498 says Müller, p. 65, a Bohemian deputation of the Waldenseans were present in Upper Italy as spectators, when Savanarola was burned for his faith in the mild doctrine. In this year under Pope Alexander VI this faithful and powerful Christian was strangled to death and then burned to ashes. He helped to preserve in large part the faith which the Waldenses kept inviolate and handed down to the Mennonites, who in the next century gladly received it.

And thus ended the 15th century amid blood and martyrdom. Those who first about the year 850 in a weak way announced their dissent from the Church of Rome, and their approval of what they understood to be the plain simple teachings of the Savior, found themselves greatly strengthened about 1175 by the sect of the Waldenseans. These spread throughout Southern and Central Europe in swarms and through fire and the sword and all manner of persecution and death turned upon them, defended the doctrine until the end of the 15th century and into the 16th, when about 1527 the new sect of the Mennonites accepted the same from the old Waldenseans, and also defended it and died for it as we shall see through two full centuries and more, in face of both Catholic and Reformed tortures against them; and finally taking it to Holland and the Palatinate for safety, handed it down in all its purity to the new world in the beginning of the eighteenth century.

Before we can describe the events of that happy latter century, the blood and the turmoil, and torture and martyr-death of the 16th and the 17th centuries lie before us, which we must next proceed to narrate.

PERSECUTIONS IN THE 16TH CENTURY OF PENNSYLVANIA'S EUROPEAN ANTECEDENTS

1500—Menno Simon

This century begins with the infanthood of a notable character in religious history, — Menno Simon, founder of the Mennonites. He tells us he was born in 1496 in Witmarsum, Friedland, in Holland. See his story of his conversion in Funk's "Complete Works" of Menno Simon (Elkhart, 1871) page 3. He says, "In the year 1524, then in my 28th year, I undertook the duties of a priest, etc." Rupp, (p. 84) therefore mistakably fixes his birth in 1505. Thus the Mennonite faith dates back nearly to the discovery of America. Indeed, as we have shown before, it is several hundred years older than that, as without much modification it was and is a continuation of the Waldensean doctrine, beginning at least as early as 1170. The coming of Menno Simon simply changed the name of one branch of the Waldensean sect; and gave new strength and vigor to its believers.

1507 — Non- Resisting Waldenseans Persecuted in Hungary.

As we shall show in a later item, both Holland and Hungary were ripe at this time for the leadership of Menno Simon as the faith which he espoused when he came to mature manhood (the Mennonite Faith) was already strong in these places. Other places had their leaders, viz:—Germany had Luther in 1517 and Switzerand had Zwingli about the same date. But Hungary and Holland including Moravia, etc., had to wait for Menno Simon about 1525. We shall give more of this later. In 1507 the Waldenses of Hungary and Moravia delivered a defense of their faith against certain unfounded accusations, because of which they were persecuted. This defense they made to the king of Bohemia, (M. Mirror, p. 397).

1509—Holland Mennonites Flee to Germany.

The Congregation of Mennonites at Leer, a Prussian town on the Leeda river, at the beginning of this century was Flemish, that is, they were not native Germans, but came from Flanders, which in these early days included parts of Holland, Belgium and France. Thus the earliest centers of distinctively Mennonite faith were Holland and adjacent places, and Hungary. In 1509 they had approached East Friedland, in Holland and were settled there. One of them suffered the death of a Martyr this same year at Holstein. Persecutions at once were begun against them by the Roman Church and the Government in Flanders, and they fled to Germany and particularly to Cologne, (See A. Brons, Annabaptists or Mennonites of Europe, page 245—a German work published in Norden).

1510—Mennonites and "Reformation" Growing Up Together

From the convent of Trub in Bohemia the reformation was promoted early. The Abbott, Thuring Rust of Wahlhusen, famous until 1510 as Vicar in Lauperswyl (Austria) felt himself possessed of the new faith. He resigned the dignity of Abbott and went out to the little valley of the Trub Mountains, and married and supported himself and his wife by making shingles, and carried on the Reformation in the Valley, (Müller, p. 22). He left the Church of Rome, which forbade him as an Abbot from marrying and became a "Reformationist."

We cite this passage from Müller to show that the various branches of the Protestant Church, especially the Mennonites, Reformed, Lutheran and Moravian branches grew out of the same causes—the abuses and degeneracy of the Church of Rome. Different leaders took hold of it in different places in Central Europe about the same time. They all suffered persecution from the Established Church and State; but some defended by war while others did not resist. This difference in the manner of meeting persecution in the course of one hundred years or more caused a wide difference between these branches of the great body of Reformers and with differences of view on the subject of baptism and other questions gave rise to a new persecution by one branch of the new faith against another and thus we later find the Reformed and Lutherans, persecuting and destroying the Mennonites, more severely than Rome ever did.

1510—Conditions Which Moved Luther and Zwingli.

Brons tells us (p. 13) that as Luther when he went in 1510 to Rome became acquainted with the corruption of the heads of the established church, so also Zwingli had his eyes opened as Chaplain among the soldiers of the Romish army in Switzerland; and from being a staunch defender of that faith he turned aside to find purity; and this helped to prepare him to join with zeal and go into the cause, which the old Waldenses started and which Lutherans, Reformed and Mennonites were now carrying on. He and Luther differed widely on the question of the sacrament and their followers differ today on the same point.

1515—The First Fierce Effort to Destroy the Holland Mennonites.

About this time the Bishop of Utrecht caused thirty-five towns in Holland to be burned, to purge the Country of the Waldensean descendants (who a few years later were called Mennonites). This was the condition under papal power. While it may astound us to learn that a Bishop could do this, we must not forget that such was the power of the State Church, that almost anything it asked of the civil rulers, those rulers gave the Church power to carry out. About the same time came floods and conflagration and famine; and the people believing that this was a punishment on them for leaving the Romish church, again went back to it for consolation; but they found no consolation. Instead they found continual demands for heavy payments of money to pay for spiritual benefits as they were called. No wonder says Brons, (p. 397) the people lost faith in the church and lifted their hearts and minds to Heaven. Thus suffered these Waldensean parents of the Mennonites in Holland in the beginnig of the 16th century.

1515—Zwingli Still Adheres to Romish Church—Not Friendly to the Mennonites.

In 1515 Zwingli a second time went with the banner of the Canton of Glarus as chaplain to Italy. The Swiss troops were to drive out the French who had made a stand at Milan. But here bribed by French gold, they made a disgraceful treaty with the French. Zwingli now preached with wrath against this bribery and want of fidelity to Keiser and Pope and the honor of Switzerland, (Brons, p. 13).

We jot down this item simply because it gives us a view of the attitude of Switzerland and particularly of the Canton or State of Glarus at this time. We remember that Glarus was the ancient home of a branch of the Herrs. The Reformer Zwingli, who later found many of the same faults with the Church of Rome as did the Mennonites had not yet renounced papacy, though as we noticed in a former article, he denounced many of its doings.

1516—Zwingli Begins Approving the Waldensean Faith.

Zwingli now accepted a position as preacher in the Abbey of Maria Einsielden, and he found rest though still a Catholic. He now began to preach to the pilgrims who came for forgiveness of sins. He told them they must not rely on indulgences and that all outward service is in vain—that the picture of Mary has no power—and no priest could forgive sins. Many a seed corn did the pilgrims carry away with them from his speeches, (Do.)

Then too, Erasmus from Rotterdam published a Greek new testament for the priests as the language of the priests was in Greek.

1518—Wicked Condition of Zürich.

In 1518 Zwingli accepted a call as secular priest in Zurich. There were there delegates and foreign powers and Swiss soldiers to be enlisted. Money flowed in streams to Zurich. Zwingli saw here that there was great looseness of morals—great joy, delight and pasttimes. Gentlemen and boys took to drink, gambling and courting. Some of the first families took the lead in this abandon. Zwingli saw that the heads of the Church made sport of the commandment to fast and on Palm Sunday they made pig roasts. These things influenced Zwingli. He says on these festive days the people played, fought, gambled, drank and committed mortal sins. If one mended shoes during this holy season, he was called a heretic; but not if he did these things. For all this he says the State Church was the fault.

We insert this item simply to show the condition of Zurich at this time just about the time the Mennonites began to grow in this sink of iniquity, where religious degeneracy was rank and the government winked at it.

1519—Swiss Government Frowns on the Rising Reformed and Mennonite Doctrine.

Egli in his Züricher Wiedertauffer Zur Reformationszeit, a German work published in Zürich, he says, (p. 7), that it has been said when Zwingli came to Zürich in 1519 to preach the new doctrine the Government powers were in his favor—blamed the wickedness of the place on the Roman Church and wanted to get rid of it. But he says it would be wrong to say the heads of the State were with him, for the Council of that day were anxiously working against his novelties. And he says the Council forbade attacks upon the Romish doctrine.

This is added here only to show the difficulties the Reformed Christian thought, of which the Mennonite was one phase, had to encounter at all times in the places of its origin.

1519—Mennonite Faith in Bohemia.

In 1519 John Schlechta of Gostelek had written to Erasmus, concerning the Bohemian brethren, (Moravians). He was told that they choose out of the laity and not the learned Greek bishops and priests to teach them. Their ministers married and had wives and children—they called themselves brethren and sisters and recognized only the Old and New Testaments as sacred, despising all other teachers. Those who joined the sect were obliged to submit to baptisms with ordinary water, (not Holy Water). They regarded the sacrament as a memorial of the sufferings of Christ. They regarded petitions to priests, pennances, auricular confessions as out of place. They kept Sunday, Christmas, Easter, etc., (Müller, p. 56).

These people we see were Weldenseans of Bohemia, a species of Mennonites in early times, afterwards Moravians.

Who were the Weldenseans asks Müller? Then he says, "The Catholic Church called the Weldenseans the old Evangelicals, who gradually gathered in the valleys of the Piedmont and around Mt. Visa, on the borders of France." By the same name the Catholic Church called all the Evangelicals of Germany and Switzerland, who like the Piedmont brethren before the reformation adhered to the old Evangelical principles in opposition to the Romish Church, (Müller, p. 56). They stretched from Southern France and Bohemia and Northward and Southward across the Alps.

1520—Mennonite Faith in Holland.

Says Müller, (p. 159) the Dutch Baptists (or Mennonites) derived their origin from the Waldenses who lived there. He also calls our attentions to a letter spoken of by Brons from the Swiss Baptists (or Mennonites) in 1522. This shows the connection of Swiss and Holland Mennonites very early.

Other authorities relied on by Müller prove that from 1520 to 30 Swiss refugees were already present in Amsterdam, Holland with their Mennonite brethren. The Reformation movement in the Netherlands from the beginning had all the marks of being led off by these Baptists or Mennonites, says Müller (Do.). Menno Simon a little later became the leader through his serious reflection upon the execution of Sicke Schneider, who was thus executed because he was re-baptized, deeming his infant baptism in the Roman Church of no avail.

1521—Decree Against Mennonites. Zwinglians and Lutherans.

This year, under permission of Emperor Charles V of Germany, a decree was issued forbidding anyone to read, buy, carry, give or have possession of any book containing the doctrines of the Mennonites, Zwinglians or Lutherans. This decree was not made by the State; but by the mother Church, yet tolerated by the State. An old writer calls it, "the first prohibition or decree concerning religion and brought into the Netherlands without the consent of the State—rather tolerated than confirmed by the State". The reason for this decree is explained by Brons, (p. 57). Congregations of the mother church were fast going to pieces and something had to be done. He says, "The movement (Anabaptism) was going on. The churches became empty, the sacraments neglected, children not baptized, monks and nuns were leaving the convents and the preachers became indifferent to the mother church. Thus Charles V ordered those who were indifferent to be punished."

1522—Swiss Became Religious Refugees.

Brons speaks (p. 53) of fifty congregations, presumably Swiss, out of which the delegates, elders and teachers, numbering 600 had gathered at Strasburg about 1522. At least, he says, most of them were Swiss refugees, while other Swiss joined the Bohemians and Moravians, within the Wald as ancient documents show. The Canton of Switzerland, South of Zurich is called Unter Walden. Luther had correspondence with these Waldensean or Mennonite refugees in 1522.

1522—The Waldensean "Reform" in Berne.

Says Müller, "In Berne we find a vigorous reform spirit in the aspiring element of the citizens, or the progressive, intelligent and business classes. Especially in all the guilds. The Munster Cathedral stone masons showed themselves full of it." It is supposed that we generally know that about the end of the middle ages the guilds or lodges of cut stone masons and mechanics were very intellectually and artistically advanced and that they had a monopoly of all Cathedral building in Central Europe, (Müller, p. 20).

Müller continues that when in 1522 the dean of Münsingen prosecuted the Minister York Bruner in Kleinhochstetten before the Council of Berne, the Council took the side of Bruner and sentenced the Chapter of Münsingen to pay the costs. Bruner's offense was that of speaking publicly of the Pope, cardinals and bishops, as devils and anti-christs and the priests and monks as cheats, seducers and oppressors of the poor; and wolves who kill and destroy body and soul.

Of course if the Government of Berne would dismiss such charges as not heretical, it shows that the Council and all the heads of the Berne Government at this time were approvers of or at least not opponents of the reformed doctrines of the Waldenseans and Zwinglians, which were taking root here.

Müller also tells us, (p. 159) that in 1522, these Anabaptists were in different parts of Switzerland and wrote letters encouraging other sections.

1522—Early Hold of the Mennonite Doctrines in Berne.

The Bible in the time of the Reformation had a wide circulation and this was the same in Berne as elsewhere. In a Shrove Tuesday play or drama in 1522 written by Nicholas Manuel, the monks in the play complain that the farmers know all about the New Testament. Among the Weldenseans the Sermon on the Mount and the apostolic administrations were regarded as the law of those Christian communities. Müller continues (p. 54) and says the chief question as to the Reform in the early fifteen hundreds is whether there is only family or race relationship between the Baptists or Anabaptists of the time and the old Waldenseans or whether both these conceptions of the Reform movement are different phenomena of one and the same religious community.

Thus Müller argues that there is a close relationship between the early Baptist or Mennonite views and the Reformed and Lutheran views, and that both have many points of belief, identical with the ancient Waldenses. But whether these beliefs were inherited ones or beliefs merely adopted and just happened to be similar to the ancient Waldensean belief, he does not undertake to say. However this be, our ancient Mennonite faith grew up out of the same soil as did that of the followers of Waldo in 1170.

1523—Melchoir Hoffman's Religious Labors in Zurich.

Melchoir Hoffman born in Swabia, (anciently the Northern part of Switzerland; and as we have seen, home of a branch of the Herr family) was a tanner by trade about 1523, in Waldshut. When the movement of religious reformation began, which emanated from Zurich, inspired him with the contents of the Bible which many common people now first began to read, he became a great student of it and learned it. In the Wald, in Switzerland, he began to make his faith known. Even in Zurich as Zwingli says, in a letter dated 1523, this pious Anabaptist's work and activity were felt. Hoffman went further than Zwingli. He did not stop with the "Reformed" principles but embraced what were then Anabaptists' views, similar to the new Mennonite non-resistant doctrine. Zwingli says of him, "The good-for-nothing fellow who dresses hides has turned up here as an evangelist and has brought me under suspicion." Contemporaries speak of Hoffman as a man of strictly moral walk and conversation,—having great eloquence and holy zeal for the cause, (See Brons, p. 373). I mention him because his is a familiar Lancaster county name; and because he seems to have been a vessel filled with Mennonite doctrine in and about Zurich, the home of many of our eastern Pennsylvanians' ancestors.

1523—Zurich Officials Favor the New Religion, But Fear the Established Church.

In Dr. Emil Egli's Zurichter Weidertaufer (p. 8), it is stated that the Government was in sympathy with the great mass of people rising from the corruption in religious matters and freeing themselves to do their own thinking as the Bible taught them; but against the Roman Church as an institution did nothing. The Government went only so far as the public compelled. The Government held back as long as it could says Egli, and therefore so much more jealous became the Reformers. Zwinglians, Lutherans and Evangelicals all had strong friends in the Government officers.

1523—The Anabaptist (Mennonite) Movement in Zurich.

Says Dr. Egli, (p. 10), the Evangelicals showed as much zeal as the Reformed and Lutherans. Simon Stumpf of Hongg, near Zurich, began teaching the mild doctrine; and Rouplin seems to have taught the same doctrine in Wyttikon, Switzerland. At least the Council in the Spring of 1523 took action with regard to the tithes of his congregation. That is, that unlike the Lutherans and Reformed, (who while they did not longer practice the doctrine of the Roman Church, continued to give tithes for the use of the buildings in which they worshipped, as they were the property of the Catholic Church), Rouplin asserted that his congregation was cut loose entirely from the Roman Church and that the buildings belonged to this congregation. So they refused to pay tithes and they not only ceased worshipping, but took down and removed the pictures of the Virgin and various saints. Thus we learn that soon a radical party was gathered, and opposed this delay of the Government. From this foundation the Zurich Anabaptism or Mennonitism took its rise, says Egli.

1523—Jacob and Klaus Hollinger, (Taufers).

In 1523 we find two more now familiar Lancaster county names in Switzerland. Egli tells us (p. 11) that the delay in the Zurich Government to recognize and encourage the reformed spirit made the Evangelicals all the more insistent, especially the zealous Jacob and Klaus Hollinger, who preached the Mennonite faith and aroused the county of Zollikon in Switzerland. In June, 1523 they demanded the communion in both forms, and insulted the priests. In September, Klaus Hollinger taught in Statehoffen that the pictures of the virgin should all be taken down and later became a thorough Baptist among a company of them in St. Gallen, and was very bitter against the "pictures". Soon after Jacob began making most dreadful expressions about the mass. They created a great public explosion in religion by 1524. And says Egli, (p. 13) Stumpf, of whom we have spoken above continued his "awkward preaching and other matters" so much that he was entirely banished from the city and country.

1523—William Reublin Becomes a Mennonite at Wittikon.

This Reublin says Brons (p. 23) had become pastor at Wittikon in Zurich. He left papacy and was publicly married. And at Wittikon at the Corpus Christi he proceeded the procession, with a beautifully bound Bible, with the proclamation, "This is your Venerable—this is your Sanctuary—all else is dust and ashes." The "venerable" is the bread and wine after the prayer.

1523—Zwingli Converts the Government Officials.

Brons tells us (p. 17) that Zwingli was now exercising such power that the council orderd that he might give a public disputation of his religion. Therefore, the Zurich authorities issued a proclamation that such disputation would be allowed January 3, 1523. Upon this permission Zwingli worked out 67 theses in which he clearly set forth his doctrine in an emphatic way. The opponents did not reply and so the council ordered it made public that "since no one rose against Magister Huddrich Zwingli to prove his error, or with divine Holy Scripture to overcome him, the burgomasters, council and great council of the City of Zurich have resolved after mature consideration and it is their will that Zwingli continue as he has done hitherto to proclaim and preach the Evangelical Gospel and scriptures according to the Spirit of God. And the other ministers of the word also in City and country shall teach and preach nothing else than what they are able with the Evangelical doctrine and authority of the Holy Scripture to prove. And all insult to this religion is forbidden under penalty."

This surely was no mean triumph in the cause of the old Evangelical faith, first given to the world by the Waldenses and handed down by them to the Mennonites and to Lutherans and Reformed.

The doctrine had also spread by 1523 into Holland, Brabant and Flanders and also a year or two later into the Netherlands, where Menno Simon was its great advocate, (Brons, p. 60).

1523—The Beginnings of a Mennonite Confession of Faith.

While the first confession of faith set forth in the Martyrs' Mirror is dated 1625, there are to be found some of the rudiments of a confession one hundred years earlier.

In 1523 as Brons tells us (p. 53) a catechism of the Bohemian brethren appeared in German and Bohemian language, in which it was taught that it was not lawful to worship the sacrament of the Altar. This was about the same time that Michael Sattler (M. Mirror) was accused of the new custom of eating and drinking the bread and wine.

This catechism caused Luther to issue a "broadside" with the title "A Little Scripture Concerning the Worship of the Sacrament of the Holy Body of Jesus Christ to the Brethren of Bohemia and of Moravia, known as Wald." In this broadside we read at the beginning, "There is a little book issued by your people in German and Bohemian to instruct the young children in a Christian way, in which among other things it is said that Christ is not independent and natural and the altar is not to be worshipped, which almost moves us Germans, for you must know how I through your delegates requested you that you should make this article clear also in a little book for our people."

Brons tells us also (p. 420) that the Moravians had entered into relations with Luther who issued a broadside to the Moravians, know nas Waldenses. Many Catholics went over to these Mennonites of Moravia and permitted themselves to be baptized again and thus brought upon them great persecution.

In all this we see that the founders of the Mennonite faith were as early and as active as those of the Reformed and Lutherans, etc.

1523—Early Martyr Manuscrpits in the Mennonite Congregation Library at Amsterdam.

The following information is taken from two anonymous German old Baptist Manuscripts of the Mennonite Congregational Library in Amsterdam.

The first is quarto in size and is entitled, "History Book of the Martyrs of Christ, who in this our time in all places of German Lands for the sake of the faith and Godly truth have been executed with fire, water and the sword. What was transacted and endeavored in many ways with them. How they steadfast and comforted were. Also what German persecutions and trouble the congregation has suffered in this last time." This writing extends from 1523 to 1618.

The second is Octavo and has the following title, "Description of the History Briefly Comprehended, How God Has Acted with his Faithful to His own Fame and Praise, from the Beginning of the World and has proved Himself Mighty till the Present Time." This extends to 1594. (See Brons, p. 419).

These are the earliest manuscript accounts preserved of the sufferings of the ancient Waldenses, Old Evangelicals, Old Baptists, Anabaptists, etc., out of whom grew the Mennonites, the Reformed, Lutherans and Moravians, etc. They have no doubt all since been printed.

1523—Anabaptists Separatists in Zurich Compelled to Pay Papal Tithes.

We have shown before that what distinguished those of the general Reformation from those called the Brethren (in doctrine Mennonites) who also joined the reform movement was that, the latter refused to pay tithes to the papal church for use of the church buildings. The Government thought that these tithes should be paid and the great Council of

Zurich passed a resolution, January 22, 1523, that the right of the church to demand tithes must be enforced. All who use the churches must pay the tithes. So these Anabaptists or Mennonites had to do so, (Müller, p. 8).

1523—An Old Anabaptist Belief That Children Should Not and Need Not Be "Taken Into Church".

A different conception toward the church was entertained by these Anabaptists from that of the Reformed. The church of the Reformed was viewed like the Roman church by its believers as a lawful communion, to which the children and minors belonged. The congregation of the Mennonites (or Brethren) was according to old tradition, customs and practices, a voluntary union of the faithful. These must have the right to receive and also expel members. The church of the Reformed was held by them as an institution for learning and Christian and intellectual growth for all, and they therefore held they did not dare refuse the children or anyone else the means of grace. The Reformed believed in children coming in as children to be taught and the church as a school; but early Anabaptists believed only in adults being admitted, (Müller, p. 9.) So their ways naturally parted more and more. Also when in October, 1523, the question was raised as to abolishing the mass, Zwingli wanted to place the decision in the hands of the Council while Pastor Simon Stumpf (Mennonite) protested against this, saying "You have not the power to do this, to give the decision into the hands of the lords of this or any other place." The Zwingli party was successful, and in this way the form of a state church was preordained, whose forms and procedure the State Council commanded. Henceforth union between Reformed and Mennonites was impossible. The former became the state church and the latter the refugee body, (Müller, p. 9).

1524—Early Difference Between Lutheran and Mennonite Forms, Etc.

Ernst Müller says (p. 11), that Luther in his book concerning baptism published in Wittenberg, in 1523-25, retained all the Roman church ceremonies. They were as follows:— the child to be baptized was first exorcised through breathing upon him—salt was then put into his mouth—the cross was made upon him—his nose and ears were touched with spittle—the head was anointed with oil and in doing all this a burning candle was held in the hand. Even in the book of Concord the formula is found. "I conjure thee, thou unclean spirit in the name of the Father, Son and Holy Ghost that thou come out from this servant of Christ."

In this report concerning the consecration of the Minister of Basil unto the Anabaptists there, whom he recently joined, Kalonford, a former Lutheran Reformer, says, "It was thrown up to me that we performed ceremonies in the baptism of children—that we conjured the Devil—that we gave the children salt—burn a candle—that we used spittle, etc. I did not want to defend this or excuse it for I, myself, don't approve of it at all."

Now from the beginning the Anabaptists or Mennonites refused to make use of these ceremonies of baptism or believe in them. Their baptism was as simple as possible. Justus Menius Pratorius and other Lutheran theologians however, expressly attributed great importance to the exorcism.

But Hans Denck broke off from this belief and he and his followers came to the Anabaptism belief saying that the new born child is pure and not possessed of the Devil. And this is often expressed in Baptist writings, (Müller, p. 11).

1524—Early Anabaptists or Mennonite Poems.

Among the Bernese Productions appear, these two lyric Anabaptist poems, which show how in early days the Mennonite views of baptism then existed in Switzerland. By a free translation and reversification, I render them as set forth below. The first is directed against exorcism in baptism of children, and is as follows:

So that our God might be despoiled,
  of his great name;
As if could be in his pure offspring
  Found a blame;
A little child, without a sin;
Which God into this world has sent;
And new created pure within;
"Its soul is lost", their cry is spent.
They take it quickly in their power
And say, "Expelled and out of it we clean
Sin and Devil from this hour."
Though they themselves are steeped in sin.

And this also is found on the subject of Christian Companionship:

In the inner light from our God we can see
  Into every one there now cometh a ray;
And the soul that is bright with these beams shall be
  The chamber of Christ and his spiritual way.
All they who receive this light from the giver,
  Shall have joy and day in their souls forever.

1524—Revolt Against Infant Baptism in Zurich.

Egli tells us (p. 18) that from the spring of 1524, Ruplin had begun to preach against infant baptism, and parents began to be opposed to it because of these sermons, and quit bringing their children. Finally about August, the Town council summoned two fathers and demanded of them why they do not have their children baptized. One had a boy about a year and a half old. These parents appealed to Ruplin's sermons and said they believed what he preached. One of the parents said that Ruplin declared that if he had a child he would not have it baptized, until it came to years of understanding, and could choose its own sponsors. This father also appealed to his neighbors who followed his course. Ruplin was put in jail, and a commission was appointed to examine his doctrine. It consisted of preachers, the Abbot of Kappel, the Clerk of Küusnoch (Ecclesiastical clerk), the provost of Embrach and four delegates of Council. In addition to investigation they were to have all unbaptized infants immediately baptized.

1524—Münzer, Greybel & Manz, and Mennonitism.

The last named author says (p. 19) that the time and place when and where their doctrine came from are not definitely known; but it is believed that the widely circulated writings of the German head of the Anabaptists, Thomas Münzer were much read in Zurich, for when in September, 1524, Münzer travelled in Walshut and remained eight weeks in Griessen, the restless spirits of Zurich, especially Conrad Greybell and Felix Manz visited him and frequently they took in the Anabaptism preached by Münzer. Münzer, however, became a war anabaptist and believed that they who believed in the new faith ought to fight for it.

1524—Materials for the Martyr Book Collected.

About this time, too (says Brons, p. 237), there was a great deal of material collected about the sufferings of the early martyrs, as a means to increase the faith and the courage of those who were suffering now. Hands and hearts were in it and many old matters and rhymes were found and made new. Some preachers of the "fatherland" at whose head was Hans de Ries, undertook to make a new edition with increased contents. These collections were made into a book, at Hoarlam, a large quarto with ten pictures, bound in leather with copper hooks and corners. The title was, "History of the Martyrs or the True Witnesses of Jesus Christ Who Witnessed the Evangelical Truth Under Many Tortures, and Established Them With Their Blood, since the year 1524." Their confessions of faith were also added and their disputations which express their living hope and mighty faith and love to God and his Holy Truth.

1524—Mennonite Growth in the Netherlands, (Holland).

By the last quoted author we are told also, (p. 244) that the number of those who had left the Roman church in the Netherlands, as early as 1524 through the influence of the writings of these fathers of the faith (considerable of it being because of Luther's writings) according to the report of Peter of Thabor, (in Mönch, in the Cloister of Thabor, or Thires, near Sneek a contemporary of Menno Simon) had become so great that the Pope the same year called a secret council in regard to the matter. It was resolved and proclaimed by the Council that in Holland the Pope would grant all backsliders for God's sake, absolution of all their sins, without money if they would come back and come to confession, keep the feasts, pray according to prescription of their church and not neglect the sacrament of the altar.

This item is highly interesting to us in Lancaster county because it gives us light on the condition in Holland at the beginning of the Mennonite faith, the country where it started. It tells us of the vigorous hold it had on the people; and how anxious the Catholic Church was to stop it. That not simply a bishop or other high church officer was moved to bring back the Anabaptists, but the powerful pope himself, shows that it was regarded very seriously by the Church. And that such a wonderful concession was made to forgive all those people their sins without them being required to pay for it, when by the ordinary course of things the forgiveness of the sins of such a multitude would have meant thousands of thalers (dollars) out of their pockets and into the pockets of the priests, shows how it was viewed. But the ancient fathers bravely withstood this munificient offer from the head of their former Church, having since learned that salvation is free to all "whosoever will."

1524—Münzer's Anabaptists Attacked.

About this same time says Brons (p. 31) Zwingli published a broadside against the turbulent Münzer and in it alluded to Greybell and Manz. Thereby Greybell was induced to send out of jail a defense to the Council of Zurich in 1524. He did not want to be considered as a person who incited to riot in his religious teachings, or spoke anything that would lead to it. Münzer as we have seen as an Anabaptist was of so determined a nature that he taught the people should defy opposition to God's truth as he saw it and Greybell did not want to be considered any other than, the mild and defenseless Mennonite. Interest is found in this item from the fact that it contains the well known prominent and honorable Lancaster county name, Greybill.

SATTLER'S EXECUTION: THE GRAYBILL MENNONITES

1525—Michael Sattler's Efforts in Anabaptism.

Michael Sattler of Stauffen was a monk of St. Peters in the Black Forest and had gone over to Anabaptism in 1525 in the region of Zurich. He was expelled from that place but continued his work in his home and was the founder of several congregations at Horb and Rotenburg. He is described by Swiss and Strasburg preachers as a highly honorable, quiet and learned man. "Golden Apples in Silver Pitchers" an Anabaptist book of 1742 contains his farewell letter to the congregation in Horb, the events of his trial and, his parting song. In 1527 he was cruelly executed and his wife was drowned. Unshelm, the Berne writer of the chronicles described the cruel execution in a tone very pathetic and pays a noble tribute to Anabaptism. Unshelm was a fellow sufferer as he was also a prisoner, but whether an Anabaptism or Lutheran is not clear, (Müller, p. 38). Sattler's death is also described in Martyrs' Mirror, p. 401.

1525—Early Anabaptists of Berne.

Müller tells us (p. 23) that in Berne there were Baptists in 1525 of whom the ministers of the Council tell. Mention is made of them in a letter of H. Bullinger which he wrote from Kappel, Switzerland to Heinrich Simler in Berne. John Jacob Simler dates the letter about 1525; and he says according to the manuscript or letter Bullinger writes, "In order that you may not get into the community of the society of Baptists, etc.," which is conclusive that the Baptists existed about Berne at this early date. The letter also sets out, "It has come to us through the common report of many people, how with those also at Berne the doctrine of Anabaptists has been introduced and which renders me friendly to the efforts there, etc."

This item is of interest to the people of Lancaster county because Berne is the place from which the first settlers of this county came two hundred years ago—Swiss Mennonites who were the descendants of those Anabaptists spoken of in 1525 and descendants of similar believers in and about Zurich.

1525—More Zurich Anabaptists Examined.

A very zealous stranger who had come to Zurich was a man of peculiar habits called Blaurock. He was to be taken by ship with his wife to his home in Chur and there he was to be kept and if he came again about Zurich he was to be tortured into silence, His doctrine was to be passed on by three secular preachers and six members of Council at Zurich, among whom were Hans Hager and Ulrich Funk; and the two schoolmasters were also to take part in examining him. Bullinger reports that the Baptists in the disputation proved no more than before. Zwingli appealed to Graybill who behaved himself as if the Savior was present. And others tell of the testimony the Baptists gave of the joy and relief they felt after they were baptized over again, (Zur., p. 30).

1525—The Graybill Anabaptists or Mennonites of 1525.

The congregation of Anabaptists had by 1525 had so far now become established that they caused the Council of Zurich to admit they were beyond control. There were by this time thirteen different religious Reformed bodies that had broken off the Catholic Church and nearly all embraced some part of the Anabaptist faith. One branch was called the free or rude brethren who condemned infant baptism and baptized their adherents anew. Aside from these was the party of Graybill Anabaptists known as the quiet Baptists who kept themselves aloof from the other Mennonites or Anabaptists. But Zwingli said he much feared in the end they would combine. This was away back in 1525, (Brons, p. 25).

1525—Anabaptism Gaining from Lutheranism.

About 1525 when Anabaptism began to spread whole town and counties which did not adhere to Luther began to flock to Anabaptism and thousands who had been Lutherans went over into their camps. They showed an enthusiasm and a courage to the death that had for its example only that of the times of early Christianity and its martyrs. This was the condition throughout Germany, (Müller, p. 14).

1525—Eastward Spread of Anabaptism or Mennonitism

Müller tells us (p.93) that in Zurich the powers greatly reduced Anabaptism by force which had in 1525 and 6 spread over Schauffhausen, Basil, Wald and other parts of Switzerland, from the neighboring Cantons. But it found entrance into Swabia and in the Tyrol in early times. Especially when Zurich began to drown the Anabaptists and when the fall of Wald brought new threats to the itinerant messengers of the Baptists who looked for a new theatre. Blaurach especially from Zurich turned to Graubünden when he had established a congregation of Anabaptists at Manz; and from there to Tyrol to gather a flock for the Lord. Ruplin and Sattler went to Alsace and on to Swabia where they found the soil ready by the Augsburgers (Lutherans) labors—and in a short time stood at the head of seven congregations of Anabaptists or Mennonites. Hatzler promulgated Anabaptism in Nuremburg, Augsburg and along the Rhine; Jacob Gross of Wald in Strasburg, etc. In Passau, Regensburg and München congregations of Anabaptists arose who kept themselves in communion with the brethren in Swabia and Upper Rhine and pressing forward to the Danube, established the same in Austria, Slazburg, Spener, Lenz and Stein. Even Vienna had congregations of Anabaptists.

1526—Jacob Gross's Mennonite Labors in Strasburg.

For a time in Strasburg there was a disposition not to incline either toward Wittenburg and Lutheranism or to Zurich toward Reform Religion; and this gave Mennonitism a chance. And thus it was that Jacob Gross was able to lead an Anabaptism movement in that region. Gross' main doctrine was that the Gospels teach there should not be infant baptism but that baptism should be given only to grown persons as a seal of their faith. He also taught that one must not take an oath. Thus he was a leader of the faith there. (Brons 408).

1526—Graybill and Manz Give the Reasons for Their Faith.

These Anabaptist leaders were several times examined for their faith. At one of the examinations in 1526 Graybill said that a careful study of the scriptures had brought him to Anabaptism. He held that no Christian could defend by the sword. The warlike Anabaptist, Blauroch from his prison wrote that Graybill and Manz and himself were acknowledged Anabaptists as early as 1526 and that they were all ready to die for their principles. He went so far as to write that the Pope, the Lutherans and Zwinglians and Judas were all the same class, that is murderers of Christ. He said baptism of children comes from the Evil One. This same Blauroch time and again

VARIOUS ANABAPTIST REFORMERS 21

declared he wanted to debate with Zwingli, and such a debate was arranged but Egli says he departed a confused man. (Zur. 54).

1526—Zurich Tries to Get the Anabaptists Back to the Former Faith.

Brons tells us (p. 47) that the Council of 200 tried in 1526 to bring the deluded Anabaptists or Mennonites back to the former faith because their movement hurt the government, and tended to the destruction of order, and to bring this about they put several men and women to prison. Also there was a proclamation issued that nowhere in the land henceforth shall any one presume to baptize again a person who has once been baptized; and any one who should violate this decree was to be tried and drowned.

1526—Advance and Growth of Anabaptism in Netherlands.

Brons tells us (p. 60) that in 1526 about Zurich an announcement or public proclamation was made in substance that as many of the subjects have been reading the writings of the new Reformers in religion that now no one shall secretly or publicly assent to the opinions in the books of Luther, Romerani, Karlstadt, Melanthon, Lamberti or others, and that all these books are to be gathered up within three days and be burnt. (Brons 60).

1526—Menno Simon Not Disturbed by the Above Order.

Says Brons at the same page Menno Simon did not suffer himself to be disturbed in the least by this order; and his fellow preachers also paid no attention to it—but they all kept on reading these interdicted writings and especially in regard to baptism. And it is laid down that Menno Simon said "these men taught me that by means of Baptism children were made clean of hereditary and original sin. I tested it and found by the scripture that such doctrine is contrary to the teaching of Christ. Afterwards he says I went to Luther, and he said children are to be baptized on their own faith. This was wrong. Then I went to others and they said the child should be baptized to make parents more careful. This Bucerrus told me. Then I went to Bullingerus and he called my attention to the old covenant of circumcism and said infant baptism was to be used istead of that; but I found this would not stand with the scriptures." Then Menno Simon took a view different from all these and what he felt accorded with the scriptures. (Do.)

1526—Some Other Mennonite Reformers at This Date.

Müller tells us (p. 194) that in 1526 when Reuplin, Gross, Sattler, Denck, Haetzer and Kautz and finally Hoffman in a united way were carrying on Anabaptism in Strasburg and surrounding countries, there was in spite of temporary banishment of former leaders a good footing gained. This kept on growing so that in 1555 there was at Strasburg the first important synod of the Baptists or Mennonites held, which brought unanimity to the leading spirits in the inflamed times that were to follow.

After many more items on early times we will hasten to the times that more nearly concern America.

1527—Anabaptism or Mennonitism Among the High Germans.

About the year 1527 Baptist congregations had become established in all the regions of the High German language, and the new religion had become fixed in those places. There was a network of small congregations from Alsace to Breslau, and from Kessen to Etchland. The center of this region was Augsburg. Neither in Germany or in Switzerland can the growth of this vigorous Mennonitism be considered as growing from any particular center—it grew from different centers at the same time. In cities it took hold and there was soon intercourse from city to city by visiting brethren. The whole of Zurich was at this time a center of Anabaptism—and also were Basil—Zollothurn, Berne, Freiburg and other cities of Switzerland. Müller (20).

1527—Hupmeier, Banished for His Mennonite Faith.

Müller tells us (p. 94) that Dr. Hupmeier, now Hoofmeier or Hoffmier about 1527 was banished from Zurich, on account of his faith and he went to the wilds of Switzerlnad and founded an asylum for those who were determined to carry on the Evangelical or Anabaptist religion. He found that the opposition to him was not so much from the Catholics as from the Zwinglians or Reformed people—and in Walshut the overcoming of the Rebellion party, led by Blauroch and others who professed the Mennanite faith, but still who were "resistants" made it impossible there.

1527—A Primitive Anabaptist Synod Begun by Sattler.

The same author quoted above (p. 10) says that at two small synods held at Augsburg in 1526 and 7 the Swiss took no part; but on the other hand in 1527 at a meeting of the south Germans, who were under the leadership of Sattler there were such gatherings held at Schlott on the Rand and at Strasburg, at which Swiss Mennonites as well as Germans were present.

1527—Lutheranism Rises Up Against Mennonites or Baptists.

Shortly before the beginning of the year 1527 Luther had a sermon printed in which he attacked the Baptists says Brons (p. 411). In his eyes the rise of these Baptists involved liberty of conscience, the very thing he fought for and yet he denied it to them. The result of it was that at Strasburg an order was issued against the Baptists or Mennonites and they were exiled. Their enemies of the town of Strasburg followed up Luther's lead by publishing a document in which they warned the people against Kautz, a Mennonite leader. The title of the book was "A Faithful Warning of the Servants of God at Strasburg Against the Sermons which Jacob Kautz, a Preacher in Worms has Published." Thus by this early date a fact almost incredible appears,—that the different branches of the new religion were at odds with each other.

1527—More Anabaptists Trouble About Zurich.

We are told (Zur. 62) that at the end of 1527 about 30 Baptists met at Hein, and the report was spread their next meeting would be in a church— that they now had friends and funds enough to own a church. When the council of Zurich (Zur. 64) sent its delegates in 1527 to the General Assembly they were instructed to bring up the subject of whether Christ's teachings were not that all were subject to the government, and whether the Anabaptist movement was not spiritually wrong. When it was found that five Baptists known of old had gone there too as delegates from Zollikon it aroused suspicion and the council of Zurich were doubly angry. These Baptist delegates confessed that they had themselves sent as delegates so that they could know whether their brethren were to be decreed to be drowned, according to the desire of the council, so that if that was the decision reached they would know it early and could go and visit the brethren and comfort them so that they should be firm, for Christ had taught clearly that they should visit the brethren in prison.

The Council at Zurich now tried suasion (Zur. 64). They invited the confederacy of Baptitsts from Berne, Basil, Schaffausen, Chur, Appenzel and St. Gallen, all in Switzerland to meet at Zurich, Monday after St. Lawrence day in 1527, stating that it could be shown to them that their aim was the destruction not only of true righteousness and inner faith of the Christian Religion but also the outward ordinances of Christian and orderly government, against brotherly love and good morals. (Do. 65).

1527—Zurich Decree Against Mennonite Street Preaching.

In the latter part of 1527, (Zur., p. 70) a decree was sent out to the Bailiffs or Sheriffs about Zurich, dated the 16th of December, to spot out all the Baptist or Mennonite preachers who were preaching on the corners of the streets and trying to get the people to withdraw from the Catholic Church. Some of these preachers were foreigners from Holland and parts of Germany. The decree was that they were to be arrested and taken to Wellenberg, but to be dismissed on paying 5 Pound penalty. Following this decree there were several arrests in the Lowlands. From this we see a new difficulty arising that often appears in the Baptist movement in this that there was corruption among the clergy; and these Baptist preachers were accused of some of this corruption. But the truth is that the corruption was not among them but that the established Church needed stricter discipline. Egli says at the same page that this section of the country is the chief hearth or location of the third period of the Baptist movement, that is, in and about Zurich.

1527—Great Martyrdom of Anabaptism About Worms.

In Brons' work, (p. 180) he tells us that according to recent research among the "Staats-Archivars", that is, the Archives in charge of the government, by Dr. Keller, that in Münster where a work on Anabaptism came to light, that Hans Denck who in Worms in 1527 sought refuge, was perhaps the most important of the teachers of the German Baptists of that time. He further says that Denck found here, as he had in Augsburg enthusiastic adherents, who recognized in the man there a gospel messenger of genuine gold. One of his adherents, a Lutheran preacher, named Kautz, affixed a series of theses to the theological Cloister at Worms, June 9, 1527. Challenged by this the Lutherans and Catholics arrayed themselves against the Baptists and the whole city went into uproar.

The Baptists in Worms were in such large majority that Wolfgang Capito, four days before the theses were fixed, wrote to Zurich that the City of Worms had by a public agreement seceded from the word of God, that is, he meant there were so many of these Anabaptists and Mennonites about that it looked as if they were about the only people in the district. This Capito was not a Baptist; he was a Lutheran, but in some ways agreed with Denck.

Soon, however, the opponents of the Baptists succeeded in stirring up the Elector against them, which was a hard task. All they had to do to these defenseless people was to reward them as the same kind as the Münzerites and the Zwickauerites, who disregarded infant baptism and so made it appear that these real Baptists belonged to the same class. We remember these Münzerites and others were not regarded as sincere and were looked upon more as persons who simply took a delight in making trouble; Münzer, their leader, was always trying to quarrel; henceforth the Baptists in the Palatinate were persecuted by the united spiritual and worldly powers in such a terrible manner that in a short time 350 of these harmless people were executed. This aroused many who did not agree with these Anabaptists or Mennonites but who were impressed by the steadfastness and who had read many writings of Hans Denck. Among these friends of the Mennonites was a preacher named John Odenbach and he wrote a letter to the Judges and said, "Behold with what great and patient love and devotion these pious people died— how knightly they withstood the world and how they can not be vanquished because of the truth. They have suffered violence but they prosper because they are the holy martyrs of God."

1527—Ancient Authority of the Anabaptists on Baptism.

The same author, last mentioned (p. 44) tells us that the Anabaptists or Mennonites' view of baptism as it was in 1527 is expressed in an old work as follows: "At his baptism by John Christ called baptism a righteousness and when the Publicans were baptized by John he called it a Council of God, therefore, children are not to be baptized because they need no repentance and know nothing of righteousness and Council of God; further Christ says after his resurrection, he who believes and is baptized shall be saved but he who does not believe will be damned." Thus it is said by this writer that no one could be baptized except those who understand and believe and therefore children can not be baptized. This work further says for this reason children will not be condemned and the Savior only speaks of those who understand to know good and evil shall be in danger after they do the evil but as to the rest he says they are simple minded and must be aware that false prophets do not lead them astray. So to them baptism would only be an outer sign and would not mean anything.

1527—Death of the Mennonite Patriot Manz.

We are told by Brons, (p. 40) that when Felix Manz, of whom we have spoken of before was taken out on the ship to death by drowning "and when he stood there ready to be martyred, beneath him the floods of the Lake of Zurich—above him the blue sky— around him the great mountains with their sun-illumined summits — his soul raised itself in sight of death above these and when on one side a preacher sympathetically spoke to him that he should be converted to the Catholic faith again, he scarcely heard it; but he heard the voice of his mother standing on the other side and his brethren with her, who at the same time prayed that he should remain steadfast; and he sang when they fettered him, with a loud voice and said, 'Into thy hands, O Lord, I commit my spirit' and soon after the waves covered him from sight." This happened in January, 1527. Brons gives us a very vivid picture of the event, etc.

1527 — First German and Austrian Mennonite Leaders.

The same author says (p. 412) that in this year Sattler, Denck, and Haetzler had gone from Worms to preach the Anabaptist or Mennonite doctrine. Sattler went to Rotenburg in the Necker and the other two went to Augsburg. Here they met Kautz, Jacob Gross and Jacob Dascher and Sigmund Salminger and other friends, all important men, who asserted a great influence on the congregations; and all prepared to risk their lives for their faith in the certainty that that faith was according to the genuine spirit of the doctrine of Christ. Christianity seemed to them a power of God that rendered men capable to be a follower of Christ as it had also rendered the first Christian martyrs. Therefore, they had courage to stand up for their convictions in spite of

SECOND PERIOD OF MENNONITISM

disgrace and contumely—in spite of torture and death. They were convinced that their affair was God's and that they were the leaven for later generations. This kept them steadfast through the horrible events in which they saw everywhere the brethren, singly and in groups, robbed, expelled and tortured and killed women as well as men.

In Austria they were smoked out of the caves and camps, burnt as fast as convicted and the officers who arrested them got their property. It was horrible there. Haetzler was overtaken too. In one of the old manuscripts the death of Haetzler is told. He was learned in several languages and in holy scripture. At the time of his departure he made a beautiful speech, which moved many to tears, and he composed a song which is still in use in Switzerland and other places.

In this we see some of the earliest attempts to act as a group of ministers or a collective body to give the new Anabaptist religion its organization.

1527—King of Denmark favors a Mennonite Leader.

The same author says, (p. 377) that Hoffmeier about 1527 attracted the attention of the King of Denmark, who examined his doctrine and made him preacher in the province of Kiel; and he soon had his own printing press, which the King assisted him in securing as he had no means himself but it excited the envy of other preachers. Brons tells us later, however, that this Danish Mennonite let his fancy and zeal carry him away. And whenever he had time he got to reading that part of the Bible which excited his fancy and led him into hallucinations, viz:—the tabernacle of Moses, the dress of Aaron, the Priest, the Exodus of the Children of Egypt, etc. From these he deduced the number four as the sacred number, which disturbed his idea of the Trinity for a time. Thus he said we had the four gospels. And he preached about the four rivers—the four colors of silk—the four horns of the Altar and the four animals of Ezekiel—and these he made more important than the gospel. "So he got a little off." Hoffmeier brought about much evil. His agreement with Luther was kept and Luther, therefore did not bother about him because he did not attack Luther very much. Luther however, wrote to Kiel to his friends there that Hoffmeier was not right and that they should not heed his doctrine.

In this we see that there was danger of the early zeal carrying the early fathers away as well as in these later days.

1527—The Second Stage of the Anabaptist Religion and Its Leaders.

The history of Anabaptism in 1526 to 1528 enters into its second period at Zurich. After the victory in Zurich had been decided by the State and the Baptists had been oppressed, the stronger of the Baptist leaders bring the Anabaptist religion into its second period in which the defeated found as leaders, and supporters such strong men as Balthaser, Hoffmeier and Johann Denck, the recognized new leaders.

At that time Sebastian Frank, Capito and Kessler in Saint Gallen recognized fully the difference between the Swiss brethren and Anabaptists in the narrower sense when in 1527 at Signau in Northwest Moravia, the difference came openly to light. The type of the Swiss brethren is more that of the early martyrs, whose valiant stand for their new Christianity was brought out more prominent by persecution, (Müller, p. 10).

It is shown us in this item that there were really different branches of Anabaptism or Mennonite faith in early times. The preachers throughout Switzerland being the more reliable and serious. In parts of Germany and in Denmark we have noticed that the leaders were inclined to try to do something odd and create excitement.

1527—Hans Seckler's Enunciation of Principles.

During the year 1527, Hans Seckler had come from Basel to Berne, both in Switzerland. Hans Dreier and Heinrich Seiler were present at the Baptists' meeting or convention of 1528, and were, according to a manuscript in the Berne Library, drowned in the Berne Lake in 1535. A minute of the hearing against these people is set out in the old books and the main points that Seckler insisted upon were as follows: (1) Baptism of children is a bad practice and can not serve any good purpose. (2) Though we do not take part in Government we ought to be subject to Government, and we are. (3) The word of Christ must remain and govern all things—we are not to swear at all—what Govenrment commands we will do as long as it is not against God. (4) The heart belongs to God and not to men (he was surely not a Socialist). (5) Paying taxes is all that is imposed upon us and this a Christian will always do. (6) As to paying interest we hold it the same as paying tithes; if interest is usury so is paying the tithes. (7) As to having several wives, he said that more than one wife is wrong, but that he knew of some Anabaptists who had several wives in common, but most of them did not believe in this doctrine, and now I believe that all who used to follow are very sorry for it and that it is stamped out. (8) As to the mass and pictures of the Virgin and as to why they do not enter churches in which there are these pictures and idols in the church, he said, he does not complain about it and those who want to do so, may; neither do we say that the women should not go into the Church. (9) Infant baptism has no foundation in the gospel but it was only begun by the Pope. This does not make it a gospel rite; because no Christian practice can exist that is not planned and set up by God himself, (Müller, p. 42).

1527—George Wagner's Execution; Also Others Put to Death.

In Martyr's Mirror, (p. 401) is given the following account of the execution of George Wagner in 1527.

"George Wagner, of Emmerich, was apprehended at Munich, in Bavaria, on account of four articles of the faith. First, That the priest can not forgive sins. Secondly, That he does not believe a man can bring down God from heaven. Thirdly, That he does not believe that God or Christ is bodily in the bread which the priest has upon the altar; but that it is the body of the Lord. Fourthly, That he did not hold to the belief that water baptism possessed any saving power. As he would not renounce these articles, he was most severely tormented, so that the prince felt great compassion for him, and personally came to him in the prison, and earnestly adminished him thereto, promising that he would call him his friend all his lifetime. Thus also, the tutor of the prince, earnestly admonished him to recant, and likewise made him many promises. Ultimately his wife and child were brought before him in prison in order, on this wise to move him to recant. But neither was he to be moved in this way; for he said that though his wife and child were so dear to him that the prince could not buy them with all his dominion, yet he would not forsake his God and Lord on their account. Many priests and others also came to himffi but he was steadfast and immovable in that which God had given him to know. Hence he was finally sentenced to the fire and death.

Having been delivered into the hands of the executioner, and led into the middle of the city, he said: 'Today I will confess my God before all the world.' He had such joy in Christ Jesus, that his face did not pale, nor his eyes show fear; but he went smilingly to the fire, where the executioner bound him on the ladder, and tied a little bag of powder to his neck, at which he said: 'Be it done in the name of the Father, the Son and the Holy Ghost;" and having smilingly bidden farewell to a Christian who was there, he was thrust into the fire by the executioner, and happily offered up his spirit, on the eighth day of February, A. D. 1527. The sheriff however, surnamed Eisenreich von Landsberg, while returning home from the place of execution, travelling on horseback, purposing to apprehend others of the brethren, died suddenly in the night, and was found dead in his bed in the morning having thus been removed through the wrath of God.

Melchior Vet, who was a companion of George Blaurock of whom we have spoken before, was also burned at the same time that Michael Satter was executed. Leonhard Keyser, the same year, was drowned for having accepted the doctrine of the Aanbaptists, (Martyrs' Mirror, pp. 403 and 405). The same year, Thomas Herman and 67 others, and also at the Hague and at other places in Holland, about 150 more were executed, (M. Mirror, 406-9.).

1527—Berne Asks Zurich How They Exterminate the Mennonites There.

On the 14th of September, of this year, the Berne authorities wrote to Zurich and informed them that they had published a decree against the Anabaptists or Mennonites to the effect that they must stop practicing the faith or leave the country, and warning them that if they went into any other part of Switzerland and keep on their doctrine, they would be punished wherever they are.

About the same time Berne asked information from Zurich how they managed to reduce the Baptists to such a small number so early, stating that they wish to follow the same method. Zurich said the best method they found was to kill them, (Müller. p. 28).

In this item we observe two points, (1) that Zurich got through her persecutions against the Mennonites earlier than Berne did. It is likely that many of them fled from Zurich to Berne and into the Emmenthal or valley Northwest of Berne; and (2) we notice that Zurich was much more severe than Berne in its treatment of these people.

1527—New Mennonite Strength in the Emmenthal.

In 1527 Berchtold Haller, (likely today Heller, the common Lancaster county name), the reformer from Berne wrote to Zwingli that the valley of the Lower Zimmenthal is on his side and further he also hears that the subjects from the Emmenthal and particularly about Langnau and Ruederswell have turned for the right, that is have become Anabaptists and have given up the mass and have petitioned the rulers of the country that they should let them practice their religion unmolested. They said also that they could show by the scriptures that the mass was a blasphemy. The Council agreed to let these faithful people go without observing the mass now until further notice. This was the same also as to the congregations of Bollingen and Rohrbach, (Müller, p. 23).

1527—Anabaptists Acted Unwisely at Zolothurn, Switzerland.

The agitation, which was in 1527 carried to Berne in favor of Anabaptism frightened the friends of the reformation in not a little degree and it was a year before the victory of the reformation was known to the friends at Berne. At this time there were some restless and foolish dreamers among the Anabaptists and this created disorders in Zurich and the news spread to Berne and did there cause much harm. Also in Germany they caused trouble and now it was carried to Berne and the Catholics took a delight is this dilemma. Zehner in 1531 reports and says the reformation movement at Zolothurn, Switzerland, that the beginning was so good that the whole reformation should have grown very strong in Christ, but he heard that everything was spoiled by these Anabaptists, who were tolerated with pleasure by the Catholics, because they saw it held the cause back and so the true servants of the gospel are not now counted anything in that section, (Müller, p. 25).

1527—Mennonite Congregations Growing in Different Parts of Switzerland.

Doctor Hoopmeier, expelled from Zurich found an asylum in Nickelburg, Switzerland, and there for a long time he was not hindered in the Anabaptism doctrine, which he believed and which Zwingli prevented in Zurich. Others came to this Asylum from St. Gallen and the Upper Mountainous regions of Switzerland. They had the powerful protection of County Lichtenstein and in a little while 40 to 50 households had turned to Anabaptism out of a population of 12,000. These formed the kernel of the Baptist congregations in that section, known as the conservative Baptists or Mennonites. There were also communities of Baptists there who were very excitable and they were called the enthusiastic Baptists. Then there were also the Swabian Baptists in the Upper Necker Valley, and they agreed to seven articles of faith about the year 1527, (Müller, page 94).

1528—Reformation Movement in Switzerland Retarded by the Mennonites.

A great discussion or debate was held in January, 1528, in Berne for the purpose of having the people decide which branch of the reformation they would cling to, that is, whether the reform under Zwingli or the Mennonite or Anabaptist faith and it was to be decided according to the result of this debate. Everyone could speak out what he desired. But the Bishops knew the opinion in Berne and remained away. Whether the Baptists would take part in it and defend their views or whether they wanted to take advantage of the excitement simply to push on their doctrine is not known but it was soon found that their appearance there would be disastrous to the success of the discussion and might have ended the debate because now all the strength of the powers or Government were to be held together to strike against Rome. And it was feared that a debate instead of getting all the reform preachers together, would just result in splitting them up more. Therefore, the foreign Mennonites who had come to attend this discussion were kept back in a cloister until the discussion was ended. Then when they came up it was decided they could say whatever they pleased. At this time also a spirit commenced to arise to punish any of those Anabaptists or heretics as they called them, who were sent out of the country and were now beginning to come back. A great effort was now to be made to gather together all the reformers and make a move against the Catholic Church and because the Mennonites and Anabaptists were splitting up this reform movement by not accepting Zwingli and Luther views, the Reformed and the Lutherans now turned against them as fiercely as possible, (Müller, p. 28).

1528—Martyrdom in Salsburg.

During this year 18 persons in one part and many others were executed for their Mennonite faith in Salsburg, Germany. The most reliable account is as follows:

"These eighteen persons, besides many others, were kindled with zeal in the fear of God, and had turned to God from the world and its idolatry, and been baptized upon faith in Christ, entering upon obedience towards his holy gospel. This the adversaries could not endure; these eighteen were therefore apprehended, and finally, as they, under many tortures, piously adhered to their faith, were also sentenced to the fire, and burned on the same day, at Salzburg, about the year 1528." (See M. Mirror, p. 411.)

All of these showed the greatest readiness to die for the sake of their faith and left inspiring tributes to strengthen their brethren and sisters. Speaking of the state churches, they say they have hid the truth for more than 500 years, seduced the multitudes with false doctrines and trampled the word under foot.

They then proceed and say that all this has been witnessed at Salzburg not a lamentable matter, viz.:—that eighteen persons should be burned in one day for the doctrine of Christ. That they suffered a great deal before they were burned, to wit.—they could not buy or sell land nor own property, because they did not believe in the State doctrine.

1528—Seventy-one Persons Martyred in the Valley of the Inn, Bavaria, Germany.

In the year 1528, "Leonhard Schoener of Becklasburg was apprehended. He was a minister of God, and was well versed in the holy Scriptures, and also in the Latin language. He faithfully taught the true baptism of Christ and his apostles, the true Lord's Supper, and the articles of the Christian faith; yea, the word of God. He also testified against infant baptism, the abominable sacrament, and other abominations of antichrist. He had originally been a barefoot friar for about six years, but beholding the impurity, wantonness, hypocrisy (Matt. 7:15), and viciousness of the monks and priests, and judging their lives by the word of God, he left the monastery at Judenburg, Austria, and went to Nurenberg, learned the tailor's trade and then traveling about as a journeyman tailor, he came to Nulasberg, in Austria. There he heard of Balthasar Huebmeier and his baptism, and learned that a number of the same faith formed a little society at Veyen. He sought them out, came to them, heard them, and, led thither by Oswald was baptized. After this he went to Steyen to work at his trade; where he taught and baptized, having been elected teacher by them; and thus teaching and baptizing, he proceeded through Bavaria, as far as Rothenburg, in the Valley of the Inn, where he was apprehended for his faith, disputed much with his opposers, and was examined. Previous to this he proposed: that, if they regarded his faith and doctrine as wrong and heretical, they should produce learned persons, doctors, monks and priests, to dispute with him concerning the matter. Should he, in dispute on true scriptural grounds be found to be in the wrong, they should punish him as unrighteous; and for still further confirmation of the truth, he offered, in order to confirm his assertion and his writings, that, if any of the learned could convince him with the truth of the word of God, that his doctrine was not comformable to the holy scriptures, he should, as having been vanquished be severed limb from limb by the executioner, and, when deprived of all his limbs, have the ribs torn out of his body, until he should be dead. But if he should not be able to obtain and hearing and disputation, and they should judge and put him to death unheard, he asked all the witnesses of his death, and all those standing by, that they be his witnesses before God, in His Judgment at the last day. But by virtue of the mandate of the Emperor, and the edict of the King of Hungary and Bohemia, he was condemned, delivered to the executioner, beheaded, and burnt to ashes on the 14th day of January of said year, at Rothenburg, for the testimony of Christ, from which he would not depart. After the death of this Leonhard, about seventy persons bore witness with their blood in the same place. Leonhard Schoener, among others, left an admonition for the consolation of all those who suffer for the name of Christ." (See Mirror, p. 409.)

By this we can see that the religious agitation was in great ferment in the central part of Germany at this time; and that the Anabaptist or Mennonite Church was slowly rising through blood and turmoil to become a great religious power in central Europe.

1528—Hans Schlaeffer and Leonhard Frick Martyred in the Valley of the Inn, Bavaria, Germany.

"In the year 1528, Brother Hans Schlaeffer, formerly a Roman Priest, but afterwards a teacher of the word and Gospel of Christ, a highly gifted man, was apprehended at Schwartz, in the Valley of the Inn, and with him Brother Leonhard Frick. They tried him greatly with many severe tortures, and disputed with him, through the priests about infant baptism; but, he orally as well as in writing, showed them his defense, as it is commanded, and as it will be found throughout the entire New Testament, namely: That the word of God must first be taught, and that only those who hear, understand, believe and receive it, are to be baptized. This is the true Christian baptism, and no anabaptism. The Lord has nowhere commanded to baptize infants; they are alrcady the Lord's, and as long as they are in their innocence and simplicity, they are not to be condemned at all. The also asked him, in what the foundation of these anabaptistic sects did properly consist. To this he replied: 'Our faith, practice and baptizing is founded on nothing else than the command of Christ: Go ye into all the world and preach the Gospel to every creature. He that believeth and is baptized will be saved' (Mark 16:16; Matt. 28:19); and many other Scriptures.

They also asked what design was concealed under this baptism, since they had thus exhorted them to raise a new uproar and sedition. But he replied that it never entered his heart, to make an uproar; neither had he ever approved of it in others; yea, he had fled fom a house in which they lived in contention, which he could prove by all with whom he had ever lived. And there is no other design concealed under it, than to amend the life, and to forsake the viscious ways of the world; so that in the doctrine which he teaches, this is not the least commandment that we are in duty bound to be subject to the authorities in all good things; how, then, should he raise and purpose uproar and sedition?

Thus Hans Schlaeffer of Schaeffer was asked what had caused and induced him to forsake his office and priest. Concerning this he told them, that he had done it for conscience's sake, because he knew that he was in a place of a prophet, and believed that God had sent him.

They would also know of him, who told him to go into Germany to plant the evil seed of Anabaptism. He told them, that no one had ordered him thither; but that, since he had no abiding place as yet, and had to go about in misery, he came there to one of his friends, with whom he stayed, and thence came to Schwartz, where he was apprehended, according to and for the will of God. As to the evil seed of which they spake, he knew nothing at all; but he intended nothing evil, but much rather the pure divine truth." (M. Mirror, p. 410).

1528—Other Executions of Mennonites or Anabaptists.

During this same year Leopold Schneider was beheaded at Augsburg for his faith. He died with songs of praise on his lips, (M. Mirror, p. 411). Also Hans of Stotzingen was condemned to death for the Evangelical truth, in Zabern, Alsace, (M. Mirror, p. 412). And the same as all the rest he seemed to show no fear at all and was glad to meet his torture and death.

The same year (Do.) two ministers of the Evangelical gospel were destroyed in the city of Brueem, Moravia. When they were being tried, one of them said to the Council who were trying them, to be careful that they do not shed innocent blood, when one of the Council being pricked in his heart named Thomas Petzer arose and pretended he were washing his hands, saying, 'Thus shall I wash my hands in their blood and think to do God service.' But a few days later he was found dead in his bed, so that he died and passed away before those whom he helped to condemn. In the same year Hans Feierer, (M. Mirror, p. 412) and five of his believers were condemned and burned at Munich, in Bavaria, and in addition three sisters being wives of three of these men, were drowned and all of them seemed ready and willing to die for their father. This name Feierer is much like our Lancaster County Feree, which at certain times spelled Ferree, and may have later been changed into Forry. And we also have the name Fiero. All of these names seem to come from the same stock and these people may have come from

1528—Growth of Mennonitism.

This year, according to Dr. Egli's Züricher Wiedertäufer, Zwingli found great difficulty in keeping his brethren from leaving the Reformed church and going over to the Mennonites or Anabaptists. He remonstrated with them but they did not heed and took such means as they saw fit. Then the Government came to his aid and compelled the people to follow Zwingli's teaching or suffer a penalty if they joined the Anabaptists. In certain places the Anabaptist strength grew so that in one town there was only one woman left in the Reformed church, the rest of the neighborhood having turned Mennonites and held their meeting in a barn, (Zur., p. 80).

They now, however, began to have difficulties among themselves and this retarded the growth somewhat, (Zur., p. 87).

1528—First Migration of the Mennonites into Germany.

The Anabaptists begged that their opponents should examine the Baptist faith more closely and their teachings and they offered to submit them to the Council of Berne but they were refused. Council said they would not accept any opinion the Anabaptists had but their damned wrong teaching about not baptizing until the children were grown up must be rejected entirely and also their dotcrine of not assisting the Government. They further said that the Anabaptist view that no Government was necessary was dangerous and the steps taken by the officials to enforce the Anabaptists to change their views so disgusted them with the fatherland, that they began to migrate to other lands. This migration was partly caused by the reason that the great Mennonite leaders, viz:—Greybill, Stumpf and others were expelled—Hoffmeier was taken captive by the Austrians and burned at the stake in Vienna, Ludwig Haetzer of Küsnitz and also Denck were submitted to tortures; and thus they began to move onward like sheep without a shepherd. The Mennonites from Schaffhausen may have gone down the Rhine about this time. Some went to the Netherlands, some went to Alsace in the Pfaltz and yet others to Hassen, (Brons, p. 47).

1528—Debate on Mennonite Principles at Berne.

This year, according to Müller, (p. 45) the Anabaptists were invited to come to Berne to discuss the religious principles and to see whether those who were imprisoned might have their liberty again. After the regular convention was held there was an informal discussion with these Anabaptists who were present and there again the Baptists re-asserted their principles more strenuously than before as is shown by an old book published in Zurich. The objections brought against them were, they do not say the "Ave Maria"—nor pay taxes or tithes—and that it is a shame that these "devilish, brazen Anabaptists are not ashamed of thmselves for refusing honor to Virgin Mary since God himself, gave her honor by making her the mother of the Savior though she remained a Virgin." This book goes on to say, "why will they call themselves Christians, if they do not give her the honor which the Arch Angel Gabriel gave to her, saying, 'Hail, Mary, full of grace; thou shall be the mother of the Savior,' etc.—

yet these people do not give her any honor."

It is related that the city clerk of the Council was an Anabaptist and he and his wife said something against the Virgin and were heavily fined; but he would not take absolution from the Priests. The Anabaptists or Mennonites were further accused, because it was charged they would not observe the Apostles' creed, since that was not in the Scripture; also they were charged with holding that there should be no authority exercised, except what was given in the Bible, and the Bible says a sword could be used, they claim that it can or should not.

1528—Imperial Austrian Decree Against the Anabaptists.

Müller says, (p. 32) that during this year, there was pronounced an Imperial decree by Austria against the Anabaptists; and in 1529 another. These decrees made it the duty of every citizen to exterminate the Anabaptist movement. This movement went into Germany and appeared in many places there as communism and looked to be detrimental to the State. Therefore, they were much persecuted about ths time; their religious sincerity was not believed in and they were looked upon as a new form of civil government much like socialists because of their peculiar views concerning Government. For this reason Zurich, Berne, St. Gallen and many other Cantons of Switzerland and other places decreed that it must be exterminated. The main question they asked however was "how shall these stubborn heretic people be exterminated?" Switzerland found that question harder to answer than to ask. By the middle of 1529, it is shown by Müller, that this movement was very strong all over Switzerland, (Müller, p. 30).

1528—Anabaptist Tortures in Switzerland, Bavaria and Germany.

Müller, (p. 17) tells us that in the latter part of 1528, in Swabia (which was anciently the Northern part of Switzerland) they had 500 to 1000 horsemen to go all over the country and without trial or judgment, kill Taufers like wild beasts and take their property. George Ausbach, who was a friend of the Anabaptists, protected them against this. Just as hard were the persecutions in Bavaria. Here Duke William gave the order that all who do not repent must be burned and their limbs be pulled out from their bodies. Some were fried to death on hot pillars of stone—some were tortured with red hot tongs—some were locked in houses and burned with the houses—some burned at the stake—some hung on trees—and some died by sword and water—some were gagged and taken to the place of death and killed. But in spite of all this they continued to grow.

1529—Anabaptists Nearly Exterminated Near Groeningen.

In this year there was such a severe measure in the district of Groeningen, that only two small letters remind us that the Anabaptists were not wholly swept or wiped out. One decree was that the Sheriffs and their Deputy Sheriffs were all compelled to see to it that these Baptists went to the Catholic Church; and those that were not found there were condemned as heretics. In spite of all this a good many kept themselves hid and did not appear at the Catholic church for two years, (Zur., p. 83).

1529—Pious Old Hans Müller's Labors and Troubles in Switzerland.

At the end of this year the authorities had new troubles on hand with the Anabaptists. In the Aathal was Hans Müller of Medikon (Switzerland). In this place he was put to jail on account of debts but he was also held on account of his Anabaptist or Mennonite views. When the promise given about going to church was offered to him, he said he wanted to have an interview with his people before he would answer, as he was one of their leaders. The Council were at the same time Judge and Jury in important matters; and he seeing that their methods were unfair said to them, what you want people to do to you you must do to them. He petitioned the Council that they should have fatherly mercy, that they should not compel him to violate his conscience or make his persecutions unbearable on account of his faith because faith is a free gift of God, and as everyone has not the same faith which the scriptures tell about, they ought all to be dealt with according to their individual faith. He went on to say that faith is not of the will of the flesh but born of God and because they have the spirit of God are the children of God—that all that comes from God is good—that the mysteries of God are hidden like a treasure in a field and no one can find them unless God shows them to him, therefore he said, "You servants of God, I beg of you let me and my faith free."

In a similar manner he expressed himself in a petition in which he asks for patience until God gives him light to decide and said he, faith is not to be taken up as a stone but must first be found.

Müller made an effort to break out of jail and his excuse was very simple and unsophisticated. He said, "Beloved do not let this surprise you that I wanted to break out from this Castle or jail, because the hardship here compels me to do it." Dr. 'Egli goes on to say that if his supposition is correct, this Hans Müller of Medikon or Edikon is the same as the Müller from the Aathal or Mathal, according to a letter of the Sheriff of Greoningen in the beginning of 1530, who interrupted the pastor in the church, because he would proclaim "Ave Maria." Edikon he says, is no other place than Medikon in Aathal, noticed as early as August, 1528, when Sheriff Vogt Berger wrote and said that one, Hans Müller has strong Anabaptist views but otherwise he was a quiet and pious man, very willing to be taught; and afterwards he said of him, "He is a fine pious fellow." It seems also that the title page of an early Hymn Book used by the Early Anabaptists contained some fine allusions to the good qualities of this Hans Müller and Egli thinks that Sheriff Berger copied them in praise of Müller. The title of the Hymn Book is, "A Collection of Nice Christian Hymns Composed in Prison of Passaw and in the Castle by the Swiss Brethren and Other Righteous Christians." Some of the hymns were composed by Blauroch and Mans. And it is plain that Hans Müller copied them and frequently quoted from them.

1529—Estimate of the Number of Mennonites at This Time.

Müller tells us (p. 17 that Sebastian Frank, estimated the number of Mennonites who were destroyed in two years by sword, water and fire was about 2000. In Tyrol there was about 1000 up to the year 1530. In Ensensheim in Austria, 600—in Luitz, 73—in Bavaria and the Palatinate up to 1529 350. There were also others in Munich and other sections. Among them were Michael Sattler of Rotenburg, whose tongue was cut out. So too there were prominent people in other sections.

1529—Melchoir Hoffman's Debate On the Lord's Supper.

This year as we are told (Brons, p. 381), Hoffman declared that if the Government of Holland does not yield and allow the Anabaptists peace, they will bring on bloodshed as they grow stronger. This he said after the great debate at Kiel, Germany, where today the great war vessels are gathered.

Hoffman was looked upon as an agitator rather than a harmless Mennonite. His enemies tried to have the ruler of Holland turn against him, but he could not do so.

On the question of transubstantiation, Hoffman said, had Christ more than one body? Was he not sitting at the table when he said, "This is my body?" He did not mean it in that sense. Neither can priests make the bread his body blessing it. No, said Hoffman, "The bread is only a symbol." On this subject Luther and Zwingli could not agree either; but they did agree on all other points by a special effort, (Do., p. 390).

1529—Decree Against the Baptists.

In 1529 the Emperor of Austria decided that all Baptists, men and women who have reached the age of understanding and who are stubborn, reproachful and inciting others not to recognize any government, may be put to death by fire and sword without trial of any kind. This was called the "blood edict" and it drove many out of the country because at this time there were a great many Bohemians and Moravian Baptists going over to Prussia. This edict was by the Emperor of Austria (Brons, p. 176).

1529—Early Holland Martyr Book.

These Baptists or Mennonites from an early date distributed papers, books and other writings to advance their religion. These were later gathered into a book. The Government began to have them destroyed, when they found the Baptists were making an effort to save them. The book was finished in 1562 and called the book of the sacrifices for the Lord. Five years later a second edition of the book came out and the Spanish Government tried to destroy it. But it was printed the third time and accounts of many later persecutions added. The first edition had only the persecutions up to 1529. The next one those up to 1559 killed in Holland, (Brons, p. 236).

1529—Luther Adopts Parts of Baptist Catechism.

The Bohemian and Moravian Waldenses, got up a little catechism about this time and Luther studied it and called attention to what he considered their mistakes; and in answer these Bohemians and Moravians tried to prove that Luther was wrong. Luther did not answer their attack; but it seems he copied much of it, changed it somewhat and published it as his catechism in 1529, (Brons, p. 53).

1529—Torture of Hans Hut (now Huth).

Brons, (p. 425) tells us of the torture of a Baptist in 1529 who bore what is now a familiar Lancaster county name—Hans Hut or Huth. Hut went to Augsburg in Bavaria and his brother John to Würtenbug. He was arrested there and taken to the tower. He tried to escape by a rope but fell off and lay as dead. A burning candle set the straw of his bed on fire which nearly suffocated him. In this half dead condition they took him to Court. He was condemned and burned, as the author who first wrote the narrative says he heard from the victim's own son. His offense was "free speech." This Martyrdom of Hans Hut is also found in Martyr's Mirror, p. 417).

1529—The Weidman Faction of Mennonites. (The Staff Mennonites and the Sword Mennonites).

Brons tells us (p. 424) that in Nickelsburg, there was a convention in 1529 of teachers. Hoffmier was chairman it seems. But there were present also Hans Huth, Oswald Vlait, Hans Pitmaier, Christian Rothmantel, Hans Werner, Strahl Weidman, Jacob Weidman and others. We see here the forbears of Lancaster county citizens. This convention was held under protection of Lichenstein, a Count of Germany, who had come over to the Mennonite doctrine. They discussed whether a Christian could go to war, carry weapons, pay war tax and similar subjects; but no conclusion was reached. Huth and Weidman were against it. They differed in opinion from Lichenstein, who thought patriotism made these things necessary. Huth was captured because he was against Lichenstein, but afterwards a friend helped him and let him down on a rope and he escaped. Lichtenstein wanted to bring Huth to his way of thinking.

This debate brought about another split and gave rise to two new parties or factions of Baptists. One was of the belief that weapons could be carried and that war taxes should be paid and the other that it should not be so. Those who split off, on the doctrine that Christians should not carry weapons, or pay taxes, followed Jacob Weidman to the number of about 200 to the great disgust of Count Lichtenstein, the powerful friend of the Mennonites and a believer in part of their doctrine. Still Lichtenstein went with his dissenters to his boundary line and gave them a drink and let them go.

They went to the Count at Austerlitz and begged him to take them and help them and he said he would if there were even a thousand of them, and he did help them. This party was called the "Staff" party or pilgrim Baptists or Mennonites and the other party the "Sword" party.

Men of power began to sympathize with the Mennonite movement, especially about the Wurtenburg in South Germany where these events happened.

There was a midle party also who were against war and carrying weapons and going to war but who were willing to pay war duties. To this latter party belong the Swiss Mennonites.

As the Baptists grew, the Catholics Church complained more and more and as a result the German emporer commanded Lichtenstein and Hoffmeier to come to Vienna, the capital of the German Empire, at that time.

As soon as Hoffmeier arrived he and his wife were captured and taken to the Castle Gravenstein and afterwards he gave out a statement that as far as bearing arms was concerned, he believed the same as Count Lichtenstein. Later however, he regretted yielding so far and said he was guilty of not being firm enough in the faith and wrote to the Nickelsburg congregation that he had become too weak but that they should hold fast to the faith? Soon afterwards the congregation received the sad news that their dear teacher was burned to death and that his wife was drowned. But it seems Lichtenstein escaped punishment.

1529—Baptist Rally at Emden, in Germany.

Brons tells us (p. 390) that, the fall of this year some preachers came together at Emden, most of whom were Baptists. They tried to come to a definite view on the principal doctrines, especially on the Lord's supper. But by this time the Lutheran view of the same had grown very strong. The Baptists semed to become more divided. They differed much from their leaders, Hoffman and others too. They said their views were right. They were an extreme branch of Baptists about Hanover, Germany.

Melchoir Hoffman baptized 300 people in 1529 about Emden. He was a valiant worker. This was the only place outside of the Roman Empire, except the neighboring territory of East Freidland in the Duchy of Albrecht in Prussia where the Baptist faith could feel any safety. Hoffman came there and worked and baptized all these people. Shortly after his arrival he baptized them in the Ancient Church. They did not seem to be quite settled. He came to this place (Emden or Embden) in August, 1529. He had two opponents against him, (Brons, pp. 385 and 386). One spoke against Hoffman from the pulpit and another preacher Olmsdorf followed his example. Also the preacher of the Danish Crown prince was against him. Hoffman challenged them all to meet him in public debate but they refused.

At Keil in Northern Germany on the Baltic Sea in the Gray Cloister, Hoffman debated the Lord's Supper, April 8, 1529. The whole place was filled. After Burgenhagen, by order of the King, had made the first speech, the Crown Prince and all of the people present fell on their knees to pray. Burgenhagen was the great theologian of the Crown Prince, (Brons, p. 379).

Six clerks were put on oath to take the debate in writing correctly or lose their souls. All the learned people and the aristocrats took seats near the Crown Prince, while those disputing were standing.

Hoffman was asked why he called all the preachers false prophets in his books and he said because they all preached a wrong view of the Lord's supper. And then a long debate followed. Hoffman here alone against the learned theologians of Northern Germany, opposed the doctrine of transubstantiation. This Bungenhagen was a great friend of Luther, the same as Melanchthon. This part of Denmark was, in those times part of Germany, (Brons, p. 381).

1539—The End of George Plauroch or "Strong George"—A Mennonite Father.

Müller tells us (p. 30) that Blauroch was the best known and best loved in 1520 of all the leaders of the Mennonite people. He labored in Chur (Switzerland) and could bring the doctrines down to the common people's understanding better than any other man. He labored in different places in Switzerland for the Baptist faith, and was driven out of Switzerland February 2, 1529. He was a reformer of Tyrol also, till August 30, 1529 and was then burned to death. So ended the beloved "Strong George" which was his lovable nickname by the people of Tyrol and Switzerland. He was a second Paul in the view of these Baptists or Mennonites.

1530—Familiar Lancaster County Names About Zurich.

In 1530, besides Müller there were the following Mennonites about lower Switzerland, toward Basel: Balthaser Stall and Hans Ruschacher (may be now Ricksecker) the tile maker of Eglisan, north of Zurich—Gabrill, the brickmaker of Tossriedun, near the same place—Casper Killer, Hans Nespler, Konrad Sewer (Sower), Jacob Schmidt, Burkhard Henry, Margaret and Ursula Myers, Appollonie Schnider and Ann Margaret and Julia Wiener, all of Bülach, a few miles almost directly south of Eglisan — also Musterlis Bub of Oberglatt, a few miles south, slightly west of Bülach— Hans Flumer of Wuningen, a few miles northwest of Zurich—also Jorg Stephen, Joder Ann and Eva Myers and Margaret Melcher of Watwill, near Keppel, far east of Zurich—Elsie Muchli or Oberhasli, a few miles north of Zurich—Margaret of Mettenhhasli, Adelaide Schwarz (or Black) of Dallikon, both near Oberhasli—Regula and Verona Kern of Nussbaumen, southwest of Zurich and Ann Fürst of Watt, north of Zurich. Working with these were foreign Mennonites, among them, Henry Spattig of Dottikon, among the mountains of the South; Hans of Horb in Wittenburg, Germany; Ann Sittler of Zug and several persons named Berkhald. Of these whole families were imprisoned —husbands and wives separated and the sect in Zurich greatly reduced. Dr. Egli also mentions with these, Hans of John Bruppacher. Thus we see that at this early period there were living in the Canton of Zurich, both in the lowlands north of the City of Zurich and in the mountains to the south, the ancestor families of the Common Lancaster County and eastern Pennsylvania names familiar today, viz:—Stoll, Ricksecker, Keller, Sowers, Schmidt Burkhard, Myers, Schneider, Weiner, Yoder, Schwartz, Fürst, Sittler, Burkholder and Brubaker. I have set this item out at such length because of this fact, (Zur., p. 87 and 88).

1530—Conrad Winkler—Leader and Martyr.

There was also Conrad Winkler of Wasserburg, southeast of Zurich among the hills. Dr. Egli (p. 89) tells us that Winkler was for several years leader of the Anabaptists in the lowlands, north of Zurich and came to visit them from the mountains of the South. He was drowned January 20, 1530 by the State authorities.

1530—Schwenkfeld, Working With Hoffman.

Brons tells us (p. 392) that in Strasburg, Germany, Casper Schwenkfeld was in close touch with Hoffman. Both of them asked to be allowed to give a public debate on their principles. They were accused of being heretics and Schwenkfeld in his petition asserts he is no heretic nor seducer and he wants protection. He was against the State Church. He was the father of the Schwenkfelders of today and of the last nearly four centuries.

1530—Factions Cause Religious Excitement and Fear of "End of the World."

Brons tells us (p. 58) that in 1530 the Diet of Augsburg was opened to the Lutherans of Germany. At this Diet the Anabaptists or Mennonites were particularly, severely condemned, because of opposition to infant baptism. Under these conditions the common people thought the "world was coming to an end" and there were all kinds of literature on the subject. Then Hoffman came out and wrote that the revelations are being fulfilled, and he explained how this was the case. Hoffman was leader of the principle faction of the Mennonites, as we have seen. He attacked Luther and said Luther makes himself a new God who can save or damn at will and that he calls all who do not believe as he does "Heretics.'

1530—Morals of the Anabaptists Compared With Other Reformers.

In 1530 Müller (p. 2) Philip of Hessen wrote, "I find these Baptist people who are called dreamers and heretics are purer than those that are Lutherans." This he stated in a letter dated February 18, 1530 to his sister, Elizabeth of Saxony. Capito goes further and says that the most of these Anabaptists were in his opinion anything but bad—they possessed fear of God and Holy Zeal. And he considered them, as dear brethren, even though he was not wholly one of them, but was an Italian, partly proselyted.

1530 — Anabaptist Movement Toward Berne.

Müller tells us (p. 46) that about 1530, when these Anabaptists had gained some freedom, they gathered in great numbers and moved toward Berne from the Zurich tortures. Berne began to deplore the fact; for they were now giving trouble there. October 13, 1530, Pfister Meyer complained to Baden that the Taufers or Anabaptists were being badly used in the new regions and they demanded protection. But they received none, of course. "Pfister" is a name met with in Lancaster county today.

The growth was such now, that in January, 1530, a general conference was held by delegates from Zurica, Bern, Basil, St. Gallen and Constance, and they unanimously held that the Taufers or Anabaptists were becoming very dangerous and that there was a great falling off noticed from the true Christian Church—that is, the Reformed Church. It was decided that a report should be made, so that at the next meeting they would know how to go about curbing and breaking up those "erring ones" by common concerted action.

1531—Hoffman's Followers Proselyte In Holland.

Brons tells us (p. 396) that this year there were nine men proselyting to the Anabaptist faith in Belgium and Holland. They were taken from their beds and put into the Hague prison. Their main offense was rebaptizing those baptized in infancy. November 15th, they were beheaded in Brussels. Thus it happened these ambassadors of Hoffman were executed without accomplishing their desire.

1531—"Taufers" Go Into Prussian Lands.

This year saw the beginning of the Taufer or Anabaptist movement into Prussia, where it was safe for them. They began to go into East Friesland also about this time. These parts of Germany were asylums also for people from all sections, persecuted for the sake of their religion, (Brons, p. 243).

1531—Early Labors of Menno Simon.

This year a girl from near East Friesland, about 12 years old was in a convent and she heard of people being burned at the stake on account of their religion and it made such an impression on her that she secured a Latin Bible to get a clear notion and when she grew up her views became known. She was pronounced a heretic and imprisoned a year. Then other nuns interceded for her and the Superior allowed her to escape disguised as a milk maid and go to Lecr. Here she found a Mennonite Home and she joined them. Then she went to Linworden and associated with a Mennonite woman named Hadein. She was the widow of a man who at the beheading of Siche Drerick Schnider, beat drum so that his dying speech could not be heard. This widow was soon afterwards convinced of the correctness of the new faith and was one of the first ones baptized by Meno Simon. (Brons, p. 109).

1531—Mennonite and Reformed Debate at Berne.

In April, 1531, there appeared in print the report of a debate between Pfister Myer and several Reformed preachers on the subject of second baptism—oaths—taking part in Government and other Mennonite articles. The report was called, "A Christian Discussion Held at Bern, Between Pfister Myer and the Reformed Preachers. The report states that Myer was compelled to disavow some of his doctrine. This was the same Pfister who was complained against by the Bern authorities as being so strong. (Müller, p. 46).

1531—Bern Orders Zolothurn to Punish the Anabaptists, (Mennonites).

Bern, which is west of Zurich, now began to feel the influence of the Mennonites coming from Zurich and the east where they were driven. Reports came in from the smaller towns, and Bern ordered the authorities of one of them named Zolothurn to punish them, or if they were not able, to allow the Bern authorities to do so. These Mennonites were holding meetings. It was feared the new sect would get a stronghold on the country. Zolothurn answered that April 1st, all the Sheriffs were ordered to drive them out everywhere; and besides it was forbidden under a penalty of 10 pounds fine, for anyone to give them shelter. Zolothurn reported that if the few leaders can be gotten hold of, the movement will cease. And thus said this town, there is no need that Bern authorities should come and help (Müller, p. 32).

1531—Death of Zwingli.

This year too, at the Battle of Kappel in Switzerland, Zwingli, the "Reformed" leader, who was also chaplain in the army at Zurich, was accidentally killed. He fell a martyr to the dangers of war.

1531—The Name "Taufer" or "Mennonite" Used Contemptuously.

So odious and yet so strong had grown the Anabaptist or Wiedertaufer or Mennonite cause at this time in Switzerland, that whenever anyone showed an extraordinary zeal in any view different from the Lutheran doctrine in Germany, he was called in derision a "Taufer" or an Arch-Taufer. Weitzel in a letter dated 1531, tells us this, (Müller, p. 6). About the same time Hans Ballinger of Zurich, a minister of the Reformed church, wrote a book against the Mennonites calling it the "Brazen Faced, Shameless, Wicked, Erring and False Teachings of the

1561—Close of the Reformation in Zurich.

The Battle of Kappel, October 11, 1531, closed the Reformation in Zurich, but for the next two years there were a great many mandates and orders directed against Anabaptists, (Zur., p. 90).

1532—Mennonite Progress About Berne.

The Anabaptists (Mennonites) now continued to grow in the Canton of Bern. August 17, 1532 the Baliiiff of Sumiswald about twenty miles northeast of the city of Bern, reported that these Baptists now continue in their activity without letup and the Council went on to say they expected good results from the printed reports of the debates, in which they felt the Mennonites could not and did not successfully uphold their side. This little book or report the authorities throughout the canton or State of Bern, ordered to be read before the congregations against the Taufers or Mennonites. But during all this time the council heard continual reports that these Taufers or Baptists won their case or debate at Sumiswald and the people were beginning in great numbers to believe in them and this gave Council great uneasiness. In Zofingen, about 35 miles northeast of Bern, the Mennonites preached publicly without much fear, since they had most of the people with them, (Müller, p. 69).

The growth about the city of Bern became so great, that orders were in 1532 also sent out to the Sheriff of Aarburg, a town about three miles northwest of the last named town, to check their growth in any way they could. So the officials began to hunt up and arrest them. In Solothurn, a large town about 18 miles almost directly north of Bern City, the brotherhood was very strong. Haller wrote to Ballinger (an enemy of the Taufers) that there these Mennonites had the upper hand and they met openly and freely. Therefore Berne sent orders to them to prevent it or allow Berne to do so. Berne complained that Solothurn seems to take no interest in trying to stop their growth, (Müller, p. 72).

1532—Spread of Anabaptism in Berne.

Müller tells us (p. 72) that after 1532 the Taüfers (or Mennonites) spread into and over the state or Canton of Berne very extensively. And in August of that year, orders were sent to the Sheriffs of Aarburg, 30 miles northeast of the city of Berne, of Thun, 12 miles southeast of Berne —of Unterseen, near the same place —of Interlacken about the same place—of Hasti six miles northeast of Berne and to the Sheriffs of the whole Upland—to the Sheriffs of Trachseiwald, 10 miles almost directly east of Berne, of Signau, also close by—and in January, 1533 and in other times during the year, to the Sheriffs of Zolothurn, Summisvil and other places all about Berne, commanding all of them to bring these Anabaptists into subjection, calling attention to the fact that prior orders were not effectively carried out.

1532— Extinction of the Taüfers or Anabaptist Mennonites About Zurich.

Dr. Egli in his work says (p. 91) that after the battle of Kappel, October 11, 1531, that the reform movement in that section closes, although the next two years a good many orders and mandates were issued. But a change had come, and the state did not prosecute those that were left, so hard as before.

He also says that these Taüfers were up to this time in three principal centers—the Zurich district—the Groeningen district 15 miles southeast and in the low country 25 miles north of Zurich. And these were large centers. But now they became broken up into many smaller centers, and small Anabaptist meetings were held all around, over the whole country. There were many small bodies of them in the Knonow district, about 20 miles southwest of Zurich, where the movement against them ended in 1533. These Baptists, it seems, in both the parts of this country, got new strength—new adherents sprang up when the war was ended. But the Catholic Church yet was their enemy; but they did not do much of importance against them, except cause two executions.

1532—Early Baptist Doctrine in Hymns.

In 1532, Otmar Rote or Roth of St. Gallen, composed a fine hymn, which is set forth by Brons, (p. 173). And in this hymn the chief elements of the Taüfer or Mennonite belief of that time is expressed. The substance of this as shown in the hymn is, that we must live true and right, that sin brings pain, we must be righteous, clean and humble. It declares that we must not imitate the worldly ones —that we must not talk about evil nor become familiar with it—we must be just—that no sin will be allowed to be unpunished—we must fear God —ask for grace early and late and not repel by force, but submit, as the Savior taught.

1532—Bohemian Anabaptists or Taüfers Preach from Palestine and Egypt to Switzerland and Westward.

We are told that the Anabaptists of Bohemia and Moravia rejected infant baptism—did not give their ministers any salary, but furnished them food and provisions—required that they should all follow some trade and make their living in that way so as not to be paid for teaching God's word. These Bohemian Anabaptist or Mennonite preachers, traveled and preached throughout Asia, in Palsetine and Egypt and other places in Africa. They also came into Switzerland and other places to the West in Europe, about 1532, (Müller, p. 56).

1532—Taüfers (Mennonites) Spread to the Baltic.

By this date says Brons (p. 245), quoting Duke Albrecht, very many Anabaptists or Taüfers had reached the Baltic region. Their spreading had become a very serious matter. The Duke did not understand their mild nature and he feared the excesses and boisterous conduct of that branch of adventurers led by Münzer some time before, farther South, who were rebellious and warlike and hurt the cause, would be repeated. Menno Simon in his defense was very careful to impress upon the rulers the fact that he never had any sympathy with the Münzerites, though he was accused of it.

Duke Albrecht, therefore, wrote to Luther and asked him what to do with these masses of new religionists who were now rising on the Baltic—these Taüfers or Mennonites. He called them a sect of factious and restless spirits or sacramentarians. Luther replied that the Duke need not especially fear them for all adherents of adult baptism are the same. He said he was afraid the Lutheran interests would suffer by too many divisions among the Reform people. They should all try to get together he said, as he still has serious war with Catholics. So, said Luther, "There will be no end to dispute and discussions and the best thing is not to irritate these people but rather to shun them and not interfere with them."

1532 — Hoffman's Writings Comfort Holland Taüfers.

In 1532, Hoffman was again in Strasburg and there he continued to write. His writings reached Holland and were a great comfort to the Taüfers there in the Netherlands. They took heart and hope again. Many of them now were fugitives in the Netherlands and they were encouraged to know Melchoir Hoffman, their leader, was still fighting the cause. Holland was early through with her persecutions and cooled off sooner than some other countries. She became an asylum for persecuted Mennonites from Germany and Switzerland toward the end of the 16th century and remained so (Brons, p. 396).

1532—Taüfer Debate at Soffingen.

Müller tells us (p. 35) that from July 1st to 9th, 1532, there was a big debate at Soffingen, Switzerland on religious matters, and also the same year in St. Gallen Canton, Switzerland another debate. Twenty-three Taüfer or Anabaptist debaters met all opponents who desired to come. But when it was found they were getting the best of the arguments, they were kept closed up in a barn.

Froschaur of Zurich had the proceedings printed however, and they are very full of interest. There were many more prominent Anabaptist debates too; and some of the principal Mennonite or Taüfer or Anabaptist debaters named are Martin Weninger, Hans Hock, Simon Lantz, Michael Utt (the tailor or schneider), Christian Brugger (Bricker).

The prominent debaters against the Taüfers were Micahel Haller—Bechtold Haller, Casper Megander, Sebastian Hoffmeister, George Stehle, Heinrich Linkey (Lincki), Sutzer of Basil and Henry Morider. The discussion ended at a session at Aarian, where the minutes were revised to print them.

The opponents told the chief debater for the Taüfers, Brugger or Bricker that he shall declare whether he will confess himself convinced they are wrong and secede from them. And he declared neither he nor any other of them would do so. He was told then they must all leave and if they come back they would be "geschwimmt" that is, swimmed or drowned. He did come back and his arrest was ordered, and he was likely drowned.

1532— Taüfer or Mennonite Demand for Separation of Church and State.

Ernst Müller, (p. 34) states that in this year at Soffingen (Switzerland) the Taüfers or Baptists held and sent forth the demand that the state must not interfere with matters of faith and conscience—that the state has nothing to do with religion. They set forth as the state had been so cruel to them, they never found cause to be enthusiastic about the Government nor show any patriotism. They stated that their ideas of justice were Evangelical and come from the scriptures. Their views of justice they said were according to apostolic models rather than those of the statutes and those enforced by the police, the inquisition, the dungeon, the galleys and the piles of fagots and fire.

1532—Taüfers or Mennonites Win the People.

When the minutes of the debate of 1532 got into circulation, there was trouble. Finally it was arranged that printed reports of it were to be given out to the sheriffs and officers. The rumor became current that the Anabaptists had gotten the better of the argumens and therefore the government sent out printed copies of the debate much modified to deny the rumors, that the Taüfers had succeeded. (Müller 70).

1532—Casper Swenkfeldt and His Followers.

Casper Swenkfeldt moved to Strasburg in Germany in 1532 and labored for religion in that section. He wrote from that place to Leo Judä, the Anabaptist and to Hoffman that he does not longer patronize them and their doctrine except to that extent which is consistent with the spirit of Christ, according as he interpreted it. He began therefore his new faith and sect, which also have lived down to our day. He seems however to have had intimate spiritual intercourse with Hoffman; and to have had a quieting effect on him. They both asked the established (Catholic) church to have a debate with them. Swenkfeldt was accused of being a worse heretic than Hoffman, and thus in his petition for a debate he avers that he is not a heretic and challenges all mankind to prove him one. A discussion was held by Swenkfeldt and Hoffman on June 11, 1533 jointly against the Church of the State, which seems to show that even at that date Swenkfeldt had not split very far off the Mennonite Church and faith.

Both these champions of non-resisting Christian religion had a hard fate. Hoffman was condemned to prison for life and died there. Swenkfeldt did not fare so hard. He was orderd out of town. Although he split from Hoffman's faith, he had deep sympathy for him, which he showed in his letter to Leo Judä July 3, 1533. In the same letter he also replied to his critics who accuse him of denying both Christ and God and shows that he is as orthodox as the most fervent can be in that regard (Brons 402).

Hoffman languished in jail several years. In 1534 Swenkfeldt and Martin Zell and Casper Medio visited him and found him sick in body and in spirit. He was badly treated and they asked that he be treated more kindly; but it seems that neither he nor his friends made application to get him out of jail. Their requests for kinder treatment of him were not heeded; and he died after being in jail six years about 1540, rather than give up or even change his religion one iota (Brons 405). I speak thus at large of Hoffman, because his is a common name in our own county today.

1535—Three Hundred Anabaptists Imprisoned in Holland.

Müller tells us (p. 159) that a group of fugitives, 300 in number besides women and children were barricaded or imprisoned in a convent near Witmarsum, the home of Menno Simon, in Friesland, Holland, this year, after they had been overwhelmed. Subsequently they were tortured and the women drowned, under the cruel edict of Charles V of Spain and Emperor of Germany, who ruled Holland as well.

1535—Charles V and the Münsterites —Enemy of Baptists.

Müller tells us (p. 159) that in many places and particulars the "reform

COMPLETE CONVERSION OF MENNO SIMON

movement" was nipped in the bud by the activity of Charles V against it. Charles took advantage of any circumstance he could to condemn these people, and especially any shortcoming or fault in the movement he was ready to turn to its disadvantage. Therefore great hurt was brought about to the Anabaptists or Taüfers by the rebellious followers of John Matthias and John Bockelsohn of Münster. These people, called Münsterites were rebellious, law-breaking and often of immoral conduct and practice; and they tried to make it appear that they were genuine Anabaptists and paraded in the garb of the same, much to the disgust of both the government and the religious forces. Menno Simon tried his influence with them, but it only resulted in them trying to besmirch him too. And in his history of his life and works, he takes great pains to inform the reader that he never belonged to the Münsterites although he says he was accused of it. They were wild agitators and they cruelly persecuted all others who did not believe as they did. On their banners they carred emblazoned all of the warnings and dire threats of the Revelations (Müller 159).

1535—A Nuremburg Translation of the Bible.

This year says Müller (p. 68) a translation of the Bible was made at Nuremburg, at a great expense and sacrifice by the descendants of the Waldenses, which Waldensean doctrine the Anabaptists or Taüfers or Mennonites largely carried out and continued from early days. The translation was into German.

1536—Menno Simon Completely Leaves Catholicism.

In 1536 Menno Simon severed his connection with the Catholic church and changed his care-free life for poverty and distress and lived in the fear of the Lord and sought out people of like mind to associate with him. By devoting himself to his cause, he found peace, says Brons (p. 65). About a year later says the same author, a body of men who were Taüfers called upon him near Witmarsum; his home, and said they were disgusted with the different upstarts who uesd to lead them and that therfore, they had now come to him and they pleaded with him and begged him that he should take to heart the leaderless condition of the Anabaptists or Taüfers and the hard lot under which they suffered. They complained that the men who assumed to lead them were too mystical and fantastic and were impracticable idealists—they called them "Schwärmers" or rovers—they said these leaders were constantly falling into fanaticism and reveries and withdrew themselves away from people and became monastic and did them no good. Menno's heart was touched by this, says Brons; but he said he doubted his ability to meet the educated opposition against the Anabaptists and also that he was of so shy and modest a nature he feared he was not the man to lead them. He said he was too "blödigkeit" or bashful and did not have the "fähigkeiten" or capability to do the work. He told them, however, to be patient and he would consider the matter in prayer and if it was God's will that he should lead them he could no more refuse to preach and teach than Paul who said, "Woe unto me if I do not preach the Gospel." And says Brons, he decided it was his duty to lead these people; and from that time on they stood as solid as a rock in the great movement of reform, which was now active all over Europe like the great wakes and tides of the ocean. Then numbers gathered around him and they were rebaptized. He began now to teach fearlessly and he sent many encouraging doctrinal letters to many places to help others.

The three events that made Menno Simon the leader of the Holland Wiedertaufers or Anabaptists were, first, his meditations over the execution of Sicke Snyder about 1528 because he was re-baptized—then the shutting up of 300 or more of these Baptists in a prison-convent near him, and the destruction of them for their faith, and finally the request of the Anabaptists we have just mentioned to him, to lead them.

1536—Combined Action in All Switzerland Against Anabaptists.

Müller, tells us (p. 34) that a meeting of the officers and political powers of the towns of Zurich, Bern, Basel, Schoffhausen, St. Gallen, Mühlhausen and Biel, all places in Switzerland, was held at Basil in 1536 and there they composed and worked out a common form of confession, including several articles against second baptism and against the Taüfers or Mennonites, etc. The 24th articles of this was that there must be a common proceedings or movement against second baptism and the Wiedertaufers and declaring that all who separate from the Holy Church (Catholic) must be punished as a duty to God, by the high authorities of the Church and the State and must be prevented from polluting the people and poisoning their minds with their doctrines. Officers were then appointed at this convention of the above chief cities of Switezrland, to see that the demand of the "Holy Church" was carried out.

1536—Bern Mennonites Flee to Moravia and Russia.

Müller tells us (p. 93) that about this time many of the oppressed Weidentaufers of Bern in Switzerland moved to Moravia and Russia. Therefore the Mennonite Church in Russia is also very old. They found Moravia, he says, a new Jerusalem and a haven of peace and rest from their torture. There they remained in peace a long time. Then calamities arose among them there from State and Church, but they endured until 1622, when they received a fatal blow, which almost exterminated them, from Russia. But during nearly all this time Moravia was an asylum until suddenly in 1622 they received there also the "todesstosb" or death blow.

1536—The Berne Mennonites Go to Help the French Huguenots.

In 1536 Harry Frantz Nageli (no doubt a remote ancestor of the Negleys of our county and State) at the head of the Berne army of great mass of Taüfers at Waadt conquered much of the opposition against the sect. November 29th, he in company with a fellow christian named Yost, of Diesbach were sent as messengers to France to speak and plead for the Huguenots and their religion. He labored to have persecution against them cease. For these reasons Müller speaks of Nageli as a leader of and at the head of the Bern Taüfers or Mennonites at this time. Nageli had difficulty to make the French King understand as Naegli's language could not be understood in

France. But he did manage to explain to the King the cause of the rise and organization of the Taüfers or Anabaptist Mennonites and especially laid stress upon the point that the priests and leaders of the Catholic church had become corrupt in early days and also that the subject of infant baptism also caused the secession, (Müller, p. 83).

1537—Berne Executions (Lancaster County and Pennsylvania Names)

About this time among others the following people were executed for their faith, in and abount Berne. In 1537 Bernard Wälti (now Welty)—John Sweitzer, Serf Hoffer, Ulrich Bichsel (now Bixler)—Barbara Willher (now Weiler)—Catharine Friedley, Berna Steli (now Sthely or Staley). In 1538 Peter Stecker, Ulrich Huber, Hans Willer or Weiler, Elizabeth Rupser or Rupp, Peter Bestmiller, Stephen Ricksecker and Rudolph Staley. In 1539 Lawrence Haberly, John Shumacker, Peter Unter —in 1543 Christian Oberlin, John Unter and Waldi or Waldo Garber.

Nearly all of these we recognize to be familiar Lancaster county and eastern Pennsylvania names of people living among us today; and our neighbors are no doubt relatives of these ancient martyrs for conscience sake. This shows again what a large number of our southeastern Pennsylvania families came from ancestry who 400 years ago lived in the mountains of Switzerland, before their later generations moved down the Rhine into the Palatinate, (Müller, p. 78).

1537—Berne Again Demands Solothurn Anabaptists to Be Crushed Out.

In 1537 says Müller (p. 73) messengers were again sent from the Council of Berne to the authorities of Zolothurn and declared that at Ettigen and Lusbligen there are many Anabaptists or Mennonites; and that if the Zolothurn authorities do not kill them according to orders, Berne will take a hand in it. Zolothurn was a center where the people were shown favors and mercy. Those who came from Zolothurn to Berne were sent back to be disposed of. In the early Waldensean times before the days of the Reformation the Waldenseans had gained a foothold in Zolothurn and therefore we must remember that even in 1737 this faith was 200 years old them. That is why they had such strength there. There were persons high in authority there who were Anabaptists or now Mennonites, whose ancestors going back several generations planted the faith there. This is why the State or Canton authorities at Berne were so anxious about it. Solothurn or Zolothurn is a good sized city nearly equidistant between Berne and Basil, being about 15 miles almost directly north of Berne.

1538—New Tortures in Berne and Basel.

Right after the religious discussion or debate in Berne which was held in 1538 the feeling against the Anabaptists or Taüfers reached its high water mark. The debate was won by these baptists. The authorities now knew that all former means to suppress them had failed. And the movement went on. So henceforth a forcible extermination was decided on and there were many executions of which there are no public records. If they were in prison every means was used to make them give up and when these failed they were killed. The order was if they do not yield to ordinary questioning, "You must interrogate them with a rope." But this was not to include women. It was also ordered that the property of the Baptists who have no children must be taken by the State at the death of the owner. In August 17, 1538 the Catholic Bishop of Basel sent out an order that no Anabaptists were to be allowed in his bishopric at all. They must leave or be killed, (Müler, p. 82).

1538—The Name "Haldeman" Appears.

This year in Eggvil, Switzerland, we find the name "Haldeman" so familiar to us and so prominent in Lancaster county and Eastern Pennsylpania, used the first time. This is about 375 years ago. Müller tells us (p. 75) that Thüring Haldeman was ordered this year to "walk the plank" or be killed. That is, he was to go on board a vessel and leave or suffer death.

1538—Houstten (or Hochtetten) and Signau Demand Another Religious Debate.

In February and March of 1538 says Müller (p. 79) a discussion on religion was demanded by the above towns. The attempt was made to prove the Old Testament equal to the New. This was an argument against the Taufers, who largely avoided the Old. At this debate Rappenstein and Pfeister Myer, the converted Baptists or Taufers, who in Soflingen had done good work, were present and entered the debate. The minutes of this decussion are still extant in two copies in the State Archives in Berne. Strange Baptists were present also and some of them spoke a great deal. Michael Utt (the tailor)—Matthias Weiser—Henry Weninger of Schloffhausen. There were Hans Hatz, George Trasser of Bavaria. Of these, Weiser, Trasser and Hatz spoke most. From the Berne neighborhood, there were John Vogt, and Hans Luthi who spoke. There were also present from Eggvil, Bernard Vergerter, Ulrich Wenenschwander, Bernard Jenruy, Christian Salzman—Waldi Gerber of Rotherbach—Ulrich and Klaws Rupp of Stauffen—Hans Schellenberg, John Krahenbuhl (Graybill), Friedli Dieboldswiler, all of Signau — Peter Schwendimann and Felix Shumaker of Big Hochstetten—Casper Kalb or Kulp and Andrew Shindler or Shindle of Thun—Casper Zugg, Frantz Oberly and John Haslibach—Jos. Meischer, Uli Flickinger, Christian Bricker, Jacob Sutter, and Jacob Caspar of Aarburg—Uli Hunsicker, Hans Gusper, Michael Zink, Hans Snyder and Beit Herman, and others were present. Amongst these we find many names today familiar in Eastern Pennsylvania. All of which shows us where our ancestors lived and moved nearly 400 years ago and where they were even before Columbus sailed on his voyage of discovery.

The four presidents who managed this debate (Müller, p. 80) had the minutes compiled and reported to the Council of Berne and it was ordered that four copies be made and the same be put in the library. The Mennonites wanted a copy of the minutes too but it was refused on the ground that it was a report and not a discussion for the public. This explains how those ancient books got into the library where they are today. They would not allow extra copies to be made for the Baptists.

THE EMMENTHAL FILLS UP WITH MENNONITES 49

1538—Mennonites Drifting Into the Emmenthal.

In 1538 a conference between Berne and the Bishop of Basel at Münster was held. The inhabitants of Münster were subjects of the Bishop of Basel and since 1486 they were also connected or had certain city rights in Münster. Wattenbach and Ferrell in Münster introduced the Reformation here and in the valley of the Emmenthal. This is important history, especially to citizens of Lancaster county, because it was to the valley of the Emmenthal, northeast of Berne a short distance, that the persecuted Mennonites gathered, from whom and from whose descendants, came from that place, the first ten or twelve pioneers who reached Amsterdam in March, 1710—London about May, remaining to the end of June and finally reached the Pequea, now in Lancaster county, in October, 1710.

The result of the conference at Münster was that both Berne and Basel should contrive to wipe out "this damned sect." Berne said to the Bishop of Basel, "What shall we do to wipe them out? The Sheriffs and Officers lead such bad lives they can not punish anyone." The answer was get other sheriffs. But said Basil, "It is your own question to deal with; we do not want to interfere," (Müller, p. 235).

1538—Herrs, Graafs, Mylins, Landises and Others Become Mennonites.

Ezra E. Eby of Berlin, Ont., in his book on the Eby family says: The Ebys belong to the Celts, an ancient Asiatic race. During the early ages lived in Northern part of Italy and were brought from heathendom through the Vandois (Waldenes). From the 8th to the 11th Century these Vandois became numerous. The Church of Rome tried to exterminate them. In 1453 the whole Valley of Luzerne was laid under an' interdict. In 1487, Innocent the XIII began an order of extermination against them; a large number fled and went to the Northern part of Switzerland. They finally settled in Bern, Luzeren, Zurich and Schweyz. Among the Vandois (Waldenes) who settled in these countries were the "Ebees." These Swiss Waldenes when Menno Simon founded the Mennonite Church in 1538 joined hm. Among those who joined were the names of Herr, Graaf, Mylin, Shank, Witmer, Landis, Eby and others. Some of these are of Teutonic origin which proves the Waldenes had accessions from that source, after arrival in Switzerland.

1538—Offreus Greisinger Destroyed.

Greisinger is a common Eastern Pennsylvania name, numerous in Lancaster county. Thus I give this item on his sufferings and death. The Martyrs' Mirror, page 432, tells us that, in 1538, a Greisinger resident of Tyrol in Austria of the same stock as the Swiss and Germans, after being sought in mountain and valley was caught, after a large reward was offered for him. He was a preacher among the Taüfers and kept many of them encouraged to hold on. They tried to make him recant but he declared he would "endure all pain unto death."

Then they drew him up by a rope about his neck, but quickly let him down and threatened hm saying he would be torn limb from limb. He said, "I am in your hands." Eight days later they drew him up again and let him down but he would not recant. Eight days later they threatened him again but did nothing. Then he was sentenced to death and placed in the fire and burned to ashes, on Halloween, 1538.

1538—Michael Weidman's Sufferings and Death.

The same book tells us, page 433, that, "About this time also Brother Michael Weidman or Beck was apprehended at Ricten, in Allegau, together with some other persons, which others persons, however were sent home, while this brother was put in prison for the faith. Many things were resorted to with him, and he was admonished to renounce, but he had a good assurance of his faith in Christ, and said: "When I was living with the world in all unrighteousness, in sins and wickedness, no one admonished me to renounce, but I was considered a good Christian before the world." After being imprisoned almost half a year, he was beheaded and burned. Here we find another old German or Swiss martyr of nearly four centuries ago, whose surname is common here in Lancaster county today.

1538—Caspar Schumacher's Sufferings.

In the same book the sufferings of another remote ancestor of a large Lancaster county and Eastern Pennsylvania family of today are given, page 433, as follows: "In the year 1538, the brethren Martin of Vilgraten, and Caspar Schumacher, were both apprehended for the divine truth, at Michelsberg, in Priesterthal, and after steadfastness, sentenced to death, and executed with the sword, thus manfully persevering in the faith unto the end. They were of good cheer in their bonds and tribulation and held fast to the love of God, from which they could not be separated through tribulation, fear, persecution, hunger, nakedness, or danger.

1538—Our Mennonite Ancestors Suffered Also Under English Decrees.

In the Martyrs' Mirror, page 434, it is stated: "After manifold tyranny, persecution and putting to death," writes P. J. Twisck, "in various countries and kingdoms, against the Christian flock, also in England, a decree was proclaimed December, to the ordianance of Christ. By virtue of the same, they, right in the face of cold winter, were banished from the country, and had to flee whithersover they could. Thus it came, that some of them fled for refuge to Holland, and having come to Delft, they were there spied out by their enemies, and fell into the hands of the tyrants; and, after manifold trials, and steadfastness in their faith, they were sentenced to death for the truth, at said place, and, on the 7th of January, A. D. 1539, put to death. Sixteen men were beheaded with the sword, and fifteen women drowned.

1539—Häuser Mennonites in Stainerbrunn, Austria.

A part of the Häuser Baptist who went under Brother Häuser to Hungary were named accordingly Häuser Baptists or Mennonites. They were understood to make great and strong profession. Some of them later went to Prussia. A little party who came from Stainerbrunn, Austria, lived unmolested there until 1539. But when they had grown to be a numerous congregation, then the Catholic Priests informed the King and they had officers with armed men and on horseback sent against them. December 6, 1539 some of the officers appeared before the houses of the brethren and took every one of the male members prisoners. The Catholic mob robbed whatever they could. The main purpose of the expedition was to get the treasures of these people. The overseer of the congregation of Austerliz was taken prisoner; and he with all the others were taken to the Castle of Falkenstein. This happened near Stainerbrunn in Austria as we have said. They took 150 priosners and among them were some who had not been as yet baptized or taken up into the congregation, (Brons, p. 431).

1539—Täufers or Mennonites Buried Paupers in Potter's Fields.

It was decided in 1539 in Berne that the Baptists ex-communicated from the Catholic church should not be buried on holy ground. The theory of the church was that whoever in his life time was not in the church, could not be buried in holy ground. According to an order of 1539, they were not allow to be buried in any of the cemeteries, and this decree was in force until 1695, (Müller, p. 362).

1540—Our Mennonite Ancestors as Galley Slaves.

In the early times the maritime nations had to have slaves in their galleys to propel them before steam engines were invented; and scores of strong men were captured constantly and chained to the oars of these war vessels. They used to take all convicts and people whose lives were of no account and make them propel the galleys. Some of the Swiss cantons agreed with the Republic of Venice and with Italy and France by treaties to supply them with slaves for the galleys. So they took these Mennonites and sent them. This saved Switzerland the trouble and expense of their prisoners and the sea countries were glad to get them. Venice had great wars with Turkey and needed them. Her ambassadors requested Swiss galley slaves and this made the Swiss officers very active to do this for them, particularly because it would rid the country of these Baptists. The Swiss got their idea from France. In this way France treated the Huguenots. Berne furnished many Mennonites for the galleys; it was decided that only these big mountain Baptists were fit to go to the galleys. As early as 1540 there were 90 of these Mennonites bound to King Ferdinand of Austria and taken to Trieste to be sent to Venice. They escaped from the Tower of Trieste but 20 were re-arrested and sent on. This began as early as 1540. And as late as 1613 Hans Landis, and Galli Fuchs and Stephen Zehnder or Zehner were sent to the galleys by Zurich but they escaped. Zurich tried to spread the galley punishment to Basel and other places; but it was condemned as too severe and went out of use, (Müller, p. 215).

1540—Täufers or Mennonites in the Principality of Basel.

The Täufers or Baptists now called Mennonites, had for some time been settling around the Emmenthal, which is in Switzerland, northeast of Berne. They became numerous there and spread throughout the Valley. They were very successful farmers and were the leaders in that region in agriculture and stock raising. But in the Canton of Zolothurn they found refuge first and then moved to the Jura in the Emmenthal. Some came to the section north of Biel and settled in the valley of the Monto. Some went to the great Münsterberg. the entrance to the Jura and then went west. About 100 years later they went to Neuberg. Many of them came from Bucheggberg. Among the first of the emigrants that came from Bucheggberg we find the family of Gerber and Neusbaum and Tanner. This happened between 1540 and 1570. But the first Baptists in Jura on the Emmenthal were not from the neighborhood of Berne but came from the north regions, in the neighborhood of Staasb, from where they were chased. There were about 4000 of them as early as 1535, (Müller, p. 235).

Of these on the 4th of June, the Berne authorities wrote to the Catholic Bishop that it must be known to him what trouble these people are making and that they must be punished. That he should punish them— these Täufers. It was also stated that the treaty with the Münsterites would be renewed as they were enemies of the true Täufers. The Bishop promised that he would punish and exterminate them. Then the agreement was made that the Münsterites should help to get rid of the Täufers. The Berne Reformed authorities and the Catholic authorities were willing to work together now to put the Täufers or Mennonites out of the way, (Müller, p. 236).

The authorities of Thun, Switzerland, some distance from Berne, sent word that they are chasing these Täufers day and night and that they had the Sheriff of Signau to help them, (Müller, p. 82).

1540—Mennonites in Moravia.

There were congregations of Swiss brethren in Popitz and Mähren; and three brethren from congregations of Thessalonica appeared in these Moravian towns, hunting for other brethren of whom they learned. They received information in different parts of Moravia in 1540 stating that these brethren had been taken by the Turks and sold as slaves. They did not find the brethren of their same faith there but they found these Swiss brethren who had emigrated there. One was Hans Pech. They could not speak to him in Latin. They also learned that Hans Führman and twelve others had been nine years in prison at Passau in Bavaria, (Müller, p. 101). The name Führman is familiar in Lancaster county and other sections of Eastern Pennsylvania and we call attention to it to show the close relation between Southeastern Pennsylvania and these ancient lands.

1540—More About Hoffman.

Brons in his book, (p. 405) states some of the hardships of Melchoir Hoffman, of whom we have studied before. He says that Hoffman was a good man and that he had written several religious works, some of which he dedicated to his Christian brethren in the Netherlands. He refers to a Martin Butzer. Butzer was against Hoffman. Their difference seemed to be on the subject of infant baptism. Butzer in a tract, after discussing Hoffman, says, "Now you can see how Hoffman is in the bonds of Satan." It seems that both these men were of the Baptist or Mennonite faith but that Butzer told many untruths about Hoffman. Hoffman was one of the greatest powers the early church had. He died in prison in 1540.

1541—Täufers or Anabaptists Defend With Guns.

An extract from a writing dated December 20, 1541, cited by Müller (p. 83) requests that consideration shall be shown to the Täufers who are backsliders. It seems some of them finding mild methods did not avail, defended themselves with guns and sent word that if the Sheriff of Interlacken was coming with force against them, they would meet him with force, as they had guns. Müller also states that in Stettler's Chronology under the date of 1545, it was stated that in 1541 the Baptists should have separate burial because in life they separated themselves from other Christians. Nagely, one of these Baptists, had travelled to France and he learned a great deal there. When he came back in November, 1541, he spoke in a manner to which the people were not accustomed, that is in Latin. He said the reason of the growth of the

MENNO SIMON—GERMANS FOUND VENEZUELA

Täufer sect was the low morals of the different religious bodies. Those who had resisted the government and were then overcome were garrotted; but as others promised to be good citizens they were left go.

1541—Thüring Haldeman's Bravery.

In this year there was a mandate condemning many Anabaptists to death but Thürman Haldeman refused to submit. He was one of the spokesmen and teachers of the people and the most disobedient to the government. He was erratic and was ordered beheaded. They told him that if he would publicly swear an oath that he would obey the order, he would be left off. We can not find what happened. In this and the preceding articles we find again familiar Lancaster county and Eastern Pennsylvania names, those of Butzer, Nagley, Haldeman, and Stettler.

1541—Menno Simon's Boldness and Labors.

About this time the persecution against Menno Simon became acute. An edict against him personally was passed in which all people are forbidden under loss of life to hand him anything or read anything that he wrote. A reward of 100 guilders or florins for his capture was offered. In addition he had trouble with a false brother in faith, who gave his persecutors track of him. But he escaped to the town of Groeningen, a safe place. This was a privileged town under Charles V and later under his son. The son was friendly to the quiet Baptists. For this reason the Catholic monks accused the Emperor's son of being faithless to the church. The Bishop of Utrecht was also tolerant. In spite of this Menno Simon, as the most prominent of his brethren, was not safe—his life was in hourly jeopardy. This curtailed his activity in the Netherlands very much but he did not leave; but he did go to Emb-den. From there to East Friesland. Several of his faith had escaped and gathered into a congregation. Countess Anne was ruler of East Friesland and she and her people about this time went over to the Protestant faith and they gave Menno Simon's people a haven of rest, (Brons, p. 70).

1541—Venezuela—First German Colony in America.

In the year 1541 there was as adventurous journey from Germany and Switzerland to America. An active traffic for years existed between Germany and Spain, and it happened also that, frequently, German soldiers were in Spain. The adventurous spirit of the Spaniards began to fill the Germans. Some of them, hearing the stories of Spanish discoveries in America also set out and arrived at Venezuela, in 1541, which was the first German settlement in America. As they approached they saw an Indian village on an island or on several islands near the coast and they exclaimed "Venezuela" which means Little Venice and so the mainland was named Venezuela. A rich banker in Augsburg in Bavaria had loaned Charles V of Spain twelve "tons" of gold and the repayment of this sum was a hard task for the Emperor. The banker Weltzer in lieu asked for Venezuela and received it. Thus the country of Venezuela was originally a proprietary province owned by a German banker but under Spanish law. This country Americus Vespucius discovered and in this way Spain became entitled to the Government thereof in 1499.

When Charles V began his agitations and persecutions against Luther, a lot of German followers of Luther sailed to Venezuela, and began gold hunting. In 1526 the first settlment took place. This Weltzer Banking and Merchant firm as owners of Venezuela became more powerful than the Castilian kings. While it was a hard matter for the Spanish government to furnish three small ships for discovery, the Weltzers in a short time built three good sized ones themselves and in 1526 set sail with Ambrose Olfinger from Ulm in Wittenburg in command. They quickly built a city and a fort and began trade with South America. Later when their trade had grown, the Weltzers sent 500 German soldiers to Venezuela, but they became a pest and brought about all manner of mischief and lost their lives, (Löher, p. 15).

1542—A Relic of Täufer or Mennonite Persecution.

Müller tells us, (p. 251), that there is an old folio of the New Testament or rather a comentary on the New Testament by Christian Froschauer in Zurich; and that a considerable part of this book is perforated with a bullet, a memento of the times when Baptists or Täufer were being hunted down for their lives. This book is in Bion above Lachsfelden. These places are in one of the principalities of Basel.

1542—Cleaes Meliss and Hans Huber Destroyed.

In the Martyrs Mirror (pp. 448 and 449) an account is given of the death of two Täufer of the same name as many in modern eastern Pennsylvania. One is Dutch—Meliss,—which may be the Dutch form of Meiley. The Papists killed him and several companions in Holland in 1542.

The same year Hans Huber (a distinct Lancaster County name) also called Shumaker was imprisoned at Waserburg in Bavaria. He was burned to death.

1543—Christian Oberlin and Waldo Garber Executed.

This year according to Müller (p. 78) the above mentioned persons, both bearing well known Lancaster County and eastern Pennsylvania names were executed in Berne, on the 17th of September. Also John Anken with them. This gives new evidence of how large a number of our ancestors lived in and about Berne.

1543 A New Decree Against Menno Simon and the Mennonites.

The Mirror (p. 449) citing an ancient Dutch work says that this year a dreadful decree was proclaimed throughout West Friesland where Menno Simon was taking refuge. By its terms all malefactors and murderers were promised pardon for their crimes, the favor of the Emperor and 100 Carl guilders if they would deliver Menno Simon into the hands of the tormentors and executioners. This shows the extreme wickedness of the west Friesian Regents. It made murderers superior to the devout Christians.

1543—Dirk Philip's Täufer Writings.

This year Dirk Philips, who had written a book or manuel of the Christian doctrine (and which later ran into five editions) had it translated into French. He also issued a work on Christian marriage, which was highly praised, (Brons, p. 74).

1543—Menno Simon's Learning and Debating Ability.

Brons tells us, at the same page that Menno Simon was a consummate Latin student, in 1543, and both wrote and spoke Latin; and that as to his knowledge of the Bible, none of his opponents could surpass him. He was therefore, in the latter part of 1543 requested to enter into a debate or religious discussion at Embden with several leaders of the Catholic Church at Francis Convent. It lasted three or four days. Menno spoke for the Täufer or Mennonites; and his chief opponent was a man named A'-Lasco. They discussed the two natures within us—Christian baptism—original sin—ordination of preachers

— sanctification, etc. Both sides claimed victory. And then Menno promised at a future date he would prove his side so that no one would doubt. He then withdrew to a quiet place and went to work and there composed several treatises.

1544—Mennonite Leaders Print Many Books.

This year as we are told in the Mirror (p. 454) John Claess was condemned to death in Amsterdam, for the crime as the clerk read it, "That he had caused to be printed at Antwerp, six hundred books which he had concluded with Menno Simon and scattered abroad in this country containing strange opinions and sectaranisms; and had kept school and held meetings to introduce errors among the people which is contrary to the decree of our Emperor, and our mother the holy church".

The same year certain Anabaptists in Germany printed over fifteen hundred religious books and that throughout Germany the sect increased greatly (Müller, p. 83).

1544—Menno Simon's Followers First Called Mennonites or "Mennists."

This year says Müller (p. 160) the name "Mennonites" was first applied to the followers of Menno Simon. Mr. Smith in his new book says the name was first used by Countess Ann of East Friesland. Though the Mennonites had to suffer, this did not retard their growth. About this time there was a discussion of several days between the Netherland Mennonites and the other Baptists. This and other causes brought Charles V to begin a counter reformation against the Catholic Church. This fight, which he as Emperor had against the Catholics, made times easier for the Mennonites.

1544—Menno Simon's Exegeses at Emden.

In 1544 Menno Simon wrote "A Brief and Clear Confession and Scriptural Demonstration on the Incarnation and Teachings of Christ to John A'Lasco and his Fellow Laborers at Emden. (See Menno's Works part 2 p. 325 to 350). This was written in East Friesland in Holland. In this he refers to his debate with them at Emden in 1543. Those to whom he wrote this were his opponents. He discusses the use of the sword and says only spiritual weapons are allowable. He then takes up a learned discussion of the Incarnation. He says he wandered about for days without food, pondering and praying over this subject. He then answers the objections.

The second part of this treatise is an admonition to A'Lasco, ArchBishop at Emden, East Friesland and to his brethren on how preachers "should be minded". He rebukes them as wordly—as sellers of the Word of God—they are blamable in doctrine—buried in "filthy lucre"—produce no fruit of the spirit—have no fear of God—no brotherly love—and finally he says they are not the true messengers of God. Therefore he says he cannot hear nor attend their preaching or partake of their supper. Then he follows up and tells the Catholic Arch-Bishop what ails their Church, etc.

1545—Mennonites Wander Along Northern Coasts.

From 1545 and during the next 5 years the Mennonites everywhere had great difficulty to form congregations. They were now chased and harassed. They scattered through Danzig, Elbing, Könegsberg, along the northern coasts and the Weichsel river. Therefore, they only gathered in small bodies of 2 or 3 and met in private houses for worship—sometimes in barns. Their plan at meeting was a preacher behind a small table and on each side of him the deacons and in front the members, women on one side and men on the other on benches, (Brons, p. 248).

1546—Menno Simon and His People Flee to Baltic Coast and Finland.

Menno Simon this year found a haven of rest in Cologne in Prussia. Under elector Herman of Wied, all Mennonites were given refuge in the principality until the Elector was defeated by the Arch bishop under Charles V's. Counter Reformation. (Müller, 160.) But after these events Menno and his sick wife had to flee to the Baltic Coast and were overcome in and around Cologne by the new Catholic forces; and the Elector was deposed by the Catholic Archbishop. This was a blow for the new teaching. Strict Popery held sway again. Menno in his wanderings on the Baltic came to Liefland where he found many of his faith and he formed a congregation there and baptized many and administered the sacraments. This was in the region of Finland and says Brons (p. 77) fruits of Menno's work there 370 years ago are still seen in the form of a large Mennonite Settlement in territory, where he had labored so long ago. The followers of that faith have existed there from that time to the present.

The next year Menno Siman was in Wismar (1547) and a theological doctor opposed him with great animosity —and said he would rather have a hatful of Menno's blood than a hatful of gold. This theologian Smedistedt, by name, also induced the authorities to compel the Baptists to get out of the country, (Brons, p. 77).

1546—Local Hardships Of, and Prejudice against Menno Simon.

In his complete work (p. 8) published in Elkhart by Funk in 1871, Menno Simon relates that in 1546, at a place in Holland where it was boasted the Evangelical Christians or Baptists predominated, four dwellings were confiscated because the owner had rented one of them for a short time to his (Menno's) sick wife and children. This severe persecution compelled him to move to a place between Hamburg and Lubeck, where there was formely a large forest, owned by a German who though cruel otherwise was much inclined toward the Holland martyrs. This he did in defiance of the King. After Menno settled there exiles from all sides came there too and shortly there was a large colony of them.

1546—Leonard Schneider and Dirk Peters Executed.

This year these persons bearing eastern Pennsylvania and Lancaster County names were executed for their faith, the former in Vienna and the latter in Amsterdam. Peters we have frequently referred to.

1547—The Diet of Augsburg.

This year says Brons (p. 88) it was lucky for the Protestants that when Charles V was successful over them all, he at the same time had serious difficulties with the Catholic Church. We remember he, though a Catholic, undertook to regenerate it. To reconcile the difference of views he called the Diet of Augsburg September 1, 1547. Over the deliberations of the Diet he had two Catholics and one Protestant theologians as moderators and they got a creed framed up; but the Protestant was out-voted by the Catholic.

1547—Lutheran Hatred of Menno Simon.

This year says Brons, (p. 77) a Lutheran Minister named Vincentius appeard in Wismar and preached so vehemently against Menno that he was smitten by a stroke of apoplexy. But Menno was not much disturbed by it. He kept a steady home there.

1547—Menno Simon Tries to Consolidate Reform Movement.

In 1547 Menno Simon went to Embden to have a talk with the elders and bishops of the Baptists—Obbe and Dirk Philips, Gillius of Achen, Henry of Vrenen, Antonius of Cologne and others. In the meeting there were two present named Adam Pastor and Franz Cuyper, whose divergent views disheartened Menno very much, (Brons, p. 77).

1550—Menno Simon Defines Separation from the World.

In 1550 Menno Simon wrote a discussion in the form of "Questions and Answers" on doctrine. He concludes that the regenerated must be separate from others—or the world. And that those who disobey this are to be banned, and that this extends to members of the same family. Dealing with the banned should only be such as necessity requires, he declares. He then sets out who are the banned, according to Galations, Corinthians, Ephesians, etc. What Menno advises here is more nearly the "Reformed" Mennonite doctrine than the "Old". Its strict practice today would cause much consternation, (Menno's Works, part 2, pp. 276-8).

1550—Inquisition Revived in Holland and Belgium.

About this time the Romish clergy became more bitter in Holland against Mennonites and all evangelicals. They caused the Emperor to revive the Inquisition there. Old authors cited in the Mirror say that, though many persecutions were constantly inflicted in Holland earlier, yet in 1550 the hatred and ill will of the people increased to a dreadful degree and caused Emperor Charles V at Brussels, April 29th, to revive an inquisition by the church whose decrees of death the government carried out. The decree was somewhat modified later, but not before many had fled to Brabant and Flanders, (Mirror, p. 483).

1551—John Bair, of Lichtenfels, Died

Here we have another familiar Eastern Pennsylvania or Lancaster County name. The Bair or Barr family is very numerous, there being in Lancaster City, according to the Directory of 1910, by count 103 Bair and Barr heads of families and self supporting adults and in the county by 1910 directory 140 of them.

The Mirror tells us (p. 485) that the above John Bair was imprisoned 23 years in a tower at Bamberg in Franconia on account of his faith, that is from 1528 to 1551 when he died. In 1548 he wrote a letter as he states in a dark dungeon at Bamberg. He states that he has received six pens, writing tablets, accounts of the doctrine (religious tracts) but a Bible he has not yet received. And this after 20 years' imprisonment. In the letter he pitiably begs for release without being compelled to change his belief. But it was not to be; and he died three years later. Franconia was an old dutchy, now the grand duchies of Baden and Hesse and Kingdoms of Saxony and Bavaria,Germany, (Webster's Dict. Gaz.).

Menno Simon Writes His People's Complaints.

This year Menno Simon wrote what he called the "Complaint or Apology of the Despised Christians and Exiled Strangers, to All the Theologians and Preachers of the German Nations, Concerning the Bitter Falsehoods, Slanders and Abuses, with which they Burden these suffering Christians". In this he laments (1) the falsehood of the accusations (2) that the accusations are of capital crimes—(3) the accusations are against nature and reason and (4) the accusations are out of accord with the spirit of Christ and are animated by hate, etc. Finally he invites all to come together in a friendly discussion. (Menno's Works, Part 2, p. 115).

1552—Menno Simon's Reply to Gellius Faber.

This year Menno wrote his reply to Faber. The reply is really a book of 115 pages, (See Part 2, pp. 1 to 115, Menno's Works). He says that Gellius in a publication slandered the Christians and attempted to receive them. He then takes up each position of Faber.

1552—Menno Writes an Explanation of the Mennonite Doctrine.

In the same work last cited, part 2, from pp. 259 to 276, Menno Simon this year wrote his "Fundamental and Clear Confessions of the Poor and Distressed Christians Concerning Justification, The Preachers, Baptism, The Lord's Supper and the Swearing of Oaths, On account of which we are so much Hated, Slandered and Belied. Founded the Word of God".

In this work he takes up each of the last named subjects in an exposition based on the Bible explains them. He shows strong power of discussion in the paper.

Two years later Menno wrote a treatise on the causes and facts of his conversion, (See His Works, p. 1). In 1555 Menno also wrote a series of letters, found in the same book, pp. 277-83.

1555—Great Religious Convention at Strasburg, Germany

Brons tells us (p. 52) that this year a great meeting of Menonites and Evangelicals generally was held. Some of the delegates traveled 150 miles. One delegate was present in whose house Michael Sattler 30 years before made an agreement on religious subjects. Sattler was then an active Anabaptist teacher. Another delegate was present who stated that he had been on the rack eleven times, but escaped. But he reported that many of his brethren died. There were 50 delegates here, made up of elders and teachers, representing 600 members of different congregations. Many were Swiss. Some descendants of the old Waldenseans were here too.

1555—Edict Inspired by Lutherans.

This year says Brons (p. 86) a new edict in Germany, not only against Mennonites but against all Reformed bodies was promulgated. It seems the edict was issued by the Lutherans or at least the Lutherans of six large towns advocated it; and the government followed their suggestion.

1555—Mennonite Strength and Synod at Strasburg, Germany.

In his chapter on Taüifers in Switzerland, the Palatinate and adjoining countries, Müller says under the date of 1555, that the Swiss through persecution were driven over the north boundary of that country and found asylum with their brethren in the Palatinate. He says at the beginning of the Reformation, the Mennonites then known as Baptists or Anabaptists were of nearly the same numerical strength as the Reformed. They were both living in and about Strasburg as early as 1526, when the Baptist leader Reublin appeared in Strasburg. Hoffman also helped them there, and through him the Baptists gained an equal foothold there in spite of persecution. In 1555 in Strasburg, Germany, took place the first important general synod of the Mennonites as they were later caller, (Müller, p. 195).

1555—Calvinism at Geneva.

This same year says Müller, (p. 76), Zorkinden wrote a letter to Calvin that the differences between the various branches of the "Reformers" could never be wiped out. It seems from this that Calvin, who began his branch of the Reformation, (known as Calvinism, later a form of Presbyterianism), about Geneva, hoped to have his doctrine accepted by several branches of the Reformation movement. He was a contemporary of Zwingli and one of the great Swiss religious powers.

1556—Menno Simon Issues Several Works.

This year Menno Simon issued a series of letters (Menno's Works, pp. 277 to 284),—one to his followers in Holland pointing out the errors of papacy there—one of consolation to the Amsterdam brethren—one to his brethren in Friesland (Holland), rebuking them for their dissentions, and one to the Church at Emden on the subject and effect of separation in families of the Christian members and the "worldly" members, which doctrine caused much grief, in many homes. The same year he wrote a work on the Anti-Christ doctrine as he called it, (Do., Part 2, pp. 351 to 422). This work is entitled, "A Very Plain and Pointed Reply To the Anti Christian Doctrine." This was a reply to a false account given by Martin Micron of the Discussion between himself and Micron in 1553, on the subject of the incarnation of Christ. This is an interesting work, written with fairness; but it lacks the learning which Menno shows in other works.

The same year he published a work on the subject of Excommunication, the Ban, Exclusion, etc. In this he discusses fully "the separation from the world" as the phrase is. The same year he wrote a work on the nature of the "Resurrection" (Do., Part I, p. 229), or the "Heavenly Birth." In this he shows considerable learning. The same year there came out his "Fundamental Doctrine From the Word of the Lord", exhorting all to the "Heavenly Birth", etc. (Do., p. 165). In this he attempts to set people right, he says, from the discussion of learned men perverting the truth. He attacks, of course, the tenets of practice of the Romish church in these particulars. This treatise is well worth reading by all. He also wrote his dissertation on " True Christian Faith" and his "Consoling Admonition Concerning the Sufferings, and Persecutions of the Saints" the same year, (Do., pp. 103 and 179).

1556—Philip II of Spain, Imitating Charles V, Issues Bloody Edicts.

This year says the Mirror (p. 530) Philip II, son of Emperor Charles V, following his father's footsteps, caused all the former bloody edicts of his father to be renewed against the Anabaptists.

The decree forbid all persons to read or discuss the scriptures, especially all doubtful points, except theologians versed in divinity and spiritual law. This was to apply to all those who try to seduce persons away from the holy mother church. Those who do so teach were to be punished as seditious persons, and be executed, viz.: the men with the sword and the women to be burned alive and their property to be confiscated. The decree recited that as especially the Anabaptist violated all decrees and moved about secretly, none of the inhabitants of Holland should be allowed into the territories of Philip, except bringing a certificate from the priest. All having knowledge of Anabaptists were compelled to disclose them. The decree forbid the Judges to mitigate the punishment in any particular. The above is cited from the Great Book of Decrees of Ghent, containing all the decrees of Charles and Philip, collected by William I, Prince of Orange in 1569.

Müller commenting on the same wicked decree (p. 161), says, that after Charles came, Philip as ruler of Netherlands and with the assistance of his hangmen, during the Inquisition, 1000 Evangelicals or Anabaptists were destroyed. Alone in Holland, outside of Friesland, in these few years, one hundred and eleven

Mennonites were executed. He also executed the Calvinists, until the execution of Duke of Egmont and Horne. Then a general religious war broke out. In six years the Duke of Alba, known as Philip's hangman, executed 18,000 people and then left for Netherlands. Goethe has written a tragedy of Eggmount. It likely depicts this awful time in Holland. Alba was to Holland, what Weyler was to Cuba.

1557—First Mennonite Gathering Into the Palatinate.

Brons tells us (p. 181) that in 1557 the persecuted of Holand and especially of Switzerland began going into the Palatinate, that is, the Rhine country in Germany, then the province of Frederick II, Elector Palatine, who was a protestant, (Rupp, p. 68). They did this to escape their terrible ordeals under Philip.

1557—Anabaptist Translations of the Bible.

From 1525 onward to 1557 more than 25 translations of the Bible appeared in Holland and the Mennonites and Anabaptist genrally helped to do most of it. After 1557 the Anabaptist helped in many more translations. Up to 1723 there were over one hundred editions of the Bible in differnt sizes issued, and made up from Biestken's translation alone, whose work was completed in 1560 at Emden, (Brons p. 57).

1557 — Persecutions Begin in the Palatinate.

This year there was a renewal of persecution against the Mennonites and Anabptists generally, and it extended into the Palatinate. The discussions of Menno Simon when he was there in 1555 was the seed which a couple years later brought on the fruit, (Brons, p. 93). The result was that in 1557 sharp mandates against the Mennonites were issued throughout the Palatinate. Elector Frederick had a discussion at Pfeddersheim that year with the Mennonite and Anabaptist leaders and the edict was the result, (Do., 185). We notice above the striking similarity between the name of the Paltinate town Pfeddersheim and that of our well known Petersheims in eastern Lancaster county, adherants of the Amish Church. It is likely their names are derived from that of the ancient German town where ancestors of the family may have dwelt in olden times. It was a more or less general custom to name citizens after the towns, as is instanced in the Oberholtzers, who were first known in Oberholtz, a town of the Wald in Switzerland.

1558 — Conrad Shumaker and Peter Creamer Suffer.

This year Shumaker and Creamer, names very commonly met with in our county and state, were executed. Shumaker was a Swabian, a section anciently comprising northern Switzerland. He journeyed with his people toward the Danube and was taken at Stein and imprisoned in Vienna. Here he suffered torture and hunger. He was brought before Emperor Ferdinand, who was attending a great diet at Augsburg, and theratened with execution before daylight so that the people should not be excited in his favor. He would not yield though the executioner was by his side. He was remanded and brought before the Bishops and his monks and priests three days later and threatened without avail. Then the Lutheran preachers of the King interceded and he was released, (Mirror, p. 552).

Peter Creamer did not fare so well. He lived in the Duchy of Berg, was arested and brought to Winnick. He was imprisoned a long time. When brought to execution he appeared so upright and pious that nearly every one wept—the steward, the judges, the deputy, the executioner and the common people. The Steward begged and begged him to come back to the Romish church; but he refused. And at last he was executed standing with the Sword, (Do., 586).

1559—Menno Simon's Last Works and Death.

It would sem that this remarkable man worked, and wrote expounding and defending his faith and that of his followers up until his death. According to Funk, who published Menno's complete works, Menno wrote and finished on January 23, 1559 his "Thorough Answer to the Slanders, Defamation, Backbiting, Unseasoned and Bitter Words of Zyles and Lemmekes" concerning the Mennonite doctrine, especially on the subject of the "Ban Separation or Shunning", (Menno's Works, Part 2, pp. 283-295). This doctrine of separation from and shunning by the church, of those who are "of the world" is more or less strictly adhered to today by one branch of Mennonites. They contend that they are the only true followers of the doctrine of the Bible as explained by Menno Simon. In this answer, carrying his arguments to the point where parents and children and even husband and wife must be baned from and must shun each other if one has accepted the doctrine of Menno as he defines it, and the other has not, his reasoning leads to very cruel conclusions and no end of family discord.

According to Brons, (p. 102), on the same day Menno finished this thesis he died—January 23, 1559, a true example of "faithful unto death". But some writers say he died in 1561. Brons says he was buried on his own estate or farm, in Germany, known as the "Wuestenfelds" or Wastefield, because when he first acquired it the place was a barren tract. He made it fertile. The place of the grave is not known. His followers, some time afterwards, continued to resort to his premises, and it seems, cultivate it and use it making it very fertile, until in the 30 years' war it was again devastated. The place is near Leibeck a free city of Germany on the Baltic.

1559—Philip the Cruel and Frederick the Generous.

We remember that Charles V of Spain abdicated in favor of his son Philip II. He was very cruel to all Anabaptists. But they (and especially the Mennonites) had a friend in elector Frederick; and he defended them against Philip's hatred. March 7, 1559, Philip writes that he has read Frederick's defense of these people but that he still thinks most of them an antichrist sect like those of Münster, who made trouble wherever they were found. But he says there are some good communities of them, who are a plain peaceful people and not crazy like the remainder. The Münsterites asserting themselves to be Mennonites and yet full of war and rebellion and sedition and not having Mennonite principles at all, mislead the rulers and make a hard road for Taufers or Mennonites in all sections. Their central habitat was Münster. Philip then said, "Those plain, harmless ones should be tolerated, under cautious surveillance; but as to all the active and troublesome ones, take the sword and slay them. As to the mild ones they simply err in faith and efforts should be made by reason and charity to get them back. Listen to them and argue. Put out and destroy their teaching but you may as you desire save their lives". Philip was now King of Spain and as Spain was very powerful at this time he also ruled Holland, parts of Germany and adjacent country; and thus Frederick the elector, was under him.

1559—Margrave Albrecht of Prussia Orders Banishment of Mennonites and All Wiedertaufers.

"Wiedertaufers", we remember means, those who have received second baptism, on the belief that their baptism while infants was of no avail. All who held this view, among whom most prominently were the Mennonites, this year by edict were ordered out of Prussia. But the persecution was mild there and more tolerant and the order was not obeyed, for 20 years later the Mennonites petitioned the authorities for free permission to settle in Koënegsburg and other places in the Duchy, on the Baltic sea. The same time they submitted their articles of faith. This latter request in 1579 was again made as we shall see later to Margrave George Frederick. He said he was compelled to refuse their request, as the Government policy was that the peoplse since the Reformation, that people should be all Lutherans; but he told them this kindly and as he said regretfully, for he found them otherwise very good people.

1560—The First Edition of the Biestkens Bible Issued at Emden.

Emden is a German city in the province of Hanover on an arm of the North Sea, on the line between Holland and the German Empire. Here in 1560, says Brons, (p. 57) the first Biestkens (Van Diest) Bible was issued. Brons introduces this chapter by telling of the rise of Anabaptism in Holland. She tells us that before the Reformation the ground was prepared by the early Evangelicals or Fraternals. These were followers of Waldo —the Waldenseans. Some of the early leaders were Thomas of Kempis, John Wessel and the great Erasmus. Kempis wrote four books on the true Imitation of Christ. He was of Rhenish Prussia—a priest or monk. But his works extended into Holland. These works are famous now in many languages and libraries. The writings of Luther followed and soon spread everywhere.—in Germany, in Holland and in Switzerland. Through this agitation the translations of the Bible were very numerous, but of all places, they were more numerous in Holland than anywhere else. And so it happened that a Hollander named Van Diest in Emden, just across a little gulf from the Holland line, issued the Bible above referred to in 1560.

1560—Beginning of Mennonites in Prussia.

This year it became known that there were three large Mennonite congregations in Prussia, Germany. It is believed that Menno Simon and Dirk Philip organized them. They were the first known there. From that time onward there were many of them. These three had one bishop and formed the first conference district. From that time a register was kept there and it was complete at least down until the time, Anna Brons of Norden, wrote her work on "Taufgesinnten oder Mennoniten" in 1884. The first bishop was Hans Von Swinderin. Dirk Philip died near Emden. The next bishop seems to have been Quirin von der Meülen in Dantzig. He printed a Bible at his own expense, called the Schotlandische Bible. Then there was a bishop named Hiltze Schmidt, (Brons, p. 251).

1560—Holland Mennonites Form Conference Districts.

Between 1560 and 66 the congregations of four cities, viz: Harlingen, Francker, Leeuworden and Sneek of Friesland, now in Holland combined into conference districts, etc., by a compact of 19 articles, so that by the efforts of all they might help those who had fled to them from other places, where they had been persecuted and robbed. A good many of these refugees came from Flanders. The compact did not last long, because a large faction of them contended that Christ would not favor so much organization and machinery in the Church, (Brons, p. 133).

Here can be seen the early stages of the Church simplicity and opposition to anything which looks like self aggrandizement, which simplicity still shows itself today. These people always had a zealous care that their church government, form of worship and church property should all be simple and plain and not exalt their manner of religion into a magnificence and ceremony that would make men forget their humility. They have thus for more than three centuries been called the "plain church".

1560—Bollinger, Becomes a Mennonite Historian.

We have written of Bollinger's activity for the Anabaptists or Mennonites, of which he was a member. In his now later and maturer life he wrote a work on the origin of the Mennonites, which he published this year. In it he tells how Moravia had become the New Jerusalem of the persecuted brethren of Zurich and Berne and Switzerland generally. Dr. Hupmeier of Zurich was active in organizing and founding an asylum there, (Müller, p. 94). Bollinger also wrote up the Mennonites in 1531, nearly 30 years earlier. Froschower printed it for him, (Do., p. 3).

1560—The Eby or Eably Family Move to Zurich.

In the History of the Eby Family, written in 1889 by Ezra E. Eby, of Berlin, Ontario, he says, "The Ebys belong to the Celts, an ancient Asiatic race. During early ages they lived in the Northern Parts of Italy and were converted from heathendom through the Valdois or Waldenses, who from the 8th to the 11th century became numerous. The Church of Rome tried to exterminate them; and in 1453 the whole valley Luzerne was laid under an edict. In 1560 a large number of them fled and went to the Northern part of Switzerland. Among the Waldenses who settled there were the Ebees. These Waldenses joined Menno Simon in 1538".

1562—Death of Caspar Swenkfeld.

We have written before of the rise of the Swenkfelders under Casper Swenkfeld. This year he died at Ulm. Ulm is in Wittenburg, on the Danube and it is famous for having the highest spire in Germany. The first followers of Schwenkfeld were in Silesia, Germany. Silesia is where Schwenkfeldt was born. His followers never had any relaton to the Swedenborg doctrine, as asserted by Löher. The capital city of Silesia is Breslau. The Lutherans prosecuted the Schwenkfelders severely. The Catholics tried also to punish them and to to get their children back to the Catholic faith. They endured all patiently without any signs of restlessness, when suddenly in 1725 the Silesian colony departed by night for Saxony and in 1734 came to America leaving everything behind. They had quietly made arrangement with England to land here, (Do.).

1562—The Swiss Catholics of Waadt Want Anabaptists Suppressed.

The persecutions about Berne are now beginning to be agitated. This year the leading Catholic powers of Waadt asked for severe rules on the Mennonites to suppress them. They asked to have Bollinger suppressed. The fight was now on between the State church (Catholic) and the Anabaptists. Twenty-four Anabaptist preachers left the neighborhood of Waadt and emigrated toward Berne, (Müller p. 49).

1564—Berne Decree Against Emmenthal Mennonites.

February 16, this year the Swiss authorities in the Canton of the Emmenthal had a decree passed and proclaimed from the Catholic pulpits in Signau, Trachelwald, and Brandis to the effect that all Mennonites are to be fined ten pounds each if they do not stop printing and reading books of their own invention. They were active printers of their doctrines about the Emmenthal, (a locality in Switzerland east of Berne) ever since 1551; and the result was that the whole territory about Hoechstetten and the Emmenthal showed a big increase in their growth. Soon a stricter order was issued, to the effect if they continue in their heresy they will be punished in body and in possessions. But the threat was not then carried out. In 1566 the subject was brought before the authorities again and a decree of banishment was passed. But it was of no avail. They continued to increase.

1564 — The Meulens or Melins of Ghent, Belgium.

There is an account in Martyr's Mirror (p. 640) edtailing how Peiter Von Der Meulen of Ghent for defending his faith as an Aanbaptist, was put to death. I speak of this only because the name seems to have some relation to the family so famous and so numerous in eastern Pennsylvania and in Lancaster County,— Meilin, etc. A well known home of the ancestors of our present day Meilins was Switzerland. The present item may establish that there was an ancient home in Belgium also.

1565—Conrad Koch of Berg Executed.

We now call attention to another name quite common in Eastern Pennsylvania and in Lancaster County,— Koch. This man seemed to live in Berg, Germany, in the region of the Rhine river. The record shows that when the light began to shine along the Rhine, Conrad Koch embraced it. He lived in the little town of Hauf. He was imprisoned in the Castle of Loemenburg about a year and then executed, (Mirror, p. 659).

1565—Fire of Calvanism Arouses Holland Against Papacy.

In 1565 the nobility of Holland got together, on the question of abolishing the Spanish inquisition in Holland. Holland belonged to Spain at this time. Charles V abdicated in favor of Philip, his son. Charles had sympathy for the Netherlands, but Philip did not. Charles was born there. Philip, however, had not the least interest in the Dutch people—he was a Spaniard. When he was crowned in Brussels that sealed the doom of thousands in Holland. So the inquisition was introduced in Holland; but in spite of all this the Mennonites flourished greatly there, and they were found in all places. Next to them were the Calvinists. Their preachers spoke on the street, in the fields, and implored the people to desert papacy. They ridiculed the Catholic Church and its Pope; showed the bad morals of the monks and priests and worked the people up into a frenzy so that the crosses along the road sides and on buildings were demolished and the graves of prominent Catholics desecrated. In three days 300 churches were demolished when Calvinism started, — Catholic churches. This was the answer of the people to the establishment of 14 new dioceses under the papacy of Cardinal Granvella. But regent Margaret, wife of Philip was herself dissatisfied and asked milder treatment for the Mennonites and all dissenters. But just the contrary resulted—the Inquisition. Then in 1565 the nobility got together and protested against its further use and declared they would stand together and if necessary lose all they had to abolish the inquisition; but it was of no avail, (Brons, p. 106).

1566—Executions About Berne at This Time.

The Mirror relates that up to this time, in Berne, 42 persons were put to death for their faith. The information is found in an extract of a document by H. Vlaming, a resident of Amsterdam, citing a document drawn up in ancient times by the elders of Alsace. In it they say: As regards the brethren who were executed for their faith in the Berne Country, there were executed from 1528 until 1566, forty-two persons, among whom were eight women. We have in our possession a brief abstract of their names and the year of death, (p. 675).

Gruner relates that this year (1566) too, a Mennonite was beheaded in Berne, who was so invincible that he vehemently declared with his last breath that no one of his enemies should pray for him. He declared he was praying for himself. Of him Zehnder says, he was the most prominent teacher of the Berne Mennonites. He was executed July 30th. A reward of 100 guilders was offered for his arrest and thus he was captured, (Müller, p. 75).

1566—Mennonites Quit the Elbe District.

Löher says, Mennonites and Quakers in the 17th century gathered about Wastefield in Holland, of which we have written before. The Mennonites by the middle of the 16th century were leaving the neighborhood of Hamburg and the Elbe district. They were going into Holland where numerous congregations of Mennonites found peace, as persecution with the decline of Philip and the uprising of the people ended there before 1570. But in Switzerland their troubles were never ended. Even in Holland, Menno's death had great effect. His congregations divided and only a few remained on the Elbe river. They scattered into Denmark and Germany, (Löher, p. 56).

1566—Berne Drives Mennonites to Zolothurn.

This year a company of Mennonites came from Zolothurn, about thirty miles away, to Berne; but Berne sent them back again. Zolothurn was never so severe on them as Berne and companies of them went to Berne for the purpose of helping their brethren there and adding to their strength by securing conversions. Berne determined to stamp this out, (Müller, p. 73).

1568—Moravian Mennonites Print a Book.

This year (Brons, p. 77), the Mennonites of Moravia and Bohemia issued a book called the Golden Portals of Heaven, published by Gabriel Ackerman of Neweustadt. In it is set forth their doctrine, explaining why they do not have any pictures of the Virgin in their churches. They say they are reproached for this omission; but they count it only proper not to worship the Virgin.

1569—Great Slaughter of Anabaptists in Belgium, Flanders, etc.

According to the Martyr's Mirror, (pp. 708 to 800) this year scores of Mennonites or Anabaptists were slain in Belgium, Flanders and parts of Holland. None of the names is familiar in Pennsylvania, except those of Hasbourke and Dirk Williams. Hasbourke is a New York name also.

1571—Hans Hasel or Haslibach of Haslibach.

October 20, this year, Hans Haslibach, teacher of a congregation in the Sumiswald in Switzerland was killed. He composed a famous hymn reciting all about his trials, and reciting that he had a vision in his sleep that as a sign of God's anger over his death, as soon as his head was cut off it would leap into his hat and begin to smile, the sun would turn red and the creek nearby would flow with blood. The Mirror recites page 851, the same supernatural events upon the execution of Hans Misel, which may be our same Hans Hasel. The Haslibach Hymn is one of the most famous pieces of the old Swiss Religious Poetry. It is found in the "Ausbund" or ancient Song Book of the Mennonites published about 1620, and also in the Mirror (p. 1069). The hymn had 32 verses, detailing the incidents in the capture, hardships and death of Hans Haslibach or Hans of Haslibach. He was to the Sumiswald, (a region 15 miles northeast of Berne), in a religious sense, what William Tell was to another part of Switzerland in a patriotic sense; and in many ways the two were alike. Governor Pennypacker in 1904 translated this hymn and the same is found in the Mennonite Year Book for 1911. About this time there was a movement against capital punishment. The putting to death of these brave people; and their bravery in meeting death had a wonderful effect in making the common people believe in them. And many were heard to remark that they wished they were as sure of salvation as the Mennonites. Thus capital punishment was simply making more adherents of the faith, (Müller, p. 77). Haslibach's death and the declared fulfillment of what he predicted about his head, the sun and the little river, gave renewed belief in the Mennonite faith.

1572—Tortures Again Rage in Holland; United Netherlands Formed.

Philip and Duke Alba, known as his executor or hangman, this year alone in Holland executed a thousand Evangelicals or Anabaptists, Mennonites, etc. Holland was in an uproar. Mennonites and Calvinists were martyred until the execution of Eggmont and the war for liberty broke out. August 15, 1572 the foundation of the United Netherlands was laid and the Prince of Orange elected Governor. In 1573 Alba left Netherlands, having resided there six years, and in that time murdered 18,000 people. The same year the Prince of Orange joined the Calvinists. Thus there are the Dutch Reformed who followed Calvin and the Swiss Reformed who followed Zwingli, (Brons, 16).

1573—Berne Prevents Mennonites from Converting Moravians.

This year says Müller (p. 96) there were three edicts from Berne to prevent her Mennonites from going into Moravia as missionaries. Nor were missionaries allowed to come to Berne. Each year after "bread breaking" these missionaries were sent.

1575—Bylers of Flanders, Tortured in England.

This year several Mennonites from Flanders fled to England because of persecution and lived in simplicity about London. Their religious services were spied out by a constable and he drove them to South Fort on the Mersey River. They were given the alternative · of subscribing to transsubstantiation — to oaths—to infant baptism—to the bearing of public offices, or being put to death. Some they put on board ship for Gravesend and some they killed, by burning alive. One named Gerrett Byler, after much misery, escaped.

Byler is a well known eastern Lancaster County name as we know. He tells of his ordeal in England this year.

1576—Zurich Issues New Decrees.

Zurich followed the example of Berne in 1576. It was found that the Mennonites and other Evangelicals were quietly leaving with their wives, as the result of the efforts of the "exciters from Moravia" as they were called. Particularly from Aargau the migration was felt. These Aargau citizens secretly sold their goods and prepared to leave. They were ordered watched and taken prisoners, (Müller, p. 96).

1576—Mennonites of Zurich Fight Against a State Church.

This year was published another edict against the Mennonites about Zurich, Switzerland and this brought on in earnest the fight against a State Church. Their congregations separated from the State Church and demanded not to be interfered with. Many congregations moved from Zurich into Moravia. But they fared no better there, and came back having lost all. The Sheriffs were to stamp out the migration. But there were no results; and in 1580 there was another Zurich decree stating they were getting more and more numerous; that people were adhering to them; and warning all that they should shun them, (Brons, 192).

1576—The Familiar Name "Bender" Appears.

The Benders are prominent and numerous in Lancaster County and Eastern Pennsylvania. About this time Matthias Bender or Binder a Mennonite minister of Wurtenburg in Germany, was arrested and taken to Stuttgart prison on account of his faith, and later imprisoned in chains. He was examined and threatened by the doctors of theology, the representatives of the Prince and by the abbott. He was then sent to the castle of Hohenwithing and remained two years, when in 1576 the Castle was burned to the ground. He was then released because of his brave conduct about the fire, (Mirror, 973).

1577— Liberty of Conscience Gains Foothold in Holland.

King William I called William of Nassau, January 26, 1577 at Middleburg (in the southwest corner of Holland on the North Sea) issued a letter of privilege to the Anabaptists or Mennonites, reciting that these citizens complain their shops have been closed by the magistrates. because these people would not take oaths, though they have always paid their taxes, etc. This. the letter says is against liberty of conscience and it has just been decided by the people of Spain against their sovereign that liberty of conscience must be allowed, especially as these Hollanders helped to gain liberty of conscience for others deprived of it; that the oath is used as a means to drive these good people out of the country, and not only those residing in Middleburg, but those in innnumerable other places in Holland and Zealand. The letter then proceeds and says these petitioners are ready at all times to offer their tender "Yea" in place of an oath and agree that those who transgress the "Yea" shall be punished as perjurers.

He then ordains that those people shall be allowed to use their "Yea" in place of an oath; but if they transgress, they shall be punished as perjurers. This was a great sin by the Mennonite Doctrine, (Mirror, 1000).

1577—Holland's Ruler Protects the Mennonites.

This year a deputation of Reformed preachers met at Dortrecht in Holland about ten miles southeast of Rotterdam; and asked that the Mennonites be restrained. But the Dutch authorities now refused to interfere longer with them. The Prince of Orange said personally that they should not be interfered with and more than that, their "Yea" should be acepted as an oath. This shows how they were regarded as to truth telling. The Prince further expressed his dislike that the civil authorities should assume to control matters of conscience. He also said to the Reformed Churchmen who made the above demand that, they should remember how the Catholics had abused them and not, in turn abuse these Mennonites in a similar way, (Brons, 117).

1579—Mennonites Settle Among Lutherans in Northeastern Prussia.

Brons tells us (p. 249) that this year the Mennonites handed in a request to settle about Koenigsburg in northeastern Germany on the Baltic Sea near the Gulf of Dantzig; and handed over their articles of faith for inspection. George Frederick, the ruler and successor of Duke Albrecht said reluctantly that the Constitution of Prussia required all should be of the Lutheran religion there, otherwise he would allow it. He ordered them to go to the consistory and be questioned about their faith and if they did not want to join the Lutheran church they should leave, in four months. But the order was not carried out. The Mennonites remained there and took deeper root. They could feel that Frederick at heart was favorable to them. Wherever they settled they made the land very fertile.

1579—Berne Declares Mennonite Marriages Void.

About 1567 it was decided in Berne that if married couples do not go to the state church they shall be considered as living together illicitly as if the marriage had never been performed; and their children should be illegitimate— the right to inherit should be denied to them. This remained an edict not carried out for 12 years; but in 1579 messengers were sent among the Mennonite congregations warning them that the old edict was to be enforced and that those who do not choose to obey shall leave within three months or be punished in their possessions and lives.

1581—At Berne, Negley a "Reformed" Praises the Mennonites.

Müller tells us (p. 84) that in 1581 a large synod was held at Berne. There Negley announced as a Reformed adherent that the many accusations against the Mennonites were unjust. He said his own people, the Reformed, ought to study their own faults. He showed that great moral rottenness existed about Berne, but not among the Mennonites. He said that each individual of them was pure and set an example for others. He said that most of them were poor and their preachers taught without pay and did various work to support themselves. We call attention to the fact that the name Negley is a common Lascaster County name.

1582—Prominent Norwegians Join the Mennonites.

This year Anslo, a Norwegian, joined the Mennonite church in Holland. He founded a large cloth business and his sons became prominent in it. They were the head of the cloth makers' guild. One of his sons, Cornelius Claes Anslo was a prominent preacher of the Mennonites and his portrait was painted by Rembrant, and a poet named Vondel wrote some complimentary poetry under it. It is now in the gallery of the Lord Holland. Other great men about Amsterdam joined the Mennonites too, about this time, (Brons, 158).

1584—Wenish Keller from Austria Joins the Swiss Mennonites.

Austrian historians tell us that this year seven brethren were sent out of that country. They went to the Swiss. One of them was Wenish Keller. He labored about Berne nine year and his death was reported in 1593, (Müller, 97).

1585—Berne Mandate, Ordering Mennonites Out.

This year, says Müller (p. 182) there was a mandate ordering the Mennonites to get out of Berne or suffer imprisonment or death. But execution by the sword was not allowed as in the past. It provided that those who were teachers should be branded. Hans Stence and Mart. Berger were two of them. After a long effort to cause them to recant they were expelled. Stence returned and was compelled to sign a covenant agreeing that if he came back again he should be beheaded. He was then sent away again; and never came back.

1585—Moravian Missions Successful in Switzerland.

So many people followed the Moravian missionaries in Switzerland that they could hardly all be taken in. A good part were accepted. In 1686 many Swiss joined the Moravian Mennonites. Moravia had her trouble nearly 100 years before Luther led by

Huss, who was burned at the stake in Constance, beginner of the Moravians, began his work. So here was an asylum for the Mennonites, (Müller, p. 98).

1586—Five Great German Mennonite Congregations

By this time, in face of all edicts, the Mennonite strength was amazing in Germany and throughout central Europe. The largest German congregations of Mennonites were at Marburg, at Niederulm or the Swamp of Weichsel, at Thom, at Gradens and at Danzig. They were the strongholds there, in spite of the edict of Danzig prohibiting any strangers there, by Whitemtide, (Brons, p. 251).

1586—Edict Against Anabaptists in Prussia.

The great tortures inflicted by Papists upon the Anabaptists of various countries drove many of them into Prussia, in the hope that these Lutheran sections would be more mild than the Catholic ones. This hope was partly inspired by the fact that Prussia boasted of her liberality. But in this hope the Anabaptists or Mennonites were sadly disappointed. The Government of Prussia, November 12, 1586 issued a decree that they must all leave or be tortured, but not killed. George Frederick, Margrave of Brandenburg issued the chief edict, (Mirror, 1006). The next year there was a similar decree against all the Baptists of Koenigsburg, (Do., 1007).

1588—Severe Integrity of Early Anabaptists or Mennonites.

A remarkable instance of Mennonite discipline is shown in 1588. A brother named Bintgens bought a house from a neighbor for 700 guilders, who was a spendthrift and a drunkard. The deed expressed 800 guilders. The church found this out through a deacon. He brought it before the church as being a device that would deceive the next purchaser as to its value. The church also found out that the drunkard should not have had the money because his creditors were entitled to a part of it. They held Bintgens should have protected the creditors. Bintgens asked to purge himself before the meeting. He said that he was sorry and that he would personally pay the creditors their claims. Then some of the elders who did not trust him went and asked his wife whether he did it. She said her husband did not act honestly. Then the whole congregation was called together for an opinion and the elders of the surrounding congregations were invited to join in the opinion. This meeting divided the churches far and near—some were for Bintgens and some against him. Then his opponents felt injured and wanted him to resign as teacher. Jan. 1589 there was a big meeting of delegates from churches far and near to talk it over. The Amsterdam brethren asked Bintgens again if it was true that there were 100 guilders more expressed in the deed than he paid. He said "Yes", but that he paid the 100 guilders in linen. Then a second meeting was held and all the prominent Mennonites to be found were pressed to be present. It was urged that Bintgens be expelled. Others wanted it decided by a vote in all the congregations of Holland. Others wanted delegates called from all the congregations and that they decide. Others wanted to proceed according to I Timothy Ch. 5, verses 19 and 20. July 3rd, there was a special meeting called to decide the method of procedure only. Then the churches of Holland divided on the subject. The Haarlem churches led one faction and the Amsterdam churches the other. The Amsterdam faction was against Bintgens. Then the factions agreed to refer it to the church authorities of the congregations of Groeningen, Emden and Cologne. At a later meeting in Haarlem this was done, and Bintgens was partly exonerated. Then the Amsterdam enemies accused the Haarlem people of covering up the facts. Bintgens had denied the Groeningen Mennonites and East Frieslanders the right to take part in his dispute. Bintgens and his adherents then left. Then the Haarlemites were put on trial by the Amsterdamers. Haarlem appealed to the whole Anabaptist or Mennonite world to show they did wrong. And so the matter ended in crimination and recrimination.

The public result is the most interesting. It was that the Haarlemites did act in underhand and inferior ways toward the Amsterdamers; and the latter gained in public esteem and in the esteem of the King as well. The Haarlemites gradually lost public favor. In Groeningen and East Friesland Bintgens people fell in favor and were called "bankrupters" and "house buyers" in odium and finally they lost greatly in public favor. All this came from Bintgens sharp trick, which innocent in itself was supposed by the brethren to be meant to deceive. The result was he and his party were much shattered for years throughout Holland. So the right won says Brons, (p. 122).

1592— The Familiar Name "Myers" Appears.

This year at Wier, in Baden, Matthias Myers was arrested through the espionage of a priest. The priest had a servant maid go to Myers and pretend she wanted to join the Anabaptists. In this way they got evidence against him. And thus they drowned him in a most horrible way, putting him under water for some time repeatedly and drawing him out to induce him to recant, which he would not do. He died steadfast, (Mirror, p. 1032).

1595—Lutherans and Reformed at Odds.

This year at Emden, a house in which the Lutherans held services was closed by the Reformed. They fought over the Lord's supper. Finally the Reformed allowed the Lutherans to preach at certain times but only under governmental supervision and under conditions. One condition was, the collection was to be handed over to the Reformed. To this, and to other conditions they had to agree; and did so in writing, signed by 108 persons. Only under the Prussian government did the Lutherans get permission to build the Church that stands in Emden today.

1599—Berne Edict against Anabaptists.

This year, March 10, there was a mandate promulgated by Berne, demanding that the Mennonites must leave without their property. Their real estate was confiscated to the Government. If they sold it before going, the purchaser would be compelled to pay it again. This was a severe edict, (Müller, p. 131).

This ends the annals of the sixteenth century.

1600—An Extensive Mennonite Confession of Faith.

About this year, says the author of the Mirror (p. 360), a Mennonite confession of faith was adopted, consisting of 33 articles. It contains the doctrine as to the Father, Son and Holy Ghost—the Creation— Fall — Restoration—Free Will—Election of Believers—the law of Moses and the Gospels—Saving Faith— Regeneration— Incarnation—Death and Resurrection —Office of Christ—the Church—Ordinances of the Church—Baptism—the Lord's Supper—Feet Washing— Good Works — Marriage — Swearing and Oaths—the Ban—Second Coming of Christ and Kingdom of Heaven. Just where this was adopted is not clear.

1601—Groeningen & Sneek Decree in Holland against the Mennonites.

The following decree was issued by the Dutch authorities of Groeningen and Sneek by the Reformed

Church authorities, who controlled the government now, against the Mennonites. The Reformed seem now to have forgotten the fierce decrees of the Catholics in former centuries against them and in turn they now persecuted the Mennonites, who differed from them. This decree is found in Martyr's Mirror, (p. 1043) and is as follows:

The burgomasters and the council make known: Whereas it has come to our certain knowledge that not only many in the city and in the jurisdiction of the same presume to exercise and practice, contrary to the treaty sworn to and made with the city, A. D. '94, another religion than the Reformed, to the adulteration of the word of God, to the misuse of his holy sacraments, and to the offense and seduction of many persons; but that also nearly all disorders and abuses in and without the marriage state, and also others contrary to the Christian church regulations established and customary here, creep in and are practiced; and we by virtue of our office recognize it our duty to meet and check all this with proper penalties; therefore, we have ordained, and do ordain and decree by these presents, as follows:

Firstly, that the exercise of all other religions than the Reformed is herewith again strictly prohibited.

And if any one be found to allow his house or place to the Anabaptists, contrary to the church regulations of this city, for the purpose of preaching, of holding meetings therein, he shall each time be fined ten dollars.

The preachers, as aforesaid, if found to be preaching, shall for each offense be fined ten dollars, or be imprisoned two weeks on water and bread; and when detected in thus preaching the third time, shall be expelled from the city or the jurisdiction of the same.

And all that shall be found attending such preaching or gatherings shall each time be fined two dollars.

Whoever shall be found to have rebaptized anyone, shall be fined twenty dollars; and when detected the second time, shall be imprisoned on water and bread, and expelled as aforesaid.

Again, unbaptized children shall not receive inheritance, according to the city statutes.

No one shall be admitted to any administration or office, public or private, nor be accepted as a witness, except he render the solemn oath required for it.

And all that refuse such oath shall be punished as is proper acording to law.

1601—Calvinists Try To Destroy German Catholics and Lutherans.

In the Mirror (p. 1044) under the date of 1601 we are told that, "In the year of our Lord sixteen hundred and one it occurred that Johann von Steyn, Count of Witgensteyn, Lord of Hamburg, being a member of the Calvinistic church, purposed to abolish the Romish and Lutheran doctrine, and at the same time laid his hands on the defenseless sheep of Christ, which were contemptuously called Anabaptists, and put them into prison.

Among these are mentioned by name, Huybert op der Straten, Trijnken, his wife, Pieter ten Hove, and Lijsken te Linschoten, which latter, as we have learned, was an aged woman of over seventy years.

The first three mentioned were imprisoned twelve weeks, the latter seventeen days, she having been apprehended much later".

1601— Zurich Mennonites Migrate to Moravia, Believing It "The Promised Land".

Ernst Müller in his excellent book tells us, (p. 98), "Repeatedly we hear complaints from the Canton of Zurich concerning the Moravian emissaries, who invited the people to emigrate. The pastor of Wald even reports in the year 1601 that 25 Moravian Brethren are traveling about the country two by two (Ottins, p. 192).

The tidings of the "Promised Land" in Moravia and of the "New Jerusalem" at Nikolsburg even penetrated to the prominent circles of the City of Berne. On the 20th day of March, 1601 Samuel Oachselhofer and Jacob Vogt are to pass over to the Treasurer 4000 pounds from the state of their mother and sister-in-law, Agatha Pfauderin and two children, who had secretly left the country for Moravia, this payment to be made to "His Grace" for his rights of confiscation". There are Vogts in Lancaster county.

Müller then tells us more of these banishments (p. 99), as follows: "If ever one of these children was to return, then its share would be given back to it. (R. M.). Very soon thereafter Elizabeth Oachselhofer, presumably a near relation of the above named Agatha, with her son removed to Moravia as a Baptist, leaving behind a very considerable inventory, which was taken on May 17, 1605, and contained enumerated goods and chattels and the rich wardrobe of a lady of the highest rank, (K. A., Vol. 80, No. 19).

This inventory was estimated to be worth 8000 pounds and should revert to "His Grace". But there is to be kept an account in the interest of the son, should he ever return.

1603—Reformed Swiss Church Oppresses the Mennonites.

Brons tells us (p. 132) that in "1603 a Reformed Synod resolved to request of the government, the latter should prohibit the bishops of the Mennonites from traveling from one place to another, preaching and baptizing; in 1604 a resolution was passed in like manner that they (these bishops) should be prohibited from educating young preachers; 1605 the Calvinistic predicants handed in a request that the Mennonites be forbidden to build churches. And thus it went on through the whole Seventeenth century at 55 Reformed Synods".

1605—Bollinger or Bolsinger of Bavaria Executed.

Under this date the Mirror contains an account (p. 1044) of the execution of Hans Bollinger or Bolsinger, while traveling through Bavaria, Germany. With him was Marcus Eder, too. I use this item simply to show the Bollinger home in Europe. It is well known that there are several prominent families bearing that name in Eastern Pennsylvania and in Lancaster county. They too, were strong in their Mennonite Faith and died for it. The Bollingers came to this country about 1730. The now much paraded name Ballinger may be a form of it.

1605 — Mennonites Tortured in Hungary.

Many Mennonite people were in Hungary, when in 1605, during the Hungarian War, the ruffians were raging in Hungary and Moravia, pillaging and burning towns, torturing to death the people. On May 4th, they led 42 persons and on June 28th, 112 brethren and sisters, as slaves to the heathen lands and to the galleys. (Müller, p. 99).

1607—Mennonite Church Re-Organized in Strasburg.

There were certain rules and regulations for the conduct of the Mennonite church in Strasburg, Germany as early as 1568. But in 1607 the congregation was re-organized and many regulations passed, upon the duties of elders, ministers and bishops. In addition to the regular church duties, rules were laid down upon their duties to visit, console and comfort the distressed and the bereaved and the strangers. These missionaries endured many hardships (Müller p. 90).

1608—Progress of the Mennonite Church in Holland.

The Holland Mennonite brethren had taken vigorous possession of Tiegenhof, had constructed dykes and canals and had achieved such remarkable success that the proprietors made contracts with them for forty years, which were thereafter always renewed. Consequently their numbers increased to such an extent that the Bishop of Kuhn complained in the year 1608, that the vicinity of Marienburg was filled with Mennonites and Samosatenes. Against this the town governments of Daniz, Thorn and Elbing protested, referring to the Warsaw Confederation of 1585 approved by King Sigismund, which says:

"We promise among us, for us and for our posterity forever under oath of our fidelity, honor and conscience, that we, who differ in religion one from another, will keep the peace among ourselves, and on account of the different creeds and the changes in the churches, we will tolerate no bloodshed, nor punish anyone by the confiscation of his goods, injury to his honor, imprisonment or banishment from the country, nor will we assist any authority or official to do such, etc."

Here again the industrious character of our Mennonite forefathers is shown. We also have here another view of King Sigismund's ideas of justice toward these people and his faith in their willingness to abide by the government. On this faith he promised the protection which we have stated, (Brons p. 255).

1610—Switzerland Confiscation of Mennonite Property.

Ernst Müller (p. 131) refers to the confiscation of the possessions of the Baptist or Mennonite brethren by the State, viz: "If the Baptists who have emigrated (from Switzerland) had previously sold their possessions, then such shall be taken from the purchaser and be confiscated, and the purchaser must look to the seller for his rights." (Mandate of April 23, 1610). The hardships of the Mennonites in Switzerland we see at this time are still going on.

1610—Berne Government Teaches Anti-Mennonitism.

All through the 17th century the authorities of Berne, Switzerland continued to do anything in their power to harass the Mennonites on the one hand, and on the other hand to encourage and give strength to the Reformed religion. They held meetings with those who believed in Anabaptism or the Mennonite doctrine to get the weaker ones by argument, to turn away from that faith, but they did not succeed to any great extent. The Protestant authorities of Berne, as the head of their church, left no method untried in order to guide and control the hearts and minds of their subjects. Among these methods was the censorship or censure. Hans Jacob Poll, of Zofingen, had written a tract, in which the doctrine was defended that no one should be prosecuted on account of his faith or belief. This tract was printed in 500 copies at Basle, and therefore the authorities of Basle were requested to confiscate this edition, "for the sake of God and His beloved Church." (Mis. January 31, 1610).

We have here another picture of the continual harassing of these non-resistant people in the Berne district. But the church kept on growing there. We remember that it was the Ementhal, a little valley northwest of Berne, from which the Lancaster County pioneers came in 1710. Their ancestors in earlier days had lived about Zurich. (Müller, p. 104).

1610—Switzerland Restrains Baptists from Going to Moravia.

Ernst Müller (p. 99) tells us that this year means were taken to prevent our Mennonite forefathers from getting out of the country of persecution and going to Moravia. Speaking of the instances of this he says: "These cases were by no means singular or exceptional. An order of the Council to Seekelmeister and Venner, which promulgated means for the prevention of the secret removal of Baptists to Moravia, bears date of April 3, 1610 (K. A.).

At page 18, Müller says, "Some were (so writes the author of the preface to the History of the Martyrers of Christ, 1610) racked and pulled or torn to pieces; some were burned to powder and ashes; some burned to a crisp at the stake; some torn with red-hot tongs; some penned up in houses and the whole burned down; others were hanged on trees; some were executed by the sword; others were pushed into the water; many had gags put into their mouths in order to prevent them from speaking, and thus lead to their doom." This is Ernst Müller's way of stating the dreadful experiences of our Swiss ancestry.

1610—Elbing (Prussia) Mennonites Made Citizens.

Brons tells us (p. 255) that Elbing, in Prussia near the Gulf of Danzig, was a district where the Mennonite people were required to exercise the privileges and also to undergo the duties of citizens. As early as 1610 he says they were given the franchise of citizens and had to take upon themselves the duties of citizens.

1611—Eldest Mennonite Deacon in Altona, Germany.

Brons tells us (p. 263) that "a certain Paul Rossen, who in 1611 had come from Fresenberg to Altona before the devastation of the place during the Thirty Years' War and the scattering of the congregation there, in whose midst Menno had spent his last days, was eldest deacon of the Mennonite Church or congregation at that place, viz: Altona opposite Hamburg in the province of Holstein, Germany."

1613—Swisser Hans Landis's Troubles Begin.

Müller tells us (p. 216) that "Zurich had in 1613 condemned Hans Landis, Galli Fuchs and Stephen Zehender to the galleys and led them bound and fettered to the French Ambassador at Solothurn, where with the assistance of Brethren from Berne they found the way out of prison (Ottins, p. 216). Hans Landis was beheaded September 29, 1614 at Zurich". We merely make a note of this at this date. We shall have considerable more to say about this prominent old patriarch Hans Landis under the year 1614.

1613—Mennonite Colony in Elbing.

Brons tells us (p. 255) that at this time there lived at Elbing, sixteen Mennonite families. This was apparently the extent of their growth in that section at this date.

1614—Mennonite Troubles in Zurich and the History of the Martyrs.

Of the condition in Zurich we possess extensive Baptist sources in the chapters pertaining thereto in the Martyr's Mirror of Tielman Van Bracht. Here we find the history of the martyrdom of the Baptists or Mennonites; and a large number of tales of sorrow and suffering in the persecution of Zurich at that time, etc. (Müller, p. 165).

The above work was published in 1615. The work is divided into three books, of which the first closes with the year 1566, the second with 1573, and the third with 1614. The last martyr recorded therein was the Swiss Hans Landis, (Brons, p. 237).

1614—The Sufferings and Death of Swisser Hans Landis.

An important teacher of the Baptist minded or Mennonites was Hans Landis, who, against the prohibition of the government preached before large meetings in forest and field, baptized and solemnized marriages. He was, for that reason, taken prisoner and as he would not promise to cease such activities in the future, condemned to six years' punishment

SUFFERINGS AND DEATH OF HANS LANDIS

on the galleys. The Swiss authorities made use of the galleys of the Italian Princes as penal institutions. On the galleys he sawed his chains by means of an instrument which the brethren had smuggled to him, escaped and returned to his country, (Switzerland). But soon after that he was again taken into custody, whereupon he was ordered to depart from the country; but he refused stubbornly to obey the orders, saying: "God favored me with this land as well as all others and the earth is the Lord's." Besides, he would remain in his native country, as he did not know where to go. Furthermore he said he was now aged and did not fear death. And, indeed, he could verily say, he did not know where to go to, for in the adjacent Austrian countries the Baptistminded or Mennonites were persecuted since 1601 unto death by Emperor Rudolph, who had again put in force the decrees of Ferdinand. In consequence he (Landis) was condemned to death by the Great Council of Zurich and beheaded in 1614, (Brons, p. 200).

The Mirror (p. 1045) gives us the following account of Hans Landis's death:

This account states that Hans Landis had gone up the river Rhine where he had his place of residence, to feed and refresh the people with the word of God.

"When the Council of Zurich learned of this, they instigated by the disposition of the envious scribes and Pharisees, could not tolerate this, but instantly caused it to be forbidden him, as though they had thought thereby to hinder the true progress of the word of the gospel. But he, who knew with Peter, that we must obey God's commands more than the commandments of men, had such love to the truth and to the young suckling's on Zion's breasts, that no human threats could induce him to forbear feeding them with the true food of the soul. Hence the enviers of the same apprehended him, and sent him ironed from Zurich to Solothurn to the papists, excepting that he should forthwith be sent to sea or upon the galleys; but through the help of good hearted people he was there released; but subsequently apprehended again and taken to Zurich, where he was rigorously examined concerning his doctrine, and when he would in no wise desist from his godly purpose or from his faith, they showed in him, that their decree of eighty-four years previous was not forgotten, neither had the spirit of it died of old age; for, according to the import of the same, they sentenced him from life to death, and hence, in the month of September of the aforesaid year, 1614, for the sake of the truth he was beheaded as a true follower of Christ. Which they nevertheless would not acknowledge, but pretended and persuaded the common people to deceive them, that he was not punished and put to death for his religion, but for his obstinacy and disobedience to the authorities."

The Mirror further states (p. 1046) a certain letter dated July 29, 1659 at Zurich, sets out that the writer was present at the execution of Hans Landis; and the following extracts are made from the letter.

"Hattavier Salr, witnessed the beheading of Hans Landis, which I also still remember well, having seen it myself in the Wolfsstadt, the whole transaction being as fresh in my recollection as though it had happened but a few weeks ago.

Continuing, he speaks of his personal appearance and the manner of his death, saying.

"Hans Landis was a tall, stately person with a long black and gray beard and a manful voice.

When he, cheerful and of good courage, was led out by a rope, to the Wolfsstadt (being the place made ready for his execution), the executioner, Mr. Paull Volmar dropped the rope, and lifting up both of his hands to heaven, spoke these words:

"'O that God, to whom I make my complaint, might have compassion;

that you, Hans, have come into my hands in this manner; forgive me, for God's sake, that which I must do to you.'"

Hans Landis comforted the executioner, saying that he had already forgiven him: God would forgive him, too; he well knew that he had to execute the order of the authorities; he should not be afraid, and see that there was no hindrance in his way.

Thereupon he was beheaded. After his head had been struck off, the executioner asked: 'Lord Bailiff of the Empire, have I executed this man rightly according to imperial law and sentence?' (Otherwise it was customary to say: 'This poor fellow', etc.) as though he believed he died saved and rich.

The people were of the opinion that the executioner by dropping the rope meant to indicate to Hans that he should run away, it was also generally said; that if he had run away, no one would have followed him. to stop him. So far the aforementioned extract.

Further Statement.—It is also appropriate to give here what has been stated to us through credible testimony, namely, that when the aforementioned Hans Landis was standing in the place of execution, to be put to death, his dear wife and children came to him in mournful crying and lamentation, to take a last and final adieu and leave from him. But when he saw them he requested them to go away from him, in order that his good resolution and tranquility of heart for the death awaiting him might not be disturbed or taken away by their weeping and grief; which having been done, and he having commended his soul into the hands of God, the quickly descending stroke of the sword put an end to his life."

1615—Berne the Ancient Home of the Shenks, Hoffers, Baumans, Etc.

A brother Stoffel Schenk of Rehogk in Switzerland, died in the Lord this year, says Müller (p. 99). In Moravia and other Austrian counties in these early times there were many families that had emigrated there from Berne in Switzerland. Some of the names in the Moravian-Mennonite communities that could be traced to the Ementhal near Berne, in Switzerland were Gerber, Shenk, Hoffer, Schlechter, Born, Amster, Bauman, and others. Therefore as early as the year 1600 the Berne district of Switzerland was the home of these well known now Lancaster County and eastern Pennsylvania families.

1615—The Holland Government Saves the Mennonites from a Flanders Decree.

This year at Aerdenborgh in Flanders the enemies of the Mennonites, principally the Romish Church, began a series of decrees and hardships against the Taufers or Mennonites of that place.

This sad beginning would to all appearance, have culminated in greater mischief to the aforesaid people, had not their High Mightinesses, the Lords States General of the United Netherlands, who had received information of this, opposed it with a certain mandate, whereby those who were the cause of sad oppression were prevented from proceeding with the execution of their aforementioned prohibiton, and on the other hand, liberty of religion was granted to those that were oppressed. The contents of the aforementioned mandate are as follows:

The States General, etc., to the Bailiff, Burgomasters and Judges of Aerdenborgh.

Honorable, etc.: We have learned with surprise, that, contrary to our order or resolution announced to Your Honor by our order by the clerk, Jan Bogaerd, you still hinder the members of the community called Anabaptists or Mennonites, residing in Aerdenborgh and the parts under its jurisdiction, in the freedom of their assembling and the exercise of their religion in Aerdenborgh, and trouble and oppress them, by prohibiting their assembling, by arrests and fines.

Whereas we desire that the aforesaid members of the community belonging to the Anabaptist persuasion be allowed to enjoy just as much freedom, with all quiteness and modesty, in their mind, conscience, assembling, and exercise of their religion, in Aerdenborgh as is the case everywhere else in the provinces, cities and places of the United Netherlands, without contradiction or resistance,; except that you may exercise an oversight over their gatherings, as far as they deem it well, and that they, to this end, may inform you every time that they desire to assemble. Hence we command you, to govern yourselves precisely in accordance with this, to the better maintenance of tranquillity, peace and unity in the aforesaid city; without causing the apprehension or execution of the aforesaid members for any fine or contraventions, because of previous gatherings. Upon this we shall rely, and, etc. Given this first of May, 1615, (Mirror, p. 1046 and Müller, p. 187).

In November 16, 1619, the Holland Government was compelled to repeat its orders to Aerdenberg, who had not fully complied with the former demands, (Müller, p. 187).

1616—Berne Renounces Condemnation to the Galleys.

Müller states, (p. 216) that this year the cities of Basle, Berne and Schaffhausen, all prominent points in Switzerland, sent protests to the Zurich government against allowing any Swiss citizens, Mennonites or any others going to the Roman Galleys. And Berne particularly came out and said that the sending of the Mennonites or Weidertaufers, as they called them, to the galleys was a punishment too severe and not to be longer allowed.

1617—Groningen (Dutch) Mennonite Leaders Warn Their Flock against Becoming "Worldly".

The old plain mode of living of the Mennonites was gradually changed to a more modern, finer way of living. The ban had been mostly abolished toward the end of the seventeenth century. The ban compelled the Anabaptists to shun those not of their church and not hear any of their preaching. Nevertheless care had to be taken and watchfulness exercised in order to curb at once any possible derelictions; for instance, the presidency of the Groningen Society in the year 1617 had published and printed a warning against the "getting worldly" (worldly mindedness) of the flock, and had the same sent to each congregation, (Brons, p. 149).

1617—About 70,000 Swiss and Other Mennonites Crushed Out of Moravia.

Brons tells us (p. 178) that 10 years prior to 1617, many Swiss brethren had fled into Moravia; but, that (quoting the Chronicler) though fully 70,000 Swiss and other Mennonites were recently in Moravia, they were by 1617 all exterminated there. Many of them fled to Sylvania.

1619—Moravian Mennonites Ravaged in the Thirty Years' War.

Says Müller (p. 100), speaking of 1619 and onward, "The following years brought levies of war and the passing through the troops, and in 1619 the horrors of the thirty years' war. First the soldiers of Dampierre ranged in Moravia, with murder and arson in their trial, and by them that year 38 brethren were slain".

1619—Reformed Church Have Trouble Over Their Confession of Faith.

Within the confines of the declaration of faith of 1619 there began considerable agitation among the Reformed; parties were formed that tried to break down these confines; the minds became heated, and there came a clash. Here there were Remonstrants and Counter-Remonstrants, Labadists and Socinians, who could not be held for the church and who began to form their own congregations, (Brons, p. 133).

1620—Moravians, Polocks, Etc., Butcher Menonites.
(Hans Gerber and Sharach Huber Slain.)

In the year 1620 came the "Polocks" and massacred under terrible tortures 72 brethren. And after the battle at the White Mountain, the Baptists in Moravia were without justice or protection, a prey to their enemies. A number of horrible massacres was the sequel. According to the records, there were killed on April 17th, at Sabatisch, among others, a Hans Gaerber and a Sadrach Huber. It was altogether an awful, fearful, terrible time, yea, a time full of suffering, anguish and evil, and neither words nor pen can describe the cruel, barbarous tyranny and devilishness in this diabolical war, which were inflicted on our country people, on men and women folk, women in confinement, young boys and girls—by the Spaniards. Neopolitans. Walloons, Crabatians, Polocks and the like Imperial war hordes. The Chronicle enumerates 234 persons of the congregations of the Lord who were put to death in these five years, (Müller, p. 100).

We call special attention here to the two now familiar Lancaster County and eastern Pennsylvania German or Swiss names, Huber and Gerber or Garber.

1620—Deventer Edict against the Mennonites.

In the Mirror, (p. 1047) the following edict is set forth under the above date:

"The magistrates of the city of Deventer prohibit all citizens and residents of their city; that no Mennonists, etc., shall hold any secret or open assembly or meeting where preaching......marriage, or any other exercise of religion is practiced; under whatever pretext the same may be done; on pain that those who shall be found to practice it shall forthwith be banished from the country forever; and every person that shall be found at such a place or in the assembly, shall forfeit the upper garment and twenty-five guilders in money; the second time, the upper garment and fifty guilders; the third time to be punished arbitrarily. And he that lends his house, for the purpose of holding such gatherings, forfeits a hundred guilders; the second time two hundred guilders; and the third time he shall be banished forever."

1620—Rudolph Philip Forrer (Forry).

Müller (p. 18) gives us the first knowledge of the Forry also called Ferry, and at one time called Ferree family of Lancaster County and Eastern Pennsylvania. The early records in the Recorder's Office as well as Rupp the Historian, mention the name as "Ferree." But the Recorder's records twenty-five years later spell the name Forrer. Whether the two names are identical or not we can not tell. The Ferrees were Huguenots; and the Forrers were Bernese, in Switzerland. They may have come from the same family stock. The subject of the title of this sketch was a Forrer, prominent in the Mennonite ministry.

"Out of the atmosphere of the dungeons, court rooms and council chambers we wander into the verdant Emmen Valley and stop in at the parsonage of Langnau, the wooden structure which at one time stood below the church, and listen to the recitals of the pastor with regard to his troubles with the Baptists. The pastor, Johann Rudolph Philip Forrer was born in the year 1598, became in 1620 only twenty-two years old, pastor in Langnau, etc. He showed a lenient forbearing spirit in his dealings with the Baptists. His efforts to induce some of them to resume their church visits and attendance at the services were not without success." (Müller, p. 18).

1621—Mennonite Families of Langnau, Switzerland.

Ernst Müller (p. 119) gives us the following list of Mennonites living at this time in and about Langnau. The names of these Mennonite ancestors of many of our present day Lancaster County and eastern Pennsylvania, Swiss and German descendant families were: Fredley Baumgardner from Mülibach and his wife, to whom he had been married ten years—also a Baumgardner of Dürsrütti and his wife but no small children; Oswald Probst or Brobst and wife, married six years; Fred. Moritz and wife; Simon Bichsel or Bixler and wife; Oswald Ruch or Reich; Michael Studer, a powerful youth; Tschoffen Elsi; Stinnis Gibbel's daughter living in the family of Christian Yost; Hans Utzenberger's wife; Klaus Yost and wife; Barbara Dellenbach; Benedict Raeber's or Reber's wife; Anna Kreyenbuel or Graybill; wife of Benjamin Baumgardner; wife of Hans Gerber or Garber and the wife of Uli or Eli Rothlisperger.

Among these it is not necessary to do more than call attention to the familiar eastern Pennsylvania Swiss names we find viz: Baumgardner; Probst or Brobst, Ruch, Yost, Raeber or Reber, Kreyenbuel or Graybill, Bixler, Gibbel and Garber. Müller, the author, was himself a preacher in Langnau as he states in his title page of his book. Langnau is a city with a population of 7,000 about 18 miles directly east of Berne. in the Emmen Valley, which valley extends from the northeast to the southeast of Berne.

1621—Bichsel or Bixler Above Named, Gave His Reasons for Leaving the Reformed Church.

Forrer or Ferry, asked Simon Bichsel why he left his old Church and came to the Taufer or Mennonite Church this year. He answered that this is a very bad world and many people of the State Church in Langnau are corrupt. He said that at the last "Fair", there he saw these who called themselves Christians and who were members of these worldly churches, in the upper tavern, clubbing each other and cursing and swearing—even the young boys—that the young people of those churches dance and are gay, and reckless and so are the older people —that they "sauffen and fressen", that is eat and drink to excess and are not Godly minded. Forry then asked him, "If God staid among sinners, why could your people not do it too?" This he did not answer, (Müller, p. 121).

1621 — Uli or Ulrich Baumgardner Gives His Reasons for Being a Mennonite.

Forry then tells us he asked Baumgardner, also, why he is a Taufer. He answered that the State Church is full of wickedness. Baumgardner lived in Dursrutti, in Switzerland and some of the Baumgardners live there today; but they belong to the State Church. In March, 1621, Michael Miller, Daniel Stroedel and Forry went on a journey to make converts back to the State Church, and took a New Testament along so that if the Mennonites would question them, they could answer by Scripture. Miller was the best scholar and he was sent to Baumgardner to argue the religious stand that Baumgardner took. Miller, Stroedel and Forry belonged to the Reformed Church. These men argued upon the right way to be saved, but each held his own opinion. Miller made some converts away from the Mennonite faith, but not many. Ulrich Baumgardner was a very strong teacher among the Mennonites, (Müller, 122).

1621—Holstein Rulers Champion the Mennonites.

In Frederickstadt in Holstein, the ruler took up the Mennonite side about 1621 A colony of Holland Mennonites moved over to Holstein (Germany) and had permission to build a town there and they called the town Frederickstein. The town had a complete Holland appearance. These Mennonites built a dyke to keep out the sea about this town. They lived quietly, attended to work and were good citizens. They kept no writings, (Brons, 265).

1621—Holstein Mennonites Given Liberty of Conscience.

These Holstein Mennonites soon became famous cattle raisers. Many others came to them, and soon they were all granted liberty of conscience. They were allowed to testify on "Yea" and "Nay". And when this privilege was once granted, every Duke thereafter renewed it. This was one of the first places in the world where the Mennonites were equal to every other class. The Government ever recognized their preachers. Preachers came to this congregation from Hamburg and from other parts of the Palatinate, (Brons, 265).

1621—John Philip Rudolph Forry's Efforts near Berne, Switzerland.

We have shown that Pastor Forry of the Reformed Church at Langnau about 16 miles east of Berne, was exerting great zeal in 1620 (the time the Mayflower reached Massachusetts) to stop the Mennonite growth. His arguments with them in the Langnau debates in 1621 he had printed in a work called, "What Was Discussed Answering the Taufers in the Church and Parish of Langnau in 1621". This work may be found today in the Bapt. Bible Archives of the Historical Society of Canton, Berne, No. 12-2, (Müller, p. 119).

The same author says at same page, "Forrer, soon after his promotion to the pastorate of Langnau, had heard of the Baptists there "that they through wrong and perverted zeal did absent themselves from Christian Church attendance and hearing the sermons, and held themselves aloof". He determined to seek an opportunity to do his duty in this matter, because the sect was increasing from day to day, and had many secret adherents and protectors, particularly because "they are mightily connected among each other".

He goes on and says with horror, "Some of them are living together in matrimony without attending church as Christans should, and have big unbaptized children, and finally the Fatherland, too is (in the great, dangerous war expeditions of these times) in danger, that the "enemy will beat our head full".

Forrer, thereupon brought his request under extensive or elaborate reasoning in God's name to the attention of the Church tribunal. February 21, 1621, with the plea, "no one should attribute sinister motives to him, even if it were to concern his own".

1625—King Sigsmund Complains That the Mennonites Do Not Take Oaths.

This year, Sigsmund, a petty king in Germany or Poland, complained that the Mennonites were given the privileges of subjects without taking oaths. He insisted that, at least they should make oath of allegiance to him. The town of Ebling particularly contained large numbers of Mennonites. But his order had no effect. The Mennonites continued to prosper. In 1631 some of them got a privilege to begin the silk business. Yost Van Kampen carried it on. His father and grandfather had similarly done so before in Elbing. Another Mennonite, Zachariah Jonsen also obtained a license to carry on the wine business. These were considered rare privileges to be granted to persons who would not take an oath of allegiance to the Government (Brons. p. 255.)

1627—Bohemian Mennonites Merge with Reformed Church.

This year at a synod at Ostarz, the Bohemian brethren or Mennonites were swallowed up by the Reformed Churchmen. who were very strong there. So they united with them rather than to continue to struggle against them. This ended their existence as Bohemian Taufers. This happened during the struggle of the 30 years war lasting from 1618 to 1648, (Müller. p. 65).

1629—More Trouble for Ulrich Baumgardner of Langnau.

September 25th, of this year Ulrich Baumgardner was arrested in the evening aid taken to Trachtelwald and held until the beginning of October. Then October 6th, he was taken to Brene. As they were taking him along the road he told them God would send a great punishment upon them and a little later in the day, at sundown, a great blazing and hissing meteor shot through the air and all became terrified; but nothing more happened. December 2nd, he was put on the rack because he would not divulge the names of the Mennonite leaders of the Langnau district. David Amman, Herr Heinberg, Court Clerk, George Langhams and Jacob Fenner of the Reformed Church had charge of his torture, and they quoted scriptures to him to prove to him that the word of God required him to disclose the names. When that failed they used the rack to convince him that he should tell. But he refused.

About the same time a Benedict Baumgardner composed a Mennonite Hymn. It appeared in a few years in three different versions and was a pretty general use among the Swiss Taufers, (Müller, p. 123).

I set this out because the name Baumgardner has played a large part in the business world of Eastern Pennsylvania, particularly in Lancaster, and Dauphin Counties, etc. We find them here, at early dates.

1629—Mennonite Exodus into Hungary.

We remember that in 1622 the Mennonites were driven out of Moravia by the Cardinal of Dietrichstein under order from King Ferdinand II. In October out of 24 villages began the exodus. They went to Hungary and Sylvania; but here also they were harassed. The Turks and the Tartars came and carried away 26 people, among them a family of young girls named Gerber. While in Hungary they elected two ministers whose names have come down to us and are familiar today — George Gaul and Hans or John Albrecht. These two men were Swiss too, just the same as most of the exiles who first went to Moravia from Zurich and Berne and other Swiss towns, and then went from Moravia to Hungary. We may pause her to note that Caesar speaks of Gaul in his "Helvetian War"; and thus it is not remarkable that "Gaul" should be the surname of some Swiss families. Here in Lancaster County we have the Golls, the Galls and others perhaps modifications of old Swiss ancestral names, (Müller, p. 101).

1632—Myers—Egli—Bender and Other Swiss Names.

We have called attention to the familiar names of Gerber, Gaul and Albright, in their ancient evironments of nearly 300 years ago. So too, now other common eastern Pennsylvania names were found in Switzerland and the Countries that became asylums for them about the same time—most of them Mennonite leaders then and likewise pillars of that church now hear at home.

In 1632 there appear such Swiss as Hans Myer and Hans Egli, mentioned by Jacob Emsler—also Andreas Bender, sicklemaker. They were elected deacons and ministers of the early Mennonites. They were found in Hungary, too, refugees from Switzerland. Between the kings and the people and the Turks they had a hard life. The Turkish War of 1665 nearly wiped out entirely the congregations of Mennonites in Hungary, (Müller, p. 101).

1632 — The Dortrecht and Earlier Mennonite Confessions of Faith.

This was a jubilee year in the history of the Mennonite cult. Their first great confession of Faith or Creed was completed and issued to the world from Dortrecht, Holland on April 21st.

This was not the first confession of Faith of this people. At Amsterdam, September 27, 1627, a code of "Spiritual Instruction" which was virtually a primitive confession of faith, was drawn up. It was more nearly a primitive catechism—in the form of questions and answers.

There was also another confession drawn up at Amsterdam, October 7, 1630, taking up belief in God and the proper manner of living. At the end of this confession it is recited that it was done by the "undersigned ministers, teachers and elders of the United Friesic and High German Churches" for themselves, as well as their fellow-brethren and strangers assembled at Amsterdam—subscribed to by the fourteen persons, heads of the church for them and for all the churches whom they were sent to represent. The "Friesic" churches were those of Friesland, Holland.

Then came the Dortrecht confession of 1632. This work takes up:

I. God and the Creation.

II. The Fall of Man. This sets forth the belief that man by the "fall" became ruined, separated and estranged from God and that all would have been eternally lost had not God made provision otherwise.

III. The Restoration Through Christ. Here is set forth a belief in the fore-ordination of salvation through Christ.

IV. The Coming of Christ. Here they say that the word at the proper time was made flesh.

V. The Law of Christ, i. e., the Holy Gospel. Here it is confessed that before ascension, Christ instituted his New Testament and sealed the same and left it to the disciples.

VI. Repentance and Reformation of Life. Here it is declared that the imaginations of all men's hearts are evil and that faith and repentance are necessary to all.

VII. Holy Baptism. Here they set forth that there can be no effective baptism, before years of understanding are reached. Only penitent believers may be baptized. This was one of the chief beliefs that brought thousands and hundreds of thousands of these people into torture and death through perhaps 500 years.

VIII. The Church of Christ. Here is set forth, belief in the "visible church," viz: those who repent and are baptized. They alone are the "chosen royal priesthood."

IX. Election and Office of Teachers, Deacons and Deaconesses. "Christ instituted offices and ordinances and gave himself as the chief shepherd and bishop of our souls." He provided ministers, apostles, evangelists, pastors and teachers, whom through the Holy Ghost he had chosen and such he meant should be continued successively. Also that honorable aged widows should be chosen deaconesses.

X. The Holy Supper. This is an ordinance in "remembrance of him." It is not his actual body and blood.

XI. Washing of Feet. This is admonished to be literally done, as a mark of humility.

XII. The State of Matrimony. This shall be only between free believing persons. A churchman is not to marry any one not of the church.

XIII. Secular Authority of Officers. Here it is distinctly taught that secu-

THE DORTRECHT CONFESSION OF FAITH

lar authority and government and civil officers are instituted by God and are to be obeyed by all; that no one must despise or revile officers of government, but honor them; must faithfully pay taxes and customs; all must pray for them and for the prosperity of the country.

This is important to notice because a more or less false notion pervails that these people oppose government and decay it. This is not the fact. Certain brances of them do not take part in the operations of government; but they all heed it and support it.

XIV. Revenge. It it admonished there must be no retaliation.

XV. Swearing of Oaths. Here it is required that swearing of oaths is abolished by the Savior and that there shall be no more than the sanction of "Yea" and "Nay" to any statement.

XVI. Ecclesiastical Ban. Those who violate the church law must be separated from it and purged out of it reproved before all. This is for example to others. But on amendment they may be re-admitted.

XVII. Shunning the Separated. Here it is argued that those who persist on being wicked separate themselves from God and must be held separate from God's people and must be shunned. Yet if the shunned be needy, thirsty, hungry and sick he must be ministered unto. This shunning is without distinction and extends to members of the famly.

XVIII. Resurrection and Last Judgment. Belief that all who have died shall awaken at the last day is asserted, and they with those who are then living shall be changed in the twinkling of an eye.

The confession is then concluded by the statement that this was done in the United Churches in the City of Dortrecht, the 21st day of April, 1632.

It was signed by delegates, from Dortrecht, a city now of 33,00 people about 30 miles southeast of the famous Hague; delegates from Middleburg, now a city of 17,000 on the almost extreme southwest corner of Holland; delegates from Vlissingen, now called Flushing, only a couple of miles from the last place, a town of 13,000 people; delegates from Amsterdam now containging 400,000 people, the great Dutch City on the Znyder Zee, and among these delegates were David ter Haer, Peter Singel, Tobias Govertzs, Peter Moyer and Abraham Dirks; delegates from Haerlem, a city of 50,000, about 15 miles directly west of Amsterdam; delegates from Bommel, a small place; from Rotterdam. a city of 200,000 people, about 20 miles southwest of the Hague, among whose delegates were Shoenmacher and Michaels; delegates from the upper parts of the County; from Krevelt (Crefeld) in Westphalia, Germany, near the Holland boundary, one of whose delegates was the famous Herman Updegroff; delegates from Zeeland, among whom was Cornelius Moir (Myers); delegates from Schiedan; from Leyden, Holland, 22 miles southwest of Amsterdam; from Blackziel; from Ziericzee; from Gorcum; from Aunhum and from Utrecht. Utrecht has 40,000 people and is about 15 miles south of Amsterdam.

Most of these places are in Holland and most of the Churches assembled and represented were Holland Mennonite Churches, but the western borders of Germany were also represented, (Mirror, p. 36).

The prominent fact is, however, that at this time and at this gathering in Dortrecht, the Mennonite Church took on its great constitution and laid the general foundation of its doctrine and has been, in the main, the model of the church as in later years it spread to other countries and grew in strength and numbers, until this day.

There is only one thing of importance to add to the above, and that is that this Dortrecht confession of Faith, as the foundation of the Mennonite Church, was in 1727 translated into German and English and adopted in America in 1727, by a conference of 15 Mennonite ministers of Skippack, and Conestoga, here in Pennsylvania, among whom were Hans Burkholder, Christian Herr, Benedict Brackbill, Martin Baer of our county and others. And thus was planted here among us almost a hundred years after its adoption in Holland, the same confession of Mennonite faith that guided the fathers for centuries, (Müller, 369).

1632—The Mennonites of Alsace Join In Dortrecht Confession.

Soon after the Dortrecht confession was signed, the faithful of other sections joined in it also. Throughout Alsace—Lorraine the churches approved it. By 1660 thousands of the Huguenots embraced it. The Palatinate also received it both before and after the great Swiss immigration of 1671. Among the prominent Swiss who signed it there were Jacob Schnebeli and Rudolph Egli. So too, the Schmidts, Scheiders, Fricks and others signed, (Müller, p. 195).

1634—The Palatinate Comes into Religious Prominence.

A writer about 1709 at the time of the German Exodus into England, said, "The poor Palatines who are objects of our present charity inhabitated lately a principality in Germany called the Palatinate, which is divided into the Upper and Lower Palatinate. The Upper belongs to the Duke of Bavaria and the Lower to Count Palatine of the Rhine. It takes its name from the Count Palatine, who formerly owned the whole and administered justice in the Emperor's name. The city of Philipsburg was first the chief city of the Palatinate. It was in the upper part on the Rhine river. It was taken six times; by the Imperialists in 1633; by the Swedes in 1634; by the Imperialists in 1636; by the Prince of Conde in 1644; by the Germans in 1676; and by the Dauphine in 1688; but it was restored to the Empire by the Treaty of Ryswick." (Palatinate Refugees in England, p. 26). Into this Palatinate, therefore, as early as 1634 and earlier the persecuted Mennonites of Switzerland flocked because the Count Palatine allowed much freedom of religious thought and practice.

1635—A New Persecution of Mennonites about Zurich.

After the execution of Hans Landis in 1614, the persecutions in Switzerland died out for about 20 years. But in 1635 the old hatred against the non-resisting sect of Christians broke out afresh from the Reformed Church, and then the State Church in Switzerland. This persecution led by the Zwinglians was not new; because in 1525 Zwingli himself pronounced decrees against them—over 100 years before the persecutions of 1635.

The cause of the persecution was the conversion of a rich and influential citizen of Zurich named Henry F———. He was chosen ensign and requested to serve as an officer in the army. But being a believer in the Mennonite or Baptist faith he refused to perform military duty and instead entered the Baptist convent. This enraged the Government against the Mennonites.

A mandate was issued from Zurich that all must attend the State Church —the Reformed Church—or lose their liberty. They refused and toward the end of 1635 many of them were arrested and also imprisoned. Many broke jail; but the prominent ones remained confined. Rudolph Egli, Uhli Schmidt and Hans Müller. They were let out on a month's probation; but not willing to yield their faith, were put back again, (Mirror, p. 1049).

1636—Progress of the New Swiss Persecutions.

This year in August and September and in the beginning of 1637, nearly all the Taufer or Mennonite brethren and sisters of Switzerland, but principally in Zurich, were summoned before the political authorities as well as before certain ecclesiastical authorities, whom the Government delegated for the purpose.

First they were summoned to the Castles of Wadischwyl on Lake Zurich; of Knownau about twenty miles south of Zurich; and of Groenigen, 20 miles east of Zurich, and compelled to give their names, surnames, residences, ages, ancestry, etc., so that they could be watched.

A second time they were summoned to the same place and ordered to attend the Reformed services.

They were next summoned to Zurich (especially all leaders) and commanded to give up their views and cease teaching their beliefs as to infant baptism, the Lord's supper and the discipline of ex-communication.

A fourth time they were compelled to appear as under arrest and give complete inventories of their properties and estates, especially all movable property, and cautioned not to dispose of any of it. After having all their property registered they were placed under arrest.

A fifth time they were sent for and brought to the castles and given the alternative of attending the Reformed Church or being lodged in jail. They begged permission to leave the country with their goods. This was refused. (Mirror, p. 1050).

Müller (p. 70) gives substantially the same account, except that he tells us that a commission of Reformed Church-men rode about on horseback to the various towns and sought out the Mennonites and had them sent to the Castles to be intimidated out of their religion, etc.

1637—Brubakers, Landises and Egles in Zurich Jails.

In 1637 a perfect swarm of beadles, bailiffs and sheriffs were sent throughout all Zurich to spy out Mennonites and apprehend them. The fire of persecution was now raging. Without ceremony they entered houses of believers, took whatever they wanted and abused women and children. Scores of men they imprisoned among criminals. A damp prison at Othenbach was the worst place.

Of those captured were Jacob Rusterholtz and Peter Brubach or Brubacher of Wadischwyl; also a Hans Landis (the second) a minister of the Church of Horgerburg and his daughter Margaret Landis. She remained in Othenbach prison about 60 weeks. While they were in prison the authorities sold all of their property for 7000 guilders.

Rudolph Egly was again imprisoned at Zurich, his children driven out of the house, the house destroyed and everything confiscated to the Government, (Mirror, 1051).

These facts were written up by Martin Meyli, a Mennonite historian, who himself passed through these tortures of 1635 to 1660 and wrote of personal knowledge. He is quoted by the Mirror also.

1637—The Meylis, Mylins or Meilens Suffer.

The ancient European home of the Meilins now Mylins, seems, to have been in the Canton of Zurich. Mr. Schnebeli, a present day Swiss historian tells us this. There was a Claes Meiliss in Holland in 1542 (Mirror, p. 448), and a Peter Von der Meülin in Ghent in 1564 (Do., 640). Whether they were the same family as the Meilins, we can not tell.

Reliable history of the ancestry of our present Lancaster County Swiss Mylins exists from 1637. In the Knonow Bailiwick in Switzerland the persecution raged; and aged Hans Meyli, a Mennonite minister was imprisoned that year. They also took his son Martin's wife. She was imprisoned a long time at Ottembach, about 8 miles southwest of Zurich and treated severely. They took all of the elder Mylin's property. About a year later they caught two of Hans Meyli's sons, Martin and Hans, Jr. and imprisoned them at Zurich where they were held in chains and handcuffs.

Their children (grandchildren of Hans Meyli, Sr.) as poor forsaken orphans were put out among strangers. One of these, Martin by name, a son of Hans Meyli, Jr. and a nephew of Martin, the Swiss historian cited by the Mirror was one of the band of pioneer settlers of Lancaster County in 1710 on Pequea Creek,(Mirror, p. 1052 and Rupp, p. 74).

1639—Hans Herr, Lancaster County Pioneer Born.

This year, Hans Herr, leader of the Pioneer band of Lancaster County, which settled near Willow Street in West Lampeter Township, Pennsylvania, was born on September 17, near Zurich. He died in 1725 and was buried in the Cemetery of the Brick Mennonite Church just east of Willow Street (Herr Genealogy, p. 1).

Following the title page of the Herr Genealogy occurs the statement:

"The race of Herr descended from a very ancient family;—is free that is to say, of noble origin;—likewise from time immemorial its knights were brave and worthy—possessing in Schwaben vast and rich estate, the name which was called and written, Herr von Bilried. The father of the race was called the Schwabish Knight Hugo, the Herr or Lord of Bilried.

In the year 1009 flourished and was known to all, the family from whom that of Herr is descended. But in the fifteenth century several of the race resigned their nobility and settled as citizens. They, however, retained their noble name and their coat of arms, and in the year 1593 John Herr as Lord of Bilried obtained from the Emperor Ferdinand in Schwabish Hall, a written testimonial proving for his flourishing family their coat of arms, their free and noble descent and the possession of their race to the latest generation; and the coat of arms yet rightly belongs to the present living family of Herr.

E. B. VIEN.

Recorded in the Register of Noble Families, with their coat of Arms, Book 5, page 258.

1639—Barbara and Elizabeth Meylin and Others Suffer for Their Faith.

The Mirror (p. 1053) relates that this year Barbara and Elizabeth Mylin and two other sisters in the faith, Ottila Mülerin and Barbara Kolbin suffered for their faith. They were not executed, however, for they managed to escape from the prison of Ottenbach, the location of which town we have mentioned. They were also relatives of the aged Hans Mylin.

1639—Another Hans Müller of Canton Zurich, Suffers.

We have set out the troubles of a Hans Müller of Medikon, Switzerland under date of 1529 (See Supra., p. 34). More than one hundred years later the name Müller again comes into prominence, through persecution in cruel Switzerland. The sufferer again is a 'Hans" Müller.

The Mirror under date of 1635 (p. 1050) refers to this pillar of faith as defending the "poor fund" of the Church, which they tried to make him give up. His home was in Grüningen, about 12 miles southeast of Zurich. He was released but 4 years later was again imprisoned, viz: in 1639. He was a powerful factor in the Mennonite Church and so zealous were the officers to find him a second time, that like ravening wolves they ran through his neighbors' houses to find him. He had escaped from his house and when they came to it and broke it open and found he was gone, they broke open chests and drawers and took all the property they could get. They threatened his little children with bare swords that they would kill them if they did not reveal his whereabouts. They took his wife and put her bound in the loathsome Ottenbach prison. Then a proclamation was announced in the Reformed churches of Zurich, that no one would be allowed to lodge or give food or drink to Hans Müller, from the Groeningen Bailiwick under severe penalty.

Then they deceived him and sent abroad a proclamation that he would be allowed a three weeks' safe conduct to argue with him, if he came forth. He trusted this and went to the convent specified to discuss the matter but as he was about to leave he was arrested in breach of faith and taken to Ottenbach; imprisoned 60 weeks, of which he spent 16 weeks in chains. (Mirror, p. 1053).

As to the Müllers, Zurich always had and now has many "Müller" (Millers). Mr. Schnebeli says a branch of the Müllers came in the early times from Zurich; but the Müllers were early distributed in Berne and in Germany and elsewhere. However, he says the whole Canton of Zurich is full of Müllers. Among the dead in the battle of Kappel in Affaltern, Canton of Zurich, where Zwingli was killed on October 11, 1531, were found nine Müllers, from Wipkengen, Zollikon, Kussnach, Thalvil, Affaltern. Lzattiken, Hetlingen, Wetzekon and Gollikon, all in Switzerland. Mr. Schnebeli say that the Müllers have always held prominent offices, did valiant and distinguished services for the state at home and abroad, and produced many able statesmen, such as Müller of Friedberg, of St. Gallen, and the historian Müller, of Schaffhausen. He says, also, that the President of Switzerland in 1909 was a Müller.

1639—The Amans, Egles, Snyders, Webers and Zehnders Suffer.

It is perhaps known to all that our Amish brethren are so called because they followed a dissenting Mennonite named Aman, in Europe. In 1639 we find that Burkhard Aman who lived by the border of Lake Zurich, was arrested for his faith, taken to Zurich and condemned and then taken to the Ottenbach prison where so many Mennonites suffered. But his year in prison was so cruel that he became ill and shortly after his release died. The Amish abound in Lancaster County and other southeastern Pennsylvania sections, (Mirror, p. 1054).

The same year Jacob Egle of Gruningen district, near Zurich as we have before stated, was arrested and after a short trial at Zurich was imprisoned in the Ottenbach dungeon, during a year and a half. He was so miserably treated that he died in prison, rather than give up his faith, (Do.).

The same year George Weber, an old man of Kiburg, a city 15 miles southeast of Zurich on a branch of the Rhine, was arrested for his faith and taken to Ottenbach dungeon and fed on bread and water. He also became sick and died soon after his release. Besides being imprisoned, both Egli and Weber were sentenced to pay 500 guilders annually as fine to the authorities, which if not paid was to be levied on their property until it was all consumed; unless they gave up their religion, (Do.).

Webers and the modern Weavers are very numerous in Lancaster County. They first located here about 1711, just 200 years ago. Hans Weber having bought the Rudolph Bundely tract containing 530 acres, forming the north-eastern section of the original settlement of 6400 acres in our country, (See map following page 75, Vol. XIV, Lancaster County Historical Society, Reports or appendix, to said volume).

The same year Ulli Snyder from Wadischwyl, about ten miles southeast of Zurich on the south side of Lake Zurich and four miles beyond Horgen suffered imprisonment because of his faith. They tortured him to compel him to embrace the Common or Reformed mode of worship. He died steadfast in jail, (Do., 1055).

The same year Stephen Zehnder of the Mennonite Church at Knonow was imprisoned in a damp cellar of the Ottenbach jail and so treated that he died of exposure and hardship, (Do.).

The above we all recognize as common Lancaster, York, Berks and Lebanon county names. The item seems to show that while it is ordinarily said that the forefathers of this section of Pennsylvania are of German descent, that such tradition is not strictly accurate. They are originally Swiss. Many of our ancestors, however, were pushed by prosecution from Switzerland into Germany and particularly into the Palatinate on the Rhine and lived there some years, migrating from that place to Eastern Pennsylvania.

1639—The Hess Family Appear in History.

Here we have one of the earliest notices of the Hess family also numerous in this county and in southeastern Pennsylvania and from Pennsylvania distributed far and wide—numerous in the Virginias, in the middle West, many of them in Chicago and in sections beyond as well.

The Mirror (p. 1056) notes Hans or John Jacob Hess in 1639 as a Minister of the Mennonite Church in Switzerland, and earlier. The account states that he was arrested and imprisoned three times, first in 1637. The third imprisonment lasted 88 weeks. But he, with others escaped. The account says that he was stripped and confined in prison, in chains 16 weeks with fellow prisoners. While he was in jail they arrested and imprisoned his wife for her religion, in the Ottenbach dungeon. There she got consumption and died after 63 weeks incarceration, (Do., 1056).

The account also states that the property of Jacob Hess was seized and sold by the authorities and sold for 4000 guilders without giving any of it back. A guilder is worth 40 cents in our money. Thus they took $1600 from this man. The exact home of the Hess family mentioned is not shown; but it was in the Canton of Zurich somewhere.

1639—Netherland Intercedes for the Swiss Menonnites.

It must not be concluded that the Mennonites had no friends and helpers during these awful days. The persecution against them in Holland which raged 100 years earlier had cooled and they were held in favor there long before 1639. In the Mennonite Archives of Zurich there is an extract of the event of church affairs from 1639 to 43; and also similar matter in the Bern Archives. Casper Suter of the Mennonite Church kept these records.

Holland sent a commission to Zurich inquiring about these matters and stated that reports in Holland were to the effect that 20 people were being cruelly treated and imprisoned in Ottenbach—that some of them are supposed to be subjects of Holland; and that they remonstrate in a friendly way for all of them; but insist on the release of any Dutch subjects that may be imprisoned. There are reports by Ottibus also about these matters. Other inquiries were made later by Berne. of Zurich asking how they treat Mennonites. We shall see, however, that a little later Berne began a series of persecutions as fierce as those of Zurich, (Müller, p. 166).

1639—Zurich Tries to Explain and Apologize to the World for the Treatment of the Mennonites.

This apology was issued in 1639, and was called out by the fact that the cruelties inflicted by Zurich moved a large part of Europe to protest. Holland lead the protests. The Swiss authorities, incited by "the so called Reformed Church" to which the officers of the government belonged, gave as their chief excuses for torturing the Mennonites the following reasons. That "they separated themselves from the obedience which they owed to the Christian Church"; that they refused to allow baptism to be performed upon little children which endangered their salvation; that they would not help defend the government against its enemies; and that they were disobedient to the authorities, refusing to help support the government and obey its laws. This apology was intended to influence the nations to believe that Zurich and indeed the whole of Switzerland was compelled to take the measures they did, for the alleged reason that the foundation of the government was endangered by these Taufers or Mennonites and the established religion in danger, (Mirror, 1056).

1639—Reply of the Swiss Mennonites to the Zurich Manifesto.

The Mennonites of Switzerland immediately made reply to the apologies and explanations of the government officials and Reformed churchmen against them.

As to separation from the Christian Church, they said this is not a fact, but that they adhere and always have adhered to the pure Word of God, and for this reason could not possibly be members of the Reformed Church, their chief persecutor now. They say also that the original leaders of the Reformed Church held the same views as the Mennonites still hold, when they were both persecuted by the Catholic Church; but that now the Reformed churchmen have entirely drifted away from the old beliefs while the Mennonites have still held on to them.

They then take up the subject of baptism and show that originally the founders of the Reformed Church held the same view the Anabaptists or Mennonites now hold. They cited Zwingli himself and Baltzer Hubmor or Huffmeier, saying that at a conference in the Graef in 1523 they, as founders of the Reformed Church declared that infants should not be baptized; and that Zwingli made this the 18th Canon in his Book of Articles. The same, they say, was held by Oecolampadius in a letter to said Huffmeier or Hubmor. They declare that Sebasitan Hoffmeyster, an early Reformed Church preacher wrote to Hupmeir and said that at a council at Schaffhausen that infants must not be baptized. These are all Reformed founders. Schaffhausen is a city of 12000 population about 20 miles north from Zurich.

They also cited that Christopher Hogendorf, Cellarius, both Reformed fathers, and the early Reformed Church preachers at Strassburg, Germany; Wolfgang Gapito, Cester Hedio, Mathew Zell and others agree in this writing that originally there was no infant baptism.

Concerning war or retaliation, they say that Lutherans who in the beginning were Calvinistic Reformed and the Reformed churchmen or Zwinglians, in the beginning believed the same as do the Mennonites. Among the earliest were Andrew Carlstadt who in his book dated 1524 wrote that war is against God's law and must not be entered upon. They also cited Luther in the twenty-second article or a tract written by him in 1520, explaining why he burnt the "pope's books" as follows: Because he (the pope) teaches that it is right for a Christian to defend himself with violence against violence contrary to Matthew 5:40.

They show that in a tract printed at Wittenberg in 1522 it is set forth that Luther taught opposition to all war and against suits at law. They concluded that Luther believed these views until he was "Seduced to another belief by the Jesuits even as Sleydonus (a Jesuit) testifies", (Mirror, 1056 to 58).

They go on to show that all the foremost Reformers against Popery in 1520—in 1530—in 1540 were opposed to war and resistance and to oaths and to infant baptism.

As to the charge that they do not support the government they deny it wholly. Thus they show that it was not they, the Mennonites, who departed from the Christian Church and its doctrines; but that the Reformed and the Lutherans departed from those first principles approved by all who opposed the Catholic Church, while the Mennonites have held on to those principles to this day.

1639—Charges against and Answers of the Mennonites, Printed.

Müller tells us (165) that the Burgomeisters and the Great and Small Council of Zurich called the Council of 200 drew up formally the Mennonite situation there in 1639 stating the acts of Zurich against them, the form of the judiciary by which they tried them and the impartiality of the justice visited upon them. The state paper was printed by Dr. Humberger the same year in Zurich. It is a quarto volume of 71 pages. It is found also in Leonard Meister's 'Helvetian Scenes of Visionariries," as he calls it.

1639—Holland Mennonites in Conference Adopt Ethical Rules.

Mrs. Brons in her book, which I have often referred to says (p. 135) that, this year there was a conference held by the Mennonites of Holland to formulate a code of moral rules for daily guidance. A year or two earlier there was a similar conference of the Mennonites of four Holland cities; but now the conference was general. Peter Van Twisk seems to have brought it about. The Friesland churches led off. The principal meeting was on a day called the 'Landsdag"; and the elders who attended as delegates were called the "Landsdienaren". The purpose was to organize rules for the encouragement and protection of the faithful. Moral rules adopted to guide them. A society was organized also to admonish all to the performance of these rules, and to keep before all the necessity of living pure lives and taking care of the poor, of aiding the preachers, etc. The society however did not keep any minutes of its proceedings until 1694. But there is plenty of evidence that it existed as early as 1639; and as late as 1716.

The 12 chief articles or rules adopted by them which were to be read in all the churches once a year were as follows:

1. When a brother or sister marries a second time they should settle on the children of the first marriage an inheritance; and obey all the laws of the land.

2. All costly and elaborate weddings must be avoided. All must be moderate and in the fear of God, after the example of Tobias so as not to dishonor God.

3. Young men and women must not be allowed too much freedom in their association. They must not "keep company" with each other nor engage themselves to marry without the consent of their parents or guardians; such a step must not be taken without that serious consideration which becomes a Christian.

4. Those who are about to marry from another place or town shall be required ot produce a good recommendation from the place in which they dwell. This shall show whether they are still free, also whether the bans have been published. Under the law of Switzerland at this same time, bans were allowed to be published in the Reformed church only; and no other but Reformed ministers were allowed to perform the marriage ceremony.

5. In trading and in doing business all are to avoid taverns as much as possible, because there one seldom learns anything good, and is very likely to become drunk.

6. No one must have business so tangled up that he will not be able to pay on the day and the hour when he should. The word pledged in business, must be kept, otherwise a person gets a bad name and so does the congregation.

7. No one is allowed to buy or receive stolen goods. They who do so, share the sin of stealing or robbing.

8. No one shall engage himself to go on an armed vessel. As soon as it is ascertained, it is armed the Christian must get off. (This might be pretty serious.)

9. No one should use tobacco unnecessarily, or make it a habit, for time and money are wasted by it; and it is offensve to others. This evil is getting so great in Holland since trade is open with America that instead of hymn books to edify, many go for the tobacco pipe. (About this time tobacco and wigs were introduced and the church said that they were introduced by Satan.)

10. No ornaments are to be allowed on or in houses or ships but all must be made plain. By external ornaments the internal ornaments of the soul are spoiled.

11. If a brother or sister move to another town they must get a recommendation or a certificate of good character from the place or congregation from where he or she come, to show that he or she is decent.

12. No one must neglect to talk to and admonish the struggling brother who is "going wrong". This must be done in brotherly love and sincerity. There must also be reprimand, but in a loving way and by taking the brother alone.

These, says Brons, were the 12 main articles of conduct of the Friesian Mennonites; and we can see what fine lives they exacted from all believers. Those who violated these rules were "set back", and not allowed to participate in the rites of the church until they repented. They bear the caption "Twelve Articles. Promulgated in 1639 by the Conference of the Congregations, and for the Preservation of Good Morals among Themselves".

All I need add to the above is to call attention to the fact that our Swiss, German and Holland ancestors were not crude in thought, but refined. It was a more or less commonly held opinion here in our country for many years that, our ancient stock of Eastern Pennsylvania Germans were gross and voluptuous, and not concerned about the appreciation nor the practice of the delicate and refined. This has been an injustice to them and a slander. While their taste has not always been standard, they have always been, in reality, sensitive and cultured.

1640—Canton Berne Begins Persecution Anew.

Jan. 17 this year, the Berne authorities in Switzerland sent out a mandate to Aarwangen Soffingen, Aarburg Kiburg, Thun, Signau, Brandis and Trachelswald that on Jan. 23 there should be an inquisition upon the Mennonites for the purpose of finding heresy charges against them and violations of the laws and customs of Berne and the Reformed church. It was decreed that the time had come for severe measures because their superstitions, service and intolerable practice kept on prospering and their sect kept on increasing, in spite of all that had been done against them thus far (Müller 132). Most of the above places are between 10 and 20 miles east, northeast and southeast of the city of Berne, in and near the famous Emmenthal or Emmen Valley, the particular location from which the pioneers came directly to the Pequea and the Conestoga in 1710, and later. About 1630 they had come into the Emmenthal from the Zurich region.

1640—More Eastern Pennsylvania Ancestry Suffer.

About this time and afterwards, the following persons suffered throughout Switzerland for their religion's sake. Among them were Werner Phister of Walischwyl who was imprisoned at Othenbach; Gallus Snyder of the same place, put in the same prison; also Rudolph Bachman a very old man of the same district who was bound to a sled and dragged to the same prison, where he was placed in chains until his death; also Henry Schnebli (now Snavely) of Knownow who was imprisoned for his religious views with criminals in Zurich; about the same time Hans Rudolph Bauman (or Bowman) of Horgerberg, imprisoned in Zurich,after having been robbed by the State church and the government of his property worth over 3000 guilders; about the same time Ulrich Müller of Kiborg first imprisoned at Zurich and, then thrown into the dungeon of Othenbach where he died; at the same time also Oswald Landis who with his wife and two daughters-in-law were imprisoned in the Othenbach dungeon; also his son Jacob Landis, and his entire family, imprisoned in the same place; about the same time Henry Fricken and Hans Ring of the neighborhood of Knowow; a year or two later Felix Landis of Horgerberg (son of Hans Landis who was beheaded in 1614) who was imprisoned at Othenbach and nearly starved to death after robbing him of 5,000 guilders; in 1643 Elizabeth Bachman of Gruningen and Verena Landis also suffered threats and imprisonment; also at the same time Barbara Neff and Barbara Ruff or Rupp of the Knowow district; also Martha Lindne and Anna Blau, (afterwards married to Moneth Meylich with whom she moved to the Palatinate), were imprisoned. (Mirror 1059 to 1062).

All of the above names we recognize as quite common among the generality of Eastern Pennsylvania and especially Lancaster County populace today. These incidents are meant to throw a clear light on the particular location of the sturdy ancestry of the neighborhood nearly 300 years ago. The places mentioned above are, none of them, far distant from the two main centers of tyranny and torture—Berne and Zurich.

1641—Amsterdam, Holland, Becoming a Powerful Supporter of Mennonites.

Müller relates (p. 166) that, this year Amsterdam received news of the persecution of Mennonite brethren by Zurich and began another examination. Zurich contended that the reports were exaggerated. The Amsterdam authorities sent Isaac Hataver, an influential merchant of the Reformed or Lutheran church of Holland to investigate. In the year 1642 Godfried Hattonus who was pastor of the French church at Amsterdam began the agitation for investigation, by writing to Zurich about the terrible reports that came to Holland. He received an answer from Antistis Breitinger, telling him the facts pretty fairly. Then pamphlets were printed and circulated in Holland calling public attention to the furious conduct of Berne and Zurich. A pamphlet was started, a strong monograph came out against the doctrines of the Baptists or Mennonites, alleging it to be a heresy calculated to overthrow the government by Petros Bontemps, minister of the "Gallicana" in Harlem (Holland). To this Yost Hendricks (perhaps an ancestor of Laurens Hendricks whom we shall mention later) made reply, painting the Swiss persecution of the Mennonites as black as night. In 1643 Bontemps replied, in which he made it appear there was no persecution going on at all. Then three strong pamphlets were issued by the Mennonites of Amsterdam, Rotterdam and Haarlem respectively, showing that in truth the Swiss persecutions were terrible. Several editions of these were printed, and greedily read until Holland was aflame wth indigation against Switzerland. There were other productions calling attention to the suffering of the defenceless Christians; and this brought on the appeal from the Holland government. Holland was a power in those days, to whose voice all European nations paid attention.

1641—Prominent Hamburgers Became Mennonites.

On the extinction of the Shumberg line the succeeding king, Christian the IV of Denmark, who at the time was Duke of Holstein became a friend of the Mennonites; and the congregation of Altona opposite Hamburg, and in Hamburg also gained privileges. In spite of the raillery of the Lutherans, the Mennonites grew. Some of the principal Hamburg families, namely the Roosen and Goverts families who had large warehouses, became Mennonites. (Brons 256.)

1642—The Dantzig and Elbing Mennonites of the Baltic Become the Best Farmers of Europe.

Until 1642, the Mennonites of northwestern Prussia were left in peace; but then a new storm broke loose, especially about Elbing in Prussia. The Chamberlain of the king Bladislaus the IV, namely Willibald of Hexburg made the king of Prussia suspicious about the Mennonites; and he got a warrant or written authority from the king, to drive the Mennonites out, because they hurt the trade of the other people in Dantzig and Elbing. This paper allowed the officer to seize the Mennonites' goods and to use them for himself. He started to carry out the instructions, and then arranged that if they would give him a sum of money instead, he would not interfere with their goods. These Mennonites, many of them, lived in the "Vaterns" —that is, on islands on the delta of the Vistula River or on swampy land; and because they did not serve in the army they were made to pay very heavy fines or rents to the government, because of the false accusations the chamberlain made against them. They had to pay fifty gulden rent, per hide. A hide is a small piece of land, enough for two persons to live on. The whole sum collected from those who dwelt in the swamp land was about fifty-thousand gulden; and from Dantzig several thousand.

The Mennonites complained of this suffering and the Land Court took it up and relieved them from these grievances. The king of Prussia saw that the chamberlain had deceived him, and gave them new privileges. He also compelled his officer, the chamberlain, to destroy the written authority he had given to him. After that, their condition was happy in the neighborhood of the Dantzig, and they took new heart and built dykes, drained the swampy land, and cultivated that which was desolate. The government protected them in their rights. The king said that the dykes which they built along the Drausees and the Sogat Rivers were splendid examples to posterity. These Mennonites located in the northeastern part of Prussia when they were driven out of Holland. The king also gave them exemption from war taxes forever. (Brons p. 256).

1642—Rupp's Account of Mennonite Sufferings at This Date.

We have given in a prior item from other sources the names of Lancaster County ancestors, who suffered from 1640 onward. Rupp in his history of Lancaster County (page 72) says that, among those who suffered was Hans Miller, Hans Jacob Hess, Rudolph Bachman, Ulrich Miller. Oswald Landis, Fanny Landis, Barbara Neff, Hans Meylin and his two sons. He says that these sufferings occurred about 1643.

1643—Joost Hendrick's Account of Suffering in Zurich.

This year, when thirty men and women of the Mennonite faith were in the Ottenbach prison of Switzerland, a Christian man of Holland named Joost Hendrick wrote about their sufferings. We have spoken before of the series of pamphlets written upon these hardships; but we now quote a part of Hendrick's letter written to Bontemps whom we have also mentioned before. He says, upon the refusal to leave their lands, persecution and imprisonment followed; and in a short time these people were compelled to pay about eighty-thousand Reichthalers. They were also imprisoned in a horrible manner—so horrible it cannot be described. About Easter there were thirty of them imprisoned in a small, dark dungeon. Most of them were so sick that they looked like dead. They even had women fast in chains.

This is the condition about Zurich. A man named Isaac Hattaver, a Mennonite elder in Amsterdam, also states they suffered, the greatest in Netherland, and were in great excitement and offered prayers for their Swiss brethren daily. They are satisfied the worst representations were the truth. So they sent their brother Hattaver to call on business friends in Zurich and get the truth. He did so, He got a letter to the prisoners; and admonished them to be mild; and they may get permission to leave. He says "They hope to come to Holland. We can get about to $200.00 to help them. Zurich claims that the Mennonites were disobedient and must be treated harsh. Our brethren say they did make a hole in the wall and broke out of jail; it was so bad they could not stay. They say the people are joining the faith and this is why Zurich is punishing them. Something must be done to help these people."

This is what Hendricks wrote about the condition at the very time the suffering was going on. (Brons p. 201).

1644—Another Futile Mandate from Zurich.

This year a final mandate was issued against Mennonites preaching throughout Switzerland. After this mandate and its failure there was a season of freedom allowed the Mennonites.

This edict demanded that there should be no more Mennonite preaching—that no one should attend any services the Mennonites attempted to hold—nor should any person harbor or give aid to any of them. All judges and magistrates and sheriffs and Reformed preachers and elders and adherents and God-fearing people were to help execute this edict under penalty.

A final effort was made to put the former decrees of 1585 and 1597 into execution, in 1644 because as they said the Mennonite heresy was taking deeper root than ever (Müller 136). Efforts were particularly directed against the teachers and leaders.

The authorities were first to reason with the offenders and if that did not bring the result to imprison them confiscate their goods and do whatever may be needed. Those arrested were to be sent to Zurich. (Do. 134.)

1644—The Prominent Swiss Names, Stauffer, Zug and Neuhauser Appear.

In an edict promulgated throughout the region of Berne April 11, 1644, a demand was made upon all loyal adherents by the Reformed Church to capture the leaders of the Mennonite "heresy" throughout the land. Among these the mandate ordered particularly that Christian

GROWTH IN BERNE—GOCHNAUERS APPEAR

Stauffer, Uli Neuhus (or probably now Neuhauser) and Uli Zuagg (likely now Zug or Zook) should be captured at all hazards. Their names we recognized as that of a numerous progeny now throughout eastern Pennsylvania and Lancaster County. It was ordered that these were "seducers" of the people should be sent to Zurich. But their homes seem to have been in the neighborhood of Thun, Trachelswald and Soffingen, places in the Berne district. (Müller 132 and 133. It was declared Oct. 26, 1644 that theretofore there had been much "winking" at the mandates; but now they were to be enforced rigidly.

1644—Mennonite Growth in the Berne District.

The Mennonites of Aarau and Lenzburg near Berne were becoming particularly prosperous. Also near Zofingen or Soffingen, about half way between Zurich and Berne on a branch of the Rhine, there were many of them. Of their principal ones there were Hans Stentz, a teacher in Ober-Culm, Rudolph Kunzli (now Kunzler or Kinsley), also Hanz Yeagli of Adra, Hanz Dester and Solomon Yeagley (Müller 105 and Ottius).

Three of the Aarau Mennonites, when they heard of the new edict, declared they were ready to go and defend their religion. It was arranged that they should be heard by the clergy of the Reformed Church; and were assured they would have safe conduct granted them, to come to the hearing and to go back again. But no Zurich brethren would be allowed to come and be present at the debate and proceedings to hear whether they made an able exposition or not. All Zurich Mennonites must get out of the country. But to allow the Berne Mennonites to see their wrong, the mandate would be suspended till May 27, 1644 and they could decide after this examination was ended, what they would do.

It appears that Yeagley and all the other Mennonite leaders first above mentioned were at this examination. Their chief inquisitor was, Rev. Mark Ruttimyer. The principal Mennonites examined were Hanz Tester and Hans Glur. They declared for themselves and their followers that:

(1) They will persist in separation because of the ungodly life of the state church.

(2) Such separation is demanded by Holy Writ and the state church does not compel it.

Because of this stand taken by these Mennonites their free and safe conduct was violated; and Tester, Peyer and Yeagley were all imprisoned. (Müller 105).

1644—Respite from Persecution in Zurich

Says the Mirror (p. 1063) that from 1644 to 1654 persecution abated. And in that time there is no record of any having died in prison of bad treatment or bad food.

1644—Gochnauers, Hubers and Baumgartners Suffer in Zurich

About this time, according to the Mirror (p. 1064) Mennonites or Anabaptists of Zurich of the names above specified suffered for their religion at the hands of the Government, which was now in the charge of the Reformed Church.

Jacob Gochnauer from Groeningen Bailiwick about 10 miles southeast of Zurich near the famous field of Greifensee was first driven out of the country, his family separated, and all his possessions sold. On his attempt to return and find his children he was caught and thrust into the horrible prison of Ottenbach about 6 miles southwest of Zurich on the Reuss River, deprived of his clothes and dressed in a gray coat and fastened with chains. Hans Huber from

Horgerburg was also imprisoned in the Ottenbach dungeon with eleven other Mennonites and was fasteued with chains and his wife and sister driven into exile.

Jacob Baumgartner an old man of 70 years had been imprisoned for his faith 5 times and each time escaped, but was now again apprehended and thrown into Ottenbach prison. He was fastened to chains. deprived of his clothes and clad in a gray coat, fed on bread and water, put in irons and hand-cuffed and his property sold for 500 gilders and the money taken by the government.

These are all familiar names in Eastern Pennsylvania and also in other parts of the United States, whence they have migrated viz.: to Indiana, Illinois and Kansas; and also in Canada. I insert this article in this series to show the ancient home of the ancestors of our people having the same name and now prominent in many sections and in many walks of life.

1644—Interesting Letter From David Shaar to Uli Zaugg or Zugg.

In the district of Diesbach, about 10 miles northeast of Berne lived Shaar and Zaugg or Zugg, above named. According to Müller (p. 117) Shaar, for some reason not revealed, was excommunicated from the Mennonite Church of Switzerland, and (it seems) Zaugg was instrumental in having this done. Shaar thereupon wrote him the following letter:

"Dear Friendly Uli Zaugg:

For your treatment of me, I will pass no invidious judgment for the high arch-angel Michael did not dare to judge any, only over Satan; but I will tell you a parable and submit it to your judgment. There was a master who had bought a sheep, as he did many times. It was not as fine as the others, but he gave as much for it as any of the others. He gave this one to the charge of the hired man. And the poor ignorant sheep went out after its nourishment on the pasture many years. After long time it was hurt by a thorn and it bled a little. This was noticed by the shepherd and he cried out it shall hurry and come to him. He set the time, the hours and the day and said "if it did not come, its injury might not be healed at all." Now this poor sheep is old and weak and the road is long and uneven and it thought to itself "How will it be if this shepherd does not have the right salve to heal if you do go to him; for many times before when you were hurt and wounded your Lord and master who had bought you healed you himself". Consequently he went to the Lord and found some relief. Then the hired man cried more and more that it should come to him and his colaborers if it wants to be healed. Now it did not want to despise the undershepherd and gave an account verbal and written of what had happened to it; and how it got hurt, but all was of no avail. The undershepherd could not cure it. The undershepherd then complained that it stayed out too long; and he made the injury seem so great and incurable. He then resolved with them it was not worth any more than that it should be killed and its misery ended. Therefore, the shepherd said, he does not want anything more to do with the sheep. But the poor sheep was not content with this and could not understand why it should be adjudged that his life be forfeited.

When the master of this sheep shall come and give these shepherds their wages and when he asks of this shepherd what he deserves, what do you think, Uli, you would give him as pay for what you did in this case? Now I pray thee, you will be judge in an impartial manner when appealed to by the Lord over all, whose judgment you will have to bear.

Herein I place you under the benign protection of our Lord. And I, too, will stay with my Lord who has bought me with his blood, and not with gold or silver. Therefore I will stay right with the universal church whose head is Christ. At times I will gladly go where the Holy Gospel is read, taught and preached. But with respect to unjust courts and judgments and power, which the people sometimes, adjudge to themselves or usurp, to that my heart and conscience and my mind will never be bound. Should the Almighty God—the benevolent God, in Heaven will it, he will give them all the wisdom to do these things, that they may govern with righteousness and justice, because they do not only hold Court by the people and account to them; but they must account to God also, who will finally be the judge of all of us. May he be merciful to us all, through Christ. Amen.

This, I, David Shaar wish to all who are ingrafted in Jesus Christ not only by baptism of water; but by a true and living, simple and pure faith. Herewith I will close, this date—next Sat. before day of St. Margaret, this year 1644. God give us his grace and his blessing for temporal and eternal life. Amen.

David Shaar.

I quote the letter in full, first, because in it, Shaar tries to make Zaugg feel that his church is as bad as the churches of "the world" because it exercised a cruel judgment upon poor David; and secondly, because the names Shaar and Zaugg or Zug are both common in Eastern Pensylvania.

1644—The Rack Used on Berne Mennonites.

Müller tells us that there always was a more or less strict censorship of the Mennonite publications. But now their enemies began to use the rack. About Aarau the activity against them became active now. This, says Müller, was because Mennonites were very numerous now throughout the Berne district, and especially in the three counties of Aarau, Lenzburg and Soffingen, (Müller 105).

1644—The Berne Mandates Begin

In December of this year a mandate was promulgated. It was ordered to be published particularly in Thun, Burgdorf, Langenthal, Brugg and other places. The authorities in these places were compelled to make a list of the children not baptized; and of the marriages entered into and not completed in the state church. It was decreed that all children of such marriages were illegitmate. To the under-sheriffs orders were issued to make an inventory of the possessions of all these Mennonite people; and to arrest all obstreperous ones and bring them to Berne to the jail and their children to the Orphan Asylum (Müller 167). It was also decreed that all their teachers, preachers and leaders were to be branded with a hot iron (Do. 182).

Müller records (p. 128) that the day the mandate was read in Berne and throughout the land, and at the very hour, a thunder storm raged all over the country; and that in the church at Berne a great stone fell on the chair of the Burgomaster and mashed it. So God was on the Mennonite side they said. This created such panic and fear that for a few years persecution ceased. But later when another fierce decree was read a bountiful rain began to fall and it rained a great deal and saved the crops of the oppressors which were drying up. So God seemed to favor the oppressors this time. This was in 1692. (Müller 182).

1645—Mart. Mylin and Jere Mangold Chronicle Mennonite Troubles.

We simply call attention here to the fact that the Mennonites had some able writers among them. According to Rupp (72 and Müller 165), Bracht the writer of the Mirror got considerable of his matter from Mangold and Mylin, especially the record of the sufferings in Othenbach prison. Bracht shows this also by citations.

1645—Swiss Mennonites Call on Holland Brethren to Pray For Their Deliverance.

The following statement is made by the Mirror (p. 1062) of the despair of our Swiss Ancestors in 1645.

"Now when some brethren and sisters in the Swiss dominations had died in prison, of misery, want, hunger and grief, but five still lived in confinement, the remaining ones who were yet out of bonds, when they were threatened, especially by th se of Berne, that they should expel them all from the country, and seize their goods, and sell them, had recourse, next to God, with an humble and friendly letter, to their fellow believers in Holland and elsewhere in the Netherlands, requesting that they should everywhere fervently call upon God the Lord in their behalf, for comfort and grace, to the end that they might patiently endure that which might come upon them according to the flesh, for his holy name's sake.

The letter was written the 22nd of July, old style, in the year of our Lord 1645, and was signed by

Hans Duster, at Baltzen, an elder in the word of the Lord.
Ruth Künstel, at Müchem, a minister in the word of the Lord. } From the Berne Jurisdiction

Ruth Hagen, an elder,
Hans Meily, a minister.
Hans Stuss, a minister. } From the Zurich Jurisdiction

What followed therefrom, and how it subsequently went with those who were imprisoned, can be seen in a subsequent account, in a marginal note, in connection with Ully Wagman."

Here again we meet familiar names in Eastern Pennsylvania today; particularly, Hagen, Mülley (or Meiley) and Wagman or Wagaman. Thus we find they also came to the eastern countries of Pennsylvania from that numerous hive of Switzerland.

1645-8 — Hans Stentz and Martin Burger Labor and Suffer For the Non-resistant Faith.

These two fathers of the faith came into prominence, according to the records by being thrown out of Berne about the end of 1644. On account of their faith (Müller, 182). One was a teacher and the other an exhorter. It seems that for their proselyting power they were expelled by the Government under the Reformed Church. They were compelled to take a solemn oath that they would not return. If they did, they would be executed as perjurers. But about 1646 or 1647 they did return and had a discussion with the State Church authorities; and set forth tenets they would not retract. An old sheriff named Freshling (Do. 107) and a sheriff named Marlott were deputed to watch them. Two members of the State Church named Venner and Hummel met them and tried to win them back. The sheriff and the last named Venner and Hummel asked Stentz and Burger to have a prayer with them, that God would give them as light. Then they began to interrogate them and the two held to their faith.

In substance, Stentz said he was born in Stezwyl and had a house at Qulm—that he was married and had five children—that he was a farmer—a member of the Mennonite Church which he had joined a couple years earlier—that he was called a teacher by his people, a position which he fills without pay, being called by lot to it according to the will of God, though he accepted it against his own will be cause he felt unfitted for it.

But he said if he took pay or refused to teach after the call he would be thrown out of the sect entirely.

Martin Burger said he was born in Burg Castle—that he married at Rynack and has six children—three years before he joined the Mennonites and a year before stopped going to the State Church entirely and that he was a farmer.

These men were given, in 1648, several questions to answer as an ultimatum. If they answered these favorably they would be released; otherwise not. (Müller 108). As to why they separated from the State Church they said, the immorality in the established religion was the cause —cheating, fraud, adultery, etc., were common—that there was no spiritual life or devotion in the church. On doctrine, they said they do not live by the Old Testament, as much as by the New and have not read it as much. As to infant baptism, they said it has no power; but they say it does no harm to do it. As to government they said it is ordained of God, though they take no part in it. Yet a Christian may take part so far as it is not inconsistent with God's will. All are bound to pay taxes, but as to war, it is wrong. As to oaths, they say an end shall not be made of things by an oath; and nothing is justified but "Yea, yea" and "nay, nay."

Jan. 15, 1648 (Müller 115) it was decided finally that Stentz and Burger were unsafe and they were ordered to be expelled, and to be sent to Venice as galley slaves. But for a time they were to be held in the Zurich jail to try to convert their souls back. They broke jail and were caught and expelled from the country. Stentz said he would gladly leave his country rather than yield his faith. But says Müller (p. 216) after these men were in jail it was decided they should be banished to some island rather than be sent to the galleys, as that was too severe. And so they were banished and nothing more was ever heard of them.

I write thus in extenso in this case because "Burger" is a name of prominence in our county and city and in eastern Pennsylvania and elsewhere. Stentz is also a name more or less familiar here.

I may add that about 1671 the tyrants of Berne and other parts of Switzerland overcame their horrow of sending Christians to the galleys, and did it freely as we shall see later.

1648—Mennonites Accused of Socinianism.

This year a new danger befell the Mennonite faith. The doctrine of Socinianism arose and many influential men took to it. Socinianism was the name of this doctrine after the founder Socinian. It started in Poland; and in connection with the Arian doctrine. It denied the Trinity, and did much damage. Council of Nicae at Constantinople was held, in 300 A. D. and the Arians seceded from the Catholic Church and led this movement off. These Arians attracted the Socinians to them. Some of the Mennonites were suspected. It was held that the Government should confiscate Mennonite property the same as the Socinian; but the King would not allow it. This was largely in Poland under King Kasimir.

1648—Switzerland Declares Her Independence of the German Empire.

This year an important historical event, vitally affecting Switzerland occurred—her Declaration of Independence from the German Empire. It vitally affected the Mennonites and their worship, in that Switzerland was now holly unrestrained in her cruelty. We shall see that she began a new series of persecutions henceforth and continued them until these defenseless Christians migrated, into the Palatinate and finally fled across the Atlantic (Lippincott's Gazeteer).

1650 — Schaffhausen Edict Against Anabaptists or Mennonites.

About this time the persecutions that had been confined about Zurich as a center, suddenly burst forth like exploded powder from one place to another. Principally in Schaffhausen, a Canton on the extreme northern boundry of Switzerland, about one-sixth as large as Lancaster County, containing about 40,000 people today, whose chief city is also Schaffhausen, located about 20 miles north of the city of Zurich,—principally in this canton—the persecutions now broke out afresh. The non-resistants here, were banished. (Mirror 1063). This is the section where many of the Millers, and the Herrs, Goods and Hubers lived. A very large percentage of our Lancaster County ancestry came from there, moving first into the Emmenthal, the Palatinate and other sections (Rupp 72).

1650—Netherlands Puts Forth A New Defense of the Swiss Mennonites.

At the time when all authorities vied with each other in their persecution of she Baptists or Mennonites and Emperor and Empire led the way with mandates and persecutions, it transpired about the middle of the seventeenth century, for the first time that state and city auhorities officially undertook the protection of the persecuted; and strongly mediated in their defense. The sorely tried people of the United Netherlands had learned the value of freedom of creed (or belief) at the time of the reign of terror under the Duke of Alba. She had, by the blood of her noblest citizens gained this freedom of belief, and the joint sacrifice of the martyrs blood, had reconciled the adherents of Menno Simon and the followers of Zwingli and Calvin, etc. It appears that the congregation of Amsterdam protested against the persecution of the Bapists or Mennonites in Berne and other places in Switzerland; but without success. Thereupon, the States General, of Netherlands and the Magistrates of Amsterdam took the matter in hand and remonstrated with the Swiss authorities, asking of them to allow the Baptist or Mennonites unmolested to leave the country with their families and belongings, etc. (Müller 164).

1653—Mennonites Blamed for Inciting the German Peasant War.

About this time it was thought that the Mennonites had something to do with the peasant war. This peasant war broke out all over Germany— and lasted a long while. Two generals were ordered June 10, 1653, to take up all Mennonites, and see whether they had helped to bring on the war, as they were against the authoriies. It turned out that they had nothing to do with it. They always denied it; because it was directly against their doctrine of non-resistance.

The peasant war was a rebellion of the poor people of Germany which broke out about this time against the plutocratic land owners, who were becoming rich at the expense of their tenants. The Mennonites were suspected also, because they never showed any strong liking for those in power, but on the other hand an aversion against them. Müller 135).

1653— Hollanders Help the Persecuted Mennonites Who Fled to the Palatinate.

Müller tells us that the first help for the Mennonites who fled into the Upper Palatinate in and about Strasburg came about this year from the Netherland Authorities and Brethren, which country a century earlier went through the same terrors. Müller 206).

1653—The Neuberg Mandate Against All Anabaptists.

This year those non-resistant christians who were forced to flee from Switzerland and established themselves in the Principality of Neuberg, Germany found that the Jesuit authorities of that place succeeded in turning their former friend Prince William Wolfgang, against them and in causing him to promulgate a severe decree against them .(Mirror 1063).

1653—The Neuberg Victims Go to Holland.

According to Müller (195) these Mennonites whom we have just mentioned of Guliche and Berge, about Neuberg, when Wolfgang turned against them, went to Cleve and other places in the Netherlands to live. They came as we have seen, from Switzerland to Germany. Now they go to Holland. Shortly after this they formed their first Swiss Congregation in Holland. They were called Pfaltzers in Holland because of their temporary residence in the Palatinate or Pfaltz. They kept up their Swiss customs in Holland.

1654—Eggwyl, First Mennonite Center in the Emmenthal.

In 1654 Venner Sturler reported to the court of Berne that, there were in Eggwyl. Mennonites, who as long as there was preaching there, never have been to a sermon in the Catholic or Reformed Church. Among them are Zaug—Lichten— Hinden — Wolfgang and other Signau people. Berne asked the predicant whether it is so that none of them go to church. The perdicant investigated and sent a detailed report in which he mentioned not less than 40 Mennonites who did not attend Catholic or Reformed services, and this report was handed to the council of Eggwyl and was a hard point to controvert.

Eggwyl is situated about 15 miles southeast of Berne in the Emmenthal about five miles south of Langnau, the home of Pastor Müller. This is right in the heart of the Mennonite center of western Switzerland, the first place of refuge to which they fled when driven out of Zurich by fire and sword 50 years earlier. Zurich is about 60 miles northeast of Berne. The Emmenthal or Emmen Valley is about 50 miles southwest of Zurich and about 10 miles northeast of Berne, the Emmen creek flowing from southeast to northwest.

Here then, about 1650 or earlier congregated the Swiss forefathers of Lancaster County and of eastern Pennsylvania. At the early date of 1654 a group of 40 heads of families of these lived there in the little town of Eggwyl (Müller 338).

1658—Martin Mylin Publishes His Mennonite History.

Müller tells us (p. 165), that Martin Mylin published this year his writings. His chronicles extend over at least 30 years. Many of them are written from actual experience and observation. Bracht, the writer of the Mirror quotes freely from them. He was the grandfather of the Martin Mylin who in 1710 came to Pequea in Lancaster County (Mirror 1052).

1658—Hans Burkholder Escapes Arrest.

We now note the appearance of a name of great extension in eastern Pennsylvania—Burkholder. The Burkholders form one of the most numerous families in this section. Müller relates (191) that in 1658 Hans Burkholder was arrested; but that he took to his heels and escaped November 26. He lived in Schneisingen about 10 miles northwest of Zurich. This is the earliest mention of this name known to us. In 1718 there were several Burkholders in Conestoga.

1659 — Zurich Mennonite Sufferings In Their New Home About Berne and Emmenthal.

The Mirror tells us (p. 1065) the little flock of Christ having fled from Zurich to Berne, now found they must undergo similar sufferings there. Berne now imitated Zurich and made especial efforts to capture the leaders (Mirror 1065).

This year "seven of the teachers and principal elders of the church were apprehended, for whom special prisons were prepared, namely: Uly, Bogart, Anthony Hinnelberg, Jegley Schlebach, Hans Zuag, Uly Baumgartner, Christian Christians, and Rhode Petres.

These were for a while kept very hard at work, and very poorly fed with heavy food, spelt and rye, to make good the expenses they caused; besides much reproach, contumely and vituperation was heaped upon them.

They were first told, that they should be kept confined in this manner until the end of their life; in which they patiently comforted and surrendered themselves to the grace of the Lord. However when they saw that there was no hope of dissuading these people from their faith and religion, they determined upon another plan (according to what we have been informed from Alsace) namely, that they should have to choose one of three things: (1) To go with them to church; or (2) Be Perpetually banished to the galleys; or (3 To have to die by the hands of the executioner.

This item is given prominent place, because here we have in the Emmenthal or in Berne, near it the familiar names Slabach, Zuagg or Zugg, Baumgardner and Peters, showing where the ancestors of these familiar Lancaster County descendants lived and suffered.

1659—Berne Now Organizes a Special Branch of Government to Crush the Mennonites.

Jan. 4th of this year says Müller (p. 136) Berne organized a special bureau to take full charge of suppressing the Mennonites. They were to look into the question thoroughly and do whatever was necessary. They were to find particularly whether the Mennonites gave sympathy and encouragement to the peasant war of Germany and Switzerland The Mennonites were suspected of this because, same as the peasants they opposed power and monopoly; and because the peasants showed such a liking of the Mennonites and joined them cordially. The committee or bureau made a report that Lenzburg particularly was a Mennonite hot bed. Lenzburg is a city about 16 miles directly west of Zurich. Sixty Mennonite families were found there. The council accordingly issued an edict punishing by a fine of 10 guilders any one who gave any encouragement or aid or held any communication with these Mennonites. All people were ordered to report any neglect to attend services of the State Church. The edict was to be proclaimed from all pulpits. The motto adopted was Titus, 3:1. (Müller 173).

1659—Amsterdam Edition of Martyr's Mirror Printed.

Brons tells us (p. 240) that, this year a complete copy of the Martyr's Mirror was printed at Amsterdam. The author says that this book next to the Bible was the most generally used of all books by the Mennonites of early days both in Switzerland and in Conestoga.

The stories of the sufferings of the Waldenses, of Menno Simon and the death of Klaus and Jacob Hollinger and Graybill and Manz and Hupmier and Denck and Wagner and Müller and Hoffman and Hochstetter and Blauroch and Hasel and Meylin and others were familiar stories to the children of our pious forefathers.

1659—Bendict Baumgardner's Hymn

Müller tells us (p. 123) that this year Benedict Baumgardner composed a hymn in which he relates his troubles growing out of his persecutions and as well the sufferings of his people for conscience sake. Some samples of its verses freely translated are as follows:

Lord, for thy grace, I, Thee, beseech
  In chanting a new song.
Without thy grace naught we can reach,
  Help, God, my heart along.

Our Savior in the mountain taught,
  In beatitude sublime;
So we the mount Dursrutti, sought,
  In sixteen fifty nine (1659).

And we the doctrine there proclaimed,
  Which on the mount, the Lord
In holy lessons sweetly named,
  From the beloved "Word."

And as our blessed meeting charmed,
  There came into the room,
Stern men with dreadful weapons armed,
  And sealed our horrid doom.

One Simon, fierce and foremost came,
  And with him many more;
And our poor Brethren, prisoned them,
  And vexed their hearts full sore.

Then horsemen and rough halbreders,
  Bared swords in every hand,
Rushed, cursed and swore; excited fears
  In all our Christian band.

Then ropes were brought, and in the sight
  Of children dear, and wives,

Two fiends named Shriner, left and right,
  Bound brothers 'gainst their cries.

And then the teacher of the flock,
  Who glad himself confessed
They took, and hastened to the block
  And threatened so, the rest.

So, Ully Baumgardner, the head,
  Went fettered to his death;
"Fear not, Oh little flock, nor dread"
  He said with parting breath.

To Trachselwald they first were lead
  Whose bailiff waiting stood;
And took them then, in fear and dread,
  To Berne, to shed their blood.

And there in prisons, vile and foul,
  With other brethren thrown;
Two ancient shepherds of the soul
  Cheered all, their Lord to own.

The jailer sought to wean away
  These Christian, from their faith;
But Ully straight declared their stay
  Was God, of Heaven and earth.

Cruel and false accused were they;
  To strange lands driven far;
But yet by grace of God they pray;
  His love their guiding star.

They trusted not in human aid;
  But built right on the "Rock."
And crowns and scepters ne'er dismayed;
  Nor e'en the headsman's shock.

Yet none of these their duties cease.
  Imposts and tithes and taxes gave;
And served their country well in peace;
  Prayed God, their rulers save.

1660—Holland Forms a Swiss Mennonite Relief Committee.

In 1660 (Müller 206) a large number of worthy people of the Netherland cities of Dortrecht, Haarlem, Leyden, Amsterdam and Rotterdam, met and formed a committee to help

MENNONITE CHARITY AND EMIGRATION COMMITTEE FORMED.

the Swiss Mennonite cause. This was a valuable aid to our suffering forefathers. This committee did as much toward settling Lancaster County and eastern Pennsylvania as any one of the three or four factors producing that result. The committee lived at least 75 years, and during the dreary time of the edicts of 1671 and 1690 and later, and the dark days of the expulsion down the Rhine into the Palatinate as late as 1700 and the days of embarkation to America from 1707 to 1735 and later the Amsterdam Mennonite Charity and Emigration Committee, gave encouragement, made provisions with monarchs and rulers and furnished much of the moneys by which the Swiss and German Mennonites found relief in the New World. A remarkable fact is that while Holland was more thickly settled than Switzerland and Germany, few if any of the Holland Mennonites came to America. The design of this item is to set out conspicuously, the beginning of that noble organization in Holland in 1660 which did so much during the following three quarters of a century to aid the oppressed and persecuted forefathers, of the most numerous nationalities of our imperial county and of eastern Pennsylvania.

1660 — List of Ancient Lancaster County Ancestors in Berne Jail.

Under the year 1659, quoting from the Mirror p. 1065, we noticed that the Mennonites driven from Zurich migrated westward toward Berne, and fell into afflictions there too. Müller (p. 179) now tells us that in the beginning of 1660, the Holland Committee or Mennonite Relief in Switzerland found a considerable number of these Emmenthal Mennonites in Berne jails.

The minutes of a meeting held by the committee Jan. 20, 1660 reports the following in jail:

1. Rudolph Wertz, from Lenzburg, not yet an avowed and declared Mennonite.
2. Anthony Himmelsburg, from the Congregation of Wattenwyl.
3. Jacob Schlabach of Oberdiesbach.
4. Ulrich Baumgardner of Lauperswyl.
5. Hans Zuagg of Signau.
6. Jacob Gut (Good) of Offtringen, of the Soffingen Congregation.
7. Hans Jacob Mumprecht of Rueg- san.
8. Peter Frider of Bigler.
9. Benedict Baumgardner of Langnau.
10. Christian Christians of Langnau.
11. Mathias Kauffman of Kriegstetten in Zolathurn district.

We observe in this list the names of Kauffman first appears—an ancestor. no doubt of the prominent and familiar family of that name here now.

1660—A Congregation of Swiss Mennonites in Alsace.

Feb. 4, 1660 there was a Mennonite congregation in Alsace, the leaders of which had moved there from Switzerland. On that day this congregation assembled and signed the Dortrecht Mennonite Confession of Faith—formulated and adopted originally at Dortrecht. in Holland April 21, 1632. Among the Alsace brethren signing the same in 1660 were Jacob Schnebly of Budlenheim—Rudy Egli in Kunenheim, Swissers and perhaps also Schmidt, Schneider and Funck. Thus before 1660 there was an immigration into the Palatinate or upon its borders. However the great inrush was 'n 1671 (Müller 195).

1660—Walloons (of Belgium) Friends of Mennonites.

From very early times there dwelt in Belgium in the region of Luxembourg and parts of Brabant, a Romanic people. In and before 1660 they showed a marked friendship for the persecuted Mennonites. In 1660 one of these Walloons wrote a book in French, dated Feb. 29, (which year must have been a leap year) interceding for them, addressed to the opponents and persecutors of Mennonites and to the pastors and other leaders of the French church, at Berne. We cannot ascertain much about the book—its name or contents (Müller 183).

1660—Amsterdam Intercessory Letter For the Mennonites.

Apr. 16, 1660 a certain Harry Fleming in Amsterdam wrote an letter of nine pages, folio to William of Dieszbach interceding for the Mennonites and for better treatment of them. He bases the letter on passages from the Gospels and on a historical presentation of the manner in which freedom of religion had won victory in the Netherlands and finally on the statement that wherever toleration gained a foothold it brought blessings with it and persecutions always brought misfortune to the persecutors (Müller 179).

June 7, 1660 an intercessory letter of the cities of Amsterdam, Rotterdam and by the Holland States General carried by Adolph de Vreed, was persecuted to the Berne persecutors, and prmission was given to de Vreed to meet the committee of the Swiss Government (whom we have seen before, had entire charge of the Mennonite question in Switzerland) and treat with them in the presence of the great Council and Burgesses. In this letter a beautiful testimony of noble character is given the Mennonites. They were declared to be a people who had lived in the cities of Holland and in the country, in perfect peace, many years, under the government; they always gladly contributed whatever was demanded and levied of them in support of the Republic of Holland and fulfilled their duties as citizens; they always showed an extraordinary beneficence toward the Reformed Church in Holland though not belonging to it; and they, shortly before, on the recommendation of the Holland Government collected 7000 pounds Holland money for the persecuted Waldenses?

The letter then continues and says "We durst therefore not, deny our dear fellow citizens the favors of interceding with you in favor of their brethren in your country—Switzerland, that if you cannot resolve to let them live as we do here in the cities and country of Holland, that it may please you to treat them kindly after the example of those of Schaffhausen or even after that of the Roman Catholic prince of Neuberg, by giving them time to depart with their families and their goods. Dated at Amsterdam and Rotterdam, Holland, June 7, 1660 (Müller 184).

This is a most extraordinary example on the part of one nation for citizens of another, who were in no way connected with the intercessory nation except by the ties of common humanity and of religion. It is an example (238 years earlier) of what the United States did toward the Spanish butcheries in Cuba.

It is very strange that there should be such a marked difference between the Reformed Church of Holland and the Reformed Church of Switzerland. Holland evidently was without fear and apprehension of any danger coming from the Mennonites at this date, while Switzerland—particularly the great canton of Berne—was full of fear because of them.

1660—Lancaster County Ancestors Banished From Berne.

Quoting above from the Mirror (1065) and from Müller (170) we cited a list of Emmenthal Mennonites as being in the Berne Jail in 1660.

Under the same date Müller (p. 191) mentions the same list with some variation of names as being banished Sept. 10, from Berne and taken to Brug, Holland, in a ship. He mentions Anthony Weber (Weaver) Jacob Schlabach, Ulrich Baumgardner Jacob Gut, Hans Jacob Mumprecht. Christian Christian, Rudolph Wertz, Benedict Baumgardner, Hans Zaugg, Peter Freider or Fridy, Mathias Kauffman and Hans Wenger. He adds that this was the first small emigration to Holland, to which other Mennonites afterwards joined themselves (Müller 191).

Müller adds (192) that the Hollanders continued to care for the Berne brethren continually. There existed a regular correspondence between them up to 1681 as a letter in native Dutch on the subject shows.

1660—Mennonites Pay Heavy Bounties in Lieu of Assisting in War.

During the wars of the middle of the 17th century in Europe, heavy drains were made on the public revenues and upon the men of Switzerland, of Germany and of other countries. Since the Mennonites would not go to war, they were compelled to make up large sums of money, and to contribute that instead. The general mass of Swiss Mennonites were poor. They gave all they could possibly gather up; but that was far short of the demand on them, and for the shortage they were imprisoned. Their friends in Holland contributed for the Danzig Mennonites in 1660, for the Poland Mennonites in 1663, for the Moravians in 1665 and in 1678 for those in the Palatinate. The whole sum raised for the Palatinate, mainly by Holland, in the last year was 30,000 guilden which was at least $12,000.00. The latter part of the same year they raised 20,000 guilden more. They also sent them several shiploads of goods. The sense of obligation to help the struggling brethren is shown here very beautifully (Müller 162).

1660—Reply to the Holland Intercessions.

The authorities of Berne, on June 15 of this year make reply to the requests of Holland complaining that Switzerland should give the Mennonites better treatment.

Berne says that rulers are bound to preserve good order and peace in the nation and also to preserve and defend the true Reformed Evanglical Religion, pure and unadulterated; that the disobedience of the Mennonites has given much offense to the government; and ways and means must be devised to root them out entirely now as weeds, for they set bad examples; that it was intended to do this with great patience and good nature, but the evil kept on growing and growing instead of abating; that finally twelve of the principal leaders and teachers have been arrested and placed in confinement, but not in jail, and that a room has been furnished for them so that the imprisonment shall not be too severe; that the government authorities, who are all sworn to support the Reformed Faith held friendly discussions with these Mennonite leaders and reasoned with them so that they might be won back, but all this was of no avail; that nothing is left but to clear the land of them entirely, since they are so stubborn; they cannot be tolerated at all; that their goods and possessions must be taken from them because property is always a source of power and so long as they have property they can do harm; and besides, a just punishment for violating the law is deprivation of property.

All this was decided upon, declare the Swiss authorities; but as Holland has so strongly intervened they declare they would modify the decision somewhat and not absolutely confiscate the Mennonite property; but only take it and hold it for their use and

SWISS MENNONITES MORE STRICT THAN HOLLAND MENNONITES.

give them the income for it, that was left after expenses were taken out; and at the death of the owner the principal would be paid out to his wife and children if they obey the government and the religion of the country. If not, then it should go to such relations as did adhere to the Reformed Religion (Do. 186).

1660—Berne Withdraws Mennonite Permit to Migrate.

At one time the Swiss Government gave to Mennonites who migrated from the country, certificates as to their character, citizenship, etc. But later this was stopped. Then the Holland authorities were satisfied with the baptismal records given to the Mennonite immigrants by their church authorities. The Berne government in 1660 ordered this to be stopped, so that the Holland authorities should deny entrance to the Mennonites. But in spite of all this, Holland received and comforted these persecuted Swiss brethren (Müller 191).

1660 — Holland Mennonites Interest Holland Government in the Swiss.

For some time the Mennonites of Holland tried directly, to influence Switzerland to be more mild to their brethren, about Berne and Zurich. But they would do very little. Then they appealed to their own government (Holland) authorities to intervene. The Holland government then appointed De Vreede as a special agent of the government to intercede in Switzerland. Amsterdam and Rotterdam took a leading part in the movement (Müller 167).

June 21, Adolph De Vreede having spent some time in Switzerland asked to inspect the jail where the Mennonites were imprisoned. He was shown their sleeping apartments. They were allowed to have a friendly conference with him and he counselled them to be patient and to trust to the Holy Spirit for comfort (Do. 186).

1660—Holland Mennonites Not So Strict as Swiss Mennonites.

Adolph De Vreede, as we have seen, admonished his imprisoned Swiss brethren to be patient. He told them also that they should not be obstreperous; and that they should yield in minor points, so that the Swiss government officers (who were of the Reformed Church) would let them out of prison. But while they greeted him with friendly salutation, and in christian fellowship, they would not yield any of their principles, at all. De Vreede, as was the case with Holland Mennonites, generally, was quite liberal in his views. The Holland Mennonites, by becoming liberal soon found many favors and much protection from their government. They wanted the Swiss Mennonites to modify their views also, and to compromise with the government's request. De Vreede told them that they should give up a lot of their fogyism. But they would not do so. They preferred to suffer, rather than violate their conscience. Rev. A. D. Wenger, who visited the Mennonites of Switzerland, of Germany and of Holland a few years ago, says the Holland Mennonites today are more liberal and worldly than the Swiss and others (Do. 186).

1660—Concessions Demanded by Holland for Swiss Mennonites— Swiss Answer.

De Vreede had with him six certificates of concessions, granted to Mennonites by the Holland Government; and he urged that Switzerland should grant the same to her Mennonites. They were: (1) The ordinance of Jan. 1577, by which the Mennonites of Middleburg were relieved of all forms of oaths, because that was a matter of conscience; (2) A prohibition by the Prince of Orange, Earl of Nassau, of July 1570, restraining all persons from interfering with Mennonites, in their trade, and freeing them from all fines in pursuing trade; (3)

An acknowledgment of the last named concession, by Maurice of Orange, in 1593; (4) A reprimand by the States General to the City of Aerdenburg (Holland) May 1615 because that city interfered with the Mennonites in the exercise of their religion; (5) A repitition the order of Nov. 16, 1619 granting them freedom from interference in trade; and (6) An order of the States General of Aug. 1651, according to which marriage contracts solemnized by Mennonite ministers shall be as valid and binding as if done by State Church authority, which custom was allowed Holland Mennonites over sixty years (Müller 186).

Their demands for concessions after being presented were heard by the inferior court or council. But instead of deciding the matters they certified them to the Superior Council in Berne as the highest body, and they gave opinion that:

1. No concession can be granted until it is decided whether the government will modify its orders against the Mennonites or not.

2. It is not advisable to modify the edicts preventing Mennonites from emigrating to Holland. The orders cannot now be revoked, taking away the Mennonite property from them (except a small interest) because the Mennonites of the country of Lenzburg and of Eggivyl are gaining every day in numbers and they declare the government is yielding.

3. The complaint that the Mennonites are persecuted barbarously are not true.

4. That Adolph De Vreede, while he will be allowed to continue to converse with the Mennonites in the jail, must first declare what and how he wished to speak to them and must speak only in the presence of the Swiss authorities.

This shows pretty clearly, the attitude of these two antipodally disposed nations toward the Mennonites, about 1660.

1660—Elbing, (Prussia) and the Mennonites.

Elbing is a city in West Prussia on the Gulf of Danzig of 42000 people today. In this town, Mennonites flourished nearly 400 years ago. For over 100 years, or down to about 1660, they were compelled to hold their meetings secretly here, and in private families. They were at last allowed to build a church in 1660. The same privilege was allowed to the Friesian Mennonites, living on the borders of Germany and Holland, about the same time. They were also allowed to build hospitals for the poor and sick. Thus their privileges began about this time (Brons 260).

1660—Musical Instruments Not Allowed in Early Mennonite Services.

Brons tells us (p. 260) that as the early Mennonites held services secretly, they did not have either instrumental or vocal music as part of their worship, since it would reveal the congregation and endanger arrest. This writer also says that about 1660 when the Danzig, and the other northern Mennonites were allowed to build houses of worship, they omitted organs and instruments from their equipment partly because they feared to make much noise in connection with worship, and partly because of a prejudice against instrumental music in service from the long custom of having omitted them. They thought it wrong to have them. However, soon after 1660 the Friesian Mennonites installed a pipe organ in their church. They were the first of the European Mennonites to use organ music in their service. This innovation was very offensive to the Flemish Mennonites, who lived near them in Flanders, who were more strict. Yet later the two congrega-

A SOCIETY TO ASSIST MENNONITE EMIGRATION.   109

tions amalgamated into one.

We may perhaps, here have some light upon the cause of the great mass of the Mennonite church not having musical instruments in their churches today. The prejudice against instruments of music must have been very strong, when such great music lovers as the Germans, would not allow them to be used.

1671—Renewed Intercessions By Holland.

There is a letter dated Feb. 26. 1661 written by the Hollanders, thanking the Swiss authorities for finally allowing the persecuted Mennonites to leave; but the letter, at the same time, complains that the time given them to go is entirely too short, since they cannot sell their property in that time, except at great loss, not settle their obligations. Thus they ask that the time be extended.

These intercessions, were recorded also by each of the six largest congregations of Holland, viz: those of Dortrecht (where the Mennonite Church really was born), Leyden, Gouda, Haarlem, Amsterdam and Rotterdam.

The signers for Dortrecht were William Broithhunsen, Thielem Van Bracht (Author of the Great Martyrs' Mirror) John Zorn Byghhoom. Geisbert Rees. Cornelius Dirchson of Soferyl and Klaus Cornel.

The signers for Leyden were Jaques Van Gamerslagh, Anton David Kop. Abraham Jackson of Limburgh, John Bogl, Henrich Van der Doeck and Ludwig Peter Caelvert.

The signers for Gouda were Henrich Giesbach, Adrean Kahlor, John Gillis. Cornelius Abrahamissen, Paul Gillissen and Wouhert Daemen.

The signers for Haarlem were Peter Marcus, Boudebin Doom, Isaac Snep, Conrad Von Bollenborn, Lambert Colen and John Everson.

The signers for Amsterdam were Tobias Wingert, Hubert Wingert, Isaac Van Limburg, Gerrett Kuysen and Frans Stevens.

The signers for Rotterdam were Andreas Jacobsen, Jean Boanes, Bastian von Weehingen, Guil van der Sluys, Mathias Müllen and Hendrick Doeman of Reet.

I mention the names of these leaders of these six chief Mennonite congregations of Holland, because, while scarcely any of them are familiar Lancaster County names, they are the very men who and principally whose sons, throughout Holland did very great service from this time onward to 1710 and later, in gathering money and means and in moulding the influences which enabled the persecuted Mennonites of Switzerland and of the Palatinate, (Germany) to get started to Pennsylvania and to our county. Holland early formed an emigration society to help our Swiss and German ancestors to America (Müller 192).

1666—Mennonites Furnish Holland Money to Defend Groningen.

In the northern part of Holland, on the Reit Diep River is Groningen a city of 56000 people. It was bombarded in 1666, and the citizens lacked money. The government called on the Mennonites of Holland; and 12 small congregations raised in a few years 149,810 guilden toward a government loan. A few years earlier the town was bomdarded also by 2,-4000 French with 60 cannon or mortars. The whole cost was 8 tons of gold. The catholics were not allowed to take part in the defense. This is the first time in history that such mortars were known. Those that the Dutch captured were exhibited in the museum for money. (Brons 145).

1668—Differences Between Palatine, Swiss and Mennonites.

This year, in the official conference between Holland and Berne, a comparison is made between the Anabaptitsts of the three countries. The Berne authorities say to Holland that the Holland Mennonites are different from the Swiss branch. There in Holland are well off and pay taxes willingly and contribute to the Reformed Churches as well as their own and have farms, etc.; but the Swiss Mennonites are of the poor classes and exempt from taxes and do not help to defend the Fatherland or show anything of a public spirit at all. In recent disturbances they were not peaceable; but were carrying on all manner of secret intrigue. Besides no pressure can be brought on them so as to affect their conscience. (Müller 193).

1669—Burkholder and Gingrich Escape.

This year Christian Gingrich and Hans Burkholder escaped from the jail of Berne. Müller tells us (p. 146) that the Berne jails were all full of these people now, and that the watch had become careless and there were several escapes, among them the two mentioned above. He says that they even allowed some of them to go walking and they were even known to go out and preach alone. They came back in the evenings.

Isaac Lefever, Lancaster County Pioneer Born.

Rupp quotes approvingly, Mr. Conyngham, that Isaac Lefever was born this year (Rupp 97). The Penn Land Commissioners confirmed to Isaac Lefever 2000 acres of land in the Pequea in 1712, being a part of 10,000 acres first allowed to the original colony of Mennonites who settled in our county. Martin Kendig, who had first right to it, asked it to be laid out to Maria Warenbuer and she asked it laid out to her son-in-law Isaac Lefever and to Daniel Ferree. The Lefevers were French Huguenots, who fled into the Palatinate from persecution. They dwelt in the town of Steinweiler, Germany. Mr. Conyngham, in an address delivered July 4, 1842, on the early settlers of Pequea valley, spoke eloquently of the good qualities of the Lafevers and Ferrees. (Do.)

1670—Doris Eby and Hans Haldeman Condemned.

This year it was ordered by the authorities of Berne, that no one was to visit the Mennonites in that Canton, particularly those of Zofingen and Canalsingen, under a penalty of 200 pounds. Two Mennonites who were ordered banished, were particularly to be shunned—Doris Eaby from Trachselwald and Hans Haldeman man from Hotchiken. It was ordered that if they are caught they are to be branded with hot irons and be sent away. This last punishment was ordered by the mandate of November 5, 1670. There was also a mandate of November 28, the same year. It was ordered that the Mennonites who are going about in the Swiss country, preaching should be found out, and a list be made of them, so that they may all be arrested. They are to be publicly whipped and be expelled. If they come back, they are to be burned with irons. Their teachers are to be delivered to the dungeon. (Müller 144).

The authorities of Berne declared, the beginning of this year that the former orders were not obeyed and that this Mennonite faith was becoming a grat stumbling block and must be removed (Do. 139). Several other mandates were issued this same year (Do. 137).

Doers Aeby is an early form of our familiar name. Toris or Theodorus Eby, earliest settler of upper Mill Creek, Lancaster County where he had a large mill. Hans Haldeman is a representative of the numerous and prominent family of that name in Eastern Pennsylvania and elsewhere today.

GREAT EXODUS INTO THE PALATINATE.

1671—Poverty Stricken Condition of Our Suffering Swiss Ancestors.

About this year the condition of the nonresistants became unbearable in Berne, which city now persecuted them more severely than Zurich. This was because Zurich had practically exterminated them. We are told (Brons 226) that both individuals and whole congregations of Berne Mennonites had to be assisted about this time. This was so, especially, right after the Armies of Louis XIV (who reigned over France from 1643 to 1715) had devastated the Palatinate in his fierce wars. which raged about this time.

1671—The Great Swiss Exodus Into the Palatinate.

This year begins the last act of the bloody drama of centuries, which prepared our Swiss and Palatinate Ancestors to come to Pennsylvania in 1710 and later.

This year (1671) the distress of the Mennonites of western Switzerland became so great that about 700 persons, young and old, men and women, were compelled to turn their backs towards the "Fatherland". Some authorities say there were "700 families" and not only 700 persons.

They migrated to the Palatinate—that is the Rhine country—a region of wide extent. A few of their brethren had gone there as early as 1527, and kept up a couple small congregations there. This was at the beginning of the Reformation, when Luther had set the world afire and when Zwingli was fanning the flame and when Menno Simon felt the cords, of the faith which had hitherto bound him to the Catholic snap, and give way.

In 1672 Van Bracht. the chief Mennonite historian and teacher of Dortrecht, visited the Berne Mennonites and found their condition very poor and miserable. He found the reports even worse than they were reported by Jacob Everling of Obersulzheim. Copies of Everling's letters we will give in a later item. (Müller 195).

1671—Swiss Reformed Church's View of Swiss Mennonites and of Galley Torture.

In the year 1671 the Reformed clergy again mediated and went before the Council with a petition which shows their view of the Anabaptists or Mennonites, and which we reproduce here in abstract.

"The great privilege accorded the Baptists four years ago to leave the country—free with goods and chattels, has been an honor to the powers that be, and has also shown how far the spirit of the Reformed Church is removed from the spirit of the Antichrist. It is to be deplored that these poor, erring people did not take this benefaction sufficiently to heart, but have returned to their native land contrary to the orders of the authorities, partly for the love of home. and partly for the honor of their doctrine. For this they have deserved punishment. But as David asked of the Lord that he might punish himself, and he not be given over into the bonds of his enemies, therefore we intercede in behalf of these deluded persons doomed to punishment that they may not be delivered over to strangers (or foreigners) and enemies of the justice of Jesus Christ, viz: to the galleys, and thereby be thrown not only in great danger to lose their soul, but also to suffer untold misery and pain (since it is known what cruel methods are employed on the galleys to make these victims turn apostate). The confessors of our faith (the Reformed) who have just been released from these implements of torture can relate plenty thereof. By the awful vices and atrocities which are daily perpetrated, not only before them. but very often on them, practically in Italy, all possiiblity for a true and contrite Christian spirit is cut off. We are not only concerned, on account of these people, but also for your own sake and for the sake of your other subjects. You are by divine authority given power over these people; but God has limited this power. The door to a penitent, returned for the redemption of his soul may not be closed against man, if the country is to enjoy the blessings of God. It has pleased an all-wise God to make these erring people, so to say, a thorn in the flesh of our high authorities and the clergy as a punishment ever since the Reformation, which thorn could so far not be removed, no matter what means were employed. Once before the galley punishment was used in spite of the intercession, at that time; but God did not want to sanction this method, and the evil became even greater, until lately when by the clemency shown, the greater part of these people were removed from the country. This method will have continued success without using such extreme measures, of which Reformed institutions have such horror, that they not only have abolished such slavery among themselves, but have never handed over any one for such punishmnt.

It is known, however, that the enemies of truth use this as one of the most powerful methods to force the confessors of truth to a revocation of their faith; what would we have to bear from them if we were to hand them over to such, who allege a 'principium religionis' for their obstinacy for torture?

What would be more pitiable than if these poor people (should they be sent thither, but which God in his grace may prevent), be induced to deny their faith, which, as we are told, some of the others have done? Should they, however, remain steadfast and loyal, this would be a matter of triumph to the others, and would cause great defection among the peasantry, who regard these Baptists as poor people, anyway. Although we are otherwise not so bold as to interfere with your business, we could not let this opportunity pass to discharge our conscience in this matter which is of such great importance to the salvation of souls, and the honor of our church.

And although no one suffers more from these people, separated from us by error, and arrogant peculiar holiness, than the servants of the Reformed church, we, nevertheless, will not cease to minister to their salvation in a spirit of impartial Christian love, and to avert in the measure of our power all that may be harmful to them, wherefore, we plead for a change and modification of this galley punishment inflicted upon them, for the sake of the honor of God, and for the salvation of their souls, as well as for the good name of Jesus Christ in whom we glory and after whom we are named. Amen (D. E.)"

For this honorable and candid expression the clergy received no laudation and thanks from their strict superiors; but a high official reprimand was given them.

It thus seems that while the Reformed church was now the state church of Switzerland, and while the rulers were Reformed churchmen, yet the clergy of that church were horror stricken that the government should inflict galley torture upon the Mennonites (Müller 221).

1671—Twelve Swiss Mennonites Condemned to Venetian Galleys.

Müller states (p. 216) that, at a conference of several Evangelical cities and St. Gall, held at Aarau April 5th to 7th, 1671, the honorary ambassadors from Berne stated, for what reasons they were compelled to condemn 12 of your obstinate Baptists to the galleys. Two of them had promised obedience, four had declared their readiness to quit the country. These six were not shipped, but the other six, who had remained stubborn and obstinate were fettered and sent to Venice in charge of a lieutenant and two muskateers, with the concession, however, that they could change their mind en-route. They were condemned to two years and were to be kept together on the galleys. (Fv. A.)

This method of punishment came into use in the year 1671, when the extermination of the sect was to be carried out with full force, at the time when the great expulsion into Alsace took place; in the year when the Council in Berne was occupied in almost every meeting with the affairs of the Baptists.

1671—Swiss Emigrants Into the Palatinate Support Those Following.

The numerous Swiss who had settled about the year 1671 in the Palatinate, and in Alsace were, in the following years the support of all those who, either voluntarily or by force had left Switzerland. The Count of Wied or New-weid also showed this constant willingness to receive exiled Baptistst or Mennonites. The Palatinate and Alsace, too, were not far distant from the old home. Thus there were always communications between the new abode and Switzerland in person and by letter. A certain Binzelli of Schwarzenburg, took Mennonite children from there, as well as from Pohleren and Blumenstein to the Palatinate for instruction and afterwards called for them again to take them home. (Müller 206).

1671—Jacob Everling of Obensuftzen Describes Mennonite Suffering in Berne.

Müller (pp. 196 et seq). Rupp (p. 72 etc.) and the Mirror (p. 1066) all give extracts from several letters written by Jacob Everling from April 1671 to January 1672, describing the condition and suffering of the Anabaptists or Mennonite brethren about that time in and about Berne, Switzerland.

In the first letter of April 7th among other things he says: "As to the request of the friends, concerning the situation of our Swiss brethren in the Berne dominion, the facts are, that they are in a very sad condition, as we have learned from the lips of the fugitives that have arrived here, some of whom are still in my house. They say, that they are daily hunted by constables, and, as many as they can get, taken prisoners to the city of Berne, so that about four weeks ago about forty, men and women, were in confinement there. They have also scourged some, and banished them from the country, one of whom has arrived here. They also scourged a minister in the word, and then conducted him out of the country, into Burgundy, where, when they arrived there, they first branded him, and let him go among the Walloons. However, as he could talk with no one, he had to go about three days with his burnt body, before his wounds were dressed and he obtained some refreshments; being in such a conditon, that when they undresed him for the purpose of binding his wounds, the matter ran down his back, as a brother who helped dress his wounds told me himself. This friend arrived in Alsace together with two women and a man, who had also been scourged and banished. Hence they proceed very severely, and, as it seems, will not desist from their purpose until they shall have utterly banished from their country and exterminated this harmless people.

It also appears that nothing further can be done in favor of these persecuted brethren; for besides that the friends of Amsterdam and elsewhere labored for several years in the matter, so that several favorable letters of recommendation from the Lords States of Holland, as also in particular from the city of Amsterdam, and also of other persons of quality, were sent thither to the magistrates; also, in the year 1660, an Express named Adolf de Vreede, was sent to them; however, he did not effect much for the benefit of our friends there. Hence, I cannot see that the friends at present will be able to effect anything that would tend to the relief of our persecuted brethren there. We will have to await with patience the deliverance which the Lord our God may be pleased to grant them." (Mirror 1066).

1671—Letters of Jacob Everling of Obersultzen, (continued)

In his letter of May 23d, he says: "The persecution of our friends continues as rigorous as before, so that we are surprised, that they do not make more speed in leaving the country. Now and then one or two come straggling down; but the most of them stay above Strasburg, in Alsace. Some go into the woods and chop wood; others go to the mountains and work in the vineyards, in the hope, as it appears to me, that by and by tranquility will be restored and that they might be able with the greater convenience to return to their forsaken abodes; but I fear, that it will not pass over so soon, and that they will find themselves greatly deceived in their hope.

The magistrates at Berne caused six of the prisoners, among whom was a man with nine children, to be fastened to a chain, and to be sold for the sea, to be used as galley slaves between Milan and Malta; but as to what they propose to do with the other prisoners, cannot really be learned. One of the prisoners, an old man of about eighty years, died in prison. May the Lord comfort them in their sorrow, and strengthened them in their weakness, so that they may patiently bear the cross, and strive faithfully unto the end, for the truth of the gospel, and thus be enabled ultimately to obtain the promised salvation and crown of life. Amen.

In his letter of October 13, to Henry Backer or Baker he says, "Hendrick de Backer, most esteemed friend and beloved brother in Christ, I wish you and yours much grace and peace from God our Heavenly Father, through our Lord Jesus Christ, as a friendly greeting. Amen.

This is in reply to your request touching the condition of our persecuted Swiss brethren. The facts are, that on the 11th ult., it was resolved in the full council at Berne, to send the male prisoners that are young and strong also upon the galleys, even as they have before this done to six of them; but the old and feeble they would either send elsewhere or keep them in perpetual confinement. Learning of this resolution, and being moved to compassion, a certain gentleman in Berne went to the magistrates, and requested that they would be pleased to postpone sending away the prisoners until he could go to their fellow-believers, residing in Alsace, and see whether they would be responsible for the prisoners, by promising that the latter, after leaving the country, should return no more without consent? This he obtained, and coming into Alsace to our friends, he presented the matter to them, who, as soon as they had heard it, forthwith accepted the conditions, and promised, in case the authorities at Berne should be pleased to send the prisoners to them, that they would be responsible for them, and aid them in obtaining other abodes. This our friend, as I understand, promised this gentleman (his name was Beatus), not only orally, but also gave it to him in writing. Thereupon he promised them again to do his best with the authorities of Berne, and hoped to obtain so much from them, that they should bring the prisoners as far as Basle, from where the friends might take them away with them. Hence, we long to meet them, daily expecting to hear that they have arrived in Alsace, or that they shall come over here to us.

At this moment there have arrived at my house, four Swiss brethren with their wives and children, who say, that also many others are on the way, since the persecution and search are daily increasing. Concluding herewith, I commend you, after a Christian and brotherly greeting, to the Most High, for your eternal salvation. Your affectionate friend and brother in Christ. Jacob Everling."

In his letter of November 2, he says "Concerning our Swiss friends, they are now coming this way in large parties, so that there already arrived over two hundred persons, and among them are many old, gray-headed people, both men and women, that have reached seventy, eighty, yea, ninety years; also a number that are crippled and lame; carrying their bundles on their backs, with children on their arms, some of good cheer; some also with tearful eyes, particularly the old and feeble persons, who now in their great age are compelled to wander about in misery, and go to strange countries, and many of them have nothing on which to sleep by night, so that I and others with me, have now for about two weeks had to make it our regular work, to provide shelter and other necessaries for them.

We are also in daily expectation of still more, so that we hope, that when the people have mostly left the country, the prisoners also will be released. Farewell. (Mirror 1066).

Referring to their "coming this way" means coming from Switzerland around about Berne, toward Obersultzen, which is a small town, where Everling lived, about 10 miles northwest of Manheim on the Lower Rhine in the very heart of the Palatinate, into which the Swiss Mennonites were now swarming.

1671—Letters of Jacob Everlinig of Obersultzen.—(Continued)

In his letter of Jan. 5th, 1672, he says: "There has arrived in the region above Heidelberg, a man being a minister in the North, having twelve, mostly very young chilidren, but having, as I understand, brought with him only four rix-dollars in money, and a very poor horse. Some others have brought with them some money, but many have nothing at all, so that after close examination there was found among two hundred and eighty-two persons one thousand and forty-six rix-dollars. And in the Alzey Bailiwick, there were found one hundred and forty-four persons; but as to what their means are I have not learned; but from appearances I judge them to be most indigent. In short, we find that their number consists of about eighty full families, then further, widows, single persons, and husbands and wives that had to forsake their companions, because the latter, being attached to the Reformed religion, could not make up their minds to leave; in all, six hundred and forty-one persons, whose funds amounts to no more than the little sum already stated; so that you can easily calculate, that considerable assistance will be necessary. Besides these, we understand, there are about one hundred persons more sojourning in Alsace, whom we also expect by the fore part of the year. Farewell."

Subsequently the brotherhoods residing in the provinces of the Unitied Netherlands, in March of the same year, 1672, sent some from their midst to the Palatinate, who traveling everywhere to the persecuted brethren and hearing and seeing them, not only found the above related, to be true, but also, that already some of the last mentioned had come over from Alsace, who, bringing also, like the others, no funds with them, were, together with these, aided and comforted by the common assistance of the wealthy churches or brotherhoods of the United Provinces.

Moreover, they learned from some of the forty prisoners themselves that they had all been released, and, according to the request of the above mentioned gentlemen, been brought to Basle, and there turned over to their brethren, with whom they then together removed. But when the chiefest of them were asked why they had not left sooner and sought such places, where they might have lived with more freedom according to their conscience, seeing the authorities had not prevented their leaving, they gave different reasons for it, of which the following ones were not the least.

1. They said that they say that the churches greatly waxed and increased, so that, though under the cross, they nevertheless flourished as a rose among thorns, and that further increase could daily be expected because many persons manifested themselves, who saw the light shine out of darkness, and began to love the same and seek after it; that the ministers considering this in their heart, found themselves loth to leave the country, fearing that thereby this promising harvest might be lost, and thus many fall back from their good purpose; and hence, they chose rather to suffer a little than to leave in order that they might yet rescue some souls from perdition and bring them to Christ.

2. A second reason was, that they could not so easily take their departure to other countries, because there are among them many divided families, of whom the husband or the wife is in the church, while the companion still attended the public church, in which case, if the latter would not follow their persecuted companions, also to forsake everything and leave the country, it caused great inconvenience and sorrow; that there were even divers ministers not exempt from this difficulty, and there were also two ministers there in the Palatinate, who had wives that were not in the church, and whom they (having secretly been warned by a good friend), also had had to leave by night, and take to flight, without knowing as yet whether their wives would follow them, or whether they, loving their property more than their husbands, should remain there in the land, and forsake their husbands. That such cases created the more sorrow and difficulty, because the authorities granted liberty to such remaining persons, whether women or men, to marry again and seek other companions. These and other reasons had prevented them from departing uncompelled out of their earthly fatherland; but induced them rather (as they had now done), to wait until they should see that they could no longer remain there and preserve a good conscience." (Mirror 1067).

The only excuse for devoting so much time and space to these letters is that, the people of whom Everling (now perhaps Eberly) writes, are the ancestors of at least 90 per cent. of the German and Swiss descendants forming the back bone of our country today.

1671—Berne Holds Mennonites as Hostages.

Not only did the exodus into the Palatinate suddenly grow to great proportions during this year, but Berne began the custom of compelling the Mennonite congregations in that part of Switzerland, to send hostages to compel the congregations to obey the stringent rules laid down for these brethren. Each congregation was compelled to send two or three prominent men to Berne whom Berne could torture, send to the Venetian galleys or kill, if the congregation disobeyed. Three of these hostages were Andrew Mowrer of Thun and Christian Oesch and Peter Forney (Fahrni) (Müller 144, p. 339).

1671—Mennonites' Friends Find Hospitals for Them.

Flamming, a friend of the Swiss Mennonites this year wrote to Berne expressing sympathy for them. But the only effect was to offend the council of Berne. He was sent word that, his interference was resented by the Berne government and if he did not stop it, complaints would be made to his government, Holland.

Another friend, B. Fisher, however, was allowed to gather sick Mennonites together and bring them to an Orphan House in Basle (Müller 198).

1671—Switzerland Prohibits Galley Punishment.

Müller in Chapter 13, of his book (p. 215) sets out that galley punishment was useful to "men of war," that is war vessels, for many years. Criminals and those whose lives were considered of little value were condemned to such fate. Several of the cantons of Switzerland had contracts with Venice to supply her galley slaves for which Venice paid a good price. Venice had wars with Turkey and needed them. As early as 1540 Mennonites of Switzerland were sent to the galleys. In 1613 Galli Fuchs and Hans Landis were so condemned. In 1648 Stentz and Burger were also sent to the galleys. But a couple years later the government of Switzerland condemned sending respectable Mennonites to such fate. However under the pretext of punishing criminals our ancestors were so sent up to the time of the exodus in 1671. March 6, 1671 an edict was issued abolishing the galley torture (Müller 215—219).

1671—Galley Masters Show Kindness to Mennonites.

Müller tells us that toward the last, the galley Masters themselves showed kindness to the Mennonites who were sent to them to be chained to the galleys. They allowed them, as a distinct favor, to keep their beards. They were known as the bearded oarsmen, and the cruel masters of Venice said of them "Those bearded oarsmen we need not keep constantly in sight They are conscientious. They prefer to carry their fetters over the Alps to us and suffer, on distant seas, than deny their faith, of which their unshorn beards in the midst of criminals bear testimony. They are not criminals, but good men" (Müller 219).

1671—The Mowrers, Oeschs and Forneys Appear.

As shown by the above item about this year we find the above named common Lancaster County family names in and about Berne (Müller 339). Müller says that these men were made to suffer financially more than bodily. It was announced that if this does not make the Mennonites go a great number of hostages would be taken.

1671—The Eggwyl Congregation To Be Wiped Out.

May 3, this year the bailiff of Signau was instructed to tell the Mennonite congregation of Eggwyl that they, (who are well known to them), were to be taken at once and be imprisoned in the Orphan Asylum, and if they do not come and surrender themselves within 14 days, armed men would be sent for them at the expense of the congregation. But up to Sept. 26, nothing was done to deliver up these Mennonites of Eggwyl.

Then another method was tried, which was effective in some places. There were twelve of the wealthiest people of the congregation to be sent to Berne to be kept on the expense of the congregation until the Mennonites were either delivered up or quit the country. Oct. 4 they were given eight days more; and as to the 12 hostages, six were to be sent away to exile or the galleys, and after eight days the other six were to suffer. These twelve were in addition to two, prior ones who were to be executed, because their congregation did not obey.

The result of this was that the whole Eggwyl congregation took their departure as is shown by the testimony of their minister. Then the hostages were discharged and their expenses were refunded to them as a special favor. But the congregation was compelled to pay some expenses. Hostages were also demanded about the same time from the congregations of Guggisberg and Schwarzenberg and from Thun (Müller 339).

1671—John Floss's Account of Swiss Mennonite Suffering.

On December 19, the Mennonite congregation of Crefeld wrote a letter to the congregation at Amsterdam, the sense of which is as follows:

"Our brother John Floss informs us that on October 21, coming from Heidelberg he met about 20 brethren at Manheim in the Palatinate who had arrived there the day before from Berne; and they offered a pitiable appearance. Mostly they were old people of fifty, sixty and even seventy years of age. Many were bare and naked, and for more than a year they had not had a night's rest in their house. He says they told him their distressing and pitiable condition with bitter tears which was very sad and touching. After they had received his sympathy and alms, with tears in their eyes they fell upon his neck and showed their gratitude. They further related that they could no longer remain in Switzerland on account of the strict and cruel mandates and the anxiety that caused. They expect about 40 more persons to arrive if they have not been intercepted, as the roads and passes are well guarded, because the Swiss authorities do not want to let them get out of the country. Many were sent to the galleys, and others were scourged and whipped and burnt with branding irons. Among them was an exhorter who died a few days after being branded. Others were cast into prison where they suffered misery and hunger. (Müller 199.)

1671—Palatines' Account of Similar Sufferings.

This year an account was given by the Mennonites who had reached the Palatinate, of the suffering of their brethren in Switzerland. The account states that fully 100 families have fled. The Palatinate was now overrun by the refugees; and the brethren now in the Palatinate are too few and poor to help the fugitives very much. Many who arrive, even in the cold winter are nearly bare and naked. The Palatinate brethren find themselves under the severe necessity of calling upon the well-to-do Amsterdam Mennite congregation and people to help clothe and feed the Swiss sufferers now flocking into the Palatinate. (Müller 199.)

1672—List of Swiss Refugees Near the Palatinate.

Müller (200-204) gives the following list of Swiss Mennonites near the Palatinate in 1672 as found by Valentine Huetwol and Lichty between Brehm and Bingen.

There were: George Lichty (or Light—Hans Borchalter (Burkholder) and his wife—Michael Oxenheim—Adam Burkholder—Christian Immel—

FAMILIAR LANCASTER COUNTY NAMES IN THE PALATINATE.

Melchoir Brenneman—Margaret Beiler—Babbie Schappe—Frona Engler—Ulrich Enders—Barbara Reusser (Risser)—Michael Schnebeli (Snavely)—Daniel Snavely—Hans Van Giente—Margaret Biery—Mary Ummel—Babbie Reauformet—Anna Reumschwanger—Hans Reuscher—Hans Eucher—Daniel Reuscher—Frona Robel—May Anthony—Christian Robel—Catherine Dinzeler — Christian Reusommet — Hans Reusommet—Christian Stauffer — Peter Reigshoerer — Hans Matti (Maili)—Ulrich Strom—Ulrich Bitner—Christian Klari—Babbie Kingelsbecker — Magdalena Luthi — Peter Walte — Mary Bauman — Christian Stauffer — Anna Stauffer — Daniel Stauffert—Hans Stauffert — Barbara Lehman — Ulrich Lehman — Ulrich Küehner — Elizabeth Einsberger — Michael Shenk—Hans Shenk—Babbie Staller — Nicholas Kieffer — Hans Jurien — Magdalena Krapf — Babbie Weilman — Michael Müller — Ulrich Stauffer—Katharine Kuene (Kahni)—Bets Bachman—Hans Müller—Christian Shenk — Ulrich Laubel — Babe Burki (Burkey) — Hans Egmann — Hans Egman (son)—Hans Röet (Rupp or Roth) — Hans Schneider — Babe Ruesser (Risser)—Christian Wenger—Stephen Luechtie (Lichty or Light) — Ulrich Lichty — Peter Boomgaert (Baumgardner)—Maria Kraebel—Barbara Fredericks and Barbara Schenk.

All these persons were found in 1672 between the places mentioned above, Brehm and Bingen, a territory near the Palatinate, but somewhat above it toward Switzerland. This fact proves that our persecuted ancestors at this time were migrating slowly out of cruel Switzerland (and away from Berne) toward the Palatinate where in 1671 over 700 of their brethren had gone.

This item is of interest to us because in the list set out, appear many of our present day numerous Lancaster County and eastern Pennsylvania names. Among these are Burkholder, Breneman, Schup or Shoff, Stauffer, Maili, Strom, Bauman, Shenk, Miller, Bachman, Snyder, Wenger, Kraebel, Bauman and others.

1672—Galley Punishment Generally Fatal.

In the Amsterdam Archives there is a statement that the lot of the Mennonites were on a certain galley ship which had gone to the Island of Corfu, and that it is supposed that will be the last that will ever be seen of them. They are hardly ever known to come back. (Müller 219).

1672—Swiss Refugees State Their Own Miseries.

This same year the Swiss refugees in one of their own petitions to Amsterdam ask for help. They also had prominent Amsterdam people approve the petition and among them we find the names of Valentine Hutewoll—George Lichty—Jacob Gut—Christ. Peters—Uly Seyler (now Saylor) and Hands Loescher (now Lescher). Lichty and Gut are Swiss names however. The petition runs as follows: "Beloved brethren and sisters in Holland and elsewhere and particularly our friend Hans Flamming—We wish to report to you that our people here are driven out of Berne and came to the Palatinate where our brethren were already there to receive us; and we are staying with them, and they are supplying us with food, clothes and drink, but because there are so many of us who have nothing, and our brethren here are not well off, we are a great burden to them—and too heavy a load for them to carry. We find ourselves compelled to write you in the Netherlands, and there are so many charitable people of our faith, that we ask them to give us alms which we sorely need. No doubt Jacob Everling has told of our conditions; and we therefore believe you will understand our petition, dated January 1, 1672."

This petition was indorsed by Everling, whose home we have noticed before was about eight miles northwest of Manheim. (Müller 205).

1672—Everling Statistics of Mennonites Residing about the Palatinate.

Müller (p. 205) states further the statistics of Jacob Everling which he sent from Darmsteiner County or conference district to the Netherlands, detailing the Mennonites situated in the Rhine valley, east of the Palatinate, being near to it. He says that in that year 1672, in Darmsteiner section, the number of Mennonites, counting the women and children was 144—in Hilsbach round about Heidelberg 250—among whom there were 19 widows and unmarried women—of women who left their husbands and children and remained with the Reformed religion 4—in Manheim are settled 11 making a total east of the Rhine of four hundred twenty-eight. In the congregation at Alzey, among which are people of the Town of Obersultzen, Chriesum, Osthoben and other places, according to Huetwold's register which places are west of the Rhine, and in the upper part of the Palatinate, there were 215 Mennonites. This makes a total of six hundred forty-three persons just above the Palatinate and just east of it. The Swiss authorities compute that there were about one hundred Mennonites in Alsace at this time. Among these latter, there were twelve teachers of the faith. Henry Funk was one of them. In the Amsterdam Archives there is an account of the moneys paid for the relief of the Swiss settling above the Rhine country, which states the sum to be 11,290 florin, which in our money was about $4500.00. The account is Number 1198 in the said archives.

1674—William Penn's Interest in the Mennonites of Emden.

This year William Penn wrote a letter to the Magistrates of Emden, counselling them to kindness toward the Mennonites and preaching the Gospel of Peace. Brons says that he also visited this section of Germany. They were much impressed by him, and some of them were the first to come to the new world. Several letters of these people are in the Amsterdam Archives, in which letters they plead for more toleration. One of them is signed by a member of the Mennonite congregation by the name of Von Ravenstein. It was in consequence of these letters that William Penn wrote to the magistrates. Penn's letter was written partly in Latin and partly in English; and was sent to a business friend of his in Amsterdam to have it translated into German, and then forwarded to the sufferers. It seems that the original letter, in a very bad condition, as well as a copy of it, are printed and preserved in the Archives of the City Hall in Emden. It is so classic that it is worth while to rescue it from oblivion says Brons (p. 223); and she has the letter complete in German in her book as a supplement, page 435. Emden is a city of about fourteen thousand people in the state of Hanover, Germany, bordering on Holland on an arm of the North Sea.

1678—Holland Helps the Mennonites in the Palatinate.

This year the Holland Mennonites furnished 30,000 florin and also sent ships up the Rhine toward Switzerland to bring the distressed brethren down into the Palatinate and into Holland where they would not be subjected to such suffering as the Reformed Church was heaping upon them; and a short time later 20,000 more were collected for the relief of the hundreds that were lately come into the Palatinate. This shows in what distress they were. (Müller 162).

1678—Jacob Telner Comes to the Delaware.

Müller tells us (p. 364) that, this year Jacob Telner came to America from Crefeld, Germany. He had, for some years been interesting himself in the welfare of his brethren. The outcome of his visit was that a little later 13 families from Crefeld consisting of 33 persons followed him and landed October 5, 1683. This was the beginning of Germantown. Telner remained from 1678 to 1681, says Brons. (p. 221). He bought 5000 acres of land on Skippack Creek in 1682 and the next year six more came; and each bought 1000 acres.

1680—Mennonite Alleged Secrets Exposed.

This year Seyler wrote a work. the purpose of which was to expose the Mennonites, as he said, being an alleged exposition of their secret rites. He was of the Reformed Church, much opposed to the Mennonites. He was pastor at Basle, (Müller, 3).

1680—Jacob Telner and the Five Hundred Year Comet.

The great comet whose appearance occurs once very 500 years and which appeared in the time of Caesar again appeared in 1680. It is the most important of all comets known to astronomers. Jacob Telner was deeply moved by its appearance and concluded that it had appeared as a guiding star to lead the suffering of Switzerland to freedom. And every night as it hung in the West, he concluded that it beckoned them to America. (Pennsypacker's Settlement of Germantown, p. 126).

1682—Early Germans Beg to be Naturalized.

At a very early date these Palatines felt their disadvantage and on the 6th of December, 1682, we find them together with the Finns and Swedes presenting a petition to the Assembly asking that they may be made free as the other members of the Province, and that they might hold and enjoy land and pass it to their children the same as others; and that they might be naturalized. The Assembly recommended this (Vol. 1 of Votes of Assembly, Part 1, p. 3). These Palatines of course, were the pioneers of Germantown and were not in Lancaster County at this early date. It was the law, however, that no foreigner could be naturalized unless he paid taxes to the extent of 20 shlings; and the Palatines complained very loudly against this, for in those days it was a large sum.

1682—"Lambister" and "Sonnister" Factions of the Mennonites.

About this time according to Müller (p. 162), a large part of the Holland Mennonites divided into two factions over a doctrinal difference upon Christ as the "Son of God" and Christ as the "Lamb of God"; and the factions were called the "Lambists" and the "Sonists." The question of the "Ban" or separation from the world began to cause more trouble. One party tried to tear down the meeting houses built by the others. The separation grew wider and there were all shades of belief from the Strict Flammingers to the liberal Frieseners and the more liberal Waterlanders. The Holland church has always been strong and has 40,000 souls today. Her theological faculty is inter-denominational. There are 120 preachers that are University men, (Do.).

1683—Germantown: The First Permanent Mennonite Settlement in America.

In Kauffman's Mennonite History, p. 126, it is stated that the first Mennonite settlers made up of 13 families reached America on October, 1683;

and that a few days after their arrival, fourteen divisions of land were measured off to them, and they proceeded to the cave of Pastorius, in which he lived at this time, on the banks of the Delaware and drew lots, each family taking one lot, and the fourteenth for Pastorius. They began to dig cellars and build huts at once. Some of the first ones were Hendricks, Cassels, Rittenheisens, Van Bebbers and Updegraffs. The colony was so poor for a while that it was named Armentown, which means in the English, "Poor Town." This custom of living in caves was one which the old Swedes established about forty years before. When trade began to grow so that wharves were needed along the Delaware river, the people who had their caves built along it would not give them up. They did afterwards give them up, and now their descendants are living in very elegant mansions on Spruce Street and Pine Street in Philadelphia. These Mennonite families came in the ship "Concord." They did not mingle with the Swiss Mennonites on the Pequea, who came later. It seems that the Germans and the Swiss being of distinct nationalities, also kept their settlement separate.

1684—A Company of German Palatines Arrive in Philadelphia.

This year a lot of German Palatines who had a special invitation from William Penn arrived in America, according to the statements set forth in the petition of Johannes Koster found in Vol. 2 of the Col. Rec., p. 241. This petition is dated 1706 and in it, he says that 22 years before many of his German brethren encouraged by William Penn came here and their industry changed the uncultivated lands into good settlements, and behaved themselves well; and that they always will be ready to do anything for the welfare of Pennsylvania, that they can.

1687—Basel Mennonites Print a New Testament.

This year the Mennonites printed a New Testament in Basel. It was at once denounced as false by the authorities of the Government at Berne and ordered to be suppressed. The mandate also said that all of the Anabaptist or Mennonite meetings should be suppressed for the honor of God and His church. However, as late as 1692 we find the authorities trying to get rid of this New Testament, (Müller, p. 104).

1688—Mennonites Forced Into the Militia.

One of the first instances of the Anabaptists or Mennonites refusing to serve in the army or do any sort of military duty, occurred in 1688. This enraged the Council of Berne. The Government decided that there should be militia musters several times a year and that all men of the Canton of Berne were compelled to wear a short sword at their side to indicate that they were loyal to the Government. The purpose in this was to find out who were Taufers or Mennonites, and by the absence of this sword this could be told, (Müller, p. 132).

1688—Mennonites' New Code of Religious Rules and Practice.

This year the ancient articles of faith from those of the times of Hans Seckler about 1528 down to this date, were gathered together and augmented and re-adopted at a meeting held at Obersultzen, March 5th. Some of the principal landmarks in this code were the minutes of the meeting in Starsburg in 1568—the minutes of the Strasburg meeting of 1667, and others. This was not the real confession of faith because the old Dortrecht confession was still in use; but this collection was rather a code of rules for the moral welfare of the Mennonites. Among the common directions given in them was that: the church should follow only the practice laid down in early Christian times by the apostles —brethren and sisters should meet three or four times a week and when gathered they should read something about the scriptures and explain it, and they should read the Psalter daily —all scandals should be suppressed— that there should be separation from the worldy—that servants, elders and deacons should go through the different congregations and find how they fared spiritually and look after the widows and the orphans. A rule was enforced that the rich should educate the poor—that, at the breaking of bread all must kneel—that in parting the brotherly holy kiss of peace should be given—that those who were tailors or mechanics should not make any fancy garments or articles of any kind, for the brethren or any one else, because it would help the worldliness along—that money should be gathered up and given to the deacons and elders to relieve suffering—that if any one owed his brother or sister money, they should demand it and set a time for payment, but never enter any suit or issue any execution for it—that in villages where the Government compels people to be watchmen at night, brothers should be willing to be watchmen or sentries, but they should not have any guns or weapons in their hands, because they might hurt somebody—that the brother could hire a substitute for watchman if he wished to—and that money could be loaned out at interest, but only in case of necessity should any interest be taken, that is, if the party had needed his interest to live on.

These were some of the main rules that were re-adopted by the primative brethren for their peaceful conduct and life in early days. The main difficulty was that being surrounded by the wicked conditions, all manner of advantage was taken of these brethren, so that they had not only the displeasure of the Government but the disadvantage of being imposed upon by the people, (Müller, p. 52).

1688—Jacob Telner's Continued Afforts on Skippack.

Müller devotes chapter 22 of his book to the Swiss Mennonites in North America, (p. 364). In this chapter he states, after telling us about the founding of Germantown in 1683, that Jacob Telner in 1688 from Crefeld, became very much interested in this place in America for the Mennonites. Telner eventually got up a colony of these brethren and landed them on the Skippack creek, one of the early Mennonite centers in America, near the Schuylkill.

1688—The Mennonites First Regular Pracher in America.

This book on p. 127, Kauffman informs us that in 1688 William Rittenhuisen was the first minister. He was born in Holland in 1644 and died in Pennsylvania in 1708. He moved to New Amsterdam about 1678 and reached Germantown in 1688 and began preaching. In 1690 he built the first paper mill in America at Roxborough near Germantown. He was ordained the first Bishop of the Church in 1701. His descendants are still among the active workers of that church. Also see Müller, p. 364.

1688—The Mennonites the First to Protest Against Slavery.

Kauffman tells us in his book and page 127 that in 1688 the Mennonites of Germantown sent their protest against slavery to the Friends quarterly meeting. This was the first known public protest in America against human slavery. It is not improper to notice that in 1712 the Assembly of Pennsylvania moved by a big petition passed an Act against slavery, (See Vol. 2 of the Votes of Assembly, p. 110) and also (Vol. 2 of the Statutes at

Large, p. 433). How different might have been the history of America if these early protests of the Mennonite Brethren and the pious pioneers of Pennsylvania had been heeded.

1689—Sixty Mennonites Imprisoned at Lensburg.

This year about 60 persons were persecuted by the Berne authorities (who were Anabaptists or Mennonites). The Sheriff of Lensburg was ordered to make a register of all the Anabaptists and to deliver the list to the authorities at Berne, who determined to make an effort to convert them. Graffenreid mentions the list of the persons found, but Müller does not give them, and we have not any access to the Graffenreid list. (Müller, 167).

1690—Decree that All Mennonite Marriages are Void.

This year it was decided in Berne that Anabaptist or Mennonite marriages are absolutely void—that their children shall not inherit—that the inheritance shall fall to the authorities—that the property coming to those who were minors should be held by guardians appointed by the Government until it would be found out which way these minors would lean and what church they would embrace when they became of age— and that if they joined the Mennonites the property should not belong to them, (Müller, p. 135).

1691—Mennonites Declared Enemies of the Government.

This year complaint was made against the Mennonites throughout Switzerland, that they refused to swear fealty to the Government, and are therefore, dangerous and must be considered as enemies of the Government. This was a revival of the old mandate of 1671. It was further charged that they make a practice of condemning the authorities—that they refuse all military exercise which is necessary to protect the fatherland from its enemies—that they are a detriment to the public and that they must all be driven out. This mandate the different Sheriffs are ordered to execute, (Müller, p. 145).

1691—Daniel Grimm of Langnau Declared a Special Enemy.

Müller tells us (Do, p. 145) that this year Daniel Grimm of Langnau, living in the village of Geibel, was declared a special enemy of Switzerland because of his strong Mennonitism, and the Sheriff of Langnau and the authorities of Trachelswald were given strict orders to watch him and arrest him upon the least proof of his violating the ordinances.

1691—Berne Complains against Mennonite Growth.

Müller tells us at the page last mentioned, that this year Berne and other parts of Switzerland, lamented the fact that the Mennonites had increased greatly and especially that their big congregations in the district of Konolfingen; and that they are so disloyal that the Government must reform them, and that they are so numerous that it is impossible to get any militia company together in that neighborhood, because those who are not Mennonites take their part and refuse to do military duty.

1691—Division of the Confiscated Mennonite Property.

This year on the 17th day of November, there was issued a mandate decreeing that the fines, the forfeitures and all moneys raised by penalties upon the Mennonites or Anabaptists should be divided into three parts, viz: one-third to be given to the Government authorities for support of the poor—one-third to the expenses of the special court that was created to take charge of the Mennonite violations of law—and one-third to the judges and officers who tried the cases against the Mennonites. This was a provision very well calculated to make the propaganda against the Mennonites effective and the officers zealous and active, (Müller, p. 132).

1691—The Palatines Promise Allegiance to the King and Fidelity to Penn.

The petition of Joannes Koster states that on the 7th of May, 1691, over 60 of these German Mennonites had in open Court at one time promised allegiance to King William and Queen Mary and fidelity to William Penn; and that many others have done the same since and that all are willing and ready to do so, (Vol. 2 of Col. Rec., p. 241). Those items give us a hint of the difficulties under which the early Mennonites labored, and make their patience, loyalty and industry all the more commendable to us. Living as we do when liberty is universally enjoyed this discrimination against them seems very unjust indeed as in reality it was.

1691—An Early Mennonite Father Secures Land on Susquehanna.

In the Second Series of the Penna. Archives, Vol. 19, p. 72, it is set forth that William Penn on the 16th day of July, 1691, granted 375 acres of land toward the Susquehanna River to Henry Maydock of Holmholl in the County of Chester (Lancaster County having been originally a part of Chester County) and that he could take up the land at once. Afterwards his son, Mordecai Maydock got a patent for it.

1691—The Dutch Minister Desires to Move from Long Island to This Province.

On the 28th of November of this year De Lavall and Albertus Brantam reported to William Penn's commissioners of property that the Dutch minister of Flatbrush upon Long Island desires to settle himself in Pennsylvania and that there would be about two hundred families with him, and that they would like to have 40,000 acres of land. He stated that if they could not be accommodated in Pennsylvania they would go to New Castle in Delaware or to Maryland. It was represented that the colony were all sober and industrious. The authorities answered that they would be glad to have these German people come and that they would look for a tract for them, and report to them in two days. Accordingly on the 30th the Commissioners of Property gave a report in writing to De Lavall and Brant, that Pennsylvania would encourage their people to come and that they had several tracts that would accommodate them, and also that they should come and view the tracts, (See Series of the Penna. Archives, Vol. 19, pp. 78 and 79). On the 26th of December the Dutch Minister wrote and asked what would be the lowest price for the land and how far from Philadelphia they could settle and how far from a navigable creek. The Commissioners replied that they wish the German settlers would send some one to view the land, that there were several tracts and different prices, but that they could have it all near the Schuylkill River if they wished, (Do., p. 80). I can not find any further record of this proposal so that it does not seem likely that the Germany colony settled here.

1692—Incidents of Mennonite Faith Preserved at Langnau.

In the collection of Baptist or Mennonite manuscripts at Langnau (which is a town in the Western part of Switzerland near Berne), dated 1692, we find the following items jotted down by Johannes Mozart, the Reformed minister at that place, giving the following facts as to the attitude of the recently converted Mennonites toward the Reformed Church.

He states that he often visited Ully Krieg (now Krick), a recent convert and that he was very strong.

Of Hans Snyder of Trub, he says that Snyder became stubborn about the baptism of his child and said that there are so many views about baptising children that his child will not be baptized until it grows up.

Of Michael Burkholder, he says that Michael was an old Baptist or Mennonite and so was his wife—and that they lived at Maettenberg. She had been a member of the Mennonite Church forty years. Michael said that it was God's will that they should not any longer go to the Reformed Church: but that his son Jacob goes and as his father, he (Michael) did not have anything against that, if Jacob wanted to go.

Ully Fisher, he says was an Anabaptist or Mennonite at Signau and when he asked him why he stopped going to the Reformed Church, Ully said, "What will I do in that grand stone pile?" He also said, "Why do the people say 'My Lord' to you? Only God should be called 'Lord'; and priests should not be called 'Father' either. Your grand stone pile is too full of pride. We must be humble."

Mozart said he talked to Fisher's sister and she said, "Yea, verily, I would join the Anabaptists but I am not worthy to be one of them—they would not accept me because they are a holy people. My brother, Ully Fisher was formerly a Godless man when he was in the stylish church, but since he is a Mennonite it is altogether different with him, like when Paul was converted and enlightened." Mozart says she did join later and so did her mother and sister Magdalena: and he says that when he asked Magdalena about falling off from the State Church, she said that she is going to try to live a righteous life, and that God does not dwell in temples made by hands.

Mozart says that he reasoned with Dan Grimm and Hans Burkholder; they said, "We object to the Church because you preach that we must honor people and rulers and that doctrine we have renounced." Mozart says further that Grimm was one of the leaders in the peasant war in younger days.

In Mooshad, Mozart talked with an Anabaptist preacher and showed him a spiritual hymn he had composed; the Mennonite or Anabaptist said it had some good in it but "you should see what I composed." Mozart asked him what he and the other Anabaptists thought of the state church and he answered, "You are with the world."

Christian Wahley said to Mozart that since he became a Mennonite he could not go to the Lord's Supper in the state church, because the members are too careless in their habits and that they drink and have frolics, and such persons must not put their lips to the Lord's cup.

Ully Steiner's wife said that since she became an Anabaptist or Mennonite, she had found a short cut to Heaven: that she is sure she is on a direct way now.

Michael Gerber, one of the same sect from Wannethal said that he would rather suffer death than go back to the State Church. Mozart asked him what would become of those Anabaptists that do go back again to the Reformed Church. He said, "God have pity on them, they will find out what will become of them."

Mozart further says that this year (1692) there were in Langnau, 28 known Anabaptist or Mennonite families, and that nearly everybody was well disposed toward them. In fact, he says they had such influence there at that time that even our own members do not want to hear us preaching

LIST OF MENNONITES DRIVEN OUT OF LANGNAU.

anything against them, and that the public opinion was with them, the prominent people being very sorry to see them moving away. He says several of them left but the most of them had to be driven out by force. They were first sold out as bankrupts and then driven out, (Müller, p. 125).

1692—List of Mennonites Driven Out of Langnau.

Müller tells us at the page last cited, that the following Mennonites among others were driven out of the Langnau district, because of their religion about this time.

1. Ully Gerber and his wife, Katharine of Wissenhollen; and a son Peter and daughter Elizabeth.
2. Michael Gerber's son Michael of Wannethal.
3. Oswald Bracher's wife Barbara (Sterchi) and himself of Frittenbach.
4. Jacob Wissler of Eyschachen and his four children, Christian, Peter, Katharine, Levi, and his wife Magdalena.
5. Michael Burkhalter, the shoemaker of Maettenberg, an old man, and his wife, who had been a Mennonite for forty years.
6. Dan Grimm of Geibel and Hans Burki, his neighbor, the first of whom before he became converted to the Mennonite Church was a petty Judge and the latter, a Poor Warden.
7. Jacob Schwartz, in Moss and his wife, Elizabeth Schenk Schwartz and their son Ully; also Peter Schenks and Barbara, the sister of Elizabeth.
8. Also the old fish woman, Elizabeth Aeschman and her two daughters, Magdalena and Elsa.
9. Ully Brasers' wife and Christian Tanner's wife, both from Wallistolen. These last two have permitted themselves to be persuaded to the Mennonite faith by their brother Ully Fisher, a very dangerous Anabaptist of Signau,—in fact one of the worst of them.

10. Ully Aeschlimann's wife Magdalena (Herman) of Rigenen.
11. Ully Bieris's wife of Katzbach, who was Maria Hoffer. She became a Mennonite or Aanabaptist in Trub and came with her husband to Langnau in 1692.
12. Ully Steiner's wife. She went at one time in distress to Caspar Luethi, a minister of the Mennonite Church at Langnau, and he proselyted her to that faith.
13. Anna Blaser Müller, wife of Michael Müller. Her husband ran away but she stayed.
14. Anna Gysler, whose maiden name was Mülten.
15. Young Hans Gerber of Yngey, who was a son-in-law of Caspar Luethi.

These are among the list who were banished from the region of Berne and Langnau and perhaps a larger section of Eastern Switzerland in 1692 for their faith. The people said that God would punish Switzerland for doing this and as it did not rain for a couple of months, the people said, "Now God is punishing this cruel country for what it has done," (Müller, p. 125). We will all observe here that nearly all of these ancient Swiss names are also present prominent Lancaster County names.

1693—Local Surnames in Thun, Oberhoften and Burgdorf, (Switzerland).

It was now decreed that all sales, transactions and obligations of the Anabaptists or Mennonites, were to be void—that in the said districts, the whole military force must come out and register, that is, all the males from fourteen and over—that all must take the oath of allegiance, and that all who refuse will be considered Anabaptists or Taufers. The payment provided for apprehending an Anabaptist teacher was $25.00 if a resident, and $50.00 if he was a foreign teacher.

There was a mandate a few weeks later, in May, declaring that these Anabaptist or Mennonites (who went to church Saturday night, and would often be compelled to wait until Sunday night to go home, so as not to be caught) should be closely hunted about Berne, and all suspicious persons be arrested, (Müller, p. 157).

Following these instructions there were discovered in the towns of Thun, Oberhoften and Bergdorf, a large number of these people. The following aged people were excused by the authorities:

From Thun, Christian Schneider—Anna Neuwhouss—Christian Müller—Hans Kropf—Michael Müller—Abram Stayman—Anton Kropf and Jacob Neushousen.

From Oberhoften, Hans Wolf and Madaline Ammon.

From Bergdorf, Hans Kohler—Jacob Schüppack (Shaubach) — Christian Yawh—Adam Reist—Barbara Sterchi (Stirk)—Oswald Bracher — Elizabeth Schank — Michael Burkholder — Ita Ross—Kaspar Luethi (an old teacher) —Peter Weidmer (Witmer) and Christian Walti.

I have mentioned these names because we recognize again in them, ancestors of our Eastern Pennsylvania Swiss-descendant families of today, (Müller, Do).

1693—Origin of the Amish Mennonites.

This year there was a division among the congregations of Mennonites in Berne. A faction of them followed Jacob Ammon, and the remainder remained under the leadership of Hans Reist. The factions were known as the Amish and Reist factions. The parting was quite bitter; each party putting the other under the ban. The division was deep and painful.

The Reist party were the Emmenthalers—that is, their stronghold was in the Thal or valley of the Emmen creek, which lies a short distance northeast of Berne. They held that there should be no emigration or at any rate that they should neither emigrate nor mix with the Amish, who were the "Oberlanders"—that is, they lived on the Ober or upland regions in Switzerland. This split was not on fundamental doctrines; but upon the question of strictness versus liberality of rules. It really had its origin in Holland where a discussion arose upon the question of discipline and behavior, especially with reference to worldliness and association with the worldly. When the same question was taken up by these brethren in Switzerland, the feeling became more intense than it was in Holland, and resulted in those who believed in strict literal adherence and severe unworldliness following Jacob Ammon, and those who took the somewhat more literal view, following Hans Reist.

The Dutch Ambassador, Runckel, reasoned with the Amish but they would not be convinced. The Reist Mennonites claimed that they were the old original Mennonites and became as bitter against the Amish as the Amish did against them, and for a time took the stand that if the Amish migrated out of Switzerland, they would not follow them. Nevertheless, it was the Reist Mennonites who first reached the Pequea valley here in Pennsylvania. They also tried to get others to break away from the "Oberlanders," as they called them, that is, the Amish. It seems that when the Amish were sent down the Rhine, some of the Reist Mennonites were forced into the ship with them, but they left the ship near Alsace and Upper Palatinate and did not go on to Holland.

This division was carried from Switzerland into Alsace and into the Palatinate, and also to America where it is preserved today.

There are manuscripts upon the division and the discussion resulting from it at the time, in the library of the Reist Mennonites in the Emmenthal or valley. These documents among others, consist of:

1. The separation letter or history of the division, by Christian Blanck.

2. A report of the said division or schism, by Peter Geiger, dated 1693.

3. A confession of faith of the Amish, gotten up by Jacob Ammon and written into form by Hans Gut in the Palatinate.

4. A letter to the Swiss brethren written from Markirch in the Palatinate, December 13, 1697, by Hans Rudy Nagele (Negley) — Christian Pleam—Rudolph Husser—Peter Leemann and Christophel Dohltan.

5. A report of the happenings in the division movement during the year 1694.

6. A letter by Hans Rudy Nagele of May 6, 1694, to Jacob Ammon and his adherants.

7. A letter to the same by Jonas Lohr from Alsace, dated September 28, 1695.

8. A letter by Gerhart Rossen in Hamburg, dated December 2, 1697, to the Alsace Mennonites.

9. A letter dated October 19, 1699, by Jacob Gut (Good), in the name of all the congregations of the Upper Palatinate to Rudy Husser—Peter Leman—Christian Dollam—Hans Meier—Christian Neucomet (Newcomer) —Hans Rudy Negele—Rudy Blotchan, Reist Mennonites in the lower Palatinate; and to Peter Hapegger (Habecker)—Peter Geiger and Hans Burki, of the Emmenthal in Switzerland.

10. A declaration by the servants, elders and deacons from the Palatinate and from Switzerland, who adhered to the Reist faction and who called themselves, "such as can not be in accord with Jacob Ammon, and therefore, his opponents," containing conisderable doctrinal controversy. This is signed by those Reist Mennonites who are mentioned in No. 9 above, and also by Hans Reist—Ulrich Kolb — Nichlaus Baltzli — Doerse Rohrer—Jacob Schwartz—Dan Grimm and Ulrich Baltzli, from the Emmenthal; and by Jacob and Hans Gut— Peter Zolfinger—Benedict Mellinger and Hans Henrich Bar, from the Palatinate.

11. A letter of the 26th of February, 1711, by Hans Bachman and others in the Palatinate.

12. A letter of the 23rd of December, 1697, by Peter Lemann and Rudy Husser (Houser) from Manheim.

13 to 15. Treatises on the subject of feet washing and smoking tobacco.

During the year 1693, Jacob Ammon, while this subject of separation was uppermost in his mind, with several other believers in Switzerland went from congregation to congregation to get converts. By what authority he did this is not shown; but the proceedings, as we have said before were generally believed to have gotten impulse from the Netherlands, where the Mennonites were discussing for many years, the question of strictness and liberality. Ammon considered himself the head of what he called, "The Real Christian Order." He said that he would not have his followers build temples either grand or modest, but they would worship God in the old way as did Abraham and the patriarchs and the early disciples, that is, in the homestead. He also said that the Bible compels him to introduce keeping aloof from the world by being strict.

Therefore, he held that all former members who were expelled should be avoided—if, of a married couple, one was under the ban, the other must separate from him or her—and members of his family must not be allowed to eat with other members that are under the ban.

Müller tells us that a few years after this separation, feet washing was first introduced by the Amish; and later practiced by the Reist Mennonites, who did not do so before. He says that the Reist party objected to the ban because it was too sharp and strict a law, was not Christian and would cause misery in, and break up families, separating husbands and wives, parents and children. Müller says further that, Ammon got most of his followers in the beginning from the Berner Oberland; but that he had one strong leader in the Emmenthal, and that was Isaac Kauffman, (Müller, p. 315).

We find here again the location of the ancestors of our Lancaster County and Eastern Pennsylvania families.

1693—The Germans Adhere to Fletcher; and Do Not Side With the Quakers.

Because the Quakers would not heed the demands from Great Britain to organize a military in 1692, William Penn's Government was taken out of his hands and Benjamin Fletcher of New York was made military Governor of Pennsylvania. While the Germans were against anything warlike as well as the Quakers, they were glad of an opportunity to take sides against the Quakers when they had a chance, because the Quakers put them to much inconvenience and expense on account of being foreigners. This year they sent a paper to Fletcher promising him to adhere to him and his requirements and to rebuke the Quakers for their opposition to him. (Vol. 1 of Votes of Assembly, p. 71.) However, John De Lavall with seven Quaker members of the Council sent an address to Fletcher protesting against his rule in Pennsylvania; De Lavall, we remember, was a German. (Vol. 1 Col. Rec., p. 370.) Francis Daniel Pastorius, the leader of the German colony, accepted the office of Justice of the Peace and showed his willingness to break away from the Quakers and help Fletcher. (Do., p. 371.)

These and other events show that the Germans took the opportunity of Fletcher's presence to show their dissatisfaction with the Quakers.

1694—Plockhoy, Sole Survivor of the Ill-Fated Mennonite Colony on Delaware, Reaches the Village of Germantown.

In Cassel's History of the Mennonites, p. 88, it is stated that, in the year 1694 an old blind man and his wife came to Germantown. His miserable condition brought much sympathy from the Mennonites there. They got him naturalized free of charge and gave him a plot of ground to build a little house on and make a garden, which he could use as long as he lived. They planted a tree in front of it and the minister took up a collection to build him a house. He was Peter Plockhoy, leader of the Dutch Mennonite colony of 1662, who after thirty-one years of wandering from the South, where it seems he was sold into slavery, reached a resting place with his brethren at Germantown.

1696—Hans Graff Arrives in Germantown.

The famous Hans Graff, one of the founders of the Lancaster County settlement, first appeared in Pennsylvania in 1695 or 1696 and joined the German colony at Germantown. He remained there for some time and joined the German-Swiss settlement in the neighborhood of Strasburg about 1709. (Lyle's History of Lancaster County, p. 63.)

1698—Henry Zimmerman Arrives in Germantown.

Rupp in his history says on p. 126 that another old father of the Church by the name of Henry Zimmerman (or Carpenter) arrived this year and inspected the brethren at Germantown. He then went back to Europe for his family and brought them over in 1706 and settled first in Germantown and then removed within the bounds of Lancaster County in 1717. His descendants are especially numerous and respectable.

1701—Cornelius Empson's Colony.

This year Cornelius Empson applied for 20,000 acres of land along the Octoraro. An account of it may be found in the Sec. Series of the Penna. Archives, Vol. 19, p. 245. Empson seems to have been a minister or at least he was acting for twenty families who desired to settle together. On p. 280 it is stated that he renewed his request, and the names of the people are given. They do not seem to be German, however, but some of them seem to be Huguenots, whether they were Mennonites or not I can not tell. The method, however, of applying for land was very much like that impressed by Mennonite leaders for their people.

1701—Mennonite School Started.

This year a school was started in Germantown with Pastorius for teacher. Some time later Christopher Dock commenced his celebrated school on Skippack. Further particulars about these events may be found in Kauffman's Book, p. 129.

1701—The Germans Petition to be Free From Taxes about Phila.

This Francis Daniel Pastorius, the leader of the Germans, by a petition signed by himself in behalf of the whole German population in Germantown, asked the Council of Pennsylvania to exempt the Germans from paying any taxes, for the reason that they were a corporation of their own, that is that they were chartered as the Germantown Colony. He sets forth for his brethren that, William Penn had especially requested his German people to come here; and also that they are now conducting the affairs of Germantown without any help from the rest of the County. The Charter of Germantown was then sent for and it was soon seen that the Germantown people had full power of holding their own Courts and trying all their cases but had no right to have anyone represent them in the Assembly. And they objected to taxation without representation. The Council however said that they had the right to choose members as well as the rest of the county and they ought to bear their part of the taxes; and that they enjoy the roads and bridges built around them, and must help to support them. They answered that they had their own roads and bridges to build and the rest of the county was enjoying their roads. The question was not solved at this time but was to be taken up at another time. However, no further action seems to be shown. (Vol. 2 Col. Rec., p. 13.)

1701—Hans Binggeli (Binkley) a Teacher.

This year a man by the name of Binggeli or Binkley appeared in Schwarzenberg. Müller in an item (p. 207) says that he took the children from Schwarzenberg and from Pholeren and Blumenstein to the Palatinate for instructions in the Mennonite doctrine. He left them there for a term and then brought them back again to their homes. He seems to have been conducting a school to advance Mennonite principles, similar to the modern Mennonite Sunday School.

1701—Some Germans May Have Located Near Susquehanna Temporarily At This Time.

In the Treaty made the 23rd of April, 1701, with the Susquehanna and Conestoga Indians there are references to the conduct that the Indians should observe towards the Christians inhabiting near or among those Indians. But it is not likely that there were any Germans lving here then but that the provision was to be made for the Germans that were about to come. (Vol. 2 of Col. Rec., p. 15.)

1702—Hans Burkholder, Mennonite Teacher.

In Geraldsheim in 1702 there was a Hans Burkholder, a teacher among the Mennonites. He taught several years, and about 1710 we find him begging the Holland authorities for 500 gulders for the family of Christian Wenger, impoverished through cattle diseases. He also states that the Mennonite congregation at Geraldsheim had been subject to an extra contribution of the 1000 gulder for the coronation of the new elector and that taxes ranging from six to ten gulden a head were levied upon the Mennonite brethren (Müller, p. 208). It will be observed here that the familiar names of Burkholder and Wenger are mentioned, giving us some knowledge of the locality from which they came.

1702—Skippack Settlement Begins.

Quoting from Pennypacker's Settlement of Germantown, we observe that he states (page 140) the Skippack Mennonite settlement began in 1702, in the present Perkiomen Township in Montgomery County. Some of the Skippack pioneers were William and Cornelius Dewees, Hermanus Keister, Christian Zimmerman, and others.

1702—New Testament Printed by Mennonites in Basle.

This year a New Testament was printed by Yohon Jacob Gevoth in Basle in octavo form and it was considered dangerous by the State Church. These New Testaments were discovered at a book-binder's shop in Bergdorf. They were ordered to be seized and sent to the Court of Switzerland having charge of Mennonite matters or Baptist affairs. It was found that Peter Geishbühler was the binder and had six of these books. Finally in 1705 Basle was given orders to suppress the work (Müller, p. 353).

1702—A Mennonite Hunt Throughout the Emmenthal.

The edicts against Mennonites in the Emmenthal did not have the desired result. The people sympathized with them and gave them warning by various signals when any officers were about. Ully Dummersmuth for a long time harbored baptists and gave them room in his building for their meetings, though he was not a Mennonite himself. He lived in Rotachen. Anna Wenger, and the two brothers, Christian and Hans Dummersmuth were caught and imprisoned twenty-four hours for being obstreperous against the officers. Ully had to pay 159 pounds and the costs of the chase and capture and work in the work house. He gave battle to the chasers. One of the men who was employed and hired to hunt down and chase these Mennonite brethren and harass them was Christian Rupp. He later came under suspicion of blackmail by the Swiss Government, extorting large sums of money from these Mennonites and then letting them go. There was some testimony that he pointed a gun at the brethren or at the breast of some of them and threatened their lives if they did not pay (Müller, p. 341).

1702—The First German Tract of Land Located.

It seems that about this time some of the German Mennonites contracted for land about Conestoga or somewhere in the Conestoga or Pequea valleys because it is stated in Vol. 1 of the Penn and Logan Correspondence, pp. 148 and 149, that there is a fear that the Indians would disturb the remote settlers, such as the "New German Tract" which they say has not been purchased from them by the white people. I can not say where this new German Tract was located as early as 1702 but the Indians referred to are the Conestogas and it is so stated. So that at this time it is certain that a German Tract was decided upon and contracted for with Penn's authorities, even though the Germans themselves had not actually located on it.

1702—The Skippack Mennonite Settlement Again.

Kauffman says in his book, p. 129, that this settlement was an extension of Germantown. It is in Montgomery County and it began by Matthias Van Bebber securing 6000 acres of land there which he immediately began to colonize with Mennonites. The principal families were the Kolbs, Zimmermans, Pannebeckers, Jansons, Zieglers, and others.

1703—Swiss Suffer and Perish Crossing the Ocean.

Our ancestors in the beginning of the century suffered with what was known as Palatine fever. It is said that the children under seven years of age rarely lived. Mittelberger says he saw no less than thirty-two children thus dying and being thrown into the sea (Kuhn, p. 71).

1703—Swiss Baptist Property Confiscated.

This year in Switzerland the farms of a lot of Mennonites who had been banished were sold at auction. We have no record of how many there were, but at least quite a number. They brought 5576 pounds. Of this money 220 pounds went to the Judge of the Court and the balance was divided among the Mayors of the towns off Steffisburg, Schwarzenegg, Ober-Neiderstachten, Blumenstein, Balsringen, Ruegsau, Trachelswald, Trub, Lauperswyl, Schangnau, Hutwyl, Criswyl, Hasli, Schofftland, Diesbach and other towns, whose officers were to hold the same in trust and pay the interest to the heirs of the exiled Mennonites. But as generally the children went with the parents, the principal fell to the Governments (Müller, page 358).

1703—Stephen Funk Preaches Before King Charles XII of Sweden, at Thorn.

Many Baptists or Mennonites at this time lived in Poland in the town of Thorn. They were compelled to furnish supplies to Charles XII in his wars. Among them was a leader named Stephen Funk from Moravia. King Charles XII's chaplain on one occasion held services and Funk was present and listened attentively to the chaplain's sermon and took notes. This was brought to the attention of the authorities and State Church dignitaries and Funk was asked why he took notes. The author was brought before the King and he asked Funk who he was and why he took notes of the sermon. He said to see if it were correctly spoken. The King said for that act Funk must preach a sermon to him, the King, and asked, "When can you do it?" Funk said, "In fourteen days, but you must keep me safe from harm." The King promised. The day came and Funk appeared and went to the tent of the King. The provost and generals, prominent and petty, were present. The King told all that he had ordered the sermon to be preached and that all should give attention. At the conclusion, none had any objections to offer. The King said to Funk, "You have proved your position in all points except you should not condemn war." Funk said, "War can not be upheld by anything in the Bible." The King said, "Is there no permission given at all in the Bible for war?" Funk replied, "If a King should be attacked in his country he could defend by war, but he must never go to another country and devastate it." This ended the matter. This was King Charles of Sweden. He compelled the Mennonites to furnish supplies to carry on his wars. This happened in Thorn, now in Prussia; or formerly in Poland (Brons, 330).

1703—Jacob Telner and Skippack Mennonites.

Telner at this time was zealous in the Skippack project. He was on the ground and spent part of his time in Philadelphia. Penn in a letter to Logan, the 6th of June, 1703, writes, "I have been much pressed by Jacob Telner about Rebecca Shippen's business in the town. I desire that truth and righteousness may take place" (1 Penn and Logan Corr., 189). Pennypacker says that Telner had a right to five thousand acres and took up the bulk of it on Skippack Creek. It comprised a township.

1704—Germans Not Allowed to Own Land Absolutely.

Without naturalization the Germans could not pass the land which they lived on, to their children by will or otherwise even though they improved it by buildings and tilled it. In order to have the same right as the English people they complained to the Assembly asking that their titles should be as good as anybody else's. Their first petition seems to have been filed in 1704. (Vol. 1 of Notes of Assembly, Part 2, p. 26.)

1704—Theodorus Eby Moved to the Palatinate.

This year an old patriarch, ancestor of a large Lancaster County family, Theodorus Eby, who was born in Zurich on the 25th day of April, 1665, moved to the Palatinate and resided there until 1715, when he came to Philadelphia and thence to Eby's Mill on Mill Creek, afterwards Roland's Mill, south of New Holland on the line between Earl and Leacock townships. (History of Eby Family, p. 5.)

1704—The Lancaster County Mennonite Pioneer.

Rupp in his history, pp. 54, 55 and 70, says that this year Louis Michelle, a Swiss miner, was in America looking for a convenient tract to settle a colony of his people on. He was among the Indians near Conestoga about 1706 and 1707 in search of mineral ore. It is thought that he built a fort several miles above Conestoga. These performances do not look much like the Mennonite actions, especially the building of warlike defenses, yet in those days a defense of that kind was as needful as an ordinary house just now. It is safe to say he was interested in the Swiss Mennonites because the statement that he wanted a tract to settle the "colony of his people on" indicates that he was acting for his distressed brethren.

1705—The German Palatines Apply for Naturalization.

This year several Germans filed a petition in the Assembly asking that they might be naturalized, not only so that they could hold their lands, but have all the other privileges of other citizens in Pennsylvania. (Vol. 1 Votes of Assembly, Part 2, p. 47.)

1705—Frederich de Redegelt, a German Palatine, Takes Land on the Susquehanna.

This year it is stated in the Sec. Series of the Penna. Archives, Vol. 19, p. 468, that John Henrich Kursten showed a deed translated by Daniel Pastorius, from Frederick de Redegelt, for 750 acres of land, part of the 10,000 purchased of William Penn in England by Redegelt, to be taken up, rent free for seven years, near Susquehanna. So it appears from this that this friend of old Pastorius and likely member of his church had secured land about Susquehanna at this early date.

1705—Swiss Prepare to Settle in Lancaster County.

In a letter written by William Penn to Logan, the 16th of February, 1705, he says, "I have a hundred German families preparing for you. They buy 30,000 or 40,000 acres; and no longer than yesterday Sir Charles Hedges discoursed me upon a Swiss Colony intended thither (eo Pennsylvania) by request of our envoy in the Cantons; but keep this close for many reasons" (1 Penn & Logan Corr., p. 352). Thus we see that this year preparations were taking shape to people the section which afterwards became Lancaster County.

1705 — Some Toleration by the Reformed Toward the Mennonites in Switzerland.

By this time the Swiss Reformed Church began to allow toleration to the Mennonites; but even this year a legacy left by a member of the Mennonite congregation for its benefit was confiscated by the Government authorities and State Church. By this we see that toleration had not made much headway in Switzerland around Berne.

1706—Familiar Names at Skippack.

Among the Mennonite land buyers of the Skippack settlement is to be found under the date of 1706 the name of Edward Beer (Bear). Among the preachers a little later were found two Hunseckers, two Landises, a George Detweiler, a Christian Hunsberger and a Hans Witmer, (Brons, p. 369).

1706—German Palatines Petition again for Naturalization.

This year Johannes Koster and about 150 other High and Low Germans presented a petition, stating that though they came over here by Penn's invitation and many more had also done the like, they feel insecure in their estates, as they are considered as foreigners; and they beg that a law may be passed to naturalize all the Germans that come, and to give them the right to hold and enjoy land and to sell it or pass it to their children, and to give them the right of voting and of being elected to serve in Assembly or other offices. They also set forth that they are Mennonists and that they as well as their predecessors for over 150 years past could not on account of conscience take an oath. And they ask that they should have the same rights as the Quakers about this matter, as the Quakers are not required to take an oath. (Vol. 2 of Col. Rec., p. 241.) The Assembly thought this was perfectly reasonable and that these good people ought to be secured in their estates and titles and have the other rights they ask for. And the Attorney General was instructed to draw up the proper act of Assembly to be passed.

But these poor Mennonites had to wait three years before the Act got through Assembly, when finally on the 17th of August, 1709, some of them appeared with an act drawn by the Attorney General and begged the Council would urge the Assembly to pass it into a law; and the Council agreed that they would request the Assembly to act on it. (Vol. 2 Col. Rec., p. 480.) From this we see that matters moved very slowly towards giving these German Palatines any well-deserved relief. The matter was now dragging along, and on the 31st of August the Council decided that this bill of these Germans required dispatch, and the Council read it and returned it to the Assembly and instructed the messenger that the Assembly is requested to consider carefully whether it is safe to make this naturalization so extensive. (Do., p. 488.) But finally it was passed.

1707—Swiss Settlers Come to Pennsylvania.

This year it seems there were Germans or Swiss who came into Pennsylvania "under a particular agreement with the Honorable Proprietor at London"; and took up lands under him, and a couple of years later moved up to Lancaster County. They had not followed the formalities necessary on the part of foreigners to get complete title, and thus on the 16th of June, 1730, they asked the Government, who called them "several Germans now inhabitants of the County of Lancaster" for the rights and privileges of British subjects. The Governor says they are all of so good a character for honesty and industry as deserves the esteem of this Government. (3 Col. Rec., p. 374—Old Style p. 397.)

1707—First Germans in Jersey.

One of the first settlements of Palatines in New Jersey was that in what was named German Valley, in the Counties of Sussex, Passaic, Essex and others. These Germans intended to go to New York, but the ship leaked, and they stopped in the beautiful valley of a little river in Jersey. They were, however, a Reformed congregation from Germany. In the year 1705 they got to Neuwyl on the Rhine, from which they went to Holland, hired themselves for Dutch settlement in New York and were sent over in 1707. (Löher, p. 70.)

1707—Swiss Mennonites Secure Naturalization in Germany and Threaten Swiss Authorities.

In the year 1707 Mennonites were permitted to leave Switzerland on payment of a fee. Some left and went to other lands, became naturalized in those countries, and then came back as citizens of other countries and made trouble for Switzerland. (Müller. p. 349.)

1707—Swiss Mennonites Not Allowed To Be Employed.

Some of the Cantons of Switzerland, by a mandate of June 29, this year, gave the Swiss Mennonites until November 20th to leave the country. It was also enacted that a fine of fifty pounds would be inflicted on anyone who hired a Mennonite as a servant or leased any land to Mennonites as tenant farmers, except such as could show a certificate from the Judge that they were honest, law-abiding citizens and obedient to the authorities of the country and had made an oath of allegiance. Whoever did not have certificates were given orders by the Government to leave and were deported if they did not leave voluntarily. (Müller, p. 349.)

1708—Accession to Skippack and Germantown.

About this time some of the principal leaders of the Germantown colony arrived in Germantown and at Skippack. By the 23rd of May, this year, there were 43 members in the Germantown and Skippack congregations. Among them were Herman Kasdorp and Martin Kolb, who were chosen their preachers. (Pennypacker, p. 174.)

1708—Swiss Settle Newbern, N. C., and Are Destroyed.

In 1708 a colony of Swiss went to North Carolina and founded Newbern. Others came to the colony a little later from Pennsylvania. Most of them were Mennonites and were induced to go to colonize that neighborhood by Michelle and Graffenreid. They cut down the forests to make their settlement. The Indians allowed them to build their huts and to build a fort in their midst. Graffenreid purchased 15,000 acres there for them. He was also kindly treated by the Indians for a time. Later they captured him up the Neuse river and decreed that he should be burnt. The chiefs sat in two rows in front of him, and behind him the savages were dancing the death dance. Graffenreid told them fairy tales and tried the expedients of Captain John Smith upon the savages, and they let him go; but Lawson, his partner, they burned to death. Graffenreid then left his colony for five weeks, and when he came back it was all destroyed by the Indians. (Löher, p. 51.)

1708—Dunkards Secede from the Mennonites.

This year Alexander Mack, of Schwarzennau, in Westphalia, founded the Dunkard denomination. (Kuhn, p. 179.) About twenty families of them in 1719 came to Germantown, Skippack, Oley and to the Conestoga. Their leader was Peter Baker. It would seem from the similarity of their creeds that they were formerly Mennonites.

1708—Kocherthal Colony of Palatines.

On the 28th day of April, 1708, a number of the German Palatines were sent under Kocherthal in a colony from New York on a Government vessel, accompanied by Lord Lovelace, the newly-appointed Governor. ("Die deutschen im Staate N. Y." by Kolb.) I cite this from Diffenderffer's German Exodus, page 7, in which he also says that the Board of Trade records (Appendix B.) state there were ten men, ten women and twenty-one children in this colony.

1708—Mennonites Granted Permission to Leave the Palatinate.

By a paper dated March 10, 1708—set forth in Rupp's History, p. 93—it is provided that the several Mennonites mentioned in it, with the view of improving their conditions, wish to reside in "The Island of Pennsylvania." It is further stated that they have requested a certificate of the authorities to set forth that they are free and not subject to vassalage and have paid all their debts, and that they have behaved themselves piously and honestly. It then states that they have the permission of the Council or of the Palatinate to leave and go to the New Country. The same day, as shown on p. 95 of the same book, they also got the permission of their Church and a certificate that they were Christians and had the record of the baptism of their children. So, with these blessings they departed for America.

This company went to New York, but their religious customs not being approved there they finally drifted across into Pennsylvania. They were some of the first fruits of Mennonite migration.

1708—First Mennonite Church in America.

Mr. Kauffman says in his book that the Mennonites held their services in private houses or in the open air until 1708, when a log house was erected for public worship in Germantown. He says that Christopher Dock, the Mennonite preacher, taught school in this house for several years. He also tells us that it was rebuilt in 1770 and is today the oldest meeting house in America.

1709—A Lot of the Palatines Naturalized.

The petition we spoke of before was finally passed September 29, 1709, and by virtue of it 82 of the Palatines of Philadelphia County and one of Bucks County were naturalized. Among them were Pastorius, the Conrads, Shuemakers, Vanbibbers, Gattschalks, Stolls, Kesselberrys, Hoffs, Smiths, Scholls and others. (2 Col. Rec., p. 493.)

1709—New Attempt to Banish the Anabaptists or Mennonites From Berne.

The Berne authorities again endeavored to get rid of the objectionable Anabaptists (all other means and measures having failed) by shipping them to America; since it became known that the Queen of England was desirous of obtaining colonists for her transatlantic possessions. There appeared at Berne about this time a forwarding merchant, or agent, named Ritter, with some associates, who was about to embark for America. They declared themselves willing to take with them "poor families" and capable persons of the Anabaptist religion, who were to be deported from the country. Negotiations were opened with this Mr. Ritter, by the authorities; and it was decided that he was to receive for the 101 persons to be deported 500 Thaler (Dollars); and for the Anabaptists 45 Thaler per person actually landed in America. The Anabaptists were to pay for their own transportation, the money to be taken from the funds obtained by confiscation of their possessions. Return to the fatherland was prohibited on pain of death.

The Swiss Ambassador at The Hague, Holland, Francois Louis Pesine, Seignueuer de Saint Saphorin, interested himself in Ritter's undertaking by asking the Dutch authorities to be watchful lest some of these deported Anabaptists might make good their escape while en route through Holland or at their re-shipment at Rotterdam. The Anabaptists of Holland had received word of their Swiss brethrens' plight; and as they were influential and were held in high esteem in that country, they were determined to have them set free as soon as they arrived in Holland. There had been several conferences with the Ambassador, Saint Saphorin, by the Dutch authorities, the Ambassador of England, Mylord Townshend, and a number of Brethren and friends of the deported Swiss. These friends sent word to their brethren in Rotterdam to have a watchful eye, lest the deported Swiss be secretly shipped over to England.

As the efforts of the Swiss Ambassador at The Hague to secure passage for Ritter's expedition had become known, letters were written by Messrs. Hendrik Toren and Jan von Gent (good fellow-believers in Amsterdam) to the Burgomaster, von der Poel in Briel; to the passenger lists of the packet boat at Hellevoet, and to Mr. James Dayrolle, Secretary of the Queen of Egnland at The Hague, asking to inform them, should anything about the prisoners be reported from England. Mr. Torne (who reported this on March 31st, to Mr. Vosterman in Amsterdam), also told Vosterman of a certain Mr. Machielse, who appeared to be a servant of the Swiss Ambassador. This is very likely the heretofore-mentioned Mr. Michelle, who was in Lancaster County, in 1705. Preparations were made to go to Nimewegen, to meet there the Swiss prisoners, and to furnish them, if possible, with a ship for their transportation over to England. (Müller, p. 269.)

1709—Mennonites Prepare to Come to Pequea Valley, Lancaster County.

Rupp tells us (p. 71) that a lot of Mennonites reached Pennsylvania and also some, North Carolina in December, 1709. He says that "a respectful number of Mennonites left Strasburg, in Germany, where they had come overland, and sailed for America." Page 74, he also tells us that they first made a bargain with William Penn, that is the Swiss Mennonites, and then came to Lancaster County, reaching it in 1709. He quotes this from Benjamin Eby's "Geschchten Der Mennoniten," p. 151; and the statement Rupp sets forth from that book is that in the year 1709 the first families from the Pfalz reached Lancaster County. Rupp also bases this date on papers belonging to the ancient Herrs and Mylins.

Rupp says the tradition is that these Mennonites made improvements and cleared land here in Lancaster County before they got their first warrant for land, that they felled trees and made cabins. Their warrant was dated October 10, 1710 (Rupp, p. 76). He says that the warrant last mentioned in 1710 would prove that they came and settled early because it states on its face that these different families had lately arrived and had settled and selected land twenty miles easterly from the Conestoga, near the head of Pequea Creek. Then on p. 96 he says that they reached America in 1709.

He also sets forth Letters Patent, dated 1708 by Queen Anne, to the ancestors of the Mennonites of Eastern Lancaster County and shows that they arrived and registered in New York the 10th of August, 1709.

On p. 97, he sets forth an extract from an address by Redmond Conyngham on "The Early Settlement of Pequea Valley." This address was delivered July 4, 1842. Conyngham was a very famous historian and can be thoroughly relied on. He tells in the address of the wanderings of Issac Lefever, the head of the Mennonites in that section of our county.

Much that is highly interesting could be said here upon the beginnings of this fist colonly in the Pequea Valley, but that must be reserved for our discussion under date of 1710, which we will shortly enter upon.

1709—Important Swiss and Palatinate Item of 1709.

The Ferrees, now Ferrys and Forrys who reached Lancaster County in 1711 and 12, according to Rupp (p. 91 to 101) reached New York in 1709, and were very Godly people.

Rupp also tells us that some of the Pequea Colony of 1710 (the first settlement in Lancaster County) lived in Germantown before coming here. They lived there in 1709. He does not mention the names of those who did live there and I do not believe the fact can be established. The Germantown and Skippack pioneers always seemed to live separate from those of Pequea—they were Germans. The Pequea settlers were Swiss. A letter written in London in 1710 by our Pequea ancestors proves they were not in Germantown in 1709 nor in 1710 either, any considerable time. (Rupp's 30,000 Names.)

In 1709 the Germans of Germantown who had come over a couple of years before were naturalized. We find no Lancaster County names among them. (2 Col. Rec., p. 480-483.) Indeed they had made application to be naturalized in 1706, and the matter was delayed three years (2 C. R. 241).

Bishop Benjamin Eby, who about 1805, moved from Lancaster county to Canada, in his "Geschicten der Mennoniten" p. 150 and 151, says that in the year 1709, there moved several Swiss families from the Palatinate and settled in Lancaster County. (Rupp 74.) We will show, by many evidences, that the date of their arrival was 1710.

1709—Berne Mennonites Write Complaint to Holland of Swiss State Church Persecutions.

The following letter written in 1709 by one of the Mennonite elders describes the condition in Switzerland at that time.

Switzerland, June 22, 1709.

"To the Brethren of Holland:

We greet you most friendly in the Lord, and return thanks to you in general for all the fidelity and love which you have showed to our brethren in the faith, in the Palatinate and in other places. The Lord will reward you in time and eternity. We as ministers and elders in Switzerland wish this to you. First we make known to you that we are all in mourning because of how the government treats us. In the year 1708 they sent hostages to Berne out of the parishes, in which we lived, that had to be maintained at the expense of the parish, in order that they might help to hate and expel us; and gave council that even children must report their parents; and the brother report against his brother that he is a Mennonite. Friends and neighbors, such were their commands, must expel each other out of the bailiwick of Berne and of the whole government, and must then bring report and testimony to the government that they are quite gone. Among others, they have carried away to prison on a cart, poor old people who could travel with difficulty. The sick and the faint were brought prisoners to Berne. Some were compelled to leave family and all else back. They had to give promise they would not come back again. If they came again, they had to keep themselves concealed. The government sent out men to search all the houses, and with their swords, they thrust into the hay cocks and hit the minister of the congregation, who had concealed himself in it and he came out with another brother; they brought them both to Berne. The minister had a chain put upon his feet in the severe cold; and he is still a prisoner with others. It also happened that where there was any property, they divided it among the children, who joined the State Church and the portion which would come to the Mennonite children was paid to the Reformed Church. From some who had no children, they took everything and made large bills of cost, in favor of the Court House officials, who carried out their work. This was paid out of the Mennonite property."

This edict is a renewal of one issued fifteen years before, which commanded that all persons must go to the court of Sagnau and make a promise that if any one should see a Mennonite, they must bring him to the bailif, or the officer of the court, to deliver him into the hands of government; and those who harbored them, if found out, must leave the country. Where the husband goes to the State Church and the wife to the Mennonite, or vice versa, the one that is Mennonite was to be called before the court, known as the Mennonite Chamber, where he or she would be punished. It happened that where a man harbored his own wife, who was a Mennonite and he was not, that she was ordered to leave the country, and had to pay 300 pounds fine; and a father for harboring his Mennonite son was ordered by the Mennonite Chamber to pay 500 pounds fine.

This simple letter is sent to you to make known to the congregations in all Holland to stand by us your servants and elders in Switzerland.

We pray to God that He may be counsel to you that your labors may succeed for us, according to that which seems good to Him. You know better than we can write, how to interecede so that the government may treat us a little milder, which would be happy news to our breasts. It seems too, my brothers and sisters that it would be better if we were at peace with each other and there were no divisions and our government would have no reason to accuse us of trouble among ourselves. I believe that if the ministers and elders would come together, as they did long ago, at Strasburg, much division would be stayed and we would be reunited. Oh, that the dear God might grant us his grace that this should happen. (Müller 255.)

Amen.

1709—The Frankenthal Mennonite Addition to Skippack and Vicinity.

The error of some historians in stating that the first Lancaster County seatlement arrived in 1709, arises from confusing the Skippack German Mennonite Colony of 1709 with the Swiss Lancaster County Colony of 1710.

A settlement of German Mennonites came to Skippack on the Schuylkill in 1709, as an accretion to an earlier colony there. They may have been a branch of the great German Exodus of 1709. (Kuhn 26.) But this is not certain. They were Strasburg people. (Rupp 71 and 79.) But they may have come by way of London. Those of the Exodus left from London for America. These Strasburg people went to Skippack.

April 8, 1709, a letter coming from the committee on Foreign Needs at Amsterdam, states that nine or ten poor families from Worms had come to Rotterdam, asking for help to be transferred to Pennsylvania; but the committee advised them not to go (Pa. Mag. of Hist. and Biog., Vol. 2).

August 6, 1709, Jacob Telner wrote of them from London, that eight families had gone to Pennsylvania and that there were six more Mennonite families in London, too poor to pay passage. He asks the brethren in Rotterdam to come to their assistance. And this year also the yearly meeting of the Quakers at London voted fifty pounds to help Mennonites to go to America (See Smith's Mennonite History 145).

It is these people no doubt, says Prof. Smith, of whom Penn wrote to Logan as having gone to Pennsylvania. The letter is dated 26th of fourth month (June) 1709; and in it Penn says "Herewith come the Palatines whom use with tenderness and love and fix them so that they may send over an agreeable character for they are a sober people—divers Mennonites and will neither swear nor fight. See that Guy uses them well. (P. & L. Cor. vol. 2, p. 354).

Prof Smith says "They reached America and located on Skippack." (p. 146.)

The Telner letter about them of August 6, 1709, addressed to Amsterdam is in part as follows:

"Eight families have gone to Pennsylvania from here; the English friends called Quakers helped them. The truth is many thousand persons, young and old, men and women, have arrived here in the hope and expectation of going to Pennsylvania, but the poor men is mislead in the matter. If they could transport themselves by any means, they might go when it pleased them, but because of inability, they cannot do it, and must go where they are ordered. Now as there are among all this multitude, six families of our own brethren and fellow believers— I mean German Mennonites —who ought to go to Pennsylvania, the brethren in Holland should extend to them the hand of love and charity, for they are poor and needy. I trust and believe, however, that they are honest and God fearing. It would be a great comfort and consolation to the poor sheep if the rich brothers and sisters from their superfluity, would satisfy their wants and let some crumbs fall from their tables to these poor Lazuruses." (Vol. 2, Pa. Mag., p. 122.)

Telner by speaking of "all the multitude" refers to the great German Exodus of 1709 in England, of which we shall presently speak. Only six families of Mennonites were, so he says, in that Exodus. These six families and perhaps a few more with them, came from Worms and Frankenthal and reached Skippack. They were Germans: not Swiss. The Lancaster County pioneers were Swiss.

Pennypacker in his "Settlement of Germantown" also notices this settlement. (p. 126.)

1709 — Dr. Hoop Scheffer's Views on the German Mennonite Emigration to Pennsylvania in 1709.

"Dr. J. G. De Hoop Scheffer, of Amsterdam Mennonite College, in an article on Mennonite Emigration to Pennsylvania, written in 1869, vol. 2 Pa. Mag. p. 117, says (inter alia p. 120) on this subject:

One of the oldest communities, if not the oldest of all in Pennsylvania, was that at Scheeback or Germantown. The elder of their two preachers, Wm. Rittenhouse, died in 1708, and two new ones were chosen. The emigration of the other brethren from the Palatinate with Peter Kolb, were men enabled to make the journey by the aid of the Netherlands and gave a favorable prospect of growth. Financially, however, the circumstances of the community left much to be desired. In a letter written to Amsterdam, dated September 3, 1708, from which these particulars are derived and which was signed by Jacob Godschalk, Herman Kaasdorp, Martin Kolb, Isaac Van Sintern, Conradt Jansen, they presented a long and friendly request for some catechisms for the children, and some little Testaments for the young."

It is no wonder that half a year later, April of 1709, the Mennonite Committee on Foreign Needs cherished few hopes concerning the colony. They felt, however, for nine or ten families who had come to Rotterdam, according to information from thence, under date of April 8, 1709, from the neighborhood of Worms and Frankenthal, in order to emigrate and whom they earnestly sought to dissuade from making the journey. They were (said the letter from Rotterdam), altogether very poor men, who intended to seek a better place of abode in Pennsylvania. Much has been expended upon them heretofore, freely, and these people bring with them scarce anything that is necessary in the way of raiment and shoes, much less the money that must be spent for fare from here to England and from there on the great journey, before they can settle in that foreign land." The committee who considered the matter useless and entirely unadvisable, refused to dispose in this way of the funds entrusted to them." The Palatines understood the situation well. If they could only reach Holland without troubling themselves about the letters the committee would end by helping them on their way to Pennsylvania. The emigrants in April, 1709, accomplished their object; though it appears through the assistance of others. At all events, I think they are the ones referred to by Jacob Telner a Netherlands Mennonite, dwelling at London, who wrote August 6, 1709, to Amsterdam and Haarlem."

1709—The Great Palatinate Exodus into England.

This year a great number of poverty stricken Germans from the Palatinate (also Swiss, who earlier had moved into the Palatinate) rushed like madmen into England. There were several causes for it. First: Queen Anne of England had issued a glowing prospectus of the great opportunities in Pennsylvania and invited the Palatines to go there and take up the rich farm lands. Second: there was great hardship and poverty in the Palatinate, resulting from its over-crowded condition (but the people who flocked into England in this Exodus were not suffering any serious religious prosecution, because they were Catholics, Lutherans and Reformed, who were not the people per-

GREAT PALATINATE EXODUS OF 1709

secuted for their religion). The number in the exodus has been stated at various amounts, from 14,000 to 33,000. Their ultimate object was Pennsylvania. But when they flocked into England they learned that there were neither money nor ships to take them there.

The most authentic account of it is given in a report made to the House of Commons in 1711. The report in part states: "In the Spring of 1709, great numbers came down the Rhine and did not stop until reaching Rotterdam, Holland. Their destination was England. By June, the number in England reached over 10,000 and the Queen's government became alarmed. Orders were sent to the English minister at the Hague to check it. Advertisements were put into the Dutch Gazettes, that no more would be allowed to land. But three thousand more came. England issued a proclamation in December, that all would be sent back; some were sent to the West Indies and Ireland; but those coming after October were sent back. Holland also tried to stop the tide. The English Board of Trade and Plantations met twenty times to consider the matter, in May, June and August.

Queen Anne ordered help to them and 19,838 pounds were provided. They were lodged in ware houses, etc.—on the commons—in large buildings of business men—and fed.

The Commons Committee says that most of them were farmers and vine dressers, but many had trades.

Finally, 3,800 were sent to Ireland in August, 1709, and February, 1710, there were 800 more sent—600 were finally lodged on Black Heath, 650 were sent to North Carolina (to New Bern), where Michelle and Graffenreid had bought 10,000 acres of land—800 (those who were Swiss) were induced to go back to Switzerland—3,200 were taken by Col. Hunter to New York, in May, 1710.

The whole subject is written up in a masterly way by Dr. F. R. Diffenderfer in his "German Exodus of 1709"; and is entrancingly interesting.

The great bulk of them were Lutherans and Reformed Their Lutheran minister took 3,548 of them back to Germany and 1,600 also went back, who were to go to Scisily Islands; and 746, who were ordered to go to Ireland, went back to Germany; and 800 who had gone to Ireland, came back and returned to Germany, making nearly 7,000 in all going back. The elector Palatinate protested against the report that religious persecution drove these people to England. He says they were not persecuted.

My only excuse for writing at such length on this subject is to show that while all of these 14,000 or more, poor Palatinates intended in 1709, to come to Pennsylvania, the only ones who did arrive here were the few who reached Skippack in 1709. And none of our Lancaster County pioneers came here from the Exodus. The British government ordered the Lutheran and other ministers, in England, to take an accurate census of the hordes in England, and make a record of their religious faiths. This was done to the number of about 6,520. The record has been recently copied in England, brought to America, and printed by the New York Genealogical Society. Before the record was printed the writer went to New York and tabulated the list. It was found that 1,784 were Lutherans, 2,257 were Reformed, 44 were Catholics, 10 were Baptists, only six were Mennonites; and the remainder were of various faiths.

Our Lancastr County pioneers were Mennonites. Beside, of all the 7,000 names, not more than a dozen or twenty are familiar Lancaster County names (See N. Y. Gen. Rec. Vols. 40 &

41). It is indeed, most remarkable that out of 14,000 to 17,000 persons intending to come to Pennsylvania in 1709, having accomplished their journey to England, only a little handful reached the province of Pennsylvania and none at all reached Lancaster County, though they were of the Swiss and German stock, who, the next year, began to settle here and who, in the next ten years, had settled here to the number of many thousands.

1710—German Colony in Ireland.

In our article on the Exodus from the Palatinate to England, we noted that a large number of the refugees were sent to Ireland. Dr. Mitchel, who visited the Palatines in Ireland in 1840, says that it is very odd to find the names Baker, Miller, Ludwig, Madler, Pyfer, Strine, and Shirk in that section of the world, where all those about them are full blood Irish. About 1895 or 6 an article in the Philadelphia Record also dwelt on this situation. (Diffenderffer on the Exodus 81.)

1710—Dutch Ambassador Runckel at Berne. Tells of the Mennonite Conditions There.

A letter written by ambassador Runckel to J. Beets in Hoorn (Holland) January 22, 1710, explains itself. It is as follows: "Your letter of Oct. last year has come to me. I have not been able to answer sooner, because I have been detained to the present time in Lyons and Geneva and other places in Italy. Yesterday I came back here again and have informed myself as far as possible. I have heard, with compassion, that the so called Mennonites are persecuted so severely as has not been the case for years; and that since one named Willading has become Mayor of Berne, who is a Godless man and an enemy to all the pious, has that been the fact. However, there are yet some good men in the Council who did not want to approve this persecution. But on the other hand, the unspiritual clerics have mightily supported the Mayor. Also, one of these Godless preachers has not been ashamed to tell him that one should cut off the heads of some of them, then the others might come to their senses. In the meantime, the Council has written to Zurich in order to ascertain how they got rid of the Mennonites there. Whereupon, they answered that they had ordered some to be killed; and after that they had thrown as many as they could, into prison. Some have been transplanted forcibly into the war in France. Others had been sold to the galleys—others had been banished and forbidden to return. Of these latter, some had returned and have given their persecutors occasion to let their wrath loose against them, so that they are now persecuted more than ever and are hunted down in every possible way and thrown into dire imprisonment. They pay money to informers, whereby a large number have come to prison. How many and who, I cannot tell but hope soon to do so. Although it is strictly forbidden to let any one visit them in their prison, yet I hope through the aid of good friends to be able to speak to them myself. In the meantime, it is reported they are very patient under this affliction, edifying one another, and have increased their friends greatly through this persecution. Within the last month, two of the best teachers were caught whom they could not get before, until two prisoners who were in jail, because of thieving, promised to bring them to jail, if they would obtain their liberty for doing so. This bold purpose they carried out in delivering up these two good men, whereupon, they received $200 in specie, as a reward. But that some of those had died in prison I cannot tell. They say that of those

RITTER'S PROJECT OF DEPORTATION TO AMERICA

now in prison some are to be sent to Pennsylvania.

Now there was in Berne a Mr. Spezieria Ritter, and fellow associate, who were of a mind, soon to take their journey into America; and offered of the very poor families here and those Mennonite people, who were of good reputation to be gotten out of the country, to take them along. Arrangements were made with this Ritter that he was to receive for 101 persons who were to go along with this expedition $500; and for the Mennonites $45 a person actually landed in America. The Mennonites were to pay the transportation by wagon themselves, to the boat which was to be taken out of the Mennonite property of the congregation to which they belonged. Return to the fatherland was prohibited on penalty of death. Ritter was to accompany them to Carolina. This was made in 1709; and supplemented the following year, to the effect that Ritter obtained some advance payment and the town Council provided for good ships themselves. These Mennonites were required by the Queen of Great Britain for the peopling of their American islands and colonies. There must therefore have been agreements and transactions with Great Britain; and passes were provided from there also. Everything was ready for the departure on the 18th of March, 1710. In the last hour, a French Ambassador, Counte Du Luc, asked for a pass. The Imperial Ambassador, Herrn Feontianmansdorf, also asked for a free pass and passage on the Rhine and the places along the same. (Minutes 11th March.) The Council and authorities of Basle, were asked to appoint a walled place situated not far from the Rhine for the passengers (Min. 15th March). They had their thoughts wholly set on getting free pasage through the Netherlands and necessary passes for embarkation to America. March 12, 1710, was set for the departure from Berne. Shortly before that date, a letter from th Chancellor to the Bernese Ambassador in Holland, Mr. De St. Saphorin, announced that the French and English passes had been given to Mr. Ritter in order to secure safe transport of the people from their plight. (So they did not need to flee.) Now St. Saphorin took care that the States will impart to the police officers the necessary directions along the route, in order that not only free foreign passage but also the necessary assistance be given to the leader of the expedition against any accidental escape at the embarkation of the Mennonites at Rotterdam. The necessary writing together with instructions, St. Sapharin is to send to Ritter in Cologne, to the address of Mr. Deitrich Kaester, export merchant. He is also to get into communication with the authorities in Rotterdam. St. Sapharin is a perfect diplomat, in the true sense of his time; and one of the finest and most skillful of men."

1710—Swiss and Holland Correspondence on Mennonite Persecution in Berne.

In the item just cited, found in Müller 257-259, we set forth the Dutch Ambassador Runckel's letter.

We now give the substance of further correspondence on the same subject between the two nations.

May 13, 1710, the Swiss authorities wrote to Holland saying:

We do not doubt that if your Highness were acquainted with the condition of our Canton, you would approve of our proceedings in this matter and find, with us, that, this kind of people cannot be tolerated in our land, without danger. All the more because we, as a case of necessity, must arm our subjects, and unlike some other of the federated nations, have no foreign troops in our pay. This we must do to keep the treaties made by the confederation." (Müller 264.)

Another letter is noteworthy. It is the reply of the Dutch Ambassador to the request of the Berne authorities, asking the Dutch to take an interest in banishing Mennonites to America. The reply dated March 22, 1710, is in part as follows:

"In religion, freedom must be allowed to every man to believe and profess that which in his judgment is necessary to his salvation. No one may be persecuted and punished for such faith and such profession,if his life and doctrines do not tend to the injuring of the state.

And as to these Mennonites, it is well known that they have at all times conducted themselves as good inhabitants and subjects. Therefore, the Holland authorities cannot in any way, lend a hand to the forcible transportation and banishment of Mennonites to America; nor do anything whereby they might give color of approving even indirectly, such proceedings as have been inflicted upon the Mennonites in the Canton of Berne." (Müller 265.)

1710—St. Saphorin, the Mennonites' Friend Still Assists Them.

Obstacles arose and largely prevented Ritter's project from realizing any important results. Louis Michelle (who before, had been to America, both in what is now Lancaster County, Pa., and in what is now the region of New Berne, North Carolina), was assisting Ritter in the project of taking the Mennonites down the Rhine and it fell to him to tell them that there was no home in Holland for them and no funds to take them on to America. It thus became necessary to persuade those who were in Holland to find means to go on to America and also those who were coming on to Holland to do the same.

St. Saphorin then succeeded as he says in a communication, dated March 28, 1710, in arranging for a temporary stay for them in Holland where Holland Mennonites were prevailed on to take care of them, for he says "they cannot be expected to go back to Berne and be killed." March 29, 1710, St. Saphorin wrote to the English Ambasador at Hague (Holland) Lord Townsend to win him over. Müller says, the manner in which he presents the project does him great credit as a diplomat.

He says among other things "Some private individuals of good family of Berne, have purchased from the Queen of Great Britain a considerable portion of land in North Carolina and seven thousand acres in Pennsylvania in order to found colonies there under the mild government of the Queen. More than eighty families belonging to a religion, according to their consciences from the Canton of Berne are on the way there. Besides these, there are fifty Anabaptists or Mennonites who are in prison because they will bear no arms for the defence of the Fatherland—will not obey the sovereign nor recognize him—and who have been given their liberty on the condition that they bind themselves to settle in America where their sect is tolerated. And on the condition that they go to America, they have been allowed to sell their goods. And favorable contracts have been made with the owners of the land; and the state of Berne has assumed to pay all expenses from Berne to America. All this was carried on with Mr. de Stanin the Ambassador of the Queen of Great Britain. It will be of great advantage to the kingdom of Great Britain if the American colonies became populated with these people, in part, as both the families of these brethren in faith, who are going thither from Switzerland and all Mennonites are very good farmers and industrious people. And as in large part they are provided with money, they will be brought into the colonies without cost to Great Britain. Thus all will be of great advantage to her."

"My lord Townsend," he says, "is therefore requested to intervene with their high mightiness the Holland states general, that they grant to all those who are in Holland a free passage who hope to emigrate from Switzerland to America." (Müller 266.)

The Mennonites, seeing the transactions of Berne simply religious persecution by which they meant to send their subjects to America by force just as they previously sent them to the galleys of Venice, were about to alarm their brethren in faith then in England, to interest the Queen in the cause of their Swiss brethren, when St. Saphorin took up their case as above. (Do. 267.)

1710—Hans Funk Leads a Colony Out of Switzerland.

There is a brief note in Müller (p. 206) stating that about 1710, apparently, Hendrick Funk led a colony of 12 exiled Mennonite families out of Switzerland.

1710—Burkholder, Zellers, Brackbill, Rupp and Donens at Amsterdam, Plead for Help to Transport Swiss Mennonites to America.

This year, according to Dr. Scheffer of the Mennonite College at Amsterdam (Holland) in his article on Mennonite Emigration to Pennsylvania in Vol. 2 of Pa. Mag. of Hist. and Biog. pp. 117-126, five Swiss Mennonite leaders, Hans Burchi or Burghalter, Melchoir Zeller, Benedict Brechtbuhl, Hans Rupp and Peter Donens were in Amsterdam pleading for their people in Switzerland. The majority desired to live in the Palatinate but found great difficulty in accomplishing it. The Palatinate community were generally poor and much hardship they endured there for want of religious liberty. They were subject to the humors of the elector, or worse, of his officers. For nearly seven years they waited, often supported by the Netherland brethren, always hoping for better times. Finally, at a meeting of the Elders at Manheim, in the Palatinate, held Feb. 1717, it was decided to call upon the Mennonite brethren of Netherlands for help in carrying out the project of going to Pennsylvania, which they had long contemplated, and which at last came to maturity. And the very land to which in 1710, they were to be forcibly exiled, they adopted in 1717, viz. Pennsylvania—particularly the Pequea and Conestoga Valleys.

The actual numbers coming here in 1717 we will treat of under that year. I may note here too, that this same Hans Burchi, or as Dr. Scheffer calls him Burghalter in 1727, was a Mennonite preacher at Conestoga. Also according to Rupp, Brechbuhl translated the Wanderland Seele into the German from the Dutch.

1710—Swiss Mennonites the First Settlers in Lancaster County, Pennsylvania.

We now enter upon a most interesting item, locally—the first settlement in the Imperial County of Lancaster. This settlement was the Mennonite colony on Pequea Creek near Willow Street in 1710.

Müller says (p. 365) that among the emigrant Palatinates to Pennsylvania, there were a large number of exiled Bernese. Bernese emigrated not only out of the Palatinate (where many had prviously settled) in 1710 to America but also directly out of the Emmenthal. They were two months on the ocean and experienced all the hardships of first settlers.

Müller says further "Bernese Mennonites are mentioned in a letter written by Toren van Gent in Rotterdam to Jacob Forsterman in Amsterdam, dated March 31, 1710, which Mennonites had gone to England on their way to Pennsylvania and whom the Rotterdam brethren had helped with money to reach London. And says Müller (p. 366) they are likely the same six Swiss Mennonites, who on the 27th of June, 1710, wrote from London to their brethren in the faith in Amsterdam.

That letter quoted in full by Müller, p. 366, is as follows:

"Worthy and Beloved Friends:

"Besides wishing you all temporal and eternal welfare we have wanted to inform you how that we have received that financial aid which the dear friends out of their great kindness of heart have given toward our journey. And this kind contribution came very opportunely to us, because the journey cost more than we had imagined. God bless the worthy friends in time and eternity; and whatever may be of good for the body and wholesome for the soul may the merciful God give them and continually be and remain their rewarder. But of our journey we report that we were detained almost ten weeks, before we were put on board ship; but then we actually entered into the ship on the 24th, were well lodged and well cared for, and we have been informed we will set sail from here next Saturday or Sunday from Gravesend, and wait there for the Russian convoy. God be with us, and bring us to land in America as happily as here in England. Herewith we commend you to the merciful God; and, should we not see one another in this life, may God permit us to see one another in eternity. Wherewith we commend you all to the merciful God (together with courteous greetings from us all) and remain your true friends. London, the 24th of June, 1710.
    JACOB MILLER,
    MARTIN OBERHOLTZER,
    MARTIN MAILY,
    CHRISTIAN HERR,
    HANS HERR,
    MARTIN KINDIG."

These six pioneers came from London in the Mary Hope, a small ship having ninety-four passengers on board (one of whom was the famous Quaker preacher, Thomas Chalkley), with John Annis, master, and left London early Friday, June 29, 1710, in the morning, and later the same day left Gravesend for America and reached the Delaware in September.

We base our belief on Chalkley's Journal, page 74, where he says: "I took passage in the Mary Hope, John Annis master, bound for Philadelphia; and on the 29th of the 4th month (June), 1710, at Gravesend, we set sail and overtook the Russian fleet at Harwich and joined them and sailed with them as far as Shetland, northward to the Isle of Orkney. We were two weeks with the fleet, and then left them and sailed to the westward for America. In this time we had rough seas, which made divers of us sea sick. After we left Shetland we were seven weeks and four days at sea before we saw the land of America. We had sweet and solemn meetings on the first and fifth days; had one meeting with the Germans, or Palatines, on the ship's decks and a person who understood both languages interpreted for me. The people were tender and wrought upon, behaved sober and were well satisfied."

He also says the ship was small and was well loaded, with ninety-four on board; and all were brought well and safe to Philadelphia in September, 1710; and that the Palatines were wonderfully pleased with the country, mightily admiring the pleasantness and fertility of it."

It is not known that in the fall of 1710 any other Palatines than these who signed the London Letter, came to Philadelphia. Chalkley's ship left Gravesend, and was under convoy of the Russian fleet, just as the Mennonite letter says they expected to do; it had Mennonites on board; it left Gravesend (which is fifteen miles from London) on Friday, June 29, almost the day the Palatines wrote they expected to leave. They expected to go Saturday, the 30th, but to catch the Russian fleet, they had to sail a day earlier. We find that the 29th of June, 1710, was Friday, because in 2 Col. Rec. p. 533, June 16, 1711, was said to be Tuesday, and the 25th was thus, Tuesday, and the 25th of June, 1710, therefore, Monday, which made the 29th on Friday.

\This traces up these six pioneers of Lancaster County settlement from Amsterdam (where prior to March 31, 1710, there were gathered), to their arrival in Philadelphia in September, 1710. Other fragmentary evidence makes it fairly clear that, in the winter of 1709 and 10 they fled out of the Emmenthal near Berne and went to Holland to collect means, etc., from wealthy Mennonites there and make arrangements to go to Pennsylvania. Lancaster County thus owes a debt of thanks to Holland for helping the opening up of this county and for helping so good and God-loving a class of early settlers here.

We shall next trace the movements of this handful of settlers from Philadelphia to Pequea Creek, their steps to acquire land there and bring it under their dominion. While only six are signers of the letter quoted, it is certain that several more were in the colony.

1710—The Pioneer Swiss Colony Secures Land on Pequea Creek, Lancaster County, Pa.

Shortly after arriving in Philadelphia in September, 1710, the Colony just mentioned secured the right to take up land on Pequea Creek.

They procured for themselves the following warrant, which is No. 572 of the Taylor Papers, in the Historical Society Building at Philadelphia.

Phil.   ber 16, 1710.

By a warrant from   dated the 8th day of Oct.   Lord, one thousand seven hundred and   is authorized and required to survey and lay out to   Rodolph Bundely   and company ten thousand acres of land with reasonable allowances for roads and highways on the northwest side of a hill, about twenty miles easterly from Conestoga and near the head of Pequea Creek, and   thereof with my office.

JACOB TAYLOR.

To Isaac Taylor Surveyor of the County of Chester."

The blanks above are occasioned by reason of the fact that the original paper has partly crumbled to pieces because of age. There is no full copy of it.

In Vol. 19, Sec. Series of Penna. Archives, p. 529, may be found certain minutes of Penn's Commissioners of Property of their meeting held Sept. 10, 1712, making reference to the same tract. It is there stated that, the Commissioners granted ten thousand acres of land to the Palatines, by warrant dated ——ber, 1710 and that part of it (2000 acres) was laid out to Martin Kendig.

Rupp, in his history of Lancaster County (p. 90) quoting the same minutes says, the warrant was dated the 6th of October 1710. The copy which I give above of the original, found

150 FACTS ABOUT ORIGINAL SETTLEMENT IN LANCASTER COUNTY

in the Taylor Papers seems to be dated the 8th of October as I state; but the date is so indistinct that the 6th may be correct.

Rupp (p. 85) sets out another paper, apparently not in the archives, stated to be a document signed by former commissioners, which states that those former commissioners by a warrant bearing date the 10th of October 1710, granted unto John Rudolph Bundely, Hans Herr, and divers other Germans, late inhabitants in or near the Palatinate of the Rhine, 10,000 acres to be laid out on the north side of a hill, about twenty miles easterly of Conestoga, near the head of Pequea Creek" etc.

Thus we have the 6th—the 8th and the 10th of October, declared as the date of this first title of land in Lancaster County by our Swiss-German ancestors.

There is an order to survey according to the Taylor Papers (No. 573) dated October 16, 1710, which sets out that by a warrant dated 11th day of eighth month (October) 1710, there was given to John Rudolph Bundely 500 acres of land adjoining the 10,000 located or to be laid out to the Palatine Company.

Thus the true date is not later than October 1710.

These pioneers at once journeyed to the head of Pequea Creek but did not find that point to meet their desires and journeyed down the stream until they arrived at a point on the creek directly east of present Willow Street and there took up, on both sides of the creek 6,400 acres of this land and had it surveyed Oct. 23, 1710 and divided the 27th of April, 1711. This may be found in a map called "Plot of Original Tract of Old Rights in Lancaster County" in the Office of Internal Affairs at Harrisburg. The remainder was divided later. (See Mennonites of America by C. Henry Smith, p. 146.)

The division was as follows: Beginning on the west Martin Kendig 530 acres—Martin Mylin 265 acres—Christian Herr 530 acres—Martin Kendig 264 acres—John Herr 530 acres—John Bundely 500 acres—Christian Franciscus 530 acres—Jacob Miller 1,008 acres—John Funk 530 acres—Martin Kendig 1,060 acres. The tracts extend nearly north and south and are of regular parallel form, the whole plot reaching from West Willow on the west to Strasburg on the east.

Upon this tract also are the remains of the original settlers in the private grave yards on the same—one on the bank of Pequea Creek, known as Tchantz's Graveyard, afterwards called Musser's, where are found tombstones (practically intact today) over the resting places of the Mylins and Millers—one adjoining the brick Mennonite Willow Street Church, where lie the Herrs—and one just east of Willow Street, where repose the Kendigs and some of the Mylins.

The division lines of the old original farms, determined the public road of today of that whole section of ten square miles, five miles from east to west and two miles or more from north to south; these roads being located precisely on the old property lines. Much of the original tract is today owned and occupied by descendants of the original owners.

1710—Record of Subdivision of Pequea Tract.

In the record of warrants at Harrisburg the subdivision of the great tract mentioned above may be found. Among other facts, it is set out that "Martin Kendig late an inhabitant of Switzerland, had surveyed to him 1060 acres of land in Strasburg township, bounded by Mylin, Herr and Funk—another of 530 acres and another of 265 acres. Recorded Sept. 1711.

ANCIENT HOME OF OUR COUNTY PIONEERS

Likewise Christopher Franciscus of Switzerland 530 acres bounded by Miller, Bowman and Bundely—in 1710 Funk had 530 acres founded by Kendig and Miller, surveyed Feb. 28, 1711. Bundely of Switzerland had 500 acres bounded by Bowman. surveyed in 1710 and Mart. Mylin 265 acres—Christian Herr 530 acres and John Herr 530 acres—all recorded July 3, 1711; Wendell Bowman 530 acres recorded July 7, 1711. Warrants for all of these are dated 1710. (See Rupp 79.)

1710—Membership and First Steps of Pequea Colony.

We have mentioned above six of the members of the Pequea Colony—those signing the London Letter. Rupp says that in addition to them, Hans Mylin, Michael Oberholtzer and others (whom he does not name), were in the Colony. (Rupp 75.) He says their warrant was recorded and the land surveyed Oct. 23, 1710; and that April 27, 1711, the surveyor-general, at their request subdivided it; "into so many parts as they had previously agreed upon."

In warrant book 1700-1714 p. 229, Shippen, Griffith Owen and Thomas under date of Oct. 10. 1710, Edward Story—Penn's land commissioners—order Jacob Taylor, Surveyor General, to survey to those named above the full quantity of ten thousand acres, with allowances for highways into as many small tracts as they (the purchasers) shall agree or appoint to each of them his respective share to be holden by the purchasers, their heirs and assigns under the rents reserved, of one shilling Sterling yearly for every hundred acres. They were to pay 500 pounds Sterling for the land—one hundred pounds each year so that in six years they should pay principal and interest in full. (See Rupp 75.)

1710—Lancaster County Ancestors Banished From Berne This Year.

Prof. Kuhns (p. 46) in his "German and Swiss settlements of Pennsylvania" states that, in 1710 among those banished out of Berne were the names of Brechbühl, Baumgartner, Rupp, Fahrni, Aeschliman. Maurer, Ebersold and others and that as surely as these are of Bernese origin, the names of Landis, Brubacher, Meiley, Engli, Ringer, Gut, Gochenor and Frick are from Zurich.

The particular Swiss home of the pioneers of Lancaster County may claim our brief attention in this item.

The ancient Herr home we have discussed before.

Martin Meiley and his ancestors, says Mr. Schnebeli, of Obfelden, came from the Canton of Zurich. And he says the ancient home of Meileys was at Hedingon in Canton Zurich; and that there are doctors and professors of that name there now.

Of the Kendigs, Oberholtzers and Millers, this same authority also says they were from Zurich. He says too that, the name Müller is most numerous there (as it is here) of them all. In Canton Glarus there are many Herrs and Tschudys.

Mr. Schnebeli says that "It is probable that two of the six signers of the London letter were from Zurich Oberland (that is southeast part of the Canton—mountainous part). They are Martin Kendig and Martin Oberholtzer.

Jacob Müller was from Zurich, for a certainty. There were nine dead Müllers on the battle field of Keppel where Zwingli met his death Oct. 11, 1531. The Müllers are most prominent in Switzerland.

They have been statesmen, domestic and foreign. The president of Switzerland in 1909 was a Müller.

152 ATTEMPT TO FORCE MENNONITES INTO PESTILENTIAL SWAMPS

A branch of the Oberholtzers came from a village called Oberholtz near Wald. There are families of that name there today.

Speaking again of the Mileys. Mr. Schnebeli says, there was a Colonel Meiley in late years. There is today a Rev. Meiley and a Dr. Meiley there too.

Other now familiar Lancaster County names are found in the County of Obfeldon and says Mr. Schnebeli, "At the beginning of the 18th century several Obfeldon residents moved to Pennsylvania, such as Huber, Landis. Ringger, Gut, Funk. and others."

He concludes by saying that the best authority on these subjects is Dr. Weber, the High Librarian of Canton Zurich.

1710—Projected Lithuanian Colony of Swiss Mennonites in Prussia.

As early as 1526 there were Mennonites in Marienberg, Prussia, asd thus that section of the German Empire was not a new country to them. When this nation had become depopulated by pestilence and what Müller calls the northern war (Müller 329) King Frederick of Prussia, in 1710 asked Berne to send a colony of the persecuted Mennonites there. The Prussian Ambassador Von Bundeli was consulted by Berne as to the matter. The Prussian King also opened the matter with the Ambassadors at the Hague and at Hamburg and reported that the Dutch and the Hamburg Mennonites thought this would be a good place to locate some of the persecuted. But these Dutch and German brethren advised that by all means a committee of Mennonites should go and view the land to see whether their Swiss brethren would like the place.

King Frederick thought well of the project and told his Berne Ambassador, Von Bundeli, to give all the aid he could and report to the leaders of the Swiss Mennonites that they would have religious freedom there and be exempt from war. The States General of Holland told their Ambassador at Berne to help the project also. The letters which passed between Berne and King Frederick's officers are said to be very interesting, but we do not have copies of them. They are dated July 31, 1710—Sept. 26, 1710 and Nov. 14, 1710. They may be found says Müller 330 in Schaerers History, etc.

Müller, however, goes on to tell us that from the correspondence, it is plain that the following conditions were laid down by Prussia:

1. That Berne should allow the Mennonites full freedom to depart with their goods.

2. They should be brought free—that is without expense to the Prussian boundary.

3. That before they came, a committee of Mennonites of Germany and Holland were to be allowed to examine all the conditions of the country and see whether it would be satisfactory to and suited to the needs of the brethren.

Berne agreed Nov. 14, 1710, to the projects in the following manner:

1. That ten per cent. of the estates which the Mennonites took with them was to be given up to be applied to the expense especially to the expense of the needy ones; and that all who went were to forfeit Swiss citizenship.

2. Berne undertook to see that those who were paupers should be landed at Frankfort.

3. Berne would not have a committee of Swiss Mennonites go to view the land—the Holland and Prussian Mennonits should do that.

4. Berne expressed the hope that the Mennonites would find a comfort-

able place there so that none of them would attempt to come back.

The particular place in Prussia where these Mennonites were to be settled was in a district on the eastern border of Germany called Lithuania. This is a former grand-duchy, later sub-divided between Russia and Prussia.

This colony of Mennonites was to be made up of a considerable number of Swiss Mennonites who had been banished from Berne and were now in Holland with the brethren there and a lot more still in Switberland around Berne, who had not yet been sent out.

The project failed. A few Mennonites from the Palatinate went but as wars were numerous in those sections then, they found that their principle of non resistance was not respected and that while they were not compelled to bear arms, they were compelled to pay large sums of money as the price of exemption. Then the Mennonites in Switzerland were not willing to go to a place which war and pestilence had once made desolate. The Swiss Mennonites in Holland were too well pleased with the happy condition of the Dutch Mennonites with whom they were living as servants, etc. (and with prospects of getting to Pennsylvania) to leave and go back east again. (Müller 329 and 330.)

1710—Benedict Brackbill's Valuable Services for His Swiss Brethren.

One of the finest and foremost characters in the Mennonite troubles of the beginning of the 18th century in Switzerland was Benedict Brackbill or (Brechbuhl) ancestor of our Strasburg Township and other eastern Pennsylvania Brackbill's of today —one of the best and most numeorus of the families of the great county of Lancaster.

According to Brons 215 and Müller 329, etc., Brackbill and two other church brethren Zahler (Zellers) and Burchi (Burgholder) March 22, 1710, appeared before the authorities of Amsterdam (Holland) to request Holland to prevent the Swiss Mennonites, whom Berne was now forcibly throwing out of Switzerland, from crossing Holland to the ocean. There three patriots found out that a ship-load of fifty-seven of these Swiss brethren (of whom we have spoken of before) mostly old people and in many cases husbands separate from wives, etc., were taken out of the jails about Berne and were being sent down the Rhine. They were sick and half starved in their imprisonment and were not fit to travel at all. By the time the vessel reached Manheim, thirty-two had to be taken off the ship or they would have died. They were left to the mercies of Manheim. They were all to be sent to America. (In a later item, see page 159, we give their names, which on inspection will nearly all be found to be our common Lancaster county names of today.)

Brackbill and his two fellow laborers agreed that these people were too weak to try to reach America and that they would all die on the trip. The Holland authorities agreed to what he asked. And thus when St. Saphorin, the Swiss Ambassador in Holland, asked for freedom of the Swiss emigrants to go on, he was refused by Holland. St. Saphorin was a great friend of the Swiss Mennonite sufferers.

When the ship containing the remainder of the fifty-seven reached Holland at Nimwegan, they knew that Switzerland could not harm them and they disembarked. They found Brackbill, Zellers and Burgholder waiting for them and they brought them before the Dutch Mennonite Congregation there for comfort, etc. There too, they gave testimony of their suffering and treatment as we have set out before. (Brons 215).

There it was too, that Benedict Brackbill got Holland interested in trying to get them to settle in Lithuania; and it seems he had been in that place of proposed settlement to examine conditions too. (Müller 330.)

Brackbill also did another service for his Swiss brethren, when he visited Holland's capital in March, 1710. They were represented by Berne as bad people and enemies of government and this was beginning to poison the Dutch against them. Brackbill explained their faith in all points and satisfied them that the Swiss Mennonites were the same good Christians as were the Holland Mennonites.

The circumstances leading up to the jail delivery in Berne resulting in the fifty-seven brethren having been sent down the Rhine are harrowing and horrible.

In February, 1710, Berne decided that the government must get rid of the imprisoned Mennonites, as their imprisonment excited sympathy and kept the cause alive. The Council acted on the matter and a large number of the body held out for executing them all; but the majority carried through a vote to send them to America. Then the Holland Mennonites determined to help them all they could and gathered up a fund of 50,000 guilden for the cause. A guilden is worth forty cents. The government of Holland too was favorable to them. All this again shows the gratitude Lancaster County and all southeastern Pennsylvania owe to Holland (Brons 215).

1710—Preparations to Send the Swiss Mennonites Down the Rhine.

The negotiations between the Swiss and Holland Government with Mr. Ritter, deporting agent, of which we have spoken before, finally bore fruit. Holland, arranged so that the journey might be accomplished. They asked for a promise on the part of the States General, that the prisoners upon their arrival in the country would be in due form declared free, so that they might go unhindered to their brethren, who would take care of them. This request was granted by Holland on April 3rd, with the advice not to allow them to return to their fatherland; for in such an event a further protection would be impossible.

At last the important information was received that the Swiss ship had arrived at Nimwegen, where the prisoners were set free by the authority of the Holland Government. Their soon-to-be-expected arrival had been heralded from Neuwied, by the teacher of said congregation. Tielman Rupp, in a letter by his son, Lieubard Rupp to Jacob Hendriks in Amsterdam, dated April 6th. Originally (the writer states) there had embarked at Berne 56 persons, who were shipped down the Rhine, among them Brechbuhl, Zahler and Burki, ancestors of famous Eastern Pennsylvania families today. Of these 28 were by reason of sickness and infirmities incapable of travelling further; and upon urgent entreaties the officer released them on the 29th of March at Mannheim. The other 28 were transported further. At Neuwied, an effort had been made to land them (which place was passed April 3rd, at three o'clock in the afternoon), but the attempt was frustrated by two officers and fifteen men of the guard. In the letter of Tieleman Rupp the Hollanders are requested to purchase their liberty. Alhough the Messrs. Von Bent and Jan Frederiksen hurried from Rotterdam to Nimewegen, on the strength of this letter, it was impossible to reach Nimewegen in time, the ship having arrived there April 6th. The banished travelers had been apprised that there existed a congregatiin of Anabaptists or

Mennonites in this port, and asked leape that some of them, ever under escort of a guard, be permitted to visit their brethren of the faith. Mr. Ritter placed no obstacles in their way. They sought out and found the place of meeting and the teacher, Hendrick Laurens, residing there. We will now let this Hendrik Laurens tell his own story of the arrival, as he wrote it to the brethren at Amsterdam.

"It was on the 6th of April that they arrived here at Nimwegen. As soon as they had heard that fellow-believers resided here, one of them came to me, guarded by two soldiers; but the soldiers went away and let the man remain with me. After I had spoken about this matter to other servants of our congregation, we went together to the vessel, and there found our Swiss brethren. We had a talk with the officer of the guard, and soon saw that some refreshments ought to be supplied to these people, as they had spent twenty days on the water in great distress and misery; whereupon we brought them into the town. Now we said to our captive brethren: 'The soldiers will not get you out of here easily, for if they should use force, we will make complaint to the States General.' But nothing of the kind happened. Now they were free, over which we felt great joy, and we showed them all token of friendship and love, to their great delight and happiness. After we spent some time happily together, and they regaled themselves with great enjoyment, they left the following day. But they could only walk with difficulty, for by reason of their long imprisonment they had become quite stiff; some of them had been confined for almost two years amid much suffering, and particularly last winter during the intense cold, when their feet were shackled with fetters. I went with them for an hour and a half outside of the town. Then with tears of joy and cheerful minds we embraced each other and parted with a kiss of peace. Thereupon they returned to the Palatinate, to seek out their wives and children, who were scattered there, as well as in Switzerland, and in Alsace, not knowing whither they had gone. They were quite confident and of good cheer in their misery, although all their worldly goods had been taken from them. There were among them a preacher and two teachers. They were by nature a very sturdy, hardened people, capable of enduring great privations and hardships, with long unshorn beards, wearing disordered, clothing, heavy shoes, made all the more clumsy by horseshoes on the heels and great nails being driven into them. They were very assiduous to serve God with prayer, reading and other works, were very plain in all their actions, like lambs and doves. They asked me how the congregation was conducted here which I told them; and they seemed to be very well pleased. But we could converse with them only with difficulty, owing to the fact that in Switzerland they had dwelled in the mountains far from villages and cities, and had little intercourse with other people. Their language was quite coarse, awkward and uncouth; and they could hardly understand anyone who did not speak their language. Two of them went to Deventer in order to see whether they could make a living in this country." Such is the letter of their host Laurens. (Müller, p. 170.)

1710—Brechbüehl, Zahler (Zellers) & Burki and Their Neighbors, Swiss Mennonites Tell of Berne's Cruelty.

The Swiss sufferers, Brechbüehl, Zahler, Burki and others, before mentioned as being at Nimewegen, afterwards went to Cleve, there to await the result of the negotiations of their brethren in Holland, of which thy had no knowledge; and then to wander further South.

When about twenty of them had arrived there (one, Bendicht Brechbuhl, upon leaving the ship had preceded them to Crefeld, by way of Cleve), they repaired to the teacher for the congregation at Cleve, Isak Vrauken. Here the emotion and pity of the liberated brethren were great. In a trice their arrival was known; one of the deacons asked the privilege of caring for half of them. The other brethren also came around, and each one asked for his portion, in order to exercise hospitality. Consequently no one could entertain more than two himself; for a teacher and a deacon remained with Vrauken. Whoever received no guest, brought clothing. These strangers could not be persuaded to lie in bed; but preferred to sleep on straw, as most of them had subsisted for one or two years on nothing but bread and water. Meats and other nutritive foods did not agree with them. They made no other request than to be taken as soon as possible to Mannheim, where their fellow-prisoners, as we have seen before, 28 in number, were left behind. When asked about the state of their purses, they refused to accept anything, saying they had partaken of more than they could ever recompense. But Isak Vrauken collected hurriedly 9 florins of Cleve money and slipped them into their hands, whilst Vice Chancellor Heine procured for them a good passport and 30 floirns, in the bargain. So they remained a few days longer at Cleve, principally upon the suggestion of some brethren at Emmerich, to await tidings from Holland which were soon expected, as two delegates had left Rotterdam on April 11th, to come to their aid with good advice. As Sunday had arrived, Vrauken's guest occupied in his stead the pulpit of the congregation of Cleve. Albeit the brethren of Cleve did not understand the sermon, it nevertheless did not likely fail to create a deep impression.

Isak Vrauken writes to the Committee at Amsterdam, he has found that these people are well versed in the Holy Scriptures, that they are very humble without any hypocrisy or deceitful show of character. Of the twenty, seventeen were married. They had a heartfelt longing for wife and children after such a long and grievous separation. None of them had a desire to return to Switzerland. They preferred rather to settle down in the Palatinate, at Mannheim or elsewhere.

On May 2, 1710, the Committee of Amsterdam transmitted the sum of 1200 florins to the congregations in the vicinity of Mannheim, who were not able to care for the Swiss who had remained there, and for those who had just returned there from Nimwegen.

The Committee of the Mennonites at Amsterdam had asked some of the Swiss, freed at Nimewegen, to come before them in order thoroughly to learn the conditions in Switzerland. In their meeting at Amsterdam on April 25, 1710, twenty-four questions were submitted to them to be answered. Of four of these questions written, answers were requested, viz: How and by whom were they taken prisoner? How long and where were they imprisoned? How were they treated then? Whether an investigation had been conducted and by whom? These Swiss were, Benedicht Brechbuhl of Trachselwald, teacher and elder at Mannheim; Hans Burki, of Langnau, deacon, and Melchoir Zahler, deacon of Frutigen. Brechbuhl had once before been expelled from the Bernese territory and gone thence to Mannheim. Returning to fetch his wife and children, he was taken prisoner and in that way got among the deported. Upon his liberation at Nimwegen, he at once traveled toward Mannheim and was then recalled to Holland. Three of these Swiss sufferers made reports in writing of their treatment.

1710—Hans Burki's Report.

For the remembrance of my descendants and of all my fellow-believers, I, Hans Burki, of Langnau, want to relate what happened to me. I had gone to the mountain called Bluttenried (Community of Langnau), in company with my wife and two sons. There a poor man came to us to whom we gave something to eat; this man subsequently went to Harvag to the authorities and told them that he saw me. Thereupon the Bailiff of Trachselwald sent the traitor with a few others to take me prisoner. They came quite early in the morning to my hut, in which I stood unawares of any evil, and when I noticed the man before the door I had him supplied with something to eat. Then I was made a captive and they took me away from my wife and twelve children and led me to Castle Trachselwald and placed me into a prison or dungeon, for four days, during which time I was taken sick. Then the bailiff with two provosts brought me on a cart into the city of Berne. There they placed me, sick as I was, in the prison, called Ahur. After two days the gentlemen called and questioned me, whereupon I confessed my faith. Then they locked me up alone in a separate hole in the Ahur, and there I lay sick about five weeks, and altogther 17 weeks, in solitary confinement. Thereupon they led me into another prison, named the Island. There I lay during the whole long and cold winter with an unhealthy body, and suffered very much from the intense cold. For a long time I was watched so closely that none of my family or anyone else could come to me, so that my friends did not know whether I was living or dead. Thereupon, at the beginning of the month of May, 1709, I was brought with all the other prisoners to the hospital, and there, too, I was kept in such close surveillance that only very few persons could speak to us. We were compelled to work on wool from early morning until late at night, viz: from four o'clock in the morning until eight o'clock at night, and we got nothing to eat and drink but bread and water. This lasted about thirty-five weeks. Thereafter ten more weeks we were treated less severely. Then the authorities had us conveyed to the ship, viz: on March 18, 1710, with the design of having us taken to America. The authorities told us that if any time and by any means we were to return to their country, they would inflict the death penalty on us. Thus the merciful Father has by his strong hand and through the medium of our brethren and friends in Holland, delivered us from our oppressors, as we arrived at Nimewegen, and came to the town where they had to release us. For this we thank the Almighty God and Father of all mercy, who will not forsake all those who place their confidence in him, but will cause them to prosper. The whole time of my imprisonment has been about 21 months, for in the month of July, 1708 I was taken captive, and on the 18th of March, 1710, I was led away from Berne. Will come to a close here.

Brechbuhl's Report.

It was in the year 1709, on the 12th of January, that the authorities of Berne sent seven provosts with a constable, early in the morning to my house, whereby we were greatly frightened so that my wife and myself tried to hide ourselves. I concealed myself under a haystack. They searched my house in every nook and corner. Finally they came to the haystack and thrust their swords in it, so that they struck me and were made aware that some one was hiding therein. Thereupon I crept out and they seized me, asked my name and whether I was a preacher, which I told them and acknowledged it. Then they led me into my room; there the constable gave me a box on the ear and tied my hands on my back and led me out of my house. Thereupon my children began to lament and cried so piteously that, as the saying is, a heart of stone would have been touched thereby. But the provosts were in great glee that they had succeeded in catching me. They led me hence to the city of Berne in company with two other brethren, and put us in imprisonment and that too, in the very long and cold winter, there we lay as prisoners. If we wanted anything warm, we had to pay dearly for wood. After six or seven days they brought me in another jail. There they put iron shackles on me. In the mean time the authorities had given those who captured me 100 Thaler, which my family had to reimburse out of my estate. After two days they again brought me in the tower and set me in a separate hole and fastened me to an iron chain. There I laid about 18 weeks. After that they led me with all the other prisoners to the hospital. There we were compelled to work from four o'clock in the morning to eight o'clock in the evening in wool and they fed us with bread and water, but supplied these in sufficient quantity. This lasted about 35 weeks. The remaining ten weeks the work was easier. So the whole time of my imprisonment at Berne was one year, 7 months and 7 days. This happened in the 44th and 45th years of my age.

Benedicht Brechbuhl, a Native of the Emmenthal.

1710—Melchior Zahler's Statement.

In the year 1709, about the month of March, the authorities of Berne had issued a commandment and a strict mandate, which they had announced from the pulpit in all their territory against the so-called Anabaptists or Mennonites, wherein all their subjects were forbidden by pain of loss of their possessions, privileges and expulsion from the country, to harbor any one of us and to give them food or drink; furthermore it was ordained that if anyone would discover or see any Anabaptist or Mennonite, he was to inform the pastor or bailiff of such fact. A reward was set, a liberal sum of money, for some 50, for others 100 Thaler of the realm, and they had their subjects make oath, that if they can get hold of any of us, be it in the houses or on the roads, or elsewhere, they should bind us and lead us all into captivity, so that the same happened about this time to myself. For when I was about to get some bread and wine for my sick and pregnant wife, now deceased, which was about between 10 and 11 o'clock at night, I was asked whether I was not a Baptist. And when I did not deny this, they told me they had to be true to their solemn promise and would not perjure themselves on my account, or they would not do this injury. Thereupon they led me part ways with much cursing and swearing. But at the same time I was released by a good friend.

After that the gentlemen of Berne had caused to be sent to the city of Berne, from all parishes wherein it was presumed that some Anabaptists dwelled, two, three or more persons; these people had to remain there for several weeks at great expense to the people of their respective parishes, so that by such loss and detriment we were to be made all the more obnoxious and hated by the peasantry, whereupon many of our people removed about that time from the country to Alsace, Mompelgard and Neuenburg, whereby the oppressed fugitives and banished, suffered great distress and poverty, since everything was taken and robbed from the most of them, so that nothing was left to them; and all this against all rights

NAMES OF THOSE DEPORTED DOWN THE RHINE IN 1710

and justice and against their own mandate.

At the same time, I, Melchior Zahler, also went to dwell in the territory of Neuenburg. Thereafter some time, my brother-in-law with a friend well known to me by the name of Hans Germann, both Reformed, requested me by word of mouth through a confidant, to come back to my possessions in the Bernese District. Thereupon I went to this well known friend, who showed me all love and friendship, and who wanted to give over to me my two children in order that I might maintain and clothe them. Then I wanted at one time to visit my brother and sister and my other children, and while I was with my brother and sister and other children, he went to the Reformed pastor and betrayed me. He divulged everything, the time, the night when I returned into the country; and of the clothing, etc. All this he told the pastor. Thereupon this pastor sent three provosts on the same evening, who took me prisoner, bound me and took me to the pastor who questioned me concerning my creed, about infant baptism, swearing of an oath, about the regulation of the ban, about the carrying of arms, about the institutios of the authorities, etc. And he ordered them to again bind me and transport me to Berne, which was subsequently done on February 27, 1710.

Once before, in the year 1706, I had been imprisoned for three weeks, and now at Berne in the hospital six weeks my right hand shackled and locked, and fed on bread and water, whereby I was afflicted during this time with much anguish, sadness and misery, for the reason that they had betrayed me so falsely, and that they had robbed me of all my children and worldly goods.

They also took away from me, besides my five children, more than 15,000 florins; furthermore banished me from my estate and ties of blood, and transported me with the following company to be sent to America without giving me a penny for the journey, viz:

Hans Burki, who was captured July, 1708—Christian Sattler, captured and made prisoner July, 1708 — Isaac Baumgartner, taken prisoner the first time........; 1709 the second time—Benedicht Brechbuhl, a teacher, on January 12, 1709 — Jacob Ulrich—Peter Zalfanger—Kaspar Bieri—Christian Janthauser—Christian Berger of Laupersville—Dan. Moser (Musser)—Ulrich Schmied of Langnau—Nicklaus Blaser of Lauperswyl—Peter Hofer of Schoenek—Peter Hofer of Lauperswyl—Christian Grähenbühl—Samuel Reber; this Samuel Reber, according to a letter of Runkel, of January 17, 1711 (A. A. No. 1301), came back and was sentenced to imprisonment for life—Ulrich Ellenberger—Peter Kohler—Henrich Wenger of Moglenberg—Christian Steiner, a deacon—Hans Jacob of Uetendorf—Jacob Schwander—Peter Thonen of Reutigen—Hans Gasser, a teacher—Hans Stubet (Stober), a deacon—Hans Rupp of Sigriswyl—Hans Murdt (Maurer) of Niederhunigen—Niklaus Hager of Niederhunigen—Ulrich Fahrni of Schwarzenegg—Hans Ramseier—Yost Kopfler—Hans Engle of Rothenbach — Durs Rohrer a deacon—Rudolph Stettler, a teacher—Michael Aeschlimann, a deacon—Niklaus Baltzer—Melchior Zahler taken prisoner February 27, 1710, and once before in May, 1706—Mathias Grähenbühl — Benedict Muster (Musser) of Diesbach—Benedicht Maurer—Hans Berain—Niklaus Moser, a teacher, who died in prison—Benedicht Nusbaum—Peter Mutrich of Trub and Niklaus Luthi—and the women folks are Katharina Ebersole — Elizabeth Gerber—Elizabeth Gerber of Signau—Elizabeth Krieg (Krick) of Hettingshem—Elizabeth Steiner of Nurzenburg

—Anna Schenk of Diesbach—Barbara Fahrni—Margaretha Engel of Diesbach—Magrith Aeschlimann—Katharina Ellenberger of Eggiwyl and Barbara Frutiger, who escaped from the Basle district.

The above named women and men folk were on March 18, 1710, transported from Berne in a ship after enduring much persecution and oppression and severe imprisonment; of these people 32 were liberated at Mannheim on the following 28th of March in consideration of the fact that they were old and feeble people, and some of them very sick. The other 26 were somewhat stronger, were taken to Nimwegen, where, on April 9, they were set free through the intercession (or intervention) of the high and mighty gentlemen of the States General and the Dutch Brethren and friends, which happened by divine will or decree."

At the close of the whole episode we enter once more the residence of the Ambassador, St. Saphorin, at The Hague, and find him busily engaged with the Messrs. Ritter and Isott, which, of course, ended to the disadvantage of that firm. In consequence thereof there remained for the master of the ship, Schinder, 12 Thaler of the money which he had received at Berne for the maintenance of the sergeant and the soldiers. As he could not enter upon the home journey with this small amount, St. Saphorin paid over to Schinder for this purpose 130 Thaler, taking a proper receipt therefor.

On April 26th, the Ambassador also received a well merited testimonial from his government for his exeertions.

1710—Brief Summary of Galley Torture

We have several times given items upon the persecution of our ancient ancestors by means of the galleys, Berne sending them to Venice and other Mediterranean countries. Müller in his Chapter No. 13, page 215, discusses the whole subject. Wars with Turkey made strong galley-men necessary. Switzerland was glad to send our Mennonite ancestors to this torture. As early as 1540 ninety Anabaptists or Mennonites were taken out of the dungeons in Austria, to be handed over to the great king of Venice for galley-service; but they escaped from the torture at Trieste. Twenty were afterwards captured and transferred to the galleys. When they arrived a receipt was given by the officer who took them and an agreement that after two years, they would be released. It was also agreed that they were to be used in one ship and not be separated. Any that would repent their religion before reaching the galley could go back.

In 1671 George Orell was in Venice collecting payments due to Zurich and Berne for the hiring of our Mennonite brethren as galley-servants. (Do. 216). He reports that Venice was greatly pleased with these people There are works devoted entirely to the subject of galley-punishment.

The great emigration in 1711 Berne thought, would rid Switzerland of the Mennonites (Müller 220); but it was found there were many of them still in Switzerland and that many more came back from Holland, refusing to be banished. This caused a split in the Mennonite religion. Jacob Ammon headed the stricter party and Hans Reist the milder party. The Ammon people, that is the Amish, were willing to go; but the Reist wing were not, and were put under the ban by the Amish. Berne now determined to send the obstinate Reist people to the galleys, because they came back from Holland; and thus it happened that this year about fifty-two were sent.

Berne now selected from those who were expelled in 1710 and 1711, (and

ATTEMPTED DEPORTATION TO AMERICA.   167

had returned), six of the most prominent, to be sent to the galleys—to be sold to the king of Sicily, but only four were found fit to go, the other two were too old. They were Hans Luithi, Nicholas Bumgardner, Peter Weitrich, and Joseph Brobst. These were of Trub. Much influence was brought to try to have the government re-consider; but to no avail. They were strong men about fifty years old and had to go (Müller 220). They were to be fettered with irons. Some time in 1711, Jacob Schnebeli (Snavely) of Manheim wrote to Jacob Frey and others at Amsterdam and stated that he had news of these deported from Turin by letters—that they were to remain there over winter—that they were kept in a vault together with ninety criminals, who had been sold to a man named Hackbrett for their crimes—that they were daily taken out to do some hard work. Schnebeli further wrote that by Spring they would go on the high seas to the galley. They presented a petition to the Duke of Savoy to release them. The Duke said he was satisfied but it was all in the hands of the officers at Berne. When at Turin the prisoners received some aid from their Mennonite brethren in Holland. A little later Berne agreed to release the prisoners, provided they would not return to Switzerland.

The original letter from these galley-slaves, dated at Balermo, September 16, 1715, signed by Christian Liebe, Peter Whitrick and Joseph Brobst is found in the archives of the Mennonites or Baptists at Amsterdam (Müller 226).

In this letter they complain of great tribulation and distress and that one of them died that year, another one the year before, at Turin, so that only three were now left. These were Nicholas Bumgardner and Hans Luthi. A little later the king of Sicily ordered them released (Do. 230). The king agreed to transfer the men free to Nice. An influential Swiss friend named Frey of Torren, succeeded in getting them liberated and he gave them money and clothing and conducted them back to Switzerland (Müller 231 and 232). They had the shackles taken off of their feet, and they started to walk to Turin but got very sore feet. From Turin they proceeded through Savoy and Geneva to Neuenburg. They were met by the bishop of Pruntret, in whose neighborhood some Mennonite friends had settled and got together a small congregation. Here they were given earnest advice not to go back to Berne. All of them but Christian Liebi (Levy) remained there; but he went on alone to the Palatinate.

1710—Scattered Items on Attempted Deportation to America.

Müller devotes Chapter 15, page 252, to an attempted deportation to America. Much of this we have already discussed. The question before Berne was, "What shall be done with these Mennonites?" All orders had been partly futile. Whenever the Mennonites were forced over the Swiss boundaries, they were sure to return. This was made worse about 1710 by a famine that had broken out in Alsace, where some had been sent. So they went back to Switzerland. Many were in the jails and were a burden. The galleys were too dreadful. Many were old and weak.

The idea of deportation to distant countries began about 1699; and on the 17th of May, that year, the East India Company at Amsterdam were requested to take ship-loads of them away. (Müller 253.) The city of Berne sent a long communication to the company, stating how obstinate these people were; that measures harsh and mild were of no avail, and that nothing would do but to send them to a far-off land. Thus Berne urged the East India Company to take a lot of them to the Islands of East India.

One of the foremost leaders was Isaac Kauffman; and it was arranged that he should be taken to the Company at Amsterdam and be sent to India. The company paid no heed to this.

The idea of deportation soon again was taken up as the number of prisoners was increasing in Switzerland. This time the Court, erected to take charge of the Mennonite matters, known as the "Baptists Chamber" was informed of the affairs in April 17, 1709 and directed to start vigorously to clean them all out of the country. So vigorously did this Court take hold of its work that shortly, more than five hundred were driven out of the country and it was hoped that soon they would all be gone. It seems that two places where the Mennonites had been imprisoned were in the "Upper Jail" and on the "Island." Among those mentioned are Benjamin Brackbill of Troxelwald, Christian Krayenbühl of Norben, Hans Wager (Wenger) a weaver of Wattenweil, Peter Thouen of Reutigen, Jacob Neueuschwanger (Newswanger) of Stocken, Hans Burki of Gibel, Christian Steiner of Grafenbühl, Elsbeth Steiner, his sister Catri, Aebersold, Anna Shenk, Hans Gerber's wife; a baby, Catrina Leuenberger of Wytigen, Peter Rubeli's wife of Aesehlen; Elsbeth Gerber, Peter Gerber's wife of Zimmerzey; Christian Danzler, an old bedfast man, Babi Forni, an old woman quite deaf. To the Baptists incarcerated on the Island were added Rudolph Stettler of Stettlen; Durse Rohrer of Ittigen and Hans Rupp of Gunten. (Müller 253.)

These and others were people not able to do galley-service, and therefore, Berne asked the Baptist Chamber to see that they were sent to the East or West Indies and Pennsylvania.

The other steps in this attempted deportation to Pennsylvania we have already had in former items and I have simply added this at this time because it was omitted heretofore. We recall that the principal step taken to deport to Ameirca was that in 1710, when fifty-seven were put in a boat and sent down the Rhine, of whom three gave their story and testimony to the Dutch Mennonite preacher, Hendrick Laurens, at Nimewegen. We have also heretofore given the names of them.

1711—The Pequea Swiss Tract Subdivided.

We have stated in a prior item that in 1711 the tract of 6,400 acres (part of the 10,000 acres taken up) was sub-divided among the different owners. This happened on the 27th of April; and the surveyor general at the request of the purchasers made the actual division I hope to append a map of this subdivision to these annals which will show the particular lines dividing the large tract. (Rupp 75.)

1711—First Swiss Birth in the Settlement.

According to Rupp 83, on the 22nd of January this year, Samuel Miller was born on the Pequea, son of Jacob Miller, a pioneer. He was the first child born to our Swiss ancestors in this county.

1711—Interesting Conference Between the Governor of Pennsylvania and the Pioneer Colony of Lancaster County.

In the Colonial Records. Vol. 2. page 533, there is an interesting account of a treaty at Conestoga on the 13th of June, 1711. The Governor of Pennsylvania, together with four of his most noted members of Council

NEW BERNE SETTLEMENT—REIST AND AMMAN FACTIONS. 163

were present at this treaty. It took place at the fork of the Little Conestoga and Big Conestoga Creeks. As far as it relates to the German-Swiss settlement of this county, we simply note that under date of Tuesday the 18th, in the forenoon, the Governor in his speech to the Indians says that he intends to present five belts of Wampum to the Five Nations and with them the Conestoga Indians, he required their friendship to the "Palatines settled on Pequea." This is conclusive proof to show that the Pequea settlement of the Swiss was in existence at that time. To this the Indians made answer "As to the Palatines, they are in our opinion safely seated." This gives us some little side light upon the conditions in which our fore-fathers lived.

1711—Palatine Colony of New Berne Killed.

According to Rupp in his 30,000 names of Swiss and Germans coming to Eastern Pennsylvania he says, page 3, that in 1709 a considerable number went and found New Berne, N. C., about 150 families; and that Sept. 22, 1711, one hundred of them were killed by the Tuscaroras. The New Berne Colony do not appear to have been Mennonites. New Berne exists today.

1711—Condition and Size of the Pequea Colony.

Jacob Taylor, surveyor for Penn, in a letter to James Logan, the 20th of the 5th month (which was July) 1711, concerning the Pequea Colony of Swiss writes "Many people are desirous to go backwards to settle land. Six or seven families of Palatines are settled at Pequea; and more desire to go there next winter. In another part of the letter he says that there is "a great want of commissions to sell the proprietor's land and that many people desire to go back to settle." (Taylor Papers No. 2796.) We state this item simply to show the condition of the first colony. toward the end of its first year of residence in this county; and we can gather from Taylor's letters that it consisted only of a few families. But that many more families were interested in coming there to settle. And that generally they were prosperous. is also evident.

1711—The Reist and Amman Factions of Mennonites on Emigration.

We have before stated that Jacob Amman led off a branch of Mennonites from the regular church on the doctrine that they were not strict enough. When the question of suffering, persecution or emigrating to America came up, it seems that the Amman faction were more willing to emigrate than the Reist faction. At least we are told by Müller (page 220 and 221) that the Reist people resisted being sent to America and either remained at home or left the ships wherever they could to return home and join their brethren in faith in the Palatinate. Therefore, the wrath of the authorities was more fierce against the Reist people than against the Amish. The Berne Government called them "the most contrary people known." The government also declared that all those who were banished and came back would be sent to the galleys or imprisoned for life. Among those sent to the galleys was Hans Gerber.

1711—Holland Mennonites Take Up Berne Mennonite Cause Before Berne Ambassador in Holland.

About this time a deputation of eight leaders of the Holland Mennonites, who had brought with them four Berne or Swiss Mennonites, one of them a preacher, came to try to induce the Berne ambassador in Holland to new efforts, to influence Berne. The Bernese Ambassador to Holland tried to thwart this. The four Bernese Mennonites were taken before him. The Holland Mennonites said that they regretted that Berne was again imprisoning their Brethren and that the wives and children of those banished, had been kept back. (Müller 281.) They represented that these Brethren do not hinder the state in any way and only ask the right to serve God, according to the dictate of their own consciences.

St. Saphorin relates as follows: I deemed it proper to answer the Holland Mennonites with asperity. I told them "I am astounded to hear you speak in such a manner after you had yourselves an opportunity to know the Bernese Baptists. These people had the permission to sell their possessions, but only upon the provision not to enter any more upon the territory of their Excellencies in Switzerland from which they had been banished. Not only did they return to the land but they also tried to convert to their notions as many of the inhabitants as they were able which under the Constitution of our State would lead to nothing less than the annihilation of its defences. They could have been punished with the severity which the law prescribes against those who break their banishment; but instead arrangements had been made with the minister of England by which they were to be received in America under the mild dominion of her Majesty, the Queen, with the same privileges enjoyed by the other subjects of their Excellencies who emigrate thence on their own accord, or voluntarily—only with this for their advantages—that those who profess the religion of their sovereign must go there on their own expense, while the Anabaptists are sent there at the expense of their Excellencies, the Swiss government. With profuse thanks they had accepted this, glad that a punishment had been meted out so little commensurate with their disobedience.

While not all could emigrate to America—although such was stipulated—yet it would have been quite proper for some who have neither wives or children to show by the journey, their compliance; but none would give in, to the admonitions of the gentlemen here who are so solicitous of their welfare. Instead, they have remained in Holland to complain of Switzerland, their Country and Sovereign. Although there is only one religion prevalent in all reformed Cantons in Switzerland, it is nevertheless not the religious dogmas which impels the intolerance of the Anabaptists or Mennonites in the territory or the dominion of their Excellencies; but because their creed contains certain things which are diametrically opposed to the State Constitution. No power can reprove us if their Excellencies (who maintain no standing army, and who impose no other burdens on their subjects, than the duty of defending the Fatherland), cannot tolerate a religion which tends to overthrow the only foundation of their security. As to the intercessions of so many different powers such as Holland, England, etc., their Excellencies know full well that all these powers have too just an opinion, as to disapprove what Switzerland demands, when they expect of their subjects the defense of the Fatherland. Besides, their Excellencies are not bound to render an account of their doings to any one; nor do they expect from any other an account of their actions. I declare that all movements by which you cause a disapproval of the attitude of their Excellencies will only have a tendency to embitter the public mind in

Switzerland, and to make the condition of your brethren in the faith all the harder."

This action of St. Saphorin defines the Bernese standpoint. The military view takes precedence of all others. The military duty is the most prominent affair of honor of the citizen; and in the storms which sometimes swept through Europe, it was not an easy matter to guard the neutrality of the country which, in addition to other duties, had to defend the Reformed Faith against the Catholic, making it a country with weapon in hand; and one whose best forces were hired to foreign countries as mercenary soldiers. The speech did not fail to have effect.

1711—Holland Mennonites Arranging to Help Swiss Brethren Out of the Country to America and Elsewhere.

After St. Saphorin had delivered his lecture to the delegation of Dutch Mennonites and their Swiss brethren present, just set out, the delegation made the following requests:

1. For the free departure of the wives and children of those who were banished and are being banished to America, so they may join them.
2. For milder treatment of, and liberation of, those recently imprisoned so that they can emigrate out of Switzerland too.
3. To stop the horrible practise of Mennonite-hunting and rewards for their capture, so they can come out of hiding, collect their possessions and leave too.

St. Saphorin replied that the first request would be granted, on condition these families would not settle down near the boundary line of Switzerland; and that Holland should see to it that none of the ship-load sent down the Rhine in 1710, of fifty-seven persons of whom thirty were put off at Manheim and twenty-seven at Nimewegen, Holland, should return to Switzerland as they threatened to return; and that a bond be given to guarantee this. If this be done, the detained wives and children may go to them. The delegates also state that as to the property of these divided families, they be allowed to turn it all into money and take the money with them; but the Ambassador said all he could do was to see that the wives' dowry rights were respected, as the husbands' share had already been forfeited.

As to the milder treatment of and liberation of the Mennonites, then in Berne jail, all St. Saphorin would say was that, the act of the first ship-load, violating their agreement to go on to America, and instead of that getting on the ship at Nimewegen as soon as they were in the free soil of Holland was responsible for the rough treatment of those then in jail and for refusal to liberate them and send them away free of charge; and that future severity of Switzerland would depend on whether the first ship-load sent out, would stay out or come back. The delegation then gave bond guaranteeing that this would be observed—that they would never more set foot on their native land. St. Saphorin also said he heard from what passed between prominent Dutch and Swiss Mennonite representatives and Lord Townsend, Englands Ambassador in Holland, that the Mennonites are full of hope that their religion, having been born in the Reformation, the same as the State Church of Switzerland (the Reformed Church), it will not be exterminated by Switzerland. He told the delegation they must give up all hope as to this, as the country was determined to crush it out entirely; and that if they had any love for their Swiss brethren, they should induce them all to get out of Switzerland as soon as possible.

They aroused surprise and admiration in Ambassador Saphorin's breast by saying that since the charge against them was that they were not patriots and would not help to defend Switzerland, they would try to get their Holland friends and the government too, to guarantee that they would raise money instead of troops, and thus do their duty to their native land. But he said, Switzerland does not keep up her defenses by bounty and substitutes, but by her own soldiers alone.

This ended the conference on the three subjects. (Müller 281-3.)

1711—Holland's Help to Persecuted Swiss Mennonites.

The final determination to deport the Mennonites to America brought affairs to a crisis. (Müller 279.) These Mennonites could not see extradition as in any sense, a favor to them. The Netherlands being in close sympathy with the oppressed Mennonites kept themselves advised on all these matters, and all that the Holland Mennonites did for the Berne Mennonites, the Holland government approved. The Holland Mennonites did everything that diplomacy could bring about. The great help that Holland gave the cause has never been acknowledged publicly, or at all by Switzerland.

As soon as the Bernese Mennonites who were sent down the Rhine in 1710 were liberated at Nimewegen, the crisis came. St. Saphorin, the Swiss ambassador at the Hague immediately took up the matter, with the English throne and the Mennonites also tried to get Lord Townsend to intercede with Britain to help them. Saphorin represented to England that Holland's help to the Mennonites instead of speeding them on to America made them more stubborn to return, and caused many of them to return to the Palatinate. He said they are determined to maintain their sect in Switzerland. Saphorin, while anxious to help the Mennonites to America, was against them in all other respects. He deprecated (to the British Government) any further efforts by Holland to help them, and especially that the Mennonites were trying to have Holland interfere with Berne. These complaints he made to what is called the "Pensioner," who seems to have been an officer with funds to help the Mennonites; whether English or Dutch is uncertain.

A conference was arranged with St. Saphorin and other powers of the Berne government; and the "Pensioner" demanded that the banished be allowed to take their goods with them, saying they could get rid of them quicker by so doing.

1711—St. Saphorin Announces Berne's Final Decision.

The deputies mentioned in an earlier item, it seems, were also the representatives of Holland. They tried again this year to intercede with Berne. But St. Saphorin thwarted it. Again and again these Mennonites tried to get favorable action from St. Saphorin and hoped that Secretary Runckel, who was going to Berne could secure favor at the home office. These Dutch friends tried to persuade Berne that they were trying to find settlements for the Swiss brethren. St. Saphorin praised them highly for the love and sacrifice they showed and said he was glad only five hundred were left in Switzerland, since they must suffer so severely there. He said finally he would recommend the Swiss government to give them sufficient time to go. He represented to this government that the Swiss Mennonite question is stirring the whole Protestant world.

He told the deputies that Berne is about to resort to severe torture upon those who refuse to go and he was compelled to exact a bond from the Dutch Mennonites that the Swiss would go and not return. (Müller 284.)

1711—Holland Declares the Good Character of the Mennonites.

The Dutch brethren became active, and to get all the information they could, three of the Nimewegen refugees came before them as we have seen before, April 25, 1710, at a meeting at Amsterdam. They learned the condition in Switzerland, by submitting to them twenty-four questions. It seems from Amsterdam, the Holland authorities took Brackbill, Burki and Zellers to the Hague and confronted St. Saphorin with them and from the answers made by the Swiss Mennonites, for their brethren and all else learned about them, the Holland officials and deputies entered in their "Great Memorial" on record, Vol. IX, page 106, and published in French, this defense of the Swiss Mennonite cause, in answer to all the reproaches against them.

"We, the Burgess and Council of the city of Amsterdam, make known to everyone whom it may concern and declare according to the truth that, there appeared before us Hans Burki, Benedikt Brechtbühl and Melchior Zahler, teacher and elders of the Mennonite Congregation in the honorable canton of Berne, Switzerland, who declare that they came into our city and were cognizant of the fact that they were accused upon three points of their Christian Doctrine, namely: that they denied the authorities were ordained by God, that they refuse to take an oath, and they refuse to defend the Fatherland with weapons. They, therefore, desire to make a solemn declaration of their faith, before the magistracy of this city, which would prove clearly that the above accusations originated from erroneous notions, inasmuch as their creed and that of their brethren in the faith was not properly understood, as to the three points in question. Whereupon the aforenamed Benedikt Brechtbühl, Hans Burki and Melchior Zahler, each one for himself, have before us, burgess and council of this city, publicly attested and declared that the creed after which they had lived in the Canton of Berne, in regard to the above named three points consisted of:

1st. That they believe and proclaim that the authorities were ordained by God the Almighty, to punish the wicked and protect the righteous, and that therefore every Christian is in duty bound to acknowledge it as a servant of God; and dare not resist it, so that one may be enab'ed under its government, to lead a quiet peaceful life, and that, therefore, one must render that which he owes—toll to whom toll is due, fear to whom fear is due and honor to whom honor is due.

2nd. They believe that, according to the teachings of Christ (Matthew 5), it is not incumbent upon them to swear an oath, but yea whatever is yea and nay whatever is nay; and that by this they feel themselves as strictly bound as all others who take an oath, and that they, when they break their word are just as amenable to the punishment of the authorities as a perjurer.

3rd. That they are ready to pay to the authorities taxes on imports for their protection and safe-guard, as much as may be levied against them, according to their means, and which they may be able to render, and that in times of distress they would be willing in lieu of military service to participate in the works of defense, as much as lay in their power.

4th. The deponents humbly pray that we might register this, their public declaration in order to serve as a testimony for all times, whenever it would be necessary.

"To this document we have affixed our city seal and have had it signed by our secretary." (Müller 285.)

1711—Brackbuhl's Further Services For His Swiss Brethren.

After numerous conferences and visits to Holland as we have seen before, the three Bernese Mennonites, Breckbuhl, Zellers and Burki, took their leave on June 6, 1710, with a Christian and brotherly farewell, and supplied with a present of fifty florins as traveling money, returned to Manheim. Brechbühl was there again active as elder in his congregation, as we now show. He was the mediator and confidential agent between the Mennonites of Berne and Holland and in many cases, rendered his brethren in the faith many services in those years. He writes under date of January 4, 1711, from Manheim to Holland:

"Report to the friends that some time since I received a letter from servants and elder in Switzerland with reference to their exodus to Prussia; they write me that they do not wish to go there; but want to await the mercy of God, and wish to remain in their land as long as they can. They who were in the ship thank you most friendly and cordially for all the great love and fidelity shown to them. I understand also from their letter that, the brotherhood in Switzerland do not deem it well that I, because of fear of men, do not help foster the small flock of Christ; and express the opinion that I should not forsake their people. But until now, I have not deemed it feasible, however, to help more than I am. In the Springtime I mean to undertake the trip up, to fetch my children. For this reason I had written some time ago to the Canton Berne to have them show me the grace and privilege of receiving me with favor, or at least to grant me a passport so that I might return for some time to the country, since I have made the promise in the past Spring to the friends of the committee, while we were at the Hague, that I would not travel up to Switzerland without their knowledge and consent. Therefore I will try to get the government to release me of my promise; for I cannot very well have my children and other things brought out (or called for) by some one else. It is my friendly request to the friends to write me whatever may be your pleasure in the matter. Furthermore, I report that, I am able to earn my board and keep, by my hands; consequently, I am well content. But, as yet I know of no place where I can dwell with my people. I trust to the Lord, however, that he will not forsake his people (for whoever does His will the Lord will not forsake), but will furnish me with a place of abode.

I have also received word a short time since that, the authorities of Berne have promised those who were made prisoners that, if they would promise to appear whenever they were wanted, they would be released; but when this would be, only time will tell.

As to the two morasses (swampy tracts in Luthania where the German King wanted to induce them to settle in Germany, vacant because of pestilence), I would report that I have heard from good authority that it would entail an almost impossible expense to make them fertile, or productive, therefore, I know not what further to write on this subject. Although I would like to write much on account of the unbroken love for the friends with which I am imbued. But

EFFORTS TO COLONIZE SWISS MENNONISTS.

as I have nothing further in particular to relate, I will let this short intelligence suffice, and commend the friends, together with their whole families to the gracious protection of the Almighty, remaining herewith your affectionate friend and brother in Christ.

"BENEDICHT BRACHTBUHL."

On May 17, 1711, Benedicht Brachtbühl writes to John Willink, that his three children have arrived hale and hearty from Switzerland, that they, however, have brought the word that the congregations there are so greatly eager to have him come that he intends to yield to them, and requests a speedy release from his promise or vow. (Müller 286 et. seq.)

This letter, so full of love and trust in the Lord under the difficulties he details, ought to put to shame the dissatisfaction we so often feel and the mistrust of God we show whenever the affairs of our lives do not wear the rosy tint we unreasonably expect. It may be found in the Mennonite Archives at Amsterdam, No. 1299. The project to send the small company of Mennonites at this time left about Berne, to the bogs of northern Germany to a place where war and pestilence had destroyed all the inhaibtants, and the powerful influences behind the project ought to make us appreciate how narrowly the ancestors of many of us here in Lancaster County, escaped being sent to another section of the world, from which they never would have reached Pennsylvania. By a similarly narrow margin, we remember they also escaped being taken to the East Indies by the East India Company. Benedict Brackbühl was a strong factor in preventing both of these fates of our people. Isaac Kauffman also rendered service to prevent the East India project.

The oppressed Mennonites of Switzerland and the Palatinate turned to the Quakers of England, through the advice of their Holland brethren, to have them intercede with the English government; but, the queen's authorities refused to interfere with Swiss affairs.

They then turned to the king of Prussia in a petition; and he gave it as his opinion that there would be no help for them unless they all leave Switzerland. In a letter dated July 5, 1710, the king wrote that these Swiss sufferers should settle themselves in the district of Brandenburg, at such places where extensive dairies could be operated, or in Prussia, where there were good chances of success. In Prussia, the raging epidemic completely depopulated many villages in the most fruitful region; but houses and cattle and agricultural implements were still there ready for people to use them, said the king. If the new settlers come at once they would profit from the rich harvest, as the former settlers had died after planting the crops. The king promised further, that everything that would help these good people would be done (Huizinga, page 25).

This act on the part of the king of Prussia was hailed by the "Amsterdam Courant" of August 9, 1710, with delight and it spread the news that the king had already written to the canton of Berne, that he would receive these people, Baptists or Mennonites, without any exception and would help them to make a living. (Müller 288.)

Müller further says that, even a narrative of the Amsterdam committee's acts in behalf of their Swiss brethren in faith would be too long to recite complete. A recital of all the journeys from Amsterdam and Rotterdam to the Hague; and the numerous conferences, with influential delegates and the letters sent make up a large catalogue in the Mennonite library at Amsterdam.

The Holland Ambassador at Berne, Runckel, used all means with the Berne government to have the hard measures against the Mennonites stopped; and to secure freedom of worship for them at home. His next plan was, if this was not allowed, to secure a few years chance for these Mennonites to sell their goods and land. But Runckel had a hard struggle in this effort; and July 12, 1710, from Berne, he wrote to the committee in Amsterdam, that though he had no further orders from Holland to assist the Mennonites, yet that of his own accord, he had inquired carefully into the condition of them; and in this inquiry he states that he found in Switzerland some people who felt that the Swiss government was entirely too severe; and who were full of pity for the poor Mennonites. (Müller 289.) But he says for every one of these, there are two or three who wish them all the pains the government has given them and no remonstrance can influence them. He states that the government especially makes it a point of honor that all they have done was right and for the welfare of the government and the glory of God. He says it is most certain the Berne officials have no idea what kind of people these Mennonites are and what difference there is between them and the Munster Anabaptists, who stirred up trouble for the government in earlier times. These people believe everything true that is charged against the Mennonites, he says; and that he knows no way to overcome it, unless the pamphlets that have been printed in their faith in Holland, and their creed, be translated into High-German and be printed, and especially that a great lot of such pamphlets be scattered throughout Berne. He says that the more he things of the subject, the more he is concerned that these poor people must be helped to escape the heavy storm which is hovering over their heads and seek a home somewhere else until the wrath has subsided. He concludes his letter in part as follows—"I believe, therefore, the greatest act of love which could be done for these people will be to seek out some place of abode for them and that they should completely leave Berne. The princess of Nassau and the count of Newweid are willing to receive some of them—such as are artisans and mechanics; but as these people are mostly farmers and stockraisers, the above offer was of no value, as Holland has enough farmers. By the last mail, I have reported to Amsterdam that more than twenty of these poor people are again in prison and the rest were scattered and chased into the neighboring countries. I will endeavor to talk with these poor prisoners myself and to comfort them as much as possible in their bondage. (Müller 290.)

Joahn Ludwig Runckel."

1711—Further Plans to Deport Mennonites—Holland the Final Asylum.

In Müller (page 290), may be found a list of the prisoners (mentioned in a letter from Alsace), who were in the jail of Berne, July 27, 1710, consisting of twenty-three brethren and seven sisters, of the Anabaptist or Mennonite faith. They are as follows: Peter Gerber, a servant in the Word of God,—lies in chains.

From the dominion of Trachselwald: Peter Blaser, Hans Wisler, Hans Schneider, Clauss Baumgartner, Ulli Bear, Peter Hertig, Peter Leuti, Ulli Brachbul, Hans Grasser, Joseph Probst, Daniel Rotenbuler, Hans Zahn.

From the dominion Sumiswald: Ulli Trüssel, Ulli Schurch.

From the dominion Brandiss: Hans Flückinger.

From the dominion Signau: Martin Stramm, Christian Gouman, the younger, Hans Holtzer, Leupersweil (bailwick of Schnottweil); district of Solothurn. Hans Kuoubuler from the dominion of Diessbach. Hans Frutiger from the dominion of Thun. Niclauss Haberli of Buchsi.

The sisters imprisoned are: Verena Aeschlimann, Catrina Bieri, Christina Trussel, Margret Scher, Margret Oberli, Anna Brentzighoffer, Anna Moseri.

There is a letter in existence stating that these thirty prisoners were also to be sent down the Rhine to Holland, in a ship, the same as a former party were. The letter is as follows: Cunonheim in Alsace, July 26, 1710. "Have received a letter from Switzerland, and understand from it that twenty-three brethren and seven sisters are imprisoned at Berne, and that they are willing to take them down the Rhine on a ship, therefore, we, the undersigned deacons and elders in Alsace beg of your deacons and elders in the Palatinate, namely, Tillman Kolb and Hans Jacob Schnebeli, very friendly to pay attention and see to it, when the ship arrives at Breisach. But we may not know when they will arrive. We are willing, however, to send people to Breisach who will let us know as soon as they arrive there. We ask of you kindly if it be your pleasure that you will write to the friends in Holland. We are afraid if they have a further passport from the king, we can hardly accomplish anything.

In haste
MARTIN EGLI.
HANSS BLUMM,
CHRISTIAN RUPP."
A. A. 1269.

On all sides, it was agreed that emigration was necessary. But where should these people be sent to? They would be received with open arms in Prussia. The Mennonite committee, therefore, requested Benedict Brechbühl in Manheim on July 18, 1710, to use his efforts to persuade his countrymen to accept this offer; and that they, as obedient subjects, submit to the demand of the authorities to quit the country. Brechbühl replied on August 27th that he communicated this suggestion to the brethren in Switzerland and that those residing in Manheim were too well pleased with their condition there to think of such a thing.

As the Baptists or Mennonites in Switzerland could not be enthused over the emigration to Prussia, it seems, Runckel on August 30, 1710, broached another subject to the Committee at Amsterdam. The Baptists or Mennonites might be colonized on Bernese territory on the two great marshes, which could be drained and by cultivation, would make excellent land for tilling and grazing purposes. As a recompense for making these morasses arable, the Bernese government should grant freedom of religion. But much money would be needed for this enterprise, which the Holland and Hamburg Mennonites would have to furnish. Brechbühl, being interrogated by the commission on this subject, on September 26th, held the project of the great morass to be absolutely unacceptable. Runckell wanted to consult with an engineer on the matter.

He did so and October 4 he secured the opinion of engineer Bodurer in Amsoldingen that was unfavorable. Then this project was dropped. The engineer, however, informed Runckel that between Romainmotier and Romont, on the boundary of Burgundy, a great tract of untilled land was in possession of Berne, which would be used as a place of abode for the Mennonites. He hoped to be able to submit a chart and an estimate of the cost by October 25th. Such well-meant but impracticable plans were soon discarded; and it became clearer and clearer that the Netherlands must be the haven of refuge for the Swiss brethren. To this end preparations in Holland were now made to receive them. (Do. 292.)

1711—Joyous Swiss Mennonite Exodus Into Holland.

Holland now became the goal. To transport the suffering Mennonites there, a new collection of money was needed, the same as in the years 1642, 1660, 1671 and 1694; and now greater sacrifices were demanded. Of the 20,000 florins which were collected in the last named year for the fugitives in the Palatinate, nothing was left. For the balance, namely; 1200 florins, Brechbuhl, on May 2, 1710, gave his receipt at Manheim. Therefore, the Committees at Amsterdam on August 12, 1710, dispatched a circular to all Mennonite or Baptist Congregations in the Netherlands. This appeal was signed by the Amsterdam brethren Willem von Maurik, Harmanus Schijn, Jan Willink Jansz, Adr, Jacob Fries, Jacob Vorsterman, Frans von Aken and Cornelis Beets. A general assembly was held on November 5, 1710, at which detailed reports were made by the thirty-seven brethren present. The Committee received power of attorney to dispose of the money to be received at their discretion. In important questions the commission should be augmented by two delegates, each of the cities of Zaaudam, Haarleh, Leiden and Rotterdam. Then the various projects for the rescue of the Swiss were thoroughly discussed, and further information requested of Mr. Runckel.

Of the Swiss liberated at Nimewegen, two, Hans Rupp and Peter Tenne (Thönen) had gone from there to Deventer, and were now brought by S. A. Cremer to the assembly. They reported to the meeting, in detail, everything which they and their brethren in Switzerland had to suffer innocently; and that of them all (as badly as they were treated), only one, Niklaus Rügen, had apostatized his Mennonite faith. They related that their split into two parties: viz.—that of Hans Reist and that of Jacob Ammon, largely concerned the "Ban"; that they could not calculate the number of their church members, but one faction estimated them at 600, the other at more than a thousand.

The report of Vorsterman contains, under date of December 2, 1710, a touching letter of consolation by the Committee at Amsterdam to the brethren and sisters imprisoned at Berne, and as an answer thereto dated January 8, 1711, from Peter Blaser in the name of his fifty-two fellow prisoners.

Of the condition of these prisoners, Runckel writes from Berne to the Committee at Amsterdam under date of October 1, 1710, as follows:

"The day before yesterday, September 29th, I, at last, found an opportunity to visit the prisoners and to console them in their sorrow as much as lay in my power, and to encourage them to submit to God's will and obey the authorities in calmness of Spirit. In this, two local citizens, Messrs. Knoll and Wagner, have given me much assistance. (Müller 293.) In the so-called 'Island' prison, I found eleven men and six women, but without chains or fetters. Among the first named, three sick. The men are idle, the women spin hemp and flax to while away the time. In the upper hospital are sixteen men and fourteen women, among whom are also some sick and weak. The men are all penned up together in one room, but without any fetters or chains. These must earn their bread by carding or combing wool or by other trade with which they are familiar. The women, too, are in a separate compartment, but not alone; and by reason thereof not confined as strictly as the men. They must in conjunction with other women who are imprisoned for other causes, pass their time by spinning wool. As much as I could observe, they are permitted to read the Bible and some other books, and, as I am informed, there is no lack of food and drink, though of course, everything, as well as the sleeping places, are very poor.

Among all these prisoners, there are very few who have any means, and even if they once had anything, it is to be feared that the costs of the prison and other things connected therewith, have already consumed that. Those who associate with these poor people declare, too, that there are (generally speaking) not as many wealthy among them as among those sent away a year ago. I spent more than three hours with them, and conversed with them. I heard from them that they are willing to leave their fatherland and go away, but that they are not able to forget it at once, and to take leave forever. Besides it is very much to be feared that they will raise difficulties when they learn that His Royal Majesty of Prussia wants to settle them in a county bereft of its inhabitans, caused by a terrible pestilence. When I hinted this, they protested most energetically against such a proposition, and earnestly requested to be spared from it. They would rather be sent to some other place, which scruples, I and the above-named affectionate God-fearing citizens endeavored to remove to the best of our ability; and will use every endeavor in the future to remove. A list of the prisoners incarcerated on September 29, 1710, contains the following names:

In the upper hospital, men: Peter Hertig, Hans Gasser, Peter Lüthei, Ulrich Trüssel. Daniel Rothenbühler, Peter Gerber, Hans Zahn, Hans Schönauer, Hans Frutiger, Heinrich Schilt, Uli Brechbühl, Daniel Neukomet, Hans Wissler, Michael Rüsser, Hans Kreybühl, Bauman the Younger. (Do. 294.)

The women are: Gertrud Rügsegger, Barbara Rüugsegger. Margrit Gerber, Elsi Brast? (Graf?), Barbara Steiner, Luzia Wymann, Barbara Rohrer, Margret Schürch, Elisabeth Aebersold, Gertrud Pärli, Vreni Aeschlimann, Stini Trüssel, Anna Salzmann. Anna Moser.

On the "Island," men: Hans Schenider, Uli Bear, Joseph Brobst, Claus Baumgatrner, Christian Gaümann, Christian Gaümann the Younger, Martin Strahm, Peter Blaser, Benedict Lehmann, Ulrich Schürch, and Hans Flückiger.

Women: Anna Brenzikoffer. Anna Habegger, Vreni Rubin, E. Heimann, Anna Bear, and Margret Oberli. (AA)

1711 — Joyous Swiss Mennonite Exodus into Holland—Continued.

Runckel took upon himself the further task of ascertaining the number of Mennonites set at liberty out of the jails, and their residences, in order to induce them to emigrate. Of course, this was no easy undertaking, since they all kept themselves in hiding as much as possible. The only sources from which anything could be learned, were the prisoners at Berne. But these, too, showed themselves distrustful. He (Runckel) secured the services of Messrs. Kuoll (or Kuoff) and Wagner to mediate; but they, too, failed to induce the prisoners to make any disclosures. So Mr. Runckel had to try the thing personally, being accompanied by the aforesaid two men. He convinced them of his intentions, and upon his promise to observe their urgent request for secrecy, he received on November 17, 1710, the desired information that there were at present in the Bernese lands about 295 men and women, not including the husbands and wives and children who must still be counted with the Reformed. This is reported under date of November 19, to the Committee at Amsterdam. By the aid of confidential messengers he procured, as nearly as possible, the lists of all participants.

Runckel learned and communicated to the Committee, under date of December 3, 1711 (A. A. No. 1290) that the Burgess Willading of Berne, formerly a bitter enemy of the Mennonites, was now engaged in an effort to effect their speedy departure. He directed (December 10th) a memorial to the Bernese authorities. Based on the proposal of the King of Prussia and the Netherland Mennonites, he now submitted, in the name of the latter the following request: (1) The Swiss are to have the privilege of making a choice between the two offers. (2) A general amnesty is to be published so that all Mennonites, who have heretofore secreted themselves, may without danger to themselves, appear openly and sell their possessions. (3) That they be permitted to name some one who shall have the right to dispose of their possessions for their benefit, even after their departure. (4) That those who are still imprisoned be liberated at once. (5) That the Reformed who are wedded to Mennonites, be permitted to emigrate with their spouses and also to take their children with them, and (6) That they may be exempt from the fee exacted until now, as a tax on emigration, when they leave the country.

Of this proposition, Mr. Runckel informed the Chancellor of the States General, Mr. Fogel, whereupon the States General by resolution of December 30, 1710, empowered Mr. Runckel to urge also in their name, the granting of the demands of the Mennonites.

The matter was considered. But Runckel writes on December 17th, with indignation, the exhortations were met with many fines and penalties, so that the Bernese government seems to act as if they wanted to retard the departure of the Mennonites, because of these requests. In the meantime, the desire to emigrate grew stronger. To Prussia, they did not want to go, as they feared the pestilence and had an aversion against the system of serfdom still in vogue there.

On January 7, 1711, the delegates met at Amsterdam. They deliberated about the places where the Swiss might be taken; passed resolutions to the effect to bring further pressure upon the Bernese government in favor of the wishes already submitted to it; and remitted to Mr. Runckel, in addition to the 300 Reichstdalern, which he had at his disposal for the brethren, 1000 florins more. At last, information was given out that the amount of the collection now had reached a total of 50,000 florins, as per detailed statement (in Huizinga, page 99).

What transpired in the meantime in Switzerland on the subject, Mr. W. J. Willink in Amsterdam, wrote on March 6, 1711, to Mr. H. Toren in Rotterdam, as follows:

"After much vexation, at last thirty-six of our brethren in the faith in Berne have already been set free from the prison under bail, and we hope to hear before long that the fifteen still in prison will be liberated too. Further, that the proclamation of amnesty will soon be promulgated, in such manner that all will receive permission to sell their estates by the end of June and to leave the country with the proceeds thereof, together with the concession that, whatever they, themselves cannot accomplish in that time, they can have attended to by their authorized agents, to which end, it is hoped, there will be granted them a term of one year. We now deem it necessary to consult with the committees outside of our city, and to find ways and means to transport and settle down these poor down-trodden people. For a place of settlement, the King of Prussia is making very generous proposals, such as we cannot offer. He places all his various provinces at the disposal of the oppressed, they to choose whichever they want. He agrees to furnish them there at once with comfortable houses, cattle and supplies, hired help, utensils and implements, and whatever else may be necessary for their calling, without great expense, so that they may be installed in their new places without delay. He even agrees to grant them great privileges in preference to the natives. But he wants also the rich as well as the poor." (Müller 296).

The King had a suspicion that the Hollanders wanted to keep the rich with them and to saddle the poor upon Prussia. Mr. Runckel endeavored to set the King's too great expectations about the wealth of the Swiss Mennonites aright, by mentioning the fact that according to his investigation they mostly belonged to the lower order.

1711—Holland Doing Everything Possible for the Mennonites.

There is a long list of documents in the Archives of Amsterdam showing what trouble and expense Holland expended to help our ancestors to flee from the wrath of Berne. Ambassador Runckel led off in the task.

In Runckel's letter of Jan. 3, 1711, he speaks of the repeated return of the Baptists or Mennonites who had been deported the previous year. This made their condition worse. Among those returning was Samuel Rebar, 75 years old. He was imprisoned for life, or so condemned. Also Hans Burki.

Through Holland's continued intercession however an amnesty proclamation was made Feb. 11, 1711, by Berne.

It set forth that, as all past efforts to rid the land of the Baptists had failed, and the sect increased—and as they will not take the oath of allegiance — nor bear arms — and as they did not take advantage of the right to depart because as they say no fixed place has been provided for them to go to, where they could enjoy what they call "liberty of conscience," that, the government of Berne has finally made arrangements with the government of Prussia by its consul Bundeli, and with the Government of Holland, by their Secretary, M. Runckel, to take over these persons. They are therefore allowed now to go to Holland or Prussia if they do not return; except they must not go into Neuenburg or Valendis. But those already condemned are not at liberty to thus depart. Those in prison will be at liberty to go too if they furnish bail. They are allowed to the end of June, 1711, to go, but not after—and no fee for departure will be exacted. The journey is to be at their own expense. Wives, children and husbands of these Mennonites or Baptists, who belong to the Reformed Church may go too if they desire. But all will lose their citizenship. Whatever is not reported to the Baptist or Mennonite Chamber in time will be confiscated. In the meantime all Mennonite meetings are prohibited under penalty. All who leave will be severely punished if they return. Runckel reported that by Feb.

14th at least 18 Mennonites secured release from prison by giving bail, and departed out of the Canton Berne under this amnesty. They went to Holland. Thirty others were promised freedom.

March 18, at Amsterdam, the conditions of this amnesty were discussed in a meeting held under government authority. Runckel was given a vote of thanks for his good work; and he was given general charge by Holland of the departure, etc.

At the meeting Dr. Herman Schijn read the draft of a letter, he favored sending out. It was approved and ordered translated into German, and to be sent to Runckel to be distributed throughout Switzerland. This letter urged Mennonites everywhere to take advantage of the permission to depart, and end their misery. They were to come to Holland.

The King of Prussia, too, soon after, Feb. 1711, granted special privileges to these people and welcomed them. Agents of the King, Steven Creamer and Alla Dirks, invited them to come; but the meeting decided it best to wait until the Swiss arrived— and then let them select whether they would take Holland or Germany to live in.

Runckel complains in his letters that it is very hard to find among these Swiss men who can be of much help to him in arranging for their advantage, and their departure. Dan. Reichen he says seems to be the only man who can help much. He complains that there is a good deal of distrust among the Mennonites. He says arrangements are made that lists of those who will take advantage and depart, and the names shall be sent in at once or by Feb. 20, 1711. Announcement is to be made in all pulpits. Berne promulgated a mandate April 17, 1711, that everything is to be done to assist these people to depart. There was a mandate of April 29, 1711, that all people of Berne in whom the Mennonites have confidence, whether Reformed or otherwise, who will assist the departure shall receive instructions and the thanks of the government. (Müller 296-7.)

1711—Exodus Into Holland (Continued).

Now that the movement into Holland was to become a fact, a list was to be made of the property and possessions of these Mennonites. But toward the beginning of Summer in 1711, these people had not yet made a statement to the authorities; and the Berne government now began to feel that they would be accused of embezzling the estates of the oppressed.

The authorities, therefore, decided that heavy penalties must be inflicted, and did so, by mandate of the 11th of May. requiring the statements. On the second of June the mandate was repeated.

June 22, 1711, there was a mandate issued by Berne that the wives, husbands and children of Mennonites or Baptists, who belonged to the Reformed Church and who are going to Holland with the Mennonites, should lose their Swiss citizenship. And those who are not members of the Baptist or Mennonite families, should pay, in addition, ten per cent. of the "departure money." Mandate of June 24.

Ten thousand florins of the moneys collected by the Dutch for the Swiss were now put at the disposal of their needs.

July 15, a meeting was held by the government at Amsterdam and the Dutch Mennonites, as the Swiss were soon expected to arrive there, at which meeting full report was made of everything that had transpired during the last few weeks. Mr. Runckel reported that with the consent of the committee he had persuaded Mr. G. Ritter from Berne, who managed the expedition of 1710, to take charge of the transportation of this expedition of 1711 that his first duty as arranged, was to provide five vessels for conveyance of about five hundred persons (the number estimated who would migrate) that the vessels were built in Berne—that the cost of them with all necessary furnishings amounted to one thousand six hundred and fifty-six reichsthalers (or dollars of the realm).

Upon the advice of Runckel, the committee secured the intercession of the States General—that is the governing officers of Holland — whereby the migrants are to be accorded at Vasal, Treves, Cologne, Hesse-Cassel and Prussia, unhindered passage on the Rhine and exemption from toll or duty. They also had instructions issued to Runckel to continue his stay at Berne. Runckel reported that the crews of the ships demanded higher wages than they did in 1710; and that the cost of the crews and the board and expenses would reach about three thousand two hundred and fifteen reichsthalers.

It was reported that there would be hardly five hundred members, because the faction of the Mennonites led by Hans Reist decided that they would not go, because Switzerland was their home and no one had a right to drive them out. But the faction led by Jacob Ammon (that is the Amish Mennonites) were likely all to go. Runckel reasoned with the Reist Mennonites a great deal but they had not yet made up their minds. (Müller 299). Runckel further reported that he felt quite indignant at this resolve, as he had done everything he could for these people. He was disgusted further because, he said old Hans Burki, disregarding all danger, had come back to the country, after having promised not to do so, and had brought a company of brethren back with him and they were all again thrown in jail and a dark future in sight for everybody.

The Mennonite committee in Holland extended their thanks to the Swiss Ambassador at the Hague (M. St. Saphorim) and also to the King of Prussia for the interest they took in these oppressed Swiss Brethren. The King was so interested that he visited the Holland authorities and leading Mennonites at Amsterdam on the 16th of June, 1711, to learn more fully what he could do for them.

1711—Mennonites Depart for Holland.

The departure of the emigrants was fixed to take place on the 13th of July. Runckel had given information that according to the latest estimates, the number who would go was 307, together with fifty-two, who had been imprisoned. But it was not known whether any members of their family would accompany them or not. It was recommended that, it be earnestly insisted on departing, that they must obligate themselves as the Berne government wishes, never again to return to their country. It was arranged that they should not disembark until they reached Amsterdam. The necessary instructions were to be handed by Abraham Fortgens, the pastor or teacher of the Mennonite congregation at Emmerich to Mr. Ritter, who had charge of these Christians. The place they were to settle when they landed was to be referred to a meeting to be held a few days prior to their expected arrival in Amsterdam. By that time minute information about colonizing in Prussia was expected to be available. The committee had sent, early in July, three Swiss Mennonite experts, Benedict Brackbühl, Hans Ramseier and Uly Bauer to the different places from which so many reports and good prospects had been held forth, to investigate and see the condition with their own eyes, and make report. It was also reported at the meeting by the delegate from Freisland, the northern province of Holland on the North Sea, that Mr. G. von Aylva, a notary or Court Officer at Bakkoveen (a town in Holland twenty miles southwest of the town of Groningen in the swamp country, about fifteen miles from the north coast of Holland), was willing to place part of his lands, on which peat or soft coal could be dug for two hundred years, at the disposal of these Swiss Mennonite members and to all others of them who should come, for the sum of two thousand florins. Others reported in favor of colonizing in the Groningen country, the north eastern province of Holland, on the North Sea. The investigation of these proposed sites progressed some time but the final decision was not to be rendered until the Swiss did actually arrive. (Müller 299.)

1711 — Exodus Into Holland (Continued).

We now glance again at the events transpiring in Switzerland. Berne agreed, though unwillingly, upon pressure being brought against her by Prussia and Holland, to grant amnesty to the persecuted Anabaptists or Mennonites; but did so only upon payment of twenty-five reichsthalers, expense money for every one released from prison. Berne also insisted that these payments should not be taken out of the charity funds collected in Holland. (Müller 300.)

The ships of which we spoke before, were ready to sail, but now it appeared that the emigrants delayed making preparations for the journey, though they had given in their names and the names of their children and wives to be placed on the list that were being made out under Runckel's orders, after great difficulty. They had no confidence in the promise of the government; they felt suspicious about whether their teachers and leaders would be included in the amnesty — about whether their children could be taken along or whether the government would keep them back and train them up in the State religion. The Hans Reist people, since they split from the Amish people were quite stubborn about going. A great deal of trouble arose about separating the goods and property of families, between the members who would go and those who would stay. A great deal of time was necessary to make the sales and transfers of property. The notice was really too short. And the fact that such an emigration could be accomplished at all is evidence of the sacrifices that the people were ready to make for their religion and how hard the intolerance which they suffered, bore upon them. We may add that, without the great ingenuity and services of Runckel, the exodus to Holland in 1711 could not have been possible. Nor must we forget the great services which George Ritter and Daniel Richen rendered Runckel in this matter. Richen was in banishment in Neuenberg at the time, and only on the 23rd of May, 1711, by the earnest efforts of Runckel, was he given permission to return to Switzerland, on the first of July.

Runckel received from the Anabaptist or Mennonite Chamber all the moneys of the emigrants who were to go to Holland and transmitted the same by a draft to the Mennonite Committee in Holland. The sum he remitted was twenty-eight thousand five hundred florins, which on the 17th of August was receipted for by Jacob Vorsterman and John Honnore at Amsterdam, to be repaid by them later to the proper owners on presentation of obligation which these owners held and which had been issued to them as an evidence of what sums they were entitled to. The sum paid to each owner was the same that he had been required to pay in, upon entering the ship, so that it would be impossible for him to turn back with his money. These receipted obligations are still on file in their original completeness in the Archives of Amsterdam.

In addition to this, the sums of money which the Swiss themselves carried with them in drafts and in cash, according to Runckel, amounted to six or seven thousand reichthalers.

Zehnder estimates the amount of capital taken out of Switzerland up to this time by departing Mennonites was about six hundred thousand pounds. The whole sum which Runckel received for the aid of the Swiss and for which he rendered an account on March 29, 1713, in Amsterdam amounted to thirty-eight thousand one hundred and thirty-three (38,133) florins or fifteen thousand two hundred and thirty-three (15,233) reichthalers.

By the beginning of June, the difficulties and hindrances had become so great that it seemed to Runckel, as well as to the Committee, that the enterprise would be impossible. In the second week of July, the five ships (four of which had been constructed at Berne) were all ready. As the five hundred emigrants could not be gathered together, other passengers were accepted (Do. 301).

Finally embarkation took place July 13th in Neunberg, as well as in Berne.

The ships joined one another at Wangen. Here one of the former prisoners, Henrich Schilt, of Schangnau, absented himself, contrary to his vow. On the 14th the journey was continued to Lafenburg; and on the 16th, all arrived safely at Basel. Runckel had reached this place a day before by a land route. The open vessels were here furnished with awnings and the necessary supplies were put on board — additional passengers were taken on board here. Shortly before the departure from Basel, on the 17th of July, two Mennonites, Hans Burki (or Burkholder) and Samuel Reber, were released from imprisonment and brought by the government of Berne to Basel and put upon the ships. These men had been condemned to severe punishment because they sneaked or stole back into Switzerland. Through the efforts of Runckel they were allowed to board the ships at the last moment.

1711—Exodus Into Holland (Continued).

The Baptist or Mennonite teacher, Daniel Grimm, had been arrested at Langnau with Hans Burki (or Burkholder), and was to have been transported to America the previous year. But, upon his liberation in Holland, he became one of the three trustees or men of confidence of the Mennonites in the Netherlands, though he had, as we have just stated, violated his pledge and returned to Switzerland. Burkholder's action caused great difficulties; and the more so because all of his children, in company with Uli Gerber, his hired man, as well as the ten sons of three other Mennonites, Peter and Daniel Grimm and Christian Neuenschwender, armed themselves with pitch forks, sticks and clubs and made a stubborn resistance to either being thrown out of Switzerland or being arrested. (R. M. July 9, 1711.) Upon this opposition to the authorities, proceedings to punish them were instituted. Burki and Grimm particularly angered the government of Switzerland because they endeavored to dissuade the

Mennonites in the mother country from going to Holland. (R. M. June 10, 1711.)

At Basel it was plain that the travelers could be transported in four ships. Therefore, the fifth vessel was left behind here to be used, perhaps, later for similar purposes. After it had lain there for a year, the people of Basel had it dismembered and removed, though it was the property of the friends of the Mennonites and was worth at least one hundred florins.

The command over the flotilla was confided to George Ritter and his two superintendents, Gruner and Haller. He was also to be advised in important matters by two prominent Mennonite Brethren, Daniel Richen and Christian Gauman, the elder, who had been appointed for this purpose. Besides this there were on the ships a few brethren entrusted with the supervision and care of the emigrants— Hans Burki, Jacob Richen, Emanuel Lartscher, Michael Lusser, Hans Meier and Peter Zehnder. (Müller 302.) Each vessel had its experienced helmsman or pilot, and the necessary crew from the brethren, of whom twenty reported as experienced oarsmen. Experienced pilots were taken along from one place to another according as they were familiar with the river at different points.

The embarkation took place in good order. Runckel tells us in a letter, however, of July 18, 1711, which he wrote from Basel to the Committee, of the trouble he had with Hans Burki and Samuel Reber, who said they positively would not go along to Holland. He said they had the rudeness, in company with a number of others whom he names, all of whom had been imprisoned and whom he had gotten out of prison with great difficulty—that they had the rudeness to inquire of him in a public place in the presence of Mr. Ritter and other prominent men, whether he (Runckel) intended to take them away as prisoners or free men. He answered them that they were certainly to go as free men but the order was, they must go on to Holland, where full liberty would be granted them. Burkholder reported that the Burgess of Berne, when he delivered him up to the ship merely told him that he must keep away from the Berne territory in the future and did not say that he must go to Holland. He now insisted that here at Basel, he was outside of Berne territory and was at liberty to go wherever he pleased; and further that he did not intend to go into the ship again; but says Runckel, Burkholder finally submitted, after being informed that he (Runckel) would get the aid of the Basel government to order him locked in irons and to be taken to Holland in that manner, if he would not go willingly, according to his vow and pledge. Runckel says further, that he lectured Burkholder very severely for his opposition to all that was being done for his and others' best interest. By energetic action, Runckel says he nipped great difficulties in the bud which later could not have been prevented or overcome. Some of the emigrants subsequently made their escape from the ships in order to go back to Switzerland and were again arrested and locked up. And after having now broken their promise several times nothing could liberate them.

Runckel inspected every ship and made a careful and correct list of those who undertook the journey; issued the necessary orders; entrusted the care of the whole expedition to Mr. Ritter; and after the departure of the ships, returned to Schaffhausen. (Müller 303.)

EXPENSES OF DEPORTATION OF 1711.

1711—Exodus Into Holland (Continued).

The following items of expense, taken from Runckel's account which he rendered on November 30, 1711, from Schaffhausen to the Committee at Amsterdam, throws considerable light on the expedition:

1710

Oct. 6—To Maid Jenner, prison-keeper at Berne, for necessaries and habiliments for the Baptists who had been imprisoned on the Island, on account; twenty ducats or 25 Reichsthaler. Oct. 6—To Mister Bembard Wagner for the same purpose for the prisoners contained in the upper hospital, thirty-five ducats or 26 Reichsthaler and 18 batzen or cents, of which he had used only twenty-six. Oct. 20—Journey to Amsoldingen to Mister Boduer, to consult with him in reference to placing the poor Baptists on the bogs of Aauburg, Yoerdon and Orbe, spent in three days with an hired man and two horses, 7 Reichsthaler and 25 batzen (cents). Feb. 4, 1711—To the poor Baptists on the Island for their necessities, 10 Reichsthaler. Do.—Gave separately to Samuel Reber who had recently been re-arrested 3 Reichsthaler.

Do.—To the so-called "Schneckemuttzer" (snail mother) who had attended to the wants of these Baptists, and who had usually opened the prison doors to us, as a tip, two dollars. Do.—To the poor Baptists in the upper hospital for their necessities, 62 dollars. Do.—To the so-called "Spinnmutter" (spinning mother) who had attended to the wants of these Baptists and who had usually opened the prison doors to us, as a tip, 2 dollars. Feb. 5—To the messenger of the Chancery who had delivered to me the decision for the liberation of the above mentioned Baptists, tip, 15 batzen or cents.

March 5—Paid to the Baptist Chamber at Berne for prison expenses one hundred Reichsthaler. Of these were refunded by:

Niklaus Haberli	16 Reichsthaler
Elsbeth Aebersold	15 "
Barbara Rohrer	15 "
Katharine Balli	15 "
	61 "

Leaving a balance on account of thirty-nine Reichdollars.

March 11th, paid further to the Baptist Chamber for prison expenses for Heinrich Schilt of Schangnau, 25 dollars; Hans Kuenbuhler of Diessbach, 25 dollars. March 12—To Mrs. Langhaus, attendant at the Baptist Chamber, for various services on account of the imprisoned Baptists; particularly at the time of their release, by request of the Baptists, 1 Louisdor, 3 dollars and 24 cents. (Müller 304)—March 30. To Peter Blaser of Lauperswyl, who was sent into the judicial districts of Trachselwald and Sumiswald, in order to induce the Baptists residing there to emigrate, as travelling expenses, 1 dollar and 15 cents.—May 13, To Peter Shenk of Trub, a member of the Reformed Church but who was kindly disposed towards the Baptists, and who distributed the printed circulars in the Emmenthal, a gratuity for his trouble, 1 dollar.—May 18, Mr. Bernhard Wagner, who was sent into the Emmenthal to persuade the Baptists residing there for Heaven's sake to get themselves in readiness for departure and for this purpose to have their names written down, since he refused absolutely to charge anything for his trouble and expense, a gratuity of four Louisdor paid him, 15 dollars and 6 cents.—June 15, To Samuel Reber, preparation for the Journey, 25 dollars.—June 13, To the four provosts, who had brought Samuel Reber and Hans Burki from the jail to the ship, 2 Reichdollars—July 14, On the journey to Basel, nights lodging in Wangen for Mr. Bernhard Wagner's postillion and horse, 1 dollar and 16 cents.—July 16, To printer Thurneisen in Basel, for the printing of seven hundred copies of that circular, 9 good florins, 4 dollars and 12 cents.—July 19, Paid in Basel for board and lodging for Mr. Wagner's postillion and horse for 3 days, 8 dollars and 16 cents.—For his return home, 12 dollars and 15 ecnts.

1711—Exodus Into Holland (Continued).

Various writers have described how the exiled protestants of Salzburg, bearing their scant effects, journeyed over the mountains of their country, and with tearful eyes, cast a last glance upon the valleys of their native land. It has been related too, how the columns of French emigrants wandered toward the boundary line of their fatherland, singing psalms. Of our exiles from the Emmenthal and from the highlands of Switzerland, no countrymen of theirs has made mention in sympathy and sorrow, none have described the feelings of these pople when they set their eyes for the last time on the spires of the cathedral of Basel, and the wooded crests of the Jura and saw their native country recede from view. On the boxes and bundles piled up on the deck of the ship, old men, the weak and infirm are seated. In other parts of the ships, the young and strong are standing together and looking with wondrous eyes on the shores, as the ships glide along. Sometimes hopeful, sometimes full of anxiety, they glance to the North, and then again and again to the South to their home country, which they were compelled to give up, the country, which had driven them so cruelly into exile—but whose verdant hills and silver-crested mountains, they nevertheless could not forget. And (their hearts, heavy with sorrow) they intonated a hymn which gave them solace:

"O Lord, we Thee implore,
  Guide well our hearts and minds
According to Thy Holy Word,
  Through Thy great mercy kind."

Kindle in our hearts
  A fervent love to Thee.
Watch o'er us and defend us;
  Or sundered we shall be.

Who loves his life shall lose it;
  But who for Him leaves wife and child,
And home and friends and country.
  Gains Christ and Heaven mild!

The winds are blowing tempests;
  The flowing streams swell high,
Yet these we freely brave,
  And to God, our Savior cry.

Whoe'er avows the truth;
  And keeps his soul from sin;
Though haunted down and seized,
  Has joy and peace within.

The Lord two groups will form,
  On the stern judgment day,
Come blessed of my Father,
  To the righteous he will say.

Ye suffered taunts and outrage;
  Left home and Fatherland of old,
He gains who struggles wage,
  A hundred thousand fold.

No man can speak it out,
  No bond can it portray,
What God will give his own,
  On the great Judgment Day."

Hans Burki took the first opportunity to leave the ship at Breisach, taking with him twelve companions; and when Mennheim hove into view, the haven of refuge of so many friends and acquaintances, Samuel Reber, and thirty others too, decamped. Mayence, Coblenz, Cologne, Düsseldorf and Wessel were passed. At Emmerich, Abram Fortgens brought all greetings of welcome, and informed them on behalf of the Committee that, Amsterdam was to be the end of the journey. Now the boundary line of Holland had been reached. Utrecht was passed, and at Nüiden, the ships were docked. From Utrecht on, two envoys from Amsterdam accompanied the transports. In Amsterdam Jan Frederiksen on August 2nd, gave notice of the arrival at Utrecht. In Nuiden they were bid a cordial welcome by a number of gentlemen of Amsterdam.

On the same day, (the third of August, 1711) Mr. Honnore gave a glowing report of the arrival of the Swiss at Nuiden, to his friend Bennings at Rotterdam, saying they would be in Amsterdam by evening, and adding the information that, their number was three hundred and forty, among whom were one hundred and fifty children, eighty to ninety men and ninety to one hundred women.

1711—Exodus Into Holland (Continued).

The Swiss, who actually did arrive on the evening of the third of August at Amsterdam, were given quarters for the night in the large rooms of the warehouses on the "Zaudlock," which was part of the malting plant, and which had been placed at their disposal by one of the gentlemen. This building had been transformed within the last few days into huge barracks and had been supplied with the necessary bedding, blankets, utensils, victuals and beverages. Everything that was needed was brought in large quantities, and the sick and infirm received special attention. It was a hospitable reception in every sense. Great was the love and cordiality mutually exhibited. And the citizens of Amsterdam came in such great throngs that it became necessary to put the entrances to the quarters under police protection. The boxes placed at the doors contained charitable offerings to the amount of one thousand and forty-five florins. For two weeks, the Swiss were here the guests of their brethren in the faith. It was indeed an arduous time for the Committees at Amsterdam. The best we can do in the way of belated thanks, is to present the name of the Holland leaders for future perpetuation. The members of the relief committee were William van Maurik, Hermanus Schyn, Jan Willink, Abraham Jacob Fries, Job Sieuwerts, Jacob Vorsterman, Jan Honnore and Cornelis Beets.

The most accurate knowledge of the doings of the relief committee is obtained by examining the account of Messrs. Vorsterman and Honnore. We find therin the entire total daily consumption of the emigrants, the furnishing of the barracks, the service, the gifts and money. We learn, too, the names of all who furnished supplies. (Müller 307) The entire account is contained in Huizinga, pages 100 to 102. The orphans were placed in homes and their board paid. A young Christian was admitted into the Orphanage of the Baptist congregation for seventy-five florins annually.

The fugitives who had arrived at Amsterdam were most part members of the Amman faction, that is the Amish. The adherents of Reist had nearly all decamped en route.

In the "Emmenthaler" ship most of the prisoners had been placed. The Overseers were Hans Burki, Christen Gaumann the Elder and Jacob Richener.

Martin Strahm, of Hohsteten, left the ship at Breisach; so did Hans Burki of Langnau, Peter Hartig of Lauperswyl; Peter Gerber and wife and Verena Aeschlimann of Langnau; Joseph Propst of Lauperswyl; Daniel Rothenbubler of Lauperswyl escaped at Mannheim; so did Hans Schwarzentrub of Trub; Ulrich Beer of Trub escaped at Breisach; so did Hans Gasser, teacher and his wife, Katrina Stauffer, and a young son of Lauperswyl. Hans Zann escaped at Mannheim; so did Hans Flückinger of Lützelflüch and Niklaus Baumgartner of Trub, and Niklaus Haberli of Lüchsee, and Ulrich Trüssel and his daughter Katherina of Sumiswald. Chr. Gaumann the elder and his wife, Anna Brenzikoffer of Hoctstetten. Chr. Gaumann the younger and his wife, Katharina Streit, with two sons, five and eleven years of age, respectively, and two daughters of six and three years of age respectively, of Hochstetten, arrived at Amsterdam. Daniel Neukomm, of Eggwyl, escaped at Mannheim. Hans Wisler of Langnau escaped at Breisach. Verena Kohler and daughter of Rothenbach, escaped at Mannheim, Hans Schönauer and his wife Elsbeth Aebersold of Hochstetten, Hans Snyder of Trub, and Samuel Reber of Trub, escaped at Mannheim. Ulrich Schurch and his wife, Barbara Grunbacher, with three sons and one daughter, of Sumiswald, Katharina Haldimann, of Hochstetten and Katrina Galbi of Hochstetten, and Lucia Weinmann, forty years old, weaver of Hochstetten, arrived. (Müller 308.) Barbara Rohrer, forty years of age, her husband, and Veit Sagimann, of the Reformed Church, and a son twenty years of age, not a member of the congregation of Bolligon, arrived. She died shortly after the arrival at Amsterdam. Marg. Schurch, widow, and a daughter twenty years of age (not a member) of Lutzelfluh, arrived.

1711 — Exodus Into Holland (Continued).

Marg. Oberli, of Ruderwyl, escaped; so did Kath Bieri of Trub; and Mary Kling of Trub; and Anna Habegger of Trub; and Hans Shellenberger and his wife, Elsbeth Neuenschwander of Trub. Among the expedition were Daniel Becker, Ulrich Hugo, student and Andreas Jeggli a tanner. Besides these the following voluntary travelers had been placed on the ship: Rudolf Stettler and his wife, Elsbeth Widmer, with two young sons, thirteen and fifteen years of age respectively, a weaver of Stettlen, who went through to Amsterdam. But Jacob Richeuer and his wife belonging to the Reformed Church, with five children eleven years down to five weeks old, respectively, of Ruppertswyl, escaped at Mannheim. Hans Kohler. thirty-nine years old, and his wife, a member of the Reformed Church, respectively, stonecutter of Wimmingen, arrived at Amsterdam. So did Madg. Gisler. widow, with two children, aged ten and six years respectively, seamstress forty-six years old of Sumiswald; and Ester Bohlen. single woman. weaver of Rueggisberg; and Barbara Shar. widow, with two children, eleven and eight years old respectively, of Sumiswald; and Barbara Joost, with a daughter, of the Reformed faith. twenty years of age. of Sumiswald; and Katharine Müller, single woman. forty-four years of age, of Melchuan; and Anna Heiniger. single woman. thirty-five years old, of Duenroth; and Kathrine Heiniger. thirty-two years of age; Magd. Heiniger, twenty-eight years of age; and Elsbeth Heiniger, thirty-four years of age, of Dunenroth; and Elsbeth Somner, single woman, thirty years of age, of Sumiswald; and Elsbeth Kaner, single woman. twenty-two years of age, straw hat maker of Dunenroth; and Elsbeth Althouse,

DEPORTATION OF SWISS IN 1711.

widow, fifty-six years of age. and daughter. twenty-three years old, not a member of Sumiswald; and Christ Brand, an orphan. eleven years old. of Sumiswald; and Elsbeth Kupferschusied, of Sumiswald. In the "Ementhaler" ship, there were altogether about eighty-nine persons. (Müller 309.)

On another list there are the following names and facts: Hans Ogi and wife, thirty-four years old and daughter five years old farmer, arrived at Amsterdam; so did Hans Schallenberg, of Neunberg, and his wife, Marg. Richen, and four daughters. Christian Kroff, his wife and three sons, aged ten, two and one years respectively, shoemaker, arrived; and Hans Hauri, weaver, wife and two sons, from the judicial distrist of Leuzburg; arrived. Hans Lang, weaver, thirty-five years old, his wife, Barb Gerber, twenty-seven years old and one child, arrived. Hans German, farmer, his wife, Magd. Schallenberger, and two children died. Ulrich Roth, miller, fifty-five years of age, his wife Elsbeth Steiner, a son of fifteen years, and three daughters and Anna Müller (or Moser) widow, sixty-six years of age, lame, arrived, and so did Daniel Gerber, husbandman, and wife, Magd. Richen, forty-six years old. In the ship, "Oberlander" (people from up the country), there were: Overseers—Daniel Richen. inspector general, and Emanuel Lortscher; and Emanuel Lortscher, husbandman, of Erlenbach, his wife, Anna Andres, and four children, from six years to six months of age, respectively, who reached Amsterdam; and Anna and Duchtly Teuscher, forty years old, single women, weavers; and Marg. Kallen, of Frutigen, seventy years of age, lame, and daughter, twenty years old, Reformed (her husband stayed behind); and Magd. Schmied, fifty-four years old, Baptist, of Latterbach, and eight children, Jobam, Abraham, Jakob, Isaac, David, Hans Rudolf, Susanna, Salome, all by the name of Lortscher, and all children of the Reformed faith; and Hans Thonen, fifty years of age, husbandman, of Frutigen, Reformed, and wife, Kath. Reichen, with three sons and six daughters, from twenty to three years of age, respectively, and Hans Schmied, Reformed, and wife, Baptist, with one son and one daughter, nine and seven years of age respectively, of Frutigen; and Chr. Schlapbach, Reformed, of Frutigen, his wife, Kath. Bohner, and four children, eight and two years of age, respectively; and Anna Schmied, single woman, thirty years old, of Frutigen. They all arrived at Amsterdam. Magd. Schmeid, single woman of Frutigen, was the only one to join the party en route. Melchoir Kratzen, husbandman, of Aeschi, forty years of age, Reformed, (his wife) Elsb. Graf. (Baptist) who had been imprisoned with four sons and three daughters, fourteen years to six months of age, arrived at Amsterdam. So did Verena Barben, single woman, thirty years of age, of Spiez, seamstress; and Kunggold Kropfli, of Spiez, with one son and one daughter, 12 and 10 years of age, respectively. (Müller 310.)

1711—Exodus Into Holland (Continued)

Christ Stutzwann, farmer, of Spiez, thirty-four years of age, and wife, Magd. Stuck, thirty-seven years of age(he a member of the Reformed faith, and she a Baptist); and Barb Gerber of Thun, escaped at Manheim, but Elsbeth Wenger, of Fhierachem, single woman, thirty-eight years old, arrived at Amsterdam. So did Maria Bogli, of Herzogenbuchsee, single woman, twenty-five years old; and Dan Richen, teacher and husbandman, of Frutigen, thirty years old, and his wife, Anna Blank, three sons and one daughter, aged from six to one year, respectively. According to this list, there were in the ship "Oberlander" sixty-eight persons.

The following names appear in another list: Christ Neuhauser, husbandman, thirty years of age, and his wife, Marg. Plank, with one child, who arrived at Amsterdam.

In the Thün ship were overseers—Michael Reusser, Hans Meier;—also passengers—Hans Meier, tailor, of Sigriswyl, forty-one years old, his wife, Dorothy Frutiger, thirty-four years of age, two sons and two daughters, from seven to six years of age respectively; also Ulrich Frutiger, husbandman, sixty-eight years old, Deformed, his wife, and one daughter of thirty-six years, who are Baptists; also Hans Frutiger, farmer, of Sigriswyl, forty-four years of age, his wife, Maria Konig, forty-seven years of age, three sons and one daughter of thirteen years to six years respectively; also Hans Ruff (Ruff or Rufener) vinegrower of Sigriswyl, forty-five years of age, Baptist, his wife, Elsb. Thommen, thirty-nine years old (Reformed), three sons and four daughters, sixteen to three years respectively; a'so Christen Ruff, farmer, of Sigriswyl, thirty-nine years of age, his wife, Magd. Konig, thirty-nine years of age, and one child of four years; also Stephen Reusser, of Hilterfingen, seventy-six years of age, his wife, Anna Buhler, thirty-eight years old, and one son of twelve years, still Reformed; also Michael Russer, twenty-seven years old, teacher, son of Stephen Reusser (who had ben a prisoner), these all arrived at Amsterdam; also Vereva Ritschard, single woman, thirty years of age, of Hilterfingen; also Ulrich Bryner, forty-two years of age, his wife, Maria Ruff, one son and one daughter, four and two years of age respectively; also Blasius Sorg, of Schaffhausen, his wife Magd. Meier of Hilterfingen, a son and a daughter, of three years and six months of age respectively; also Anna Jenni, of Hilterfingen, thirty years of age, widow, with one daughter, one year old; also Hans Schlappach, farmer, of Eriz in the judicial district of Thun, fifty years of age, Reformed, his wife, Verena Duchti, forty-two years old, four sons and four daughters, from two to eighteen years of age respectively; also Elsb. Eicher, of Schwarzenburg, country servant, twenty-six years of age; also Christ Steiner, farmer, of Diesbach, deacon, sixty years of age, and his wife, fifty years of age; also Hans Krenbuhl, hired man, of Diesbach, who had been imprisoned; also Anna Kuenzi, called Seiler, of Diesbach, single woman, twenty two years old; also Peter Krahenbuhl, of Diesbach, thirty seven years of age, Reformed, his wife, Anna Wenger, thirty-eight years old, Baptist, and three sons from six to three years of age respectively. All these arrived at Amsterdam.

Anna Rubeli, of Diesbach, escaped at Mannheim; Barbara Ruegsegger, of Diesbach, who had been imprisoned, escaped at Breisach; Kath, Ruersegger, of Diesbach, who had been imprisoned, escaped at Briesbach. Anna Aeschbacher, widow, thirty years of age, of Barbers, of the judicial district of Schwarzenburg, with two sons and two daughters, from fourteen to five years of age, arrived at Amsterdam; also Christ Stockli, husbandman, fifty years of age, unmarried; also Barb Gerber, twenty-five years of age, single woman, lame; also Elsb. Huber, forty years of age, of Frutigen, widow, with a son six years old; also Els'b Tsihbald, of Steffinburg, widow, fifty years of age, a son of sixteen years and a daughter of twenty years. These last reached Amsterdam.

DEPORTATION OF SWISS IN 1711.

Although in the ship "Thuner" there were seventy-one persons. On another list are the following names, etc:—Hans Buhler tailor, thirty-nine years of age, who arrived at Amsterdam; also Peter Streit, widower. rope maker, thirty-four years of age; also Adam Gautschi, shoemaker, seventy-two years of age. and his wife, sixty years old; also Hans Gautschi, thirty two years of age, his wife, Barbara Hafele. twenty-six years old, and two children; also Jakob Peter, carpenter, forty years old, Reformed, his wife. Maria Stadler, thirty-eight years old and three children. All reached Amsterdam.

In the ship "Neuenburger" were Hans Anken, husbandman, teacher and elder, of Spiez, thirty-seven years of age, his wife thirty years old, one son and two daughters, who arrived at Amsterdam; also Peter Lehner. husbandman, of Oberhofen, thirty-four years of age, and wife; and Ulrich Roth. his wife, two daughters and one son, of Diesbach; and Niklaus Gerber, husbandman, of Thun. thirty-four years of age, his wife, Magd. Yenger, twenty-four years old, and two sons; also (Müller 312) Peter Wenger, husbandman, of Blumenstein, seventy-nine years old, and his wife, Kath. Wyler, seventy years old; and Melch Zahler, deacon, husbandman, of Frutigen, forty-one years old, and his wife, Anna Richen, thirty years old; and Mathys Aeschbacher, husbandman, of Diessbach, seventy-five years of age, and his wife seventy years old; also Math. Aeschbacher. Jr., wine grower. twenty-six years of age, his wife. forty years old, and one daughter; also Peter Krebs, glazier, of Reutigen, thirty-two years old, his wife. twenty-four years old, and one daughter; also Martin Richer, husbandman, of Frutigen, thirty-four years of age, his wife, Barbara Turner, twenty-five years old, and one son; also Peter Thonen, shoemaker, of Reutigen, twenty-five years old; also Hans Krebs, husbandman, of Reutigen, thirty-two years old, and his wife twenty-two years old; Peter Krebs, Jr., husbandman, of Reutigen, twenty-four years old, and Barb. Rubi, eighteen years old; and Steffen Simon, husbandman, of Reutigen, thirty-nine years of age, his wife, Ursel Fahrni, and a daughter; and Peter Aeschbacher, farmer, of Lauperswyl, widower, thirty-nine years of age, and three children; also Abr. Lauffer, tailor, of Zofingen, twenty-four years of age, his wife, Kath. Richen, a son and two daughters; and Hans Schallenberg, of Erlenbach, and his wife and four daughters; and Hans Gasser, husbandman, of Schawrzenburg, seventy-five years of age, his wife, fifty years old and three children; also Jakob Stahli, husbandman, thirty-five years of age, of Hilterfingen, his wife, thirty-five years of age and one daughter; also Bevd. Stockli, forty-two years of age, of Schwarzenburg, his wife, Anna Glaus, forty-four years of age, a son and one daughter; also Hans Furer, forty-five years old of Oberhofen, his wife, Magd. Kampf, a son and four daughters; also Hans von Gunten, of Sigriswyl, fifty-five years of age, his wife, Kath. Isler, thirty years old, two sons and one daughter; also Hans Bauer, vine grower, of Oberhofen, forty-one years old, Reformed, his wife, Anna Willener, thirty-four years old, two sons and two daughters; and (Müller 313) Kath. Rubi, of Frutigen. sixty-seven years old, and a daughter. Magdalena. twenty-six years old; also David Lauffer, tailor, of Zofingen, seventeen years of age; also Peter Maier, shoemaker, of Siebenthal, thirty-eight years of age. Reformed; also Peter Tschageler, (?) husbandman, of Barometer (?) in the judicial district Thun, twenty-five years of age, Reformed; also Nikl. Hoffman, cooper, of Affoltern, thirty years of age, Reformed; als Hans Zurcher, forty years of age, cripple, of Frutigen, and his mother Barb. Germann, widow, seventy years old, knitter; also Anna Trachsel, of Frutigen, thirty-four years of age, forsaken; also Verena Kallen, country servant, of Frutigen, twenty-nine years of age, single woman; also Christina Kallen, country servant, of Frutigen, thirty-two years of age, single woman; also Anna Bucher, of Reichenbach, weaver, thirty years of age, single woman; Barb. Frei, of Hilterfingen, country servant, thirty-nine years of age; and Elsb. Binggeli, of Schwarzenburg, thirty-eight years of age, Reformed; Hans Lortscher, wine grower, of Hilterfingen, unmarr'ed, thirty years of age; and Hans Aeschbacher, husbandman, of Lauperswyl, twenty-three years of age. All these arrived at the end of the journey.

On another list is recorded Hans Schmied, Reformed, thirty years of age, Elsb. Schmied and two children, who arrived at Amsterdam. There had departed, therefore, altogether:

67 men	among them	14	Reformed
76 men	"	2	"
21 single men	"	2	"
35 single women	"	3	"
147 children	"		"
346 persons	"	21	"

Of these, who had been imprisoned, there escaped at Basel, Ulrich Brechbuhl and Peter Blaser, of Lauperswyl, Peter Luthi, Anna Einmann, the wife of Smaule Roth, from the parish of Diessbach, with her Reformed husband Heinrich Schilt had already decamped at Wengen, making a total of six.

Two women returned to Switzerland to their husbands — Katharine Moser and Barbara Steiner. With the permission of the authorities of Berne, two of the prisoners remained in the county on account of old age; Christen Dubach and Benedict Lehmann. There is a record of forty-nine names of persons who had reported themselves willing to emigrate, but who failed to appear. On the other hand, twenty-three went along who had not been advised, or reported, and who are enumerated in the foregoing register. At Breisach, thirty more persons embarked. These are in part the same who are mentioned as being recorded on one of the lists above mentioned.

The complete record is undersigned "Schaffhausen, the 23rd of July, 1711. Johann Ludwig Runckel."

(A. A. No. 1396, Huizinga page 113, etc.)

1711—Goal of the Emigrants to Holland.

The emigrants to Holland intended to push on to America. A large number of them never reached America, however. (Müller 319.)

We remember many of them were housed in the Daudhoek near Amsterdam. They, as well as others in Holland, were looking for a place in Prussia; but as we have seen before, the persons sent to view the land, reported against them going. Richen, Anken and Zahler were asked their opinion, as representatives of the Swiss, but they said the country would not suit. A landholder of Groningen offered to take twenty families of about one hundred persons and see that they got a suitable place. Abraham Cremer undertook to find a place for the rest at Kampen and Deventer, till the following May at least. How to maintain these Swiss Mennonites for the winter was a question. The deputies of Friesland (Holland) said they would take a number of them for the winter. Mr. Ritter was voted two hundred reichthalers for what he did.

DISTRIBUTION OF HOLLAND EXODUS.

On the 20th of August, the vessels left their mooring in the presence of a large crowd (who were deeply moved at their departure) and carried the Swiss out on the angry waves of the Zuider Zee, to distribute them. Twenty-one went to Harlingen —one hundred and twenty-six to Groningen—eighty-seven to Kampen and one hundred and sixteen to Deventer. total 356 persons. It is observed that this distribution was made by water—some of the Swiss being landed at the first coast point to these towns, and then escorted to the town.

The expense of those who went to Groningen was taken care of by the committee. largely of the elders of the old Flaninger congregation and of the Vaterlander congregation. They rendered a detailed account on the 30th of March 1712. In it they show that the board and lodging amounted for the first few days to five thousand seven hundred and eleven florins, in Groningen. (Müller 320.)

Authorities of the town had very little information when the Swiss arrived. and called upon Runckel to explain all about the causes of this emigration and the kind of people these were. Runckel praised them highly and succeeded in having conditions all favorable to them in the town. The price of land there was low, because the crops had failed in 1709. but there was demand for labor now.

Lists of names and accounts are still in existence, from which we get a good idea of the settlement. Names and numbers of families are given. and the expense of the trip. Also the points they touched on the road— the amount of money brought along by each—the allowance granted to each out of the general fund.

The full details would be too long but the names of the heads of families and some of the individual persons may be given with profit.

1711—Swiss Leave Holland's Shelter.

The names of the heads of families and individual persons referred to above are; the families of Peter Lehner, Ulrich Roth, Jacob Stahli, Christ Stutzman, Niklaus Teuscher, Hans Tschabold, Peter Krahenbuhl, Hans Bauer,—and the single, Elsbeth Tschabold, settled at Saperneer. In Hoogkerk, also near Groningen are the families of Emanuel Lortcher, Hans Furxer, Hans von Gunten. In Helpen, the widow Magdelena Schmidt, with her family, purchased an estate; in Vinklaus, Steffon Simon, with his family was located—the rest of the people were in and about Groningen, namely, the families of Hans Meier, of Ulrich Frutiger, who in December 1711, lost his wife in Groningen; Anna Eesclebacher; of Kringold Kroffli; Matheys Aeschebacher; Christ Stucki, Christ Schilling, Elsbeth Rubin, Peter Krebs, and Peter Thonin. The other unmarried persons are, Niklaus Hoffman, Vreni Barber, Hans Knenbuhl, Hans Aeschbacher, Peter Tschaggeler, Hans Lortscher, Anna and Tillie Tuscher, Anna Kunzi, Elsbeth Binggeli, Elsbeth Wenger, Barbara Frei, Katharina Schmied.

In the year 1721, the information was sent from Groningen to the committees at Amsterdam, that none of Swiss were in need of any further assistance. Some of these in later years emigrated to Pennsylvania.

To Kampen came thirty-five children, three widows and seven children, and eight single persons, with a total amount of ten thousand nine hundred and seventy-eight florins. These were domiciled in the same manner as those of Groningen by Steven Cremer of Deventer, who bought the rights of citizenship in Kampen for six families, for one hundred and forty florins each, which carried with it the privilege of pasture for six cows and two horses each. They are the families of teacher Michael Reusser, Stephen Reusser, Melchior Zahler, Hans Long, Hans Jacob Burki, Hans Gerwanni Hans Ogi, Hans Schmied, Hans Surer (?), Hans Buhler, Hans Gautschi, Peter Aeschbacher, Benedict Stockli, Hans Grasser, Blasins Sorg, Anna Muller, Marg. Galli, Chr. Schlappach, Daniel Gerwanni, Adam Gautschli, Jacob Petri, Chr. Stockli, Peter Meier, Peter Streit, Math. Aeschbacher.

The above named brought one hundred and six persons to Deventer, namely, the families of the teacher Daniel Richen, Martin Richen, Peter Richen, Hans and Peter Krebs, Abraham Lauffer, Hans Schellenberger, Hans Thonen, Chr. Neuhauser, Ulrich Bryner, Elsbeth Althaus, Daniel Gerber, Peter Wenger, Chr. Krebs, Margret Giseler, Barbara Schar, Kath. Rubin, Elsbeth Kufferschmied, Anna, Elsbeth, and Margaret Heiniger, David Laufer, Anna Bruger, Verena and Christian Galli, Marie Bogli, Peter Thonen, Elsbeth Koner, Kath Muller, Esther Benli, Barbara Gerber, and student Daniel Becker.

The Swiss experts, who, headed by Benedict Brechbuhl, were to investigate and pass on the Prussian offers, wrote under date of August 12, 1711, from Danzig to Amsterdam. They gave a description of their experiences in Luthania, praised the remarkable fertility of the soil, the favorable inducements of the king, and the great love and affections which were shown them by their brethren in the faith, in Danzig and Elbing. The houses, very naturally, did not suit them, but they had the royal promise of the permission to fell the needed lumber from the forests of the domain free of cost. There were to be had 62 farms of 30 acres each. These journeys and a visit to Berlin, where they went upon invitation of the king, delayed their return to Amsterdam, until the 8th of September. By that time the Swiss had already gone to their new places of abode in Ireland, and there was a question whether, on the strength of the favorable reports of Brechbuhl, they could again be induced to wander to another place. For that reason three delegates to their brethren in Kampen; but neither there nor in Groningen and Deventer did they find a willingness again to emigrate, inasmuch as there was a prejudice against the plague, which had a short time before decimated those countries. Brechbuhl reported on September 20, 1711, from Deventer in like manner as two days later Russer, Anken, Richen. Steiner and Zahler, who gave the assurance that they would no longer be a burden to the commission, but would endeavor to earn their bread. Brechbuhl was quite enthusiastic over the colonization in Prussia, and no doubt, through his efforts, there were in later years, founded Swiss congregations there, which, howveer, in 1720, and particularly in 1730, became greatly distressed and later on, mostly emigrated to Germany, the Netherlands and North America.

1711—Wanderings of a Portion of the Exodus.

From the year 1711 on, more emigrants followed almost annually, since the persecutions did not cease, and which found renewed expression in the proclamation of March 24, 1714. In this year there emigrated from Goutenschwyl near Lenzberg to Holland—Hans Gautschi, his wife, Barbara Hafele and his daughter, Jacob Peters and his wife, Marie Stödler; Samuel Peter and Barbara Frei; Rudi Peter and Anna Erisman; Samuel Peter Stulzer and his wife; Samuel Leutswyler, single; Rudolph Peter and Verena Aeschbach and Rudolph Wurgler.

Samuel Peter and Barbara Frei were called Neuhauser from their estate Waihaus, near Goutenschwyl, and are the ancestors of the very large and flourishing Neuhuizen, whose family tree Huizinga has worked out in great detail. Very likely they were induced by relatives who were among those who settled in Groningen, to make this the destination of their journey, and they remained in Kalkivyk at Hoogezand, near Groningen. At Sappeneer and Groningen, small independent Swiss emigrations were formed. Prior to 1671, fugitives of Swiss orign (M. 323) had come from the Palatinate into the country about Groningen, and were called Pfalzer (inhabitants of the Palatinate). This was applied to the arrivals of 1671, as they amalgamated into a congregation which held their services in a house in the "Achterunner" in Groningen. As founder of this congregation, their first teacher, Hans Anken, may be regarded as principal; soon thereafter, assisted by Daniel Richen and Abraham Stauffer. It would have been considered too good a fortune if these Swiss could have been without dissensions in their new place of abode! Hans Anken had bought a house for himself, called the "great cloister." Abraham Lauffen deemed the style of architecture too vain, and insinuated to the owner to change the same. Anken did not take kindly to this suggestion, and this difference of opinion was sufficient cause for a split in the congregations into "Old" and "New" Swiss.

1711 — Mennonite Division Into Old and New Swiss Factions

The heads of one congregation of forty to fifty members were Hans and Peter Kreb, the heads of the other congregation of fifty to sixty members were Daniel Richen and Abraham Lauffer. This split lasted from the year 1720 to the last quarter of the century, and extended to the congregation at Sappeneer. The stylish house of Anken's led as supposed to this split. It is very likely that the showy or conspicious house which Anken had bought was only a pretended motive to bring to a focus a deeper rotted difference—a difference which ever and ever shows itself among the Baptists, between the strict and severe and the less strict.

1711 — Emigrants of 1711 Exodus Reach Lancaster County Eventually.

We have in a previous article given a description of the transportation of the Berne Mennonites down the Rhine in 1711. Kuhns in his work (page 46), calls attention to the fact that the names of many of those Swiss emigrants are identical with our Lancaster County names and those who went down the Rhine in 1710 are identical with our Lancaster County prominent names also. Among them he mentioned Gerber, Gaumann, Schurch, Galli, Haldiman, Burki, Rohrer, Schallenberger, Oberli, Jeggli, Wisler, Hauri, Graf, Wenger, Neukomm, Fluckinger, Rubeli, Ruegsegger, Krahenbuhl, Huber, Buhler, Kuenzi, Stahli, Rubi, Zurcher, Bucher, Strahm. Among those exiled in 1710 were the names of Brechbuhl, Baumgartner, Rupp, Fahrni, Aeschlimann, Maurer, Ebersold and others. All these names —which, more or less changed, are common throughout the State and country today—are of Bernese origin. The Landis, Brubacher, Meili, Egli, Ringer, Gut, Gochnauer and Frick families came from Zurich.

This would argue that (while Müller does not trace any of these emigrants of 1711 to Lancaster County) many of them eventually reached this county.

1711—Brethren Join the Pequea Colony of 1710.

According to Rupp, it would seem that as soon as the winter of 1710-11 was passed, the Pequea colonists sent one of their members back to the Old Country, to bring on members of their family, who were left behind.

Rupp described very vividly, pages 80 and 81, how this came about. Quoting from a source which he does not mention, he says, that before the ground brought forth its first crop, they made preparations to bring the balance of their families over — that after the lot fell to Hans Herr, it was decided that Mart Kendig should take his place and that he, accordingly, went abroad and brought a company of Swiss and Germans back with him. He tells us that the party consisted of the balance of families already here and of Peter Yordea, Jacob Müller, Hans Tchantz, Henry Funk, John Hauser, John Bachman, Jacob Weber and three others, whose Christian names are not given, Schlagel, Wenrich and Guildin. It would seem that Schlagel's name was Christopher, because in 1713, he had established himself on the Conestoga creek, and complained of the Cartledges interfering with his mill.

1712 — Large Palatine Possessions in Lancaster County.

This year a tract of 3330 acres in Strasburg Township was ordered to be surveyed to Amos Strettle, for the occupation of Swiss Mennonites. It adjoins the original Herr tract of 1710 on the east. The warrant is dated the 5th of July 1712, and the survey was made November 1st, the same year. This tract was divided during the next twenty years among the following holders, viz.: Henry Shank, Ulrich Brackbill, Augustine Widower, Alexander Fridley, Martin Miller, George Snavely, Christian Musser, Andrew Shultz, John Foutz, Jacob Stein, John Hickman, John Bowman, Valentine Miller,Jacob Hain, John Herr, Henry Carpenter, Daniel Ferree, Isaac Lefevre, Christian Stoner, John Beiers, Hans Lein, Abraham Smith, John Jacob Hoover, Septimus Robinson, Samuel Hess, Samuel Boyer, John Musgrove.

It is intended a little while later to make a map of the original tract and show the present sub-divisions thereupon, setting forth the name of the owners of the present farms carved out of the same. Mention of this tract is made in Rupp, page 77.

1712—Poor Ragged Palatines in England.

Ralph Thoresly in his diary under date of June 1712, published in 2 volumes in London in 1830 says that on his return to Hyde Park, he saw a number of Palatines in England and that they were the most poor and ragged creatures that he ever beheld. (Diffenderfer's Exodus 86.)

1712—Growth of German Skippack Colony.

We are told that by this year, on April 6th, the Mennonites of Skippack numbered 99. They had additions in 1708 and '09. (Pennypacker's Germantown 169.)

1712—Ferree and Lefevre,Mennonites, Take 2000 Acres of Land in Conestoga Valley.

In the minutes of the Pennsylvania Board of Property, under date of September 10, 1712, it is stated that "at a meeting of the commissioners that day held—the late commissioners having granted 10,000 acres of land to the Palatines, by their warrant, dated 6th of 8th month, 1710, in pursuance thereof there was laid out to Martin Kendig, besides the 2,000 acres already

ADDITIONS TO SWISS SETTLEMENT.

confirmed and paid for, the like quantity of 2,000 acres, towards Susquehanna, of which the General Surveyor has made a return. The said Martin Kendig now appearing desirous that the said land may be granted and confirmed to Maria Warenbuer, for whom the same was taken up. But upon further consideration of the matter, it is agreed among themselves that the said land shall be confirmed to Daniel Fierre and Isaac Lefevre, two of the said widow's sons, and the consideration money, viz £140 at £7 per 100 acres, by agreement having been for some time due, but is now to be paid down in one sum. 'Tis agreed they shall only pay £10 for interest, that is £150 for the whole. (2nd Series Pa. Arc., Vol 19, p. 259 and Rupp, page 90.)

This is the large section lying north of the Herr and Strettle tracts; partly in East Lampeter Township and partly in Strasburg Township. The Fierres are the ancestors of the present Ferry or Forry family. Neither the Lefevres nor Forrys were pure Swiss, as there was French extraction in their race. This tract was subsequently divided among the following persons — Henry A. Carpenter, Forre Brinton, John C. Lefevre, Joseph L. Lefevre, Jacob Hershey, Christian Leman, Henry and Jacob Brackbill, Theo. Shertz, John Shertz, F. S. Burrows, D. Lefevre. (Rupp 102.) I hope to have a map of the sub-divisions of this tract also.

That it lay partly in Strasburg Township is shown by the fact that Maria Warenburger, mother-in-law of Isaac Lefevre paid a quit rent on 2,000 acres in Strasburg Township, the same year. (Rupp 107.) Ferrees and Lefevres came from Steinmerster into the Palatinate. (Rupp 85.)

1712 — German-Swiss Reach the Conestoga Valley.

It appears that, this year, the German-Swiss immigrants in Lancaster County reached Conestoga in their settlement for under the name of the "Dutch" it is stated in First Pa. Arch., Vol. 1, p. 338, that they had been living at Conestoga during the past 20 years. The date of the letter is 1732. In some of the proceedings of the Conestoga Road, as it was laid out from time to time, there is a reference to "The road up to the Dutch settlement on the Susquehanna" in 1712. This makes it plain that there was a settlement that year, including road improvements up to the River. This refers to a road "that leads from Philadelphia to the Dutch settlements at Conestoga" found in Volume one of the original road papers in Chester County, p. 50. The public are indebted to the industry of Gilbert Cope in Chester County for the compilation of these road papers.

1712—Further Swiss Additions about This Year.

According to Rupp, in his "Thirty Thousand Names," about 1712, additional tracts of land were bought by Pequea settlers. The settlers living in the Pequea Valley at that time (1712) he gives as follows: Johan Rudolph Budeli, Martin Kendig, Jacob Müller, Hans Groff, Hans Herr, Martin Oberholz, Wendel Bauman, Martin Meylin, Samuel Gulden, John Rudolf, Daniel Herman, John George Trulberger, Hans Mayer, Hans Hagy, Christian Herchy, Hans Pupather, Heinrich Bar, Peter Lehman, Melcher Brennen, Heinrich Funck, Michael Schenck, Johannes Landis, Alrich Honench, Emanuel Herr, Abraham Herr, Melchoir Erisman, Michael Müller and Christopher Schleagel.

1713—Rapid Additions to the Mennonite Colony.

This year Isaac Lefever purchased 300 acres of land adjoining the other settlements made by his countrymen near Conestoga and received a warrant for it. And Samuel Guilden, who had lately come from Berne, in Switzerland as a minister to the Switzers, desired 800 acres in Strasburg with the rest of his countrymen and a warrant was signed to him for the price of ten pounds per 100 acres, Pennsylvania money, 80 pounds or 60 pounds of English money. (2d Ser. Pa. Arch., V. 19, p. 669.)

1713—The Mennonites Build Their First Grist Mill on the Conestoga.

This year we have an account of a remarkable German Mennonite on the Conestoga. In Vol. 19 of the Sec. Series of the Penna. Arch., p. 569, it was stated at a meeting of the Land Commissioners, held on the 8th of October that, Christopher Schleagel, late of Saxony, being desirous to settle near the Palatines about Conestoga and build a mill on a run, running into the Conestoga Creek, wishes to take up 1000 acres of land there and build such a mill for the accommodation of his neighboring inhabitants; and it was agreed that he could have the 1000 acres for 100 Pounds. And if he built the mill immediately 20 Pounds were to be thrown off. He did build the mill, because a year later I shall show he made complaint that people were interefering with his mill race.

Schleagel had some trouble about his land and at a meeting held on the 18th of March, 1718, Edmund Cartlidge claimed to own it by having purchased from Schleagel, the right to a tract of land and an ordinary grist mill on a branch of the Conestoga; and it is stated that Schleagel did not comply with the terms, when he first bought, he lost his right. It is, however, set forth that Cartlidge has since built a good mill on the same land and he desires 400 acres to be laid out to him, including his buildings and improvements. A warrant was accordingly given him, (Do. 644). Rupp also notices that Christopher Schleagel in 1712 took up this land to build a mill and he finds the place not far away from the land granted to the Palatines, (Rupp, 115).

113—The English are Moving in Among the German Mennonites

We have just noticed that Edmund Cartlidge, the Indian agent, seated himself on Christopher Schleagel's land and in addition to this, we have the account that a patent was given in 1713 to Thomas Story near a settlement of the Palatines at Conestoga, and that he had a right to it as early as 1711, (Vol. 19 of Sec. Series of Pa. Arch., p. 572). There are also signed the same year, a patent to John Marlow for 260 acres on Pequea in the rights of Gilbert Mace. These last are English names and show that the English were interested also in settlements in this section.

1714—Scheagel's Mill is Now Serving the Mennonites

The mill which Christopher Schleagel said he was about to build he evidently erected as may be seen in the Taylor papers, No. 2827. Schleagel went to Philadelphia, and made complaint about the English claiming his mill; and James Steele gave him a letter dated the 24th of September, 1714, which Schleagel carried to Isaac Taylor, surveyor for the Penns, who was surveying at Conestoga. In this letter, Steele states that Schleagel complains that a certain person has seated himself near the mill he hath lately built at Conestoga, by whose means the Indians that are thereabout are likely to be troublesome and dangerous to him. This letter then further states that Isaac Taylor shall order the people there interfering with Schleagel's mill to remove and that 300 acres belonging to the mill

FORCIBLE DEPORTATION OF SWISS TO PENNSYLVANIA.

should be in quiet possession of Schleagel.

1711—George Leonard Takes Land in Octorara.

A patent for 300 acres on the Octorara Creek, dated 15th of September, was also executed to George Leonard. (Do. 572.)

1714—Additional Settlers Come to Pequea Colony.

In Rupp's "Thirty Thousand Names," page 10. he sets forth a statement by Johnathon Dickinson, under date of 1719. in which Dickinson says: "We are daily expecting ships from London which will bring Palatines, in number, about six thousand to seven thousand. We had a parcel that came over five years ago, who purchased land about 60 miles west of Philadelphia, and proved quite industrious." Reference may also be found to this addition in Colonial Records, Vol. 3, p. 29 and 228.

1714 — More German-Swiss Locate in Our County.

This year the following order for passes to deport some of our ancestors was issued, "We, the Mayor and Council, of the City of Berne, herewith notify you that we, being the persons in authority and especially appointed for this purpose, having power and command to transport five stubborn Mennonites and one celebrated thief out of the country to Lausanne, under guard, with all necessary secrecy, on the 10th day of August, to be delivered to our Chief of Police, do command you and all people to allow them to pass safely through, and unhindered, and to give all aid to our State Officers conveying the said Mennonites. that lies within your power." (Müller 224.) These Mennonites (who were called stubborn) to be sent to Lausanne, according to Smith, were to be sent to the galleys.

1714 — Benedict Brackbill's Letter to Fries.

In Müller, p. 224, the following letter written by Benedict Brackbill in Manheim to Jacob Fries of Amsterdam appears:—

"Some time ago, a brother came from Switzerland and told me the present condition of the Swiss brethren. The government still keeps up its persecution against our people. They have given their police power anew to take our people to prison, and on one day about fourteen persons were taken and conveyed to prison, whose names, as well as I know, are Casper Ammann, of Reugan —Benedict Mowrer, who was previously a prisoner with me and who also was gotten free with me at Nimwegen, three years ago. At present he is in prison without his wife. Babbie Steiner. They have robbed him of everything that they were able to find. They also imprisoned a poor H———— R———— of Signau, and Oswald Otzerberger of Hochstetten—Christian Wagsel (Wochtel) from Eggwyl, also Has Luthi and his son-in-law — also Elizabeth Zeuricher from Lauperswyl—and Barbara Yost from Landau, and three of the Amish side or branch. They are in a city situated far from us, in Savoy, hired out as slaves. One of them died on the way, by the name of Niklaus Baumgartner. At the end of the year they are to be set free. Some say they are to be set free and to be given some money." Dated Nov. 14, 1714. (Müller 224.)

Müller goes on to say that Brackbill made a mistake here, because the fourteen prisoners were not taken away to Turin, which he called Savoy, as can be shown.

1714—Another Brackbill Letter.

The substance of another letter written by Brackbill, this year, is as follows:

"Under date of February 6. 1714. Brackbill reported to Holland that conditions in the Palatinate were most deplorable, owing to the war. The gift of 400 florins was received with pleasure. Many are fleeing back to Switzerland, and are there again taken into captivity; others have gone into Alsace and to Zweibrucken." (Müller 207.)

This shows again the interest that Brackbill displayed for his people. In the Historical Society at Philadelphia, among a lot of letters called "Dutch Copies" are several in German. written by Brackbill.

1714—Swiss Mandate against Mennonites.

The attitude of the Swiss government toward the Anabaptists found expression in the Great Mandate of May 24, 1714. It provided that those who were then in captivity, some of them teachers, and those who had been expelled under pain of punishment, corporal and capital, and who in spite of their oath, nevertheless came back, who were fit for work should all be sent to the galleys, for life, as they have well deserved it. Others were to be confined in Berne, in imprisonment forever. (Müller 221.)

1714—Christian Leiby or Liebeck Tortured.

Müller gives the following account: Christian Liebi (R. M. "Liebegg") who came from the Palatinate under the dominion of my liege lords, and admitted that he had intended to visit Mennonites in Berne here, to console and comfort teachers, and if chance presents itself, to baptize several of them; who declared that the inhibitions of the authorities were known to him, was condemned with no less punishment than the native teachers, and, therefore, he was sent to the galleys, in company with the teachers already sentenced and as a terror to other strange teachers. (R. M. June 6, 1714.) (Müller 228.)

Jacob Schnebeli's Testimony on Mennonite Torture.

Information was given by Hans Jacob Schnebeli in Mannheim to Abram Jacob Fries and Company in Amsterdam, he learned by the deported Mennonites at Turin that they must remain there during the winter. They were confined in a vault, in company with 90 miscreants and good-for-nothings, who were sold on account of their wickedness to a certain man named Hackbrett, of Turin. They were daily taken out to hard work. "I fear," writes Schnebeli, "that by springtime, they will be sent to the galleys on the high seas." A petition had been presented by certain persons to the Duke of Savoy, to which answer was given that the Duke would be willing to grant their release, but that this matter was wholly a concern of the gentlemen of Berne. (A. A. No. 1371. December 1, 1714.) (Müller 225.)

As we notice above, this letter is still preserved in the Amsterdam Archives, and is number 1371. It was written by Jacob Snavely.

1714—Further Light on Brackbill's Letter.

In a former item, Bennedict Brackbill's letter of Nov. 26, 1714, is set out. Müller states (p. 225) that Brackbill relates one of the brethren died on the way to a distant city in Savoy—Nicholas Baumgartner. This letter is preserved in Amsterdam and is No. 1371 of the Amsterdam Archives. It is stated that Brackbill got the prisoners and the deported confused, because these prisoners were never taken to Turin in Savoy.

1714—Reformed Clergy Sympathize with Mennonites.

Müller relates (p. 223) that under date of July 19, 1714, the clergy of the State Church, criticized the government for the cruel treatment of the Mennonites. They uttered very commendable and honorable sentiments. But the government severely reprimanded them. The government officials said that the sentences imposed are no concern of the Church, and that these Anabaptists are so stubborn, that sentences must be severe.

1714—Persecution On the Deported of 1710 and '11 who Returned.

We have noticed above that an edict was issued by Berne to send to the galleys, such of the Mennonites, who were deported in 1710 and '11, as returned to Switzerland. Some of these who were deported in 1710 and '11, reached Lancaster County. The edict, condemning to galley punishment, required that until they should be sent to the galleys, they should be put in the jail of Titligen. It seems that on account of their age and weakness, only four were found fit for galley service. They were Hans Luthi, the teacher of Schaufelbuhl, 54 years old—Nicholas Bumgartner of Trub, forty years old—Peter Wüthrich of Trub, fifty years old and Joseph Brobst of Trub, fifty years old. These were to be given over to Col. Hackbrett, who was to force them on to Silicia.

1714—A New Flood of Swiss Emigrants Moving Toward Pennsylvania.

Müller tells us (page 322) that, beginning in the year 1711, with the exodus of four shiploads of Mennonites down the Rhine, there followed emigrations every year, west into the Palatinate and into Holland, intending to reach America; but he says a new impulse was given by the mandate of 1714; and that the severity of that mandate sent an emigration that year from Goutnschwyl, near Lensburg, to Holland; among others, Hans Goutchi and wife, Barbara Hafeli, and daughter—Jacob Peters and wife, Maria Stattler — Samuel Peters and his wife, Barbara Fry— Rudy Peters and his wife, Anna Erisman—Samuel Peter Stultzen and his wife—Samuel Lentzwyler, single — Verena Aeschbach and Rudolph Würgler. It will be noticed that the maiden names of the wives are given here. That seems to have been the custom. We may notice also, that Samuel Peters and wife are ancestors of a very large family in Neihuizen, and also of Groningen.

1714—The Means of Baptist Persecution.

Müller inquires, (page 352) "With what means had the campaign against the Baptists to be carried out?" He then answers, before 1714, "the state church was blamed," that is, the Reformed Church. An effort was then made to inculcate the Orthodox doctrine into the minds of the young, through the land, so they would grow up in the State Church and not embrace the faith of their Mennonite ancestors, who were tortured and suffered all manner of penalty; and the government and the State Church tried to secure teachers throughout the land to do this.

1714 — Another View of the Edict of this Year.

The efforts to deport in 1710 and '11 and help to get these Mennonites out of Switzerland and to America, did not have the result Switzerland expected. They hoped that these Mennonites in America would draw all the others over to them, but there still remained many powerful members of that church in Switzerland, who refused to go. The amnesty offered by Switzerland in 1711, to all who would go, did not have the result intended. Therefore, this severe edict of 1714, imposing life imprisonment and galley service for life, was issued.

1714—A Battle Growing Out of the Edict of 1714.

Müller relates (page 344) how the officers trying to carry out the edict of 1714, were very roughly handled near Sumiswald, a town of now 6,000 people, about 15 miles northeast of Berne. He relates that several Baptists or Mennonites had been arrested there, but that a party of 60 or 70 neighbors rescued the prisoners from the officers. In this struggle, these Mennonite hunters were handled roughly and beaten in a bloody way. The government punished some of the perpetrators and a hunt was made for all the others who beat the constables. Several were arrested and they had to pay the expense of the officers sent to catch Mennonites, and fines to the extent of $100, for each one. Andreas Sommer in the Nüenwatte, was the chief leader of this rescue. He was ordered to pay $100 or be banished. This banishment was annuled in 1715, by him furnishing bail. There was another Peter Sommer, a horse doctor, that harbored Mennonites. He was sent, for a year, to one of the French provinces. Benedict Widmer (Witmer), the school master, who was in the fight, was sent for a year and a half to Brassu in Romainmaister—Benedict Risser in the Lengenwalt, who sent his two sons with bludgeons to this fight, was banished until the next November to St. Croix,

and the two sons were fined heavily. Peter Sommers, the son of the horse doctor, was banished a year to St. Cerge, and Jacob Christen, the hired man, who had a hand in this fight, was sentenced to eight days imprisonment. His term was made short because he had a large family. Some of those condemned had behaved themselves obstinately and were impudent before the Court and were to be kept under the eye of the Sheriff. Some were sent to the galleys. One of them, Christian Wachsel, was pardoned.

1715—A Few More Warrants Given to the Mennonites.

In Vol. 19 of the Sec. Series of the Pa. Arch., p. 597, under this date, it is set forth at a meeting of the Land Commissioners at the end of the year that several warrants were signed at sundry times at ten Pounds a 100 acres and One Shilling, sterling quit rent, all in Chester County. The whole is 2800 acres but the only Mennonites among the number were Hans Graeff, 200 acres—Benedictus Venerick, 200 acres — and Joseph Hains, 100 acres. At the same time there were 250 acres laid out to John Funk at Strasburg, (Do) and 1000 acres to Herman Richman in Strasburg.

1715—Ambassador Runckel's Letter.

Müller recites (p. 360) that under the date of March 7, 1715, Runckel wrote to Holland about the destitute condition of the prisoners and the rest of the Mennonites whose determination to stay in the country, brought upon them. They are losing friends by it. He says he does not feel satisfied that Holland owes them much more sympathy and assistance.

1715—Disposition of Fines on Mennonites.

Müller (p. 356) informs us that the fines collected from the Mennonites, and the moneys raised from their confiscated property, was divided up; and that one-third of it went to the Court or Mennonite Chamber, one-third to the Lords of the land and one-third to the Sheriff for his activity and vigilance in the matter.

1715—Efforts to Release Mennonites from the Galleys.

Müller (p. 288) recites the petition of the mother of Christian Liebe (or Liebeck) for the release of her son, who had been sentenced to the galleys. The petition was received by the authorities but nothing particularly was done on the subject. On the subject of galley torture, information was sent, 15th of October, 1715 (Müller 229) of the release of the Swiss Mennonites from the galleys, under a proviso that they would not go back to the Berne territory. At the same time, attempts were made to secure the release of 40 prisoners, who were being prepared to send on to Venetian galleys, provided they would promise to leave the country and never come back. It was further reported that if money was needed, there was an English Arch-Bishop, ready to place a large sum at their disposal.

1715—More Condemnations to the Galleys.

About the same time, Daniel Knopf, in Berne, sent word to Mennonite friends at Amsterdam, that a friend of the Mennonites named Freytorrens, at Berne, offered his services and had a plan to raise moneys and send to the prisoners, now at the galleys. He stated that the Swiss authorities would be willing to do this, if pledges were made that when released, these people would forever leave the country. There were subsequent letters on this same point. One proposed that the petition be submitted to the king, in the name of the authorities of Berne, asking for the release of all prisoners. There was also a letter from the Burgess and Council of Berne to the king, giving their views upon this subject.

Müller recites (p. 232) that at a meeting of the committee on the welfare of Mennonites at Amsterdam, it was stated that four prisoners had been condemned by the Government of Berne, to the galleys; and 40 more had been imprisoned. The aid of the Holland Government was invoked; and the Holland officers took up the matter with Switzerland, and secured full freedom for all of them. Former efforts to the same purpose were without avail.

1715—More Galley Torture and Trouble.

Müller sets forth, (p. 226) that even in Turin, these prisoners, ready for the galleys, were aided financially by the Dutch. Goosen Goyen, in Krefeld, wrote to Van Woorst, that he had received moneys for these Mennonites and had forwarded the same. He also wrote that Freytorrens (a man referred to in the preceeding article, p. 229) was a fanatic or Mennonite, and that he was interfering too much with affairs at Berne. He also says that he has false doctrines on religious matters, and was supposed to be the author of a shameful tract or treatise, on religious subjects. Finally he was placed under arrest. His political activities were to be looked into. He states that it is expected that he will be banished from the country as an undesirable foreigner, if some one pays the cost of his release. Müller continues and says that his noble efforts on the part of the oppressed Mennonites who were suffering galley torture, was looked upon with jealous eyes.

At another place Müller recites that there are original letters in Amsterdam, written by Christian Liebe, Peter Wetrich, and Joseph Brobst, dated at Palermo, September 16, 1715, relating to the efforts made for their release, in which they promise that if they are released from the galleys, they will never go back to Swiss territory again.

The same page, Müller tells us again of the efforts of Gabriel of Wattenwyl, to get these people out of prison. He also states that if some one would be willing to go to Turin to intercede for the release of the prisoners sent there. Berne is ready to give a written pledge that they will take up mediation on the part of the friends of these people, provided they would never come back to the old home.

1715—Eby Family Come to Lancaster County.

The Eby family is numerous in this section, and the original home seems to be on Mill Creek, at a point known as Eby's Mill. Theodorus Eby was the ancestor. According to Bishop Benjamin Eby's records, found in the "Eby Family," pages 2 and 3, Theodorus Eby was a son of Jacob Eby, and came to America in 1715. Peter Eby, a nephew of Theodorus, came in 1720; also Nicholas Eby. These are all Swiss. But it is said that earlier generations of the family came into Switzerland from Northern Italy. Menno Eby, a young lad living near Terre Hill, is the 9th generation descendant of Theodorus Eby.

1715—Land Taken Up on the Susquehanna.

In the 2d Ser. Pa. Arch., Vol. 19, p. 602, there is an account of a warrant being issued to John Salkeld for 400 acres of land. This is made up of 375 acres formerly granted to Richard Hyde and 25 acres new land. It was warranted on the Susquehanna. (See also p. 575.)

Page 594 of the same book, there is an account setting forth that the land commissioners of Pa. had an application for 1,000 acres of land in Strasburg from Harmon Richman, late of Hamburg, Germany, and that the commissioners have decided to give him a part of that land which was first laid out to John Bundeli in Strasburg. The account states also that he wants 100 acres more and the same was assured to him by a warrant dated Oct. 22, 1715. This same year, the commissioners of property signed a patent to George Pierce for 600 acres in Sadsbury Twp., dated May 24, 1715, in right of John Hennery. In Harris's History will be found an interesting record of Strasburg land purchased in 1691. If this is a fact, it seems to be the earliest land taken up in the present county. In the same volume of the Arch., page 600, there is a record of 650 acres of land on a branch of the Pequea Creek, applied for by Richard Cloud, for which he is to pay 78 pounds, and also 300 acres to Wm. Cloud. (See p. 597.) This year, 1715, there was also an account of several other warrants, one to Robert Hodgen and James Hendricks, for 3,500 acres at Conestoga, ten pounds per 100 acres (see p. 595) and a warrant to Henry Worley for 600 acres on a branch of a creek, whose name is not given, for erecting a mill. (Do. 595.) And one to Francis Worley for 1,000 acres in Conestoga. (Do. 602.)

1714—Land Laid Out at Strasburg.

In the second series of the Pa. Arch., Vol. 19, page 587, it is recorded that a patent for 350 acres at Strasburg, was signed to Isaac Lefever, at 10 pounds per 100 acres, dated Sept. 25, 1714.

THE GERMAN-SWISS TAKE LANCASTER COUNTY LAND.

The same year a warrant for 1,000 acres to James Hendricks, near Strasburg, at the same price, dated December 28, 1714 (See page 591) was granted. Also the same year and same date, a warrant to Peter Bellas at Strasburg, for 200 acres at the same price, was granted; and also, the same year and date, 1,000 acres to Thomas Reichman, of Strasburg.

Rupp states that the land taken up by Peter Bellas was in the neighborhood of Smoketown, that is near Bird-in-Hand, and that Daniel Harmon, William Evans and James Smith were neighbors. (p. 116.)

1716—German-Swiss Take Up Some Land in Lancaster County.

In the second series of the Pa. Arch., Vol. 19, page 607, it is set forth that in 1716, a warrant was issued to Anthony Pretter for 300 acres of land in Conestoga, dated November 16th—and page 608, a warrant dated December 9, 1716, was set forth as being issued to John Gardner for 500 acres of land on the Conestoga River—and page 608 there is a patent, dated December 10, 1716, to Thomas Dawson for 300 acres, near Conestoga. On the same page, tracts amounting to 12,871 acres, were granted to John Estauch, near Conestoga—and page 609, a tract to Columbus McNair, for 200 acres in Conestoga. In Pequea, in the year 1716 (See same book, page 609) there is a record of Daniel Fierre (now Ferry or Forry) applying for 600 acres of land near Pequea, for which he was to pay in three months, 10 pounds for 100 acres. A warrant was signed October 4th for the same.

Also note here that in 1713 (See same book, page 574) Samuel Guilden of Berne, the Mennonite Minister, asked for 800 acres in Strasburg, with the rest of his brethren. The warrant was granted January 1, 1714. We will notice this again under date of 1718, when it was patented to Martin Kendig.

This same year, a warrant was executed to Isaac Lefever, dated October 10th for 300 acres, at Strasburg, and Rupp says, page 116, that this same year, Jacob Greider or Kreider, Jacob Hostetter, Hans Frantz, Shenks and others, settled on the banks of the Conestoga. He also says that Kreider and Hostetter arrived in America earlier than 1716, visited their brethren in faith at Pequea, and then settled on the north side of the Conestoga, two miles south of the present site of Lancaster, and that here, they took up the 800 acres above referred to. He recites that their first tent was covered with tow-cloth, which they brought along with them, and that during the winter, the Indians came to secure shelter with them and sleep by their fire. Rupp does not quote his authority.

1717—A Few More Mennonite Additions This Year.

This year a patent was signed to Hans Moyer at Strasburg for 700 acres (Rupp 624). A considerable tract was also surveyed near the head of Pequea Creek, inculding the old Shawanna Town by Mathias Vanbibber for some Germans to settle. This year also, says Rupp, Hans Zimmerman came to Lancaste Crounty (Rupp 126) and Hans Graeff settled in Earl (Rupp 133).

1717—The First Ship-loads of Mennonites.

Under this date, we are given knowledge of the first ship lists of Mennonites, who were coming to Pennsylvania, and up into the Susquehanna Valley. In Vol. 3, Col. Rec., p. 29, it is stated that Captain Richard, Captain Tower and Captain Eyers(Ayers) waited on the Council of Pennsylvania with a list of Palatines or Mennonites they had brought over in their ships from London. The names are not given, but the record states that Richards had 164, Tower 91 and Eyers 108; this makes a total of 363 persons. This throws some light upon how rapidly our Swiss ancestors were coming to this section. We believe that nearly all of these settled in Lancaster County, because in the year 1717, all who came over were coming up to this region. In 1739, a list of 178 Lancaster County German-Swiss were naturalized and likely, many of these were among the list. (4 St. L. 326.)

1717—Slow Progress of the Mennonite Colonies.

The Mennonite colonies in Lancaster County seem to have made very little progress. There is a record of only a few additional land grants. The principal one seems to be the one given to Martin Kendig and Hans Herr of 5,000 acres, to be taken up in several parcels about Conestoga and Pequea Creeks at 10 Pounds per 100 acres. The Penna. Pound was worth $3.24 and, therefore, this would have been $32.40 for 100 acres or 32 cents an acre. In addition to this, there was the usual quit rent to pay. The record of this grant of land is found in Vol. 19 of the Sec. Series of the Pa. Arch., p. 622, and it states that these two men took up the 5,000 acres for settlements for several of their countrymen, lately arrived. The warrant was dated the 22nd of November, 1717. In addition to this tract, the same date, warrants were signed for 15 other persons about Conestoga for land, making a total of 6,675 acres, but this land may have been practically the same that Kendig and Herr had applied for. The warrants are set forth as follows: To Hans Moyer, 500 acres—Hans Kaiggey, 100 acres—Christian Hearsey (Hershey), and Hans Pupather, 1000 acres—Michael Shenk and Henry Pare (Barr), 400 acres—another to Hans Pupather for 700 acres—another to Peter Leaman for 300 acres—another to Molker Preneman (Brenneman) for 500 acres—another to Henry and John Funk, 550 acres—another to Christopher Fanciscus for 150 acres—another to Michael Shenk for 200 acres—another to Jacob Landis and Ulrick Harvey, 150 acres—one to Emanuel Heer (Herr) for 500 acres—one to Abram Herr for 600 acres—one to Hans Tuber, Isaac Kauffman and Melkerman, 675 acres and one to Michael Miller for 500 acres.

We will see later that these were settled practically in a colony, neighbors to one another. It will be also noticed that the authorities were not slow in laying the assessment upon these newcomers, and under the year of 1718 we find the first assessment list of Conestoga sets forth these names and we have noticed that they have just arrived about this time. Christopher Franciscus was more than an ordinary man and we will notice later his activity and his encounters with panthers and wild animals about his home.

1717—The Governor Advised the Province to Protect Itself Against the Mennonites

In Vol. 2 of the Votes of Assembly, p. 217, Governor Keith in his address to the Assembly under the date of 1717, warns the province to protect itself against the great number of foreign German Palatines now arriving. Keith says to the Assembly on the 13th of October, "I must recommend to you in particular not to lose any time in securing yourselves and all the people of this colony from the inconveniences which may possibly arise by the unlimited number of foreigners that without any license from the King, or leave of this Government, have been transported hither of late, and to provide some discrete regulations to allay the apprehensions we are under, of greater numbers, which I am informed are to be daily expected from Europe." We can plainly understand that he meant the Mennonites, because Englishmen, Irishmen, Scotchmen and Welchmen were not foreigners and the only other persons coming were these German Mennonites. It will be a pleasure to notice that Governor Keith a few years later changed his opinion very much about these good people.

1717—Great Increase of the Mennonite Colony Alarms the Government at Philadelphia.

On the 17th of September of this year, Governor Keith brought before his Council the fact that a greater number of Germans have lately come into the province and that many of them are Mennonites, and therefore will not take the oath of allegiance, and that there may be some danger in allowing them to come. He gives the matter to the attention of Council in the following words:

"The Governor observed to the Board that great numbers of foreigners from Germany, strangers to our Language and Constitutions, having lately been imported into this province daily dispersed themselves immediately after landing, without producing any certificates, from whence they came and what they are; and as they seem to have first landed in Britain and afterwards to have left it without any License, from the Government, or so much as their knowledge, so in the same manner they behaved here, without making the least application to himself or to any of the Magistrates; that as this practice might be of very dangerous consequence, since by the same method any number of foreigners from any nation whatever, as well enemies as friends, might throw themselves upon us; The Governor, therefore, thought it requisite that this matter should be considered by the Board, and accordingly it was considered, and it was ordered thereupon, that all the masters of vessels who have lately imported any of these foreigners be summoned to appear at this Board, to render an account of the numbers and characters of their passengers respectively, from Britain; that all those who are already landed be required by a proclamation, to be issued for that purpose; to repair within the space of one month to some Magistrate, particularly to the Recorder of this City, to take such oaths appointed by law as are necessary to give assurances of their being well affected to his Majesty and his Government; But because some of these foreigners are said to be Mennonites, who can not for conscience sake, take an oath, that those persons be admitted upon their giving any equivalent assurances in their own way and manner and that the Naval Officer of this Port be required not to admit any inward bound vessel to an entry, until the master shall first give an exact list."

In this we see that very few of our Mennonite forefathers came over and joined the Colony of 1710 until about the year 1717. They are now coming rapidly as this extract from the records tells us.

An important regulation in the Mennonite migration started from this incident, that is, it was now made the law that hereafter every ship must give an exact list of the Palatines imported by them before they will be allowed to land. From this action by the Governor and Council, we have today the complete records of the coming of these Mennonites, including the times, the numbers, the ships in which they came and the names.

1717—Lands Taken Up By German Swiss This Year.

According to the Penna. Archives (Vol. 19 of Series 2) Dan Morris received a warrant for 1,000 acres of land at Conestoga, dated Oct. 12, 1717 (p. 621)—Mart Kendig and Hans Herr, for 5,000 acres in several parcels about Conestoga and Pequea Creek, for settlements for several of their countrymen "lately arrived" dated Nov. 22, 1717, the total of which, however, reached 6,675 acres— viz. Hans Moyer 350—Hans Haiggy 100—Christ Hearsey and Hans Prupacher 700—Peter Lehman 300—Melker Preneman 500—Henry and John Funk 500 — Christopher Franciscus 150—Michael Shenk 200—Jacob Lundes and Ulrich Harvey 150 — Abram Herr 600—Emanuel Herr 500—Hans Tuber, Isaac Kauffman and Milkerman 675 and Michael Müller 500 acres (p. 622). These foreigners were informed they should be naturalized if they expect their children to be able to fall heir to this land. (p. 624.)

1718—Our Swiss Ancestors Complain That They Must Obey Laws They Have No Part in Making.

In a letter to Wm. Penn, dated May 20, 1718, the same year he died, our Swiss (Amish) ancestors complain that they are to be subject to laws in which they have no share in making, and which they do not want, or avail themselves of. In it they say "We are subject to the laws of God—you to the laws of men. We do not go to the elections—we do not go to your Courts of Justice—we hold no offices, neither civil or military—we do not refuse to pay for our land, but we regard it as a subject for complaint that we should be subject to civil and military domination. We came to Pennsylvania to enjoy the freedom of our opinions and of our bodies, and expect no other prescriptions of the laws than such as God has commanded. Because we make no debts and need no laws to collect such, we ought not be compelled to pay for the support of other criminals in jails. We respect your rights—do you also, respect our customs. We demand nothing from you beyond what the word of God justifies."

Since their American freedom of that day and the laws were not satisfactory to them, we can easily understand how odious their attitude must have been at home in Berne. In the face of their partial dissatisfaction here, they prospered and grew, so that in 1883, they had 3,500 baptized members — 41 churches — 47 preachers and eight bishops in Lancaster County alone. (Müller, pp. 367 and 8.)

1718—William Penn, Jr., Was a Friend to the Mennonites.

In Vol. 3 of the Col. Rec., pp. 63 and 64, there is a letter dated in which he first recites (p. 63) the views of his father and then says, "I profess myself to be a minister of the Church of England and recommend to be careful of their interest and protect the clergy; but also protect in their possessions such 'strangers' as are settled among us, for the public faith is concerned in it." We readily see by the last clause here that the Junior Penn referred to the Mennonites as the strangers and he shows that, while his father was a Quaker, he was a member of the Church of England.

1718—The First Assessment List.

In the first assessment list of Conestoga, which included all of Lancaster County from Strasburg to the River, and as far North as what is now Manheim, the names of the Mennonite families living here in that year (1718) are as follows:

Martin Kundig, Martin Milan, Christian Heer, John Haer, Wendall Bowman, Jacob Miller, Joseph Steman, Daniel Harmer, John Miller, John

Funk, Henry Carpenture, Henry Hayne, Christopher Franciscus, Peter Bellar, Benedictus Venrick, Daniel Ferre, John Ferre, Philip Ferre, Isaac Lefevre, Richard Davis, Thomas Falkner, John Milen, Hans Haure, John Taylor, Martyn Berr, Imanuel Heer, Henry Kundic & Son, Jacob Moyer, Hans Steff, Hans Keague, Jacob Griter, Jacob Highstetter, John Widwer, Andrew Koffman, John Broakpather, Junior, John Broakpather, Jacob Broakpather, Peter Swaor, Abraham Heer, Melchior Arisman, Christopher Hearse & Son, John Toup, Henry Heer, Michael Bowman, Hance Bugholder, Hans Neicomer, Melchior Prenamon, George Kendrick, John Natts, Junr., Michael Shank, Junr., Jorn Natts, Senr., Henry Funk, Benjamin Wilmer, Jacob Lundus, Hance Henry Neff, Michael Miller, Felix Lundus, Jacob Kundrick, Junr., John Frame, Charley Christopher Woolrick Howry, Stoffal Prenaman, Jacob Hoober, Christian Stone, Isaac Frederick & Son, Jacob Kundrick, Jacob Lundus, Junr., Martin Boyer, Hance Boyer, John Bowman, Penedictus Brackbill, Christian Shank, Michael Shank, Senr., Rudey Moyer, Hance Brand, Hans Graff, Junr., Hans Graff, Senr., Peter Yorte, Torey Ebys, Hans Currick Moyer, Christian Shank, Hans Weaver, Woolrick Hource, Peter Laman.

The original of this assessment list is in the possession of Gilbert Cope of West Chester. As may be seen from the above spelling, the German-Swiss names were not well deciphered. In addition to these Dutchmen, as they were called, there were 43 Englishmen settling or owning property there.

1718—The Amish Protest Against Penn's Laws.

In a previous article we set forth the protest of certain Amish brethren, against the laws of Penn, concerning land, inheritance, etc. We simply call attention here to the fact that the same protest is found in volume 7 of Hazard's Register, page 151, where, however, it appears in somewhat different language.

1718—The Assembly Take Action on the Growth of Our Swiss Ancestry.

In answer to the Governor's speech, the Assembly in an address drawn up by David Lloyd, say to the Governor that the Assembly feel a great concern at the coming of so many foreigners and that the Royal Charter seems to be taken against them, especially unless they take the proper tests to show that they are not his enemies. The Assembly went on further and suggested that it would be well for the Governor to appoint a Committee of the Council to join a Committee of the Assembly and plan proper methods to remove jealousies already raised in the minds of the inhabitants concerning these foreigners; and also to prevent the inconveniences which may arise from their settlement in one place or some of them settling promiscuously among the Indians.

This conclusion left the Mennonites very little choice. They were not to be allowed to settle in one place and they were not allowed to settle promiscuously among the Indians. The Governor replied to this on the 10th of January, two days later and said that he approved of the appointing of a Committee to confer about these foreigners lately transported here; but that he would delay action at present because he had written home to England to find out the King's desire upon the matter.

The upshot of it was that the Assembly proceeded to introduce a law that the sum of 1 pence per pound and four shillings a head should be laid upon all those Palatines that are taxable. This, however, was doing nothing more than putting the same tax on them as the other subjects were taxed. (See Votes of Assembly January 10, 1718.)

1718—Large Additions to the Mennonite Colony in Lancaster County.

This year, according to the records, a considerable addition was made to the number of Mennonites in our county; but I can not find any mention of a church built by them at this date. It is likely they held their services in the different homes before they built their church, the whole body gathering Sunday after Sunday at these different places. There is no doubt that they had services because their minister was usually the leading man of the Colony from the beginning.

This year, as shown in volume 19 of the Second Series of the Pa. Arch., p. 626, there is considerable set forth showing the activity of these Mennonite forefathers. It is stated that the late settlements on and near the Conestoga Creek have made it necessary that the Indian fields about the town should be enclosed by a good fence to secure the Indians' corn from the horses, cattle and hogs of the new settlers. A patent was also granted to Isaac Lefever for 300 acres at Strasburg. And Pupather, Hershey, Shenk and Henry Pare were given patents for the land which they took up last year (p. 628). Matrin Kendig was given a patent for his 800 acres. Wendell Bowman also got a deed or patent this year for his part of the Mennonite tract which he first took up in 1710; and so did Hans Moyer, Melker Preneman, Jacob Hochstater, Jacob Kraytor and Christopher Franciscus, the land being all about Strasburg. According to Rupp, these parties all joined one another and lived in and about the neighborhood of Strasburg. The same year land was also taken up by Theodorus Eby at Conestoga. His land it seems, was located on Mill Creek, and when the road was laid out from the junction of the Cocalico and the Conestoga, down to what is now Dowingtown in 1726, it speaks of the same running by Dorus Eby's mill on Mill Creek, (Do. p. 632). Later in the year 1718, patents were granted to Hans Graeff and Christopher Franciscus, (Do. p. 639). Abram Herr also got his deed or patent—Henry Pare got his deed for 300 acres at Conestoga and Hans Shenk took up 200 acres at the same place, (Do. p. 640).

This same year, Hans Graeff took up 1100 acres more near Strasburg by a new warrant, (Do. p. 642). The same year Michael Danager, late of Germany, was given a warrant for 300 acres of land near Pequea, Joseph Stehman 100 acres near Conestoga and Christian Stone 100 acres, (Do. p. 650). This is the record as far as the Land Commissioners' books show the state of the land taken by our Mennonite forefathers at this time.

We notice at this time that a considerable number got their warrant or rights to land in 1710, nearly all about the neighborhood of Strasburg and a few about the same time along the Conestoga, near where the Little Conestoga and Big Conestoga come together, which is in the neighborhood of Rock Hill; and no patents or deeds were given, with perhaps a very few exceptions, until 1718, in which year the patents or deeds were signed and delivered, and we find many of them so recited in our records in the Recorder's Office; and also that in this latter year of 1718, a new lot of applications for land were made and a new lot of warrants given. This shows that there was a second incoming of Palatines in 1717, and between the two dates, there is no record of very many having come. The Colonial Records do not contain accounts of any arriving between these two dates. Those who took up their land in 1717 did not get their deeds or patents until about 1734.

As to the Mennonite population in Lancaster County in 1718, there is no record except the assessment list of Conestoga Township, which I have found in charge of Gilbert Cope at West Chester. This list contains 86 Dutchmen and 43 Englishmen, as being assessed in Conestoga at this time.

Therefore, averaging these early Mennonite families at six in a family, including parents. it would seem as if there were fully 500 Mennonites in Conestoga, at this date. As Conestoga, at that time, included what is now Strasburg and Pequea, we may say that it included all of the settled part of Lancaster County. Thus in the first eight years, from 1710 to 1718, the Mennonite population of Lancaster County reached perhaps the neighborhood of 600 persons. There were practically no other inhabitants in the Conestoga and Pequea Creek valleys at this time, as the Scotch-Irish had not yet come up to the Donegals. So that Lancaster County, at that time, was wholly a Mennonite settlement.

1718—Emanuel Zimmerman—A Wonderful Amish-Mennonite Boy.

The great concensus of opinion is to the effect that Hans Herr and Martin Mylin, Dr. Hans Neff and a few others were the leading spirits of the early Mennonites in Lancaster County and there is no doubt that these elderly fathers were the very back bone of the first Mennonite settlers; they managed the spiritual, financial and business affairs for their brethren. But in 1717 there appeared within what is now the bounds of Lancaster County, an Amish-Mennonite boy, 15 years of age, who was gifted with a wonderful intellect, religious spirit and strong constitution. At the early age of 16, in the year of 1718, it is asserted he drew the memorial we have just referred to, for his brethren, addressed to William Penn. He lived to be seventy-eight years of age, dying in 1780, after having served as Justice of the Peace, Judge and Member of Assembly many years. Mr. Conyngham has the following to say of him, as may be seen in Vol. 7 of Haz. Reg., p. 152:

"Henry Zimmerman arrived in Pennsylvania in the year 1698, and returned afterwards to Europe for his family, whom he brought out in 1706; and settled first in Germantown, and removed within the present bounds of Lancaster County (then Chester County) in 1717.

Emanuel Zimmerman, son of Henry, was the most distinguished of all the early settlers. He possessed from nature, an ardent love for liberty in every form, zealous and active in every pursuit. His mind was finely organized; and he enjoyed an unbounded influence over the whole settlement. Tunkers, Aymenish, Lutherans, Calvanists, and Mennonites, all applied to him in any emergency. He possessed as strong a constitution as intellect. He was born in Switzerland in the year 1702, and died in the year 1780. He lived beloved, and died lamented, by all denominations. He was in every sense an honest man—always just, liberal and tolerant. He was arbitor in all matters of dispute among his neighbors; and from his decisions, they never appealed; such was the confidence in his integrity.

The memorial of the Aymenish and Mennonites, breathes the spirit of a William Tell. It was written probably by Emanuel Zimmerman, as his name is attached to it, on behalf of the Mennonites, Amish, etc.

The memorial is dated May 20, 1718. William Penn died on the 30th of July of the same year, in England. Sir William Keith was deputy governor; and it does not appear, from any record that I can trace, that he ever acted upon the memorial." The later services of Emanuel Zimmerman I will mention under later dates.

1718—Danger from the Wild Beasts in the Mennonite Country

In the same book and page last spoken of, the following appears from the pen of Conyngham:

When the Amish Mennonites first settled on the Pequea, its woods were infested by wolves and panthers. These animals committed great depredations, especially among the sheep. The hunters would laugh at the Amish, because they would not attempt to destroy them. The Amish said in justification, "That they considered it a crime to deprive any of God's creatures of life, except those which God gave us for our use; and that to instruct youth in the use of firearms, would be to lead them to eternal ruin." "You," said an old Amish to a hunter, "pursue the deer, the fox and the squirrel, and neglect not only your farm, but your family. We give your children bread, when you leave them destitute. You are improvident—we are provident. Your race will be short—ours will be long. In the eye of the Almighty, who discharges his duty? You or I?"

1718—Customs of Early Amish-Mennites.

Mr. Conyngham in Vol. 7 of Haz. Reg., p. 150, speaks thus of the early dress of the people saying that the long beards of the men and the short petticoats of the females, just covering the knee, attracts the attention of the English settlers. He further says, "The men wore long red caps on their heads; the women had neither bonnets, hats or caps, but merely a string passing around their head to keep the hair from the face. The dress of both male and female was domestic, quite plain, made of a coarse material, after an old fashion of their own.

Soon after their arrival in Philadelphia, they took a westerly course in pursuit of a location, where they could all live in one vicinity. They selected a rich limestone country, beautifully adorned with sugar maple, hickory, and black and white walnut on the border of a delightful stream, abounding in the finest trout—here they raised their humble cabins. The water of the Pequea was clear, cold and transparent, and the grape vines and clematis, intertwining among the lofty branches of the majestic buttonwood, formed a pleasant retreat from the noon beams of a summer sun.

These emigrants were neither stimulated by the desire of distinction, or the love of wealth. They approved of an equalization of rank and property. All they required was sufficient land, from which by their own industry, they could raise produce for the support of their respective families. Tea, coffee, West India sugar, and spirituous liquors, were not considered by them, either as useful or necessary. The sugar tree supplied them with sugar and molasses. They had, therefore, no want but what they could gratify.

As land was easily acquired, it was in the power of each individual to be a large proprietor but this neither agreed with their professions and practises."

1718—Earliest Form of Administering Sacrament, Baptism, etc.

Mr. Conyngham in the same book last referred to, p. 131, gives this as the early form of baptism, which he says they had brought over from the old country, "In administering the right of baptism the following rule was observed: The person to be baptised being an adult kneels; a preacher holds his hand over him or her while the deacon pours water into the hands of the preacher, which runs on the head of the person to be baptised, after which prayer accompanied by the imposition of hands closes the ceremony."

Conyngham then goes on and gives the form that another sect practised on the same page, as follows: "One of the Mennonist sect baptise after this fashion; the person to be baptised is accompanied to a stream of water by a large number of people, attended by persons playing on various instruments of music and some singing. The preacher stands on the bank and pours water on the head of the person, who is in the stream, saying "I baptise thee in the name of the Father, and of the Son, and of the Holy Ghost."

What sect of them followed this custom, I can not tell. As to the early mode of sacrament, the form was this, says Conyngham, on the same page: "The principal ancient Mennonists pursue the mode pointed out in the New Testament, in administering the sacrament. See the eighteenth verse of the twenty-sixth chapter of St. Matthew. The preacher sends a message to a member—"Make ready for the passover." In the evening the congregation collect; and on a table are placed small loaves of bread and a pitcher of wine, and as they eat, the preacher blesses the bread (see the twenty-sixth verse) and breaks it, then hands it around the table saying "Take, eat, this is my body;" then taking up the pitcher, he returns thanks to God, then handing the pitcher to the congregation, he says "Drink ye all of it." The people partake of the Holy sacrament whilst walking around the table, talking with each other sociably; and after having finished the bread and wine, sing a hymn and then return to their respective dwellings."

1718—The Mennonite Settlement, the Thickest Settlement in the Interior of the Province.

In Vol. 3 of the Col. Rec., p. 37, under the date of the 13th of February, 1718, Governor Keith acquainted the Board of certain dangers at Conestoga by Maryland people and he says that they were surveying land not far from Conestoga, "near the thickest of our settlements" to the great disturbance of the neighborhood there. I simply quote this item to show that the Governor called this the thickest of our interior settlements.

1718—Swiss and Germans Who Came to Lancaster County Prior to This Date.

In Vol. 4 of the Statutes at Large (p. 147) there is a list of persons who came from Switzerland and the Palatinate to Lancaster County, prior to 1718. The list in part is the same as the assessment list of Conestoga Township of 1718, which we have given; but there are the following names in addition to those appearing on that list:

Martyn Mylin, Jacob Funk, Franciscus Neiff, Sr., Franciscus Neiff, Jr., Abraham Burkholder, Michael Bohman, John Frederic, Martin Harnist, Michael Mire, Henry Bare, Peter Bumgartner, Melcor Erishman, Jacob Goot, John Woolslegle, Jacob Mire,

Christopher Somers, Joseph Stoneman, Daniel Ashleman, Christopher Peelman, Abraham Hare, Jacob Biere, Peter Yordea, Peter Leaman, John Jacob Snevely, Isaac Coffman, Andrew Coffman, Woolrich Rodte, Roody Mire, Jacob Bheme, John Coffman, Michael Doneder, Andrew Shults, Christian Preniman, Mathias Slaremaker, big John Shank, Jacob Churts, John Croyder, John Leeghte, John Hampher, Peter Newcomat, David Longnicker, Abraham Mire, Woolrich Houser, John Mire, Henry Mussleman, Peter Aybe, Hans Goot, Christian Staner, John Jacob Light, William Loughman, Frederic Stay, John Line, John Shoope, Bastian Royer, Jonas Lerow, Simeon King, Joyn Aybe and Everard Ream. Conestoga was a large section in those times. This list includes residents of the whole county.

1718—Land Grants and Warrants This Year on the Conestoga.

Vol. 19 of the Sec. Ser. of the Pa. Arch. sets forth the following warrants for or grants of land in 1718 in Lancaster County. The list for Conestoga consists of 200 acres to Moses Comb, a brother-in-law of Peter Bizalion (p. 625)—patent to Hans Pupather, 700 acres—to Pupather and Hershey, 1000 acres—to Daniel Herman 450 acres—to Michael Shenk and Henry Pare, 400 acres (p. 628)—warrant to Theodorus Eaby, 300 acres (p. 637)—patent to Thos. Baldwin, 200 acres, stated as a part of the tract laid out to James Hendricks—warrant to Henry Pare, 300 acres—warrant to Hans Shenk, 200 aces, (all p. 640)—warrant to Robert Wilkins 150 acres, above Conestoga (p. 641)—warrant to Thos. Morgan, on branch of the Conestoga Creek—warrant to Gabriel Davis, 450 acres, same place—warrant to Hugh Hughes, 500 acres same place (all page 642)—warrant to William Hews, 400 acres near Conestoga, (p. 648)—warrant to Richard Carter, Conestoga 200 acres (p. 649)—grant to Joseph Steman, 100 acres near Conestoga—warrant to Christian Stone or Steman, 100 acres near Conestoga (both page 650).

We may say in reference to the tract of Theodorus Eaby that it was a grant on Mill Creek, at the point where the Old Peters Road today crosses that creek, known as the Ressler Mill. This mill of Theodorus Eaby is referred to in the laying out of a road in 1726, (the records of which are in Chester County), extending from near Downingtown, originally, to the junction of the Cocalico and Conestoga Creeks.

We note also that it became necessary at this time for Penn's land commissioners to order James Steele, the surveyor general, to prevent Maryland from surveying lands about Conestoga, among our Germans. (Do 625).

1718—The German Cattle and the Indian Corn Fields at Conestoga.

Vol. 19, of the Sec. Ser. of the Pa. Arch. sets forth that the late settlements on or near Conestoga Creek make necessary that the Indian fields about the town should be closed by a good fence to secure the Indians' corn from the horses, cattle and hogs may fence in 200 acres more for convenience of pasturage; 300 acres were of the new settlers; and the government, therefore, ordered that the fences should be made and that James Logan should pay for the same out of public funds, not over 20,000 pounds.

1718—John Cartlidge at Conestoga Allowed to Fence Off Pasturage.

In the same book, page 644, it is stated that at a meeting of the land commissioners, held Jan. 18th, this year, John Cartlidge, having seated himself between Conestoga Creek and the Susquehanna River, desires a grant of 300 acres, and also that he granted to him at ten pounds per hundredweight and one shilling sterling quit rent. The 200 acres he is permitted to fence in and hold for pasturage for the term of fourteen years, in consideration of the good services he has done among the new settlers of those parts as well as to the Indians, whose town is very near to his dwelling. A warrant for said grant is signed dated Dec. 11, 1716, for 300 acres, and for 200 acres.

1718—Christian Schlegel's Old Mill Site Granted to Edmund Cartlidge.

In the same book (p. 644) we find Edmund Cartlidge having purchased a pretended right of Christopher Schlegle to a tract of land and ordinary grist mill on a branch of the Conestoga, which the said Christopher by not complying with the terms on which it was granted, became void. But the said Edmund having since built and erected a good mill on the same land, the grant of 400 acres to be laid out to him, including his buildings and improvements for 10 pounds 100 acres and 1 shilling quit rent and was signed Oct. 1, 1717, for 400 acres.

1718—Nathaniel Christopher's Tract Above Conestoga, Granted to Peter Bizalion.

In the same volume of the Archives it is stated that Peter Bizalion, having purchased a small improvement made by Nathaniel Christopher, on the Susquehanna River above Conestoga, desires to purchase 700 acres of land to include the said improvement, the whole being for Nathaniel and his wife, daughter of John Comb, late of Philadelphia. It is agreed that 700 acres be laid out to said Martha, the wife of said Peter Bizalion, in the place aforesaid, in a regular tract fronting on said river, and to include the said improvement; to extend as far back into the woods as the place will bear, for which said Peter agrees to give 70 pounds and 1 shilling yearly, sterling, quit rent to Christopher. Warrant signed Jan. 25, 1719, for 700 acres.

1718—Maryland Encroaches on Our German Land.

In the Sec. Ser. of the Penna. Arch. Vol. 19 (p. 625) it is recorded that, Mathias Van Bebber from Maryland, taking with him Henry Hollingsworth surveyed a considerable tract near head of Pequea, including in same old Sawannah town, by virtue of warrants from Maryland and offered the people settled there under this governmnt to sell lands in right of Maryland and make good titles. Andros issued proceedings to dispossess them and ten pounds reward to any one apprehending the surveyor.

James Steel was ordered to Conestoga to present like orders there.

At the same time 500 acres near the Old Sawannah Town on the Pequea Creek was surveyed to Col. French. for the interest he took in keeping Maryland people from taking up land in the Pequea Valley, that was intended for our Germans. These operations took place evidently near the head of the Pequea Creek in Salisbury township. There was such a town there. It was the town of the Shawanee Indians. There was also one of their towns on the Octorara. near Christiana. and another at the mouth of Pequea called Sequehan.

1718—A Few Pequea Settlements.

This year, according to the same book. there were additional warrants for land on the Pequea, some to the Swiss and some to the English. Thre was a patent to Ezekial Kennett for 200 acres (p. 625)—one to William Middleton for 100 acres, (p. 640) —warrants to Owen O'Neil, John Blake and David Jones each 100 acres (p. 621)— and, also, (p. 650), there is a record of a warrant to Michael Donnager for 300 acres, near Pequea Creek, and he was to pay one shilling sterling per 100 acres yearly, quit rent. The same year a warrant was given to Thomas Edwrad for 250 acres "back in the county of Chester" (p. 651). There is a further record about the John French tract, (p. 681) the same year.

1718—Land Taken About Strasburg This Year.

In the same book (p. 628) three hundred acres were granted to Isaac Lefever at Strasburg anl the patent was granted to Hans Hawry (Howry) for 300 acres at Strasburg and fifty acres land (p. 632)—and at the same page, there is a record of a patent to Wendell Bowman for 250 acres at Strasburg, and it stated to be "part of the land granted to the Palatines in 1710"—at the same page also are recorded a patent to Hans Moyer at Strasburg for 350 acres—one to Melker Prenneman for 500 acres and a warrant to Jacob Hockstatter for 250 acres at the same place and also a warrant to Jacob Kryter for 250 acres, (p. 633)— a warrant for 200 acres to Christopher Franciscus—(p. 639) a patent to Hans Graeff for 300 acres—one to Christopher Franciscus for 150 acres and one to Hans Snyder for 200 acres, all at Strasburg and (p. 640) there is recorded a patent to Abram Herr for 600 acres at Strasburg; and (at p. 642) a warant to Hans Line, Strasburg, for 900 acres; and also a warrant to Hans Graeff for 1100 acres at Strasburg. All these warrants and patents in and about Strasburg were granted by Penn's land authorities, in the year 1718.

We remember that this year, or perhaps the later part of the previous year, there was the first big migration of Swiss and Germans to our county, after the first colony came in 1710 and 1711 and perhaps, 1712, between which two settlements. there was five years of a recess.

1718—Lands Taken Up at Susquehanna This Year.

Turning in the same book to Susquehanna, we find that a warrant was granted this year to lay out to Peter Carterer, 300 acres on the Susquehanna "where his father had settled, at his father's request" and (p. 634) a warrant to John Henry Henison for laying out 100 acres at Susquehanna, part of 10,000 acres sold to Redegeldt by his land commissioners. a part of which Redelgeldt transferred to Henison.

1719—Mart Mylin's Gun Factory.

Rupp tells us that Martin Mylin, who landed here in 1710, built a gun factory on Mylin's run in Lampeter Township in 1719. (Rupp, p. 74.) It is well known that the gun factory industry was begun in this section very early. In the time of the Revolutionary War, there was a gun factory in the neighborhood of Smithville on a run of water there, and in other parts of the county.

1719—Dunkards in Pequea, or Conestoga.

Kuhns tells us that this year the Dunkards were founded. Alexander Mack of Schwarzenau in Westfalia, began the foundation of that faith as early as 1708. Though they became perfected as an organization about 1719 and on or about the same year twenty of those famileis came and settled in Germantown—on the Skippach, Montgomery County—at Oley, Berks County, and on the Conestoga, Lancaster County. (Kuhns, 179.)

1719—German-Swiss Properties at Conestoga.

This year, according to the records of Penn's land commissioners, David Powell agreed to take 3,000 acres of vacant land back of the late survey, upon which he had settled divers families of Palatines, to whom he sold the whole 3,000 acres. This was for 300 pounds. (Second Series of the Pa. Arch. Vol 19, p. 663.) William Grimpson, "who dwells on the road going to Conestoga," is to have 100 acres that belonged to John Hendricks (p. 690). Hans Weaver was given 500 acres on the Conestoga Creek, four miles above Hans Groff's. James Letort who had taken up land between the Conestoga and the Pacstang on the east side of the Susquehanna River, at a convenient place to trade with the Indians, desired 500 acres more laid out, fronting on the river, and a warrant dated Jan. 25, 1719, was granted to him. The price was 50 pounds and 15 shillings quit rent.

1719—New Strasburg Laid Out.

In the same book (p. 652) under this date, it is stated that Edward Ream is given 200 acres of land near New Strasburg, at 20 pounds and 1 shilling quit rent. Just where this is, is difficult to tell. It is well known that Everhard Ream, about 1724, was given the first grant of land, which is now Reamstown.

1719—A Law to be Drawn in Favor of the Mennonites.

On the 11th of February of this year a motion was made in the Assembly that leave be granted to bring in a bill to settle and confirm the foreigners in their possessions and to make firm all the sales heretofore made by them. The Assembly ordered that leave be granted to bring in such a bill and David Lloyd should draw up the same (2 votes of Assembly, p. 253).

1719—Mill Creek Mennonite Settlement Begun.

Conyngham in Vol. 7 of Hazard's Reg., p. 124, says that the word "Tunkers" was a name given to the sect that broke off from the Baptists in Philadelphia and moved up the country. In the year 1719, about twenty families came to Philadelphia, some settled at Pequea, some at Germantown, some at Skippack, etc. In the year 1729, more than thirty families arrived within the province, belonging to the original church of Schwardzenau. The Tunkers were originally Calvanists and were baptized in the river Eder by Schwardzenau. The words, Tunkers in German —Baptists in Greek—and Dippers in English, have all the same signification. Persecution drove some to Holland, and some to Crefeldt. The original congregation removed from Schwardzenau to Sornstervin in Friezland, and from thence to Pennsylvania i.. 1719.

1720—Lands Taken Up in Conestoga and Strasburg by Swiss and Germans.

This year 600 acres of land were warranted to David Lewis on a branch of the Conestoga—in two parcels (2nd Ser. Pa. Arch., Vol. 19, p. 707). The same year Walter Walters and others examined the country back in the Conestoga branches to find a place to settle themselves and their families, where they desired 2,000 acres, above the lands of Evan Jones and others. They were allowed 1,000 acres. This was on the head waters of Conestoga (Do. 708). There were settlements the same year on Octoraro—to James Cotton, 200 acres near Nottingham and to John Matthews, near Musgrove's 200 acres (Do. 704-708).

About the same time, Hans Geo. Shutz and Mathias Reuger were given 500 acres of land including the old plantation, where Peter P. Bizalion lived (Do. 626) and Thomas Edwards was given 250 acres "back in the County of Chester" which was the name of this section before Lancaster County was erected (Do. 651).

Page 289 of same book, it is stated that a tract of 30,000 acres in the upper part of Chester County was laid out soon after it was first purchased in 1686.

We may also note that, in 1686, by Act of Assembly, 20,000 acres of land on the Conestoga were vested in Chas. Reed and others in trust. This, later deeds show, included practically the whole peninsula, between Pequea and Conestoga creeks, from the Susquehanna River, many miles up said creeks. (Recorder's Office of Lancaster Co., Book B, p. 213, etc.)

1720—Mennonite Children Play With the Indians.

A very interesting topic in the life of the Mennonite families in the early times is shown in 7 Haz. Reg., p. 163, in an account given by the ancient Amish-Mennonite of those early times, as follows:

"An aged member of the Amish or Ommish faith relates, that he often heard his grandfather say, that his family was one of the first of the Europeans who settled west of the Conestoga. That the Indians lived near them; and that the German and Indian children would frequently play together in the neighbouring wigwam. Some times you would see them engaged in conests of foot race; in which the Indian lads would excel although the German lads would discard their clothes, to put them on an equality of the naked savages. Sometimes with the bow and arrow, but here the little Indians would all show their superiority in skill, and accuracy of aim. In wrestling, and in most of their exercises, the Indian boys excelled; but in the mechanical arts the little emigrants had the advantage. I have often seen the chiefs reclining on the ground leaning on the arm, looking at the diversions and amusements of the children; and when the little Indian would excel, they would laugh very heartily.

It would not unfrequently happen, that the little Germans would show some degree of anger, when they were unsuccessful, by giving a blow, and taking up a stone and unceremoniously hurl it at the head of a competitor, which the little Indians would receive with the utmost complacency. I was one day amused by seeing a struggle between an Indian and a German, the former was younger, but more active than the latter, and the little son of the forest was evidently playing with the strength of his adversary; the German became heated, and exerting all his strength, endeavored to throw his adversary with some force upon the ground, but the wily Indian gave a sudden trip, which caused the German to fall beneath: who, rising angrily, seized a stone and levelled his opponent to the earth. The chiefs who were near laughed very heartily, for the little white faces did not stay to see the result, but ran hastily homewards, dreading the severe catigation. In all and every transaction, we had with the Indians, we found them mild and peaceable; and as just related, not disposed to revenge, when the act appeared to be a momentary burst of passion. I have often seen the little Brennemans, children of a Mennonist emigrant, playing in the most sportive and innocent manner with the little red faces, and I never knew or heard of one little white face receiving an injury from their red brethren; that is, no intentional injury.

1720—Arrival of a Ship-Load of Germans and Swiss Immigrants Not Officially Recorded.

In the American Weekly Mercury, under date of September 1, 1720, there is an item stating that "the ship Laurel, John Cappel from Liverpool, with 240 odd Palatines, who came here to settle" just arrived.

This is the only place where a record of this shipload of these people is to be found. It is not in "Rupp's Thirty Thousand Names," nor in any of the ship registers. Pennypacker in his preface to the reprinted first volume of the Mercury says that this is the only place any knowledge of this particular shipment of immigrants is to be found. The "American Weekly Mercury," which began publication on the 22nd of December, 1719, in Philadelphia, was the third newspaper in United States, in point of time. The first was a newspaper called "Public Occurances," first issued September 25, 1690, in Boston, then the "Boston News Letter," first issued in 1704—then the "Mercury." There was a paper known as the "Boston Gazette," issued on the 21st of December, 1719, but as that was the only issue, we may say it died the day it began, and thus, could hardly be called a newspaper.

1720—The Absence of Avarice in Early German-Swiss Life.

We are told in an article in Vol. 7 of Haz. Reg., p. 150, of a reply made by a Mennonite in 1720 upon an offer of 1000 acres of land granted to him In the year 1720, a thousand acres were offered to an influential member of the Amish faith by the proprietary agent, but he refused the grant saying "It is beyond my desire, also my ability to clear; if clear beyond my power to cultivate; if cultivated, it would yield more than my family could consume; and as the rules of our Society forbid the disposal of the surplus, I can not accept your liberal offer; but you may divide it among my married children, who at present reside with me." This individual is supposed to have been a man named Kurtz.

1720—Conrad Beissel Reaches America This Year.

According to Harris' Biographical History of Lancaster County, p. 44, Conrad Beissel arrived in America in 1720, and settled at Millport, in Lancaster County in 1729; where he and a companion built a house. His services to the early colonists in arranging Indian matters, is one of the greatest instances of life devoted to betterment of conditions to be found. About 1759, as I recollect it, there was an attempt to burn his house. Bundles of straws were laid about the doors and windows and ignited, but the fire was extinguished. It is a remarkable fact that nearly 150 years later, a similar attempt to burn that same house resulted in its destruction about 1909 or '10. This Millport, however, is now in Berks County, but was in 1729 part of Lancaster County.

1721—German-Swiss Object to Bearing Arms.

In Vol. 2 of the Votes of Assembly, p. 297, it is stated that on the 12th of October of that year a petition of a considerable number of Swiss- Palatines, setting forth the reason for removing themselves or their families into this province, and praying leave to bring in a bill for their naturalization and to be exempt from swearing and bearing arms was presented to the House and read. The Assembly ordered the bills to lie on the table so as to be examined by the members of the House afterwards for action upon it. This would be an interesting document of these good people and the early times if it could be found. I cannot find any act passed to relieve them from bearing arms but they were frequently naturalized from time to time as they applied. I am inclined to believe that they could be relieved from military service only by paying a bounty as has been the law in some later days.

1721—Mennonist Outlet to Philadelphia.

This year we find there was a proceeding to improve the road which led from the Mennonite Colony about Conestoga to Philadelphia. The record is set forth in Vol. 3 of the Col. Rec., p. 142. The petitioners state that the Judges of the Courts of Chester County lately directed a road to be laid out in the highway to Conestoga, which road runs through uninhabited land quite up to the Mennonite settlement on this side of Conestoga and they think that the change that is asked for here is not a good one. These good people had a road of some inferior character as early as 1714 and in a petition filed in the Quarter Sessions of Lancaster County in 1734, to improve it, they speak of having used it for 20 years before that date. It was also proposed to make a King's Highway out of it as early as May, 1718, and the Mennonite people around Conestoga were the leaders in trying to get this improvement, for which they signed a petition that same year. This may be seen in Vol. 3 of the Col. Rec., p. 43. This road was what is now known as the Long Lane, passing through Conestoga, Pequea and other townships to the East, beginning at Rock Hill and going through Strasburg. It was the earliest outlet to Philadelphia that these ancient people had.

1721—The Conestoga Palatines Assist in the Indian Treaty of This Year.

In Vol. 3 of the Col. Rec., p. 121, it is set forth, under date of July 5th, that year, that the Governor arrived at Conestoga at noon and in the evening went to Captain Civility's cabin. The Governor held part of the treaty at the cabins of the different Chiefs' and then adjourned to the house of John Cartlidge and continued the treaty on the 8th of July. It appeared that large numbers of the Swiss Palatines were present at this treaty and the Indians told the Governor that they would take very good care that these settlers were not interfered with, and the Governor refers to the town of Conestoga, that is, the Indian town.

We are to notice here that the Indians' dwellings are referred to as cabins and not tents; so they likely built small houses here. Some light on this treaty and the conditions about Conestoga is given in a small book published on Neath Street, Dublin, in 1723. The publisher there goes on to say that the Indian Village of Conestoga lies 70 miles directly west of Philadelphia, and that the land there is very rich and is "now surrounded with divers fine plantations or farms, where they raise quantities of wheat, barley, flax and hemp, without the help of any dung." I merely quote this so as to give a picture of the forwardness of agriculture by our Mennonite ancestors at this early date of 1723. We must remember that they had only reached this section five or six years before, and thus, that they were good farmers is clearly shown. This was in the neighborhood of what is now Indiantown, in the central part of Manor Township. The account further goes on to state that the Governor was attended by between 70 and 80 horsemen well armed and that when they arrived there, great amounts of provisions were provided. Thus, we see that our ancestors were

1721—The Taking Up of Land in Conestoga.

In the Taylor Papers, No. 3323, there is a paper indorsed "lands in Chester County" and on one of the first pages, this heading, "lands on Pequea and Conestoga, 58937 acres." I cannot tell how early this account was set forth of lands surveyed in Conestoga, for our Mennonite ancestors; but it is as early as 1721 and perhaps earlier. This shows that at that time, the immense sum of nearly 100 square miles of land was surveyed and taken up. In paper 3349, a surveyor renders a bill for surveying Conestoga Manor, which is now Manor Township 16,500 acres. And about the same time, a survey on Chickies is set forth. Taylor sets forth his authority for all of this. I cite this simply to show the activity among our ancestors at this time and in fact, from 1714 onward, in the Taylor Papers, there are letters upon letters, showing the extreme anxiety for land on the Conestoga. About this time complaint was made that nearly all the back lands were taken up and there is very little more to sell.

1721—Ores Discovered in Conestoga.

Under the date of the 17th of February, 1721, No. 2-22 Taylor, Paper No. 2975, the following letter is found:
"Isaac Taylor, Esteemed Friend:— These inform thee yt there has come into this province from New England a gentleman named John McNeal and he hath been with me and hath viewed ye iron ore and matter yt we laid out. I suppose yt I will sell to them as I have advised him to note how we shall ye most easy way come at ye land, if we conclude with business for if any old rights can be had, I incline most to make a purchase yt way; however thy opinion in yt matter is what is desired by me, and a line or two from thy hand to advise, till an opportunity present a conversation and consultation yt best measures further about ye same, which is all at present. Respectfully from the true and loving friend, John Cartlidge." The sense of the above letter is that ore was found about Conestoga, and John Cartlidge wanted to find out whether he could buy some of the land that contained the ore deposits.

1721—The Road From Philadelphia to Conestoga, Spoken Of.

In 3 Col. Rec. p. 142, is given some light on how the country was developing around Conestoga. In a petition signed by a considerable number of those people, setting forth that a new road was lately laid out and cleared in the highway to Conestoga; which "runs all along through uninhabited and unsettled lands, quite up to the Palatine settlements on this side of Conestoga"; and they then go on and ask to have certain changes made on this road and viewers are appointed etc., for that purpose. I quote this simply to show the activity of that time.

1721— Palatines Tell Why they Left the Palatinate.

In Vol. 2, Votes of Assembly, p. 297, under this date, the Palatines set forth that for religious reasons and financial difficulties, etc., they left the Rhine valley and came to Conestoga Country, where greater liberty of conscience was allowed them.

1722—Activity on the Conestoga River

In Vol. 9 of the Penna. Arch., p. 714, there is a record of 200 acres granted near Stephen Atkinson above Conestoga Manor to Edna Dougherty and (at p. 718) a return made of an additional grant. Page 720 "Casper the Smith" having desired a tract of land, is given 100 acres" where some Indians settled on Conestoga Creek, this year, asked for 200 acres, two near Atkinson's mill." On the same page it is recorded that "Stephen Atkinson requests the grant of a parcel of land lying in the barrens behind his plantation for erecting a mill and that "Logan has writ to Isaac Taylor about it; Vide book of letters." The land was given to him.

1722— Settlement Activity on Ootoraro

In the same book, p. 714, John Asler or Hassler, a tailor, is recorded as having made a settlement near Arthur Park on a branch of Octoraro -about the same time John Seager asks for a tract (p . 710),—also on the Susquehanna, Gordon Howard, two miles from Garlbseath's Mill to the northward and about four miles back of Susquehanna River (p. 713) —also Pat Cammel wants land on the Suspuehanna River (p. 715).

1722—Mennonite Hospitality and Charity towards Indians.

In Vol. 3, Col. Rec. p. 153, we find it recorded that this year the Palatines undertook to bring corn to the Indians at Conestoga as their stock seemed to be exhausted. It seems, however, there was to be a small payment for the same. This was the season of hard times—the first panic in Pennsylvania. We are told also in the same book, p. 179 and 180, that there was great scarcity of bread at Conestoga and the Governor went up to that country to find out how pressing the need was, (p. 181).

1723—Conestoga Township Divided.

The good old German-Swiss region of Lancaster County, known as Conestoga originally, included all the region from the Susquehanna River almost to the Octorara—particularly all of the great middle belt of our County. It extended south to present Drumore, east to the Gap, including the Earls, Leacocks, etc. In 1720, Salisbury and Gap and adjacent sections were organized into Pequea Township. Our present Pequea Township is no part of old Pequea Township. The inhabitants were the Davises, Powells, Galts, Clarks, Morgans, Cooksins, Collins, and others. The Lefevers and Ferrees are also mentioned; but they lived farther north than we now think. (Cope and Futhey.) This section was not really a part of old Conestoga proper.

But the northwest section of West Conestoga included what is now Donegal, Conoy, Mount Joy, Rapho, etc. In 1723, this section was cut off from the old Township.

Most of the inhabitants in the new section were Scotch-Irish; but a few Germans were also in that section,-- Ephraim Moor, Jos. Woork, John Gardner and others.

1723—John Meylin Joins Ephrata Community.

Rupp (74) makes a simple note of the fact of John Meylin joining the Sieben Taeger (Seventh Day) fraternity at Ephrata and assuming the name "Amos" or "Bruder Amos." There does not seem, at the present day, to be any branch of the Meylin family so connected.

1723—German Palatines of New York Come to Pennsylvania.

In the great German Exodus of 1709, of which we have spoken before, Governor Hunter brought 3,000 of those Palatines (who were landed and stranded in England in the Exodus) to New York. They camped or lived in New York till the fall of 1710, and

POVERTY OF THE PALATINE IMMIGRANTS.

then the Queen of England provided for their transportation to a wilderness near Schoharie, New York, where it seems one of the chiefs of the Five Nations gave a tract of land, because this chief and several of his tribe (who were in England to get England to send a force to reduce the French in Canada), saw the destitute condition of these Germans, while they lay in England in their poverty and misery.

The laws of New York did not suit the Germans—and therefore, in 1723, they asked permission to come to Pennsylvania. They were allowed to do so, and settled on Tulpehocken and Swatara Creeks—becoming the foundation of some of the best German stock of Upper Lancaster, Dauphin and Montgomery Counties. Conrad Weiser descended from them. (Rupp 183 and 4.) The petition of these people for permission to come to Pennsylvania is also found in the Colonial Records.

1723—Mary Ditcher and Palatines.

According to Hazard (See Register Vol. 9, p. 113) the first proprietor of the western end of the Hempfields, was a peculiar old German woman named Mary Ditcher. Rupp also quotes Hazard (p. 189) and says that "the land back from the River was settled principally by Germans—Forrys, Stricklers, Sherricks, Garbers, etc." Their first purchase was from an old woman, who used to go through the country making what was then called "improvements"—a few sticks piled together—a fire kindled and a pot hung over it. This constituted a first right. Those who could pay for the land had first choice; but these "improvements" were generally bought for a trifle. Mary Ditcher is described as wandering through the woods, leading an old horse, her only property, with her knitting in her hand; and clad in a garment chiefly of sheep skin. This was called Hempfield because of the great quantities of hemp raised.

1723—Weavers Take Up Weber-Thal.

Rupp says (p. 191) that while the Welsh were making improvements, some Swiss and Germans settled in Weber-Thal, south of Conestoga Creek, so called from the Webers or Weavers who took up between two and three thousand acres of land in 1723 or 4. George Weber and Hans Guth, brothers-in-law, and Jacob Weber and Henry Weber, all Swiss, were the first settlers, contiguous to the Welsh. The name "Guth" became "Good." The Webers and Goods had settled in Lancaster County twelve or fifteen years earlier and lived near the present city of Lancaster. A good account of their early movements and connections is contained in a record owned in 1842 by Samuel Weaver.

1723—Our Poor Palatine Ancestors Cannot Pay Passage.

There is a notice in the American Weekly Mercury of January 15, 1723, calling on the Mennonists of Conestoga to pay the passage money of their brethren who were then coming to the Susquehanna Valley and advising them that if the passage money was not paid, the delinquents would be sold into servitude. Therefore, before any of us became overbearing or haughty, we had better look into these ancient names and annals.

The notice is as follows:

"These are to give notice that the Palatines who were advertised to be at the head of Elk River in Maryland, are now come up to Philadelphia and will be disposed of for five years each, to any one paying their passage money at 10 £ per head. If any of their friends, the Dutch at Conestoga, have a mind to clear any of them, they may see them at this Port."

1723—A Hitherto Unknown Ship-load of Palatines.

In the Mercury of June 6th, this year, we find a brief article stating that the Brigantine that came out with the Beaver bound to Philadelphia was not Captain Lee's, but Captain Lee's Brigantine sailed out of the River a tide before Captain Fitch, being bound to Holland, to take in Palatines for Pennsylvania.

I note this item only for the purpose of recording the name of the vessel and of its captain interested in bringing our Mennonite ancestors here, as the records from official sources are not yet complete. Frequently, our people today, try to trace their family history back to the ship in which they arrived.

1724—Everhard Ream Begins Reamstown.

Rupp (p. 190) relates that this year, Ream, whose descendants still reside in the village called after him, began the settlement of the northeastern part of present Lancaster County. He states that Ream journeyed to the spot with his wagon, into the woods thereabout and unloaded his "fixtures and furniture" under an oak tree and lived there until he built a small hut on what is now known as (or was in 1843) the Lesher farm. He gives as Ream's earliest neighbors, the Buchers, Hubers, Walters, Kellers, Leaders, Schwarwalders, Schneiders, Killians, Docks, Forneys, Rupps, Balmers, Mays, Mayers, Hahns, Resslers, Boyers, Leets, Schlotts, Groffs, Wolfs, Feiersteins, Weidmans and others. He does not tell us the source of his information.

In the Second Series of the Penna. Archives, Vol. 19, p. 725, there is recorded a minute that "Eberhard Ream of Conestoga requests a grant of about 200 acres of land on a branch of that creek including a small Indian settlement called Cocalico. He had the Indians "consent to settle and can pay the purchase money down."

This is very definite. It shows that Conestoga was recognized as extending up to the region of Adamstown, etc., and this lay entirely across the present county, following up the Conestoga Creek, almost to its source. It also definitely locates a small Indian village; and shows his fair dealing and that he had means.

1724—Our Swiss Mennonite Ancestors Begin the Settlement of Salunga and Chickies.

In the book last mentioned (p. 724) we find that this year, Michael Shank requested and was allowed 250 acres of land near Checosolungas. Jacob Graeff requested the same amount near that place. Henry Work and John Garrett were also given tracts of land (the size not specified) at this time "near Conestoga or Shecossolungus." "'Shecossolungus" is our Chickies Creek.

1724—Additional German-Swiss Settlements at Conestoga.

In the Second Series of the Pennsylvania Archives (p. 721) it is recorded that Mart Mayley desires a grant of 100 acres in the "Point" in a fork of Conestoga Creek, near the land called "William Willis's," to make tiles and bricks. At p. 724, there is a request by Christian Herr for 50 acres of ordinary land in Conestoga, joining his other land. And p. 726, it is recorded that James Als Couradt, rector, requests the grant of a piece of land near Conestoga, adjoining to Frederickful. Just what and where "Frederickful" is, we cannot tell.

1724—Earliest Known Tile and Brick Yard in Lancaster County.

Referring to the last named item, we may call attention to the fact that Mart Mayley (or Mylin), very likely, made the first tiles and brick in this county. We know there were tiled houses here very early. Mart Mylin was evidently a genius. Rupp tells us (p. 74) that in 1719, he erected a Boring Mill on Mylin's Run, in West Lampeter Township, and that he was also the first gunsmith in our county.

1724—Our Swiss Mennonist Brethren Apply for Naturalization.

Rupp (p. 194) notices the efforts that our Swiss ancestors were compelled to make in order to be naturalized, to hold land and pass it on to their children, at their death; for without naturalization, they could not do so. He states that as early as 1721, they began to petition for naturalization, but it was not until 1724 that they were given permission to bring a bill before the Assembly, to naturalize them. It could only be done then, provided each German or Swiss would obtain from a Justice of the Peace, a certificate of the value of his property, the nature of his religious faith, etc.

The proceedings in 1724, for naturalization came up in April, and in Vol. 2, Votes of Assembly, (p. 388) it is related that a petition of a great number of persons who were born under the allegiance of the Emperor of Germany, setting forth that they have moved themselves into this province and their families, and have purchased lands which they are not capable to hold for them and their heirs, and therefore, they pray that they may be enabled by a law, to buy and hold lands and enjoy the same benefits as the rest of the inhabitants—was filed. The Assembly ordered it to lay on the table. The next day it was read again and debated, and it was resolved that as many of these petitioners as shall bring certificates from the Justices of the Courts, signifying the lands they hold and of what conversation they are reputed; and also have taken the oath or affirmation and declaration of fidelity and allegiance, and set forth the profession of their religious belief as the law directs, shall have leave to bring in a bill; but the Assembly orders that the Justices shall examine this matter very closely.

It seems that there was still more difficulty for our ancestors because the Register General now began to stir up strife against them, and to make it appear that they were suspicious characters, (2 Votes 391). However, they were finally naturalized in 1727. Two, however, Casper Wister and John Cartho, under the allegiance of the Emperor of Germany, were naturalized this year (Vol. 3, Statutes at Large, p. 424); and a great many others later.

1725—The Swiss Take Up Land in the Susquehanna Valley.

In Vol. 2 of the Penna. Arch., p. 734, we find that in 1725, Mathias Stauffer recommended by Christian Herr, requests the grant of a piece of land on the Checosolangas; and the same year, according to the same book (p. 729) Jacob Funk requested the grant of 50 acres adjoining his other tract in Conestoga. The same year several tracts were granted on the Octorara —one of 300 acres to John Devour near John Musgrave's (p. 726)—one to Robert Burd, 100 acres near the place called Horse Hook, formerly of Cornelius Empson (127) — one to George Carr at the head of the Octorara, where he wished to carry on tanning (p. 723) one to Hugh Morrison, Thomas Paxton, Hugh Robinson and Lawrence Small, near the same place (p. 734)—one to James Harlan (p. 734) between the Octorara Creek and the Susquehanna River and one requested by Mrs. Musgrave for John Cohalan. As these are not German Swiss people, but rather English, we will say no more about them and only metion them for the sake of regularity.

The same year lands were taken up in Pequea; but we must remember that Pequea was the region about the head of the Pequea Creek, north of the Gap, and we find in the same book (p. 729) that Robert Eyes, a cooper, was given a tract of land and (p. 734) that William and James Johnson his son, requested a tract on a branch of the Pequea Creek called Cat Tail.

1725 — Governor Keith, a Friend of Our Mennonite Ancestors.

About the year 1725, the Governor of Pennsylvania began to realize that our English laws discriminated too severely against the Germans and Swiss. In that year Governor Keith, in the message to the Assembly, found in Vol. 2, Votes of Assembly, (p. 442), among other things, states that as to the "Palatine Bill," as he called it, he is of the same opinion he was the year before—that the producing of certificates is not a proper method of securing the allegiance of these people to the king and this government, but that it is not agreeable to English liberty or to the proprietor's declaration for encouraging settlement of the colony and much less to the freedom of conscience, so much professed here, to demand other qualifications to settle any man to the right of an English subject, than what we have prescribed by law, namely, affirmation of allegiance. The provision made in this intended law to prevent these persons from enjoying privileges of this government, unless they go and take a legal qualification, is not only the best but the most justifiable method (and that we have many precedents in England); but he says that to demand a strict inquiry into private conversion and the religious faith of these people, other than what the law directs, and especially to pry into the circumstances of their private estate, would be contrary to natural and equal justice and a dangerous precedent, and would injure our reputation as a free country. The Governor, therefore, hoped that they would have a particular regard against being drawn into propositions and new emthods inconsistent with liberty. He goes on to say that he thinks it is a very hard case to deny a stranger who has purchased land in this province, the right to transmit those lands to his children; therefore, he approves of the bill, only so far as it requires a qualification to be made, but he does not approve inquiring into the religious beliefs and private estate of these people. A few days later he goes on to say that he congratulates them on passing a liberal law for the ease of conscience, and that he expects them to use their best endeavors among the people to convince them of the peace and quiet we enjoy. He then says that he wants to impress upon them the bill which lies still before them, not acted upon, in behalf of some "protestants from the Palatinate and other parts of Germany," who have a great desire for the blessing of the English Government. He also says that they have seen him personally and in the humblest manner have besought him that he should have extended to them the same terms of naturalization, granted in England to foreign protestants.

1725—Our German Swiss Ancestors Very Grateful to the Governor; and They Stand by Him.

It seems that a very stern struggle

was before our Mennonite forefathers here to secure their right to make wills and deed land over or to have it pass to their children, on their death, unless they made certain affirmations. On the 25th of November this year, there was a petition of 237 of these people setting forth the tender care and kindness of the present Governor and the many advantages of the religious and civil rights of the people that have been granted by him and especially by the creation of paper money, which is very much appreciated by them. They go on in this petition and state that they are his friends and that they know that he is grossly misrepresented in the province of Pennsylvania to the proprietor for his enterprising stand taken and that there may probably be a change in the government by a new governor being sent. They pray the house in this petition and the governor, that as they are faithful people, that their needs be recognized and that the true state of affairs concerning the blessing paper money has been to the people here shall be sent to the proprietor at home, so that their friend, the governor, may be saved from removal by his enemies and by the misrepresentations made concerning him. This petition they filed in the House of Representatives and begged the representatives to stand up for the governor and not let him be scandalized. Paper money was opposed by England.

1725—A Large Number of Our German-Swiss Brethren Desire to be Naturalized.

The records of the Assembly Nov. 24, 1725, show that the petition of high and low Germans on taking and subscribing the qualification required by law, that they may have a bill passed, to enable them to hold and enjoy lands and to engage in trade and merchandise was laid before the house. This simply means that they applied for naturalization.

1725—The Early Mennonist Ministers, Because Aliens, Were Not Allowed to Perform a Marriage Ceremony.

There was a law in the early days of Pennsylvania that only the ministers of the State Church could perform marriage ceremonies. Rev. Anthony Hinkle was arrested for marrying a pair. This was because he was an alien minister, there being a law against an alien minister joining parties in matrimony. (Vol. 2, Votes of Assembly, p. 465.) We can readily see, therefore, that so long as ministers of our Mennonite ancestors were not naturalized, they were aliens, and could not perform the marriage ceremony. These are some of the hardships in early Pennsylvania, that people hardly dream of as existing.

1726—Mennonist Neighbors at Donegal.

This year James Anderson, a Presbyterian Minister, who formerly lived at New Castle, desired to settle among the people at Donegal and asked a grant of 300 acres there, he being a person of good repute at New Castel. The Land Commissioners thought he would be of great service in this neighborhood and Secretary Logan also desired that the land be granted him. (Sec. Ser. Pa. Arch., Vol. 19, p. 745.)

1726—Mennonist Neighbors along the Susquehanna and Octorara.

This year there was granted to Mordecai Maydock 375 acres of land on the Susquehanna, which his father, Henry Maydock, had the right to, by a writing from William Penn, dated May 6, 1691. Peter Risk was also given 400 acres at the same time; and this year, Elisah Gatchell and others were given three tracts of land, "on the running water of Conowingo," where there was a vacancy; and Emanuel Grubb was given 100 ocres on the same place, on the northeast side of his former tract. James Daniel and Robert Mackell were given land by request of the Minister Craighead. James King and Charles Allen and Josiah were given land on the Octorara—also John Kirkpatrick and Moses Ross and William Evans and Thomas Jackson and James Buchannan and Alexander Allison and Alexander Montgomery. Jackson and Buchannan were given 200 acres each —Evans 60 acres and the size of the others are not mentioned. (See the book last mentioned pp. 729-740-742-744 two grants—745 two grants and 743 three different grants.)

1726—More Swiss Brethren Buy Land on Conestoga.

According to Vol. 19, Sec. Ser. Pa. Arch., this year Ulrich Burkhold, Hans Krow, and Hans Leaman requested land through Christian Herr, among the Swiss Colonists near Conestoga (Vide p. 742).

The same year Henry Zimmerman or Carpenter set forth that Henry Vinger (Wenger), who had some years ago settled on a piece of land of Henry Richmann formerly, and that Wenger died, leaving a widow and three sons. But that John Musgrove's son has settled on the land. He desires the same (200 acres) to be turned over to Widow Wenger (or Vinger), see p. 743.

The same year Henry Zimmerman requested a grant of 600 acres of land on a branch of the Conestoga (Do).

The same year John Eby requested a grant of a vacant piece of land on a branch of Conestoga Creek to build a grist mill upon as a convenience to the neighborhood (Vide 745).

This is no doubt the origin of Eby's Mill on Mill Creek, a branch of the Conestoga, because in 1728, when the old Peter's Road was recorrnized and first laid out by law as appears in the Road Records of Chester County, (which I have personally examined), one of the courses surveyed extends to Torus or Dorus Eby's Mill, this being a contraction of Theodorus Eby. Likely Theodorus was a son of John, the original applicant for land.

The same year Hans Hess of Conestoga requested 75 acres of land for his son Jacob, between a branch of Conestoga and land of Hans Ulrich, adjoining his own tract (Do. 746).

And Thos. Honenger and Phil Shong requested the grant of land for two settlements on a branch of Conestoga, the same year (Do. 746)—Also Hans Miller for 100 acres on Little Conestoga—recommended by Christopher Franciscus (Do) — also Sebastian, Beyer and Geo. Goodman requested the grant of a parcel of land; each near Conestoga (Do).

1726—Pequea Additions.

In the book last noted (p. 743) we find that this date, 200 acres of land were granted to Wm. Richardson and a like amount granted to Samuel Robinson, both located on Pequea.

1726 — German-Swiss Beginning to Take Part in Public Affairs.

In Vol. 3, Votes of Assembly, p. 4, there is mention that Ludwig Sprogle was a member of Assembly. He was active on a committee to induce England to allow salt to be imported.

1726—Our German Ancestors Again Petition for Right to Pass Land to Their Sons.

It is stated Vol. 2, Votes of Assembly, p. 461, that a large number of high and low Germans have presented a petition asking that upon their qualifying, according to law, they may be empowered to hold and transmit land and enjoy trade, etc. (See also 3 Col. Rec. 241). The Assembly replied by proposing to tax them three pounds each and then they are to be allowed same privilege in holding land as others, (2 Votes of Assembly, p. 467).

1726—Another German Minister Punished for Performing a Marriage.

Anthony Hinkle, a German minister of the Gospel, who was fined for performing a marriage for two people, refused to pay the fine and costs and was committed to prison, (2 Votes of Assembly 470).

1726—Our German-Swiss Ancestors a Mark for Vagrancy.

In Vol. 2, Votes of Assembly, p. 466, we find a complaint made this year about vagrants and horse thieves on the Susquehanna, preying upon the thrifty Germans and Swiss. The Assembly took note that a great number of convicts and some Irish servants of low character had arrived and a great many more were expected; and it was decided that there should be a fine of five pounds a head put upon all of them. This condition is noticed in the petition to create Lancaster County, which sets forth that along the Susquehanna, the people not having local government, are very great victims of robbers and horse thieves and vagabonds. On the 19th of June, 1726, a petition was signed by the citizens of Conestoga setting forth that many vagabonds resorted to that neighborhood, praying that the law be provided to suppress them. (Vol. 2, Votes of Assembly 468). In a little while the newspapers began to notice this unlawful condition and in the Pa. Gaz. of April 12, 1729, the following item occurs: "We hear that there are associated together a company of Irish robbers, the chief of whom are said to be one Bennet, whom they call their captain, and one Lynch, whom they call their lieutenant, with Dobbs, Wiggins and many others, who sulk about this and neighboring provinces; their villianies being to steal the best horses and load them with the best goods, and carry them off before the people's faces, which they have done lately in and about Conestoga. It seems their usual practice has been to steal horses from this province and carry them to sell into Maryland, Virginia and North Carolina. It is said that they begin to grow more numerous and have a place of rendezvous where they meet to consult how to perpetrate their rogueries and entertain all like themselves." This last note is three years later than 1726, but it is intimately connected with this subject, and I, therefore, insert it at this place.

1726—Trouble to Collect Taxes Among Our Ancestors on Conestoga.

In Vol. 2, Votes of Assembly, p. 491, we find it set forth that the people on Conestoga began to neglect and refused to pay their excises and other taxes to the province in their sense of immunity from being so far away from the officers of the law—the county seat being at Old Chester, 100 miles distant. It is hard to say at this time whether this complaint was made against our German-Swiss brethren or the people generally, but we can readily understand that in the face of the hardships, the German-Swiss were undergoing, because they were not allowed to hold and transmit land, they being foreigners, that they might very readily feel like retaliating, by withholding the tax upon lands which they were not certain whether they had a good title to or not.

1726—The Law to Naturalize Germans.

In Vol. 4, Statutes at Large, p. 457, we find set forth a law to naturalize several Germans who had moved to this province. They do not seem to be Lancaster County names, as their names are not familiar here; and there are only a few of them. They are Bernard Van Lear, Arent Hassert, Michael Smiths, Wm. Selliger, Arnolt Bambarger, Wm. Hilligart and Ulrich Haggeman. The Statute states that they are born under the allegiance of the Emperor of Germany.

1727—More Lands Taken Up By Our German-Swiss Brethren in the Susquehanna Valley.

Benjamin Roads, recommended by sundry inhabitants of Conestoga, was granted 100 acres near a branch of Conestoga this year. (Vol. 19, 3rd Ser. Pa. Arch., p. 748.) Henry Bear was given 100 acres, adjoining his other land on Little Conestoga, (Do. 751.) Joseph Hickenbolten and Joseph Sterman requested a piece of vacant land lying between their plantations near the Conestoga Creek's mouth, (Do.). Anthony Breller requested a piece of land near his own settlement, "near the Dutch Mill" (Do.). Killian Law requested a piece on Mill Creek (Do.). Jacob Rife, Ulrick Sauck, Rudolph Bear, Jacob Lintner, John Snevely, Jacob Snevely, John Long, Casper Hoorn, Derrick Miller and Christian Graybill were recommended by several old settlers to have land to settle upon at Conestoga, (Do). Richard Carter in behalf of his kinsman, Henry Noland, requested 200 acres on the east side of Lewis Lewis', under the barren hills some distance from Conestoga, (Do.). William Cloud requested 300 acres of vacant surveyed land on the Conestoga. Nathan Evans requested 100 acres east of his other land to erect a mill, (Do. 753). John Burkholder requested a grant of 200 acres adjoining Benjamin Hershey's land on Little Conestoga, and it is stated that he is ready to pay cash for it, (Do. 755). All of these persons received the land which they asked for very shortly after their request.

1727—More Neighbors on Octorara.

This year Hugh Morrison requested land on the Octorara, (Do. 745). Albert Edwards requested 200 acres adjoining the old settlement that Francis Warley owned, (Do. p. 747). John Musgrove obtained 300 acres but sold his right to Roger Dyer and George Legerd, (Do. 748). Abraham Emmett requested lands for three settlements on the Octorara, (Do. p. 750). Robert Wright requested land on Octorara, (Do. 750). John Tinner, from Ireland, requested land on the Octorara (Do. 751). John Creswell, for himself and Robert Stewart. requested the same, (Do.). Robert Evans requested 250 acres on the west branch of the Octoraa, (Do. 752). Robert Love requested a parcel near Octorara, (Do. 754). Hugh Berkely and George Patterson requested land on Octorara, (Do. 754). All these requests were made in 1727, and in every case the land was granted a little later.

1727—Neighbors on Pequea.

John Barnett desired 200 acres near Joseph Hinkman, (Do. 750) and Pallso Friends (a very odd name) who dwelt with Daniel Ferree, desired a tract of vacant land on the south side of Pequea, (Do. 756) and Peter Bazillion requested 200 acres of land adjoining other lands where he dwells, 100 acres at each end of his tract,(Do. 747). These requests were made in 1727 and were granted.

1727—Grants on Susquehanna.

The Commissioners by their warrant of June 2, 1718, had granted to Peter Chartier 300 acres on Susquehanna, which he afterwards sold to Stephen Atkinson, and in 1727, Penn's land commissioners confirmed Atkinson's title for these 300 acres, (Do. 749). The same year James Moore requested land on the Susquehanna,

LANDS TAKEN UP—NEW HOLLAND FOUNDED. 227

(Do. 750)—and William Brackin requested land on Fishing Creek near Susquehanna, (Do. 754). Nathaniel Newlin and Joseph Cloud requested 500 acres on the Susquehanna, (Do.). And near Susquehanna, on Chickies, John McNile requested land and has sent another letter that an order be made out to him, which was done, (Do. 747). The commissioners having prior, by two warrants, granted to Thomas Griffith the right of 1500 acres which on Chickies Creek, Thos. Griffith, in 1724, transferred his right to Isaac Norris and in 1727 Isaac Norris was given a deed from the commissioners dated April 15th for the same, he to pay 100 pounds, (Do. 749)—and also on Susquehanna near Donegal, this same year, Richard Allison requested a tract above Donegal, called "Cornish's Plains," (Do. 750)—and Jonas Davenport, having purchased certain improvements of Leonard Millborn, an inhabitant of Donegal, requested a deed for 200 acers made to him which was done, (Do. 750). He also requested 300 acres more on the upper side of the mouth of Swatara Creek, (Do. 750)—and John Galbreta requested 200 acres at the same place; and William Alexander, recommended by James Anderson, requested land to settle about Donegal on the Susquehanna. These requests were all made in 1727 and were granted.

1727—Origin of the Hans Graeff Holdings.

In the Volume last set out above, p. 746, we find under the date of 1727 that Hans Graeff requested the grant of a piece of land on the Cocalico Creek, a branch of the Conestoga, to build a grist mill for the accommodation of his neighbors. It was granted to him.

1727—German-Swiss Begin to Register About This Year.

The law was fast requiring shipowners to take a list of all the Germans and Swiss that they bring over. These lists were carefully kept and preserved and may be found in the Colonial Records from time to time. They have been collected from Rupp in his "Thirty Thousand Names." This resulted from the fact that the government authorities became frightened at the inrush of so many foreigners. Rupp stated that of course they meant these Non-Resistant Germans and Swiss. Rupp also says that in the year 1727 about a thousand Palatines arrived in this province, (Do. p. 193) and we have observed in the items preceeding that a lot of them were coming, which is shown by the land which was taken up.

1727—Pioneers of New Holland.

According to Rupp, about this year the Diffenderfer Brothers, Alexander and John, sailed from Rotterdam in the ship William and Sarah and arrived here in the Fall. John settled at SaeueSchwamm, (now New Holland) in the woods. His grandson David, who was a son of Michael Diffenderfer, lived to be high in the nineties, and he personally informed Rupp that his grandfather's household goods were brought from Philadelphia by a brother in the faith, by the name of Martin, who unloaded them under an oak tree, but a cabin or hut was built by the aid of the neighbors in a few days, and thus, settlement began in that comfortable and wealthy section, now known as New Holland, (Do. p. 193).

1727—Copy of the Declaration that the German-Swiss Were Required to Sign.

In Vol. 3, Col. Rec., p. 283, (new series) the paper is set forth which had been agreed upon and was drawn up by the authorities of Pennsylvania, which all the Palatines (and this included the Swiss as well as the Germans of the Palatinate) were required to sign, if they came with the intention of settling in the province. The paper is in these words:— "We, Subscribers, Natives and late Inhabitants of the Palatinate upon the Rhine and desiring to transport ourselves and families into this province of Pennsylvania, a Colony subject to the Crown of Great Britain, in hopes and Expectations of finding a Retreat & peaceable settlement therein, Do Solemnly promise & Engage, that We will be faithful and bear true Allegiance to his present MAJESTY KING GEORGE THE SECOND, and his Successors Kings of Great Britain, and will be faithful to the proprietor of this province; And that we will demean ourselves peaceably to all His said Majesties Subjects, and strictly observe and conform to the Laws of England and of this Province, to the utmost of our Power and best of our understanding." This shows what these good people were required to do; and we may mention here that because they and all their successors were required to sign a similar paper that it explains in a large part the reason why there was opposition among them in the Revolutionary War to fight against the mother country, England. It must be remembered that the other settlers in these provinces did not take any such oath or affirmation or make any such similar promise to stand by the British government.

1727—Conestoga Accepts Dortrecht Confession of Faith.

This year the Dortrecht Mennonist Confession of Faith (promulgated at Dortrcht, Holland, in 1632) was adopted in America by formal action. The fifteen Mennonist ministers of America in Conference, signed an Article of its approval and adoption here. Among these ministers, so signing and thus binding themselves and their congregations to that confession of faith were Hans Burkholder, Christian Herr, Benedict Hearshey, and Martin Baer (Bar) of Conestoga — Daniel Longanecker from Manatony. These are all of Berne ancestry. There was also a Henry Hunsecker and other of the Germantown Congregation.

1727—Comment on the Dortrecht Confession.

In a previous article. we noticed how the Mennonists of Conestoga this year accepted the ancient Dortrecht confession of faith, adopted in 1632. A writer of note says that the Mennonists and Aymenists refer for their principle and usages to their confession of faith, published in Philadelphia in 1727. This writer makes note of the fact that this year, to wit, 1727, they changed the method of baptism from immersion to affusion and that thereafter they were no longer known as Baptists or Anna-Baptists. It is not known generally that before that date the Mennonists believed only in immersion as the efficient form of baptism. This writer goes on to say that Aymenists or bearded Mennonists are the Amish of today (7 Haz. Reg. 124.) He also says that the Mennonists used later another confession of faith, one composed by Cornelius Riss, which was published in Hamburg in 1726 (do. 129). He gives a succinct history of the rise of the Mennonists at the page last mentioned and states that it arose largely out of opposition to infant baptism—that their main increase was along the Rhine and Westphalia, Holstein and the Netherlands. He tells of their rising and complete control of Munster, the capital of Westphalia. He speaks of the twenty-six missionaries sent out and notes that Melchior Hoffman was one of the strongest of them. He also says that in early days in Moravia, these people divided into three branches; one called the "buttoners" because they wore buttons; one called the "pinners" because they used wire pins and another the "hookers" because they wore hooks and eyes to fasten their clothes. He also mentions two or three other classes.

1727—German Swiss Immigration into Pennsylvania This Year.

In the year 1727, as we have already stated, the German and Swiss were pouring in so rapidly that the Government determined that they should be put under an oath or promise of allegiance. Ship owners were required to make accurate lists of all of these people who came over to Pennsylvania. Many came before 1727 as the County was pretty largely filled up before that time. But accurate and reliable information as to just how many there were, is to some extent wanting; but from 1727 onward we have reliable information. The Colonial Records show, that in 1727, five ship loads of these people came making a total of about 1,000 persons of whom 270 were male heads of families (3 Colonial Records 284, 287, 288, 290).

The names of the most familiar families that came over during this year are: 2 Martins—4 Bowmans—2 Bairs—2 Graybills—5 Hoffmans—2 Hiestands—4 Leamans—10 Millers—3 Sieglers—2 Siegrists—2 Stauffers—2 Snavelys—2 Swartzes and 2 Zuggs. In addition to that, there were one of each of the following prominent Lancaster County families in this year: Bixler — Diffenderfer — Frey — Funk — Gross — Good — Habecker — Hostler — Keener — Kendig — Longenecker — Landis — Oberholtzer — Swabb — Seitz — Shertz — Snyder — Strickler — Shultz — Schaeffer — Wolf — Weaver and Zimmerman.

As to the ages of these people nothing is set forth in the Pennsylvania Archives (Vol. 17, 2nd. Series Pa. Archives), and none except the names of the men are given—that is only 272 of the 1,000 persons. Beginning about 1730 we frequently find the ages given, names of women and children also and from the ages given in the lists, that are set out in full, we find that a great many of them were between 20 and 40 years old; but a great many of them were very young children also.

1728—German Swiss Immigration into Pennsylvania This Year.

In the year 1728 there was considerable falling off of German Swiss who came into our province. Only three ship loads are mentioned in the records in the Archives (3 Colonial, 327, 328, 331, also Vol. 17, 2nd. Series Pa. Archives, pp. 12 to 15). The number of the heads of families was only 152; including women and children the total number was 390. Among them occurred the following prominent names: 3 Dinkelbergs — 2 Denlingers—3 Grosses—2 Groffs—2 Keelers—4 Millers—2 Myers—2 Mussers—2 Shirks—3 Stauffers—2 Engels—2 Schmidts (Smiths) and also one each of the following representative families: Bair — Bixler — Dumbach — Ebersole — Eshleman — Frey — Hensel — Hoffer — Newcomer — Forrey — Hellar — Neff — Pheffley — Ritter — Strickler — Sellers — Schumaker and Ranch. Nothing is known of the ages of these immigrants.

1728—German-Swiss Arrivals in Lancaster County.

This year Johannes Kitzmiller of Germany, having purchased the consent of Nathaniel Evans, was given a license to build a mill on a vacant piece of land on the Little Conestoga Creek, and he was granted 400 acres there (Sec. Ser. Arch. Vol. 19, p. 757), and Jacob Huver reported 150 acres of vacant land on the west side of the Conestoga Creek, which he desired and it was granted to him (Do. 760). The same year Hans Hess was given 50 acres additional to his settlement near Conestoga (Do.);—and John Burkholder was given 200 acres adjoining Ben Burkholder's land on the Little Conestoga (Do. 755). We find in these names the beginnings of the Burkholder and Hess and Hoover families, who now inhabit the Conestoga locality so numerously. Kitzmiller is not so numerous a name at present; but the name is found frequently in Berks and adjacent counties. Pequea, in the region adjacent to New Holland, received some additional settlers this year, as well as did the Strasburg section; and on the Susquehanna. George Stewart obtained 200 acres, being a part of the land owned by Isaac Taylor, between lands of John Gardner and Robert Wilkins (Do. 759). About the same time, Joseph Jones was given the right to settle on the Conowingo Creek.

1728—England Opposed to Further Swiss Settlement Here.

We have noticed that the proprietor of Pennsylvania and the English inhabitants and owners of the province of Pennsylvania, several times became frightened less the Germans should completely crowd them out. The fear seemed to have reached England this year, because this year governor Gordon stated to the House of Representatives of Pennsylvania, in his address to them, that Great Britain demanded these people should not be allowed to come into Pennsylvania hereafter. Part of his message on this subject is as follows: "I must make use of this Opportunity to acquaint you, that I have now positive Orders from Great Britain to provide by a proper Law, against these crowds of Foreigners who are yearly pour'd in upon us, of which the late Assembly took notice in a message to me of the 18th of April last. Nor does this arise, as I conceive, from any Dislike to the People themselves, many of whom we know are peaceable, industrious and well affected, but it seems principally intended to prevent an English Plantation from being turned into a Colony of Aliens. It may also require our Thoughts to prevent the Importation of Irish Papists and Convicts, of whom some of the most notorious I am credibly informed, have of late been landed in this River." (3 Col. Rec. 342.) It is rather annoying at this late day to have the ancestors of our good German-Swiss people of this county classed with criminals or convicts. The growth of Papacy we can here also see was struck at in these earlier times. All these obstructions put in the way of the earlier settlers add additional luster and glory to their pluck in continuing to come and settle the land.

1728—German-Swiss Actively Trading With Philadelphia.

It is interesting to note the extent of the commercial and industrial activity at different stages of our local historical development. The year 1728 was the year before Lancaster County was formed, and according to Witham Marsh, was the year that the first house was built in the location, which is now Lancaster. Samuel Blunston, who lived on the Susquehanna, in writing a letter to James Logan, dated the 12th of May 1728, among other things, states that "there are a great many wagons going down this week to Philadelphia, and it is needless now to engage any more for you may have your choice." He also states that provisions were very scarce in this section. (1 Pa. Arch. 216.) The reason I mentioned the extracts from this letter is that it shows the activity of our German-Swiss ancestors in trading with Philadelphia. So many wagons moving at that time between Philadelphia and the Conestoga Creek was to give, as he says, in his letter, any one a choice of going down by one of the several wagons continually on the move.

1728—Swiss Brethren Again Ask Holland's Aid.

This year the Swiss brethren suffering for religious sake and desiring to emigrate to America, asked Holland again to aid them. There was great poverty among these suffering people at this time. But they were not all honest in their poverty—not only beggars; but also impostors. A certain Rudolph Agh, a teacher in the non-resistant church was deposed from his office for imposing on the charitably inclined. A Daniel Landes was found making collections without warrant authority, also. He operated in Germany and Holland. In Geroldsheim a Hans Burkholder, a teacher since 1702, was found soliciting from the Holland commissioners, a hundred guilders and then five hundred for the family of Christian Wenger, impoverished as he said, by reason of the cattle disease. The need was found to be genuine. He asserted that the Mennonist congregation at Geroldsheim were subject to an extra assessment or contribution of 1500 guilders toward the expense of the coronation of the new elector. Complaint was made against this by the brethren who felt that Burkholder was urging the government to extract this from his own people, for profit to himself. Numerous complaints were made about this by the brethren, also against the poll tax upon them which was doubled about this time per capita. (Müller 208.)

1728—Swiss and German Brethren Allowed to Come Into Penna. from New York.

This year a number of the non-resistant brethren, who in the Exodus from Germany and Switzerland unto England in 1709 succeeded in reaching New York with the assistance of Governor Hunter, were allowed to settle on Tulpyhocken Creek in Montgomery County and surrounding country. There were 3,000 of them who came to New York, where they lived 19 years and then finding the New York policy not to their advantage, prayed permission to move to Pennsylvania, which they were allowed to do. (3 Col. Rec. 325.)

1728—General Excitement and Alarm Continues in Penna. from the German-Swiss Influx.

The large numbers of our German Swiss ancestors now continually coming to us, increased the general alarm which had excited the people for some time. The Assembly noted that "thousands of Palatines" are now coming and held strongly that they "refused to obey" our laws. (3 Votes of Assembly 42.) It is claimed they were unlawfully on Tulpyhocken Creek. This was false (3 Col. Rec. 325). They were complained against for owning and conveying land, contrary to law, without being naturalized. (3 Votes of Assembly 42.) Many applied to be naturalized but were long delayed. (3 Votes of Assembly 43 and 45.) Reports officially made on their citizenship and behavior were good. (Do.) The government of Pennsylvania appointed a committee with full charge and control of the Mennonist or Palatinate question. (3 Votes of Assembly 46.) Governor Keith was their friend, however. (3 Col. Rec. 325-325.) More petitions to be allowed to hold land were filed by them—but the delay continued. (3 Votes of Assembly 435-436.) The subject of the treatment of our German-Swiss ancestors as to holding of land is comprehensively treated in Mr. Sache's Works and a succinct write-up of the same may be found in the Philadelphia Bulletin of Jan. 31, 1910, under "Men and Things."

1729—German Swiss Immigration into Pennsylvania This Year.

This is the year that Lancaster County was created out of Chester County. The German Swiss immigrants this year consisted, as far as the oath of allegiance is concerned, of only 2 ship loads containing 134 heads of families or a total list of 306 (3 Colonial Record 367, 368, also Vol 17, 2nd. Series of Archives, pp. 15 and 18). The ages are not given; but the names of the female passengers who were on the last ship load are given, however. Turning to the names we find that there were 2 Freys—3 Millers—2 Moores—4 Macks—2 Bossarts —3 Snyders and 2 Weavers in the list and one each of the following: Bowman — Bumgardner — Christ — Eshleman — Hoffer — Killheffer — Longenecker — Rauch—Rote and Snavely.

1729—Naturalization of our German Swiss Ancestors.

As we have written before, the subject of naturalization was a grievance which was continually affecting our ancestors. A great leader in all steps for the advancement of these brethren was Martin Mylin (Rupp 75). He was continually looking out for their welfare. This year a large number of these people were naturalized (Rupp 121). The complete act of naturalization is found in Vol. 4, Statutes at Large, page 147, and, it seems that the original document itself, which Martin Mylin so ably helped to secure, was in the possession of himself and his descendants for many years. Rupp states that 114 years it was in the possession of the Mylin family; and when he wrote his history of the county, Abraham Mylin of West Lampeter Township near Willow Street had the original naturalization act and showed it to him. The act as set forth in the Statutes at Large, omitting such parts as are repetitions is as follows: "An act for the better enabling divers inhabitants of the province of Pennsylvania to hold lands, and to invest them with the privileges of natural-born subjects of the said province.

Whereas by the encouragement given by the Honorable William Penn, Esquire, late proprietary and governor of the province of Pennsylvania, and by the permission of his late Majesty, King George the First, of blessed memory, and his predecessors, Kings and Queens of England, etc., divers Protestants who were subjects to the Emperor of Germany, a prince in amity with the Crown of Great Britain, transported themselves and estates into the province of Pennsylvania between the years one thousand seven hundred and one thousand seven hundred and eighteen, and since they came hither have contributed to the enlargement of the British Empire and to the raising and improving sundry commodities fit for the markets of Europe, and have always behaved themselves religiously and peaceably, and have paid a due regard and obedience to the laws and government of this province. ....

(Section 1.) Be it enacted by the Honorable Patrick Gordon, Esquire, (Lieutenant) Governor of the Province of Pennsylvania, etc., by and with the advice and consent of the freemen of the said Province in General Assembly met, and by the authority of the same, That Martyn Mylin, Hans Graaf, Christian Stonemen, Jacob Funk, Francis Neiff, Junior;

George Kindick, John Burkholder, John Burkholder, Junior; Abraham Burkholder, Michael Bohman, John Hess, John Frederick, Christopher Preniman, Martin Harnist, Joseph Buckwalter, Felix Landas, Junior; Adam Preniman, John Funk, John Bohman, John Taylor, Henry Neiff, Michael Mire, Henry Bare, Peter Bumgarner, Melcor Hufford, Melcor Erishman, John Brubaker, Jacob Nisley, Jacob Snevely, Jacob Goot, John Woolslegle, Jacob Mire, Christopher Sowers, Joseph Stoneman, Daniel Ashleman, Christian Peelman, John Henry Neiff, John Henry Neiff, Junior; Abraham Hare, John Ferie, Jacob Biere, Peter Yordea, Peter Leamon, John Jacob Snevely, Isaac Coffman, Andrew Coffman, Woolrick Rodte, Henry Funk, Roody Mire, John Mylin, Jacob Bheme, John Coffman, Michael Doneder, Charles Christopher, Andres Shults, John Howser, Christian Preniman, Jacob Miller, black; Henry Carpenter, Emanuel Carpenter, Gabriel Carpenter, Daniel Herman, Christian Herman, Philip Fiere, Mathias Slaremaker, big John Shenk, Jacob Churts, Jacob Snevely, Junior; John Woolrick Houver, John Croyder, John Leeghte. Martin Graaf, Peter Smith, Peter Newcomat, Jacob Bare, Junior; John Henry Bare, Jacob Weaver, Henry Weaver, John Weaver, David Longanickar, George Weaver, Abraham Mire, Woolrick Houser, John Mire, Henry Musselman, Michael Shank, Jacob Miller, Jacob Miller, Junior; Martin Miller, Peter Aybe, Hans Goot, Christian Staner, John Jacob Light, Adam Brand, Christopher Franciscus, Caspar Loughman, Frederick Stay, John Line, John Shwope, Bastian Royer, Jonas Lerow, Simeon King, John Aybe, Everard Ream, all of Lancaster County and John Negley, Bernard Ressor, John Wister, John Frederick Ax, John Philip Bohm, Anthony Yerkhas and Herman Yerkhas, of Phil. County, be and shall be to all intents and purposes deemed, taken and esteemed His Majesty's natural-born subjects of this province of Pennsylvania as if they and each of them had been born within the said province, and shall and may and every of them shall and may within this province take, receive, enjoy and be entitled to all rights, privileges and advantages of natural-born subjects as fully to all intents, constructions and purposes whatsoever as any of His Majesty's natural-born subjects of this province can, do or ought to enjoy by virtue of their being His Majesty's natural-born subjects of His Majesty in said province of Pennsylvania." (Passed February 14, 1729-30.) Apparently never considered by the Crown, but allowed to become a law by lapse of time, in accordance with the proprietary charter.)

We observe in this that nearly all of these are Lancaster County persons, and the act of naturalization, in addition to giving them the right to hold land, gives us an accurate history of the time when they came to this country, as we observe that the preamble to the act states that they came between 1700 and 1718. In this, therefore, many persons today may ascertain that their first ancestor in this country arrived here before the year 1718.

1729—Robbers Harass Our Early German-Swiss Ancestors.

A picture of the dangers which our early German-Swiss ancestors here were exposed to (in addition to dangers from Indians) is painted in an article found in the Gazette of April 12, 1729, as follows:

"We hear there are associated together a company of Irish robbers, the chief of whom are said to be one Bennet, whom they call their captain; and one Lynch, whom they call their lieutenant, with Dobbs, Wiggins and many others who skulk about this and the neighboring provinces; their villanies being to steal the best horses and load them with the best goods, and carry them off before people's faces, which they have lately done in or about Conestoga. It seems their usual practice has been to steal horses from this province and the Jerseys and carry them to sell in Maryland, Virginia and North Carolina. It is said they began to grow more numerous and have a place of rendezvous where they meet to consult how to perpetuate their rogueries and to entertain all like themselves."

This makes it clear that there were many drawbacks in the "good old times" and that the pathway was far from a sunny one with continual fear of savages and robbers and wild beasts uppermost in the minds of all.

1729—Complete Registry Kept of German-Swiss Immigrants of Penna.

From about the year 1726 onward it was the law that all immigrants into Penna. who were not subject to Great Britain and Ireland were compelled to be registered and their names, dates of arrivals and the ships in which they arrived were all taken down and preserved. Thus we have a list of about thirty thousand or more of the names of our German Swiss ancestors largely of this county, but containing some of adjoining counties. And in the Colonial Records these names may be found. Rupp's "Thirty Thousand Names" was made up from these ship lists. By this means, thousands of people today in Lancaster County can find the names of the original members of their family who arrived here. They nearly all came from Rotterdam but the ships touched at Cowes or other points in England, on the way to America. The names of these immigrants and the ships on which they came are entirely too numerous to set forth in this work as they constitute a complete book in themselves.

1729—Temporary Falling Off of German-Swiss Immigrants.

The real exodus of German-Swiss immigrants into this section occurred a few years after 1729. In the year 1728 the immigration was only 152 families, making up 390 persons. In 1729, 243 persons came and yet this number caused the English government to be much afraid of them. During 1729 there were 267 Welsh immigrants, 43 Scotch, 1155 Irish and only 243 German-Swiss Palatines; and the same year by way of New Castle there was 4500 Irish immigrants. So we can see that the number of German-Swiss that were coming at that time compared to the Irish was very small. Later, however, the German-Swiss came by thousands. (Rupp 195-196.)

Among the Irish there were some Irish noblemen, as appears in the Penna. Gazette of April 12th this year. An account of the coming about this time of our ancestors is also found in (7 Haz. Reg. 150).

1729—Conrad Beissel, the German's Great Friend, Arrives.

About 1720 there arrived in America a German native of great usefulness and power. He settled at Millport, Lancaster County, in 1729, where he and a companion built themselves a house. He gave his attention to religious matters almost entirely. He was the first in America to insist that Saturday was the true Sabbath. He contended, therefore, that the 7th day was the Sabbath. Before he moved to Millport he had published a tract on the subject which caused a great deal of excitement throughout this region. (Harris 44.)

WILD BEASTS AND DANGERS AT CONESTOGA. 235

1730—Wild Beasts—The Neighbors of Our Early Ancestors.

A graphic picture of the wild animals living plentifully about the residences of our German Swiss ancestors is given in the American Weekly Mercury of Jan. 14, 1729, and of Jan. 27, 1729. The first is a picture of a panther that was killed near Conestoga. The article states that he had been among some of the swine in the night and the owner hearing a noise went out with a couple of dogs to drive him away. The animal had gotten up into a large tree. The farmer did not know what kind of an animal it was. He made a fire under the tree and left the women of his household to watch it, while he went to a neighbor for a gun. They fired at the animal twice and the second shot broke his fore legs. The infuriated animal made a great desperate leap and fell to the ground near the people who just managed to get out of his way. The dogs seized him and after another shot he was killed. The second item is also about Conestoga and this item sets forth that at Conestoga the beginning of January, Christopher Franciscus was wakened up in the night by a disturbance among his sheep and he arose and went out and found that a wolf had been in the sheep pen but that in jumping over the fence one of his legs was caught and he could not get away. Franciscus took a strong grasp upon the wolf's neck and held his leg by his other hand; then he threw him on the ground and forced his knee on his body and called for his daughter, who came with a large knife and ripped him open, letting out his entrails. I put this under the date of 1730 because in the olden times, January and February were the last two months of the year instead of the first two—the first month being March. When the calendar was re-arranged about 1750, January and February fell in the following year, so that it was really 1730 in this case.

1730—Indians at Conestoga Disapprove the Great Inrush of German-Swiss

This year Captain Civility, a chief of the Conestogas, wrote a letter to Governor Gordon saying that when he was at Lancaster a short time before he heard much talk about the crowds of "Dutch" who were going to settle on the Susquehanna and that the Indian lands were being surveyed there to be sold to the Dutch. This he said gave his tribe much trouble and uneasiness. The Indians' road for hunting would be shut off, he said. The letter is dated September 28, 1730. (1 Pa. Archives 271.)

1730 — Our German-Swiss Ancestors Not to Be Drawn as Jurors.

According to Hazard (7 Haz. Reg. 150) the sheriffs of Pennsylvania were ordered this year, by Gov. Gordon, not to summon any of the Mennonist people nor the other non-resistant sect as jurors. This, he says, was done because they held God only could punish man and that the Courts had no right to deprive any one of liberty or life at all. Besides this, an oath was required of a juror and these people would not so qualify (Do. 152). One of the finest characters and purest minds in Pennsylvania, Emanuel Zimmerman or Carpenter, this year, framed and pushed to adoption a memorial for the Amish and Mennonists and all plain sects, asking the legislature to provide by a law passed that these people might take an affirmation istead of an oath.

1730—Our Ancestors' Good Character Certified.

In January this year the governor of Pennsylvania came out and certified to the sterling qualities of the early Germans and Swiss here on the Susquehanna in a message to the Assembly. All sorts of rumors had been afloat as to them for several years—to the effect that they were an unpatriotic and disloyal people. Thus when they petitioned for naturalization he made a careful investigation into their character, customs, etc. And on this point he says to the assembly: "Upon application made to me in behalf of several Germans, now inhabitants of the County of Lancaster, that they may enjoy the Rights & Privileges of English Subjects, & for that End praying to be naturalized; I have made Enquiry & find that those whose names are subjoyned to a Petition that will be laid before your House are principally such who many years since have come into this province under a particular agreement with our late Honourable Proprietor at London & have regularly taken up lands under him. It likewise appears to me by good Information, that they have hitherto behaved themselves well, and have generally so good a Character for Honesty and Industry as deserves the Esteem of this Government, & a Mark of its Regard for them. I am therefore inclined from these Considerations to favour their Request, & hope you will joyn with me in passing a Bill for their Naturalization."

1730—Our Ancestors Pray that Immigration Tax Against Them Be Removed.

In Vol 3 Votes of Assembly, p. 99, there is a minute account of the petition and application presented by our German-Swiss ancestors to have the immigration tax removal which discriminated against them. They failed in this, however, as the English government felt a jealousy against Germany and Switzerland on account of the strong and influential foothold they were securing in the English government in America, especially in Pennsylvania.

1730—German Swiss Immigration into Pennsylvania This Year.

In 1730 the list of immigrants was small, there being only three ship loads consisting of 147 persons or 440 all told (3 Colonial Records, 385, 386, 289, Vol. 17 Pennsylvania Archives, 2nd. Series, pp. 20 and 22). The names of the women and children are given in the last ship load and the ages of the entire lot. The oldest person was Christian Miller, 60 years old. There was another Mike Shever 50 years old and Margaret Miller 50 years old. The ages of the others would average about 20 or 22 years. The greater number by far of them being between 20 and 35 years. This shows that they were mostly the middle aged people that were coming across at this time. Among the prominent families that came this year we find 3 Bairs—2 Burgers—3 Hoffmans—3 Hesses—2 Hartmans—3 Hertzlers—6 Millers—4 Myers—4 Schaeffers and 2 Smiths. There were also one each of the following prominent families: Ammon — Good — Gross — Kellar — Keplinger — Leaman — Minnich — Oberholtzer — Shultz—Bitner and Bricker.

1731 — Our German-Swiss Ancestors Succeed in the Right To Hold and Transfer Land.

After a hard struggle lasting through several years, our German-Swiss ancestors succeeded in having a law passed allowing them rights in real estate the same as other people. The law was passed Feb. 6, 1731 (4 St. L. 208). The Act sets out that at their own cost they purchased small pieces of land in Pennsylvania and erected churches and other houses of religious worship and school houses and almshouses thereon, and enclosed burying

PARTICULAR LOCATION OF OUR ANCESTORS IN THE PALTINATE.

grounds. It then goes on and allows them the rights they prayed for. It also allowed their religious societies to hold property for religious, educational and charitable purposes.

1731—Our German-Swiss Ancestors Build Many Churches and School Houses.

The Act of Assembly last referred to shows plainly that our German-Swiss forebears built churches and schools as soon as they arrived.

1731—Residence of Our Swiss Ancestors in the Palatinate at This Time.

Müller (p. 209-212) gives us an adequate idea of where the Swiss (who came to the Rhine Valley earlier) lived in that Valley at this time. He says there were in the congregation at Friedelsheim (about eight miles from Neustadt) forty families. The ministers were Hanz Tchantz (Johns) and Hans Jacob Schneider. In the congregation six miles south of Worms 40 families, whose ministers were Hans Burkholder, Christian Burkholder, Christian Stauffer,—the last named a deacon of Ober Sultzheim. Of the congregation of Ibersheim near Worms, the minister was Hans Jacob Heistand and the deacon Abram Burkholder. In the Tribbach congregation, John Neff was minister and Hans Longanecker deacon. Altogether, says Müller, there were in the Palatinate (or Rhine Valley) 458 families of Swiss below Manheim and 160 families above Manheim—in all 618 families.

1731—Names of Swiss Mennonites in Upper Rhine Valley This Year.

Müller (page 209 et seq.) give the following persons as those constituting the Swiss Mennonite congregations above Manheim in the Palatinate in the year 1731:

(1) The congregation on the Ziehmerhof one hour (4 miles) from the city of Wimpfen on the Neckar, to the northwest. The heads of the family are Ulrich Steckley, Nich. Schnepach, Hans Loscher, Hans Wittmer, Jacob Lehmann's widow, Chr. Hodel, Jacob Kauffman, Hans Wittmer, Hans Bloetscher, Peter Gran's widow, Uirlch Gletler, Nich. Neukomn, Nich. Ploetscher. Minister of the congregation: —Ulrich Neukomm of Griembach,— Markus Frantz, and Hans Baechtel Deacons.

(2) The congregation on the Büechelhoff two and one half hours from Wimpfen on the Neckar to the northwest: Christian, Hans and Daniel Neukomm, Peter and Jacob Kraehenbuehl, Henry Engersten's widow, Nich Wagner, Hans Horsch, Peter Brand, Hans Kuendig, Tob. Hodel. Minister of the Congregation Samuel Boechtel at Unter-Gambfer, Nich Krahenbuhl,—deacon at Dreschkilngen.

(3) The congregation at Hasselbach one hour from Bischofsheim to the South Kaspar Rasy, Hans Hecht, Hans and Peter Witmer, Melchoir Bauman, Melchoir Huersch, Henry Vol Weiters (Vollen Veider's) widow, Hans and Jacob Schenk, Oswald Hofstetter, Samuel Lierstein, and Samuel Dierstein's widow, Hans Ringstbacher's (Rindlisbacher), Chr. Gaumann, David Kauffman, Peter Rasch's widow. Minister of the congregation:—Abr. Zersert on the Rauhof, Valantine Wagner, —deacon at Haselbach.

(4) The congregation at Halmstad one hour from Bischofsheim to the north, Ulrich Iseli, Henry and Hans Wagner, Christian Kleh, Andr. Diter, Andr. Schmits, Peter Neuenschwander, Peter Aebi, Nichlaus Strahm, Val. Schmitz. Minister of the congrega-

tion: Hans Schmitz at Haelmstad and Chr. Schmitz of the same place.

(5). The congregation of the Bokschaft, two hours from Ebingen to the northwest: Hans Landis, Hans and Chr. Brand, Hans Dierstein Peter Moser, David Kobel, Ulrich Burkhalter, Chr. Martin, Hans Schaerer's widow, Samuel Nysli, Samuel Hess, Samuel and Martin Meyer, Hans Huber, two Hans Schaerer, Hans Graf, Chr. Shenk, Chr. Kraitter, Chr. Oberholtzer, Peter Graf. Minister of the congregation: Heinrich Kuendig in Grambach. Martin Kreiter, deacon in Zetlingen.

(6) The congregation on the Streigenberg, one hour from Ebingen eastward: Heinrich Beer, Samuel Funk, two Hans Frei, Hans Baehr, Fr. Rohrer, Hans Hodel, Hans Funk, Jost Glnecki, Hans Mueller. Ministers of the congregation, Chr. Janw. on Streigenberg, Hans Funk in Richen, Hans Heinrich, Mueller,—deacon in Ebingen; Peter Plaettle, deacon in Streigenberg.

(7) The congregation in Wesingen two hours from Durlack eastward, Hans Chr. Ruth (Rupp?), Samuel Kraehenbuehl, Nich. Hassler, Hans Eschbacher, Hans Gut, Hans Bauman, Phil. Schneider. Minister of the con gregation; Chr. Eschbacher in Wesingen, Ulrich Schneider,—deacon in Kraetzingen. (Rupp 209.)

(8) The congregation in Meekesheim, two hours from Neckarsmond, southward: Samuel Ploetscher, Jas. Huersch, Nich. Brand, Peter and Hans Bueller, Hans and Jacob Zety, Hans Rohrer, Nich. Myer's widow, Benj. Nich. and two Hans Musselman (Mosimann?), Hans Jacob and Hans Kauffman. Minister of the congregation: David Kauffman in Dasbach, Hans Bresler in Langzael, Hch. Landis, deacon in Zutzenhausen.

(9) The congregation on the high Eckerhof one hour from Wersloch eastward. Jacob Shallenberger, Chr. Wenger's widow, Hans Gleller, Peter Allenbach, Nicholaus Gutzler, Jost Gutzler's widow, Chr. Fuchs, Nich. Bachtel, Daniel Hattel, Hans Fallman, Nat. Schenk's widow. Minister of the congregation: Christian Bachman, in Wersloch, Hans Meyer in convent Logefield, Hans Plaetcher, deacon in Mechersheim.

(10) The congregation on the Haschlof one hour from Neustadt, northward. Peter Schneider, Chr. Frantz, Andreas Moeselmann, Peter Kunzi, Daniel Gran, Ulrich Neukomn. Minister of the congregation: Chr. and Nath. Moeselmann.

(11) The congregation on the Immelthaeuserhof, one hour from Sintzhelm, southward, Chr. Buenkeli, (Binggeli) Samuel Frei, Hans Baehr, Hans Brand, Heinrich Mueller, Heinrich Schab, Peter Gut, Claus Gerber, Hans Lienhard, Jacob and Samuel Schneider, Martin and Jacob Oberholtzer, Chr. Huber. Minister of the congregation: Chr. Eicher on the Im melhaenserhof, Rudolph Linhard at Rohrbach, Peter Moser, deacon in Logefield, Hans Plaetcher, deacon in Mechersheim.

(12) The congregation in Thernheim, one half hour from Sintzheim southwestward: Jacob Meyer, Chr. Herr, Rudolph Plaetscher, Peter Brand, Hans Wisler, Hans Pfaeffli, Hans Herr, Nich. Kratter, Nich. Meii, Hans Jacob Santer, Bend. Wissler. Minister of the congregation: Rundolp Linhard of Rohrbach, Samuel Meyer,—deacon at Dirhheim.

(13) The congregation on the Rohrhof, two hours from Mannheim eastwards, Hans Schwarz, Wolfgang Hall, Hans Rudolph Schneebeli, Hans Jnerg Bachstel, Hans Meyer's widow, Hans Bachman, Melch. Hanri, Hans

Wegner, Peter Burchdalff, Hans Jacob Schneider, Hans Saurer, Greg. Stoeger's widow. Ministers of the congregation: Jost. Eschbacher, in Oelbellenheim, Melchoir Foelmann in Bruchhausen, Chr. Neukommer,—deacon in the Rohrhof making together 160 house fathers or families.

1731 — Additional German Swiss Settlements in Our County.

Rupp says, page 78, Mart Kendig built a walnut log house on his large tract of 1060 acres. This tract, as we have seen before, included all the land between Willow Street pike and the West Willow road on the east and west and extended from the property of William G. Mellinger to John Rush on the north and south.

According to the Colonial records, Volume 3, page 381, seven shiploads of German-Swiss arrived at Philadelphia this year and nearly all came to the Conestoga Valley, (See page 417). Several Acts of Assembly were passed concerning these people. They laid a duty or tax upon them because they were foreigners, (See 4 Statute at large, 135). Laws were also passed naturalizing them and enabling them to hold land. (See same book, page 20). The discussion concerning this right to hold land, as it took place in the Assembly of Pennsylvania may be found in Vol. 3 votes of Assembly, page 131. Many of them were naturalized by a later act, this same year. The naturalization is found in 4 Statutes at Large 147. We have discussed under the date of 1729. Those naturalized under the act 1731 (Page 219) were German Swiss who settled in Philadelphia County and city and Bucks County and Chester County. Some of the names prominent in the list are: Ziegler, Detweiler, Hunsecker, Zimmerman, Schmidt, Mayer, Bowman, Swartz, Andrews, Levand, Kauffman, Shenkel, Hoffnagel, Cressman, Funk, Schrack, Seltzer, Pennypacker, Hollanbiak, Reiff, Peters, Kline, Snyder, Kosdorf, Sander, Bauchman, Roth and Acker. None appear in the list as Lancaster County settlers.

1731 — Early Forest Fires and Other Items.

In the American Weekly Mercury under the date of April 15, this year the following items appear, "Last Monday (April 12) a number of wagons, coming from Conestoga to the city of Philadelphia laden with flour and hemp, etc., were set afire by burning bushes along the road. The hemp burned with such violence, that it was with great difficulty that they saved the wagon. They lost all their hemp, four bags of flour and six bags of provender."

This item shows that there was a trade between Conestoga and Philadelphia, in the hemp and flour business. The mills on the Conestoga and other Lancaster County places were manufacturing flour for Philadelphia and growing hemp. Hemp raising was so general, among our Germans, that in fact, Hempfield Township was named from it. Another thing made plain is that there were evidently, much wood and underbrush along the road in these early times, nearly 183 years ago or more.

From the Pennsylvania Gazette, under the date of May 6, 1731, there is an item reported as follows: "From Lancaster County, we hear that on the 18th past the woods being afire some people fearing that their fences would be burned, went out to save them, when a child following them wandered along the rails and being surrounded by fire the flames seized her clothes and she was burned to death." This is not an unusual item especially; but it gives some light

240   THE ESHLEMAN FAMILY (SWISS).

upon the early condition in and about Lancaster.

Another item of early German Swiss days, of Lancaster County, is that, surrounding the name of Mary Ditcher, in Volume 9 of Hazzar's Register, page 119. Mr. Conynghgam, proficient writer, states that, land back to the Susquehanna river, was settled in the Neighborhood of Columbia, by Farricks, Strickler, Garbers, and others; and that they purchased their first right from Mary Ditcher, an old German woman who went about making what she called, improvements. This consisted of a few sticks put together and a fire kindled and a kettle hung over it, which constituted her claim. She would sell out her claim for a trifle and then move and take up another claim. The article continues and says that she wandered through woods leading her horse, which was her only property, with her knitting in her hand and clad in sheep skin. The writer gives a good description of the founding of Columbia, also.

1731—The Eshleman Family.

The following receipt is found in Rupp page 75, "Received September 29, 1731 of Martin Mylin, 8 pounds, 11 shilling and 8 pence for passage and head money of John Eschellman.

Signed Thomas Lawrence."

This suggests that an item on the Eshleman Family might properly be entered at this point.

The Eshlemans arrived in America and in the Susquehanna Valley, much earlier than 1731; and perhaps the chronology of these annals would be better preserved, by this item having been entered under the earliest date of any Eshleman arrival here. But as that was omitted, this item may as properly be entered now as at any other time.

The earliest arrival of an Eshleman in what is now Lancaster County of whom there is reliable proof, is that of Daniel Ashleman, who came before 1718, as set forth in the Act of naturalization which embraced him, recorded in Vol. 4 St. L. 147. He is stated there as one of those who came before 1718 and as a native of Lancaster County. (See also Rupp 125.)

John Eshleman, above named, arrived in Philadelphia as one of a ship load of 269 Palatines, (Swiss Palatines) from Rotterdam by way of London and Cowes on September 21, 1731, in the ship Brittania and signed the declaration of fidelity to the Government of Pennsylvania that day. (3 Col. Rec. 414 and 415.) He lost no time in reaching Lancaster, for as we have stated, 8 days later Martin Mylin settled his passage and head money. Mylin lived on Pequea Creek near Willow Street. According to the same record page 367 and 368, Jacob Eshleman arrived about Aug. 19, 1729, with a ship load of Palatine Swiss of 180 persons in the ship Mortonhouse, from Rotterdam by way of Deal; and signed the promise of fidelity, etc.

And Hendrick Eshleman (Ishelman) arrived about Aug. 24, 1728, in the ship Mortonhouse from Rotterdam by way of Deal, with a ship load of 200 Palatine Swiss immigrants (See De. 327 & 328). It is evident, therefore, that the pioneers of the family here, go back to the days of the first opening up of civilization in our Susquehanna Valley—near year 1710.

There were also Peter Eshleman, Aug. 28, 1733, in ship Hope; Barbara Eshleman, and Jacob Eshleman, the same time—and several more in early years. (See Vol. 17 2nd Ser. Pa. Archives pages 13, 16, 17, 29, 30, 85, 86, 88, 90, 282, 284, 433, 439, 440 and 494.

But mention is made in European records, of Eshlemans on the move toward Philadelphia and the Susquehanna Valley much earlier than the above dates.

In the account given by Melchoir Zahler (Zeller) in 1710 of those who were being deported for America in the ship sent down the Rhine that year, he mentions Michael Eshleman, a Mennonist deacon and Margrith Eshleman. (See Ante 159 & 160.) They did not proceed farther than Nimewegen in Holland, however.

As to the old Swiss home and ancestry of the family, it appears from Ernest Müller of Langnau, Switzerland (a noted historian) that about 1550 the Eshlemans were first known in the Langnau district—a short distance southwest of Berne. In the list of Mennonites driven out of Langnau in 1692 occurs the name Elizabeth Eshleman the old fish woman and her two daughters—Magdalena and Elsa and also Ely Eshleman's wife Magdalena. (See Ante 127.) According to Kuhns in a letter written to Cyrus H. Eshleman of Grand Haven, Michigan, a few years ago, an infant Peter Eshleman, son of Benedict Eshleman, was baptized in Langnau in 1556. He states that there are few, if any, earlier Eshleman records in Switzerland than this. The Consul of the United States, at Berne states that there are 20 or more Eshleman families in Berne; and that the family may be of Bernese origin — that is in western Switzerland.

1731—The Eshleman Family.
(Continued.)

But the Eshlemans are numerous throughout the Emmenthal too, which is a short distance northeast of Berne. They are found in Trachselwald, Summiswald and Burgdorf as well as in Langnau. It seems that the family lived earlier than 1550 in the Emmenthal and embraced the Baptist or Mennonite faith during the migration of the Zurich refugees into the Emmenthal about 1530.

The origin of the Eshleman name is not clearly established. Imobersteg who published a work on the Emmenthal in 1876 says that the Aeschlimann (Eshleman) family originates from Aeschlen in "Gemeinde" (congregation) of Diesbach, in the Emmenthal. And a certain Michael Aeschlimann, nicknamed "der Bergmichael" or mountain Michael Eshleman was one of the leaders of the peasant war against the industrial tyranny and landed tyranny of Switzerland, about Berne, in 1653. This I cite on the authority of Cyrus H. Eshleman of Grand Haven, above referred to. He has a copy of Imobersteg's book.

Authorities give two or more derivations of the name "Eshleman." It is said by them that the name may mean one who came from the village of Aeschlen or Aeschi or Aeschli, receiving the name Aeschlimann to designate them after they removed to another town to denote their original home. Another theory is that an Aeschlimann was one who was an overseer of an Aesch, a section of cultivated land extending around a small town. In the old towns in Switzerland the land round about them was called the Aesch and the tenants lived in the center in a small cluster of houses. The overseer for the nobleman (owner of all the land the village was built on and extending some distance about it in all directions) was the Aesch-man. And the "li" is said to be a Swiss localism whose use made the name of the overseer the Aesch-li-mann.

Authors in the "Pennsylvania German" at different places give interesting history relative to the Eshleman family. In the number for June 1910, page 373, Kuhns, commenting on Imobersteg, says that Aeschlimann comes from the parish of Aeschli in Diessbach—he also says in number for Oct. 1906, page 311, that there are many Eshlemans in Langnau to this day—under Oct. 1906, page 610, he says he found Aeschlimanns also in the district of Meilin in Canton Zurich, etc. But the name does not appear in the Lexicon of Leu (Switzerland).

There is an Eshleman family coat-of-arms too. Ernest Müller, of Langnau, Switzerland, has considerable knowledge upon it. The description of the coat-of-arms given, is as follows: There is shown upon it a man and an Eschbaum (ash tree); but it seems that in other instances there is described a man and a fish "Aeschi." The name, however, seems to be older than the coat-of-arms. The Eshleman family hold family reunions annually. Mrs. John Flaharty, of Plains, Luzerne County, Pennsylvania is the Secretary of the association.

Hon. W. U. Hensel, of Lancaster, Pennsylvania, states that, heading the list of those who died in the old Switzerland wars, in long columns on tablets on Memorial buildings in Berne, the names of several Aeschlimanns stand at the top of the lists.

In the County of Lancaster there are 180 of Eshleman adults and heads of families noted, and in the city directory 53 heads and adults, total 233.

In America at large today there are perhaps four or five thousand of them. They are found, according to Cyrus H. Eshleman, of Grand Haven, Michigan, in the following large American cities: Boston, New York, Rochester, Philadelphia, Pittsburgh, Baltimore, Memphis, Washington, D. C., Columbus, Cincinnati, Cleveland, Toledo, Detroit, Minneapolis, Chicago, Springfield, St. Louis, St. Joseph, Kansas City, Indianapolis, Sioux City, Seattle and Los Angeles, etc.

1731—German Swiss Immigration into Pennsylvania This Year.

According to the Colonial Records and other records this year, 4 ship loads of the German-Swiss or Palatine-Swiss reached Pennsylvania. (3 Col. Rec. 410-13-14-16.) The number of male heads of families of these four shop loads was 235; and the total number of immigrants was 638. Of the most general families residing in Lancaster County we find the following: 2 Huberts—2 Leamens—3 Keeseys—2 Ritters and 6 Smiths.

One representative of each of the following families were among these immigrants: Albert — Bumgartner — Bauman — Bender — Cramer — Dietrick — Eshleman — Frey — Frieman — Fisher — Hiestand — Myers — Metzgar — Roth — Rohr — Seyler — Shultz — Snyder — Vogell — Wanamaker and Wald.

The women and children's names are given in most instances and frequently there were more women than men. In the ship-load of the vessel called "Pennsylvania Merchant" qualified at Philadelphia Sept. 11, 1731, there were 56 women above 16 and 58 children under 16. (Second Series Pa. Archives, Vol. 17, page 25.) In the ship load coming in the ship Brittania Sept. 21, this year, the ages are given and they average about 22 years, women, men and children. One child, only 5 weeks old, is reported. It was born in passage. Another child landed 15 days old. That is about all that we can collect of interest in the immigration of 1731.

1732—German Swiss Immigration into Pennsylvania This Year.

The year 1732 records the beginning of a new inrush into Pennsylvania, of German Swiss or Palatines. According to Colonial Records, (3 Col. Rec. 429, 31, 52, 53, 54, 55, 56, 57, 58. 65 and 66) eleven vessels of these people ar-

IMMIGRANTS OF 1732 TO SUSQUEHANNA VALLEY.

rived this year, making a total of 762 heads of families and a total cargo of about 1950 persons. The first vessel arrived on May 4, this year—the second in August—the next seven in September and the last one in October.

Turning to the names we find the following persons of familiar names in the list: 16 Albrights—4 Breckleys —5 Bairs (Bears)—3 Bumgartners—5 Bergers—3 Brickers—5 Benders—4 Brandts—7 Brackbills—2 Balmers—2 Berntheisels—4 Burkholders—2 Bollingers—2 Buchers—3 Basslers—6 Beavers—7 Cramers—12 Crists—6 Ebermans—3 Freys—11 Frantzes—6 Fishers—3 Gerlachs—3 Groffs—9 Hoffmans—4 Hartmans—7 Hostetters—8 Kieffers—2 Kreiders—2 Harniches—2 Hoaks—2 Hoffers—2 Keeseys—4 Kellars—2 Keplingers—2 Kolbs—7 Kuhns —2 Kauffmans—4 Klings—3 Longs— 18 Myers—7 Mumaws—48 Millers—24 Mussers—4 Peters—2 Pickels—2 Ackers—2 Andrews—2 Abels—4 Rupps—2 Ritters—6 Seylers—10 Stauffers—3 Snyders—8 Steinmans—2 Sanders—4 Saddlers—3 Schuymeyer—3 Strauss— 2 Schlaughs—2 Spanglers—6 Schocks —2 Sigmans—3 Wolfs—6 Weavers and Webers—7 Wagners—17 Zimmermans and 4 Zieglers.

There also appears one each of the following families: Sprecher — Schuman — Shaub — Shilling — Berger — Gochenaur — Gerhart — Gable — Kleinhous — Keeler — Kline — Moseman — Byerly — Brenner — Bechtold — Reinhart — Shearer — Landis — Pellman — Albert — Hostetter — Frank — Brackbill — Gerlach — Herman — Kreider — Moseman — Burkholder — Kellar — Kolb — Lehman — Zircher — Meck — Oberholtzer — Rohrer — Smith — Snyder — Schuyler — Wendel — Weaver — Ziegler — Crist — Capp and Christian.

A large number of women and children came with the immigrants on the ships that arrived in the fall. There were not many old people, as far as ages are given, among these immigrants. The ages of the men average 28 years—that of the women 27 years and of the children 7 and one-half years.

In some of the earlier immigrations the people that came were older persons; but it seems that in later years the spirit of immigration, into the Susquehanna Valley, was taken up by the younger people as the above details seem to show.

1732 — Hardships of Our German-Swiss Ancestors on the Sea.

In the Pennsylvania Gazette, the fourth newspaper published in America (which was begun by Benjamin Franklin in 1728, and which exists to this day in the form of the Saturday Evening Post) there are set forth the following accounts of hardships endured by our early German Swiss local ancestors in coming across the sea.

The first item is found in the issue of February 8, 1732, and is as follows:

"There is a letter in town from some Palatines who embarked at Rotterdam in June last in a ship bound for this place, but instead arrived at Martha's Vineyard, an island on the coast of New England—containing an account that the ship, being four and twenty weeks in her passage, their provisions fell short, and in the last eight weeks they had no bread; but a pint of grouts was all the allowance for five persons per day. They ate all the rats and mice they could catch, and the price of a rat was 18d. and of a mouse 6d. and water 6d. a quart. That seven persons died of hunger and thirst in one night; and of 150 passengers, which came on board at Rotterdam, over 100 were miserably starved to death. When at length it pleased God that a sloop should meet them and conducted the ship into Homes-Hole, a harbor of the above named island. In the first three days after their arrival fifteen more died, who had been reduced so low by famine that it was impossible to recover them. They write further that they think if they had continued at sea three days longer, they should all have died, no one being able to hand another drop of water. But the good people of the island are very charitable to them and do everything in their power to refresh them; so that many who were famished and near death began to revive, but none are yet strong enough to travel."

What was done for their relief appears in an article in the same paper, dated February 22. It is as follows:

"Governor Gordon has been pleased to write a letter to the Governor of Boston, in behalf of the distressed Palatines on Martha's Vineyard as follows:

"'Sir—On the application of several Germans and others from the Palatinate, now inhabiting this province, I am to address you on behalf of their unhappy countrymen, who, after a passage of twenty-four weeks from Rotterdam, are lately arrived at a port in your government, near R. I., as I suppose. The enclosed being an exact translation of a letter from them to a Dutch Minister here, sets forth fully their calamitous circumstances, and the horrid barbarity with which they have been treated by Lohb, the master of the vessel, who seems to have formed a design to destroy them, in order to posses himelf of their effects, which are said to have been very considerable, when they embarked. A gentleman of your goodness and humanity cannot but be moved with pity, for the miserable conditions of these poor wretches, and with a just indignation against the author of their misfortunes. And as it will be an act of great charity to relieve and protect the first, it will be no less a necessary act of justice to call the last to strict account. That if he cannot acquit himself of what is laid to his charge, he may reap the just reward of his oppression and cruelty.

"'I am with much respect, sir, etc.
"'Philadelphia, February 9, 1732.'"

And in the issue of May 18th we have a brief account of the slow progress of these suffering people on their toilsome journey from Boston to their final home with their brethren here in this land of Pequea and Conestoga.

It is as follows:

"Philadelphia, May 18. — Saturday last arrived here 34 Dutch passengers, being those who came into Martha's Vineyard half starved in December last. They have since been in Boston, where they say the people took them into their houses and used them very kindly, so that many of them were at no charge, all the while they waited for passage; and, moreover, a collection was made among the inhabitants for their relief, by which 200 pounds was gathered and given to them. The Captain who brought them from Holland was prosecuted there on their account; but the accusations against him were not made good and he was acquitted and has since arrested those five who signed the letter for damages, and they are forced to remain behind to answer his action. 'Tis said the people who arrived here complain almost as much of being abused by those five, who were the chief persons among them, as they in their letter did of the Captain."

It may be that some of our town ancestors were among that desolate body of men and women, fleeing to this land to escape persecution and poverty at home in Europe.

1732—Another Picture of Suffering and Hardships.

Another picture of the dreadful experiences which ignorant Palatines subjected themselves to in their tedious journey to our land is shown in an item of the same paper of October 19, 1732. It is as follows:

"Sunday last arrived here Captain Tymberton, in 17 weeks from Rotterdam, with 220 Palatines—44 died in their passage. About three weeks ago, the passengers dissatisfied with the length of the voyage, were so imprudent as to make a mutiny, and, being the stronger party, have ever since had the government of the vessel, giving orders from among themselves to the captain and sailors, who were threatened with death in case of disobedience. Thus, having sight of land, they carried the vessel twice backwards and forwards between our capes and Virginia, looking for a place to go ashore, they knew not where. At length they compelled the sailors to cast the anchor near Cape May, and eight of them took the boat by force and went ashore; from whence they have been five days coming up by land to this place, where they found the ship arrived. Those concerned in taking the boat are committed to prison."

Those indeed were times that tried men's souls.

This ship was the "John and William" which reached Philadelphia October 17, 1732, under Captain Tymberton from Rotterdam according to Vol. 17, Sec. Series of Pennsylvania Archives, page 72.

Turning to the list of passengers on that ship we find Martin Lorenz, George Albright, Jacob and Benedict and Hans Peter Brackbill, and John Peter Reinhart, and John Martin Schaeffer, and Jacob Weber and Gideon Hoffer, and Jacob Henrich and John George Sprecher, and John Nicholas Boshung and Philip Melchoir Meyer and John Peter Appel, and Laurens Kieffer, and Baltzer Gerlach, and Stephen Matz and John George Martin, and Ludwig John Herr and Sebastian Druckmiller, and John Shock and Conrad Getz and Mathias Musser and John Vogel and John Michael Hoffman, and John Jacob Scherr and Joseph Houbley and Michael Miller and Mathias Mentzer among the list.

We recognize all of these as common Lancaster County names. It is indeed interesting to contemplate that these persons (ancestors no doubt of present families of the same name now in our county) suffered such a discouraging experience on their journey here. What a fascinating story they must have told their children and grandchildren of their desperate plight, at sea. No wonder they mutinied! Ordinarily 10 to 12 weeks were quite sufficient to make the passage. But these people saw no land after 12, 13, yea 14 weeks of patient sailing. Then they became frightened —horror stricken. They felt that they were lost—lost on the great Atlantic Ocean, with no land in sight anywhere. They threaten the master and seamen and take charge of the ship. This they did at the end of 14 weeks or as the account states, about 3 weeks before landing.

Think of the scene on that ship from another point. According to the record there were 98 women and children on the vessel when it landed in addition to about the same number of men. What terror they must have experienced and how the children must have cried in terror. How desperately in despair were the mothers. How helpless all of them! Think too of the deaths—44 deaths that voyage. That is, one each third day dies and is sunk in the sea.

It took brave souls indeed in those days to cross the ocean and found a new land. This was, no doubt, one of many similar fated ships. And according to the preceding item, that vessel had a much more terrifying experience. These people were surely persons of grim determination; and it is not a great wonder that they succeeded in establishing themselves comfortably in a little while after they reached their new home here on the Conestoga.

1732—Ministers and Members in the Palatinate.

The name Landis appearing in the ship records of this year suggests to us that an important item, that is dated 1709, was omitted. We, therefore, insert it at this place. It is a greeting and communication from the brethren in Switzerland to the brethren in Holland, and it is as follows:

March 3, 1709.

We the ministers and elders of the Mennonite congregations here wish all ministers and elders of the Anabaptist (Taufesinden) congregation in the Netherlands, much grace, peace and blessing from God, the Father of all Grace, through the comfort and blessing of the Holy Spirit, in Christ Jesus, Amen.

It pleased, God the Lord, by his Almighty hand to call our brother Christian Phlein from this world, and thus close his earthly career. Since then his accounts, and some errors and discrepencies have been discovered, and this fact has had rather a wide circulation among the people and caused much unpleasant gossip; several have been gone so far as to enter complaint against us with you, which might cause you sadness.

That this might be avoided and that you may be correctly informed, we the undersigned have mutually agreed and thought it well to send several of our ministers and elders to you. For this purpose Peter Kolb of Knightsheim (Kriegsheim) was appointed, and Hans Bechtel from here, an ordained Deacon, has been appointed to accompany him on his journey. It is with much love that we send them to visit you and many other places. For the love and great good you have shown by your brotherly love to us and those in needy circumstances, we desire hereby to express our gratitude. Our wish and hope is that the Lord, by his holy angels, may guide them to you and back again in health. That the above may carry more weight we have with our own hands subscribed thereto.

Jacob Landis,
Samuel Meyer,
Christian Bäth,
Jacob Güt,
Hans Heinrich Ber,
Pieter Bladtli,
Michel Meir,
Samuel Meyer,
Ulrich Neiwkomme,
Hantz Chenstsy.

We the ministers and elders of the Palatinate, assembled acknowledge the foregoing to be proper and advisable, and bear testimony to the same by subscribing to it with our hands.
Ubersheimerhoff, March 13, 1709.

Hantz Miller,
Hantz Mayer,
Casper Güt,
Tielman Kolg,
Peter Leman,
Heinrich Hiestant,
Hanz Buszhaler,
Hanz Jacob Schutblÿ,
Jacob Miller,
Christian Siekommel,
Henrich Friedt,
Valentine Gütwohl,
Christian Swustut,
Hansz Brubaker,
Christian Kruntz,
Hansz Schimmer.

In these signatures we see a large number of Lancaster County names of today. This will serve to show where they lived 200 years ago—in what sections our forefathers inhabited.

1732—Naturalization of the Palatines Under the Year 1718. (See Ante 209.)

We made note of a large number of Palatines, principally from Lancaster County, who came to the County before 1718 and who were naturalized. We now make note of a company of them who were naturalized about this year. (4 St. L. 219.) The preamble of the naturalization act states that divers protestants, subjects of Germany under encouragement given by William Penn, transported themselves to Pennsylvania and have contributed very materially to the enlargement of the British Empire and have always behaved themselves religiously and peaceably, and as they desire naturalization they are now to be naturalized.

Most of them were set down as residents of Philadelphia County and a few of the city; a few of Bucks ounty and Chester County; but no Lancaster County residents are mentioned among them. There are about 100 mentioned in the list. Among them are such names as are now in and about Philadelphia as Kolb, Ziegler, Detweiler, Zimmerman, Bowman, Levand, Shenkel, Longenecker, Pennypacker, Reiff and others.

1732—Poverty of Some German Swiss Immigrants.

While some of the immigrants from the heart of Europe had means to enable them to come to this country, yet a great many of them were miserably poor. In the American Weekly Mercury, December 26, 1732, there is the following notice:

"This is to give notice to all Palatines, who came in the ship Mary, John Grey commander, who have never paid their passage nor given security for the same; that they are hereby required to come to said John Grey or to Benjamin Shumaker in Philadelphia, and there pay the passage money or give security, or they will be proceeded against according to law."

A similar notice is inserted as to the Palatines who came in the ship Pleasant.

The law which is referred to is the Statute passed by early Pennsylvania giving authority to the ship masters to sell the persons, who did not pay their passage, into servitude to make up the money to pay their passage.

According to Colonial Records (3 Col. Records 457) there were 61 Palatines on that ship Mary, John Grey commander, and of the common Lancaster County names we find: Mike and John Eberman, Conrad Miller, Christian Klenn, John Mazer, Henry, George, John and Heinrich Shissler, John Adam Miller, Andrew Mazer, Kasper Meyers, Jacob Walter, George Pickle and others. No one can tell at this late date, whether any of these were among the persons who found such great difficulty and hardship in coming over, whether they paid their passage or not.

It is not, however, to their discredit that the hand of poverty was so heavy upon them; but rather a compliment to their pluck and determination that they would face all these difficulties for the sake of religious and political freedom.

On the ship Pleasant, record of which is found in the same book, page 465, we find there were 42 heads of families and among them, Balzer and Henry Spangler, John Kellar, George Peters, George Bair, Fred Bassler, Henry Eckert, Jacob Hornberger, John Sickman, Funk Miller, John Tauber, Isaac Reidenbaugh, John Michael Hoffman, Conrad Book and others.

These all sound like Lancaster County names and it is highly probable that the ancestors of our German Swiss people, here in the County today, were among those poverty stricken sufferers, who were mentioned in the article in the Mercury as having such an unfortunate financial ending of their voyage. The holdings of their descendants, round about us today, very forcibly teach us that they have overcome the obstacle of poverty against which they struggled, in those early times.

1732—Occasional Instances of Low Morals.

In the Colonial Records, Volume 3, page 429 and 430, there is set forth a record which gives us a melancholy picture and the fact that human weakness was a factor among other German Swiss ancestors, then as now.

In fact, it would not be complimentary to civilization at all if we could not point to advancement and a rising of the moral plane, as the result of years of effort and culture. We do not believe, that by any means, all of the ancestors of whom we have been speaking, were clean and godly for there are many accounts to the contrary. The item which we are now about to give, while it shows the weakness of one individual and her sin, on the other hand, shows that the spirit of charity and humanity filled the breasts of her neighbors.

At a meeting of the Council of Pennsylvania, (which corresponds to our Senate and the Governor Cabinet combined today) a report of the Justice of Lancaster County was received, setting forth, that at the Oyer and Terminer Court, held at Lancaster, Margaret Sheets was convicted of concealing the birth and burial of her child, born to her, she being a single woman, and upon being so found she was sentenced to death, according to law. But, it appearing to the Judges that there was great doubt concerning the mother's injuring the child and, therefore, the Judges themselves ask the Council to relieve her from the death sentence.

In addition to this a petition, signed by 63 German neighbors of Margaret Sheets, in which they ask mercy to this woman, was presented. Taking all these facts into consideration, the board decided that this woman should not be hanged; but be given a much littler punishment. The names of the persons petitioning for this mercy are not given.

1732—A German Fore-Father Discovers a Gap Nickel Mine.

In Volume 2, of the Pa. Archives, page 311, under the date of 1755, there is a letter from Governor Morris to Thomas Penn in which he states that certain persons concerned in the "Gap Mine," in which Penn is interested, are inclined to go to work on it again. He says, that it may be worked to advantage by the help of a fire engine similar to the one that Schuylers have erected at their mine. He also says, that the vitrol which he is told the mine abounds in should be turned to account. He further goes on to say, that if Thomas Penn is satisfied that he, Morris, will buy or lease Penn's whole share.

A note at the bottom of 312 goes on to say, that this mine is near Gap, in Lancaster County, and was first discovered by a German named Tersey in or before 1732, and that a grant of land, made by John Penn to Governor Hamilton an account of a couple springs later discovered, was reported to the Philosophical Society of London. I simply quote this item to show that the Germans were on the lookout for ore as well as for rich ground.

GERMANS OF EPHRATA—IMMIGRATION OF 1733.

Some time earlier than 1732, in fact I think about 15 years earlier, there was considerable excitement, as the ancient records show, concerning an "Ore Mine at Conestoga."

1732—The Germans Start the Ephrata Monastic Society.

In Volume 15, of Hazard's Register, page 161, there is a historical sketch of Ephrata by Mr. M. Fahnestock. In it he says, that in the year 1732, the solitary life of Ephrata was changed into a Conventical one and Monastic Society was established. The first buildings erected for that purpose were finished in May 1732. The dress of the White Friars was adopted.

The writer goes on to say that this grew out of the Dunker movement which originated in Europe and extended to America in 1719, namely, to Germantown, Skippack, Oley, Conestoga and elsewhere.

He goes into the account much deeper than these annals contemplate.

Harris in his biographical history of Lancaster County discusses the same solitary life under his sketch of Conrad Beisel.

1733—German Immigration.

The records that we have mentioned above, 3 Col. Records, pp. 515 to 524, show that there were 7 shiploads of these German Swiss immigrants who arrived at the port of Philadelphia, during this year making a total of 444 heads of families or a total list for the year of 1183 persons.

Among the prominent Lancaster County names we find 4 Adams—4 Arndts — 6 Brocks — 3 Becks — 8 Burkharts—2 Beyers—5 Bergers—6 Burkholders—3 Bowmans—4 Christs —5 Eshlemans—19 Freys—6 Fishers 13 Fegleys—10 Fousts—5 Hoffs—8 Hallers—10 Hetricks—3 Hoffmans—7 Isemans—11 Kuhns—7 Kemps—8 Millers—7 Moores—2 Mosemans—11 Roots—7 Rushers—5 Reeds—3 Richters—2 Reinharts—20 Smiths—9 Steinmans—3 Straubs—10 Schaeffers—8 Snavelys—3 Sauders—5 Taylors—8 Trouts—15 Whitmans.

Besides these there are a large number of other common Lancaster County names of which there are one single representative. It will be observed that among these immigrants the greater number are still Swiss. The pure German names have not yet appeared in these ship lists.

1733—More Hardships and Perils on the Ocean.

From the Pa. Gazette, of Mar. 22, 1733, we cull the following item: "We hear from New York, that last week arrived there the Snow, 'Experiment' with about 80 or 90 Palatines. She came from Dover about the middle of October, beat 8 weeks upon the coast and then put away for Bermuda, in which time the master and many of the passengers died. She set out with 180 on board and brought not more than the above 80 or 90 to shore." This vessel is not among those registered as arriving at Philadelphia during the year; but, we think that the name does appear in earlier or later years. This particular trip of 1733, was to New York.

1733—German Swiss Settlers Deceived by Maryland.

In Vol. 4, of Colonial Records, page 64, there is a petition set forth, by our German-Swiss under the date of 1736, complaining that 3 or 4 years earlier, they having just newly arrived in Pennsylvania and not knowing the boundary between Pennsylvania and Maryland, were deceived into believing that the Susquehanna River was the division and that all lands west of the Susquehanna were Maryland lands. Therefore, they took up lands there and made settlements with the Government of Maryland;

but, they found that the usage and treatment of them was so different from the rest of the Government and that the small substance they had was stolen from them. They also state, that they complained, frequently to Maryland authorities but received no redress; except, that they were told that they were worse than negroes for they had no master and were not under the protection of any laws; and they were finally told that the Susquehanna River was not the boundary. They also state, that they noticed people living east of the river, further south than they do, were living in peace and without any disturbance. They also say, that they now see they were imposed upon, to answer some object of the Government of Maryland; and now, conscious of the wrong that was done them and wrong they have done to Pennsylvania by living on land and not paying acknowledgement to Pennsylvania or its laws, they have resolved to show to Pennsylvania their loyalty and spirit and ask the authorities that they should not hold against them what they did in ignorance. The Board or Council read the petition and sent a letter to the Justices and the High Sheriff of Lancaster County, in which they state they are apprized of a warlike proposition in Maryland and that, therefore, the Sheriff of the County should go to the west side of the Susquehanna River and protect our people living there. This shows some additional hardships and perils under which our people suffered in those early days.

1733—More Petitions for Naturalization.

In Vol. 3 of the Votes of Assembly, page 197-199, mention is made of the fact that many of the Palatines, are petitioning for naturalization; and their naturalization was accordingly, taken up.

1733—Oldest German Swiss Cemetery in Lancaster County.

Soon after our first settlers arrived here, and took up their home in Pequea, in the fall of 1710, cemeteries of course, became important. The oldest one, as far as records show, was known anciently as "Tchantz Grave Yard" later as "Musser's Cemetery" on the west bank of the Pequea Creek just south of Lampeter, being on the Jacob Miller ancient tract or farm of 1008 acres—now being on the farm owned by Mrs. McAllister near Neff's Mill. In that cemetery is the tomb stone yet standing of Jacob Miller, who was one of the first settlers that came in 1710 and who was one of the signers of a letter when in London on June 24, 1710, in which he and others state they "are now about to set sail for America." Right south of his grave and stone are those of his wife, Magdalena and Samuel, likely a son; next north of Jacob Miller's grave is that of Martin Mylin, Jr.; and north of his Hans Mylin; and north of his Barbara Mylin's. These persons all died at a very early age. Martin Mylin in 1732—Barbara Mylin in 1742—Samuel Miller in 1743 —Jacob Miller in 1739—Hanz Mylin in 1733.

Another cemetery, quite likely as ancient as this one, is that of the Herr cemetery, connected with the old brick Mennonite Church just east of Willow Street.

1733—Swiss and German Palatine Immigrants This Year.

According to Vol. 3 of the Colonial records pages 515-524 there were 8 ship loads of these people who arived at Philadelphia in the year 1733. They constitute 400 heads of families, making a total of 1252, and among the common Lancaster County names are the following: 4 Adams—4 Arndts—5 Brocks—3 Becks—8 Burkharts—6 Burkholders—5 Burgers—4 Christs—5 Eshlemans—20 Freys—5 Fishers—13 Fegleys—10 Fausts—5 Hoffs—8 Hellars—10 Hetricks—7 Isemans—11 Kuhns—7 Kemps—9 Klines—4 Kautz—14 Longs—6 Lutz—8 Millers—7 Moores—4 Peters—5 Reeds—11 Roots—5 Rhodes—3 Richters—23 Smiths—9 Steinmans—3 Straubs—10 Schaeffers—8 Snavelys—3 Sauders—3 Stricklers—9 Shermans—5 Taylors—8 Trouts—8 Wises—5 Wagners—7 Whitemans—9 Whitmans and one each of many other common Lancaster County names. The ships in which these people came are the "Samuel of London" of which Hugh Percy was master—"Eliza" Edward Lee master—"Hope" David Reed master—"Richard and Elizabeth" Christopher Cline master—"Mary of Dublin" James Benn master—and the "Charming Betty" John Ball master. All of these came from Rotterdam, except the last one seems to have left from London; and they came by way of Diehl, Dover, Cowes, Plymouth—some of them going one way and some of them another.

1734—Great Suffering in Conestoga from Heat This Summer.

In the Pennsylvania Gazette of July 11, 1734, it is stated, that the weather has been so exceedingly hot for a week that a great number of people have fainted and fallen into convulsions and died—and "we also hear, that a great number of harvest people fainted in the fields and in some places a multitude of birds were found dead. Since the hot summer 7 years ago, such intense heat has not been known in this country."

1734—Great Storm at Conestoga.

In the same paper, under the date of September 25, it is stated that "last Sunday, between 7 and 8 in the evening, we had the most terrible gust of wind and rain, accompanied with thunder and lightning, that can be remembered in these parts. It blew down several stacks of chimneys, uncovered several houses, some wholly and others in part, and demolished some weak buildings. The wind was so violent that we have heard of it going from Conestoga to the Bay in one-half an hour."

1734—Michael Welfare, German of Conestoga, Preaches in Philadelphia.

In the Pa. Gazette under September 25, 1734, it is stated that "yesterday morning, Michael Welfare one of the Christian philosophers of Conestoga appeared in full market in Philadelphia, in the habit and dress of a Pilgrim, his hat of linen, his beard full length, and a long staff in his hand. He declared himself sent by Almighty God to denounce vengence against the wickedness of the inhabitants of Philadelphia and to preach speedy repentance. His discourse continued about one-quarter of an hour and the importance of what he delivered commanded the attention of a multitude of people; but when he finished he went away unmolested."

Welfare, later, was one of those who joined the Ephrata community, in the days when they lived in monastaries and withdrew themselves from the world and felt themselves called upon to denounce all manner of worldliness everywhere.

1734—Baltzer Hubmier.

We have, at an earlier place in these annals (see pages 22, 25, 28, 29 and 103) referred to Hubmier and his work. We made note of his name, because the name Huffmier is frequently met with in our county, and it seems to be related to the ancient Hubmier. At this time, we refer again to him, only in form of a brief note.

A rather extended account may be found in the Mennonite Year Book and Almanac, for the year 1914, page 38. This publication was gotten up by Bishop N. B. Grubb of the Mennonite Church in Germantown, and contains a lot of historical matter which relates to the German-Swiss people in America and Europe.

Bishop Grubb's article tells of Hubmier's debates with Zwingli and his various arguments made, concerning the non-resistant faith. For a time Hubmier believed with Zwingli, yet eventually he differed with him on the subject of infant baptism and was finally firmly established in the belief, that only adult baptism can avail anything. This belief he finally held to through the preachings of Reublin. He also stated, that Hubmier introduced feet washing, imitating Christ's method. For a long time he was rather uncertain about infant baptism; but eventually he renounced it. He was a thorough scholar and wrote many strong pamphlets. Professor Wedel, who has written an excellent history of the Mennonites, says about Hubmier, that "We may justly place him by the side of Peter Waldo, Bishop Reesner, George Blaurock, Michael Settler, Hans Denk, Menno Simon and other leaders of our faith."

1734—Belief in Witchcraft Among the Early German-Swiss.

In the American Weekly Mercury, we have, under issue of January 22, 1733-34, the following account:

"The following letter was sent us by an unknown correspondent with a desire that it might be published just as it is, viz:—

"James Swafort, of Lancaster County, at Octorara, the 29th of December, 1733, had some hands helping him dress flax in one end of his dwelling house, and by some means the flax or tow took fire, and there being some quantity above stairs, which soon took fire so that in an instant it was past putting out. In the company, there was an old woman who had been spinning there and was helping to get some things out of the fire before they were burnt, and bethinking herself of some of her own clothes that were above stairs, said hastily, I'll go save my clothes if I lose my life for it. So running up stairs, she threw them out and they were saved; but the fire was so vehement that she could not return but fell upon a bed and was there burnt. It is somewhat surprising, the fire beginning at night, there was such a violent whirl-wind about the place where she lay burning that it raised the flames to such a height that it gave light above a mile. Another thing added to the surprise of the spectators; there suddenly gathered out of the darkness a company of dogs, some thought near 20 about the fire who were so fierce about the place where she lay burning that it was thought they would have leaped into the fire had they not been hindered."

The imputation here is, that the great flame shooting around where this old woman lay burning, was due to the fact that she was a witch. Also the fact that there appeared a pack of about 20 dogs, out of the darkness trying to get where this old woman lay, was also a fact which the witches brought about.

1734 — Swiss and German Palatine Immigration This Year.

According to Vol. 3, of the Colonial Records, pages 568-570, there were two ship loads of these people who arrived at Philadelphia in the year 1734. They constitute 89 heads of families, making a total of 261 persons, and among the common Lancaster County names are the following: 2 Freys—2 Housers—6 Hoffmans

IMMIGRANTS OF 1734—THRIFTY ANDREW FERREE. 253

—2 Leshers—2 Millers—3 Meisters—4 Nobles—3 Naumans—3 Reshs—2 Reinwalds—5 Shultz—5 Smiths—3 Shuberts—2 Steiners—7 Wagners—7 Youngs and 2 Zimmermans. And one each of the following: Andes, Albrecht, Bowman, Cameron, Camel, Carter, Hilderbrand, Johns, MaGee, Richter, Reynold, Ruth, Reinhold, Weber, Yager, and others. The ships in which these people came, are the "St. Andrew" of which John Stedman was Master—and the "Hope" of which Daniel Reid was Master. All of these came from Rotterdam.

1735—The Large Estate of a Thrifty German-Swiss Ancestor.

In Rupp's history of Lancaster County, p. 103, there is set forth an inventory of the estate of one of our thrifty French-Swiss ancestors, Andrew Ferree, who died that year. The name now is Ferry or Forry, and is quite common among us.

The inventory is as follows:

To wheat in the stack at 8 lb.—wheat and rye in the ground at 5 pounds.Lb.	14	0	0
To great wagon, Lb. 12—little wagon Lb. 5......	17	0	0
To a plow and two pairs of irons	1	10	0
To 2 mauls and 3 iron wedges, 9s—to four old weeding hoes, 4s........	0	13	0
To a spade and shovel, 8s—to a matock and 3 dung forks, 10s	0	18	0
To 2 broad axes, 12s—to joyner's axe and adze, 7s	0	19	0
To Sundry carpenter tools, 1 lb.—sundry joyner's tools, 2 Lb. 5s....	3	5	0
To 7 Duch sythes.........	0	12	0
To 4 stock bands, 2 pair hinges, sundry old iron.	0	14	0
To a hand saw, Lb. 2—to 5 sickles and 2 old hooks	0	11	0
To a cutting box, 2 knives, Lb. 1—to 22 bags, Lb. 2, 10s	3	10	0
To 2 pair chains, 14s, 2 hackles, Lb. 1 10—to 5 beles, 12s	2	16	0
To 4 small chains and other horse geers at....	1	4	0
To other horse geers at Lb. 1 10—to a man's saddle at Lb. 1 10......	3	0	0
To 3 felling axes at 10s—two fowling pieces at Lb. 2	2	10	0
To a large Byble.........	2	0	0
To 2 feather beds at Lb. 6—to wearing cloaths, Lb. 7	13	0	0
To sundry pewter, Lb. s 8—to a box iron, 4s.....	2	12	0
To sundry wooden ware at Lb. 1—to two iron potracks, Lb. 1............	2	0	0
To sundry iron ware, Lb. 2—to a watering pot 6s	2	6	0
To 4 working horses, Lb. 24—to a mare and 2 colts, Lb. 11............	35	0	0
To 6 grown cows at Lb. 15—to 10 head of young cattle, Lb. 13 10........	28	10	0
To 11 sheep, Lb. 3 17—to swine, Lb. 1 10.........	5	7	0
To 2 chests, 15s — to a spinning wheel, 8s......	1	3	0
To sley, 6s—to cash received of Samuel Taylor	2	8	0
To cash received for a servant girles time.....	3	0	0
	152	8	6

A hundred pounds was "big money" in those days. But besides this the man owned a fine farm also. One is attracted too by the variety of the articles. Where did he get these wagons and plows and carpenter's tools, etc.? There were certainly very few mechanics here then. He may have brought some of them with him and bought some of them in Philadelphia. We notice that 4 working horses were worth 24 pounds—or 6 pounds per head. He thus had the equivalent or value of 25 horses as his 152 pounds of personal property and that would be equal to $4,000 today as horses are worth $150 to $200 a head.

1735 — German Swiss Between Two Mill Stones in Border War.

It is known, that during the first few years after Lancaster County was organized, Maryland made unreasonable claims against Pennsylvania concerning the line. An account of this is set forth in 4 Colonial Records, 63, stating that from Lancaster County certain information was received, to the effect that, after the Sheriff of the county and some of the people were gathered near the river, the Sheriff and 200 men under officers of Maryland, met just across the Susquehanna with drums and trumpets. Then they went to the house of John Wright, where 300 inhabitants were assembled and demanded the Dutch who were in the house. The Lancaster County Sheriff asked, why they came in such a hostile manner after these Dutch. They appointed a time to discuss the boundary matter; but while this was going on, about 5 o'clock Sunday evening, multitudes of Maryland started to show a warlike disposition and they demanded, that these Dutch had come over there and settled on their lands and now they owe obedience to Maryland. Pennsylvania, of course, claimed that they were inhabitants of Pennsylvania.

1735 — German-Swiss Refuse to Pay Penn's Quit-rents.

In the Pa. Gazette of December 30, 1735, "this notice is given, that as the people have not done their duty that they are now given further notice that the subscribers, that is the Receiver general, is appointed to attend his Office at the town of Lancaster, for County of Lancaster from the 26th to 31st, of March, for the recovering of the arrears of quit-rent due there; at which place persons in arrears of quit rent are requested to pay the same, and if they refuse to pay the same, measures will be pursued against them." J. Steel Receiver appointed.

Of course, there were other parts of the State subject to quit-rent, which gave much trouble also; but our Conestoga citizens felt very much aggrieved by being compelled to pay these rents.

1735—Swiss and German Palatine Immigration This Year.

According to Volume 3 Colonial Records, pages 593 to 607, there are three ship loads of these people, who arrived at Philadelphia, in the year 1735. They consititute 85 heads of families, making a total of 260 persons, and among the common Lancaster County names are the following: 3 Brunners—8 Buchers—2 Eberharts—4 Freys—2 Hallers—3 Hubers —2 Kellars—2 Millers—2 Meyers—4 Smiths — 8 Wises — 7 Witmers — 7 Weidmans — 3 Wingers — 2 Shellenbergs. And one head of the following names: Albrecht, Appel, Eberly, Kline, Oswald, Peters, Weber, Sweitzer, and Schwab, and many other common Lancaster County names. The ships in which these people came, are the "Ship Mercury" of which William Wilson was Master—and the "Brig Mary" of which James Marshall was Master, and the "Billander Oliver" of which Samuel Merchant was Master, from South Carolina. All of these came from Rotterdam.

1735 — The Solitary Germans at Conestoga.

In Volume 16 of Hazzard's Register, page 255, we are given one of the original letters of Peter Miller. Peter Miller was one of the early patrons or founders, at least, of the Ephrata community, of which the old cloister buildings are still land marks.

After stating that he published the Chronicon Ephratense, he goes on to say, that in August 1730, he arrived in Philadelphia and at the end of the year, upon order of the Scotch Synod, was ordained in the old Presbyterian meeting house by three eminent ministers, Tennant, Andrews and Boyd.

He then says, that he visited among the Germans for several years and quitted the ministry and turned his attention to the monastic ideas. In his company he says was a School Master, 3 Elders, one of them Conrad Wiser, 5 families and some single persons, who had raised a fermentation in the Presbyterian Church.

Then he says, that they had separated and incorporated with the congregation at Ephrata in May 1735.

He further says, that at that time, the solitary brethren and sisters lived in the wilderness and caves, as hermits. "And I following in the same way, set up my hermitage in Tulpehocken and laid foundations for solitary and religious life."

He then says that after about one half a year "a camp was laid out for all solitary persons at the very spot where Ephrata now stands and where then, the President lived with some hermits."

He says, at this time charity had been their chief occupation—that Conestoga was a great wilderness and began to be settled by poor Germans, who desired assistance in building houses for them, which kept them employed several summers in hard carpenter work and also increased their poverty. At times he says the necessaries of life were wanting. Then to make things worse, a constable came into the community and demanded the single man to pay taxes. Some paid and some refused. But the Constable summoned six of these Brethren to prison in Lancaster for 10 days. But a Magistrate set them at liberty. A very venerable old Justice of the Peace, Tobias Hendrick, offered himself for their bail. He said when Court came on, the fear of God came on the gentlemen who were their Judges. When they saw these 6 men before them in the prime of life and reduced to skeletons, the Judge decided that since they were so thin, that the whole lot of them could be taxed as one family. This taxation remained in force for over 50 years; that is, all the brethren of Ephrata community were just taxed as one person.

He says further, that they erected grist mills—one of three sets of stones — paper mill — oil mill — had three wagons, printing office; and then money commenced to come in. They also gave alms to the Indians, Mohawks and others. This is about the substance of this interesting letter.

1735—Conestoga Manor Parceled Out.

Conestoga Manor was surveyed in the year 1718, and the warrant to survey may be found in the Taylor papers. It is also set forth in Rupp's history of Lancaster County (page 130), as follows:—

These are....March 1, 1717 to 1718.

While the Manor was laid out and surveyed, it was not divided among purchasers until afterwards. It seems that no patents were granted until 1723 and from that time on until 1774, different patents were issued to various Germans.

256 CONESTOGA MANOR (NOW MANOR TOWNSHIP) PARCELLED OUT.

As the patenting to different owners was at its height, about the year 1735, we are placing the list of patents under this year. It is better that they should be together in one paper, than to be distributed through these annals.

The principal ones are as follows:— Israel Pemberton held 300 acres, date of this patent is October 1, 1723. The Messrs. Wrights own 1500 acres—date of patent, December 13, 1735—sold afterwards in smaller parcels to John Herr, Andrew Stineman, Daniel Lintner, Jacob Kilhaver, Rudy Herr, Jr., John Kilhaver, Jacob Frantz, Godfrey Klugh, Mathew Oberholtzer, Christian Hershey, Andrew Kauffman — James Pattison 107 acres, November 21, 173, James Logan 700 acres, patent dated July 15, 1737, afterwards held by George Brenner, Philip Brenner, Christian Stouffer, Casper Souter, Adam Fisher, Valentine Rummel, Lawrence Cliffer, Christian Stake— Michael Baughman 489, Michael Mayer 131 acres, both same date February 20, 1738, Michael Mayer, sen., 217 acres, patent dated October 16, 1737, Abraham Steiner 63 acres May 3, 1740, John Wistler 167 acres July 3, 1741, Jacob Kuntz 166, Anna Ottila Betty Koffee, 166, Jacob Hostetter 475, John Shank 197 acres, patent dated July 30, 1741, Edward Smout 113 acres June 21, 1743, Michael Baughman 339, May 28, 1752, Abraham Hare 424 April 22, 1751, Jacob Wistler 125. Valentine Miller 140, both May 25, 1756, Martin Funk, 237, December 18, 1758, Jacob Wistler 202, Jacob Shuck 185, August 18, 1759, Abraham and John Miller 89, Valentine Haith 29, Robert Beatty 226 February 1760, Samuel Herr 247, John Keagy 188, Henry Funk 150, Jacob Wistler 173, Ludwich and Fredrick Ziegler 209 June 1760, John Witmer 77, Abraham Miller 204, Rudolph Herr 176, Jacob Witmer 77, November 1761, James M'Master, 247, April 1761, John Keagy 159; Henry Funk 177, David Hare 195, John Miller 150, George Adam Dustler 112, John Correll 209, Christian Stoner 244, all dated 1761, Michael Kauffman 116, John Kauffman 118, Jacob Kauffman 167, Christian Kauffman 163, Michael Kauffman 118, Abraham Steiner 200, John Wormley 115, Jacob Wistler 19, John Kreemer 184, Bartholomew Butt 40, John Graff 136, all dated 1762, Philip Ulweiler 39, Benjamin Miller 220, David Hare, Jr., 94, Peter Snyder 86, Henry Atkinson and Adam Bigging 49, Peter Witmer 132. dated 1763, John Miller 60, January 19, 1764, John Newcomer 109, Joseph Nelson 109, Jacob Wistler 178, Mary Wright 119, dated 1767, John Kendrick 558, James Pratt 232, 1768, Henry Buckley 150, 1769, William Wright 257, 1770, Ulrich Rebur 232, John Manning 165 1772, Jacob Ashleman 340 1774, Indian Town 414, Blue Rock 800 acres. We omitted fractions of acres.

Thomas Penn estimated the value of Conestoga Manor being 65 miles from the City of Philadelphia, 13,400 acres, 40 pounds per hundred acres, 5,360 pounds, Pennsylvania currency.

There is no date to the paper from which the extract is made. See Sparks' Franklin Volume 3, page 535. All can be found in Rupp, page 131, 132.

German Swiss Distressed by Boundary Troubles.

About the year 1736 the troubles between Maryland and Pennsylvania boundary became very acute, and our German Swiss were really between two mill stones—if they sided with Pennsylvania, Maryland oppressed them, and if they sided with Maryland, Pennsylvania oppressed them— they were non-resistants and therefore, did not take up arms to defend themselves. Maryland had asserted that the Susquehanna River was the boundary between Pennsylvania and Maryland. This was contested for 60 or 70 years before being finally settled by the Mason and Dixon Line.

Sixty families of our German-Swiss ancestors, living west of the Susquehanna River, and holding their allegiance to Pennsylvania and their titles from Pennsylvania, this year were forcibly dispossed of their land, and driven out of their homes and compelled to flee to the other side of the river. Thrilling accounts of this can be found in Vol. 4 Col. Rec. 149 and also Vol. 3, Votes of Assembly, page 288.

Cresap "a free booter" of Maryland, was encouraged by the Maryland authorities, to harass the German-Swiss because he had a great deal of the character of an outlaw, and he was very rough to our ancestors. And through a rough character by the name of Higgenbottom some of these Germans being intimidated, acknowledged the right of Maryland to govern them. Afterwards they found their mistake and then acknowledged Pennsylvania was their lawful authority. (Vol. 4 Col. Rec. 56.)

The 60 German-Swiss, who were dispossessed, sent a pitiful letter as to their troubles to the authorities at Philadelphia, renouncing their allegiance to Maryland and announcing their cleavage to Pennsylvania. (Vol. 4 Col. Rec. 57.) In fact, matters became so serious, that a particular Justice of the Peace was appointed, by the authorities of Pennsylvania, to protect these defenseless Germans or German-Swiss in this region. (Vol. 4 Col. Rec. 58.)

Maryland, among her other cruelties, sent a letter to the 60 families, threatening them anew with vengeance, if they did not acknowledge Maryland's right to rule them.

In Vol. 4 Col. Rec. page 60, there is set forth, a letter from the Lieutenant Governor of Maryland to the Governor of Pennsylvania in which he enclosed the letter signed by the 60 Germans, who he said, asked the Maryland authorities and the Government, for lands there, and that the Maryland Government empowered them to settle, which he claimed to be in Maryland, and that these people resolved, by this enclosed letter, as a combination or association, to disown their allegiance to Maryland; and transfer themselves to the Government of Pennsylvania.

The letter which the Governor of Maryland refers to, signed by these 60 people, is in substance as follows: (page 61.)

That they met with oppression and ill-usage from Maryland, very different from the treatment in Pennsylvania, and that they believe that they are not settled in Maryland at all; but in the bounds of Pennsylvania; that their troubles are so unjustifiable and so grievous that they finally fled. They concluded by saying that they, the subscribers, with many of their neighbors are truly sensible of the wrong that they have done Pennsylvania in settling on lands that are in Pennsylvania, and at the same time, paying allegiance to Maryland. They decided therefore, to do their duty and live under the laws of Pennsylvania and the Government of Pennsylvania, and that they will unanimously adhere to this till a legal decision of the disputed boundary is had.

German Swiss Distressed by Boundary Troubles. (Continued.)

The communication is dated to be on the 11th day of August 1736; and in addition to this letter, depositions were taken of Francis Kipp to the effect that he met the Master of the Sloop "Bachelor Hall," a vessel now lying in Susquehanna River. He said that a large number of men from Baltimore County with guns and on horseback, came out along the River, passing near by him. He asked the Colonel at the head of the column, if he was going to fight? But the Colonel said, that he was going on on peaceable terms. He later learned, that the Hall went up with these soldiers and crossed the Susquehanna River near the Northeast Iron Works in Cecil County, and was going up to join Cresap and get possession of certain lands the German Swiss had posession of.

The same year there was a petition of 48 of these Germans, sent to James Logan, and members of Council, stating that they are inhabitants on the west side of the Susquehanna River, opposite to Hempfield, in the County of Lancaster. In this petition they state, that three years before, many of them just newly arrived in America, were by fair promises of the Maryland authorities told to settle west of the Susquehanna River and were promised and told that the Susquehanna River was the division between two provinces. They state that they soon found the whole usage was different from the usage in Pennsylvania; and also, without any cause, they were told that they were worse than negroes, that they had no Master and that they were not under the protection of any laws. They later learned that the Susquehanna River was not the boundary of Pennsylvania. They also noticed that their neighbors living on the east side of the River, further down than they lived, were enjoying the blessings of Penn's government. Therefore, they promised obedience to Pennsylvania, if Pennsylvania would take care of them.

On receiving this, letters were sent to the Justices along the River, to protect these people against Cresap and other Maryland rogues. Vol. 4 Col. Rec. 65-67.

But things went worse. The following report was sent concerning the affairs. That a man named Tanner tried to get some of these Germans into ambush. This report was made to the Sheriff of Lancaster County. It was stated, that on Tuesday morning, a certain person went about six miles back from the River and there the Maryland people were plundering the Dutch people's houses. They were taking out of windows, cloth and other things that they could get their hands on, informing the Dutch that this was a public tax and that they owed Maryland money. They stated that these Dutch people did not pay the Government and for this reason they had the right to do this. They threatened to burn the houses. When they were asked why, they retorted, because the Dutch people had revolted against Maryland. Then they told the Dutch, if they would come back and obey Maryland law, these taxes would not be collected until they had money. One of these intruders got a leader of the Dutch to get the neighbors together and ask them, if they agreed to go back to the Maryland government, and if they would sign a paper. They all refused. Then these intruders said that they would not do anything more to molest them now; but at the end of two weeks if they did not comply with the Government of Maryland that they would come up, with an assembly of men, and put them out of their houses and put people in, who would be true to Maryland. These troubles lasted for a good many years. (Vol. 4 Col. Rec. 69.)

In the same book, (page 70), James Logan writes a letter to Mr. Blunston, one of the Justices along the river, in which he states among other things, "You may let the Dutch people know that the Susquehanna River is a part of Pennsylvania; but it is hard to keep up a large force to protect them." But he states that Pennsylvania is going to stand by them.

There were petitions sent in by the Maryland people to the Maryland Government. One of these is found in the same book page 101. In this petition the subscribers who complain, state that they hear there is some vacant land near the Susquehanna River that the Dutch families settled on. They also state that these Dutch people are disloyal to Maryland and loyal to Pennsylvania and, therefore, they asked if Maryland will allow them to go and settle on these lands and throw the Dutch out.

A great deal more on the controversy may be found in Col. Rec. Vol. 4, pages 90 to 120.

All this tends to show, that great difficulty was had and great hardships were endured by our German Swiss ancestors, in those dark early days.

1736 — Our German-Swiss Ancestors Suffer Under the Navigation Acts.

A new view of the difficulties and the burdens, under which our German-Swiss ancestors labored, in the Susquehanna Valley, and southeastern Pennsylvania generally, is shown by the following item, which appears in Vol. 4 Col. Rec. page 171:—

"A petition of Durst Thome, of Philadelphia, in behalf of himself and others, was presented to the Board, and read in these words:

To the Honorable, the President and Council of the Province of Pennsylvania:

The humble petition of Durst Thome, of Philadelphia, in behalf of himself and others, whose names are mentioned in a schedule hereunto annexed, being owners of the household goods and utensils in an inventory likewise hereunto annexed, humbly showeth:

That being protestants and subjects to the Emperor of Germany, and encouraged by the accounts that they had received from others of their countrymen in the province of Pennsylvania, of the great blessings of peace and liberty of conscience, enjoyed in the said province, under the protection of that gracious and mighty Prince, King George the second, King of Great Britain and Elector of Hanover, they thereupon, in the year of our Lord, One thousand seven hundred and thirty six, did transport themselves, with their families into this province; and having disposed of their old household goods and utensils, which were very bulky, at their coming down the Rhine, for very small quantity of new ones of the same kind, they were laden on board the ship Princess Augusta at Rotterdam. And when the said ship made report of her lading at the port of Cowes, in Great Britain, the said household goods, utensils and other things belonging to your petitioners were freely exposed to the view of the Officers of that Port, who suffered them to pass without molestation or requiring any rates, duty or customs for the same, they being for the proper use of your petitioners and not for sale. But so it is, may it please your Honors, that upon the arrival of your petitioners in the said ship at Philadelphia she, together with the goods and utensils aforesaid was seized by the collector and Naval Officer of this Port, or one of them, by which and the severity of the said Officers, your petitioners were reduced to very great straits. And notwithstanding the said ship, upon a full hearing in the Court of Admiralty of this Province, before Charles Read, Esq., then Judge of the said Court; but since deceased, was legally acquitted, yet the said goods were condemned as forfeited; which sentence, as to the condemnation of the said goods and utensils, your petitioners being advised could not be warranted by law. They thereupon, petitioned the said Court of Admiralty for a re-hearing of the said sentence as to the household goods and utensils, in which petition they humbly conceive they have sufficiently shown that the said sentence was altogether null and void; and that the same (were the Judge of the said Court stil living) could not be put in execution, as by a true copy of the said petition herewith exhibited, and to which your petitioners for greater certainty beg leave to refer themselves, your petitioners humbly conceive will manifestly appear; and as they are so unfortunate as to be deprived of having the sentence re-heard in that Court, by reason of the Death of the Judge, they do most humbly pray, as your honors are interested in the forfeiture of the said goods and utensils if they had been legally condemned, that you will in compassion to the unhappy circumstances of your poor petitioners, be pleased to grant them such relief as you, in your wisdom shall think fit.

And your petitioners, as in duty bound, shall ever pray.

DURST THOME.

It will be observed that these afflicted German Swiss ancestors said that they arrived in the Ship Princess Augusta in 1736. Upon making a search of the list of those who came in this vessel, which list is found in Second Series of Pennsylvania Archives Vol. 17, page 126 and also in Vol. 4, Col. Rec. page 72—we find among them the following general Lancaster County names, George and Jacob Myers, Jacob Miller, Jacob Bair, John Bumgardner, Philip Gardner, Charles Smith, William Huber,

Lawrence Simon, John Dubbs, Hans and Thomas Kerr, John Jacob Busch, John George Graeff (Groff), Christian Snavely (Sneiblein), Teilman Hershel, Fred Greir, John Jacob Kellar, John Rudolph Erb, John Jacob Kreider, John J. Dubbs, Fredrick Gardner, Sebastian Groff, Walter Bowman (Baumann), Melchoir Detweiler, Hans Zwalley, Peter and John Binkley, Rudolph Bumgardner, Jacob Christman, Jacob Lawrence, Nicholas Faree (Free), George Mowrer, Christian Shibley and Joseph Newell and others.

We may, perhaps, infer from this fact, that many of these people who suffered these hardships came to the Susquehanna Valley to settle. One thing is certain, if they did come up here, they came without their goods, for as we shall see in the next item, their goods were forfeited to the Government and sold. A list of their goods will appear in the next item.

1737—List of Our German-Swiss Ancestors' Forfeited Goods and Disposal of the Same.

The following petition (4 Col. Rec. 173) and the added items show how our ancestors fared in the difficulties mentioned in the preceding item.

"To the Honorable Charles Read, Esq., Judge of the Court of Vice Admiralty of the Province of Pennsylvania.

The humble petition of Nicholas Tainy, Benedict Youghly, Bastian Graffts and George Graffts, passengers, in the plea of the aforesaid Samuel Marchant, mentioned on behalf of themselves and others, the passengers aforesaid, humbly showeth:

That the said petitioners and others, the passengers aforesaid whose names are contained in a schedule hereunto annexed, were owners and now claim property in Thirty Stoves, in the in-

GERMAN-SWISS AND NAVIGATION ACTS.

formation exhibited, called Chimney backs, five hundred and ninety-six Syths, One hundred and three large Iron Instruments called Strawknives, Fourteen Iron Instruments called drawing knives, Twenty seven Iron stew pans, eighty one Iron Ladles. Five dozen and three Iron Shovels, Twenty-seven Iron pot lids, Twelve Iron dripping pans and frying pans, Thirteen axes and one hatchet, three small and one large crosscut saws, one gross of Shoemakers' and two of Saddlers' awls, six box Irons and six Chissels, Six Iron baking stove pans, Twenty three dozen of Clasp-knives, One dozen of Steels, One dozen of Plyers and Hammers, Six Iron Lamps, Six Trowels, One spade, One cask of nails and a smith's Vice, Fourten copper kettles, Five copper stills, Two dozen scissors, one packet of sleeve buttons and Studs, four Umbrellas, Four dozen and one half of Worsted Caps, Two dozen of printed linen Caps, Six pair of worsted stockings, Four pieces of striped cotton Handkerchiefs, Twenty five pieces of Tape, Two dozen black Girdles, One piece of black Crepe, One piece of striped Cotton, Nineteen pieces of Bedtick, Two pieces of brown Linen, One piece of blue and white Linen, Two dozen of ivory Combs, Two dozen and one half of tobacco Pipes with brass covers and a brass box, Two dozen of Ivory needle cases, Three handbrushes, Three dozen of Pewter Spoons, Three dozen of Spectacles, Eight looking Glasses, Eight Flutes, Six wooden Clocks, and one dozen of briarhook Sickles, in the information aforesaid mentioned; that to them they belong and were imported for their own private use, and not for sale; And say they are advised and hope to prove that the sentence against the Goods, Wares, and Merchandise aforesaid ought not to be put in execution, for that the proceedings in the cause aforesaid against the said goods are Null, void, invalid, and of no force and effect in the law, for the several causes following, viz: for that it appears by the plea of the said Samuel Marchant the goods aforesaid were the goods of those Claimants, and therefore, ought not to have been condemned without a hearing first given them, And also an opportunity of examining witnesses, by which it might have appeared to the Court here that the said goods were not liable to be condemned as forfeited; also, for that by the practice of this Court and Law in such cases, at least a third proclamation ought to have been made before the goods aforesaid could legally be condemned; also for that the information aforesaid is altogether uncertain and illegal, which has rendered the sentence grounded thereupon, altogether null and void; the said information being exhibited on behalf of the Governor or President, whereas, at the time of the exhibiting of that information, the Government, by the death of the late Lieutenant Governor and the laws of this province, devolves upon and still continues in the President and Council and not in the President only, and therefor the information aforesaid ought to have been in the name of the President and Council of the Province of Pennsylvania (in whom the power and authority of a Governor of this Province, by the death of the said late Lieutenant Governor, Patrick Gordon, Esq., deceased, is vested) and the sentence ought to have been pronounced accordingly. And even had this been done, as your Honor is a member of that very Council, and consequently interested in the event of the forfeiture, if any be, They submit it to your Honor whether it be consistent with the rules of Justice and Equity that any sentence should be given in the premises at this time and in this Court.

For which reasons they humbly pray, that the said sentence may be reviewed, reheard, and not put in execution; but that the proceedings for the causes aforesaid may be declared invalid, null and void, and that the goods, wares, and merchandise aforesaid be restored to their owners. And they, as in duty bound shall pray.

NICHOLAS TAINY
BENEDICT YOUGHLY
BASTIAN GRAFFTS
GEORGE GRAFFTS.

A schedule or list was likewise annexed to the foregoing petition, containing the names of One hundred and sixteen foreigners. Which petition and papers annexed, are contained under consideration."

Other steps taken by these unfortunate foreigners, concerning their goods, are found in the same book, page 226, where it is made plain, that all these goods were condemned and sold and the moneys given to the use of the English Government.

From these we observe, that since these German Swiss were not English and not naturalized, the goods which they attempted to bring to this country and start their life here with, were liable to seizure as the English law did not allow any goods from any other country except England, to be imported into the colonies of America. It seems that under a certain taxation and restriction, certain amount of clothing and household goods could be brought over. But they fared very badly in the incident referred to above.

1737—Ship Records of the Preceding Year.

The records of immigrants, coming to Pennsylvania in 1736, may be found in the item setting forth, the unfortunate company who arrived in the Princess Augusta, set forth (ante) in these annals.

The only other ship arriving during that year was the Perth Amboy, account of which is found in 2nd. Series of the Pa. Archives, Vol. 17, page 130. The immigrants arriving in this ship are as follows, common in Lancaster County:

Frantz — Hellar — Lambert — Steiger — Herr — Eberhart — Shultz — Haas — Rausch and Smith.

There are others arriving in this ship; but these are those of Lancaster County's common names.

1736 — Michael Welfare a German Baptist Preacher from Ephrata.

The Germans in and about Ephrata who followed a monastic religious life, produced several peculiar characters and a great many religious writings. One of these characters was Michael Welfare.

In the Pa. Gazette, in the issue of January 6, 1737, there is a notice of a book published by Welfare called, "The wisdom of God crying and calling to the sons and daughters of men for repentance."

The notice states, that this is really a sermon or testimony delivered to the people of Philadelphia Market September 1734 by Michael Welfare; together with some additional remarks on the present state of affairs concerning christianity in Pennsylvania. To be sold by Benjamin Franklin. About the same time the testimony was delivered, a notice appeared in Franklin's newspaper under the date of September 25, 1734.

This may be found under that date in the preceding item of these annals.

1737—Ship Records For This Year.

During this year we find 7 ship loads of these German Swiss people.

HORRORS OF THE BORDER WARFARE.

Among the common Lancaster County names we find the following:

Four Alberts—2 Arnolds—2 Beckers — 6 Bowmans — 2 Fishers — 2 Frantzs—2 Falcks—4 Groves—2 Garbers—6 Habeckers—2 Kauffmans—4 Longs—3 Leamans—8 Millers—2 Meyers—2 Minnichs—2 Rotes—2 Reigels—2 Smiths—4 Stouts—3 Wolfes—3 Wises—2 Wagners—2 Welches—2 Zieglers—3 Stricklers—5 Shantzs and 3 Shrivers.

We find one each of the following: Appel — Bishop — Bumgardner — Christ — Eberhart — Engel — Foust — Fink — Frederick — Grim — Hollinger — Gardner — Kline — Krauss — Melchoir — Thomas — Snyder — Ritter — Ruth — Vogel — Weber — Wetzel — Spangler — Shober — Shank —Slegel and Springer.

These German Swiss people came in the Ship "Samuel" Hugh Percy master—"Snow Molly" John Howell master—"Virtuous Grace" John Bull master—"St. Andrew Galley" John Stedman master—"Bilander Townshead" Thomas Thompson master—"Charming Nancy of London" Charles Stedman master and the Ship "William" John Carter master.

1737—Horror and Suffering of the Early Germans in the Lancaster County Border Warfares.

The Colonial Records, particularly Volume 4, contains a great many letters upon the suffering of our German ancestors by reason of the contention of Maryland along the Susquehanna River.

In that book, page 159, and continuing for several pages, there appears a letter drawn up by the President and Counsel of Pennsylvania to the Maryland Governor, on the state of affairs. And contains, among others, the following extracts, made from it:

"But what must the world judge, or yourself say, of the last transactions begun about the time of the date of your letter, and since continued by your new Captain Higginbotham and his crew, the seizing and taking at one time half a dozen quiet and peaceable German men from the human office of digging a grave to bury the dead of a neighbor's family, hurry them through the woods in the most rigorously cold season that has been for some years known, about a hundred miles on foot, and there committing them in the like weather to a narrow noisome gaol without any other subsistance than a pint of Indian corn boiled in water for the whole twenty four hours, for which pint of the value of about a half penny each man is charged by the Sheriff twenty pounds of tobacco for each day, and no fire or any other lodging than the bare floor allowed them further than as the distressed people could procure them from the humanity of others, or borrow money to purchase them. And again others of the same people yet more barbarously treated, for instance your Captain and his gang, breaking down the window fired in upon the family at one man's house, then violently breaking up both his doors then cruely beat him and his wife with their guns, until they broke two of them, and then took the man; another they took from his threshing, and being at the work very thinly clothed, his wife following him to carry his coat to him, they fired at the woman and obliged her to return; they cut down the door of the third and took the man; at another who had fled on horseback to escape them, they fired two shots; at another's house they cut down two doors and took the man; at another's they cut down three doors, two at his house and one at his mill, and took him; and then took two others who went to them with the intention to have those unhappy prisoners freed; and all these, when thus taken, they hurried down in the same manner to Annapolis and committed them as they had the others before. They have also since taken Joshua Minshal, a frequent sufferer in your gaols, for no other reason formerly than acknowledging the jurisdiction he lives under, and now for none that we can learn besides their own will and pleasure. Nor do we find anything is or can be alleged against those Dutchmen or Germans, more than that being from their own observation convinced (for they were never that we can discover, solicited or persuaded to it by any of this Government) that the place they lived in could not be in Maryland but in Pennsylvania, and therefore, they thought themselves obliged in conscience to acknowledge their rightful proprietors and accordingly let you know this, a proceeding that, on their application to some of our Magistrates of Lancaster, they were advised to as the most candid and in genuous means they could use on their return to us, which they had of themselves proposed and were determined in before."

This is simply a summing up of what our German-Swiss ancestors had to endure along the Susquehanna River in 1737 and before. And it is set forth as a mirror, which our people of the present day can see reflected, some of the conditions of the so-called "good old times." This took place in both Manor and W. Hempfield townships and also along the west side of the river.

This extract was found in Vol. 4, Col. Rec., p. 160.

1738—Ship Records For This Year.

During this year we find 16 ship loads of these German Swiss people.

Among the common Lancaster County names we find the following:

3 Beyers—4 Bowmans—2 Benders—2 Burns — 2 Funks — 3 Fullmers — 2 Fritzs — 2 Hellars — 8 Hoffmans — 4 Halls—2 Hesses—4 Jacobs—2 Klines—3 Lites—3 Longs—18 Millers—9 Myers—3 Nagles—2 Palmers—3 Reeses—11 Smiths—13 Snyders—2 Shoemakers—3 Sharps—2 Shaeffers—2 Thomases—8 Wagners—2 Walters—2 Wolfs—3 Zieglers and 3 Webers.

We also find, one each of the following:

Arnold, Abel, Burkhart, Brock, Bernhart, Bricker, Beck, Daniel, Diehl, Engle, Fisher, Funk, Fehl, Gable, Goodman, Huppart, Hartman, Hoover, Hellar, Kinzer, Haller, Kauffman, Leonord, Mitchell, Mosser, Moore, Peters, Roth, Rhode, Stout, Ruth, Shenk, Shoop, Shultz, Starr, Slegel, Strauss, Stein, Shearer, Swartz, Tshudy, Zimmerman, Weaver, Wenger, Wise, Walker, Wanamaker and others.

These German and Swiss people came in the Ship "Bringantine Catherine" Jacob Philips Master—"Winter Galley" Edward Paynter Master—"Glascow" Walter Sterling Master—"Snow Sisters" James Marshall Master—"Robert and Alice of Dublin" Walter Goodman Master — "Queen Elizabeth" Alexander Hope Master—"Thistle" John Wilson, Master — "Nancy" William Wallace, Master —"Friendship" Henry Buch, Master—"Snow Fox" Charles Ware, Master—"Davy" William Patton, Master—"St. Andrew" John Stedmans, Master—"Bilander Thistle" George Houston, Master—"Elizabeth" George Hodgson, Master — "Charming Nancy" Chas. Stedman ,Master and "Snow Enterprise," Lynell Wood, Master.

1738—Unsanitary Accommodations in Our Ancestors' Ships.

From time to time the ancient records make reference to the sick and deceased conditions of the poorer immigrants and of the necessity for hospitals and lazarettos. In Vol. 4, Col. Rec., page 306, necessity for quarantine is again brought up.

It is there stated, that Dr. Thomas Graeme, who was appointed the official visitor on all ships arriving in Philadelphia made a report concerning four ships that had just come from Rotterdam and Amsterdam. It was particularly pointed out, that the passengers on the ship Nancy and Friendship should not land, as such landing might prove dangerous to the health of the inhabitants of the province. And, it was therefore ordered, that the Masters of these ships should be taken into custody for contempt in not obeying the Governor's order, which required, that all ships must remain one mile away from the City, until they give security not to land any of the passengers, baggage or goods until the passengers have been examined and until the ships have a license to do so.

It seems that Philadelphia was afraid of small pox and other contagious diseases.

On turning to the records of those who arrived in the Nancy and Friendship, we find persons bearing our Lancaster County names, such as Hoffman, Myer, Beck, Reese, Rhode, Young, Hoover, Miller, Shoop, Smith and many others.

1738—The Progress of Our County Largely Due to the German-Swiss.

Turning again to Col. Rec., Vol. 4, page 315, we find, that at this same time, the Governor made an address to the Assembly, in which he gave his views upon the subject of the German Swiss people and their condition in this county up until that time.

Among other things he says: "This Province has been for some time the asylum of the distressed Protestants of the Palatinate, and other parts of Germany, and I believe it may with truth be said that the present flourishing condition of it is in a great measure owing to the industry of those people; and should any discouragement divert them from coming hither, it may well be apprehended that the value of your lands will fall, and your advances to wealth be much slower; for it is not altogether the goodness of the soil, but the number and industry of the people that make a flourishing country. The condition indeed of such as arrived here lately has given a very just alarm; but had you been provided with a Pest House or Hospital in a proper situation the evils which have been apprehended might under God have been entirely prevented. The law to prevent sickly vessels from coming into this Government has been strictly put in execution by me. A physician has been appointed to visit those vessels and the Masters obliged to land such of the passengers as were sick at a distance from the City, and to convey them, at their own expense, to houses in the Country convenient for their reception. More could not have been done without inhumanly exposing great numbers to perish on board the ships that brought them."

1738—Another Lot of German Swiss Ancestors Naturalized.

During this session of the Legislature the following persons were naturalized, among those, we recognize many names of our Lancaster County people of the present day, Michael Albert, William Albert, Leanord Bender, George Miller, John Bushong, Nicholas Candle, John Hagey, Charles Kellar, Stephen Leiberger, Ludowick Dettenburn, John Peter Ccoher, Michael Becker, Kaspar Stump, Jacob

Becker, Bartholomew Shaver, Tobias Pickle, Peter Rutt, George Klein, Paul Tittenhoffer, Mathias Tise, George Ludowick Horst, Sebastian Graeff, John Henry Bassler, Mathias Yung, Jacob Schlough, Henry Michael Immel, Felix Miller, Martin Weybrecht, Frederick Eigelberger, Sebastian Fink, Hans Adam Shreiner, Christian Lang, Caspar Fillar, Anthony Bretter, Hans Graff, Theophilus Hartman, Jr., Benjamin Witmer, Abraham Witmer, Johannes Binkley, Turst Buckwalter, Henry Neaf, Jr., Valentine Hergelrat, Henry Bassler, John Stettler, Leonhard Romler, Leonhard Heyer, Peter Schell, John Nohaker, Michael Knoppenheffer, Christian Leman, George Unrook, Jacob Sheffer, Valentine Keffer, Jacob Etshberger, Herman Walburn, Casper Reed, Christian Ley, Jacob Lower, Hans Moor, Johannes Blum, George Steitz, Erasmus Bluckenmeyer, George Graff: "being all of the Protestant or Reformed religion, and subjects of the Emperor of Germany, and other provinces now in amity with the King of Great Britain; every one of them was by this Act declared citizens, and all the immunities enjoyed by natural liege subjects, were to be enjoyed by them." (Rupp 271.)

1738—Another Small Influx of Germans.

Rupp, in his history of Lancaster County, page 273, says that about this year, many immigrants from the Palatinate settled in Brecknock Township. Among these were Jacob Guth, who erected the first grist mill; John Mussleman and Francis Diller, who erected the first distillery in Brecknock; Jacob Schneder, and Francis Eckert, Herman Deis, Christopher Waldhauer, William Morris and some others. This marks the opening of the northeast section of Lancaster County settlements, namely, old Brecknock Township. The number of taxables about this time were 2560, in Lancaster County.

1738—Settling of Another Lot of Palatines.

In the Pa. Gazette of Oct. 26, 1738, contains this item. "Last Saturday arrived here, the ship Davy from Holland with Palatines.

The Captain with both mates and one hundred and sixty passengers died on the passage and the Carpenter brought in the vessel. Most of the ships which bring Dutch passengers this year, have been visited with a sickness that has carried away a great number of Swiss.

We see by this, why a pest house or a similar method of quarantine was so badly needed. This ship had to be brought in by the Carpenter and apparently very few passengers were left.

Turning to Volume 17, Second Ser. of Pa. Archives, page 169, we find that this ship "Davy" was not Dutch, but German; and came from Amsterdam. The list of passengers given in the records number 94.

We observe that two-thirds of the number died on the passage.

Among the ordinary county names in this ship we find such as Kunzler, Long, Shearer, Thomas Seber, Myers, Stein, Kellar, Frey, Wise, Fehl, Shrum, Kinzer, Subert, Khehr, Snyder, Moore, Reichert, Hoffman, Beck, Lantsinger, Wetzel, Lantz, Stoltz and others.

We see, therefor, that the sufferers mentioned in this item were ancestors of people actually living in this county today.

1738—Great Percentage of German Swiss Immigrants Died En Route.

From the records we have shown of the several ships names, whose catastrophes we were able to describe, because, of the meager accounts of ancient newspapers, still on file, we are able to calculate how many thousands of those who started for America from Amsterdam and Rotterdam between the years 1700 and 1750 never reached America; but died at sea and were buried in its waters.

We cited the case of the ship that had 150 on board and arrived here with only 50 persons; and another case where one-half of the crew were lost and one-half of the passengers died; and of the ship Davy, just mentioned in which, out of 254, fully 160 were lost and only 94 reached shore.

There were many others, no doubt, in which 50 to 100 died on the voyage and no note was ever made of them. It is therefore safe to say, that the 30,000 German Swiss immigrants who arrived here from the year 1700 until the times reaching up to the Revolutionary War may not have been more than two-thirds or three-fourths of those who started to reach America. That is to say, it is wholly likely that out of nearly 45,000 or 50,000 immigrants who set sail for America in that time, 15,000 to 20,000 of them died on the voyage by diseases, hardships and exposure. And perhaps, many entire ship loads of them went down, of which we have no record in America at all. Those 30,000 who arrived here during that time, may simply be survivors of a list of nearly 50,000 who started.

1739—Ship Records for This Year.

During this year, we find 8 ship loads of these German Swiss people. Among the common Lancaster County names we find the following:

2 Adams—3 Beckers—2 Bachmans—3 Diehls—2 Gables—4 Hoffmans—3 Klines—8 Millers—2 Smiths—4 Snyders—2 Swenks—2 Stouts—2 Thomases—2 Wolfes—2 Webers and 2 Weidmans.

We also find one each of the following:

Albert, Burkhart, Brenner, Barr, Cook, Christian, Dorwart, Engle, Fisher, Frey, Fox, Gerhart, Good, Hess, Kramer, Moore, Martin, Neff, Roth, Reisser, Ream, Schaeffer, Shearer, Swartz, Strauss, Weaver, Welchans, Wolpert and Zimmerman.

These German-Swiss people came in the Ship "Bilander London"—John Pipon Commander; "Jamaica Galley"—Robert Harrison, Commander; "Snow Betsy"—Richard Buden, Commander; "Samuel"—Hugh Percy, Commander; "Robert and Alice"—Walter Goodman, Commander; "Friendship"—William Vittery, Commander; "Loyal Judith"—Edward Painter, Commander, and "Lydia"—James Allen, Commander.

1739—Many Inhabitants of Lancaster and Philadelphia Petition to be Naturalized.

In Vol. 3, Votes of Assembly, p. 334, a large number of our ancestors set forth their desire for naturalization and this action as well as the general situation in Pennsylvania on the subject of German Swiss immigration the Assembly represented to Hon. Thomas Penn as follows:

To the Honorable Thomas Penn:

The address of Representative of Freeman of said province showeth:

That we have received sundry petitions from a great number of inhabitants of Philadelphia and Lancaster Counties, which we take the liberty to lay before the Proprietor setting forth the great straits they and their families will be reduced to and the inconveniency that will arise to many others though not under their circumstances, if those poor people should be removed from their present habitations at the time limited by the proprietor's advertisement of November 23 last:

Though some of these people have most unwarrantably possessed themselves of your lands and others of them very much failed in their duty in complying with their contracts, yet we hope the Proprietor will be pleased to have compassion upon their present circumstances and rather impute their falling short in that justice which they owe to your Honorable family, to their necessities and want of knowledge and due consideration, rather than a disregard and contempt of your right or authority.

And as we are of the opinion that the greatest part of these people, under the circumstances mentioned in said advertisements, may in time become useful inhabitants,—We humbly request our Proprietor to take their unhappy condition into his consideration, and allow them such further time, under such limitations as the Proprietor shall judge reasonable, in order to pay for and get their titles to their lands confirmed; and this house, will in a proper time, readily join with the Governor in any Act that may be judged necessary, as well as for protecting the property of the Proprietor and others from such unjust intrusions in the future, and for the preservation of the Peace of the Government, as for guarding against the danger which may arise from the great and frequent importation of foreigners; and by these means we hope the Proprietor's interest will be much advanced and the poor people much relieved.

We shall see that the wish of these people was gratified.

1739—Lancaster County Ancestors Naturalized.

May 19, of this year, the following residents of Lancaster County were naturalized, Michael Albert, William Albert, Leonhart Bender, George Miller, John Bushong, Nicholas Camile, John Hagey, Charles Kellar, Stephen Remsberger, Ludowick Dettenburn, Jacob Bair, Jr., John Leiberger, Bartholomew Shaver, Caspar Stump, Jacob Becker, Tobias Pickle, Peter Rutt, George Kline, Paul Tittenhoffer, Mathias Tise, George Ludowick, Sebastian Graff, John Henry Basseler, Mattheas Yung, Jacob Shloug, Henry Michael Immel, Felix Miller, Martin Weybrecht, Fredrick Eigelberger, Sebastian Fink, Hans Adam Shreiner, Christian Long, Caspar Tiller, Anthony Bretter, Leonhart Ellmaker, Andreas Bersinger, Hans Graff, Jacob Hartman, Theopolis Hartman, Jr., Benjamin Witmer, Adam Witmer, Johannes Binkley, Turst Buckwalter, Henry Neaff, Jr., Valentine Heargelrat, Henry Basseler, Johan Stetler, Leonhart Romler, Leonhart Heyer, Peter Shell, Johan Nohaker, Nicholas Miller, Johan Hock, Thomas Koppenheffer, Christian Leeman, George Unrook, Jacob Shaffer, Valentine Keefer, Jacob Etshberger, Herman Walburn, Caspar Reed, Christian Manusmith, Nicholas Cutts, George Weyrick, Christopher Ley, Jacob Lower, Hans Moor, John Blum, George Steitz, Erasmus Buckenmeyer, and George Groff. These 78 names are all familiar ones down to this day. It is quite a satisfaction to know the date when they were thus granted full citizenship. They are spoken of in the record as of the Protestant or Reformed religion and are stated to have been subjects of the Emperor of Germany and other princes in amity with Great Britain.

At the same time a long list of Germans or Swiss of Philadelphia were naturalized. They are as follows:

Johannes Dylander, Christian Grassold, Henry Shocklier, Michael Jansen Halling, Daniel Steinmetz, Johannes Smith, David Deshler, Hans George Passage, David Seesholtz,

Stephen Greiff, Hans George Hickner, Sebastian Mirry, Rudolph Bonner, Baltzazae Ressler, Jr., Joannes Zacharias, Charles Benzel, Jr., Daniel Macjnd, Jr., Justis Reeb-Camp, Charles Reeb-Camp, Jacob Gallete, Anthony Hinkle, Peter Righter, William Rerig, Henry Stouz, Christopher Roab, Caspar Singer, Ludowick Knauss, William Hauke, Leonhart Hartline, Michawl Kline, Leonhart Kristler, Johannes Wilhelm, Ludowick Cirkel, Ludowick Hinnige, George Cressman, Fredrick Gotshall, Andreas Trombourger, Jacob Troumberger, Hartman Detterman, Philip Enghert, Jacob Coob, Henry Deinig, Johan Ditterig Bauman, Johan Kleim, Fredrick Marstaller, Mathias Koplin, Johannes Bender, Henry Deeringer, Adam Moser, Peter Jarger, Jacob Aister, Samuel Gooldin, Hans George Jarger, Andreas Kepler, Jacob Frey, Christopher Witman, Andreas Geisherts, Benedictus Muntz, John Eigster, Michael Herger, Philip Frederick Hillengas, Philip Labar, Michael Knappenberger, Michael Dotterer, George Hubner, Herman Fisher, Conrad Kolb, George Philip Dotterer, Johan Miller, Jacob Freeh, Henry Smith, Leonhart Smith, Rowland Smith, Michael Kraus, Daniel Kreestman, Abraham Beyer, Michael Good, George Good, Henry Snyder, Adam Reed, Christopher Ottinger, Anthony Jager, Nicolaus Jager, John Henry Weeber, Johan Jacob Roth, Johannes Geldbaugh, and Christian Gondy.

No doubt many of these are the ancestors of the great flourishing Mennonite Church of the City of Philadelphia, which is (among others) under the jurisdiction of that enterprising and learned father of the faith, Bishop N. B. Grubb. (See record of this naturalization in Vol. 4, St. L., p. 326.) This is the fruit of the petition set forth in the preceding item.

1739—German Swiss Ancestors Not Able To Pay Their Passage.

We have noticed in prior articles, that some of our German Swiss ancestors were held occasionally for their passage money. This difficulty they seemed to encounter continually. In the Pa. Gazette of April 19, 1739, it is stated, that "Whereas sundry Palatines are indebted for their freights in the under mentioned ships and sundry others have given their notes and bonds which have long been due; they are desired to take notice that if they do any longer neglect to come and pay their respective debts unto Benjamin Shoemaker living in High Street they may expect to be prosecuted according to law.

The ships are as follows:

The Ship Hope, Daniel Reed commander—Ship Samuel, Hugh Percy commander—Ship Mercury, William Wilson commander—Ship Princess Augusta, Samuel Marchant commander—Ship Virtuous Grace, John Bull commander—Ship Harle, Ralph Harle commander—Ship Winter Galley, Edward Painter commander—Ship Queen Elizabeth, Alexander Hope commander—Ship Glascow, Walter Sterling commander and the Ship Friendship, Henry Berch commander.

We can easily gather from this, that poverty was pretty generally the common lot of the earliest forefathers of Lancaster County. Of course, they had opportunity ahead for making money and did make money; but they began in face pinching poverty.

1739—The Dangers of Wagoning to Phihladelphia.

In the Pa. Gazette of October 25, 1739, there is an account as follows:

"On the 20th inst. as one Willmouth Brackbill, a Palatine, was driving a team on the Conestoga Road, he stepped out of the fore part of the wagon, his foot slipping the wheels went over him and he was killed."

There is nothing of importance in this item, except that, undoubtedly the road ways were in a bad condition between Lancaster and Philadelphia and they had many dangers. The traveling between the two places was quite numerous and many accidents occurred. It will be remembered, we learned that commodities of all kinds were taken to Philadelphia in wagons.

Harris in his Biographical History of Lancaster County contains notes of this death also. (P. 5.) Where he speaks of him as Ulrich Brackbill. It may be that it was Ulrich Brackbill that was killed. As Harris says, Ulrich Brackbill was one of the most prominent of our early ancestors. He was, I am quite positive, a son of Benedict Brackbill mentioned in a previous item of these annals. Benedict Brackbill was very instrumental in preventing the first ship load of Palatines from being sent by Switzerland to the East Indies. He interceded with Holland not to allow such a shipment to be sent across the Holland dominion down the Rhine and, therefore, the project was abandoned and some of the same people afterwards came to Lancaster County.

1739—Lancaster County Reformed Germans Naturalized.

In 4th Statutes at Large p. 327, will be found a list of what are called, Reformed Lancaster County Germans naturalized. This is the same list we gave in a previous item, although in that item, we did not refer to them as being of Reformed faith. It is made clear that they are not of Mennonite faith. At the Court of St. James, May 12, 1740, an Act for naturalizing these Germans came before the King's Council, and on recommendation of the Lords Commissioners for Trade and of the Privy Council the Act for naturalizing was approved.

1740—Ship Records For This Year.

During this year we find 6 ship loads of these German Swiss people. Among the common Lancaster County names we find the following:
2 Beckers—2 Freys—2 Hellars—8 Millers—3 Myers—8 Smiths—13 Snyders—4 Shoemakers—2 Walters and 3 Wolfes.

We also find one each of the following:
Arnold — Beyer — Beck — Brosius — Berger — Cramer — Casper —Cook — Fisher — Fink — Frantz — Greenawalt — Hoffman — Hall — Hersh — Hart — Kress — King — Moore — Marks — Oster — Rhode — Reinhart — Reissner — Rupp — Schaeffer — Stein — Saylor — Shaeffer — Weber — Wacker and Werner.

These German Swiss people came in the Ship "Friendship," William Vittery master—"Lydia," James Allen master — "Samuel and Elizabeth," William Chilton master—"Loyal Judith," Lovell Painter master—"Robert and Alice," Walter Goodman master, and "Samuel," Hugh Mercy master.

1740—Taxation Without Representation.

In Vol. 16 of Hazard's Register, page 253, there is an article showing the original letters of Peter Miller, who was a prominent figure in the Ephrata settlement. Peter Miller writing about the events in his letter of 1790 says, "that 50 years earlier, which would have been 1740, the subject of taxes came up and they were all very poor at that time." He further states, that at that time, a Constable entered their Camp, for they lived in the form of a Camp then, and demanded a single man's tax from each one of the single men. The Brethren differed among themselves in opinion, some paid, some refused and claimed a personal immunity, on the ground that, in the eastern countries the Monks and hermits were not subject to taxes, they simply collected every harvest by their labor so much grain as was needed for the yearly supply and have also supplied all the prisons and helped the poor and, therefore, the old Roman Emperor freed them from any taxes. They claimed these early brethren were not inferior to those of ancient times. The result was, that six of these brethren were taken to jail at Lancaster and were imprisoned 10 days but were set free, and a veneral old Justice of the Court offered himself for bail for them. His name was Tobias Hendricks.

When the Court came on and the brethren appeared before the Board, the Judges became greatly impressed with the fear of God; because these 6 men had been reduced to skeletons, and finally, the Court decided they could go and be free; but, they should pay the tax as one family, that is the same as one head of a family would pay instead of each man paying a tax.

You can readily see, that the only excuse the brethren had, was that as they did not labor for gain and lay up estates: but spent their time in helping the poor and in teaching religion, they should be freed of taxes.

1740—Historical Ephrata.

In Volume 15, of Hazard's Register, page 161, there is a historical sketch of our early German ancestors at Ephrata, stating that they came to America about 1719 and settled at Germantown, Skippack, Oley, Conestoga and elsewhere. They formed a church at Germantown in 1723 and established a church at Muehlbach; and the account details, how they grew from time to time. It is too large an account for these annals.

1740—German Migration into the Cumberland Valley.

It seems, that about this time, the low wall of mountain ridges between lower Susquehanna and the settlements following to the southwest into the Potomac and other valleys, no longer formed the western boundary of our German population.

It is stated in Vol. 5, of the Colonial Records, page 445, that about 1740, Fredrick Starr, a German, with two or three more of his countrymen made a small settlement in what is now called the Cumberland Valley.

It seems that the Delawares roamed in these parts of Pennsylvania and that they considered it a breach of treaty, for white people to come into that section. They complained to the Governor and the Governor said that he would see that they were thrown back over the mountains again.

We simply note this item as it seems to be the beginning of the Cumberland settlements.

1740 — Germans Support the Quakers in Opposing Gov. Thomas's War Spirit.

We all know that in 1740 Governor Thomas of Pennsylvania was very zealous in this Province, in gathering up soldiers to take part in King George's War—and he made no scruples of causing servants to leave their masters (who had paid for their services for a term of years), and entering the army. The Quakers opposed this; and John Wright the presiding judge of our local courts (also a member of the Assembly) was strong in denouncing the governor. The governor refused to continue him longer as a judge and dropped him. He was a Quaker.

Gov. Thomas found himself opposed and overcome by the Quakers in the Assembly, and the Quaker members held their seats by the German voters, who also opposed war measures.

The governor complained of this to England at last. In his communication to the English Government Oct. 20, 1740 (Vol. 4 St. L. p. 468) he says in explanation of why he does not succeed better, that the Quakers and Germans, "entered into consultation and came to a resolution to exert their whole power to secure a considerable majority of their own persuasion to be chosen to assembly to oppose all expense on warlike preparations as they call it." That this was not secret but publicly openly avowed. Again p. 470 he says, "There is little reason to expect provision for defense of the Province—as the same people at their yearly meeting which is now designed to direct the civil affairs of the government, instead of regulating religious affairs, were so strong that out of 30 members of the Assembly there are only 3 that are not Quakers. He then complains that "This could not have been effected had not the votes of the Germans (who are very numerous here) been engaged, by deceiving them into a belief that a militia will bring them under as severe a bondage to governors as they were formerly under their princes in Germany; that the expense would empoverish them, and that if any others than Quakers were chosen upon the Assembly they would be dragged down from their farms and be obliged to build forts as a tribute for their being admitted to settle in this Province. Many other falsehoods were spread among them in printed papers one of which falling into my hands I have enclosed with as good a translation of it as I could procure."

Further on he says that "This province is become very populous from the great numbers that have for many years past come into it from England, Ireland and Germany—and there is now 10,000 pounds interest in the bank from the interest of paper money, etc."

He also says that though only one third of the people are Quakers yet by electioneering and using the German vote they elected all but 3 Quakers to the Assembly out of 30. This article shows us several facts: —that our early German and Swiss non resistant ancestors took an active part in elections, which in some branches is not exercised today—that they were however, not independent in politics as in religion, but were used by Quaker politicians—that they were fearful of expense and extravagance—that they were numerous—that they were for peace, and fearful of arbitrary power—and that they could easily be frightened, because of their ignorance of the constitution under which they lived. The translated paper above referred to is not preserved nor set forth.

1740—Earliest German-Swiss in Western Pennsylvania.

About this time or a little earlier, our Germans and Swiss found new homes in "western Pennsylvania." In Vol. 4 Votes of Assembly p. 140 it is noticed that some Germans were then settled in western Pennsylvania and were getting into trouble among the Six Nations of that place. Thus we see that at this early date, the country toward the east was filled up and the new comers were obliged to seek homes farther west. We remember that by 1730 the whole country east of the Susquehanna River was filled up, and the migration into what is now York County began. We thus can trace the rate of growth and migration westward, of these German-Swiss ancestors.

1740—Our Germans and King George's War.

This year, war having been declared against Spain by England which later (in 1744) included France and became known as King Georg's War, the Governor of Pennsylvania ordered notice to be given to all persons in Pennsylvania, that they are invited to join Pennsylvania's expedition against the Spanish West Indies; and that the persons to receive their enlistment in Lancaster County, were Dan Cookson, Andrew Galbraith, Thomas Edwards and Samuel Smith the late sheriff. The notice further set forth that these gentlemen were not permitted to give out any person's name who would join; but to keep it secret.

This notice was published in both German and English in the papers and was designed to attract the "Dutch servants" of the Lancaster County people. See American Weekly Mercury date Apr. 17, 1740, in the Historical Society Library of Pennsylvania at Philadelphia, where old newspapers are on file.

The design of not giving out anybody's names was to prevent the owners of servants from making claim and from obtaining knowledge of where their servants were.

The fact that German servants and free Germans were enlisting is shown by the names of some of them who deserted the army, who were from Lancaster County and also by the following article:

"Notice is hereby given to all masters of servants in the Counties of Philadelphia, Bucks, Chester and Lancaster who may have in any manner suffered by the late enlisting of servants, that they immediately make known their several grievances to the constables of their respective townships, who have orders to transmit the same to Philadelphia, to the committee of grievances appointed by the Assembly." See Pa. Gazette, Aug. 14, 1740.

Though names cannot be ascertained yet there were a great many of our German-Swiss ancestors in the military operations between England, Spain and France, of these early days. We were loyal Englishmen then and fought for mother Britain against her European foes. But later we compelled her to acknowledge our independence.

1740 — A Lancaster County German Had a Genuine English Lord as a Servant.

Lord Altham, whose name was Arthur Annesley, and who was married to the daughter of the Earl of Buckingham in 1715 had a son James by her the next year. Then he had a difference with his wife and separated—soon afterwards, she died and the father became intimate with a Miss Gergory. She expected to marry the lord, and did all she could to alienate the father's affection for his son. The son was placed in a Dublin school, and in a few years the father died. Then his brother, uncle of James, to possess his brother's estate, enticed the boy on board a vessel for America in 1728. He was landed at Philadelphia a redemptioner that fall, at the age of 13 years, sold as a redemptioner, and served 12 years here in our county in rough farm labor. In 1740 when he was about 25 years of age two Irishmen found him, working for an old German, in the eastern part of Lancaster County near the "40-mile" stone on the Lancaster road. The two Irishmen found that they and the boy were all from the same locality in Ireland and they agreed to go back with him and testify to his identity and prove his lordship; and did so. In England, James was tried for killing a man, which he accidentally did soon after arriving, and his uncle tried to have him convicted. But he was acquitted. The great estate was given to the boy, but he did not live long, when his uncle again became entitled to it; but he also died soon after coming to it—a finished villian and an Irish nobleman. (See Vol. 9 Haz. Rec. 145.)

This is perhaps the only case in which a plain German Lancaster County farmer had a member of the British nobility as a farm hand; albeit, many Americans have had scores of fool British nobility sons-in-law since.

1740—An Echo From the First Settlement.

Among the first settlers on Pequea in 1710, there was one named Martin Mylin. Thirty years later his son Martin Mylin erected on the Mylin tract just east of what is now Willow Street, a fine large stone house of imposing proportions. Rupp tells us, pp. 286 and 287, that the house, compared with the modest dwellings of the times was so much a mansion that the settlement who were practically all unassuming Mennonists, were greatly excited and felt it their duty to take him seriously to task for such violations of the principles of humility which were fundamental in their faith. Therefore, they called a meeting and protested against such ambitious building on the ground that it would seriously affect the peace and harmony of the community and offend their central tenet of humility. Brother Mylin, however, mollified the brethren; and with a sober and friendly admonition against further grandeur and display the matter was dropped. The house was enduring and substantial as well as palatial and stood until a few years ago.

1740—Land Transactions of This Year.

This year Jos. Shippen and wife sold by deed of December 6, 1740, a tract of 94 and 2-3 acres of land on the Conestoga Creek, and also a tract of 100 acres adjoining it by deed dated December 9, 1740, to Oswald Hostetter. (See Recorder's Office, Lancaster, Book A, pp. 25 & 29.) These deeds recite that, William Penn on September 27, 1681, granted to Charles Jones, Sr., and Charles Jones, Jr., soap boilers of Bristol, England, 2000 acres of land in Pennsylvania to be surveyed. From the Joneses it passed Nov. 4, 1711, to Esther Shippen, wife of Edward Shippen and from them to their grand-son Joseph Shippen by will August 4, 1724. Michael Shank paid 35 pounds for his 194 and 2-3 acres.

It is described as a tract on a branch of the Conestoga and extends 130 perches or nearly half a mile north and south and 123 perches or about three-eighth of a mile east and west. The Hostetter tract lies by it.

There was a conveyance this same year on November 22, for 192 acres of land in Sadsbury Township from James Musgrove to Daniel McConnell. (Same book p. 27.)

I cite this transaction on Conestoga Creek to show the state of German-Swiss settlement at this date. And I give the history of the transaction to show the fact that the early land titles of this county run back far beyond the first deeds. In this case 60 years elapsed before a deed was given and 16 years between the warrant and the deed.

Penn made many sales of land in Pennsylvania in 1681 and 1682 which land was not taken up and settled until 1720-1725 and later.

1741—Ship Records For This Year.

During this year we find 9 ship loads of these German Swiss people.

Among the common Lancaster County names we find the following: 2 Bernharts—2 Kocks—2 Millers—2 Myers—2 Martins—2 Welshes and 2 Kieffers.

We also find one each of the following:

Arnold — Becker — Bitner — Biegler — Berger — Frey — Hess — Huber — Henry — Hertzog — Hoffman — Keiper — Kemper — Kapp — Reese — Ruth — Kapp — Smith — Snyder — Stout — Wagner and Wolfe.

These German Swiss people came in the ship "Frances & Ann," Thomas Coatman master—"St. Mark," Thomas Wilson master—"Lydia," James Allen master—"Marlborough," Thomas Bell master—"St. Andrew," Chas. Stedman master—"Friendship," Alexander Thomas master—"Snow Molly," John Cranch master—"Snow Thane," William Weems master and "Europa," Lumnsdaine, master.

1741—Contagious Diseases on Ship Board.

The question of contagious diseases among the German Swiss immigrants for some time had caused a great deal of excitement and trouble; but about 1740 and 1741 measures began to be passed to guarantee protection against the spread of the diseases. The Government appointed Dr. Graeme to make a report and investigation on the condition and upon the necessity of erecting a lazaretto or quarantine. What he did on the matter will be found in Vol. 4, Col. Rec., page 515.

The German Swiss about this time began to feel that they were quite disfavored in Pennsylvania; and in fact they had great reasons to feel that way; because every Legislature had something to say against them. They were looked upon suspiciously. This was partly because of them being aliens and partly because they began to take positions in political affairs in the Province. At least those who were naturalized. (See Rupp page 286 and Lyle's history page 126. A few years later they began to be very zealous politicians.

Now that these contagious diseases were breaking out among them on ship, they were suspected of bringing over foreign fevers and foreign ailments. They themselves asked for quarantine. (4 Col. Rec. 507.) In sloops which had been landing it was reported that great fear seemed to be rising in Pennsylvania, because they were afraid of the spread of small pox and other sicknesses. (See 4 Col. Rec. pps. 496 and 498.)

The province of Pennsylvania passed a law for the protection of themselves as well as of the Province in general, from the diseases which were being founded. (See Vol. 4 Col. Rec. p. 475.) The Governor was glad that the Assembly could agree to something favorable to these people, and he expressed himself favorably to them. (See Vol. 4 Col. Rec. p. 511.)

These German Swiss people felt that these new troubles were very likely to cause more intolerance to be exercised towards them, and therefore, that began to seek toleration. Some of their troubles can be seen in Vol. 3 Votes of Assembly, p. 347.

1741—Tremendous Snow Storm and Cold Winter in Lancaster.

In the Penna. Gazette, under the date of April 9, 1741, we are given a picture of some of the suffering of these German Swiss in the Conestoga settlement, at that early date.

The article is as follows:

"We hear from Lancaster County, that during the continuance of the great snow, which in general was more than three feet deep, great numbers of the back inhabitants suffered much for want of bread; that many families of the new settlers for some time had little else to subsist them but the carcasses of deer they found dead or dying in the swamps or runs about their houses. And although they had given all their grain to their cattle many horses and cows are dead, and the greatest part of the gangs in the woods are dead, that the deer which could not struggle through the snow to the springs are believed to be all dead, and many of those which did get into the Savannahs are also dead, ten, twelve or fifteen being found in the compass of a few acres of land. The Indians fear the winter has been fatal to the deer, turkeys, etc., in these northern parts—that they will be scarce for many years.

We also hear, that a young woman in Derry Township attempting to get home about one mile, as soon as she came within sight of her father's home turned out the horse which she had borrowed of her neighbor, as he directed her, but not being able to make her way through the snow, she threw off her clothes and attempted to return in the horse's footing, but after much struggle as appeared by her tracks froze to death."

Therefore, we have here another evidence that our early ancestors had a very rugged existence in this new country.

1742—Amish Mennonites Petition Assembly.

Hazard's Register (Vol. 5, page 21) informs us that in 1742 a number of Germans stated to the General Assembly that "They had emigrated from Europe by an invitation from the Proprietaries; they had been brought up, and were attached to the Amish Doctrines, and were conscientiously scrupulous against taking oaths—they therefore, cannot be naturalized agreeably to the existing law."

To remedy this a law was passed allowing them to be naturalized.

These people followed the leadership of Jacob Aman, originally, separating themselves from the main Mennonite Church to which they had belonged. The factions were then known as the Reist and Amman branches of the church. They believed in a more primitive form of worship and in "foot-washing" as the form of sacrament. This subject is discussed in these annals under date of 1693, page 128, ante.

1742—Germans and the Election Riot of 1742.

In the fall of 1742 there was a serious election riot, between what was known as the "country party" and the "city party" in Philadelphia. The city party secured a lot of toughs and dare-devil sailors to appear at the election and with clubs and missiles terrorize the Quakers and Germans as they came to vote. The city party asserted that the country party in recent years imported Germans from Lancaster county and other places to help swell their Philadelphia vote, and alleged that many of such persons were present at this election. At any rate, an ugly fight ensued. The matter came before the Governor and Council and also before the Assembly. The petition of the country party is found in Vol. 4, Col. Rec. 620. The proceedings in Assembly are found in Vol. 3, Votes of Assembly page 498 and also pages 564 to 575.

Some of the witnesses for the country party were Hugh Roberts who said the mayor refused to quell the sailor rowdies and to call the constables together. John Dellyn also testified and said the mayor simply said the sailors "have as much right at the election as the 'Dutchmen' you had to meet at Reese Meredith's last night."

Thomas Lloyd said about 50 sailors led the fight. He reported it to the city Recorder and that officer said he heard that 300 unnaturalized Dutchmen (Germans) had come down to the city armed with clubs and stated the sailors had as much right as those Dutchmen.

Jos. Wharton in his testimony said there was a riot like this two years before and that there are only 400 naturalized Dutch in the county and many more were at the polls (p. 568). Another witness said that one of the officers declared he would not stop the rioting sailors as they had as much right there "as the Dutch that you have brought down to vote" (do. 568). A witness said that every year they had trouble to dissuade the unnaturalized Dutch from voting and arming themselves with clubs. John Rynell (p. 571) testified that the Recorder when asked to restore order said "the sailors have as much right at the election as the unnaturalized Palatines many of whom have come down to the city to vote." A witness (Samuel Maris) said Captain Mitchell was drinking with the sailors and when spoken to, that he said it was agreed that these sailors and others should be there too, with clubs as the country party intended to have a lot of unnaturalized Dutch on hand to vote. Another witness Jo Hitchcock said he heard a gang of rough sailors going from the wharf to the Court House with sticks and asked them where they were going and they said "to knock down the broad brims." (p. 575). John Mitchell said he heard sailors say "Damn it, let us go down and knock those Dutch s—s of b—s off the steps." (p. 578). Another witness heard the city party call the country party "Broad-brims and Dutch dogs." Another witness said the City Recorder said "There are only 400 naturalized Dutch in the county and you have over 1000 of them here" (p. 586).

The Assembly having heard all this testimony decided to draw up a "humble petition" to the Governor setting forth that a pre-meditated design of disturbing the public peace of the province and terrorizing elections had been formed and that the magistrates did not try to suppress it and that the origin of the plot must be found and all concerned in it must be punished. (Do. p. 501).

This will suffice to show us that the early Germans here were subjects upon which politicians could draw to further their ends and also that many of those Germans and Swiss were zealously interested in the political affairs and in the Government of the Province; and I fear it is true that some of the unnaturalized (who did not have the right to vote) could be induced and frequently were induced to vote. We shall see that this was so, not only in Philadelphia, but in Lancaster County also. I do not know whether any of the Germans or Swiss engaged in the Philadelphia riot were from Lancaster County or not. The statement that they were "brought down" to vote may mean were brought down from Germantown to Philadelphia proper. Some may have come from other counties. But the chief grievance was that they tried to vote and did vote though unnaturalized.

The riot at any rate did not succeed in defeating the German and Quaker vote, because a large Quaker assembly was elected helped by the votes of their German friends. The action of the new assembly in resolving to punish the rioters, studiously avoids any reference to Germans voting illegally. This is ignored as if there is nothing in it.

1742—German-Swiss Ancestors Re-Assure the Government.

Our unpopular German-Swiss local ancestors were now being continually accused of lack of love for the Government in Pennsylvania. But in every instance they proved that they were wrongly suspected. Excitement ran high against them. To allay the feeling and prejudice they held a meeting and made a representation to the Governor and assembly in 1741 in part in the following words:

"Who they are that look with jealous eyes at the Germans, but the Governor has not been pleased to inform us, nor do we know. Nothing of the kind can be justly attributed to us, or any preceding Assembly, to our knowledge. The Legislature of this province has generally, on application made to them, admitted the Germans to partake of the privileges enjoyed by the King's natural subjects; and as we look upon them to be a laborious, industrious people, we shall cheerfully perform what can be expected from us for their benefit, and for those who may hereafter arrive."

To allay unfounded prejudices, the Mennonites gave a decided proof thereof in 1742, in convoking a church council, consisting of elders, preachers and the bishop, and meeting at the house of Martin Meylin, in Lampeter Township.

Martin Meylin, grandfather of Martin Meylin, Jacob Meylin, John Meylin and Abraham Meylin, all at present residing in West Lampeter township, built what was then called a palace, of sandstone. It was, in 1742 one of the most stately mansions in the country; and as the Mennonites were a plain people, and Martin Meylin an active member, the house was not only considered too palace-like, but the appearance of it might, as they reasoned, strengthen their enemies in prejudicing the Government against them—they had been virtually charged with disloyalty—"determined not to obey the lawful authority of government—that they were disposed to organize a government of their own."

The bishop, Hans Tschantz, with his elders and assistance, having repaired to the humble log cottage hard by the "stately mansion" and organized the meeting, himself presiding over the deliberations of the assembled. Martin was first questioned, upon conscience, to openly declare what his intentions were in erecting so large, so gorgeous a dwelling—reminding him of the rumor some twelve or thirteen years ago; and lately, of the prejudices excited against the Germans. He stated, he consulted only his comfort, and that he had no sinister views. Next he was reminded that, in their view, the house was rather too showy for a Mennonite. The question was, whether he deserved severe censure, if not suspension from church privileges, for this oversight. After some concessions, and mutual forbearance, by the parties, it was resolved that Martin be kindly reprimanded; to which he submitted—thus the matter ended, and all parted as brethren. (Rupp 286 and 7.)

We cannot tell at this date whether the meeting was held for the purpose of re-assuring the Government that they were a humble people and not ambitious for political power: or whether it was held for the purpose of cautioning brother Mylin that he was in danger of violating the rules of the church.

1742—The Case of Jealousy Against the German Swiss (Continued).

Governor Thomas in his address to the Assembly, concerning the suspicions that the German Swiss settlers had inspired among the early political powers of Pennsylvania, says, in Vol. 4 Col. Rec., pages 507 and 508, "Several of the most substantial Germans, now inhabitants of this province, have joined in a petition to me, setting forth in substance, that for want of a convenient house for the reception of such of their countrymen as, on their arrival here, laboured under diseases contracted in a long voyage they were obliged to continue on board the ships which brought them, where they could not get either attendance or conveniences suitable to their condition from whence many have lost their lives; and praying that I would recommend to the Assembly the erecting of a proper building at the public expense, not only to accommodate such as shall arrive hereafter under the same circumstances, but to prevent the future importation of diseases into this City, which has more than once felt the fatal effects of them.

The numbers of people which I observed came into this province from Ireland and Germany, pointed out to me the necessity of an hospital or pest-house, soon after my arrival here; and in 1738 I recommended it to the Assembly of that year, who seemed so far from disapproving it that they gave me hopes of building one so soon as the circumstances of the province should admit. I very heartily wish for the sake of such families, inhabitants of this City, as suffered in the late mortality by the loss of some who were their chief support, and will therefore feel it for years to come, and on account of the Irish and German strangers, that it had indeed been done so soon as the circumstances of the province did admit of it. But as it can profit nothing to bewail evils past, I hope you will now make the proper use of them by doing all in your power to prevent the like for the time to come.

I am not insensible that some look with jealous eyes upon the yearly concourse of Germans to this province, but the Parliament of Great Britain see it in a different light, and have therefore given great encouragement by the late act to all such foreign Protestants as shall settle in his majesty's dominions; and indeed every man who well considers this matter must allow that every industrious labourer from Europe is a real addition to the wealth of this province, and that the labour of every foreigner in particular is almost so much clear gain to our Mother country."

In this we see very plainly that while some of the English inhabitants settled here and holding offices were jealous of the growing power of the German Swiss people, that the Governor of the province was favorable to them. More than that it is evident, from what he says, that the Parliament of Great Britain had great faith in them, as a proper people to develop the resources of this province. The Assembly in their answer to the Governor, state, that a great many of these Germans and Irish are afflicted with the contagious diseases, that that is a cause to make us more cautious, and that it makes a quarantine building a great necessity.

In the last pargraph, the Assembly also tried to make it appear that they are also favorable to the Germans, for as we said in the former item, that the Governor did not tell them who the people are that are jealous of them; and further, that they, the Assembly, look favorably upon them.

This will suffice to show, that while at present the line of jealous powers of the two nationalities in this county and in southeastern Pennsylvania, has died out, that in early times there was great danger of friction. We shall trace up this growing power of the German Swiss people in southeastern Pennsylvania as these articles proceed.

These proceedings may also be found in Vol. 2, Votes of Assembly, pages 48-49 etseq.

1743—The Governor and Assembly Divide On the German Question.

The feeling against the German Swiss coming into Pennsylvania grew stronger in the Government of the province about this time. Turning to Vol. 4, Col. Rec., pages 526-27, we find, that a committee of Assembly really made charges against the Governor and the Council.

The Assembly ask the Governor why, if he has full power to employ a Doctor to examine the condition of the sickly palatines that arrive—why he asks help of them. They charge that the governor is not vigilant enough concerning these people in restraining the ships from landing for they will spread unhealthy diseases over the City.

The Assembly also discharged the quarantine doctor, so that the Governor had no physician to examine these passengers. The Governor complained that without examining these passengers and proving them dangerous, he would admit them. The Governor also observes, that the Assembly try to accuse him of arbitrary power; but he states, that the law gives him the authority to examine these vessels and he has the right to employ physicians to see whether any disease is found in them or not. He complains that they refused to pay the doctor he employed.

Further on, the Governor proceeds to consider what he calls the facts and says on page 529, that doctors appointed to examine these Germans acted diligently and that in 1738 there was a Palatine vessel with sick passengers arrived and the Assembly spread the fear that dangerous epidemic diseases were being brought but the doctor found nothing more than a common ship distemper among them. Afterwards it turned out that they had a very malignant disease.

The Governor here says that he acted as diligently as was needed and the Assembly publicly thanked him for the care he took. In this manner, the contention kept on during several years. The same subject may be found in Vol. 3, Votes of Assembly 451-2-2; also the same Volume, pages 472-500 and 501 and other places in Vol. 4 Col. Records.

1743—Further Naturalization of German and Swiss.

One of the results of landing a foreigner, was that such person still in Pennsylvania, could not will their land to their heirs, the same as natural born subjects could. For this and for other purposes, it was made necessary to naturalize them and this subject came up again in 1743. (See Vol. 4 Col. Rec., page 627.)

The proceedings to have the law passed also appear in 3 Votes of Assembly, page 505. A law was passed also enabling these people to devise their real estate to make wills, etc. (See 3 Votes of Assembly, page 514-15.)

1743—Law Passed to Establish Hospitals for German and Swiss Immigrants.

This same year a law was passed to establish hospitals for the sick immigrants. It is found in Vol. 4 Statutes at Large, page 382, the law states that as there had been a law before not allowing vessels with sickly immigrants to come nearer than one mile of any town or port, without a bill of health; but that no place was provided for the sick passengers that were on these vessels, and therefore, they started to land them secretly and they got into Philadelphia and spread diseases.

Therefore, Fisher's Island in the Delaware River was to be henceforth called Province Island, containing 340 acres, with buildings erected, and that this island together with the buildings should be under trustees to be used as a quarantine or hospital for these sick people. The buildings should be put on it for these purposes and that the buildings and fences and other improvements on it shall always be kept in repair; and that the Governor or two Justices of the Peace shall have the right to order and direct all persons brought into this province, who have infectuous diseases to go to that island and remain there until the physician says that they are free of disease. Their nursing and maintenance must be paid by the master of the vessel, that the sick people were brought in and the expenses of the master was put to, must be repaid out of the goods and property of the passengers, if they had any.

And for this purpose, the Justice of the Peace have the right to send for the master of the vessels and oblige them to give a bond that they will find proper food and nursing for the sick people, before they could land them. The law further provides, that a book must be kept in which the persons' names are entered, as sick persons. It is also provided that after the persons have recovered, they could be discharged only under the seal and certificate of two Justices.

It is further provided that no inn keeper or other inhabitants shall receive in their house, any of these persons who are known to be afflicted with any of these contagious diseases, until after discharged. A fine of ten pounds is provided for such persons.

Therefore, we can readily see that there were many difficulties to be encountered.

1743.—An Unusual Naturalization of Germans.

We have heretofore seen, that the Germans and Swiss in Pennsylvania, were naturalized by virtue of acts passed by the Assembly and the Governor of Pennsylvania, but finally, Great Britain herself passed an Act of Parliament to naturalize our Germans in Pennsylvania and in other parts of America. The complete act is found in a pamphlet known as the General Magazine and Historical Chronicle, a monthly periodical, published by Benjamin Franklin about 1740.

The January number of 1741, contains this Act of Parliament. This shows another event of Benjamin Franklin's activity. The pamphlet may be found in the Philadelphia Historical numbered Api. 228.

In conformity with that act of Parliament, the Pennsylvania Gazette reports, under the date of April 14, 1743, that "at the Supreme Court held here (Philadelphia) on Monday, Tuesday and Wednesday last, 304 Germans Protestants were naturalized by virtue of a late act of Parliament, having resided in this province upwards of seven years." It would be interesting to know the names of these Germans who were naturalized; but there seems to be no list in existence. There is no record in the Statutes at Large of such naturalization about this date. But there is, however, in the Statutes at Large, Vol. 4, page 391, an act passed in February 1743, allowing Protestants settled in Pennsylvania, not Quakers, to be naturalized on an affirmation instead of oath. And the introduction of the act recites, that there was an act of Parliament passed, in the 13th year of King George II, which is likely. The one above referred to, for naturalizing Protestants, states that after June first, 1740, all persons who have resided for seven years or more in American colonies, and shall not have been absent more than two months at a time, and should take an oath and repeat the declaration of allegiance and subscribe and set forth their Christian belief before the Judges, shall be adjudged to be the same as his Majesty's natural born subjects.

This Act goes on to say, that any foreigners who were not Quakers; but who conscientiously refused to take an oath, desired to be naturalized, and therefore, this Act allows them to be naturalized on an affirmation instead of an oath, if they have lived here seven years. But it further provides, that after the affirmation is administered, and entered in the Secretary's Office, the names of these persons naturalized must be transmitted to the Commissioners for trade and plantations in England yearly, in the same manner as the Act of Parliament is directed.

1743.—A German Paper Began Publication.

In the Pennsylvania Gazette, on the June 2, there is a notice as follows: "WHEREAS, the Subscriber has begun to publish a weekly newspaper in the German language for the carrying out of which he has received good encouragement from his country men, the Germans, in all parts of the province, So if all merchants who want ads inserted, send them to the subscriber or David Doshler, they will be faithfully translated and inserted.

Signed,
J. CRELLIUS."

This was no doubt a Philadelphia publication; but at any rate, it is pretty early and deserves mention, as one of the marks of German enterprise in an English Colonial history.

1743.—German Quarantine Again.

In Vol. 4 Statutes at Large, (382) the final steps, as to the German Quarantine building is taken. This is in the shape of an Act of Assembly to secure the title of Province Island and the buildings thereon, for a hospital for the sick passengers, to prevent the spread of contagious diseases.

As it was said before, this Island is situate "on the southerly side of the mouth of the Schuylkill River in the County of Philadelphia, adjoining on Delaware river, before known as Fisher's Island; but afterwards known as Province Island. Containing 312 acres of land and buildings." etc. Full provisions are made in the Statutes at Large, for the maintenance and regulations of the hospital. The act was passed February 3, 1743.

1743.—Act to Enable Germans To Make Wills and Give Legacies.

We have seen before that these Germans and Swiss, until they were naturalized, could not make wills, devising their lands to their descendants. Further it was (not apparently until 1743) lawful for any person to whom a legacy in money or goods was given to sue and prosecute an action to recover the legacy in Court. Therefore, particularly to assist the Germans and Swiss, an act was passed, to enable them to get property by will, and to accept it.

1743.—Crash Over Conflicting Land Grants.

In Vol. 4, Col. Rec., page 648, we have another picture of the trouble our German Swiss had to encounter, concerning their lands along the Susquehanna River. This time the Indians were mixed in the difficulty, and one of the chiefs of the five nations, made a speech to the Governor of Pennsylvania, and said that "the Dutchmen settled on southeastern Pennsylvania lands, claimed the right to the land simply because he gave a little victuals to the warriors of the Indian tribe, who were very often in need of it. The Indian then went on in his speech and said, this string of wampum serves to take the Dutchmen by the arm and throw them over the big mountains beyond the borders. The Indian chief also said, that they had given these valleys over to their cousins the Delaware Indians and to their brothers the Shawanese, and reserved some rights there to live themselves. Therefore, he repeated that the Indians will demand the Governor of Pennsylvania to remove immediately by force, all of those Dutchmen that are living on their lands. It appears, however, that this concerns lands further up the Susquehanna River, in the neighborhood of the Juniata River.

However as it is the same question of the Germans looking for further settlement, and coming in contact with the native tribes, this item has a place in this article.

This orator then goes ,on to say that he now lives on the River Ohio, harmless as a child. He could do nothing and is weak and does not intend any mischief; but that he looks for the Governor to have charge of this. He, therefore, went on to say, that the place where he lived, is over shadowed by a great cloud, that he looked with pitiful eye on the poor women and children, and then looked on the ground all along for sorrow; because of these poor women and children.

He states further, that the people were given to lies and raise false stories, and they asked the Governor to stop up their mouths, as he could do it with one word.

1743—Ship Records of 1743.

During this year we find eight ship loads of these German Swiss people. Among the common Lancaster County names, we find the following: 3 Benders — 3 Bakers — 2 Goodmans — 2 Gilberts — 2 Harts — 4 Kauffmans — 2 Hermans — 2 Krafts — 4 Kleins — 4 Kellars — 4 Myers — 13 Millers — 2 Snyders — 4 Smiths — 2 Stamms — 4 Swartz — 2 Shaubs — 2 Wagners — 2 Webers — 2 Hellars — 2 Youngs.

We also find one each of the following:
Albright — Appel — Bumgardner — Beyer — Brunner — Burkhart — Caspar — Eckert — Eberhart — Fisher — Frey — Good — Garber — Huber — Hellar — Kuhn — Koch — Kreider — Leinbach — Lehman — Landis — Neffs — Root — Sherts — Soutter — Shoemaker — Walters — Wolf — Wise and Zimmerman.

These German Swiss people came in the ship "Francis and Elizabeth," George North master — "Snow Charlotte," John Mason master — "Lydia," James Abercrombie master — "Rosanna," James Reason master — "Phoenix," William Wilson master — "Robert and Alice," Martley Cusack master — "St. Andrews," Robert Brown master — and "Snow Endeavor," Thomas Andrews master.

1744—Lancaster and Its Germans This Year.

Lancaster was an English town—it was founded by the English. It began to be built about 1728, according to Witham Marsh (Marsh's Diary), there was a sprinkling of German Swiss in the town, from its beginning; but they resided most numerously in the rural sections. An old geography of 1816 calls this, Lancaster the "biggest inland town in United States," which it was at that time (Jedidiah Morse's D. D. geography, published by Thomas and Andrews, Boston, in 1816, p. 171). The County of Lancaster at this date, was given a population of 58,927. But to come back to German Swiss element, in the little Lancaster town, which in 1744, the date of which we are now writing was 16 years old. William Marsh in his diary says, "the town was begun about 16 years earlier and has one main street." He says the "inhabitants are high Dutch, Scotch

Irish and English, and some unbelieving Israelites, who dwell very considerably in this place." Marsh proceeds to say, "that the spirit of cleanliness, has not yet, in the least troubled the major part of the people; for they are in general very great s...s and slovens. When they clean their houses, which is very seldom, they are not willing to remove the filth away from themselves, for they place it near to their doors, which in the summer time breeds quantities of bugs, fleas and vermin."

We believe that Marsh was very much prejudiced and was telling falsehoods in making these statements. The German Swiss who lived here were industrious and were also scrupulously clean, as to the scrubbing brush and broom and mop, which were almost constantly in their hands.

The leading German churchmen, who lived here, according to Marsh, at this time, were the sect of Lutherans. He also says the Dutch church was flourishing here, which is to be understood to be the German Reformed. Evidently in his opinion, the Lutherans were much more prosperous in their religious advancement, than the German Reformed people.

The houses of which he called this Dutch town, he says are mostly built with and covered with wood, except a few are stone and brick. He also tells us that he was stopping at Warrall's Hotel, which was the ancient Cross Keys, and when he went to bed he was "attacked by legions of Dutch fleas and bugs which were ready to devour both himself and the minister that he was sleeping with."

He also gives us the description of a dance held in the Court House, during which the Governor of Pennsylvania got too much wine and got very merry. He says "during the merriment two Germans happened to pass by the Court House with harp and fiddle and played for some time under the window." Then he says, "the Governor ordered them to come in and amuse us, which they did; but not with the harmony of their music, for it was very uncouth and displeasing; that they played a tune of some sort to some young Indian who danced a jig with Andrew Hamilton." He says that the Dutch girls (which he would call females, not ladies) danced wilder than the Indians, that the dancers in the party consisted of Germans, Scotch Irish and some Jewesses, and that the Jewesses were the best dancers. Finally he says, that after the Indian treaty, which he was attending was ended, he and his people mounted their horses and went away from this filthy Dutch town, to a very kind landlord at Nottingham, by the Gap road. (See Lancaster County Indians P. 346.)

We believe that this man Marsh, an Englishman from Maryland, was entirely unfair to the German Swiss people living in this town; and it is likely this feeling arose from the fact that Maryland and Pennsylvania, had for a dozen years prior to Marsh's visit, been in grievous dispute, about the boundary line, and the German Swiss people living on the western side of the Susquehanna, as we have shown earlier in these items, were the bone of contention between the two provinces, Maryland, in a very greedy fashion, claimed the Susquehanna River her northern boundary.

1744—Our German-Swiss Are Victims of Privateers.

In the Pa. Gazette of December 25, 1744, the following item appears: "That Friday last, arrived at Philadelphia, Captain Duraell, from Holland, but the last from Poole, with Palatines after a passage of thirteen weeks. Admiral Davis, with the squadron for the West Indies was at Spit Head when he sailed, and was to sail in a few days. In his passage, twelve leagues to the west of Sicilly, he was chased by a French Privateer, designed for Philadelphia with Palatines, as he sailed from Cowes, the day before he left Poole. But his vessel going very well, he got clear of the Privateer." This article is not very clearly stated in the Gazette, nevertheless serves to show us, that the Palatines, that is our German-Swiss ancestors, had a great deal to contend with besides the rough storms at sea, which frequently lengthened their voyage from 10 or 11 weeks to 17 and 18 weeks and perhaps 20 weeks. We are here given one of these difficulties, namely: "being chased by privateers." The privateers evidently found profit in robbing these poor people of what little substance they had.

1744—Conrad Weiser.

The most influential German, outside of those who lived at Germantown during the first half of the eighteenth century in Pennsylvania, was Conrad Weiser. His labors extend over a long series of years, until he died in 1760. He was the leading spirit in all of the treaties held with the Indians of Pennsylvania, and at the great treaty in 1744. He was the chief interpreter and was implicitly relied upon, by the Indians, in all matters. He made a journey to Shamokin at the instance of the Province of Pennsylvania, in 1744 (See 4 Col. Rec. 680), to investigate the murder of James Armstrong by the Indians. Among his many activities, from about the year 1730, was his leading of the Indians to Philadelphia — his interpreting at Philadelphia—his entertaining the Governors at his house—his conferences with the Indians of Ohio—his dealing with the 6 nations—his work in the Cumberland Districts — his interest in missionaries for the Indians—his conferences with Governor Clinton — his labors among the Mohawks—his opinions and activities in the Connecticut dispute — his services at the Albany treaty — his purchase of provisions for the Indians — his history of the Owandot Indians—his controversy with Sowers concerning some newspaper notoriety —his efforts to discourage scalping, and his trading business. All of these activities are found in Vol. 3 onward, of the Col. Rec.

In the first to the fourth series of the Pa. Archives are found a large number of his letters, his journals, accounts of his dealing in wampum, accounts of the transactions with the Indians, in buying and selling horses and dealing in their goods, etc., all of which are illuminating and show the wide range of activities of this man.

1744—Ship Records for This Year.

During this year we find 5 ship loads of these German-Swiss people. We find a total of 1080 people.

Among the common Lancaster County names, we find the following: 2 Bergers—2 Benders—2 Engles—2 Groffs—2 Harts—5 Klines—3 Kings—8 Myers—7 Millers—2 Michaels—2 Moores — 4 Snyders — 3 Smiths — 3 Schaeffers—4 Wagners—6 Webers—2 Wises and 4 Youngs.

We also find one each of the following:

Albright — Baker — Baer — Brown — Bernhart — Bauman — Doebler — Herman — Hartman — Huber — Kautz — Kurtz — Long — Lobach — Lintner — Metzler — Morgan — Mosser — Mussleman — Roth — Reith — Stein — Thomas — Werner — Witmer and Steinmetz.

These German-Swiss people came over in the ship "Aurora." Robert Pickeman master — "Phoenix," William Wilson master — "Friendship," John Mason master—"Carteret." —— Stevenson master — and "Muscliffe Galley," George Durell master.

1744—Indians at Lancaster Bark Trees for the Germans.

One of the results, incidentally happening, in connection with the Indian treaty of 1744 at Lancaster, was the depredation by Indians, upon the property of citizens. Among those injured was John Musser near Lancaster. July 31st, of this year, he made a complaint to the Assembly of Pennsylvania, that at the late Indian treaty he had considerable trouble and loss, by the Indians breaking several of his walnut trees, which they wanted to "bark" their cabins, and that he was told not to differ or interfere with them about it, but to hand in his bill to the Assembly, and that he now does so, and claims six pounds damage. August 2nd, the Assembly allowed him five pounds. (See 3 Votes of Assembly 555 & 6.)

Our German-Swiss ancestors also suffered by reason of the traders and others carrying rum to the Indians and then cheating them when drunk. When they became sober, these Indians were inclined to be savage and threatening to the peaceful Germans among them, even though they were innocent. (Do. p. 549.)

1744—Praise for Lancaster County Germans Agriculture.

A traveller in Lancaster County states "We have been accustomed to hear the population of Pennsylvania, sneered at and continued as vulgar and ignorant; and our Germans branded as animals. But by their fruits ye shall know them. Thus tested, they are not surpassed by any population in any country. They are intelligent and honest; they understand perfectly the business that belongs to them—they do all that they have to do in the best manner and with best results. There is no agriculture in the United States like that of the Germans of Pennsylvania— there is none superior anywhere. I have known farms on which other occupiers have starved and have been finally ejected by the Sheriff, and then they were succeeded by Germans, who, in a few years, covered the barren fields with rich crops and became prosperous and wealthy." (6 Haz. Reg. 69.)

1744—Germans Oppose War With France.

This year England declared war against France and the colonies in America became involved too. Our Germans were having a great deal of trouble with their servants, running away to war, whose time these owners had paid in advance from three to seven years. As many persons came to Pennsylvania not having money to pay the expense of their passage, our German farmers constantly bought these persons who were sold for a term of years to pay those expenses. Thus when war was declared and these servants found they could obtain ready cash for their services in the army, they joined the ranks. A great storm of opposition to the effect of war on the servant question arose in Lancaster County and throughout the Province. The trouble had existed some years, and John Wright, Judge of our Courts, was dismissed by Governor Thomas, because of his opposition to the War Governor in 1741. Then later came this new trouble. (Pa. Gazette June 14. 1744, etc.)

1744—Attempt to Burn the House of Conrad Weiser By His Enemies.

In the Penna. Gazette of December 6, 1744, the following appears: "By order of the Governor — WHEREAS some evil minded person or persons, did in the night between the 15th and 16th, inst., attempt to burn the dwelling house of Conrad Weiser in Tulpyhocken in the County of Lancaster, by means of a large bundle of straw, which was purposely laid and set on fire, upon the roof of a low building joining the house, and at the same time fastened the door of the house, on the outside, with the intent to confine the family so that they might be unable to help themselves and perish in the flames. But the same was happily prevented, through some of the family being awakened from the flames and great quantities of smoke from the straw, and the shingles beating on the roof, into the room where they lay, and alarming the rest of the family. Then with difficulty they broke open the door, which had been fastened by a strong rope, and they extinguished the fire. (This attempt did not succeed; but a few years later this house was burned to the ground, as we shall note.)

And whereas, one Adam Haines, a vile, profligate young man, in the neighborhood of the said Weiser, having committed a crime, which coming to the cognizance of the said Weiser, he as the next Magistrate, was by the duty of his office, obliged to bind him over to the Court of Quarter Sessions of Lancaster County. And refusing to accept a bribe of the said Haines, which he solicited him very much to take to suppress and keep back the recognizance, and for that and other reasons, the said Weiser having good reasons to suspect Haines and other of his accomplices, supposed to be of the same family, to have been guilty of that villanous attempt to destroy him and his family, he caused the said Haines to be apprehended by the Constable; but Haines made his escape and fled from the Constable and now absconds.

These are therefore, to give notice that if any person or persons will discover and find out, the said Haines, so that he may be retaken and committed to some of the common jails of this Province, in order to undergo a legal prosecution, in the premises, all such persons who shall cause the said Adam Haines to be apprehended and secured, shall be handsomely rewarded. And by his Honor, the Governor, special command is hereby given, that if any one of the accomplices in the said crime shall give to the Secretary of this province, the names of the rest, so they may be persecuted, and brought to condign punishment for the same, he shall secure his pardon."

It is to be observed in this article, that this good old German friend, advisor and counsellor, of the infant provinces of Pa. had his enemies for conscientiously doing his duty. Not only were there rascals among the younger people of this German Swiss ancestors here; but also among other nationalities.

Adam Haines, referred to above, seems to be a rascal. He was convicted in Quarter Sessions Court of Lancaster County, February 5th, 1745, of stealing a cow, and being found guilty August following, was sentenced to pay 50 shillings, the price of the cow, 50 shillings fine, and the cost of the suit, and to have 21 lashes, the next day, across his bare back, at the public whipping post at Lancaster.

George Haines was prosecuted for stealing a ram and a ewe—and Adam Haines was also convicted of being the father of a bastard child, and sentenced to pay a fine of ten pounds and costs, and the woman received the same sentence.

1744 — Suffering in Switzerland and Holland from Oppression, Disease and Famine.

In Earnest Müller's Anabaptist History, p. 208, he states, that in 1744 one of the old fathers, by the name of Burkholder, wrote, that he and his people were suffering indescribably, because they were compelled by England, France and Austria to furnish supplies for them in their wars, and to quarter the troops of soldiers and take care of them and feed them. He states that these soldiers became unbearable in their manner, insulting and threatening to the families of these non-resistant people, and often they had to support and quarter as many as five or seven soldiers, for a considerable time. Besides this they suffered from failing crops, and famine. There were also epidemics among their cattle, and thousands of their young cattle died. Some of the brethren lost every head of stock they had. And to make matters all the worse, they were now living the best they could, since they were compelled to flee from Switzerland, when they began to take measures to expel all these Anabaptists or Mennonites.

Now they began to turn their attention towards emigrating towards Pennsylvania, as their Brethren in distress, had done more than thirty years earlier. Therefore, we see from this, that the difficulties and persecutions, both in Switzerland and in the Palatinate along the Rhine, were continuing.

1744—John Armstrong an Early Resident Killed by Indians.

In the Pa. Gazette of April 26th, 1744, it is stated that news from Lancaster reports, that John Armstrong, an Indian trader, and two servants, were murdered by three Indians, who waylaid them as they were going with goods to Allegheny. The chief of the murderers was taken to the Lancaster jail. He confessed the fact with all the circumstances. The Indians are of the Delaware tribe. It is stated that there had been some differences and difficulties, between the deceased and the Indian, that was taken to jail.

And in the same news appears, under May 10th, it is stated that the Indian who killed Armstrong tells his side of the trouble, and says, it was about a horse. The Indian gave his horse and three belts of wampum, for goods, and found that he was cheated; and when he went to get his goods back, Armstrong would not give them up, but got mad and hit the Indian with a stick. The Indian then killed him with a tomahawk. The Indians then buried Armstrong by the side of the Juniata Creek, and threw the bodies of the two German servants into the creek. The corpses of these two fellows were found by the crows and a bald eagle, hovering over them.

1744—Swiss Mennonite Patriarch Hans Burkholder's Letters From Germany.

Among the most active of the early Swiss Mennonites, was Hans Burkholder, who nearly all his life, was a leader in everything that pertained to the welfare of our Swiss ancestors. There are records of his activities before the year 1700, and these records continue down to the time of his death. We are fortunate in being able to present a translation of two letters, written by him, a very short time before he died in the year 1744, from Heroltzheim in Palatinate, giving us again, a picture of the renewal of the difficulties that had arisen for these non-resistant followers of Menno Simon, in the heart of Europe. Switzerland had driven the most of them out by this time, and they were strangers living in the valley of the Rhine, that is, in the Palatinate. The later difficulties seem to be famine and the necessity of furnishing quarter, for soldiers, while the regular run of difficulties that grew out of their religion, while religion in the heart of Europe generally was a State matter, controlled by the State, etc.

These letters are translations from a collection of what he called the "Dutch copies" in the Historical Society at Philadelphia, and are here inserted for the purpose of giving a picture of the difficulties in the ancient home of our ancestors, from the mouth of one who was going through the difficulties himself; and one who is an ancestor of the great family of Burkholders, of our County and Pennsylvania, and other parts of the United States. These letters are written to Johannes Deknatel who was an official somewhere in Holland, likely one of the officials of that Government, who was friendly to these Mennonites; and perhaps, a member of the Swiss Mennonite commission or Chamber of Holland's Government, kept up for the sake of helping the Swiss and Mennonites, to better their condition and to go to Pennsylvania, and to America in general.

The first letter is No. 1495 and is as follows:

Heroltzheim, Jan. 4, 1744.

Bartholomeus von Lowenig together with other fellow-servants of our Taufgesindten (Mennonite congregation) in Amsterdam — May (E. L.) Your Honors be blessed.

Very dear and worthy friend and brother in Christ Jesus, we cannot well omit giving you word, Your Honors, about our sorrowful condition and of how we have found this past summer. So you must know that the French have oppressed us with many and great burdens, compelling us to give supplies which we can hardly accomplish. To comfort us, we are told that everything shall be paid, but we have not, as yet, received a single Stuber (silver coin). And besides we have been loaded with so much compulsory service (villainage Frohndrenst), that it is no longer possible to bear it. If one comes home at night, one must go away again in the morning. Besides these the English have also come and for four long weeks remained, only two hours distant from us, with a great army so that we must again, do compulsory service that can no longer be endured. After this, the army broke camp and went to Weyer. Then we have had the headquarters of the Austrians twice among us, so that Your Honors can well see how things have gone with us, and that we passed this summer in great cares and under unbearable burdens.

Now dear friend, these troubles have come to an end; but the great God has visited us with another punishment, a contagious disease and death have come among the hornedcattle so that many thousands of them have fallen and many of our brethren have not a single one left so that the poverty is very great among the friends and many know not how to help themselves. Besides the lordly (Herrschaftlich) oppressions are very great and no remission to be hoped for.

Now dearest friend, we must make known to Your Honors, yet another gloomy situation. On the death of our most gracious Elector and lord, we have, as at all times proper, made application in a moral moving petition, to the present reigning illustrious Elector, regarding the confirmation of our Confession. So far we have received no answer and have also little hopes that we shall receive a favorable one, for a command has gone forth from the the high government of all bailiwicks regarding the burial of our dead that they shall no longer be buried in the churchyards; which seems to us very hard and burdensome. I have, myself spoken about it to several gentlemen of the Government who said to me that we must have patience and first see what protection we receive from our gracious Elector. I have been myself to five of the most eminent ministers and have also spoken with them. They gave good answers, but as yet we know nothing about how the matter will end.

We beg dearest friend, Your Honors will in this give us good counsel how the matter may best be brought to a close, for we are so embarrassed in the matter. It has almost the look as if they would drive us from out of the land. The great God will have pity on us. So much for desired news of us and we hope for an agreeable answer from you, Your Honors.

Wherewith I close for the present and remain with friendly greeting and recommendation to the divine protection, your Honor's affectionate friend and brother in Christ Jesus. In the name of the other fellow workers of our Mennonite Congregation, I have written this Adieu.

HANS BURKHOLDER.

Hans Burkholder Letters continued No. 1496.

"Heroltzheim, February 17, 1744. Johannes Deknatel:

Dear and worthy friend and brother in Christ Jesus. May you be blessed. Dear and worthy friend and brother your (E. L.'s) Excellency's agreeable letter of the twenty-fourth of January has been duly received, wherein we perceive with love, that you also have duly received our letter of January fourth, the which we were pleased to know. We have also seen by your (E. L.) Honor's letter, that you are very sorry for our afflicted condition, but for this time can give us no advice, regarding our letter of protection (safe conduct). You should be informed that so far, we have as yet received no answer to our letter and request, which surprises us, as we were given favorable information by word of mouth. Also we as yet know nothing, dear and worthy friend, how it will go with us. We have to give so many promises before the Muhwaltung to the eminent minister (or so many promises of painstaking care to the eminent Minister) that we do not know well how to accomplish them, since we have suffered so much damage by the war and the death of the horned cattle, and besides, had to advance the large sum of money so that we do not know how to help ourselves while the poverty is so great here in the land, and yet no understanding or sympathy is to be expected, so that we do not know what we should do. Dear friend and brother, it is the wish and intention of some of our friends, to travel to Pennsylvania. We cannot very well advise them against it since we dwell so uncertainly ourselves and do not yet know how we shall be sustained. But we do not wish to burden and trouble your (E. L.) Excellency, in the matter. We hope that they may be able to cross and thus not trouble your (E. L.) Excellency; but we would like very much to know your advice and opinion, if indeed you could advise to go there. Dear and worthy friend, we have judged from your letter, that you would like further information of where there is the greatest poverty and need, on account of the cattle. They might each one try to help himself as much as possible, so we advise you that we do not wish to trouble you much in the matter outside of three or four families that cannot help themselves. If your (E. L.) Honor, seem inclined to help them according to your pleasure and as you deem proper, it would be very kind and agreeable. So far for desired news.

Dear friend, I am growing old and infirm and travelling grows tiresome to me. When however, we have anything to do for the Master and Mistress (Hunschaften) the other servants always think that I should take precedence. Because I am an old man and have a white head, they think that my words are worth more than theirs, which I have also discov-

HANS BURKHOLDER LETTERS (Continued).

ered, myself, but my sight and hearing are failing me fast.

(E. L.) Your Honor, you are however, by me, most cordially greeted and committed to God's good care, with which we then close for the present and remain with friendly greeting and recommendation to the protection of God, your affectionate brothers in Christ.

HANS BURKHOLDER,
CHRISTIAN STAUFFER,
JACOB HIRSCHLER."

The second is number 1499 and is as follows:

"Heroltzheim, March 6, 1744.
Johannes Deknatel:

Very worthy and in Christ beloved friend and brother, May your (E. L.) Excellency be blessed here in time and hereafter in the blessed eternity—a friendly and brotherly greeting in the Lord, Amen.

Worthy friend, the cause of this writing to you, your (E. L.) Honor, is this, that some friends and brothers of our congregation are thinking of going to Pennsylvania, as I informed you in my former letter, and as we have found from the newspaper, and also otherwise, that it is very unsafe on the ocean on account of pirates and not very promising for the journey, we desire in the most cordial and friendly manner, to beg your advice and opinion, regarding this journey and whether you approve of it, and whether it is also safe to start or not. If your (E. L.) Honor does not approve, the friends will remain here. They have sold their things and prepared themselves for the journey, but will not further trouble your (E. L.) Excellency, than to know of the safety on the sea. Please, dearest friend, be not displeased that I write to you; and write to me at once your (E. L.) Excellency, your advice and opinion that they may govern themselves accordingly.

Concerning our letter of protection, we have yet no news. I have been, myself, a short time ago at Manheim and have, myself, spoken with the president. He has given me very good news—all shall go well. So much for desired news.

I await a speedy answer from your (E. L.) Excellency, with which I close at present and remain with cordial greeting and commending you to the divine protection your (E. L.'s) Honor's affectionate friend and brother in Christ Jesus,

HANS BURKHOLDER."

I call your attention to the fact that, in connection with these letters, the sufferers could find no apparent relief from their distress, except to migrate to Pennsylvania, which many hundreds of them did about this time, although the greatest flood of immigration was over. We observe too, the danger from pirates that existed in those days, as discussed in these letters.

1744—Our Germans and the Indian Treatment.

Leher in his book (p. 104) says: That from 1744 to 1748, while King George's War was going on here, the Germans had a hard lot of it—things were so war-like here that a fort was built in the neighborhood of Lancaster he says. Further he states, that the white traders used the Indians badly and cheated them, and the Indians were very likely to take revenge on the peaceful Germans that settled in Pennsylvania and Carolina, who were innocent of this kind of conduct towards the Indians. Also he states, that in South Carolina the Mennonites who had drifted down there had to bear the burden of a great deal they were not guilty of; and further he states, that it became worse when the French began to fight the Indians.

The situation was made all the worse, because the young, strong and hearty ones, to a certain extent, were taken away from their homes and left the homes unprotected; and besides this, a good many German servants ran away from their masters and joined the army. To show the extent of military operations, he says, there were fifteen companies of soldiers that were raised throughout Lancaster County, for these French and Indian Wars.

1745—Samuel Peter Meihuisen's Letter on the Conditions and Treatment in Switzerland.

Müller, page 328, gives the substance of a letter which a Swiss father wrote July 5th, 1745, giving account of his son's trials on a trip back to Switzerland in 1745, a good many years after the father was driven out. He writes from Noogeland in the Palatinate to his brother and sister in Gautenschwyl; and a copy of the letter is found in Huizinga, a historian of those times and events.

In this letter, Samuel Peter Meihuisen praises the country as a great place to produce milk and butter and cheese and meats; but he states that so much misery and unrest and anguish exists because of the wars and the rumors of wars, and the cattle epidemic, and that it is very destructive. He alone lost 19 head of cattle. But it extends all over the country. It made many people poor. This epidemic came from Italy, was introduced into Holland and from there to Switzerland. It was all the people could do to endure it. There is no land here, too good for pasturage he says. He also has 30 sheep and young horses and cattle in the pasture. He means that pasturage is the best use land could be put to; and not good enough for farming, at that particular place. Then further in his letter he states family news and news of friends. He then admonishes all to seek the Lord.

Among other things that he says in his letter, he states, that his son Melchoir intended to see his fatherland (Switzerland) as they were now in Holland. It seems, that it was not possible for him to see his friends, which he would like to have done. Later he went to see them with one of his chums. While in Berne, they were in the great church (Cathedral). As the Apostle Peter had said "Prove everything and hold on to the thing which is good." Here he refers to the experience of his son, that is the boys wished to hear the services and learn how much good was in it. They heard the whole worship, and kept what they thought was good. Further he says his son and his friend were taken prisoners in Berne and put in the big dungeon in the Tower. Then he adds, that the Lord had said, that the child should not bear its father's sins. It was not right for this boy to bear the sin of his father, because his father fled from Switzerland years before. Whoever sins should bear the punishment himself. They must determine for themselves whether this act was Christian or not. We leave it to you to consider. Closing he exclaims, "Oh my dear fatherland that I loved so well and wish well always" (Switzerland). Müller says that Huizinga thinks their boys had not got to Switzerland and that the other writers are mistaken. But the Manual of the Star Chamber or the Mennonite Court, contains a record that two Baptists came from Holland and were again expelled. But these probably were other persons, he thinks.

1745 — Swiss Wandering in Germany and France.

Earnest Müller in his book (p. 248) states, that about this date, Jonas

Stiegler of Schutzigen near Zurich, and Nicholas Knör of Goszwyl in Buckeberg lived near France. Also he states in Päterlen about 1745 there lived Peter Lichty of Biglen, and Elizabeth Yobs of Bechigan, and Catherine Berger of Lauperville and Jacob Sprunger and his wife Elizabeth Schmedly who came from Tannegg were of similar faith, from which the other Anabaptist families that went to America, for causes growing out of the Reformation and to escape their sufferings.

At the bottom of p. 247 he says also, speaking of the year 1745, that on the 22nd of February in Perry, which seems to be a town in the Palatinate near the French border, there were fifteen Swiss families at that time, who had migrated from Switzerland. Among others were Michael and John Sieger who came from Rothenbach, and Michael Longnegger (Longenecker) formerly from Trub, John Burkholder, John Henry Turner, Jacob Marti, Peter Beck, Ulrich Lerch, John Gauler of Sumiswald, Michael Burky of Diesbach, Barbra Hertig, Michael Witmer of Lauperville, John Burky of Biglen, Christian Burkholder of Langnau, Peter Burkhart, and Witley Grenhenbuhl (Graybill) of Trauschenwald, Ulrich Burkholder of Luderswyl, Joseph Wenger of Amsoldinger. These towns, from which he says these people came are towns in Switzerland. But the place he says they were found this year, as we have stated above, are in Germany near the French border.

He adds in this paragraph, that in 1724 there were 16 of these Taufer families, consisting of 50 members from Sumiswald, Hockstetter and Langnau and other places. About 1738 five other families came. Among others were Burkharts, Burkholders, Brobsts, Millers, etc.

I cite this item to show the continual drifting of our persecuted forefathers from Switzerland into the Palatinate, and their further migration to America. From this place, additional settlers in this county, were continually coming.

Müller also states (p. 248), that in 1745 there were in Peri La Hutt, near Sonzeboz—Christian Swartz who came from Langnau, Anna Myers from Rothenbach, Durs Rohr of Solligen—Benedict Gauman and Christian Schnegg of Hochstetten, Nicholas Strohm and John Engle of Rochenbach, John Lichty of Biglen, John Bumgardner of Lauperville, Abram Newswenger of Eggville, Peter Luginbuhl of Runkhofen, Peter Sommers of Sumiswald. And that as early as 1724 there were also Catherine Berger, Andrew Bechtol or Bichsel, Eli Lehman all from Langnau. All this Müller recites under his chapter on "Im Fürstbistum Basel" (p. 233)—or the Anabaptists from Switzerland in and about the Principality of Basle. This item will show us the line of migration out of Switzerland into Germany and the Alsace, and later on to America.

He also says p. 248, "Weiter thalaufwärtz folgt Gorgemont mit der grosten ein-wanderung des St. Immerthals oder Erguel." And that in 1745, were found here the families — Christian Weidner who came from Sumiswald—Ulrich Engel of Rothenbach, Joseph Bumgardner and John Steiner of Langnau, Peter Brobst and John Newcomer of Eggville, Christian Gauman from Great-Hostetten — Samuel and James Geiser of Langenthal — Ulrich Berger of Signau—Magdalena Burger and Elizabeth Dreier of Truh; Simon Siezenthal and David Ingold of Lauperville. And that in 1729 there were Peter Siegenthaler, Ulrich Newcomer, Nicholas Luthi, Abram Bomgardner, Abram Grier, Ulrich Zolner, Hans Burky, Christian Jacob and Peter

Brobst, David Swartz and Andrew Bichsel all of Langnau—and J. Schönauer of Hochstetten, Ulrich Berger of Signau, Nicholas König of Bucksee, Simon Seigenthaler, Barb Schild, and Nicholas Erb of Rothenberg and Jacob Kommer of Jurich there. In 1738 he finds the families of Joseph Bumgardner, Christian Berger, Barbara Kuller, Nicholas Imhoff, Peter Brobst, Peter Newswenger, David Bomgardner, Christian Widmer, Elizabeth Gerber, Benedict Gauman there. And that in all there were 103 eingewanderte, or "in-wandering" persons or settlers from Switzerland, of whom 40 were Mennonites or Taufers.

Page 249 Müller says that in Tramelan in 1745 there were Barbara Gerber from Langnau — Nicholas Maurer of Desbach. And p. 328. he says about this date the Lötsher (Lesher) family and the Gerbers were numerous about Groningen.

1745—Early Execution of a Woman in Lancaster County.

It is stated in the Pennsylvania Gazette of October 24, 1745, that Rebecca Moss of Conestoga Township was executed at Lancaster for the murder of her child. There was another instance of a similar killing of a natural born child by its mother in Conestoga; but as the evidence was not conclusive a great number of the German friends of the women petitioned that her life be spared and this was done. There was a great deal of capital punishment in Pennsylvania from about 1725 onward during 30 years or more, including punishment for burglary and many other crimes. This came about because of a reign of terror and lawlessness and the killing of a couple of judges, about 1718, which excited the people to enact a very severe law.

1745—German Lutheran and Moravian Controversy in Lancaster County.

This year the German Pastor of the Lutheran Church united a portion of his congregation with the Moravians. A great ferment was excited among the Lutherans. They carried their trouble to the Governor and represented to him that they were compelled to hear a doctrine which they did not approve or resign their church. But the Governor told them he could not interfere; "that the law however, would protect them in their rights." (5 Haz. Reg. 22).

1745—Hans Burkholder's Labors

We have noticed Hans Burkholder's letters in a preceding part of these annals. We insert here another letter from him to the influential Governmental friends of his people in Holland. It is No. 1489 of the "Dutch Copies" in the Penna. Historical Society at Philadelphia. He writes from Geraldsheim and addresses Bartholemew Von Leivening and other religious friends in Holland. After religious greetings he says: "I cannot refrain from writing to you as I wrote February 27, 1742. I do not know whether you received the same." Then he says that he gave the money which the friends sent to him to the most needy of the Mennonite Brethren of the congregation and states that he set out the names and amounts.

Then he states that he heard early in 1742 that some of their brethren in the Palatinate near Heilbrom were thinking of going to Pennsylvania. He heard this from Henrick Kendig the pastor of the congregation. He says he inquired whether these people were provided with necessary means, but that the pastor said they were not. Then he asked how they could go in such dangerous times. The minister told him they had friends in Pennsylvania who would pay their passage on landing and set them free. Burkholder then says that it is against his advice that these people go without ready money to pay their own way.

Then he continues in his letter: "I have word from the minister of the so-called Amish congregation of Friesland, that some of his people are determined to go to Pennsylvania, too. I asked him if they had the money and he said they had and also had letters from Holland which told them to come and they would see that they landed safe. This seems strange to me because your friends in Holland encourage them and discourage our people. Those people (Amish) make no common cause with us; they do not associate with us, when we are in trouble. They try to bring us into dispute. They belong to the better classes. They consider themselves the best and finest people. They are very prominent. As far as I am concerned I would not ridicule anyone; but they ridicule us.

Conditions are very hard among us here in the Palatinate. Our young men cannot be received as congregation men by the authorities here. To get a letter of protection we must pay 50 florins. This is double what others pay for safe conduct. We cannot endure this much longer. We have no civil protection. Besides this, the oppression of the "herrschoft" or local magistrates is already too great—and the taxes provided by court are too heavy. We cannot provide them; let alone the money for bounty for our young men to escape army service.

I have tried to help others in my household; but I must give up house keeping and seek provision for myself elsewhere. I must get rid of my burdens because my bodily powers are failing me as I am getting so old and on account of my sight and hearing failing, I must be relieved of all burdens as I cannot hold out.

Wishing all, God's Grace, etc.—
HANS BURKHOLDER."

1746—Interesting Landes Letter of This Date.

The zeal of Bishop N. B. Grubb, of Philadelphia, in gathering up and translating information and letters from the original sources, concerning our German-Swiss ancestors, has put in form some interesting matter concerning the Landeses. In the Mennonite year book for 1914, page 38, he gives, verbatim, a copy of a letter written by Elizabetha Landes of Germantown in 1746, which letter in German, is the property of J. M. Landes. And in connection with the letter there is shown an excellent sketch of the Landes homestead in Switzerland, located at Hirzel erected in 1488.

The letter written by Mrs. Landes is addressed to her friends and relatives and especially to the children of the late Caspar Landes. She sets forth the following facts concerning the Landes family, and the following events that happened in the family:

"I, Elizabetha, the widow of Heinrich Landes, a brother to your father, Caspar Landes, a barber in Richterswil, but again married to Heinrich End, desire to inform you as follows:

When my former husband, Heinrich Landes, left Switzerland for the first time with his father, he entrusted to his brother Caspar a certain sum of money without taking from him anything in writing because he had absolute confidence in his brother's honesty; and had not the least doubt at all, that everything would be right. Twice he had received some of the amount, so that now there is a balance of about 300 Rix Dollars (about $210.00) remaining unpaid; as my dear husband Heinrich Landes, so often informed and assured me. Since then, my husband Heinrich Landes, entered orderly and publicly into the bonds of matrimony with me, Elizabetha Hirt, born in Mark-Kirch, in Elsass, the daughter of Jacob Hirt, of the same place. This was in 1709. After having resided for ten years in different places in Germany, we finally, twenty-two years ago, came to Pennsylvania, fully intending again at some time to visit you, as he had promised his brother Caspar he would, and then bringing the balance of his money home with him. From this he was however prevented by my frequent solicitation and entreaty not to go until the year 1727 when he died, leaving me a widow with four children namely, one son and three daughters.

In addition she states that she has four children living, Elizabetha, Barbara, Henry and Dorothea. She also states that the money about which she is writing could be transferred to Dr. Hollinger, the Reformed Minister in Heidelberg, who is a native of Zurich, and by him can be sent, through certain other persons to Philadelphia, addressed to certain party in Germantown by which it can be transferred to the proper owners. It is signed Aunt Elizabetha Landes, Germantown, Pennsylvania, 20th Nov. 1746. It is addressed to be delivered to the surviving children of Casper Landes (barber) at Richtersvil, three hours from Zurich.

She states that she and her husband after living for 10 years in different places in Germany, came to Pennsylvania in 1724.

The cut of the old Landes Homestead at Hirzel plainly shows it to be long and low, one story high with an attic, about one-half story high at the eaves. It seems to be of stone plastered on the exterior and stands on the side of a Commons, at least the side of an unfenced road. Just immediately to the left of it stands another building somewhat in the general shape of the buildings erected by the Amish of Lancaster County, consisting of a main house and an attachment which seems to be "shed-roofed." And then to the left of it stands a frame or externally-plastered church, with a high steeple which appears to be hexagon in shape, standing upon a high square tower. It is likely a Reformed Church. In the background there are undulating hills, dotted with a great many trees, and the whole picture is distinctively agricultural.

I find from the maps, that Hirzel is about 9 miles southeast from Zurich, on the south side of Lake Zurich.

1746—Germans Along the Susquehanna Want Maryland Line Dispute Settled.

The dispute between Maryland and Pennsylvania, over the line between them still continued. It had now destroyed the tranquility between the two provinces many years.

Certain phases of the dispute are set forth in Vol. 1, of the Pa. Archives pp. 692 et seq. From these records, the following condition appears: In August 1746 the Governor of Maryland wrote to the Governor of Pennsylvania, enclosing a letter from Virginia. A man opposite Conewago named Diggs, claiming that section to be Maryland, complained that the Pennsylvanians used him badly. The Governor of Maryland says allowance must be made for Diggs, because he is a Catholic and is opposed to the Government. Diggs replying to the charge, that he is a troublesome person says, that by a Maryland warrant dated 1727, he has settled on a tract called Diggs' choice, opposite the Susquehanna and received a patent in 1735. That he had his land surveyed and the Dutch objected to this, and he had them arrested for trespass. And since then a survey was made including his land, by officers of Pennsylvania, defying the Government of Maryland. That a man named Kittsmiller and others, threatened to shoot and kill Diggs if he did not move away. Another witness declared that he heard this land was laid out for John Lemon, David Young, Adam Messier, Adam Miller and others of Pennsylvania.

Another witness declared that when Diggs came for his land, he found some Germans plowing on it, Nicholas and Adam Furney, who claimed they owned it. Furney said he would pay no attention to Maryland officers, and went on plowing. Adam Furney said that Mr. Cookson told him, if any land officers of Maryland came, to bind them and take them to Lancaster. These friends of Furney spoke Dutch to them. The upshot was, that Furney and his friends began to beat and club Diggs and the Maryland officers, and one of the Maryland officers attempted to draw his "banger" and Furney ran to the house to get his gun. It seems that then the Lancaster County authorities took an ax and tried to use it on the Diggs party. The battle finally ended by the Maryland parties taking their band spikes and giving the Pennsylvania party a chase.

On the other side Herman Updegraff, being a Quaker, said that 5 years ago he tried to buy a piece of land from Diggs at Conewago. He said the tract lay north of the Pennsylvania line. Then too the deposition of Adam Furney was taken on the dispute. He lived at Conewago, and he said that he and several other Germans had agreed to purchase some land of John Diggs, lying at Conewago, and they found that Diggs land was of great extent there, that Diggs claimed he had 14,000 acres there. This excited the Germans as they knew it included their land.

Page 709 of the above stated record, the case between the Germans and Diggs at Conewago is set out showing the difficulties of our people at that place. It there appears that the temporary Pennsylvania-Maryland line was furnished in May 1739, and as soon as it was run many Germans took out warrants for land, from the Pennsylvania authorities, lying north of that line at the Little Conewago, over the Susquehanna, adjoining the tract claimed by Diggs. This Diggs tract was found to be wholly in Pennsylvania and surrounded by lands these Germans took up and paid for. These Germans did not interfere with Diggs; but asked him to mark his line so they could locate their land, and then he threatened them not to come near his place, etc. He warned them that their surveys were not good, as all that was Maryland property, etc. Then in 1743 Diggs applied to Pennsylvania to get as much land as would make his tract a regular square, and that this would take 1,000 acres. He was told he could have land at the same price the Germans were paying; but he could not interfere with their land. But he disregarded this and asserted title right over the German's land. See these conflicts fully discussed in Vol. 1, Pennsylvania Archives pp. 692 to 713.

1746—Ship Records of This Year.

During this year we find two ship loads of these German-Swiss people.

Among the common Lancaster County names we find the following:

Three Bohns — 2 Kauffmans — 2 Reinharts—2 Zimmermans and 2 Millers.

We find one each of the following: Beck, Herman, Pieffer, Reith, Snyder, Thomas and Wagner.

These people came over in the Ship "Ann Galley," William Wilson Master—Ship "Neptune," Thomas Wilkinson Master.

1747—More Labors of Hans Burkholder.

Among the "Dutch Copies" in the Pennsylvania Historical Society at Philadelphia is a letter of Hans Burkholder, which is No. 1510 among the said paper, and is as follows:

Heroltzheim, March 16, 1747.
Johannes Deknatel:

Much loved and worthy friend and brother in Christ Jesus, together with other fellow workers of our congregation in Amsterdam. May your Honor be blessed now in time and hereafter in the blessed eternity, Amen.

Very dear friend. I cannot in Christian love refrain from once more making known to you our hard condition regarding the marriage of our children, as also concerning the burial of the dead. We are not permitted to bury them in certain places without great expense. But we do not wish to make too much of this as we desire to attend to our own burials when it can be done elsewhere and so do not make much more of this. But concerning the marriage of our children that is very trying for us that no one will accept any one from a common or middle class family as they do not wish to increase the number of poor grave lots.

When, however, the parents have died or the housekeeping has been broken up (as I also have done myself) a boy can be brought into the father's place only with great labor and expense; for then a certificate must be procured from the mayor and other proper officials with which one enters on the office and duties of a father. And then the subordinate office directs one to the superior bailiwick, who directs the person to the high electoral government which sends him to the exchequer to a clergyman of the church, who must pass his judgment about it, and so he all the time has his hand in his pocket and by the time he has finished it costs much money as well as labor, and often it is a quarter of a year or even a half a year, before he can come to the end. Now if your honor could give us good advice in this matter, we would be very glad. Among those who cannot help themselves the poverty is very great. If things cannot be changed, we fear a falling off in the congregation among the young people. God will, however, cause all this to work for good and graciously assist us.

As concerns myself, I grow from time to time more decrepit and infirm in my body with tremblings and weakness and my calling and service become more and more a burden and yet at Easter I administered to five congregations, the Holy Communion, and had to travel three or four hours, which was very fatiguing to me. I hope with Paul, soon to lay down this tabernacle and to obtain a better, which I greatly desire. If, your Honor, is not fully opposed to me as heretofore seen, I hope your Honor will pity me, and grant me graciously, your Christian support and contribution, as you deem proper, and be to me a cordial friend in my old days. I hope the great God will again richly recompense you for all. Wherewith I close for the present and remain with friendly greeting and recommendation to God's protection, your affectionate friend and brother in Christ Jesus,

HANS BURKHOLDER.

Beloved and worthy friend, I have just learned with great astonishment that some of our friends from Ober-Pfalz (in the Palatinate) wish, in

DISEASE AND HORRORS ON SHIPBOARD.

these dangerous and difficult times, to set out on the journey to Pennsylvania. If your Honor would only give us your advice as to what is to be done under the circumstances about this journey we would thank you. I await an early answer. Adieu.

HANS BURKHOLDER.

1747—Infected Germans Were Compelled to Submit to Examination Before a Ship Doctor.

This year, the ship Vernon, from Rotterdam, arrived in Philadelphia with foreigners from Switzerland and the Palatinate. Captain Ricks, commander, reported he had on board a great number of these people, and asked an order to be given to two doctors to examine the health of his passengers. The ship landed quite a distance below Philadelphia. It could not come up to the city, and unload passengers in the city, until the examination was made. The Council sent Dr. Graeme and Dr. Bond to examine them; and gave them authority to decide whether they should be allowed to land or not. (See Vol. 5. Col. Rec. p. 100).

When we turn to the list of passengers who came in this ship, (p. 256 of the Sec. Ser. of Pa. Vol. 17), we find among the names, Christopher Barr, Jacob Lesher, Abram Funk, Samuel Witmer, Rudolph Huber, Fred Wertz, Michael Eiselman, Jacob Shavely, Peter Bowman and Henry George Schar and others. This enables us to determine that they were likely persons who were destined to settle in Lancaster County.

1747—Ship Records of This Year.

During this year we find five ship loads of these German Swiss people coming into this country.

Among the common Lancaster County names we find the following:

Two Arnolds—3 Beyers—2 Becks—2 Eberhards—2 Freys—3 Frantzs—3 Hoffmans—4 Hermans—2 Hubers—2 Kaspars—2 Lantzs—3 Myers—2 Millers—2 Rohrers—3 Snyders—4 Smiths—4 Wagners—2 Wises and 2 Wengers.

We also find one each of the following:

Adams, Alleman, Bowman, Bauman, Buck, Fox, Hahn, Kline, Kurtz, Kauffman, Lesher, Lutz, Mosser, Pieffer, Roth, Reith, Roop, Reese, Shaeffer, Steinmetz, Streiker, Wolfe, Weidner, Witmer, Young and Ziegler.

They came in the ship "Billander," Thomas Ricks master—"Lydia," William Tiffin master—"Restauration," James Hall master—"Two Brothers," Thomas Arnott master, and ———. This last ship seems to be unknown.

1748—Ship Records of This Year.

During this year we find six shiploads of these German Swiss people coming to this country.

Among the common Lancaster County names we find the following:

Three Adams—3 Diehls—3 Myers—2 Millers—2 Smiths—4 Steins and 2 Wagners.

Also one each of the following:

Antes, Brown, Eberhard, Foltz, Gerhart, Grove, Hoffman, Hartman, Heller, Hollinger, Keller, Hensel, Kline, Metzler, Mann, Moore, Shoemaker, Stauffer, Stout, Weber and Wolf.

They came in the ship "Edinburgh," James Russell master—"Hampshire," Thomas Cheeseman master—"Mary Galley," George Lawson master—"Two Brothers," Thomas Arnatt master—"Patience," John Brown master—"Patience and Margaret," John Povan, master.

1748—Crowds of These German Swiss People Emigrating, Taxes Holland's Resources.

It is related by Müller (p. 365) that the number of emigrants coming from the Palatinate, (but originally from Switzerland and other sections), has greatly increased in late years. A commission of the Mennonite brethren in or near Amsterdam, was doing all they possibly could to aid these emigrants to Pennsylvania. As these emigrants became more numerous the commission was compelled to cease its financial aid. About 1732 there had arrived at Rotterdam more than 3000 inhabitants of the Palatinate, among whom, of course, there were some Reformed and some Lutherans. A portion of these founded the congregation at Skippack (Schebach), Montgomery County, Pennsylvania. By the year 1748 they had thrived so far in their new home, as to own a paper mill and printing office. Müller also tells us (p. 369) that this year some of these people who had emigrated, had settled at Hilltown, in Pennsylvania, and among them were Christian Lederich who came in 1747 and Valentine Hunsecker in 1748.

1748—Horrors of Overloading These Poor Germans and Swiss Settlers in Small Vessels.

As the rush of the Germans to Pennsylvania became more numerous about this time, the owners of the vessels began packing them away in places entirely unfit for them, so that a great deal of sickness broke out. We shall see that in a year or two, a law was passed to prevent this. Henry P. Fairchild has written up this subject in a thorough manner, in a work called "Immigration in the Early Days." It was published by McMillan & Co. and gives a great deal of information concerning the horrible condition that existed.

Not only had these Germans become so numerous as to be the main civilizing factor in Pennsylvania shortly before and about 1750; but we must remember that as Barclay says, of George Fox, the founder of the Quakers, "We are compelled to view him as the unconscious exponent of the doctrine, practice and discipline of the ancient and stricter party of the Dutch Mennolites." (See Barclay's Religious Societies of the Commonwealth p. 77).

To this thought, ex-Governor Pennypacker adds that "To the spread of Mennonite preachings in England, we therefore owe the origin of the Quaker and the settlement of Pennsylvania." (See Pennypacker's Settlement of Germantown, p. 66).

It is no small honor to the Mennonite to have the credit of being the real founder of the province (and now the great Commonwealth) of Pennsylvania back of William Penn, whose lives and characters, as Penn viewed them, when he visited them along the Rhine Valley, which gave rise in his mind to the "Holy Experiment" and made him the father of Pennsylvania, that he was, and is held to be, to this date. As William Penn made Pennsylvania, so the ancient Mennonite Brethren in reality, made William Penn.

1748—Martyr's Mirror Published at Ephrata.

About this year, the German Brethren in and about Ephrata, who about 25 years ago, had left the Conestoga settlement and became a religious sect of their own (existing down to this day, and known as the Seventh Day Baptists), had attained such proficiency and skill, and such intellectual ability, so as to be able to publish Tielman, Van Braght's Book of Martyrs or Martyr's Mirror in German, being a work of about 1400 pages, according to the type of that time. A large edition was published running into the hundreds at least. This shows not so much the intellectual advancement to which the "brethren" had attained at that time (even though the book had to be translated from Dutch to German), but more particularly the mechanical skill and the ingenuity attained, by these people, in making presses and in procuring type of a superior character, so as to print that great work. Many copies of the Mirror, which they printed, still extant, attest the early capacity and skill of these people.

Inasmuch as the "Chronicon Ephratense" gives a minute detail of the lives and ways of these people and their history, I will not insert any of it in these annals. According to Kuhns, it took 15 men three years to complete this task.

1749 — German-Swiss First Political Efforts in Lancaster County

As soon as King George's War was ended, there was leisure in the British Empire for attention to local politics again. Factional contests began in earnest in Lancaster County and were made more intense, because the German-Swiss-Quaker alliance against the Scotch-Irish was now an established condition here. The German-Swiss now took part in earnest.

There was a keen fight for Assemblyman in 1749 in Lancaster County, between James Webb and Peter Worrall.

Worrall was the popular hotel keeper on West King Street in Lancaster Borough and Webb a prominent politician in Lancaster Township (See 3rd Series Penna. Arch. Vol. 17, pp. 83, 170 and 346). Both were members of the Assembly in 1748. Webb was English; had just finished building the stone work of the new jail and was close to the English and Scotch-Irish Lancaster County politicians. Peter Worrall was "Dutch" (German) very widely known and very popular as the principal hotel man in the county.

So the "Dutch" or Germans threw their strength to Worrall and re-elected him. Webb was defeated and charged fraud and contested Worrall's election before the Assembly.

Webb in his petition to the Assembly set forth that at the late election there were gross frauds whereby he was not elected; that the good people thereby are defeated of their privilege. Many of the voters in the County also joined in a petition setting forth that at the late election the people crowded in a body and that they stuck their tickets in the end of cloven sticks, and committed other frauds; that tickets were put in by boys; that many voted several times; that the number of votes received was more than double the number of the people who were present; that the officers did not put any on oath or call for any tests. By reason of all this they pray the election to be declared void. (4 Votes of Assembly pp. 117-18). November 22, the Assembly took the case up and heard many witnesses. The testimony was that the election was tumultuous, that no regular list could be taken of the voters' names; that votes by proxy were allowed; that illegal votes were received by inspectors especially by Christian Herr an inspector; votes from minors received that persons not legally chosen inspectors received votes as inspectors, that many people voted three, four, five and even ten times; that one of the candidates (Worrall) who is returned as elected encouraged giving in more than one vote by the same person, that the number of voters attending did not exceed 1000, though the tickets found in the box were more than 2300 (4 V. p. 122 and Rupp p. 299).

Counsel for the petitioners examined more witnesses the next day. Then Counsel for the Sheriff and inspectors examined witnesses. These are objected to because they are interested witnesses.

The defense was that only two tickets were taken by proxy, by the owners of the tickets were in view, that tickets were taken from minors to get rid of them, but they were not put in the box, that those elected inspectors soon after starting in were pulled away from their tables and that the number of voters present was as great as the number of votes cast (4 V. p. 123). The case went over to 1750, and Jan. 2nd the Assembly resumed considering it (4 V. p. 126). Several witnesses were heard the next day and the list of taxables of Lancaster County was produced showing there were 4598 to show there was no duplication in voting or repeating (4 V. p. 126). The next day the case was up again and the representative who was charged with encouraging plurality of votes in favor of himself on his oath purged himself and also by witnesses supported the same (Do. p. 127).

January 5th, a vote was taken on the question of issuing a writ for a new election because the other one was fraud; but it was voted down and the election was adjudged good and regular (Do. 127).

The next day Jan. 6th the Sheriff of Lancaster County was called in and admonished that though the proofs were not sufficient to throw out the members returned the method of managing the election in Lancaster County was very irregular and he was warned that hereafter the names of those for Assembly must be on one ballot, those for Sheriff on another and those for Coroner on another, those for Assessors on another and those for Commissioners on another, and not all on one ballot as has been the custom in Lancaster County; that inspectors must be more particular in the choice of clerks and choose only such as excessive drinking will not, as heretofore, disable them from acting; that the Sheriff must hereafter call for the list of voters and have the tally taken and preserve the tallies; care must be taken to prevent tumult and disorders by placing constables at the doors; that the fraud of repeating must be suppressed (4 V. pp. 127 and 128). After all this the Sheriff had the "cheek" to present a bill of £20 for his expenses in defending his suspicious and crooked proceeding, (4 V. p. 142).

No comment is necessary upon the extraordinary election of 1749 in the County, except to notice that Christian Herr being appointed out as one of the chief defiers of the law, it may be reasonably inferred that the Germans had control of the election and that their friends the Quakers counselled them.

We may conclude too that they knew their case would not suffer in review before the Assembly in the hands of their friends in that body, a large majority of whom were Quakers.

1749—Ship Records of This Year.

During this year we have twenty-one ship loads of these German-Swiss people.

Among these ship loads of German-Swiss people, we find the common Lancaster County names:

2 Adams—5 Appels—2 Bernharts—5 Brunners—6 Becks—12 Beckers—3 Bauers—4 Benders—2 Browns—2 Burkharts—4 Benners—8 Conrads—2 Diehls — 6 Eckerts — 6 Fishers — 2 Frant—2 Franks—5 Foxes—16 Hoffmans—2 Hertzlers — 4 Hasslers — 7 Hubers — 3 Hausers — 2 Hellars — 5 Hartmans—4 Hasses—14 Hesses—4 Hahns—2 Hagers—4 Isemans—2 Jacobys—13 Klines—3 Konigs—7 Kellers — 2 Kramers — 4 Kauemans — 3 Kuhns—3 Kurtzes—5 Longs—2 Lenharts—9 Lutzes—9 Markles—2 Messners—11 Millers—12 Meyers—2 Magees—22 Schaeffers—25 Snyders—2 Stauffers—2 Shumakers—2 Snavelys—2 Shumans—5 Schieds—3 Sprengers—

SHIP RECORDS OF 1749.

4 Shermans—4 Smeltzes—2 Steigerwalts — 6 Wolfes — 31 Wagners — 19 Webers—10 Wises—2 Wanamakers—2 Workmans—10 Weitzels—2 Yosts—2 Yaegers—11 Youngs—3 Zieglers and 4 Zimmermans.

Also one each of the following Lancaster County names:

Arndt — Albert — Albright — Berger — Brant — Baer — Barr — Bowman — Buchman — Christian — Care — Detweiler — Dellinger — Derr — Dietz — Eshleman — Erb — Eberhart — Ernst — Eckman — Fritz — Foltz — Frantz — Frey — Hummel — Hersh — Herr — Herman — Herman — Hetrick — Kiehl — Kessler — Kern — Kramer — Kieffer — Kraus — Krantz — Lambert — Lehman — Lanyz — Ludwig — Morris — Martin — Mann — Marshall — Pieffer — Pfoutz — Peters — Rohrh — Roth — Richer — Reinhart — Schwartz — Simon — Schaeffer — Switzer — Singer — Stump — Steiger — Smeltz — Stein — Steinmetz — Seitz — Stauffer — Shock — Spangler — Thomas — Tshudy — Vogel — Wissner — Waters — Witmer — Widmyer — Walker — Warfel — Weidner — Walters — Zerfoss and Zwally.

They came over in the ship "Elliot" James Adams master—"Chesterfield" Thomas Coatam master—"Albany" Robert Brown master—"St. Andrew" James Abercrombie master—"Priscilla" Wm. Muir master—"Christian" Thomas Brady master—"Two Brothers"—Thomas Arndt master—"Edinburg" James Russell master—"Phoenix" John Mason master—"Patience" Hugh Steele master — "Speedwell" James Creagh master—"Ranier" Henry Browning master — "Dragon" George Spencer master—"Isaac" Robert Mitchell master — "Ann" John Spurrier master — "Jacob" Adolph DeGrove master—"Leslie" J. Ballendine master—"Lydia" John Randolph master — "Dragon" Daniel Nicholas master—"Fane" Wm. Hyndman master and "Show Good Intent" with Benjamin Boswell as master.

It will be observed from the above records, that these Germans were coming in great hordes now. They were nearly all poor Germans at this time. The Swiss immigration had practically been ended a few years earlier. This is a period when the Germans began to push to the front, as leaders in other lines, besides agriculture in the County of Lancaster, and we shall observe from now on, (true to their nature), having once become accustomed to these matters, have never ceased, but paid every increasing attention to the subject. In the last preceding item their political activity fully appears.

1749—More Contagious Disease Among German Immigrants—Its Treatment.

At a Council held Sept. 11, this year at Philadelphia, the subject of contagion among our German ancestors was discussed again. The minutes (5 Col. Rec. 410) of the discussion, are as follows:

"The Governor having order'd Doctor Groeme and Doctor Thomas Bond to visit the Ship Francis and Elizabeth, arriv'd in the Cove below the City with Palatines on board from Rotterdam, and they having reported that she was an unhealthy Vessel, several of the Passengers labouring under an eruptive fever which they were of opinion was infectious, he had order'd the Trustees of the Province Island to attend the Council to be inform'd of the Condition of the Pest House and what conveniences there were or might soon be made for the reception and care of the Sick; and the Trustees accordingly attending, together with the Doctors, it appear'd on examination that the Place was in great Disorder, and that for want of room, Household Furniture, and suitable Apartments, the Sick cou'd be but indifferently taken care of, yet there being a necessity of immediately landing the infected the Trustees promis'd to put the Rooms into the best order they cou'd and to build some slight out Houses that might serve the present Occasion; whereupon the Captain of the Ship Francis and Elizabeth was serv'd with an order from the Governor to remove his Vessel to the Mouth of Schuylkill, as near to the Pest House as he cou'd conveniently lye, to send there all the sick and keep the well on board, and not to suffer any Persons to go near them except the Doctors, Necessary Nurses, and Servants."

1750—Law to Prevent Crowding German Immigrants in Unhealthy Ships.

In prior articles, we have noticed, that the greedy ship owners, began to overcrowd immigrants into their ships for the purpose of making money. This became so bad that the Philadelphia merchants began to object to these passengers being treated in this way and exposed to disease and, they brought it to the attention of the Assembly in 1749, as may be seen in Vol. 4 Votes of Assembly, p. 121. Conditions became so bad, that citizens began to petition the Assembly to prevent sick and diseased passengers from being imported. (Do. 178).

It was further contended, when the reason for this condition became known that not more than a certain number of these immigrants, depending upon the size of the vessel, shall be put on a vessel, and a bill was drawn for that purpose (Do. 132). This bill was granted in the Assembly (Do. 133). The Council of Pennsylvania, the higher legislative body in the Province, also took a hand in the matter. The Governor also became interested. Among other things, he said that the provisions of the new bill ought to make considerable amendment, while the law should be stronger to prevent these evils. While the Council was debating it, the Assembly agreed to certain amendments and asked a joint committee on the subject, so that the Act be sufficiently strong. (5 Col. Rec. 427). The result was that on Jan. 27th, 1750, the Statute was passed, which is found in Vol. 5 Statutes at Large, p. 94, which sets forth that it has been the practice for masters and owners of the vessels, trading in this province, to import so great a number of Germans in one vessel, that through want of room and accommodations they contracted mortal and contagious diseases, which have caused not only the death of great numbers of passengers; but infected those that have arrived, who when they landed, spread the disease. The Act then provided, that no vessel bound to Philadelphia or elsewhere in this province, shall import into Delaware River, or any port in the Province of Pennsylvania, a greater number of passengers in a vessel, than such as may be well provided with good wholesome meat and drink and necessaries; and have room for single passengers of the age of over 14 years, 6 ft. in length and 1 ft. 6 in. in width, and if under 14, to contain the same length and width for every two passengers. Upon failure to comply with this Act, the parties were to be fined 10 pounds for each violation.

Further, the Act provided, that the ship owners must know the condition and circumstances of all the passengers, and inquire whether the officers of the ship have provided them with such room and necessaries, as this Act provides. The law further provided, that if master or officer of the ship, had passengers that die on the way, leaving goods behind, that the vessel within twenty days after arrival, or after the death, should present a true inventory of the goods, out of which the costs of passage were to be taken, and the remainder should be given to some person for the benefit of the wife or children of the deceased. This Act the Government of Great Britain approved May 13th, 1751.

1750 — Gottlieb Mittelberger Tells of the Sufferings of These Germans.

We have another authority upon the condition under which these Germans had to live while crossing the ocean, in the writings of Gottlieb Mittelberger, who journeyed to Pennsylvania in 1750, and knew and experienced personally some of these conditions. His writings contain his experience in coming over and of his visit through this section of Pennsylvania. This we find in a small book in the Historical Society of Pennsylvania at Philadelphia, marked Vg. 33. Among other things he relates the state and unfortunate conditions of these Germans who immigrated.

Mittelberger was the organist at the Lutheran Church at Trappe. He says May 1, 1750, he set out from Enzwehingen, Vaihingen Co., for Heilbronn, where an organ was ready to be shipped to Pennsylvania —that he sailed with the organ down the Necker and Rhine to Rotterdam, with 400 persons, Wurtenbergs (Durlach) Palatines, and Swiss to Cowes in England. Finally he landed at Philadelphia, Oct. 10, 1750. He then says the reason for publishing this book is the grevious conditions of those who traveled from Germany, and the outrageous proceedings of the "Dutch Man Dealers" and other man dealing emissaries—that the journey from Germany to Pennsylvania is 1700 french miles, and that you pass 36 custom houses going down the Rhine. He proceeds and says, that it takes 6 weeks to go down the Rhine alone — that if a woman should die in child birth, that the dead mother and the living child are both thrown into the sea together—that 32 children died on the ship that he was on—that every year 20 to 25 ship loads of Germans and Swiss come to Pennsylvania—that in the last 4 years, 25,000 people came— that on his way to America a large shark was caught and when he was brought on the vessel and cut open, a whole man was found in him with boots and silver buckles on. He says that a trip from Durloch to Holland in open sea, takes 200 hours and often from May to October to cross the ocean—that sickness on board the vessels is horrible and terrible stench is present all the time—that people vomit continually — suffer from dysentery, headache, scurvey, cancer, mouth rot, the latter coming from old sharply salted food and foul water—that besides that, they are afflicted with damp, heat, hunger and want—that the lice are so thick they can be scraped off—that when a gale rages for two or three nights, misery is at its height, people cry and pray most pitiously—the healthy ones get cruel and curse and some time kill one another—that a woman in childbirth (because of no physician present, it was thought she would die), was pushed right into the sea—that children from 1 to 7 years nearly all died from hunger and thirst and itch.

1750 — Gottlieb Mittelberger's Description of the German Sufferings (Continued).

As to the food he says it is dirty and that the passengers get warm food only three times a week—that the water is black and full of worms—the biscuits are full of red worms and spiders' nests, and finally, that when the passengers land, they are barely able to walk and just creep from the deck, and when they reach the ground they weep for joy and pray and praise God.

He goes on to say that when the cargo is landed at Philadelphia, only those who can pay their passage can leave the ship—the others are sold—they often stay two or three weeks before any one will buy them and during this time, a good many die. As to the cost of the journey from Rotterdam to Philadelphia he says it is 10 pounds or 60 florins—children 5 to 10 years old go at one-half price—cost from his home to Rotterdam, 40 florins.

He then tells about how the passengers are sold, and tells that it begins in a market on board the ship. That every day the English, Dutch and the High Germans come from the city of Philadelphia and other places, 20, 30 or 40 hours away, (1 hour means 4 miles) and go on board the ship and select and bargain, the adults agreeing to serve three, four or five years for the amount that is due; but young children serve ten to 15 years until they are 21 as a rule. He says that many parents must sell and trade their children like cattle, for this will free them of their passage money. A woman must stand good for her husband's passage, if he should arrive sick. If the passenger dies when he is half way over, or more than half, the other members of his family must pay for him; but if he dies less than half way, he goes free.

Mittelberger then tells of some of the customs in his day in Pennsylvania among the Germans and what he learned about Philadelphia. As to Philadelphia in 1750 he says, it takes 1 day to walk around the town—that there are 300 new houses built every year—that there are 8 churches, three English, 3 German, 1 Swede and 1 Quaker—that the language is German and English. Then as to Pennsylvania he says (p. 57) that this is a very populous province inhabited far and wide—that there are new towns here, such as Germantown, Lancaster, Rittengstown (Reading). As to country weddings and funerals, as many as 400 and 500 come on horseback—neighbors give warning as far as 50 miles in 24 hours and give notice to people to come to funerals—that while coming in, good cake is handed all and a goblet of hot West India rum punch into which lemon, sugar and juniper berries are put—and sweet cider is drunk—that the coffins are made of walnut stained brown and varnished—4 brass handles are on them—and if a young man dies, 4 maidens carry him, and if a maiden dies, 4 unmarried men carry her. He said that the German Lutheran preacher in Lancaster at that time was Mr. Garack—there are no beggars in Pennsylvania—that on the first Sunday of May all make merry, those born in America deck themselves like Indians and no one else is allowed to do that. He states at that time there were pipe organs in Pennsylvania, namely in Philadelphia, Germantown, Providence and New Hanover and Tulpehocken and Lancaster,—and that they were all shipped into this country in the last 4 years.

Speaking about the people he says an English servant woman in Philadelphia is as elegantly dressed as an aristocratic lady in Germany—English ladies are very beautiful and wear their hair cut short or frizzled.

Speaking of the development of the country he says: in one day's journeying from Philadelphia, you come into wild, uncleared land; but there are three great roads — one from Philadelphia to Delaware and Frankfort, one to Germantown and Reading; and one to Lancaster.

This ancient minister and musician says considerable more in his book; but we have quite enough to give us a general idea of the conditions of the German sections of Pennsylvania at this time.

1750 — German-Swiss in Political Affairs.

In Vol. 4, Votes of Assembly, p. 153, it is stated that this year a great multitude of people, mostly Germans, came upon the regular election officers at York and with sticks and billets of wood, drove them away, and broke the windows about the place of holding the election; threw brick bats and took the ballot box away and held the election themselves. This seems to indicate that the Germans were determined that they would see that justice was done at the elections and they employed the methods of getting control, that were used by all parties during these times, brute force. There was a similar clash somewhat earlier in Pennsylvania. Account of this appears in a prior article of these annals. It appears that this was a regular election riot between the Irish and English and the Germans. The case came up before the authorities and among others, Benjamin Swope gave his deposition, which appears in Vol. two, 1st ser. of Pa. Archives, p. 51. His deposition is in substance as follows: That the election was begun and carried on by the Sheriff, in a peaceable manner, about one hour and one-half, and then the riot began and the Sheriff went out and quieted the people and then he returned. Then five or six men of the neighborhood of Marsh Creek came with clubs and another riot happened and the Sheriff tried to quell it; but he was afraid of getting hurt—that there was fighting among the people, several were knocked down—but at last the Dutch prevailed and came in a body to the number of 150 all around the house where the election was held, and the Sheriff went out the third time to quell the tumult — the election was stopped and the ballot box was locked up by the Sheriff before he went out. When the Sheriff returned the box was put on a table and he was asked whether he would not go on with the election. He said when the tumult was over a little he would go on but not at present. The Sheriff told the people if they would be quiet the election would be opened by him; but the people behaved in a disorderly manner and threatened in the German language, if their tickets were not taken immediately, they would break open the door. The Sheriff all this time was walking about the house in great fear and his friends advised him to go on with the election at once, or otherwise the people would break in. The Sheriff said he would not go on with the election that night. Then Benjamin Swope went and told the people in Dutch language that they might as well go home, there would be no election that night. The Dutch answered, that they had as good a right to vote as the others that voted, and they would vote and they began to tear down the windows, broke down the door and behaved disorderly. Then Swope tried to get the Sheriff to go on with the election, that he would surely be killed if he refused; but he said he would take the box into a private room and count the ballot. Swope said he would not be present at the reading of these tickets; because there was only one-half of the tickets taken in that were there ready to be voted. Swope went out to quell the people and when he came back the Sheriff was gone. Then the Coroner got up on the table and sat on the box, which was locked, and proposed to go on with the election; but it was decided the Sheriff must be sent for. By the time they sent for the Sheriff he was seen coming through the woods; but the people would not let him come in. Then two of the company went to get the Sheriff and he said he would not come. Then a man by the name of Nicholas Ryland said he would go on with the election and they got another ballot box and three more Judges and two Clerks were sworn in. Then the election went on and was carried on until dark of the evening, and it was again proposed to send for the Sheriff and read the tickets in his presence; but the party that went for him said he was tired and he went home. Finally they started in reading the tickets and found the ticket box was in the hands of three parties, not regular officers and none of the inspectors were present. They read the tickets in both the boxes.

This gives us again a pretty good idea of the manner in which the elections were held in those early days. That is, they were not always tumultuous like the one just mentioned. They were quite frequently disorderly, drink was sold and a good many persons got drunk. There was a great deal of fighting and intimidation.

We close this incident by saying that not only did the Germans who were refused, cast their vote, but they succeeded and won at the election.

These outrageous proceedings are also reported in 5 Col. Rec., p. 468, where it is set forth that Hans Hamilton, Sheriff of York Co., instead of presenting a return of election, presented a petition, to the Council for the Province, setting forth in substance, that he was by violence, driven from the place of election and prevented from returning and it was not within his power to preside and do his duty; therefore, he could make no return of the election. He had several of his neighbors with him at Philadelphia, where the Council sat, and they were called in and examined and gave their testimony concerning this matter, and Council adjourned the case until Monday and heard some witnesses. Just what determination the Council came to is not shown.

The proceedings are also noted in 5 Haz. Reg., p. 114, and there it is set forth that the Sheriff had 6 of the free holders give their testimony as to the persons that voted during the elections, and drew up a certificate which they signed.

The Germans gave the following explanation of their conduct, to the Governor, as appears in Haz. Reg. namely: The Sheriff did not open the polls until 2 o'clock, at which time the Marsh people assembled armed, surrounded the windows and would not let the Dutch people vote—that thereupon the Dutch people, being the most numerous, broke into the Court House and the Sheriff and the regular inspectors escaped out of the back window — that they invited the Sheriff to come back and he refused —that the Coroner took the Sheriff's place and proceeded to take their tickets—that when the election was over, the Sheriff was invited to come back to the place, and he refused, and therefore, the election went on without him.

1750—German Politics in Lancaster Borough.

About the year 1750, according to Hon. W. U. Hensel's address made at the time of the celebration of a centennial event in connection with the Old Trinity Church in 1911, (which address appears in the New Era of May 18th, 1911), the Germans took a lively part in political affairs in the Management of our Borough. Hensel said among other things, "160 years ago, the conduct of political campaigns and political elections were attended with debauchery and controlled by demoralization, which no party today could stand for." About the time Handchuh's preaching was most effective, and 250 persons attended his Communions, there was a considerable political revolution in the town. Adam Simon Kuhn of this church entered upon six year's tenure of the office of Chief Burgess. Another Lutheran, Jacob Schlough, was elected Under-Burgess, and still another Chief Constable; four members were chosen assessors at the same election, "more quiet and orderly" than ever before known in the history of the town. The pastor in his joy over the prospect of a new and more efficient civil administration forgot the fever with which he was breaking down. I am not prepared to admit, however, that the only issue in that memorable early municipal campaign was one of private or public morals for I find it recorded by Handschuh in the "Hallische Nachrichsten" that "many of the Reformed, all of the Moravians, all the Mennonites without exception and even five or six Lutherans who were afraid of proper town order and discipline, voted on the other side. On the other side, the Episcopalians, many of the Presbyterians and Irish Catholics, some refined Quakers and all the Lutherans." I apprehend it would be difficult to make municipal platforms or select candidates here today for or against whom there could be such allignment of the voters. Adam S. Kuhn began his term as Chief Burgess of Lancaster Borough in 1750-1. He also served 1752-4 and 1755-6.

1750—Germans Intended for Halifax.

In the Pa. Gazette of May 24th, 1750, there is a news item to the effect that a Boston dispatch says that "They have advices from London that a Regiment of Soldiers and 600 English settlers with 1500 German settlers would be sent over this summer; and that they would have a Man of War and two ships stationed at Halifax to protect them."

We are not able to say whether the emigrants who were thus expected to arrive, landed or not. The item is interesting however; because it shows us in addition to the natural perils of the sea voyage, these people were compelled to run the risk of being captured or interfered with by military enemies of Great Britain.

1750—Dunkers in Virginia.

According to Vol. 5 of the Colonial Records, p. 531, there were at this time "Dunker" settlements in that part of Virginia now known as West Virginia. These people were a part of the migration of Germans and German-Swiss into the Shenandoah Valley from Lancaster County. In the book and at the page stated, it is set forth that a "Dunker" from the colony of Virginia came to Logstown in the central part of Pennsylvania and required liberty of these people, to settle on the Youghiougany, a branch of the Ohio in Pennsylvania. The Indians answered it was not in their power to dispose of land; that he must appeal to the Great Council at Onandago and further that he should first be recommended by the Governor of Pennsylvania with whom all such business must be transacted.

This gives us an idea of the early existence of that branch, of the non resistant German-Swiss Christian or Mennonite that have since become so strong and influential in our state.

1750 — Mueller's Discussion of Hardships on the Ocean.

In the historical work, which we have heretofore quoted of Earnest Mueller, p. 245, he discusses in considerably lengthy statements the hardships of the German-Swiss people, in coming across the ocean. Taking these facts in addition to the ones given by Mittelberger, it makes a very interesting chapter. Mueller gives us a pretty fair idea of why it became such a distressing situation and how to correct it.

1750—Ship Records of This Year.

During this year we have 14 ship loads of German Swiss people, and we find among them the following Lancaster County names:

2 Ackermans—2 Albrights—2 Becks—2 Burkharts—2 Bauers—4 Beyers—2 Bendets—4 Beckers—2 Bergers—2 Conrads—5 Foxes—3 Freys—3 Fishers—3 Grors—4 Gilberts—2 Hogmans—5 Jacobys—2 Jacobs—3 Kellers—2 Kings—2 Longs—22 Millers—2 Martins—3 Meyers—5 Peters—5 Reinharts—2 Roths—3 Rohrers—16 Smiths—2 Sanders—2 Shaeffers—11 Snyders—2 Shultzes—2 Steins—3 Wolfes—4 Wagners—7 Wises—5 Webers—and 8 Youngs.

Also one each of the following Lancaster County names:
Arnold — Benner — Bumgardner — Bernhart — Bassler — Bricker — Cooper — Dietrich — Eckert — Eberly — Fritz — Foltz — Falck — Gerlach — Gardner — Houser — Hess — Herr — Herman — Hensel — Kramer — Leinbach — Leaman — Lutz — Metzgar — Mast — Oberly — Spangler — Shaffner — Shoop — Werner — Walters — Yaeger — Ziegler and Zimmerman.

They came over in the ship "Patience," Hugh Steele master—"Bennet Galley," Wm. Wadham master—"Edinburgh," James Russell master—"Royal Union," Clement Nicholson master—"Anderson," Hugh Campbell master — "Brothers," Muir master — "Two Brothers," Thos. Arndt master —"Phoenix," John Mason master—"Nancy," Thos. Cantom master — "Prescilla," Wm. Wilson master — "Brigantine Sally," Wm. Hassleton master—"Osgood," Wm. Wilkie master—"Brotherhood," John Thompson master—and "Sandwich," Hazlewood master.

1750—Mueller on Origin of Weaverland District.

Earnest Mueller, historian, whom we have mentioned so frequently, seemed to have kept track of the movement of the Mennonite Church in America, and seems to have studied the history of it carefully. Page 360 in his book he says in the Weaverland District, Christian Burkholder was in 1750, the first Bishop; and we also find Martins, Zimmermans, Webers, Wanners, Goods, Newswengers (Neienschwander), Hollinger, Nornings, Gerhmann (Gäumann), Baumans, Wengers, Liechtys, Metzlers, Rissers, Ebersoles, Lehmans, Stauffers, Stricklers, Snyders, Schipes, Kreybills (Krähenbühl), also among the pioneers of that district.

Christian Burkholder may have been a son or other descendant of Hans Burkholder, whom we have mentioned before,—a father in the Mennonite Church in Switzerland,—who died in 1752.

1750—New Movement to Expel Swiss Mennonite Tenants.

Mueller in his history, p. 245, under the date of 1750, refers to the movement which was inaugurated in 1730-3, to expel these "Baptists" or non-resistents or Mennonites, from the vicinity of Munster (in Alsace); but he says the movement was opposed by the "Congregation Court," where about 20 of these non-resistent religious families lived. Then he recites that this conflict, however, went on and it is summed up in the statement made to the Prince Bishop under the date of January 17th, 1750, which statement or representation, was signed and joined in by leading citizens and especially by the pastors of the Reformed Church of St. Immen and of Pery. The petition or statement recites, that the movement to expel these people, known then as Anabaptists, began about 20 years ago, by those who through wantonness and litigousness or barretry had been reduced in circumstances (became impoverished), and who hoped by the expulsion of the Baptists to get tenantry of the places themselves. To counteract this, a representation was made by the land owners to the Prince Bishop Johann Kourad which was favorably received. But the disturbance and the petition against these people did not cease until his Highness, in the interest of peace finally yielded. This measure did not benefit the petitioners; who thought that by continually complaining to the Bishop that the Baptists would be expelled. But it was found that when the Baptists or Mennonites had gone away other tenants took their places who were also Anabaptists or non-resistents.

Then this statement made to the Bishop (whether this means Bishop Kourad or not, is not very plain) proceeds and says "that now in 1750, this same movement to expel these people, is being undertaken again, and it will appear as is generally the fact, that it will affect mostly the poor people." These petitioners, who are urging this statement to the Bishop, to interfere for their sake, want this to be prevented by a counter movement. These petitioners, then, go on to state, that the Baptists are of great benefit to the country and they set forth the following, as the reasons for that opinion: In 1724 James Als Couradt (Rector) applied for land on Conestoga near Mill Creek (Pa. Arch., 2d Ser., Vol. 19, p. 726).

"By reason of their constant industry and thrift tilling the soil as well as pursuing trades, principally as weavers, by their simple mode of living, by their complete avoidance of luxury, their shunning of the tavern and of litigation (staying out of Court), they are enabled to pay a much higher rental than others." Should the owners be compelled to employ as tenants the people who have squandered their own possessions? Can it be expected that these would take better care of property belonging to others than of their own? In consequence of such a state of affairs, the owners would have to sell their lands to strangers. Among those who are protesting against strange tenants, are such who themselves are tenants, who sell their harvested crops to the strangers, even to Baptists, and thereby are attracting them. The statement that those to the manor born, would plant more corn than the strange tenants, whereby the title of the bishop would be increased, is sophistry. For since the great felling of trees in the woods on the Chasseral by which arable lands are to be gained, much colder weather manifested itself on the mountains opposite, that almost every year there are killing frosts, ofttimes only the seed being sowed. In spite of all these drawbacks, it has been proven that the tithe has been increased since the presence of the Baptists (P. A.).

And, indeed, we now hear no more of that peculiar social policy of the congregation (or communities).

From this we can see that these non-resistant people did not need to fight their battles alone; but that they had also good and influential friends in other churches, and among people who did not belong to their faith. This gives us the information, that while the extreme measure of torture we have noted as happening in earlier days in these annals, were past; yet the non-resistent, Anabaptists, were compelled continually to look out for their interests and to make every effort by all possible means, that they could, to secure anything like even the meagerest personal liberty.

1751—Ship Records of This Year.

In the year 1751 we have fifteen (15) ship records of these early settlers, coming into United States.

Among the common Lancaster County names we have the following: Two Arnolds—2 Adams—2 Becks—3 Benders—3 Bernharts—3 Burkharts—2 Baumans—3 Ehrharts—3 Eberharts—5 Foxes—4 Fishers—2 Frantzes—4 Flicks—2 Groffs—2 Gerharts—7 Hoffmans—2 Hubers—3 Hesses—3 Haases—7 Klines—1 Kings—3 Longs—12 Millers—6 Martins—11 Meyers—2 Peters—4 Reinharts—2 Roths—16 Smiths—6 Shaeffers—11 Snyders—2 Steins—2 Straubs—3 Steigers—3 Steinmetzs—10 Wolfs—12 Wagners—2 Walters—6 Wises—8 Webers—4 Youngs—2 Zimmermans.

Also one each of the following Lancaster County names:

Albright — Brant — Becker — Bucher — Decker — Eckert — Eckman — Fritz — Frank — Herman — Heller — Hahn — Hirsh — Hartman — Kauffman — Lintner — Messner—Stauffer — Sprecher — Werner and Weidner.

They came in the Ship "Anderson," Hugh Campbell master — Ship "Shirley" with James Allen master—Ship "Patience" with Hugh Steele master—Ship "St. Andrew," James Abercrombie master—Ship "Duke of Bedford," Richard Jefferson master—Ship "Edinburgh" with James Russell master—Ship "Nancy," Thomas Coatam master — Ship "Brothers" with William Muir as master—Ship "Two Brothers" with Thomas Arnot as master—Ship "Neptune" with James Weir as master—Ship "Neptune" with John Mason as master — Ship "Phoenix" with John Spurrier as master — Ship "Queen of Denmark" with George Parish as master—Ship "Janet" with William Cunningham as master, and the Ship "Duke of Wirtenberg" with Montpelier as master.

1751—Great German Wheat Crop.

This year and that of 1752 produced for Lancaster County's German farmers tremendous wheat and other crops. The Chron. Ephratense, p. 190, tells us that these mercies were not thankfully received and appreciated. They led men into excesses. Many in their wantoness destroyed this rich store of provisions and fattened their hogs on wheat. Others in various parts of the county erected distilleries and thus consumed the wheat by converting it into a poison and thereby brought great evil upon the community. See also Rupp 299.

1752—Another Christian Burkholder Letter.

Among the "Dutch Copies" in the Historical Society of Pennsylvania Library, is one written by Christian Burkholder, April 4th, 1752, from his Palatinate home. It is No. 1521.

The introducing paragraphs are of religious character.

Then he says, "I want news of Nova Scotia of England, etc., for this year many of our families want to take the journey to America, for they are promised much freedom there. I want your advice, whether our members shall go or not. Concerning the journey to Pennsylvania this year he says, there are many of those who would like to go but have no opportunity. They want to go and I feel that we must allow and assist them to go. I hope your honors will not object nor make difficult the journey. Unless they are supported by a certificate from me, under my hand, I do not advise you to encourage them. That is as much assistance as I can expect of you. Do not be displeased with my frequent entreaty. I send my cordial thanks for your condescension toward our people and hope the Lord will reward you.

If your lordship will allow a little aid, there are six orphans in our congregation of whom three are under age—very young. Three can earn their bread. They all need money for support. There is nothing left of their parents' property by the time the debts and expenses which their oppressors have put upon them are paid. We leave it all to you; but any money your honors give for these purposes will be well spent. May we expect an answer by next post.

CHRISTIAN BURKHOLDER.

To His Honor
De Knotel of Gerroldshein.

1752—Death of Hans Burkholder.

Early this year (Müeller 213) Hans Burkholder died, at a great age, after 47 years of activity as teacher of the Congregation of Geroldsheim, having gone through many extremely severe trials, and having served his congregation with loyalty and fidelity.

Burkholder was a name of great worth in Germany and Switzerland in early days. He may have been the father or uncle or perhaps a cousin of Christian Burkholder spoken of above.

1752—Germans Settle at Halifax.

An item in the Pennsylvania Gazette of April 2, 1752, informs us that "By a letter from Halifax dated 21st of last month, 700 Germans are going to settle at Mallagash Harbor, twelve leagues to the westward of Halifax early this spring. It is also said the 700 men will be put on the "Kings Works" at Halifax some time this month."

This item shows us that the German ancestors of that great horde of descendants which now so powerfully influence America, were quick to gain a foothold in all climes and quarters of this land, as soon as they had reliable knowledge of conditions and prospects here.

1752—Ship Records of This Year.

During the year 1752 we have 18 ship loads of these German Swiss people.

Among the common Lancaster County names we find the following: Three Albrights — 5 Becks — 6 Bernharts—6 Beckers—2 Baumans—3 Conrads — 4 Dietricks — 6 Eberlys — 2 Fishers—2 Gehrharts—11 Hoffmans—4 Hubers—2 Hesses—7 Hermans—2 Hartmans — 3 Kleins — 6 Kings — 3 Kautzs — 6 Longs — 2 Ludwigs — 30 Millers — 14 Meyers — 6 Roths — 21 Smiths — 4 Shaeffers — 11 Snyders—2 Shumakers—3 Wolfes—3 Walters—6 Webers—2 Wagners—4 Zimmermans —3 Youngs.

There were one each of the following:

Arnold — Beyer — Berger — Cramer — Eberhart — Herr — Hollinger — Keller — Metzgar — Neff — Reinhart — Straub — Shaub — Snavely — Weidner — Weidman.

They came over in the Ship "Two Brothers," Thomas Arnot, master—"Edinburgh," James Russel, master —"Brothers," Wm. Muir, master— "Halifax," Thomas Coatam, master— "St. Andrew," James Abercrombie, master—"Ann Galley," Charles Kenneway, master—"Richard & Mary," John Moore, master—"Anderson," Hugh Campbell, master—"President," Captain Dunlop as master—"Nancy," John Ewing, master — "Forest," Patrick Ouchterlony, master—"Snow Kettey," Theopolis Barnes, master—"Duke of Wurtemberg," Daniel Montpelier, master—"Bawley," John Grove, master—"Phoenix," John Spurrier, master—"Queen of Denmark," George Parish, master—"Louisa," John Pitcairn, master—and ship "Phoenix" with Reuben Honor as master.

1752—Germans and Lancaster Town.

In 1752 the town of Lancaster, according to Hazard's Register (Vol. 5, p. 115) had 311 taxables—that is about 1800 souls. We remember then in 1744 Witham Marshe in his journal or diary called it a filthy Dutch town. It was no doubt most largely made up of German people both in 1744 and in 1752. But at neither dates was it physically unclean. The scrub and mop were too constantly in evidence to allow slovenliness.

1753—Continuous Arrival of Palatines.

Immigration of Palatines continued to be a subject of live interest in and about Philadelphia at this date (as it had been for many years). In the Pennsylvania Gazette of September 20th, this year, it is stated: "Since our last, the Captains Russel Still, Moore & Lickty arrived here with Palatines, and the following are daily expected: Arnott — Mason — Coolan — Muir — Pitcairn — Abercrombie and Lyon from Hamburgh, Captain Brown from Maryland and Captain Crawford from New York both with Palatines sailed before Captain Russel.

1753—Burkholder's Further Advice.

From Gerroldsheim on Nov. 20th, 1753, Christian Burkholder writes to De Knatel again, and after sending Christian greetings and expressing surprise that former letters are not answered, says, he thanks all friends for helping the projected colony in Nova Scotia. He also thanks them for kindnesses, shown to his father during his life. The great need drives him to ask further favors of aid. He says their people do not have even enough of bread. He then says "I inform you I am greatly troubled to feel that you think the money is for myself. We need what we ask, for the help of others. It is Christlike to help others. He hopes that those in power will take "our part" when we are assailed, or when any speak evil against "us." He then concludes and says "Our congregation has been proceeded against again—another decree has been made against us—the Lord will turn it all to great good."

CHRISTIAN BURKHOLDER.

1753—Ship Records of This Year.

During the year 1753 we have 8 shiploads of these early German-Swiss people.

Among the common Lancaster County names we have the following:

Two Bakers—3 Bausmans—3 Cramers—3 Longs—3 Leanords—3 Fishers—3 Hartmans—5 Hoffmans—5 Millers—2 Kuhns—6 Browns—7 Snyders—3 Wagners—12 Smiths—3 Klines and 5 Webers.

Also one each of the following:

Arnold — Adams — Bernhart — Brenner — Engel — Frey — Gerhart — Jacoby — Hellar — Metzgar — Bollinger — Kast — Schied — Rudolf — Wise — Young and Ziegler.

They came in the Ship "Two Brothers" with Thomas Arnot as master—"St. Michael," Thos. Ellis as master—"Buelah," with Captain Richey as master—"Queen of Denmark," with George Parish as master—"Edinburgh," with James Russell as master—"Patience," with Hugh Steel as master—"Richard and Mary" with John Moore as master—"Leamley" with John Lackley as master.

1754—Palatines Again Contract Ship Diseases.

This year a report was made by the surgeons employed at Philadelphia to enforce the quarantine against "Sickly vessels," arriving in that city. (6 Col. Rec. 173-5). The following account of conditions is given by them. They say all passengers are liable in crowded vessels to fevers from foul air—fevers from contact with others in small rooms—fevers from infectious matters brought on board. The steam of bilge water and the breath of great numbers between decks made the air putrid and produces poisons. Animal putrefaction is added to this and also uncleanliness. The sickness caused makes the victims rage in delirium. The poisons stay in the ships after the people land.

This year (1754) we have had these fevers again, the same as in 1741. It spread from the ships to the wharves and over large areas in Philadelphia. Vessels that bring convicts and servants are the worst. Among the poor Germans it is so bad that often half of them perish. But not all by the fevers breaking out about the wharf came from the Palatines. But that their numerous arrival in such conditions do add "fresh fever" is probable. It is true that too often the state of Palatine ships is concealed from the physicians who visit them in such a manner, that it is impossible to discover it, from anything they can see on board.

Thus we see that in spite of the "humane" law of a few years prior, requiring more space and greater sanitation to be provided by ship owners, for poor passengers, great epidemics of sickness were prevalent in this ocean travel.

1754 — German Immigrants Buried in Strange Burying Grounds at Philadelphia.

Thomas Greene and Thomas Bond, medical inspectors for the Province of Pennsylvania, gave an account of the deaths, occurring largely from the contagious diseases, in a report to the Governor, this year. The subject seemed to have claimed the attention of the early Government of Pennsylvania, and in 6 Col. Rec., p. 168 to p. 176, a considerable amount of information on the subject may be found. Among other things, in their report, these surgeons state (p. 173) that they inspected the different contagious diseases on these ships, and have given their view of the cause of the same. On page 175 they state the number of Palatines who recently died from the fevers and were buried, to be 253 during the year 1754. They were buried in what was known as the "Strangers Burying Ground." They state that Alexander Stedman reports 62, Henry Keppely 39, Benjamin Shumaker 57, Daniel Benezet 87, Michael Hilligas 8. This gives us an idea of the continued difficulties under which these people suffered.

1754—Petitions of the Germans in Philadelphia.

This year the Germans who had newly arrived and who were dispersed throughout the City of Philadelphia and its neighborhood, in a penniless, sick and other unfortunate condition, had their friends draw up a petition for them, and set forth some of the evils they were compelled to undergo, etc.

The petition was read in Council, Dec. 21, 1754, by Richard Wistar, and is found in the second Volume of the Pa. Archives, p. 217, as follows:

"It's humbly requested that the Governor would please to take the present unhappy situation of ye poor Germans dispersed thro' this City and the neighborhood under his consideration.

Our complaint is not so much of such as are called sick houses, that is houses hired by the merchants for the reception of their sick, tho' we have reason to fear that there is not such sufficient provision of food, clothing and fuel made for the sick, even in those houses as their weak condition and the severity of the weather requires.

But our chief complaint is on the behalf of such as the Importers don't look upon as under their care, having as they term it, discharged themselves of them. These are people in years, others with very small children, and especially widows with small children, who not being able to pay their passages nor fit to be bound out as servants, the merchants have discharged them upon their own security, or after interchangeably binding them one for another, generally keeping their chests which contain their cloathes, tools, &c., & often best bedding as a farther security, many of these are now dispersed as lodgers in many houses in town, in the outskirts and in the small plantations near it, generally destitute of necessaries, not only to restore them to health, but even to keep them alive; such as are able to go abegging to the terror and danger of the inhabitants, who from the smell of their cloathes when brought near a fire and infectious disorder which many of them are not free from, apprehend themselves in great danger. And those who are not able to beg must inevitably perish of misery and want, as it's believed that scores if not hundreds have already done this fall. It's therefore earnestly requested that the Governour would please to direct that a particular inquiry may be made in this melancholy case."

1754 — Address of the Philadelphia German Protestants to the Governor.

This year according to Vol. 2, of the Pa. Archives, p. 200, the German Protestants of Philadelphia and the vicinity, delivered an address to the Governor of Pa., the following were the subjects, after first setting forth that they were of various religious denominations:

1. That they appreciated the excellent government under which they live, where the best privileges in the known world are established.

2. They praise the government of Pennsylvania for the "inestimable liberty of conscience" and administration of laws, resulting from the plan laid down by Wm. Penn of immortal memory."

3. They have great affection towards the King; and are thankful for the continued succession of the Protestant rulers on the British throne; and they have very great respect for the governors, that have been sent from time to time, though they have not publicly said so, heretofore, because of their people living so far apart over the province, and because they were modest and feared it would be looked upon as audacious.

4. They remind the government that in the past they were accused publicly in England, of being against the government; but they say no single instance can be pointed to.

5. That this address is the name of all classes of Protestant people, (except a few ignorant unmannerly people, who lately came among them) and these same people were always inclined to submit themselves under Romish slavery.

6. They firmly stand with the King of Britain and Parliament in their effort to overthrow the designs of the French King, who are trying to disturb our peace.

Finally they say that being confident, that the Government of Pennsylvania and of the King of Great Britain and Parliament will not be moved by the various defamations made against them, and believing in the love of justice, to Great Britain, they now do this to deface unjust clamors at home, and in England, against them and promise to prove by their loyal behavior, their affection for this government. They then sign their names as follows:

> Michael Schlatter
> George Hitner
> Mareus Kuhl
> Christian Schneyders
> Henry Keppele
> Jacob Peinerz
> David Susholtz
> Rudolph Buner
> Friedrich Mauss
> Ernest Kurtz
> Henrich Bassler
> Johannes Gamber
> Mathias Cline
> Mattias Abell
> Jacob Keanke
> Jacob Kopp
> Henry Antes
> George Hubner
> Christopher Sholtze
> Peter Pennebacker
> Henry Keck
> Henry Muhlenberg
> Michael Walther
> Mathias Hollenbach
> Christophe Rabe
> John Schrack
> Philip Lidick
> Peter Brunnholtz
> Mathias Heinzelmann
> George Graff
> Johann Caspar Rubel

The exact trouble or cause, made against them is not made very plain; but it is likely it was similar to the accusations made so many years against them, that they were not loyal to the government. See Vol. 2, Pa. Archives, p. 200.

1754—Germans and Others in Lancaster This Year.

It will be remembered that we gave a brief picture of Lancaster at least as far as the German-Swiss element was concerned, under the date of 1744, at the time Witham Marshe wrote in his diary the impression he received while visiting here.

Ten years later in 1754, (6 Haz. Reg. 28-29) Governor Pownall visited this section and he has written what he saw. I make a note of this here, because at that time, the buildings, and the improvements on property, etc., were more largely carried on by the Germans and Swiss who lived here, than by the Irish, English and Scotch Irish. He says "Lancaster is a growing town and making money—manufacturing saddles and pack-saddles and guns—it is a stage town—500 houses—2000 population. Between Lancaster and Wright's Ferry I saw the finest farms any one could possibly see. It belonged to a Switzer. Here it was I saw the method of watering the meadows by cutting a trough in the side of the hill, for the springs to run in. The water would run over the sides and water the whole of the ground. If the plan be used in England, I never saw it."

A town called Ephrata lies near Lancaster, settled by people called Donkers, Doopers, Dimplers; they are, I think, a queer set of protestant regulars.

Captain Gustavus Cunningham has given this picture of Lancaster, which he drew as an inference from Governor Pownall's Journal, "When Governor Pownall visited Lancaster there was not one good house in the town. The houses were chiefly of frame, filled in with stone — of logs and a few of stone. When Lancaster was laid out it was the desire of the proprietor to raise an annual revenue from the lots; no lots were therefore sold of any large amount; but settlers were encouraged to build and receive a lot, paying an annual sum of ground rent—hence the large number of poor persons in indigent circumstances who were induced to settle in Lancaster. The Lancaster town was therefore too large at an early period in proportion to the population of the surrounding country, and its inhabitants suffered much from want of employment as from its local situation remote from water, it was not or could it ever possibly become a place of business. The proprietor was therefore, wrong in forcing the building and settlement of Lancaster. The town outgrew its strength and looks dull and gloomy in consequence.

1753—Ship Records.

The following is an additional list of ships for this year: Ship Peggy, James Abercrombie, master, qualified Sept. 24—Ship Brothers, Wm. Muir, waster, qualified Sept. 26—Ship Windsor, Sept. 7, John Good, master—Ship Halifax, Capt. Coatam, master, qualified Sept. 27—Ship Two Brothers, Capt. Thomas Arnot, master, qualified Sept. 28—Ship Rowand, Arthur Tran, master, qualified Sept. 28—Ship Edinburgh, Capt. Lyons, master, Sept. 29—Ship Louisa, Capt. John Pitcairn, master, qualified Oct. 2—Ship Eastern Branch, Capt. James Nevin, master, qualified Oct. 3. There ships all came from Amsterdam.

The Ship Good Hope, John Trump, master, qualified Oct. 1—Ship Friendship, James Seix, master, qualified Nov. 19. These two ships came from Hamburg.

This makes a list of eleven ships, and 931 passengers.

On these ships, in which the ages are given, the average age of the immigrants is: 27 years, the oldest being 50 years and the youngest being 15 years.

On the ship Peggy, the average age in the men's list is 29 years, the oldest being 54 years and the youngest being 17 years. On the ship Brothers the average age being 25 years, the oldest being 31 years and the youngest being 20 years. On the ship Halifax the average age being 26 years, the oldest being 50 years, and the youngest being 15 years.

In the men's list on the ship Edinburgh the average age is 27 years, the oldest being 48 years, and the youngest being 16 years—on the ship Louisa, the average being 26 years, the oldest being 41 years and the youngest being 17 years—on the ship Friendship, the average age being 30 years, the oldest being 44 years and the youngest being 17 years.

The names which appear most numerously among these passengers, which are common Lancaster County names are the following: Wagner, Lintner, Berger, Brown, Arnold, Miller, Martin, Smith, etc.

It will appear from these figures that these were mostly young people.

1754—Ship Records of This Year.

The ships arriving at Philadelphia, in 1754, with Palatines, that is Germans and German-Swiss immigrants, this year, were:

Neptune, with John Mason as master, qualified Sept. 24, 1754—Nancy, Captain John Ewing as master, who took the oath Sept. 14, 1754 (inhabitants of Loraine)—ship Barclay, John Brown as master, who took the oath Sept. 14, 1754—Brothers, Capt. Muir as master, qualified Sept. 30, 1754—ship Edinburgh, with James Russell as master, qualified Sept. 30, 1754—ship Neptune, Capt. Ware as master, qualified Sept. 30, 1754—ship Phoenix, Capt. Spurrier as master, Oct. 1, 1754—ship Peggy, with Capt. Abercrombie as master, qualified Oct. 16, 1754—ship Henrietta with John Ross as master, qualified Oct. 22, 1754—ship Halifax with Thomas Coatam as master, qualified Oct. 22, 1754—ship Mary, Capt. Moore as master, qualified Sept. 30, 1754. All these came from Rotterdam.

We have the following from Amsterdam:

Friendship, with Charles Ross as master, qualified Oct. 21, 1754—ship Banister with John Dyles as master, qualified Oct. 31, 1754—Mary and

Sarah, with Capt. Broderick as master, qualified Oct. 26, 1754—John and Elizabeth, with Peter Ham as master, qualified Nov. 7, 1754.

We have the following from Hamburg:

Neptune, with Wm. Wallace as master, qualified Dec. 31, 1754—ship Adventure, with Jos. Jackson as master, qualified Sept. 25, 1754.

This makes a list of 17 ships, and in all we have 1778 passengers.

Some of the well known Lancaster County names are: Hartman, Shaeffer, Miller, Brubaker, Kauffman, Long, Smith, Conrad, etc. The names that occur most numerous are: Miller, Hartman, Smith, Weber, etc.

1755—Irish to Leave Lancaster County to Germans.

Immediately after the Indian treaty of 1755, the proprietors of Pennsylvania told their agents that "In all sales made by them, that they should take particular pains to encourage emigration into Cumberland County, from Lancaster County, as serious disturbances had arisen in consequence of dispute between the Irish and the Germans at election. The proprietaries desired that York be settled by Germans, and Cumberland by Irish."

This is cited in 15, Hazard's Register, p. 81, but the source of the knowledge is not set forth. We have noticed heretofore that the Scotch-Irish and the Germans ever since 1742, had election conflicts; and we remember in 1749-50 and 51 that those election fights were particularly bitter in Lancaster and York counties. This gave the Government sufficient cause to desire the separation of these two nationalities, that "would not mix."

1755—Massachusetts Invites the Germans and Swiss.

This year Dr. Jonathan Mayhew who preached election sermons in Massachusetts, to his congregation (just as many other ministers of the New England States did to their congregations), stated in his sermon, before the Governor and members of the Legislature of Massachusetts, that though Pennsylvania will have some inconvenience from too many unassimilated Germans coming among the people, yet the growth and prosperity of the province of Pennsylvania, has become a fact, largely because of the great number of German and Swiss people, inhabiting there. He further said, that Massachusetts had too many English now to be hurt by the ad-mixture of these foreign races, and that he advocated all proper measures to be used to encourage the immigration of foreigners from the Palatinate. (See election sermons for 1754, pp. 30 to 48, and Fairchild on "Immigration," p. 46.)

Indeed, not only Massachusetts, but other provinces invited the German-Swiss to settle among them. As early as 1726 Governor Clarke, of New York, sent a circular advertisement to Germany, which was distributed far and wide, offering to give free, 500 acres to each of the first 200 families from the Palatinate that would come to New York. The invitation did not meet with any great success. This may be partly from the fact that the Germans who went to New York with Governor Hunter 1709, (about 3000 of them), soon found the laws there not favorable to them, and about 1722 they nearly all left and came to Pennsylvania, and settled on the Perkiomen Creek. (See Doc. Col. Hist. N. Y. Vol. 6, p. 60.)

Additional light upon the influence and effect of the Germans in Pennsylvania can be found in Watson's Annals, Vol. 2, pp. 266 and 267.

1755—Crowding Germans on Ships Again Causes Trouble.

We have noticed in several prior articles, efforts were being made to prevent crowding poor Germans and Swiss on ships. In Vol. 6, Col. Rec., p. 225, a bill was entered to prevent importation of Germans in too great numbers, on vessels, and was delivered to the Governor, and he gave the Assembly a message upon the same. The Governor stated, several parts of the bill were against the principles of humanity—that more power was given to the magistrates than was consistent with justice — that in other sections they were excluded from exercising rights which belonged to them and in general the bill they intended to have passed into a law, amounted to an absolute prohibition of Germans being "immigrated," and this he said, would meet with disfavor in England, as England was now convinced these people were a great help in developing this Province.

This German bill, as it was called, came up later, and the Assembly laid another answer before the Governor. (See p. 243.) They said that they consider the bill to prevent immigration of Germans, to be of utmost importance to the health of the people, and because trouble is arising from this, they ask the Governor to make this a law, as nearly like the proposed act as possible. The Assembly further explain, that they were attempting to strike at the owners of the vessels, who were making a business of importing these people, in the same manner as you would import commodities for sale and merchandise—that is, carrying on a kind of slave trade. They insist that these are important matters on the bill; but in other respects, if the Governor wishes to amend it, they are satisfied.

The matter dragged along until about April, 1755, and then a copy of the proposed act was laid before the Council (p. 345). This copy says, in order to prevent spreading contagious diseases, it is found necessary to add to the insufficient laws; because diseases have spread all over the province. The Act then goes on to provide that no commander of any ship, having on board more than 50 persons, including mariners and all, shall bring his ship nearer than 3 miles from Philadelphia, land any goods or passengers, until the health officers and physicians examine it and the license from the Governor allows the landing. A penalty of 150 pounds is attached.

From this point on a large number of amendments and changes of more or less importance were made in the bill—the subject occupying about ten pages in Colonial Records. It then appeared to be in proper shape, but when the Governor sent it to the Assembly, they returned it and complained of the personal amendments that the Assembly demanded, the Governor refused to carry out.

1755—Emanuel Zimmerman's Political Career.

One of the greatest figures in Pennsylvania, before the Revolution, was that of Emanuel Zimmerman, the English equivalent of whose name is Emanuel Carpenter. He began his political career in 1755. He was a member of the Assembly of Pennsylvania seventeen consecutive years, up to and including 1771. Many times, he requested his fellow citizens to cease voting him into office; but they would not do it. In spite of his protests, year after year, they elected him by great majorities. When the end of his career came, a large meeting of citizens gathered together in 1772, and passed resolutions, thanking him for his great services. We shall try to give a complete account of this, at the proper date.

Besides, being a member of the Legislature, he was Justice of the Peace, President Judge of our Courts, which position he held up to his death in 1780. He shed as much luster on the early history of our county, as George Ross and some other great figures (Harris 129).

An interesting biographical sketch of his career will be found also in Vol. 7 Haz. Register, p. 152. The writer of the Register says, he was the most distinguished of the early settlers. He possessed an ardent love for liberty in every form—his mind was finely organized, and his influence was powerfull alike, over all the non-resistant religious sects, as well as over the Lutherans and Calvinists; and they all appealed to him for advice in every measure. He was born in Switzerland, in 1702—he first became presiding Justice of the Common Pleas Court in 1760 and remained on the bench for 20 years, until his death. He was also a historian and gathered up such history of the non-resistant people as he could From his race an illustrious line has descended.

1755—The Quality of the German-Swiss Now Arriving Has Become Low.

From the debate, between the Assembly and the Governor and Council, we are shown, the German-Swiss immigrants who were now coming, were very different from those who came to Pennsylvania 25 years earlier. This appears in the contest on the bill, which was attempted to be passed improving the condition of shipping, and to prevent undesirous Germans from coming.

This German bill was again considered May 14th, 1755 (See 6 Col. Rec. 382). At that time the reply to the Assembly's answer was given by the Council to the Assembly. The Governor and the Council still insist on their amendments or most of them. The Assembly sent another message to the Government, later the same day, which is found p. 384. In this message they say they are anxious to make proper provisions to prevent the spreading of diseases in the future, and that the bill they first suggested was a fair one—that many of these immigrants were perishing for want of change of clothes, room and necessities on the ship—that the Governor and the Assembly could get along very well in enacting legislation; but the Council are interfering too much and this obstructs legislation. The Assembly then go on and state that the Germans now coming are of entirely different grade from those who first came. They state that at first and for a considerable time, the families were persons of substance, industrious, sober people, who brought with them, chests of wearing apparel, and other necessaries; but that for some time past, the passengers who are thus fortunate, are sent on other vessels, so as to leave more room for crowding in the miserable Germans in greater numbers, who are now coming. They also complain, that in order to be secure for the fare, of those who died on the vessels, which was the case lately, they hold the passengers' trunks, and they are crowded in the ships without any change of clothes or any means of keeping themselves clean. They complain that the Governor has cut out of the bill, the provision the Assembly desired to change this for the better. They also state that they tried to provide for pure air which the Governor cut out.

The Assembly then proceeds and says the immigration of the Germans for some time, past, are composed of a great number of the refugees of their people, and that the jails supply some of them. Therefore, the Assembly think it reasonable to prevent all such coming — to prevent the ship owners from exacting grevious bonds or security, but the Governor cut this out. The Assembly say that from the late immigration, many numbers of these Germans are beggars from door to door, and that many of them who have bound themselves out for service, have loathsome diseases and are unfit for service. The Governor has struck this out. The result is, the matter ended in a dead-lock for a long time, and the bill failed of passage for a considerable time.

1755—Christopher Sauer's Joy in Pennsylvania Religious Liberty

Our early local ancestors were careful to send back to their old home the good news of religious liberty enjoyed here. In 1711 the first settlers of Lancaster County did so, the very first Spring they lived here. After that many glad tidings went back to the old home. One of the most prominent of the enthusiasts over the good things to live here, was Christopher Sauer. He was learned and influential. In 1756 he wrote to Governor Denny: "When I came to this province and found everything to the contrary from where I came from, I wrote largely to all my friends and acquaintances of the Civil and Religious liberty, privileges, etc., and of the goodness I have heard and seen; and my letters were printed and reprinted and provoked many thousand people to come to this province(and many thanked the Lord for it and desired their friends also to come here." (Brumbaugh's History of the Brethren).

1755—A German is Chief Burgess of Lancaster Boro.

We have noticed before that the Germans began (about 1750) to take an active political interest in our local affairs. After this lesson was learned they kept on holding "fast to that which" was "good." In 1750-1 and in 1752-4 and in 1755-6 Adam Simon Kuhn was selected Chief-Burgess of Lancaster borough, then a good sized and flourishing town. Jacob Schlauch was under-burgess and also another German was elected Constable. (See Hensel's Address, New Era, May 18, 1911).

1755—The Governor Complains Against Efforts to Disaffect the Germans.

In Vol. 6 Col. Rec. p. 621, we have the following complaint in Governor Morris's message to the Assembly:— "You have in the Message now before you, and in several other, taken great pains to infuse into the minds of the people particularly the Germans, that the Government have designs to abridge them of their Privileges and to reduce them to a State of Slavery. This may and will alienate their affections from his Majesty's Government, destroy that Confidence in the Crown and its Delegates, which at this time is particularly necessary, and render all the Foreigners among us very indifferent as to the success of the French attempts upon this Continent, as they cannot be in worse Circumstances under them than you have taught them to expect from the King's Government."

"This you may with your usual Confidence call Duty, Loyalty, and affection to his Majesty, but I am convinced it will not be esteemed such by his Majesty and his Minister, before whom all these matters must be laid, and how the innocent people of this Province may be affected thereby Time will show."

And in the same book p. 631 the Assembly reply and say the Governor knows that his charges against them of trying to turn the Germans against the Government is false and that he does not believe the charges himself and knows that no one else believes them.

1755—Primitive Church Properties of Conestoga and Pequea Secured by Our Early Mennonite Fathers.

In the Recorder's Office at Lancaster in Deed Book D. Page 296 there is recorded a Deed dated July 1, 1755, between Stephen Prinnaman & Margaret his wife and John Burgholder all of Conestoga, in the County of Lancaster and Province of Pa., of one part and John Hare, Charles Christopher and Jacob Beam each of them elders and Trustees of the Mennonist or Baptist Congregation in Conestoga in the County of Lancaster, in which the Grantors sell to the second parties their heirs and successors etc., for ten pounds in trust for the said Mennonist Congregation a certain lot of ground in Conestoga Township.

BEGINNING at a stone in line of lands of Stephen Prinnaman and extending by the same North 16 perches to a stone; thence by same land and by land of John Burgholder East Ten perches to another corner stone; thence by said John Burgholder's land South sixteen perches to another corner stone, thence by same and lands of Stephen Prinnaman West ten perches to the place of BEGINNING. CONTAINING ONE ACRE.

Being part of the land (viz. part of two tracts)—one of which was granted in fee to Melchor Prinnaman by the late Commissioners of property under William Penn, by Patent dated 30th Nov. 1717 and Recorded in Patent Book A. Vol 5 P. 295 and Melchor and his wife by deed of March 16, 1730 conveyed a part of it to Stephen Prinnaman; and the other a part of a tract granted to Martin Kendig by the said properties by a patent 31st Day of December 1714 entered in Patent Book A. Vol 5 P. 264 and Martin Kendig and wife Elizabeth by Deed May 2, 1729 granted and conveyed on interest to John Burgholder who with his wife Catherine by Deed 29th May 1733 granted and conveyed the same to their son John Burgholder and to hold the same for the Congregation "in common whole undivided and never to be divided property forever."

This Deed was acknowledged before Robert Thompson, a Magistrate of Lancaster County. It is witnessed by him and by Geo. Gibson; and was Recorded Sept. 24, 1755.

This is the church property known as the New Danville Old Mennonite Church. It has since been enlarged by additional purchases of land.

The Mennonite Congregation in Conestoga Township at "River Corner," secured their first burying ground and place of worship, about this same year from Benedict Eshleman which appears in the Recorder's Office in Book S S pages 110 and 112.

The Mennonite Congregation at Boyerland formerly in Conestoga Township (but now in Pequea Township) secured their burying ground and place of worship from Samuel Boyer or Hans Boyer about the same time. Hence it was called "Boyerland." See same office in Book R. Vol. 3 P. 549 and also in B. Vol 3 P. 153.

The Willow Street Mennonite Congregation now in Pequea Township, formerly in Conestoga Township, secured their church property very early, in fact shortly after 1710, from Christian Herr, son of Hans Herr, an original pioneer.

1755—Ship Records of This Year.

The ships arriving at Philadelphia this year with Palatines were the "Neptune," George Smith, captain, from Rotterdam, Oct. 3, 1755, and the ship "Pennsylvania," Captain Lyons, Nov. 1, 1755. This indicates that the rush had fallen off. The land was pretty generally taken up now, and a feverish war condition existed in

America at the time. This cause may have had the effect of checking the immigration.

The number of immigrants in 1755 arriving here was 106—90 on the first named vessel and 16 on the second.

Among the common Lancaster County names we find the following: Acker, Barr, Bausman, Bauman, Bertch, Buch, Dietz, Deitrich, Funk, Fisher, Gast, Henckel, Klinger, King, Keller, Kraus, Kauffman, Leity, Moser, Metz, Mayer, Miller, Messner, Reingier, Schaeffer, Shock, Schneider, Steinman, Shaub, Seitz, Scheidt, Schmidt, Schindel, Ulrich, Weise, Weninger, Wertz and Weber.

1756—"Dutch" Grain Fans First Manufactured Here.

In the Pennsylvania Gazette of July 8, 1756, the following appears:

"Notice is given that Adam Acker makes all kinds of Dutch Fans for cleaning wheat, rye and other grains. It will take cockle, etc., cut and clean 200 bushels a day."

The grain fan or cleaning-mill here referred to was the kind used in Switzerland long ago. Thus we see it was introduced among us 160 years ago. The type is still in use, though they are made much lighter now. And besides fans are attached to threshers now. In earlier times these fans were heavy to turn and it took fully grown up men to do it. One could hear them running whole days in the barns. In some sections even these heavy fanning mills were not known 75 years ago, not even 50 years ago; but men threw up the grain by shovels and let the air clean out the chaff, etc. Now all this is changed.

1756—Ship Records of This Year.

Only one vessel of Palatines is recorded as arriving in Philadelphia this year, the "Chance," under Captain Lawrence, Nov. 10, 1756. Only 42 heads of Palatine families were on board. Among the common Lancaster County names were: Conrad, Derr, Bernhart, Klunck, Hengel, Müller, Schmidt, Schoff, Haas, Wagner, Fulweiler, Kamp, Dall, Eberle, Kuhn, Weytzel, Karner, Weber, Zimmerman and Eplinger.

After this date (1756) there are no vessels carrying Palatines or Germans recorded as entering for five years, viz: until 1761. The German and Swiss immigration had truly become slack at this time.

1757—Martin Boehm Secedes from Mennonists.

This year according to Harris (in his biographical history of our country, page 49) Martin Boehm, a father of the Mennonist faith, left that section; and in conjunction with other strong religious characters laid the foundation of the United Brethren Church. Later, says Harris (page 50), Boehm's son helped to found the first Methodist Church in Lancaster County, that of Boehm's Methodist Church in Pequea Township near Baumgardner's Station, which simple but solid stone building is still standing.

1758—Lancaster County Mennonites Sponsor the Cause of Their Virginia Brethren, in an Appeal to Holland.

Among the "Dutch Copies," before referred to, is a letter dated Sept. 7, 1758, in which representatives of the Mennonist Colony in Virginia described their sad condition and hardships because of Indian slaughter; and ask Holland for help. They send John Schneider to Holland for help; and the Lancaster County brethren appoint Martin Funck one of their ministers to go with him. A very lovely lesson in service for others is here shown.

The letter, for which I am deeply indebted to Bishop N. B. Grubb, of Philadelphia (as well as for Holland's response, both of which he translated), is as follows:

"The grace of God and the love and peace of Jesus Christ, is our wish to all God-loving souls and especially to our brethren in the faith in Holland or Netherlands.
Greeting:—

Today, the 7th of September, 1758.

Herewith we authorize our brother and co-fellow in the faith, Johannes Schneyder, who until now has been a good friend to the poor, and who contemplates a journey to the friends and brethren in Holland on account of the dark times in which we find ourselves at this time, owing to the tyrannical or barbarous Indians who have already killed so many people, and have taken many prisoners and carried them away; others were driven from their homes and lands, so that many people are now in great poverty and distress.

We were thirty-nine Mennonite families living together in Virginia. One family was murdered and the remaining of us and many other families were obliged to flee for our lives, leaving our all and go empty-handed.

Last May the Indians have murdered over fifty persons and more than two hundred families were driven away and made homeless.

We come, therefore, with a prayer to you, brethren and co-fellows in the faith for help, by way of charitable aid, if your love will persuade you to show mercy to us, so that we may with God's help, and the aid of good friends, be guided through this Valley of Grief; the dear Lord will reward you for it, here in this life and finally in eternity for what you will do for us.

Further, I do not deem it necessary to write much, as our friend and brother will give you a better report than I could in my simple and imperfect writing, for, he too, had been in danger of his life with his wife and four children, and was compelled to flee and leave his all behind. He had been so situated that he could make a comfortable living. He had a nice little farm, and besides he had begun the distilling of ——— and turpentine oil. He was always a good friend to the distressed in times of need.

Further we request you to remember us in your prayers, as we are likeminded toward you, that we may have the comfort of good old Tobias, with which he comforted his son, when he said, "Even though we are poor, but if we fear God, we shall receive much good.

P. S. This our friend desired a traveling companion from the congregation to accompany him on his journey, as he deems it best not to go alone. Upon our advice and with our Best Wishes, our minister and elder, Martin Funck, has consented to go. Until now he was found true and honest in all things by all. He is, however, still a single man, and by occupation a miller. He, too, was compelled to flee and leave all he had behind. This man was found by the grace and help of God, and will be a true traveling companion to our brother, Johannes Schneyder, on his journey to Holland.

Further, in my simple-heartedness, I do not know what more to write, only to greetings from us all to all the brethren and congregation in Holland.

Signed by us and many others, Michael Kauffman, Jacob Borner, Samuel Bohm, Daniel Stauffer.

Written by Benedict Hirsche, one mile from Lancaster town, Mennist Minister."

1758—Holland's Answer to the Appeal of the Virginia Mennonists, Which the Lancaster County Brethren Sponsored.

"Amsterdam, Holland, December 27, 1758.

Michael Kauffman, Jacob Borner, Samuel Bohn, Daniel Stauffer:

Dear Friends: We have received your letter dated September 7th, but without denomination of the place out of which it is written, by the hands of your deputies, Johannes Schnyder and Martin Funck, who have given us an ample account of the calamities you had suffered, which moved our hearts with due compassion, and since we do not doubt but their narration of your troubles were true and faithful, we have opened our hands to your assistance with fifty pounds English Sterling which according to the value of your money amounted to the sum of seventy-eight pounds, eleven shillings and five pence, Philadelphia money, which you may receive upon the enclosed Creditive from Messrs. Benjamin & Sam Shoemaker in Philadelphia.

We hope that this sum will be sufficient to help and assist you until it pleases the God of Peace to restore the desired peace in America, as well as in Europe; and that you get restitution at the hands and properities you are driven out and enjoy there the same prosperities as before for ye sustentation of your families and the assistance of the Poor, which the Almighty will grant you out of his all sufficient Grace!

In the meanwhile we recommend you highly to keep fast the confession of your Holy Faith in our Savious Jesus Christ, and be always thankful for the Goodness of God bestowed upon you by our compassionate hands and hearts; for as we were unknown to you, it was only the good God who makes this impression on our bowels and gave us the power to assist you.

We hope the bearers of these, the above mentioned Deputies, will return soon and in good health to you, and find you and the other friends in a good condition. We have provided them all the necessities here and for their return till London.

We leave you to the Almighty Providence of God and our Saviour Jesus Christ, and we are with tenderest affection, Dear Friends,

Your well-wish, in Friends,
The committee of ye Baptist
Congregation in Holland.

P. S. When occasion offers we desire your answer that we may be sure that you have duly received the above mentioned money, and please to direct your letter to Mr. Hendrick Kops, Amsterdam."

1758—Müller's Observation on the Virginia Situation.

In Müller's "Wiedertaufer," etc., page 365, he gives us the following account of the Virginia Mennonists' troubles and the sympathy of their Lancaster County brethren:

"In Virginia to which colony the Mennonite colonization had extended, nineteen families were attacked and ransacked by the Indians, and returned in flight to their Brethren in Pennsylvania; but here, too, the Indians surprised and attacked the colonies. Two hundred families were robbed of their possessions, and fifty people were killed. In consequence thereof, two envoys, Johannes Schneider and Martin Funk, arrived in Amsterdam December 8, 1758, and presented to the Commission for Foreign Aid a request for assistance which was undersigned by Michael Kauffman, Jacob Borner, Samuel Bohm, and Daniel Stauffer. It may be assumed with certainty that among the inhabitants of the Palatinate who had emigrated to Pennsylvania were a large number of brethren expelled from Berne.

At this time, about the middle of the last century, brethren of Berne did not only emigrate from the Palatinate to America, but also from the Jura and Emmenthal direct. After a sea voyage of two months they experienced all the discomforts and dangers of the first settlers. Ulrich Fugel, Christian Brechbuhl and Isaac Neueuschwander write under date of December 7, 1755, from "Donigall" in Pennsylvania that Hans Jacob König, or the dyer from Souceboz, had left his wife and the younger children with a certain Abraham Herr in "Canenstogen," but that he himself with son and daughter and "Odina of Dramlingen" went up as a hired man, and together with several other households (or families) settled down on the borders of the savages, at a place called "Schamogen" (now presumably Shamokin in Northumberland County)."

1758—German-Swiss Suffer from Indian Attacks.

The sufferings of the Mennonist Communities spoken of in prior items, are further illustrated in the following news items from the Pennsylvania Gazette of June 29, of this year.

"Advice from Swatara, in Lancaster County, is to the effect that on Tuesday 20th a Dutchman was shot and scalped by Indians; and that the next day a man named Samuel Robinson was also killed by them.

Also "A letter from Fort Henry in Bucks County dated 19th giving an account of the wife of John Frantz and their children being carried off by Indians. The woman was found murdered. A son of Jacob Snavely was also killed."

The non-resistant sects being least ready to defend themselves were more frequently the victims of these outrages than they would have been, had they been always armed and ready.

1758—Swiss Settlers Help in French and Indian War.

It is stated by Rupp (p. 87) that Colonel Bouquet, a Swiss, in the employ of the English during the French and Indian War, visited Daniel Zimmerman in 1758, while his detachment of men was quartered at Lancaster.

This visit was made at or near Big Springs near "Lampeter Square," the ancient "capital" of West Lampeter Township. Zimmerman bought of Christopher Franciscus, who was one of those original Swiss-Mennonite Colony who took up 6400 acres in 11 big farms, near Pequea Creek, in the fall of 1710, their combined tracts reaching from West William to Strasburg, 5 miles from east to west and being about two miles in width, north to south.

1758—Mennonists of Pennsylvania First Opposes of Slavery.

In his "Mennonite Year Book for 1914" Bishop N. B. Grubb quotes the following article from our our deceased mutual friend, James M. Swank:

"Lucy Foney Birttinger copies the following incident from the journal of John Woolman, in 1758, which illustrates the continued aversion of the Mennonites to negro slavery: "A friend gave me some account of a religious society among the Dutch, called Mennonists, and among other things related a passage in substance as follows: One of the Mennonists having acquaintance with a man of another society at a considerable distance, and night coming on, he had thoughts of putting up with him, but passing by his fields, and observing the distressed appearance of his slaves, he kindled a fire in the woods hard by and lay there that night. His said acquaintance, hearing where he had lodged, and afterward meeting the Mennonist, told him of it, adding that he would have been heartily welcome at his home, and from their acquaintance in former times wondered at his conduct in that case. The Mennonist replied, "Ever since I have lodged by thy field I have wanted an opportunity to speak with thee. I had intended to come to thy house for entertainment, but seeing thy slaves at work, and observing the manner of their dress, I had no liking to come and partake with thee." He then admonished him to use them with more humanity, and added: "As I lay by the fire that night I thought that, as I am a man of substance, thou wouldst have received me freely; but if I had been as poor as one of thy slaves, and had no power to help myself, I should have received at thy hands no kinder usage than they."—James M. Swank on "Negro Slavery in Penna."

1759—Efforts Made to Allow German-Swiss to Make Wills.

We have seen that the law of Pennsylvania did not allow the German-Swiss, who were foreigners, to will any real estate at their deaths to any one, nor if such persons died intestate, would lands be allowed to go to the children of such foreigners. Of course if these persons were naturalized, then they could so dispose of their lands. Several acts were passed to naturalize them. It always required a special act in each case. In 1759 such an act was passed by our assembly. It is found in Vol. 5 of the Statutes at Large, page 444; and it provides that as it has happened that these people born outside of the British Empire were induced to come to Pennsylvania and here purchased lands, and died without being naturalized, therefore further provided that if they died without being naturalized, yet if any deed or will made by them in the presence of two witnesses were so executed, such deeds, wills, etc., should be good and valid, same as in case of natural-born citizens; and further if any such unnaturalized foreigner purchase such lands and die without a will the lands should go to his heirs the same as naturalized or native born citizens.

The King in Council however repealed the act, so that what Pennsylvania lawmakers did, the King undone. This he did September 2, 1760.

The King's objections are found in Vol. 5 St. L. 669 and are in substance as follows: "This act is the most infamous attempt to cast a reflection upon the proprietors that ever was invented. It supposes that the heirs and devisees of persons dying unnaturalized have suffered for the want of such act—for though estates of persons dying unnaturalized do by law escheat to the proprietors yet there is no instance found where the proprietors have refused to grant the lands to the heirs or devisees, and this is the constant well-known custom in Pennsylvania. It is therefore abominable in the assembly to attempt to take away a right in the proprietors, and is an evidence that they are so desirous of stripping the proprietors of every legal power and authority whatever, that they would debar him from the power of doing good."

"The proprietors are determined, strenuously, to oppose the law, but would consent to an act for this purpose, imitating the Legislature of England who confined naturalization to Protestants, whereas this will be an encouragement to Papists to settle in Pennsylvania in hopes of similar acts."

This sentiment, which was advanced by the proprietors, was approved by the King's Council and the act failed. Today, with the wickedness and greed there is extant in high places, we would not be any more content than our humble ancestors, to have a dangerous and impoverishing engine of power hanging over us, simply upon the excuse that while it could be used, it never would be used. We have learned too well the lesson of the need of placing an effective check on every dangerous official power.

1760—Growth and Progress of German and Other Counties Compared.

In Volume 5 of Votes of Assembly, page 120, may be found a table showing the progress of Pennsylvania by counties in acres of cleared land, taxables and amount of taxes paid, in 1760. The table is as follows:

Counties	Acres of Land	No. of Taxables
Philadelphia Co.	315,805	5687
Philadelphia City	——	2634
Chester	399,674	4761
Bucks	287,868	3148
Lancaster	436,346	5635
York	256,561	3302
Berks	208,925	3016
Cumberland	179,185	1501
Northampton	189,173	1989
	2,273,537	31,673

Counties	Rate of Land Taxable £ s. d.	Valuation £ s. d.
Philadelphia Co.	1- 3-0	6,540- 1-0
Philadelphia City	2- 3-0	5,926-10-0
Chester	1- 2-0	5,237- 2-0
Bucks	1- 1-0	3,305- 8-0
Lancaster	1- 2-0	6,198-10-0
York	0-16-0	2,641-12-0
Berks	0-16-0	2,412-16-0
Cumberland	0-16-0	1,200-16-0
Northampton	0-14-0	1,392- 6-0
Total amount		34,855- 9-0

Note.—The above is the Report of a Committee appointed at the last sitting of the Assembly, to apportion the sums to be paid annually by each county for sinking the several late grants from the Province to the King.

It will be seen that the total assessed value of Pennsylvania was 34,855 pounds at that time; and that Lancaster County was worth more than one-sixth of the whole province; and outside of Philadelphia County and City its land was valued at more than one-fourth of the province. We had 1760 as many people in Lancaster County as Philadelphia County and over twice as many as the City of Philadelphia. In fact as figures given in the tables are the number of taxpayers, we had, likely, three times as many people as Philadelphia City because our families were larger.

The taxables of Pennsylvania in 1760 numbered 31,673. The population from this was perhaps 6 to 7 times that number, or about 200,000 people. It will be noticed that the average tax was slightly over one pound—$2.66 if a Pennsylvania pound or $4.86 if an English pound.

It will be noted that the rate per head in the City of Philadelphia and in the older counties was higher than in the new counties.

I am indebted to Mr. Morris K. Turner of the University of Pennsylvania for this table, from the Votes of Assembly.

1760—Emanuel Zimmerman Appointed President Judge of Lancaster Co.

In Vol. 7 Hazard's Register, page 152, note is made that Zimmerman was appointed presiding judge of our court this year. The following sketch of his life which is seen on the same page:

"Henry Zimmerman arrived in Pennsylvania in the year 1698, and returned afterwards to Europe for his family, whom he brought out in 1706; and settled first in Germantown, and removed within the present bounds of Lancaster County (then Chester County) in 1717. Emanuel Zimmerman, son of Henry, was the most distinguished of all the early settlers. He possessed from nature an ardent love for liberty in every form—zealous and active in every pursuit. His mind was finely organized; and he enjoyed an unbounded influence over the whole settlement. Tunkers, Aymenish, Lutherans, Calvinists, and Mennonists, all applied to him on any emergency. He possessed as strong a constitution as intellect. He was born in Switzerland, in the year 1702, and died in the year 1780. He lived beloved, and died lamented, by all denominations. He was in every sense an honest man — always just, liberal, and tolerant. He was arbiter in all matters of dispute among his neighbours; and from his decisions they never appealed, such was the confidence in his integrity.

The memorial of the Aymenish and Mennonists, breathes the spirit of a William Tell. It was written probably by Emanuel Zimmerman, as his name is attached to it, on behalf of the Amish, Mennonists, etc."

1760—Newspaper in Lancaster.

In Vol. 6 of the Register, page 137, we have an item stating that in 1760 there were five newspapers in Pennsylvania, all weekly, three in Philadelphia, one in Germantown and one in Lancaster. We may state that Lancaster had a paper several years before that, the Lancaster Gazette, which was put out about 1754 and ran in two years. It contains interesting items concerning the early fairs which were held in May and October each year for the purpose of selling goods; and also items about the schools at that time. Also in the Pennsylvania Gazette on November 27th of this year there is an item stating that:

"WHEREAS in June 1759, a waggoner who lives near Reading acquainted the subscriber that he had about Christmas before, lost several bars of steel on the road between Philadelphia and Reading, and the same being advertised in the Dutch News was procured by the subscriber for the owner, who has not since been heard of, notice is hereby given the steel will be sold to defray the charge."

(Signed) Geo. Absentz.

1760 — German-Swiss Families Scattered By Being Bound Out.

The result of binding out the children of the poor German-Swiss families who came over to this country in the early days is shown by an article in the Pennsylvania Gazette Oct. 30, 1760, which is as follows:

"WHEREAS Rudolph Miller & Barbara Miller came over from Switzerland to this Province with their father Jacob Miller, since deceased, and their sister Regina; and the said Rudolph and Barbara were then bound out as apprentices; and the said Regina has never since heard of her said brother and sister; she therefore desires them or either of them, if they hear of this advertisement to direct a letter to her or to her husband Daniel Kohn living at Conestoga Ferry near Lancaster."

This is similar no doubt to many cases that happened in those early days. One would think that when there were so few people it would not be hard to find the relations of one another; but it must not be forgotten that there were no railroads nor modern conveniences and that travel was very difficult. Thus it happened people living thirty or forty miles apart did not get to see one another as often as people living 1000 miles apart visit one another now.

1760—London Company's Lands Go to the German-Swiss.

In Pennsylvania Gazette December 11, 1760, there is an advertisement announcing the sale of the land of the London Company which consisted of 15 tracts. This land was in Philadelphia County—Bucks County—Lancaster County — and other sections of Pennsylvania. The sale was advertised for April 2, 1761; but the Gazette of that year does not give any account of the sale.

From the description of the land in Lancaster County which are tracts number 12 and 13 it is seen that at this time this land was surrounded by German settlers. There is no doubt that these same Germans also bought up the land. The German-Swiss descendants occupy it today as the Germans have done in previous years.

Tracts 12 and 13 are described as follows:

1 2. Tract (2500 acres) in Lampeter and Manheim township, and partly on Conestoga Creek and on the road from the city to Lancaster and extends within a mile of that town, containing upwards of 2500 acres, laid out in plantations, now in the possession of John Kirk, David Crawford, Andrew Baisinger, James Patterson, John Rorer, Christian Stover, Widow McFilly, Mart Mosser, ——— Rudisball and others, and is bounded by land of Sebastian Grove, Michael Immel dec'd, Melchor Snyder, Leonard Bender, John & Wm. Bond, Jacob Hartman, Darus Buckwalter and others and is intended to be sold in parcels.

13. Tract (1874 acres) Strasburg Twp., on a branch of Pequea containing 1874 acres bounded by land of John & Isaac Ferree, John McCauley, John Elliott, John Huston, Matthias Slayermackers and others. It now consists of five plantations in possession of Mathias, Daniel and Henry Slayermackers, Robert Smith, John Huston, Wm. White, Isaac Taylor and others and is intended to be sold in as many parcels.

1760—High Price of Wood in German Valleys.

It seems that the German-Swiss soon learned that the good heavy timber in the rich lime stone lands which they owned was very valuable and that they had the best grade of it found anywhere. Thus as time went on they began to ask and got high prices for it. Of course hauling it was an item of expense.

In the Pennsylvania Gazette of January 10, 1760, the situation is set forth as follows:

"Help! help! help! Wood at 3 pounds and 10 shillings a cord,—a price never before heard of. The country men say we have wood enough. The boatman says he can bring two loads while he is bringing and unloading one. The merchants complain that the boatmen can bring wood at the same time they are bringing sugar. The woman hears a noise in her yard, rises from her bed at midnight and from her window sees a thief and she asks him what he is doing. He answers, that he must have wood. In the morning she views her small pile and laments the loss of half a cord. The rich engross, while perhaps 200 families have not a stick to burn. And thus it is at the very moment, that at one house two persons lie dead of small-pox.

Should not the fathers of the city do something in this extremity? Cannot our magistrates appoint an officer or officers to inspect every boat —and to agree on a price of the whole —make them distribute their wood in small quantites at a price agreed on— restrain the carmen from every other service and compel them to attend to the boats until they are unloaded? If this or something to the same purpose be not done, what may be the condition of this city before the beginning of next February?"

Here was a wood famine. We are beginning, in this 20th century, to notice that a question is rising as to coal becoming harder to get and going higher and higher in price. We are not as far on yet, in the pinching stage of the coal question, as our ancestors were in 1760 in the wood question. Thus we see that the same difficulties come round again and again. There evidently was a great deal of the mean monopolistic spirit then as now. Old King "Selfishness" would crush and destroy others for his own gluttonous self then, as now.

1761—Conditions in the Palatinate at This Time.

Mr. John C. Egly of Philadelphia has a letter written in Manheim, in the Palatinate, in 1761 by John Jacob Hackman to a relative or friend in Holstein inquiring concerning relatives there, a short sketch of his relationship and also giving something of the religious conditions and liberty there at that time. It required 8 years for this letter to reach its destination—the addressee acknowledges that he received it in 1769. The distance was only a couple hundred miles. It is remarkable that such delay ensued. We give below the sense of the first part of it; but the part concerning conditions in the Palatinate is given in full. Those interested may see the whole letter in the Mennonite Year Book of 1914, page 35.

In the letter Hackman says that he has relatives in Holstein, near Frederickstadt—his mother's brother Conrad Egly, who was born in the Palatinate. He states that during the late war the Palatines moved to Holstein, temporarily, most of them returning after the war; but that Conrad Egly and Conrad Strickler did not return.

He says his father corresponded with this Egly and his children some years; but not of late. He also says he is the only child of Ulrich Hackman and Maria Egly Hackman and lives in Manheim, the capital of the elector,—that he has eight nephews and nieces (brother's children) and that four of them have gone to Pennsylvania in America.

The balance of his letter is as follows:

"As for me and our congregation here in Mannheim, we number seventeen families and are contentd in our condition. Thank God, we have not had any great burden on account of the war. We have a gracious lordship and reasonable liberty and citizens' right to do business for a living. I distil whiskey as my means of livelihood. In our worship we are not disturbed. The meetings are held in my house. As far as our countrymen are concerned, they have somewhat heavier burdens to bear because of the war and winter quarters and forage for the army. Still we fare better than the people who have to provide quarters for the soldiers both summer and winter. This we have not had to do here in the Palatinate, for which we cannot be sufficiently grateful to the Lord. Everything is, of course, dear—food and other necessities. For the French army is stationed only eight miles away and is lying in winter quarters only two miles away. I do not intend to write much more now about the circumstances of our country.

You will already have understood our situation. I pray, therefor, dear brother, not to think hard of me for thus troubling you in taking the liberty of writing to you.

If I can otherwise be of service to you, I shall do so with pleasure. If you wish to reply to my letter, address me Jacob Hackman, at the Schwarzen Lamme, Mannheim. God bless you, and greetings and the protection of the Most High to all who read this. Commending all friends and brethren in Christ to God's care, I remain,

Your faithful servant,
JOHANN JACOB HACKMAN."

This shows again the conditions even in 1761 which made it hard for our German-Swiss ancestors to live their peaceful religious lives in Europe. The reasons are very plain why they came to the Susquehanna and Conestoga.

1761—Ship Records of this Year.

The Col. Rec. (Vol. 17, second series, page 454) record only one vessel arriving in Philadelphia carrying German Palatines this year. It was named the "Squirrel," and carried only thirty heads of families. There may have been many wives and children on board. Her master was "John Benn" and she came from Rotterdam by way of Portsmouth and arrived in Philadelphia Oct. 21, 1761.

The names of the men on board were:

Peter Mischler, Christophel Bomberg, Andreas Graff, Daniel Schaab, Valentin Anwaldt, Johann Wilhelm Serger, Joh. Nickel Hertzog, Nicolaus Schweitzer, Wilhelm Becker, Henrich Holtzapfel, Friederich Probst, John Henry Diessinger, Johann Friederich Diehl, Johan Ludwig Probst, Johann Dietrich Taub, Eberhart Disinger, Johannes Beyerele, Stephan Danner, Friederich Lieberknecht, Casper Knobalnch, Johan Simon Mayer, Johann Conrad Serger, Johan Nickel Becker, George Vogelgesang, Hans Eckardt, Joh. Jacob Vogelgesang, Georg Friederich Rohrer, Johann Jacob Hackman, Johann Nicolaus Diehl, Johan Jacob Probst.

Among them we notice many common Lancaster County names, viz: Mishler, Bomberger, Groff, Schweitzer, Becker, Brobst, Disinger, Byerly, Danner, Mayer, Zercher, Eckert, Rohrer, Hackman and others. In 1762, no recorded ships arrived at all.

1762—Early Executions in Lancaster County.

It frequently happened that capital punishment was inflicted upon criminals in early colonial times. The German-Swiss in southeastern Pennsylvania figured frequently in crimes so severely punished. We have referred to crimes that were not uncommon to the more ignorant German women's weaknesses.

We now set forth the predicament of two more Germans who were sentenced to death. Their felony was burglary. For this they were condemned to die. The record states that Anthony Miller, John Heller and Cornelius Dougherty were convicted of burglary in Lancaster County on November 1st, 1762. No application was made to the council for a substitute for the death penalty and thus on November 11th, 1762, it was ordered that the sheriff of Lancaster County execute them by hanging, Saturday, November 20th. Apparently they were hanged that day.

The horror of capital punishment shocks the senses today; but in those days it was inflicted even for burglary because people lived widely separated; and burglary was more serious than now and often resulted in death. The victims could not secure help. The swiftness with which sentence and execution followed the verdict is a noticeable fact. The "hangings" were carried out on Saturday because it was a day when hundreds could be present to witness the entertainment. See this record in Vol. 9 Col. Rec. 5.

1762—Financial Standing of Germans and English in Lancaster at This Date.

This year a law was passed providing for a night watch for Lancaster

Borough. The people, living on the outskirts of the town, petitioned to have a law passed for the repeal of the law on the ground of its expense. This led a large number of the citizens who lived in the heart of the town to oppose the repeal. These citizens say that those who want the law repealed "are possessed of little property and liable to bear very little tax" and that the greater part of the taxes fall on those who desire the law to remain.

Complaint is also made that those who want the repeal acted in a secret manner. The petitioners there conclude as follows:

"Your petitioners beg to observe that without the aid of the law or one similar the borough will be exposed to the greatest disorders by reason of the near situation of houses therein to each other—that the chief intent in applying for a law was to furnish themselves with a sufficient quantity of water, lodged in public parts of the borough to prevent fire which expense is too much for subscription; and that the useful design of the several fire companies of the borough purchasing engines, etc., buckets at great cost is frustrated by the want of water. Your petitioners beseech your honors not to assent to the law to repeal; and further that the house reconsider the bill and pass one which will allow the levy of a tax for the purpose of supplying a quantity of water in case of fire."

The signers are:

"James Burd (Chief Burgess)—Isaac Whitlock—A. Hubley—John Fellman—Caster Shaffer—Lodewick Stone—Geo. Moyer—Wm. Henry—Stofel Franciscus—Casper Shaffner (Town Clerk)—Friendship Fire Co.—Thos. Barton—Miller Albertson—Wm. White—Jacob Jeller—David Trissler—John Miller—Jas. Marchall—Philip Frank—John Grassel—Nicolas Stoner—Stofel Martin—Fred Shadel—Mary Louman—Sebastian Graff—Jocob Clefs—John Musser—Ludwig Louman—Jos. Chalye—Andrew Graff—James Sanderson—Wm. Jevon—John Ceary—Michael Diffenderfer—Wm. Montgomery—Jas. Soloman—Ulrich Reigart—Geo. Peters—Lowerntz Margert— Royer Connor—Union Fire Co.—Edw. Shippen—Adom Simon Kuhn—Christian Crawford—John Hopson—Rudy Stoner—Geo. Graeff—Christian Voght—Frederick Dombrey—Thomas Boyd—Anthony Snyder—Adam Reigart—Christ Reigart—Lenhart Kleis—John Eberman—Henry Dehoff—Balzer Keller—Mathias Slough—Jos. Simon—Nis Miller—Sun Fire Company—Martin Quay—Michael Gross—Paul Wentzel—Christ Wentz—Casper Singer—Christ Mendenball—Wm. Bausman—Christian Hayne—John Spoore—Philip Bush—John Henry—Wm. Lasch—Chely Lintner—Christian Stone—Bernard Hubly—Philip Beakler—John Epple—John Barr—Michael Fordner—John Hambright—Michael Job—Jawb Weaver—Daniel May—Simon Schnyder—Henry Hutlenstein—Christian Knerscheldt—Peter Gonder and Michael Garther."

From this list it will be seen by going over the above names that about half these petitioners (who say they are the chief men of substance in the town) are English and half are German-Swiss. The original petition and list of signers may be found in a volume of manuscripts in the library of the Pennsylvania Historical Society at Philadelphia known as Miscellaneous Papers of Lancaster County (1724-1772) on page 157.

1763—Ship Records of This Year.

Four vessels carrying Palatines arrived in Philadelphia harbor this year: The Richmond under Capt. Chas. Y. Husband from Rotterdam via Portsmouth Oct. 5; The Chance, under Capt. Chas. Smith from same place via Cowes Nov. 1; The Success under Capt. Wm. Marshall from same place Nov. 25, 1763; and the Pallas, under Richard Milner from same place via

GERMANS AGAINST PAXTON MURDER—CLEARING LAND.

Portsmouth Nov. 25. The total number of heads of families, or male adults reported in them was 248. This list may represent perhaps 800 to 1000 persons.

Among the familiar southeastern Pennsylvania names in the list are: Alsbach — Shellenberger — Kessler — Hauch — Becker — Wolf — Arnold — Schmidt — Huber — Johns — Hauser — Schwabb — Zeiner — Ebersohl — Hoffman — Behr — Miller — Weller — Gill — Bernhart — Menges — Christ — Speilman — Hedrick — Christman — Helm — Bauman — Moyer — Kuhnete — Wagner — Schoff — Wendell — Flick — Blum — Hammer — Scherer — Keiser — Pieffer — Groff — Rohrig — Burkholder — Schweitzer — Sehner — Seitz and Schreiber.

In some instances there are several of the same name in the list. These names are almost wholly sure Swiss though there is a percentage of Germans among them. (See series 2 of Pa. Arch. Vol. 17 page 455, etc.)

1763—German Tries To Stop Paxton Murder.

From the manuscript journal of the great-granddaughter of Robert Barber, one of the three pioneer settlers of Columbia; it is stated by Arthur B. Bradford in Vol. 9 Haz. Reg. P. P. 114 and 115 that "On a snowy morning in December, 1763, a German neighbour came to Robert Barber's house, and requested him to go with him in pursuit of some ones who had been at his house the night before, and whom he called robbers. They had behaved in a very disorderly manner, such as melting the pewter spoons on the stove, etc. Mr. Barber, supposing it had been some persons in a frolic, advised his friend to take no notice of it. He had scarcely left the house, when five or six men came in, very cold, their great coats covered with snow and wet. They left their guns standing outside. Mr. Barber was not personally acquainted with them, though he knew from what part of the country they came. He made up a fire to warm, and treated them to the customary morning refreshments. While they warmed themselves, they inquired why the Indians were suffered to live peaceably here. Mr. Barber said they were entirely inoffensive, being on their own lands, and injuring no one. They asked what would be the consequence if they were all destroyed? Mr. Barber said he thought they would be as liable to punishment as if they had destroyed so many white men. They said, they were of a different opinion, and in a few minutes went out. In the mean time, however, two sons of Mr. B. about 10 or 12 years old, went out to look at the strangers' horses, which were hitched at a little distance from the house. After the men went, the boys came in and said they (the men) had tomahawks, tied to their saddles, which were all bloody, and that they had Christy's gun, (Christy was a little Indian boy about their own age—they were much attached to him, as he was their playmate, and made their bows and arrows, and other means of amusement.) While the family all wondered what it could mean, a messenger came from Herr, giving information of the dreadful deed. Mr. Barber and some others went down to see the extent of the massacre. Shocking indeed was the sight!—the dead bodies of fourteen poor Indians lay among the rubbish of their burnt cabins, like half consumed logs! Mr. Barber after some trouble, procured their bodies to administer to them the rights of sepulchre."

1763—German-Swiss' Strenuous Clearing of Land.

Hazard in Vol. 5 of this register, page 22, says under date of 1763: "The rapid growth of the county by large and extensive clearings, made each year by enterprising emigrants from Germany, Holland, and Ireland, induced also many of the worthless, idle, and dissolute to follow, and therefore compelled the honest settlers to build a House of Correction for the punishment of the vicious. A large number of the Scotch-Irish, in consequence of the limestone land being liable to frost and heavily wooded, seated themselves along the northern line of the counties of Chester and Lancaster, well known at an early period by the name of the "Chestnut Glade." The Germans purchased their little improvements, and were not intimidated either by the difficulty of clearing, the want of water, and the liability to frost which at this period was experienced every month in the year. Several valuable mills were built, but altho' very necessary for the settlement, they became a subject of much irritation among the farmers on the waters of the Conestoga, as appears from a petition presented to the General Assembly, stating, "that Michael Garber, Sebastian Graff, and Hans Christy, erected three large dams on Conestoga Creek, to the great injury and detriment of the settlers on its banks; that said Creek flows about thirty miles through a woody and fertile country, of a width about 250 feet, well calculated for boats and rafts, of wood; that the price of wood in Lancaster is raised to 10s. a load for oak and 15s. for hickory; that before the dams were built, wood was lower, and they had an abundant supply; before any dams were built shad, salmon, and rock fish were in abundance, and in the tributary streams plenty of trout; before the water was dammed up, the country was free from pestilential fevers and from diseases of every kind; that in consequence of the damming of the water, the country along the Conestoga is visited by an autumnal fever, and that which was formerly healthy is now become unhealthy: They, therefore, pray that the Assembly pass a Law requiring the Sheriff to remove said dams, as there would be left no less than ten good Grist Mills, all in the distance of five miles from the town of Lancaster."

Note.—The owners of said dams altered them so as to remove many of the causes of complaint.

1763—Mennonists Help Indian Victims.

In the Pennsylvania Gazette of Aug. 4, 1763, the following item dated Lancaster, July 28, occurs:

There are certain accounts that Indians have passed the South Mountain and are gone into York County, and that some of them have assuredly been near Carlisle. The wants of the distressed refuges have been greatly relieved by sums of money collected in the different congregations in Lancaster County. The Quakers and Mennonists have been very liberal on this occasion, having raised a considerable sum and having hired men to assist the poor people in gathering in as much of their harvest as possible— and we are told that several large parties have again attempted to go over the mountains for this necessary and laudable purpose, but the risk they run is so great we cannot think of them without dread."

While this item mainly shows the Indian situation in southeastern Pennsylvania at this date, it also shows that the German-Swiss people were liberal in helping to relieve distress and gives us a picture of the "good old times" in which they lived.

1764—Mennonists Kind to Indians till Extinction.

In the Annals of the Susquehannocks, etc., page 386, published by the present compiler in 1909, the following item showing the kindness of the German-Swiss toward the Indians of lower Susquehanna Valley occurs:

"In a lonely spot in one of the back pasture fields of this Homestead (The Old Hershey Homestead) the visitors found four stone markers set securely in the ground within whose enclosure lie the remains of "Michael and Mary," the last two Indians of Lancaster County. These Indians were friendly and during their declining years were cared for by Christian Hershey, who then owned the homestead. The following document was read by Mr. Hershey at this spot, after prayer over the remains of these last Children of the Forest, by Rev. Hershey.

'Protection for Two Friendly Indians In Lancaster County, Pennsylvania By Ho'ble John Penn, Esq., &c.,

To Whom It May Concern:

Greeting: Whereas, I am given too understand that the Bearers Michael and Mary his wife are friendly Indians who formerly resided with other Indians in the Conestoga Manor, and have for upwards of fifteen months past lived with Christian Hershey, at his plantation in Warwick Township, Lancaster Co., Pa., during which time they have constantly behaved in the most friendly and peaceable manner to all his Majesty's subjects, I do hereby grant the said Michael and Mary my protection and do enjoin and require all officers, civil and Military, as well as all other persons whatsoever within this Government to suffer to pass and repass on their lawful business without the least molestation or interruption, and they are hereby also desired to treat the said Indians with Civility and to afford them all necessary assistance.

Given under my Hand and Seal at Arms at Philadelphia, the 17th Aug., 1764.'

JOHN PENN.
'By his Honour's Command.
JOHN SHIPPEN, Secretary.

Thus it will be noticed that the Hershey family is honored with decently burying the last Indians of Lancaster County and suitably marking their graves."

1764—Ship Records of This Year.

The vessels importing Gtrman-Swiss Palatines to Pennsylvania in 1764 were:

The Ship "Polly," Captain Robert Porter, from Rotterdam by the way of Cowes, September 19, 1764, carrying 56 passengers; among the familiar names in the list are: Beck—Galle—Mann — Bergman — Wenger — Konig — Eulman — Holleback — Strass — Schwaab — Grebiel — Dietrich — Moser — Wenger — Graff — Schmidt — Strass — Heibst — Bauer — Welte — Hoffman. The Ship "Sarah," Captain Francis Stanfell, from Rotterdam by the way of Portsmouth, September 20, 1764, carrying 100 passengers; among the familiar names in the list are: Bischoff — Lehman — Frick — Lichtenfeld — Keyser — Eich — Hoch — Allspach — Vollprecht — Welte — Betz — Weber — Kaufman — Hubacher — Dorr — Gass — Bintz — Lohr — Funck — Scheffer — Schaub — Strack — Thran — Hoff — Schuster — Kuhn — Sheets — Hitz — Ottershelt — Hartman — Kuhn — Raque. The Ship "Brittania," Captain Thomas Arnot, from Rotterdam, September 26, 1764, carrying 108 passengers; among the familiar names in the list are: Heger — Weber — Roth — Lamphardt — Wolker — Wiser — Schaffer — Miller — Bruckert — Ott — Pautzler — Ersterger — Weibel — Stettler — Lombach — Weiss — Gitt — Reiff — Krombach — Rau — Jager — Rup — Freiberger — Nieder — Helidz — Spitzer — Lampart — Michel — Buhler — Kaintz — Menges — Fishler. The Ship "King of Prussia," Capt. James Robinson, from London, October 3, 1764, carrying 48 passengers; among the familiar names in the list are: Muller — Apffel — Haffner — Deisert — Dippel — Mattes — Suder — Schell — Horst — Stutz — Specht — Breszler — Steinmetz — Reinbold — Fischer — Kilb — Hart — Gantz — Koster — Wagner. The Ship "Richmond," Capt. Chas. Younghusband, from Rotterdam, October 20, -764, carrying 106 passengers; among the familiar names in the list are: Jacoby — Gulcher — Kuhn — Staufftr — Schott — Seitz — Jacob — Haffner — Bardon — Kamerer — Gerhard — Rupert — Bockle — Runckel — Heiser — Gluck — Reiner — Satzler — Muller — Minger — Feikert — Thiel — Mayer — Henrich — Beckel — Harn — Muller — Knoblauch — Kolb — Pfeiffer — Henrich — Heiss. The Ship "Hero." Captain Ralph Forsttr, from Rotterdam, October 27, 1764, carrying 180 passengers; among the familiar names in the list are: Hufer — Weiss — Wolff — Muller — Ludwig — Durr — Walter — Klein — Berg — Hass — Etter — Will — Honig — Gress — Durr Bauer — Schiff — Sellheim — Wittig — Daniel — Brennemann — Lutz — Schantz — Weidenmeyer — Frietsch — Baum — Schad — Beck — Seybtrth — Brubacher — Bruchauhser — Becker — Weber — Volck — Hess — Nagel — Weiss — Peter — Buch — Unangst. The Ship "Jeneffer," Capt. George Kerr, from Rotterdam, November 5, 1764, carrying 86 passengers; among the familiar names in the list are: Kromm — Strunck — Frantz — Decker — Miller — Gruck — Reyman — Frantz — Landes — Meisset — Reutch — Klein. The Ship "Prince of Wales," Capt. James Edgar, from Rotterdam, November 5, 1764, carrying 68 passengers; among the familiar names in the list are: Becher — Muth — Booss — Happel — Hessler — Orth — Mattheis — Haerberger — Schneider — Umstatt — Duckel. The Ship "Boston," Capt. Matthew Carr, from Rotterdam, November 10, 1764, carrying 62 passengers; among the familiar names in the list are: Bertsch — Wentz — Schaffer — Lampart — Wentz — Scheffer — Bausmann — Hartman — Klein — Kessler — Bernhardt. The Ship "Snow Tryall," Capt. John Clapp, from Amsterdam, December 4, 1764, carrying 23 passengers; among the familiar names in the list are: Bender — Stein — Stauffer — Gross — Enck. The Ship "Chance," Capt. Charles Smith, from Rotterdam, Aug. 8, 1764, carrying 90 passengers; among the familiar names in the list are: Bender — Metzgar — Wanner — Grosh — Ammann — Geiger — Tandt — Vogt — Scholl — Hes — Muller — Beck — Mayer — Kemper — Scherer — Schaffer — Blum — Huber — Ringer — Strein — Descher — Hoffman — Weinberger — Schmidt — Haass — Druckenbrodt — Gebhardt — Grob — Chasseur — Wilhelm — Weniger — Zimmerman.

The total number of passengers imported on these ships were 927.

1765—Lancaster County Germans in the Hemp Industry.

The German-Swiss who crowded the valleys of the Susquehanna, the Conestoga, the Pequea and other adjacent regions, became very active near the Susquehanna in raising hemp.

Many prizes were offered by Philadelphians for the best water-rotted hemp and the best hemp prepared by other means. The ancient newspapers frequently offered such prizes for the Lancaster County product. The Philadelphia merchants were also very eager to advertise Lancaster County hemp seed. Among these an advertisement is found in the Pennsylvania Gazette of May 9, 1765, setting out that, "Lancaster County hemp seed is to be had at very reasonable prices at Daniel Wissler's store on Market Street." Lancaster County red clover seed was also advertised as a special seller by Philadelphia merchants.

SUPPLEMENT TO GERMAN-SWISS SHIPPING LAW.

1765—German-Swiss Misfortune in the Susquehanna Valley.

In the Pennsylvania Gazette of the issue of April 4, it is set out that the property of the late John Stoner is to be sold by virtue of an execution on April 6, in Conestoga Township, Lancaster County; on it is erected a complete mill with two pairs of stones fit for merchant and country business and a complete saw mill excellently situated on Pequea Creek. There is plenty of water and 200 acres of land. It is set forth that the title is good and that it is likely a copper mine can be opened on it as there is supposed to be plenty of ore there. It might be added here that up to this date 150 years later the copper has not been found.

1765—The Palatines Still Come.

In the Pennsylvania Gazette of August 29 this year it is set forth that on Saturday last Captain Porter arrived at Philadelphia from Rotterdam with 240 palatines all in good health. This is good news because usually the Palatines ships had a great deal of sickness on board, a large number of the other ships cleared from Philadelphia about the same time.

1765—Nightly Watch Established in Lancaster.

The growth of the people in the Lancaster County region made it necessary for better police protection. To meet this necessity a law was prepared September 20, 1765, found in Vol. 6 Statutes at Large 441. The law provides that the people of the borough may elect such night watchman; and provided the manner in which the money can be raised for the purpose. This item is inserted for the purpose of showing the continual growth of this section.

1765—Supplement to the German Shipping Bill.

In the same Law Book mentioned in the above item there is set forth an act that was passed May 18, this year, to better protect the Germans, that came over in crowded ships. This act sets forth that to protect these people and at the same time to enable the ship owners to recover their fares, that certain regulations must be made. Among these regulations it is set out that there must be room for each passenger, and that these rooms must be three feet nine inches high in the forepart and two feet nine inches in the cabin and steerage, and that no more than two passengers shall be put together in one bedstead except if the father and mother want their children in the same bedstead with them they may do so. These berths were 18 inches wide and six feet long. The act further provides that these ships carrying German passengers must have a well recommended surgeon and a complete chest of medicine—that the medicine must be given to the passengers free—that twice a week the vessel must be smoked with burning tar between the decks and that it should be well washed with vinegar twice a week. It is also said that neither the purser nor other persons shall sell to passengers at a greater price than 50% profit on first cost, any wine, brandy, rum, beer, cider or other liquor or any spices or necessaries for sick persons—that no person shall carry any liquor or other things more than 30 shillings worth. The act also provides that the officer in Philadelphia appointed to carry out this law shall take with him a reputable German inhabitant of Philadelphia to interpret into English the statements of the German passengers. It is also provided that the interpreter in a loud voice shall declare in German that the duties required by this act will be read to them in German and that they may inquire about any matter they may wish to know. It is also provided that the master of the ship must give each person a bill of lading mentioning the trunks, crates, chests, bales or packages belonging to every passenger except of such goods they may want to keep in their own possession. It is also provided that the ship owner must declare when starting out what goods the Germans will not be allowed to bring from their home to America, and that if they have such goods he shall declare what taxes or duties they must pay on the same, so that they will not lose them. The act provided that the fares must be fixed and certain, and that if the German passengers offer that sum the ship master must take it and dare not hold their goods to compel them to pay higher prices.

Many other provisions were made in the act; but all with the same end in view to prevent these ignorant people from being robbed.

1765—Ship Records of This Year.

The vessels importing German-Swiss Palatines to Pennsylvania in 1765 were:

The Ship "Polly," Captain Robert Porter, from Rotterdam by the way of Cowes, August 24, 1765, carrying 81 passengers. Among the familiar names in the list are: Werner — Schneck — Muller — Rhein — Dietrich — Bender — Kohler — Obermiller — Heintz — Gram — Schultz — Schwenck — Schmidt — Dietrich — Kauffmann — Mayer — Fischer.

The Ship "Chance," Captain Charles Smith, from Rotterdam by the way of Cowes, September 9, 1765, carrying 77 passengers. Among the familiar names in the list are: Grim — Roth — Hafferstock — Meyers — Muller — Mayer — Weber — Keller — Frantz — Ritter — Schmidt — Schissler — Metzger — Kurtz — Hoyer — Franck.

The Ship "Betsy," Captain John Osman, from Rotterdam by the way of Cowes, September 19, 1765, carrying 85 passengers. Among the familiar names in the list are: Gabriel — Schaffer — Betz — Zweigart — Garthner — Hiller — Gottschall — Litcht — Pfeiffer — Becker — Schaffer — Schneider — Wolff — Strauss — Ostertag — Metzger — Weller.

The Ship Myrtilla," Captain James Caton, from London, September 21, 1765, carrying 33 passengers. Among the familiar names in the list are: Schmidt — Dieterich — Frey — Naumann — Burgholder — Keller — Meyer — Wissler — Christian.

The Ship "Countess of Sussex," Captain Thomas Gray, from Rotterdam, October 7, 1765, carrying 23 passengers. Among the familiar names in the list are: Hacker — Metzler — Schultz — Vohl — Hubert — Bender.

The total number of passengers imported on these ships were 299.

1766—Lancaster County a Modern Switzerland.

In Switzerland there are many tablets containing lists of names of those who fought and died in the various Swiss wars. These lists are numerous. They are found attached to public buildings, churches, ancient residences, boulders, monuments, and on other permanent bases throughout Switzerland. They contain the names of Swiss patriots from 1766 onward, and the names of some prior to 1766. The names are particularly numerous of those who fell in the Napoleonic wars.

Hon. W. U. Hensel, who died early in 1915, while visiting Switzerland made note of many of these above named tablets; and stated to the compiler of the annals that if the surroundings did not prove to you that you were in Switzerland you would conclusively presume that you were reading the names taken from the assessments lists of the central, north and eastern parts of Lancaster County, Pennsylvania. The names are exactly the same, both the surnames and christian names, and the proportions of persons of one family name compared with those of other family names are identical with the proportion in Lancaster County. That is the family names which are most numerous in Lancaster County are the ones that are the most numerous there, such as Millers — Herrs — Weavers — Stauffers — Harnishs — Millans — Kendigs — Eshlemans — Hubers and others.

1766—Ship Records of This Year.

Five vessels carrying Palatines arrived in Philadelphia harbor this year: The Ship "Chance" under Capt. Charles Smith from Rotterdam September 23, 1766 with 106 passengers. The Ship "Betsy" under Capt. John Osman from Rotterdam October 13, with 84 passengers. The Ship "Cullodian" under Master Richard Hunter from Lisbon October 15, with 12 passengers. The ship "Polly" under Master Robert Porter fom Rotterdam October 18, with 53 passengers. The ship "Sally" under Master John Davidson from Rotterdam November 4, with 7 passengers.

The total number of passengers were 263.

Among the familiar Southeastern Pennsylvania names in the list are: Muller, Weitzel, Arnold, Locher. Schaffer, Weber, Kehl, Meister, Lantz, Hasler. Becker, Weingartner, Lipp, Gross, Conrad, Locher, Weber, Flick, Frey, Martin, Sand, Zimmerma-Ott, Shffer, Singer, Hoffman, Wolff, Mosser. Keller, Volmer, Benner, Kauffman. Wagner, Miller, Frantz, Ziegler. Eckert, Oberlander, Fisher, Meyer. Stoltzfus, Muller, Walter, Herman, Donner, Schmidt, Jacob, Schreiner, Henninger and Amecker.

1767—German-Swiss Improved Agricultural Implements.

It is shown from some early records that the German-Swiss did not lag behind in certain improved methods of conducting their affairs. Those before referred to show that the German Lancaster County Clover Seed had gained great reputation in early days. These farmers of the Susquehanna Valley made efforts to turn out high grade products. The cleaning of the grains was an important matter to them.

In the Pennsylvania Gazette April 9, 1767 there appears among the advertisements the following:

"Dutch Fans & Screens made and sold by Richard Truman at James Truman's place Elbow Lane near the Harp & Crown Tavern at Third Street, Philadelphia, also various wire work for cleaning grain and flax." Accompanying this advertisement there is a picture of the Dutch Fan; and it shows the fan to be similar to those in use about here for cleaning grains just before the combined trasher and seperator took their place.

This article is cited to show the progress made among these people at this date in the processes of agriculture.

1767—Lottery for Church Improvement.

Among not only the early Germans but among all nationalities of early settlers in southeastern Pennsylvania and elsewhere the lottery became a favorite method of raising money for laudable improvements. We have given items on this before.

Another item on the same subject is found in the Pennsylvaia Gazette of October 22, this year and is as follows:

"The Managers of The German Lutheran Church Lottery In Earl

Township Lancasetr County are obliged to postpone the drawing till the 4th of January next. And as there are but few tickets on hand those who desire to become adventurers are requested to be speedy in applying for the same."

1767—The German-Swiss As Political Leaders.

In the Gazette of October 8, 1767 it is reported that those elected to the assembly for Lancaster County were Emanuel Carpenter, James Wright, Jacob Carpenter & James Webb. And those elected for sheriff were James Webb Jr. and Fred Stone and for Coroner Mathias Slough and Adam Reigart. The Governor had the right to select the sheriff and coroner out of the two persons for each of these offices elected by the people.

1767—More Light On the Above German Lottery.

To show that lotteries in days past were perfectly legal and did not partake of the criminal nature which now brands them as public evils, I cite an act of assembly passed (7 St. L. 133) authorizing the same. The circumstances justifying the resort to lottery are set forth in the act as follows:

"Whereas it hath been represented to the assembly of this province by the Church wardens and elders of the German Lutheran Church lately built in Earl Township that not-with-standing the subscriptions heretofore made towards raising a sum of money for the erecting and finishing of said church there yet remains a considerable sum of money due for the work already done, and a further sum besides what has been hitherto raised by contributions among themselves will be wanted to complete the same and to erect a school house near the said church for the education of youth; Therefore it is enacted, etc., that Edward Hughes, Michael Tiefenderfer, Philip Martsteller, John Shultz, Charles Miller, George Rine, George Stohley and Henry Rockey of Lancaster County shall be and are appointed managers and directors of the lottery hereby instituted and to be drawn and to attend to the drawing of the lots, etc., and they shall cause proper books to be prepared in which each leaf shall be divided into three columns, on the first column shall be printed 4444 tickets, numbered from 1 to 4444; on the middle column shall be printed 4444 tickets same as first column and likewise numbered; in the extreme column a third rank or series of tickets of the same number as those of the other two columns, which shall be joined with oblique lines and in addition to the date, each ticket shall have printed on it:

This ticket entitles the holder to such prize as may be drawn against its number, if demanded in nine months after the drawing is finished subject to such deductions as is mentioned in the scheme."

And the managers are empowered to sell the tickets in the extreme or last column at 15 shillings each to be cut out through the oblique line or device indentwise and delivered so as to secure his interest in the ticket. When all tickets of the column are sold the managers shall cause the tickets of the middle column to be rolled up and fastened with thread or silk the same being cut out of the books indentwise (by a waving or saw tooth line) through the oblique lines and put them into a box marked with letter A and to be sealed, till the tickets are to be drawn; and the first column shall remain in the book to discover any mistake.

And another book of tickets in two columns of 4444, tickets in each column shall be prepared with oblique lines across; and 1519 of the tickets of the outer column shall be called fortunate tickets and on one shall be

GERMAN-SWISS CHURCH LOTTERIES.

written 112 pounds 10 shillings—on two of them 37 pounds and 10 shillings—on four of them 18 pounds and 15 shillings—upon 10 of them 11 pounds and 5 shillings—on 20 of them 7 pounds 10 shillings—on 50 of them 3 pounds and 15 shillings—on 100 of them 3 pounds—on 400 of them 2 pounds and 5 shillings—on 932 of them 1 pound 10 shillings, and a premium of 9 pounds 7 shillings additional to the first fortunate drawn ticket and the same to the last one makes 3333 pounds. Out of these prizes the managers are to deduct ratably 15% amounting to 490 pounds and 19 shillings the sum needed for the school and church. And the outside column of these tickets shall be rolled up and put in a box marked "B" and sealed, and the boxes shall be taken to a public place and the managers shall publicly cause the boxes to be unsealed and the tickets well shaken and mixed in each box. And a disinterested person shall draw out one by one the numbered tickets and another person draw out one by one tickets not numbered from other box among which are the 1519 fortunate tickets, the other 2925 being blank. If the one drawn at same time a numbered one is drawn is a blank, they shall be put on one file; if a fortunate one a clerk shall record the number and amount drawn and so on till the 1519 fortunate ones are drawn.

The result was to be published in the Pennsylvania Gazette and a deduction of 15 per cent made and balance went as prizes. Then when the expense of the lottery was taken out of the 15% or 490 pounds the balance went to the church and school house.

What fun these German Brethren of Earl had in drawing the lottery! One can see in the plan a provision to ease the conscience of the projectors and to salve the disappointment of those drawing the blanks — viz. that the lucky ones had to shave off 15% of the prizes drawn to make up the amount to be raised. It was an attractive plan indeed — 4444 persons paid in the 3333 pounds, each one paying 15 shillings for his ticket or (15 shillings for each ticket he bought) ¾ pound and then 1519 persons falling into the luck of getting the 3333 pounds in prizes and each one giving up 15% of the prize secured by him for the object intended and expenses. To add zeal to and to whet the interest in the plan one capital prize and 8 or 10 other very large ones were offered. Who would not have nibbled at such bait even today, in spite of the plan being illegal? It would almost be strong enough to divert our credulous inventors in gold mining stock, etc., from their favorite hazards, to a scheme at home where the chance of winning was more certain.

This plan from another angle is interesting. The man who drew the 112½ pounds by paying ¾ pound cleared up all the money that 150 others paid in. 1519 lucky ones gathered in all the money that the 4444 put down. This operation affecting 4444 persons and involving 3333 pounds (about $15,000) had to be resorted to and employed to raise about 450 pounds or $2,200 for the laudable purpose desired. It is small wonder that the legality of the lottery has been struck down.

Of course what I have said is no condemnation of the people who held this particular lottery. All grades and nationalities and religions and sects as well as the public itself, employed the lottery.

1767—Ship Records of This Year.

Seven vessels carrying Palatines arrived in Philadelphia harbor this year: The Ship "Juno" under Capt. John Robertson, from Rotterdam, January 13, 12 passengers. The Ship "Sally" under Capt. John Osman, from Rotterdam, October 5, 116 passengers. The

Ship "Hamilton" under Capt. Charles Smith, from Rotterdam, October 6, with 134 passengers. The Ship "Brittainia" under Capt. Alexander Hardy, from Rotterdam, October 26, with 39 passengers. The Ship "Brigantine Grampus" under Commander Henry Robinson, from Rotterdam, November 4, with 7 passengers. The Ship "Minerva" under Capt. John Spurrier, from Rotterdam, November 9, with 88 passengers. The Ship "Sally" under Capt. Patrick Brown, from Rotterdam, November 10, with 36 passengers.

The total number of passengers were 432.

Among the familiar Southeastern Pennsylvania names in the list are:

Hirsh — Huber — Sommer — Adam — Bernhardt — Detweiler — Bast — Muller — Weber — Acker — Miller — Ziegler — Hartman — Diehl — Dietz — Fischer — Beyer — Lechler — Lutz — Hoffman — Buchman — Keffer — Zeller — Kuntz — Smith — Schneider — Gramm — Butz — Smith — Hartman — Beck — Wagner — Schmidt — Futter — Hirsch — Dietrich — Steigerwalt — Nauman — Herr — Stahl — Schaffer — Fischer — Kauffman — Blankenburg — Schmidt — Pfeiffer — Dieterich — Roth — Schaub.

1767—Peter Miller's Presidency and Difficulties.

Peter Miller, at one time a prior or president of the Ephrata community, in letters, tells of his labors and difficulties. In Vol. 16, Haz. Reg. 256, speaking of the beginning of his presidency he says he followed a learned man in that position. He also says (p. 254) that soon after he arrived in Philadelphia in 1730 he was ordained in the old Presbyterian meeting house by Tenant, Andrew and Boyd. Then he served among the Germans several years and he quitted the ministry and returned to private life.

He continues his story saying that charity was their chief occupation. "Conestogues was then a great wilderness," he says, "and began to be settled by poor Germans who desired our assistance in building homes for them; which not only kept us employed several summers, at hard carpenter's work but also increased our poverty so much that we needed the necessaries of life." Then he says, tax troubles arose and that "The constable entered the camp and demanded a single man's tax; some of the brethren paid and some refused and claimed each a monk's immunity. But the constable summoned some wicked neighbors and delivered 6 of the brethren to prison at Lancaster for 10 days. But the venerable magistrate set them at liberty and offered himself as bail. His name was Tobias Hendricks. At court, when the brethren appeared, the fear of God came on the gentlemen who were to judge them when they saw the six men before them reduced to skeletons by their charitable labors and privations though they were in prime of life, and the judges granted them their freedom under the agreement, that the whole number of the brethren should be taxed as one family."

He says that in the French and Indian War a Marquis from Milan in Italy lodged a night in the convent or Cloister; and that he presented to him the former president's sermon and writing on the "Fall of Man" published in Edinburgh Magazine and requested it to be given to the Pope. The Pope greatly appreciated it.

1768—Ship Records of This Year.

Four vessels carrying Palatines arrived in Philadelphia harbor this year: The Ship "Pennsylvania Packet" under Robert Gill from London, October 3, with 19 passengers. The Ship "Minerva" under Thomas Arnott from Portsmouth, October 10, with 109 passengers. The Ship "Crawford" under Charles Smith from Rotterdam, October 26, with 85 passengers. The Ship

GERMAN FIELDS DESTROYED BY HAIL.

"Betsy" under Capt. Samuel Hawk from Rotterdam, October 26, with 102 passengers.

The total number of passengers were 315.

Among the familiar Southeastern Pennsylvania names in the list are: Linder — Brenner — Hoffman — Engel — Frauenfelder — Wagner — Huber — Wolff — Decker — Herr — Koch -- Holland — Strecker — Weber -- Zimmerman — Fisher — Dietrich — Meyer — Schmidt — Hartman — Keller — Becker — Heller — Dietz — Giehl — Fries — Diehl — Anthony — Sieber — Muller — Kuntz — Dupont — Bernhart — Huber — Gerhart.

1768—German Fields Destroyed by Hail.

A writer in the Pennsylvania Chronicle of 1768 as reported in Vol. 8, Hazard's Register, page 124, under the title of "Hailstorm in Lancaster County" says:

"I now sit down, under the shade of a friendly oak in the country, in order to give you some account of the late dreadful storm here, the effects of which I have taken pains to examine, having rid several miles for that purpose.

"On Friday, the 17th inst., about two o'clock P. M. the sky was overspread with flying clouds, apparently charged with heavy rain. The wind blew pretty fresh from the S. E. and thickened the clouds in the opposite quarter; so that about 4 o'clock there was "darkness visible" in the N. W. attended with a distant rumbling thunder, and now and then a small gleam of lightning, without any explosions. The clouds deepened more and more in the N. W. and there seemed to make a stand, being opposed by the wind from the opposite points. At half after four, they assumed a frightful appearance, and at last formed a large crescent, with its concave sides to the wind, and its inner edges tinged with a dusky violet colour. About 5 the wind veered about to the N. W. which immediately gave motion to the clouds, and discharged a most dreadful and destructive volley of hail. The storm then proceeded in a S. E. direction, at the rate of about twelve miles in an hour, attended with a most dreadful noise, something like the sounds of cannon, drums and bells mingled together. The hail stones were of various dimensions, shapes and forms. Some measured nine inches in circumference, some seven, whilst others were no larger than peas. As to their forms, some were globular, some spheroidical, surrounded with small excresences or knobs; some elliptical, and some irregular and smooth, like pieces of broken ice. Such as were globular, were endued with so much elasticity, that they rebounded from the ground like a tennis ball. This storm divided into several branches or veins, (if I may use such terms) all which kept the same course, but bent their fury most towards the mountains, hills and highlands. At Susquehannah the hail was as large as pigeon's eggs. At Lancaster about the size of peas; at Dunkertown, and in the Valley, between the Welch and Reading Hills, they were as large as turkey's eggs; in some other places still larger; and at Reading no hail appeared. The damage done by this storm is very great; the county of Lancaster alone, it is thought, has suffered several thousand pounds. In many places there is not a single ear of wheat, rye, barley, &c., but what is cut off; and nothing left but the green straw, bruised and beat to pieces. It is melancholy to see fine plantations, and extensive fields, which, a few days ago waved with luxuriant crops, now lying waste. Many able farmers, who expected to carry several hundred bushels of grain to market, will be obliged to buy bread for their families; and many of the poorer kind will be ruined, and reduced to beggary. All these people are now mowing their late promising and rich crops, as fodder for their cattle. Their distress is truly moving and alarming. At Dunkertown, it is said (with what truth I cannot say) that cattle were killed by the hail; but certain it is, that about Muddy Creek, in this county, calves, pigs, fowls, etc., were killed in that settlement; the ground in the woods, is as thick covered with green foliage, beaten from the trees, as it is with the fallen leaves in the month of October; and in many places the birds are found dead in woods and orchards. The N. W. side of the fruit trees are barked, and all the glass windows on that side, that were not secured by shutters, are demolished; and even the rails of fences visibly show the impressions of the hail upon them. In short, this storm threw every person, who saw it, into the most dreadful consternation; for the oldest man here never saw, or heard anything like it."

1769—Ship Records of This Year.

Four vessels carrying Palatines arrived in Philadelphia harbor this year: The Ship "Nancy and Sucky" under Capt. William Keys from London, September 1, with 13 passengers. The Ship "London Pacquet" under Capt. James Cook, from London, September 29, with 15 passengers. The Ship "Minerva" under Capt. Thomas Arnott, from Rotterdam, October 13, with 92 passengers. The Ship "Crawford" under Capt. Chas. Smith, from Rotterdam, October 24, with 18 passengers.

The total number of passengers were 138.

Among the familiar Southeastern Pennsylvania names in the list are: Roth — Miller — Mellinger — Weller — Bentz — Dobler — Weber — Fritz — Neff — Becker — Hess — Jacob — Weber — Schaffer — Arnold — Stumph — Ziegler — Frey — Jacob — Hinckel — Hoffman — Flick and Miller.

1770—Ship Records of This Year.

Seven vessels carrying Palatines arrived in Philadelphia harbor this year: The Ship "In The Snow Neptune" under Thomas Edward Wallis from Lisbon, Portugal, July 27, with 8 passengers. The Ship "The Brig Dolphin" under Capt. Geo. Stephanson, from London, August 29, with 9 passengers. The Ship "Snow Rose" under George Ord, from Lisbon, Portugal, Sept. 10, with 7 passengers. The Ship "Minerva" under Thomas Arnott, from Rotterdam, October 1, with 89 passengers. The Ship "Brittannia" under Richard Eyres, from Lisbon, Portugal, October 3, with 6 passengers. The Ship "Sally" under John Osmond, from Rotterdam, October 29, with 79 passengers. The Ship "Crawford" under Chas. Smith, from Rotterdam, November 23, with 26 passengers.

The total number of passengers were 224.

Among the familiar Southeastern Pennsylvania names in the list are: Alison — Miller — Dore — Kuntz — Hess — Wolff — Schmidt — Weber — Shultz — Marx — Becker — Heintz — Zimmerman — Wager — Stein — Klein — Dietz — Wagner — Petersen — Bauman — Stauffer — Gramm — Diehl — Rohrer — Hartmann — Seitz.

1770—Germans and the Connecticut Claim.

An item appearing in Vol. 9, of Col. Rec. 663 gives us information of the early life of our ancestral German-Swiss people in Wyoming Valley, of the traitorous conduct of brother Germans under Connecticut Yankees. This is the region in which massacres occurred later, perpetrated by the Indians, and the region in which during the gloom of the Revolutionary War General Hand led an expedition exterminating the Indians.

The item is a report made to the Colonial Council and is as follows:

"Mr. Tighman communicated to the Board a Letter he had just received by Express from Charles Stewart, Esquire, dated at Easton, the 2d Instant, which informs him that on Wednesday the 28th of last month, the New England Men, accompanied by a number of Germans, appeared before the Houses at Wyoming, possessed People under the Proprietaries, whooping, Yelling, and Swearing they would have the Prisoners which had been taken from them, and after expressing much abusive Language they began to Fire upon the People in the Houses, who immediately returned the Fire, by which one of the Germans was shot Dead, and thereupon the New England Men, etc., returned to the Fort, etc.

The said Letter contains several other particulars relating to the Conduct of the Connecticut People at Wyoming. (Vide Letter and its inclosures.)

The Board taking into Consideration the best Measures to be pursued on this Occasion, advised the Governor to write a letter to General Gage informing him of the riotous Conduct of the Connecticut People in taking possession of the Proprietary Lands at Wyoming, and of the Legal Measures used by this Government to remove them and prevent further Disturbances, and also requesting the Aid of the King's Troops to support the Civil Government in the Execution of its legal Authority on any future Exigency.

This was one of the raids made by the Connecticut people and some German sympathizers with them, trying to enforce the famous Connecticut claim. The claim made was that a part of northern and northeastern Pennsylvania belonged to New England Colonies. Connecticut was the leader."

1770—Spinning and Weaving of the Industrial German Women of Lancaster.

"In 1770 and before, an elaborate textile manufacture was carried on here by our industrious German mothers, God bless them. In the year May 1, 1769, to May 1, 1770, cotton, woolen and linen goods, consisting of clothing, bed clothing, curtains, etc., of thirteen varieties, made by the women of Lancaster, reached 28,000 yards reported, with materials in the looms for 8,000 yards more and many more not reported at all, as the Germans feared it was sought for taxation. One good mother alone, while at the same time she was proprietor of one of the principal hotels in the town wove 600 yards herself (Pa. Gaz., June 14, 1770).

1771—Ship Records of This Year.

Nine vessels carrying Palatines arrived in Philadelphia harbor this year: The Ship "Pennsylvania Packet" under Peter Osborne, from London, June 17, with 7 passengers. The Ship "Brig America" under William Copeland, Lattimore, from London, July 27, with 12 passengers. The Ship "Minerva" under Thomas Arnott, from Rotterdam, September 17, with 98 passengers. The Ship "London Packet" under Capt. Cook, from Lisbon, Portugal, Sept. 19, with 9 passengers. The Ship "Brigantine Recovery" under ——— Bull, from Rotterdam, Oct. 31, with 51 passengers. The Ship "Tiger" under George Johnston, from Rotterdam, Nov. 19, with 108 passengers. The Ship "Crawford" under Charles Smith, from Rotterdam, Nov. 25, with 8 passengers. The Ship "Brig Betsy" under Andrew Bryson, from London, Dec. 1, with 38 passengers. The Ship "General Wolfe" under Richard Hunter, from Lisbon, Dec. 10, with 10 passengers.

The total number of passengers were 341.

Among the familiar Southeastern Penna. names in the list are: Bachman — Rohrer — Eckman — Stahl — Hepp — Miller — Schaffer — Wentz — Kuntz — Oster — North — Wagner — Heiss — Kurtz — Wenger — Straub — Schmidt — Berger — Ackerman — Weber — Benner — Thomas — Becker — Schneider — Wagner — Apple — Boyer — Steinbecker — Martin — Marx — Weill — Zimmerman — Trexler — Wolff — Herr — Smith and Berger.

1771—Silk Production in Lancaster County This Year.

In Vol. 1 Haz. Reg., page 63, there is an account of cocoons (or silk balls) purchased in Philadelphia and among them there is mention of certain of them which came from Lancaster. Among these Lancaster producers were Samuel Davis who produced seven pounds and 8 ounces—John Ashbridge who produced 39 pounds and 8 ounces—Caleb Johnson 44 pounds and 4 ounces—William Heny 16 pounds and Isaac Whitlock; as it took a great many cocoons to make a pound, their yield as stated above was quite considerably large.

1772—Ship Records of This Year.

Eight vessels carrying Palatines arrived in Philadelphia harbor this year: The Ship "Hope" under John Roberts, from London, Feb. 24, with 23 passengers. The Ship "Minerva" under James Johnston, from Rotterdam, Sept. 30, with 39 passengers. The Ship "Crawford" under Charles Smith, from Rotterdam, Oct. 16, with 94 passengers. The Ship "Catharine" under —— Sutton, from Rotterdam, Oct. 19, with 19 passengers. The Ship "Phoebe" under Castle, from London, Oct. 19, with 6 passengers. The Ship "Sally" under John Osmond, from Rotterdam, Nov. 3, with 53 passengers. The Ship "Hope" under George Johnston, from Rotterdam, Dec. 3, with 40 passengers. The Ship "Bright Morning Star" under Georg Demster, from Rotterdam, Dec. 24, with 44 passengers. The total number of passengers were 318.

Among the familiar Southeastern Pennsylvania names in the list are: Vast — Wohler — Jacob — Ziegler — Hartmann — Beck — Miller — Bentz — Kessler — Hoffman — Zimmerman — Ziegler — Beyer — Rupp — Muller — Winter — Stauffer — Eberly — Smith — Stump — Hess — Vogel — Lindeman — Wertz — Paul — Kock — Lehman — Ostertag — Dieterich — Meyer — Hoover — Pfautz — Hentz — Richards — Hoffmann — Turner.

1722—Great Silk Production in Lancaster County.

Our German women took great pride in the textile industry, in early times. They were very industrious. In securing clothing for the family, they were compelled to do in those times a great deal that is done by machinery and in great mills now.

In silk production in 1722 in Pennsylvania for the greatest number of cocoons and best reeled silk, Lancaster County led the entire state, (Philadelphia city included) in quantities and quality, Widow Stoner herself having raised 72,800 cocoons, Caspar Falkney 22,845 cocoons, and Catharine Steiner 21,800 cocoons. All of these producers were Germans living in this county. Chester and Philadelphia counties and city fell far behind. (Pa. Gaz., March 17, 1773.)

1772—Banking and Agricultural Commerce of Our Local German-Swiss.

We are given a picture in the Pa. Gaz. of January 2, of this year of the manner of doing banking business and of marketing farm products. It is stated that "Henry Funk of Manor Township on Dec. 19, sent his wagon with flour to Newport and gave the wagoner Philip Jacobs an order to bring 40 pounds or 50 pounds in cash from James Latimore and a neighbor Jacob Genter likewise gave him an order to bring for himself and others 100 pounds from James Latimore and Jacob having received the cash bought a horse at Newport left his wagon 5 miles on this side of the town and went off. He is 30 years old "Dutch" 4½ feet high sandy hair and copper red face, white eye brows, gray eyes, large teeth and one crooked leg. Had on a blanket coat, a blue great coat leather breeches, crown boots, yarn stockings. Ten pounds reward and charges."

In this we also see that the agricultural products of the Susquehanna valley were sent by wagon to distant points—in this case to Newport on the seashore; and that long wagon trips were a common thing in those days. We also see the dishonesty of the times.

1772—"Poverty of Some of the German-Swiss Immigrants."

In the Gazette of January 23, this year (1772) there is a notice dated at Philadelphia, Jan. 20, 1772, stating that "There still remain several German families on board the ship "Tyger," George Johnston, Master, lying in the Bird-in-hand Wharf whose freight are to be paid to Willing & Morris. These families are willing to serve a reasonable time for their freight money and credit will be given to those that want it on giving bonds bearing interest." In this item we see again the extreme poverty of many of the German-Swiss immigrants who came to Pennsylvania and settled in the Schuylkill and Susquehanna valleys.

When we turn to this ship we find that it landed Nov. 19, 1771 (Vol. 17 Second Series Penna. Archives, p. 497) and that it carried 118 male passengers. There is no list of the number of females; and we are not able to tell whether the names stated in the records include only adults or children and infants also. It is certain that there were a number of females on board; but likely not as many as males. The following is a list as given in the record.

The names are as follows:

John Kreble—Nicholaus Scheuerman—Ludwig Schneider—Hans Georg Benner—Sebastian Willie—Nicholas Grunenwald—Peter Wagner—H. Jacob Wagner—Johannes Muller—Johann Jacob Beyerle—Dominicus Heyrom—Johann Lautenschlager—Peter Wasser—Henry Apple — Anthony Klein — Johnaanes Feigle—Caspar Beyer—Nicklaus Kohler—Jacob Burg—George Hann—Jonas Bleech—Gustavus Muller — Peter Odern—Wilhelm Kumpf—Johannes Ihrig—Henrich Ricker—George Eissenring — Joh. Gottlieb Steinbecker — Johann Adam Low—Johan Caspas Lorentz—Johan Wilhelm Schneider — Johann Nickel Martin—Johann Ludwig Starck — Johan Conard German — Johannes Peter Reusch—Johannes Schott—Johannes Nitzel — Georg Volck — Peter Kessler — Johannes Benner — Jacob Marx — Peter Trexler — Jacob Kessler —George Michael Weiss—Jacob Samuel Golde — Johann Michael Beltz — George Mich Raffenberger — Johann Wilhelm Fleck — Hen. Jac. Raubenheimer — Joh. Hen. Lautenschlager — George Henrich Kindle — Johannes Waltman—Johann Christ Jager—Johann Peter Weill—Johann Daniel Cleiss —Lewis Noy—Sebastian Unacht—Martin Eberts — Adam Steiner — Henry Webber — Nicholas Jost — Matheis Fauth — Johannes Motte — Friederich Foltz—Jacob Hoffman—Nicholas Hoffman—Jacob Ihrig—Johannes Lupp—Chritoph Storner—Henrich Mulberger —Martin Grahn — Johann Freiderich Dorr — Johann Peter Schrig — Johann Georg Horn — John Bernard Leyer — Hans Heinrich Zimmerman—Gottfried Kuhner—Johannes Leonhardt Henn—Johann Adam Dracker—Johann Leonhard Ragel—Coard Meyer—Johannes

Muller — Leonard Kessler — Johannes Schneider—Carle Benner—Martin Benner—Adam Grosshart—Michael Trexler — Conrad Haasee — Joh. Daniel Schwanfelder — Johann Nicolas Fuchs —John Le Port — Hans Georg Ackermann—Georg Simon Grun — Johannes Wucherer—Johannes Willmann—Niclaus Samuel Golde—George Friederich Kuchle — Wilhelm Schmidt — Johan Georg Scheuermann—Johann Michael Ihrig—John Noy—Johannes Schletzer —John Jorts—Jacob Scheibly—Adam Als—Johannes Reusch—Johann Jacob Menges—Johannes Kiebel—Hans Mich Lautenschlag — Anton Eberhardt — Philip Egle—Christ Jeremias Schmidt — Conrad Radman — Jacob Sanner — Johan Georg Lautenschlager—Conrad Von Halt—Andreas Ehmer.

Many of the above German-Swiss descendants are living today and in affluence and have not the slightest idea of the poverty of those days.

1772—Emmanuel Zimmerman Foremost Local German-Swiss.

In the Penna. Gazette of October 14, 1772, we find that, unlike most men, Emmanuel Zimmerman was elected to office again and again against his will; and begged his constituents many times to release him from further holding political office. But his reputation and character and the results which he obtained for his community and state were so great that the people would not heed his request to be released but kept on electing him. Finally in 1772 he came to a positive resolution not to hold office any longer. This final decision the people accepted but not without passing a resolution of their respect for him.

He was a citizen of Lancaster Borough and the whole Borough in its corporate capacity passed the resolution and sent it to him. His attitude toward public office and the manner in which he discharged his duty are a beautiful and splendid example to modern office-holders and servants of the public. The resolution is found in the Pa. Gaz. Oct. 14, 1772, and also in Harris' History of Lancaster County, page 130, and is as follows:—

"To Emmanuel Carpenter, Esq., late one of the Representatives in the Assembly for the County of Lancaster:

Sir: The burgesses, assistants, etc., of the borough of Lancaster met this day, at the request of a number of the reputable inhabitants of the borough, and being sensible of your services as one of the Representatives for the county of Lancaster in the General Assembly of the Province, these seventeen years past, have directed that the thanks of the corporation be offered to you, with the assurance of their approbation of your steady and uniform conduct in that station. And as you have declined serving your country in that capacity, I am charged to mention, that it is the earnest wish of the inhabitants of Lancaster that you may be continued in the commission of the peace and a judge in our country, where you have so long presided, and deservedly acquired and supported the character of an upright and impartial magistrate, &c.

By order of the Burgesses and Assistants,

Casper Shaffner, Town Clerk.
(Signed)
Lancaster, October 3, 1772."

To which Emmanuel Carpenter made answer as follows:

"To the Burgess of Lancaster County:

The appreciation you express of my conduct as a representative and magistrate for this County gives me great satisfaction. I hope to continue to deserve your great opinion by endeavoring to discharge any trust reposed in me with impartiability and fidelity.

Emmanuel Carpenter."

A similar resolution of respect and confidence was passed at the same time in compliment to George Ross; and appears in the same issue of the Penna. Gaz.; but as he is not a German-Swiss but of English extraction the article does not properly fall into these annals.

1773—Lancaster County Clover Seed Again Commended.

In the Penna. Gaz. April 14, 1773, appears the following item:—

Lancaster County Red clover seed of the last year's growth to be sold by Benjamin Paulley at the sign and "Crown of the Anvil" on Market Street above Fourth and opposite to the sign of the Conestoga wagon. This shows that at that time the German-Swiss farmers of Lancaster County were producing a very superior article.

1773—German-Swiss Redemptioners.

In the Penna. Gaz. of Sept. 22, 1773, the following notice is inserted with special reference to Lancaster County farmers calling attention to the number of young German-Swiss passengers who are willing to bind themselves out for several years to pay for their passage:—

"Lancaster Co.

German Passengers:

Just arrived in the Ship Brittenna, Johnes Peters master a number of healthy German passengers chiefly young people whose freight are to be paid to Johannes Fisher and Sons or to the master on board ship lying off draw bridge."

This gives us a view of the hardships and difficulties of the remote ancestors of Lancaster County.

1773—Establishment of Glass Factory by a German.

The Pennsylvania Gazette of Mar. 17, 1773, contains the notice that:

"The proprietor of the American Flint Glass Manufactory at Manheim Lancaster County with the advice of many gentlemen of Philadelphia City has offered a scheme of lottery to the patronage of the public to enable him to carry on a manufactory of public advantage and to raise a sum of money for that and other beneficent purposes, in the scheme mentioned."

This was the Stiegel factory, which though it had been in operation some years needed more capital than it then could command. Stiegel the famous German of whom we all know, and other early German-Swiss people whom he had associated with him made a very superior line of glassware in Lancaster County at that time.

1773—Philadelphia and Baltimore Rivals for German Trade and Produce of Susquehanna Valley

In the Gazette of April 7, 1773, it is stated that:

"There are many anonymous handbills of great complaints about the badness of the Lancaster Road by reason of which the writer says we will lose the western trade. The inhabitants of Lancaster, York and Cumberland counties carry a great part of their produce to the landings on Christiana Creek, Elk River, and Baltimore. Christiana Creek has always been a near and safe way to transport the produce of the Counties of Chester and Lancaster to the markets of Philadelphia and always will be. This trade was early encourged by some of the ablest and best merchants of the Province. The people who are most alert in keeping good roads to Christiana landing deserve the hearty thanks of the public.

You will find that there is but one main road from the back counties to Baltimore and thereby the inhabitants are able to keep it in good repair.

On the other hand by several roads being laid out from Susquehanna to Philadelphia they are all very bad and spoil trade. And the new one now to be opened and ordered by the Governor and council is laid out in sight of the old one and very erroneously laid out by those who wish to increase their land to sell. It is laid out on the worst and swampiest ground all the way to the "Ship Tavern."

Our predecessors formerly judged very right in laying out the public roads to Lancaster. They looked for the highest and best ground and made it central to the inhabitants whose interest it is to go to the "landings" and to Conestoga and Tulpehocken settlements. Let us repair the old road. It will cost only one-tenth as much as to make a new one."—A Friend of Liberty."

In this we see early road politics— also the deep concern with which Philadelphia viewed Baltimore as a rival for the Susquehanna trade. Then too we see that considerable of the German-Swiss rural development and progress in Susquehanna Valley depended on the highways to the big business centers of Philadelphia and Baltimore.

1773—Ship Records of This Year.

Fourteen vessels carrying Palatines arrived in Philadelphia harbor this year: The Ship "Pennsylvania" under Peter Osborne from London April 30, 22 passengers. The Ship "Catharine —— Sutton" under (name not given) April 30, 18 passengers. The Ship "Brigantine Dolphin" under Arthur Hill from London May 31, 36 passengers. The Ship "Carolina" under Benj. Loxley Jr. from London June 4, 8 passengers. The Ship "Sally" under John Osmond from Rotterdam Aug. 23, 114 passengers. The Ship "Brittannia" under James Peter from Rotterdam Sept. 18, 118 passengers. The Ship "Catharine" under James Sutton, Sept. 21, 14 passengers. The Ship "Union" under Andrew Bryson from Rotterdam Sept. 27, 97 passengers. The Ship "Hope" under George Johnson Oct. 1, from Rotterdam, 75 passengers. The Ship "Charming Molly" under Robert Gill from Rotterdam Oct. 22, 60 passengers. The Ship "Crawford" under Charles Smith from Rotterdam Oct. 25, 66 passengers. The Ship "Snow Neptune" under Thomas Edward Wallace, from Lisbon Nov. 23, 5 passengers. The Ship "Fame" under James Duncan from Lisbon, Nov. 24, 3 passengers. The Ship "Clementina" under Patrick Brown from Lisbon Dec. 7, 7 passengers. The Ship "Montague" under Wm. Pickels from Lisbon, 36 passengers.

1774—Ship Records of This Year.

Six vessels carrying Palatines arrived in Philadelphia harbor this year: The Ship "Snow Sally" under Capt. Stephen Jones, Aug. 15, 8 passengers. The Ship "Brigantine Nancy" under Thomas Armstrong from Hamburg, June 21, 7 passengers. The Ship "Charming Molly" under Robert Gill from London, Sept. 29, 14 passengers. The Ship "Union" under Andrew Bryson from Rotterdam, Sept. 30, 108 passengers. The Ship "Patty and Peggy" under Robert Hardie from Lisbon, Oct. 29, 12 passengers. The Ship "Sally" under John Osmond from Rotterdam, Oct. 31, 52 passengers.

1774—Local German-Swiss and the Revolution.

All readers of local history know that, beginning with 1774, the County of Lancaster in common with other counties and sections of the Province of Pennsylvania held patriotic meetings protesting against Great Britain's treatment of us and also held meetings to draw up resolutions upon the sufferings of Boston and New England in general. Among the persons who attended the meetings there was always a considerable number of our patriotic German-Swiss people; they did their part nobly in that struggle as well as others.

1775—Ship Records of This Year.

Just two vessels carrying Palatines arrived in Philadelphia harbor this year: The Ship "Catharine" under John Baron from London, Jan. 16, 7 passengers. The Ship "King of Prussia" under William Potts from Rotterdam, Oct. 9, 68 passengers.

1775—Amish Mennonite Immigrants.

In Vol. 7, Haz. Reg. 150 may be found a monograph called "History of the Amish, etc."; it is only a sketch however. Among a number of other things the author speaks of these men wearing long red capes; and the women wearing neither bonnet, hat nor capes but a string is tied around the head so the hair is kept from falling in their faces. He says that they lived in a limestone country and near the Pequea, whose water was clear and cold. As to worldly possessions he says that they desired very little and gives an instance of a brother of the faith being offered 1000 acres of land by the Penns free, to gain this influential man's favor and thereby stimulate purchase of land in that neighborhood. The writer states that the old churchman refused it saying that it was against the church as they did not believe nor approve of a man owning more land than he could cultivate.

In the same article a petition is set forth addressed by these people to William Penn or his son dated 1718 which is quite interesting and which we have mentioned in its proper place in these annals.

1775—Joseph Ferree Begins Gunmaking for the War.

In 10 Col. Rec., page 290, under the date of July 22, there was a resolution passed by the Committee of Safety as follows:

"RESOLVED That a messenger be sent to Joseph Ferree, of Lancaster County with a letter from this Committee requesting him to complete the guns wrote for as patterns, and to know how many he can furnish of the same kind and at what price." This little item is sufficient to show us that Lancaster County and its German-Swiss had a prominent position in the time of the Revolutionary War. There were others besides Joseph Ferree making guns in the towns of Lancaster.

1776—Mennonites Confession of Faith.

We have stated at a prior place in these annals something of the Dortrecht Confession of faith under the date of 1632 and of the first confession of faith in the new world at Conestoga about 1721.

We now notice that the Mennonites revised their confession of faith in the European countries about 1776. In Vol. 7, Haz. Reg. 129 it is stated that the Mennonites followed a confession of faith about that date composed by Cornelius Riss, preacher, and which was published that year at Hamburg. He goes on to say that this gave them new life in Europe and that they launched out on education; and erected the Mennonite College at Amsterdam. Considerable more is set forth in the article just mentioned.

1776—German-Swiss in the Revolutionary War.

Vol. 4, Penna. Arch. 774 we are told of the formation of the German Battalions for the War. Not only is this so but there were several German regiments in the War. One of the German regiments was very largely made up of Lancaster County Germans.

1777—Germans Against Military Laws.

In Vol. 5, Penna. Arch., page 343, we find set forth that the local German-Swiss people were very much opposed to methods which would make a military nation of America; and again on page 504 they voiced their opposition to military proceedings in very certain and positive tones. In the same book, page 396, it is recorded they refused to sell their produce for military purposes believing that the country was taking a wrong course. In the same Vol., p. 427, we find these brethren meeting and passing remonstrances against military action. About the same time in the same Vol., page 576, we find these same brethren taking a positive stand and resorting to strenuous actions at York. A similar account of other proceedings may be found, page 414; and page 768 another stand against militarism in Pennsylvania is recorded as being taken. The leaders of these Germans were wide readers and thoughtful students and their newspaper was highly respected and was subscribed for by the Government so that the authorities might be able to keep in touch with German-Swiss thought and action. Col. Rec. 11, page 409. The paper however was discontinued the next year. Col. Rec. 11, p. 573.

1778—"Dutch" Disaffection.

In the Pennsylvania Magazine of History and Biography, Vol. of 1745, page 233, there can be found an article upon what the writer terms to be the disaffection of the German-Swiss for the stand this country was taking against Great Britain. However this may be, these people did valiant service in that struggle. They did however renew their complaint against the oath which was attempted to be urged upon them. Vol. 6 Penna. Arch. 572.

1780—German-Swiss and Revolutionary War Taxes.

It seems that about this time Germans became discouraged with the long dreary war which was in progress more than four years and felt that the struggle would be lost and their treatment from Great Britain would be harder than ever. This led them to refuse to sell cattle for war purposes; (Pa. Arch. Vol. 8, page 329) and also to oppose the payment of war taxes. Do. 330. The result was a large number of them were imprisoned for this matter of conscience. 8 Do., page 343.

1780—German Society for Relief of Germans.

This year as may be seen in Vol. 10 St. L. 355 the suffering of the German-Swiss people of Pennsylvania caused a law to be passed to incorporate a German Society for contributing relief to the distressed Germans in Pennsylvania. The act says that the Germans by their numerous settlements in Pennsylvania have greatly contributed to the wealth and strength of the State; and that it is necessary to furnish relief to those who need assistance here, and teach their children the English and German languages, thereby allowing these children to finish their studies at the University at Philadelphia and to have means of creating a library. A society for these purposes was needed. The act then goes on to set forth the organization of the society and to mention its purposes, and give the names of original founders. This shows that they were enterprising for an education and general welfare.

1782—The German-Swiss Disregard the Prohibiting of Trade With Great Britain.

In Vol. 13 Col. Rec., pages 317 and 328, it is set forth that some of the German-Swiss people began selling, buying and dealing in British goods; in spite of the fact that the Colonies had determined not to deal in British trade in any manner whatever. Those who did so were severely punished as referred to in this book. Vol. 15 Col.

JACOB FRIES' TREASON TRIAL.

Rec., page 546, there is an account of the seizure of some of these goods that were dealt in by some of their people in defiance of what the patriots had decided upon. This clashing of views between those who felt it their Christian duty to live a life of non-resistance and to obey the oaths to support the British government they had taken when they were permitted to enter Pennsylvania on one hand, and the patriots on the other hand (who were determined to break the bands which bound them to British authority) caused many bold, open outbreaks. One of the most noted of these was that of the action of Jacob Fries who refused to pay Revolutionary War taxes and defied the United States Government to such an extent that he was tried for treason. The full particulars of the trial may be found in Vol. 18 of the proceedings of the Lancaster County Historical Society, page 87. There is a document connected with this trial; namely a petition signed by some of the German sympathizers of Jacob Fries asking release from these burdensome conditions, in the library of the Lancaster County Historical Society.

On the corner of the document are the initials of the President of the United States, Thomas Jefferson. Other particulars concerning the trial are found in the paper of Lewis Richards in the proceedings of the Pennsylvania State Bar Association held at Erie, 1914. It is interesting to note that Judge Chase was impeached for certain acts occurring in these treason proceedings.

It was our intention to bring these annals down to the time of the Revolutionary War. Having done so, we now conclude the series. The items set forth in the latter part of this work are simply specimen items illustrating the trend of the life of these people and their general policy. It is not pretended that all of their doings are here chronicled, but only a few of them. Many thousand items that might have been written concerning them from 1750 onward are not taken in the scope of this work. Many of the items of this volume have been gathered from rare sources and translated from the Dutch and German languages; in which languages the original manuscript which we have consulted were written.

We feel that the estimate we gave in the opening paragraph of this work is justified by the material included within these covers.

Our task is now at an end and we leave it to the consideration and judgment of those who shall read the history which, we feel that, herein we have helped to preserve.

H. FRANK ESHLEMAN.

INDEX OF ITEMS

NOTE: It is probable that some items are inadvertently omitted from this index.

Anabaptists, see Mennonites
Alsace Anabaptists 104
" Mennonites in 114
Altham - Lord - Servant of German Farmer 273
Agriculture and Mennonites...... 341
Amsterdam Library, "Mennonite". 15
" Supports Anabaptists. 92
" Interceded for Anabaptists 105
Amish Mennonites Origin......... 128
" Mennonites Documents.... 128
" Documents on Faith, 1693. 129
America, Attempted Banishment to, 1710 159
" Deportation to, 1710..... 161
Amish Protest Against Penn's Law 205
" Mennonites' Early Customs 208
" Protest Against Laws..... 204
" Mennonites Petition for Relief 276
" Immigrants 353
Armstrong, John, Killed by Indians 288
Anabaptism and Bohemia......... 11
Anabaptism's Rise in Berne...... 12
" Rise in Zurich..... 13
" Early Spread in Netherland 18
" Attack by Rival Creeds 18
" Triumph Over Lutherans 20
Annesley, Arthur, an Irish Lord.. 273
Austrian Decree Against Anabaptism 33
" Anabaptists 50
Augsburg Diet of................. 56
Avarice, Absence of............... 215
Background (European) 1
Bavarian Prominence 5
Baptism (Early Anabaptist View) 24
Bavaria and Anabaptism....... 29, 30
Baptists, see "Anabaptists"....... 35
Basel, Tortures in............ 47, 51
Bair (John) A Mennonite Father, 1551 57
" of Lichtenfels 57
Baltic Anabaptists 93
Banishment Divides Families of Mennonites 116
Banishment of 1710 to America... 159
Baptism, Earliest Form of........ 209

Banking and Financiering of German-Swiss 348
Baltimore Wants Germans' Produce 351
Beghinen, Rise of................ 6
Berne and Walderseans, 1522..... 12
Berne, Migration of Anabaptists to 39
" Orders Extermination..... 40
Berne's Decree Against Emmenthal 63
Belgium Mennonites, 1564........ 64
Berne Executions 64
" Government Teaches Against Anabaptism 73
" Growth of, In............ 94
" Jail Roll................. 104
" Decrees, 68, 91, 92, 97, 100, 102, 105, 107, 110, 116, 124
" Banishment of Mennonites. 138
" and Runkle 144
" Banishments of 1710...... 151
Beissel's Labors and Achievements 215
Bearing Arms, Objection to...... 215
Bible, Nuremburg Translation.... 25
" Anabaptist Translation.... 60
Biestkin's Bible, First Edition 1560 62
Bible, Biestkin's Translation, 1560 62
" Emden Edition 62
Bixler Leaves the Reform Church 79
Bible Testament Printed at Basel. 122
Bingelli's Colony 131
Birth (First in Lancaster County) 162
Bizalion and His Labors.......... 211
Blauroch's Death................. 37
Bloody Edicts of Charles and Philip 59
Bohemia and Mennonite Faith.... 11
" and Anabaptism 11
Bollinger, Mennonite Father and Historian 63
Bounties, Anabaptists Pay to Escape War Service............ 105
Bounties in Lieu of Military Service 106
Bound Out, German Boys......... 330
Boehm Secedes 324
Boyerland Church 323
Brackbill's Services 153
" Diary 155
" Report of 1710 Exodus 157
" Friendly Services, 168, 169
" Benedict's Letters 195, 196

INDEX OF ITEMS.

Brickmaking Among Palatines.... 221
Bumgardner, Ulrich, Reasons for
   Anabaptism................. 79, 81
Burkholder (Hans) Escapes Arrest 101
Bumgardner's Hymn 103
Burki's Report of 1710 Exodus.... 157
Burkholder, Letters of Hans...... 288
Burkholder's Labors and Letters.. 294
    "   Letters and Labors.. 298
    "   Letters and Labors.. 312
    "   (Hans) Death 313
Burial at Philadelphia of Dead
   German Immigrants 315
Burglary and Punishment........ 333
Calvinism at Geneva............ 58
    "   vs. Papacy 64
Calvinists vs. Lutherans.......... 71
Cartledge and Conestoga........ 210
Capital Punishment in Pa. (Early) 333
Cemetery, Oldest in Lancaster Co. 250
Children in Church.............. 16
Church and the Children......... 16
    "   and State, Separation of.. 43
    "   and State, Separation of
        1532 44
Charles Fifth and Anabaptists.... 44
Chronicles of Anabaptists' Torture 97
Church, First Mennonite, in America 137
Churches, First Mennonite....... 323
    "   Mennonite, Earliest in
        Lancaster County.... 323
Chalkley's Account 148
Chickies and Salunga Settlement. 220
Clover Seed, Germans Produce It. 351
Comet, The Great and Telner..... 121
Confession of Faith, Mennonites, 15, 353
    "   of Faith, Anabaptist... 70
Confiscation of Property by Swiss 73
Confession of Faith in Reformed
        Church 77
    "   of Faith (Dortrecht).. 82
Confiscated Property of Anabaptists 124
Conestoga Valley Settlement in 1712
        192, 193
    "   More Settlements..200, 201
    "   Assessment of 1718..... 204
    "   Land Grants........... 210
    "   and Strasburg Additions 213
    "   The Great Road........ 217
    "   Additions 220
    "   and Collection of Taxes 225
    "   and Dortrecht Confession 228
    "   and Wild Beasts....... 235
    "   Suffering 251

Conestoga Manor Sub-divided..... 255
Confiscations of Mennonite Goods 260
Confiscation, Mennonite Goods, 259, 260
Commerce between Philadelphia
   and Lancaster 269
Contagious Disease on Shipboard. 275
    "   Ship Diseases 315
Contagion on Ship Board, Crowding, etc. 319
    "   and Quarantine 339
"Corner" in Fire Wood........... 331
Congregations in Palatinate, 1671 332
Connecticut Claim and Our Germany 346
Cumberland Valley Migration..... 271
Denmark Favors Anabaptism..... 25
Debate on Anabaptism........... 32
Deventer Edict vs. Anabaptists... 78
Delaware Mennonite Colony...... 130
Deportation to America.......... 161
    "   of Mennonites 1711,
        List from Berne Jail 170
    "   to Holland, 170, 171, 172
Departure Money of the Banished 176
Deportation, 28,500 Florins Collected for 178
Death in Ocean Travel........... 275
Ditcher, Mary, and the Palatines. 219
Disease, Contagion on Ship....... 321
Disaffection of Germans.......... 322
    "   of "Dutch" 354
Dortrecht Confession of Faith.... 82
Donegal, Mennonite Neighbors at. 223
Dortrecht Confession of Faith in
   Conestoga 228
Dry Goods of Early Times........ 261
Dunkards Secede 137
    "   In Pequea and Conestoga 212
Dunkers in Virginia............. 309
Dutch Grain Fans Invented....... 324
Dunkers' Troubles at Ephrata.... 344
"Dutch" Disaffection 354
Eggvyl Anabaptist Colony in Emmenthal 101
Eggvyl Congregation to be Destroyed 117
Elbe, Anabaptists Flee from...... 65
Elbing Anabaptists.............. 108
Election Riots of 1742 and the German 276
    "   Funds of 1749.......... 301
Emmenthal, Earliest Anabaptists of 27
    "   Drift Into, 1538....... 49
    "   Suffering 102
Empson's Colony on Octoraro.... 131
Emmenthal Hunt 132

INDEX OF ITEMS.

Emigration Tax Opposed by Mennonites 236
" to Lancaster Co. of 1717 203
" to Pennsylvania Opposed 230
" to Pennsylvania Creates New Alarms... 231
" to Lancaster, 1731... 239
"End of World" Scare............ 38
English Decrees Against Anabaptists 50
England and Poor Palatines...... 192
Ephrata Monastic Society Begun.. 249
" Community Solitary Life 255
" Community Historical Note 271
" Dunkers' Troubles....... 344
Eshleman Family........ 240, 241, 242
Ethical Rules of Anabaptists.......90
European Background............ 1
Evangelical Doctrine, The Rise of 5
Everling's Letters 114, 115
" Statistics of 1672...... 120
Executions of Anabaptists at Munich 31
Exodus to England of 1709....... 142
" on Rhine in 1710......... 154
" Hymn (Exodus into Holland) 182
" of 1711 190
" of 1711 Reach Lancaster County 191
Executions in Lancaster County.. 333
Farmers, Anabaptists Excel as.... 93
Faith and Conversion of Anabaptist Fathers............... 125, 126
Fares and Expenses of Immigrating 269
Families Separated 330
Feierer as a Mennonite Father, 1528 31
"Foot Washing" Among Amish... 276
Finland, Anabaptists Flee to..... 56
Fines, Disposal of................ 198
File Making Among Palatines.... 221
Filthy Condition of Ships........ 269
Financial Progress of Germans... 333
Flanders Decree, Holland Intervenes 76
Forrer (Forry) Philip Appears... 78
Forest Fires, 1731............... 239
Frankenthal Colony and Skippack 141
French & Indian War, German-Swiss Oppose 286
Fries, Jacob, Tried for Treason.. 355
Fraud at Election of 1749........ 301

Funk Preaches before Charles XII of Sweden 133
" Stephen and Charles XII... 133
Galley Slaves (Anabaptist)....... 51
" Torture, Berne Renounces 77
" Torture and Reformed Church 111
" Torture in 1671........... 112
" Torture of Mennonites, 1671 114
" Torture Prohibited 117
" Masters Show Kindness... 117
" Punishment Fatal 119
" Torture Summed Up....... 160
" Torture on Mennonites.... 199
Germans (High) and Anabaptism. 21
Germany, Migration Into, Anabaptists 32
Geneva, Birthplace of Calvinism, 1555 58
German Peasant War, Anabaptists Accused of 100
Germans Adhere to Fletcher..... 130
German First Settlement.......... 132
" Reform Exodus to England in 1709............ 143
" Swiss Trading with Philadelphia 230
" Swiss Victims of Robbers 233
" Swiss Thrift and Industry 265
" Swiss Emigrants, Poverty of 269
" Reformed Christians Seek Naturalization 270
" Swiss on the Election Riots of 1742.......... 276
" Swiss Supporters of the Government 277
" Swiss Newspaper in Penn. 282
" Swiss in Lancaster in 1744 283
" Swiss and Indian Depredations 286
" Swiss Agriculture Very Successful 286
" Swiss and the Indians... 291
" Swiss Mennonites Murdering 292
" Swiss Woman Executed for murder 294
" Swiss and the Quarantine 299
" Swiss and Politics....... 307
" Swiss Politics in Lancaster County 308
" Immigrants Poor and Needy 315
Germans and Irish to be Separated 319

INDEX OF ITEMS.

German Swiss Limited to Massachusetts 319
" Swiss in Politics........ 320
" Swiss Quality Declines... 321
" Swiss Disaffection....... 322
" Swiss Help French and Indian War 327
Germantown Brethren Oppose Slavery 327
Germans as Aliens............... 328
German-Swiss Increase in Penna. 329
Germans Get London Company Land 331
" Oppose Paxton Murder. 335
" and Last Two Indians.. 337
German Mills Sold by Sheriff..... 339
" Swiss and Lotteries...... 341
" Lutheran Church Lottery 341, 342
" Swiss Political Leaders.. 342
" Crops Destroyed by Hail 345
" and Connecticut Claims.. 346
Germans and Glass Making....... 351
German Produce, Baltimore and Philadelphia Customers 351
" Swiss Gunmakers 353
" Society for Relief of Germans 354
Germans Disregard Navigation Acts 354
Glass Making Among Our Germans 351
Gun Making in Lancaster County. 353
Grain Fans, "Dutch" Invented.... 324
Graft in Stove Wood............. 331
Good's Account of Suffering Mennonites in 1672................. 119
Government Declares Mennonites Enemies 124
Golden Book (Queen Anne's)..... 143
Greybill, Munzer and Manz as Mennonite Fathers, 1524............ 17
Graybill Mennonites 19
Gross, Jacob, as a Mennonite Father, 1525 20
Groeninger Attempts Extermination 33
Greisinger, a Mennonite Father, 1538 49
Greisinger's Death............... 49
Graef (Hans) Arrival............. 130
Graffenried's Expedition with Mennonites 143
Grist Mill (First in Conestoga).. 194
Gun Factory, Mylin's............ 212
"Haldemann" and "Hochtetter"... 48
Haldeman as a Mennonite Father, 1538 48

Hauser a Mennonite Father, 1539. 50
Haslibach, the Hymnist.......... 65
Hambergers Turn Anabaptists.... 93
Hamburg Mennonites, 1641....... 93
Hardships of Sea Voyage......... 243
" of Sea Travel, 17 weeks 245
" on Ocean 249
Halifax, German-Swiss Intended for 309
Hardships of Ocean Travel....... 310
Halifax, Mennonites at........... 313
"Hangings," a Public Event...... 333
Hail Storm in Lancaster County.. 345
Hershey's (Benedict) Letters..... 325
Hemp Industry and Mennonites... 338
Herr as a Mennonite Father, 1538 49
Hendricks' Account of Suffering.. 94
Hendricks, Jacob, Dutch Preacher, Diary of Rhine Expeditions.... 154
Heat, Great Heat in Conestoga, 1734 251
Hempfield, Its Hemp............. 338
History of Anabaptists Published 101
Holland Mennonite Refuge....... 9
" Mennonite Faith in 1520.. 11
Hollinger, Jacob and Klaus, Mennonite Leaders, 1523........... 14
Hoffman, Melchoir, as a Mennonite Father, 1529................... 35
Hoffman's Followers in Holland.. 39
Houstetter as a Mennonite Father, 1538 48
Holland Refunds Anabaptists..... 67
" Anabaptist Progress in.. 72
Holstein Anabaptists of.......... 80
Holland Helps Anabaptists........ 100
" Relief Organized 103
" Anabaptists Not Strict... 105
" Anabaptists Help Swiss Brethren 107
" Intercession 109
Hostages, Berne Holds Anabaptists 116
Hospitals for Anabaptists........ 117
Holland Helps Palatine Anabaptists 120
" Persecutions 139
Holland's Friendship 145
Holland at Nimewegin Rescues Departed Mennonites 155
" Brethren Care for Rhine Expedition Refugees... 156
" Mennonites Befriend Their Brethren..163, 164, 165, 166
" Exodus, List from Berne Jail 170
Holland's Valuable Help.......... 175

INDEX OF ITEMS.

Holland Migration Divides Families 176
" Exodus Into (Names of People) 185
" Exodus, Those on Board Ship Thun 186
" Another List of Exodants Into 186
" Exodus To, 172, 173, 176, 177, 178, 179, 180, 181, 182, 183, 184, 185, 186, 187, 188
" Exodus, Those in Ship "Neumburger" 187
" Exodus, List Summed Up 188
" Exodus, List of Heads of Families 189
" Mennonites Leave 189
" is Asked for Aid......... 231
Horse Stealing Mennonite Victims 233
Household and Farming Utensils of Early Times................. 261
Hospitals for Contagious Diseases Among German Swiss......... 280
Holland Oppresses Mennonites.... 287
" Overtaxed in Exporting German Mennonites 299
Horrors of Ocean Travel......... 304
Holland Helps Virginia 324, 326
Hupmeier as a Mennonite Father, 1577 22
Hut (or Huth) as a Mennonite Father, 1529 35
Huguenots, Anabaptists Aid...... 46
Huber as a Mennonite Father, 1542 54
Hungarian Mennonites in 1629.... 81
Hungary, Exodus Into............ 81
Huguenot Mennonites (Lefever) 1669 111
Hunter (Colonel) Cargo of Mennonites to N. Y. 143
Immigration of 1729............. 142
" Floods Towards Pennsylvania 197
" and Contagious Diseases 303
" and Crowding of Ships 319
Infant Baptism, Revolt Against... 17
Inn, Valley of, Martyrdom........ 29
Inquisition in Holland........... 57
Integrity of Anabaptists......... 69
Indian Treaty and Mennonites.... 216
Inheritance Law Favoring Mennonites 224
Industry and Thrift of Our Ancestors 265

Indians Among German-Swiss.... 286
" Attack Mennonites 327
Inheritance, Germans Allowed.... 328
Indians Helped by Mennonites.... 336
Irish Palatine............... 143, 144
" and Germans to be Separted 319
Jails in Early Times............. 263
Jealousy Against the German-Swiss 278, 279
Jefferson, Friend of Germans..... 355
" President, and Jacob Fries' Trial 355
Jersey, First German in.......... 136
Jury Duty and Mennonites........ 235
Judge Zimmerman Appointed..... 329
Keith, Governor, a Friend of Mennonites 222
King, Fidelity to, by Anabaptists.. 125
" George's War and the Mennonites 272
Kocherthal Colony 137
Lancaster County Names in Zurich 38
" County Names (Berne Executions) 47
Landis', Hans, Suffering and Death 74
Langnan Colony of Anabaptists... 79
"Lamb" and "Son" Anabaptists... 121
Langnau Expulsions of Anabaptists, 1692 127
" List of Mennonites Expelled from 1692...... 127
Land Ownership 134
Lancaster County First Settlement 147
" County Pioneer's Graves 149
" County Palatine Accessions 192
" County Additions 193
Land, The Right to Hold......... 236
Lancaster Trade With Philadelphia 269
" County's Great Snow Storm of 1741........ 275
" County Election Riot, 1742 276
Land Grants, Conflicts Over...... 282
Lancaster in 1744................ 283
Landis Letter 295
Lancaster County Germans and Politics 301
" Town and Germans.... 314
" Germans in 1754, etc... 317
" County to Send Irish to Cumberland 319
" German Burgess....... 322
" County, Acres of Tilled Land 329
Land Cleared and Tilled in Pennsylvania 329

INDEX OF ITEMS. 361

Land Valuation in Pennsylvania..	329
Lancaster Newspaper	330
" County Like Switzerland	340
Land Clearing by Germans	335
Liberty of Consciene, Rise of	67
Lithuanian Colony of 1710	152
List of Those on First Rhine Expedition of 1710	159
Liberty Reigns in Pennsylvania..	322
Lord's Supper, Debate On	35
Long Island, Mennonites Move From	125
London Company Lands	331
" Letter	148
Low Morals Rare in German Pioneers	248
Lotteries and German-Swiss	341
" and the Church	340, 341
Loyalty to Government Pledged by German-Swiss	316
" to Government Pledged by Mennonites	316
" of Germans to America..	352
Lutheranism, Rise of	8
Lutheran-Mennonite Differences..	16
Lutherans Try to Crush Anabaptists	22
Lutheran Hatred of Anabaptists..	56
" Exodus to England in 1709	143
" and Moravian Controversy	294
Martyrs, Lancaster County Names	5
" The Burning of	5
Martyr Manuscripts	15
Manz, Greybill and Munzer as Mennonite Fathers, 1524	17
Martyr's Mirror, Beginnings of	17
Martyrdom of Wagner	26
Marriages, Anabaptists Void	68
Mangold, a Mennonite Historian..	97
Martyr's Mirror, Amsterdam Edition	102
Manheim-Rhine Expedition Halted	154
Maryland Encroachments	211
" Border War	254
" Boundary Troubles	256, 257
" Boundary Oppressions	257
" Border Struggle	263
" Line Dispute	296
Martyr's Mirror Published	300
Massachusetts Invites German-Swiss There	319
Manheim Glass Works	351
Mennonites, See "Anabaptists"	
" Descendants of Waldenseans	5
Mennonite Faith in Bohemia, 1519	11
" Faith in Holland	11
" Doctrine's Early Foothold, 1522	12
" Fathers and Founders,	13, 14, 17, 18, 19, 20, 21, 22, 24, 25, 26, 28, 30, 31, 34, 35, 36, 37, 38, 42, 48, 49, 50, 52, 56, 57, 60
" First Confession of Faith	15
" Library. Amsterdam	15
Mennonites, Early Torture	19
" Graybill Faction	19
" Reformers	21
Menno Simon, the Mennonite Founder, 1526	21
" " Persecuted	21
Mennonites' Synod	22
Mennonites and Hupmier	22
Mennonitism, Second Stage of	25
Mennonites, Attempt to Exterminate	27
" Retard Reformation..	28
" Number of, in 1529	34
" Catechism	35
" Rally at Emden	37
" Success in Berne	41
" Extinction in Zurich.	41
Menno Simon Renounces Catholicism	45
Mennonites (Berne) Flee to Russia	46
" (Berne) Help French Huguenots	46
" To Be Crushed	47
" Executions	54
"Mennonists" First Appearance..	55
Menno Simon's Death	61
Mennonite and Reformed Merger.	81
Mennonites as Vine Dressers, 1671	114
Mennonite Refugees' Poverty and Suffering	115
Mennonites, Early Large Families	115
Mennonite Refugees (Statistics) of in 1672	120
Mennonites (Swiss) Number in the Palatinate	120
" First Settlement in America	121
" Enemies of Government	124
Mennonite Marriages Void	124
Mennonites and Fletcher	130
" Not Friendly to Quakers	130
Mennonite School at Germantown	131

INDEX OF ITEMS.

Mennonites Beg to Escape Taxes. 131
Mennonite Leaders, 13, 14, 17, 19, 20, 22, 24, 25, 30, 34, 35, 36, 49, 52, 60
" Teachers 132
" First Church in America 137
Mennonites Banished from Berne in 1709 138
" in Exodus to England in 1709 143
" Sent to Ireland, 1709 143
" Banishments from Berne 151
" Good Character...... 167
" Rescued from Berne Jail 174
" Old and New Swiss Factions 191
" Large Shiploads Arrive 201
Mennonite Colony of Lancaster County 206
" Emigrants Prior to 1718 209
Mennonites Franchised 213
Mennonite Children and Indian Children 214
Mennonites Assist Indian Treaty. 216
" Fond of Keith....... 222
" Victims of Vagrants.. 225
" and Taxes 225
" Victims of Robbers... 233
Mennonite Emigration Falling Off, 1729 234
Mennonites and Jury Duty....... 235
" High Character Certified 235
" Oppose Emigration Tax 236
" Names of, in Rhine Valley, 1731 237
Mennonite Immigrants Poverty... 247
Mennonites Deceived by Maryland Government 249
" Goods Confiscated 259, 260
Mennonite Household Utensils, List of 261
" Migration Into the Cumberland 271
Mennonites Friendly With Quakers 271
" and King George's War 272
" and the Election Riot of 1742 276

Mennonites Industrial Prosperity 279
" Oppose French and Indian War 286
Mennonite Swiss Wandering in Germany 292
Mennonites Treatment of, in Switzerland 292
" in Maryland Line Dispute 296
" and Ship Travel Horrors 300
" and Political Activity 301
" and Political Affairs.. 307
Mennonite Tenants 310
" Wheat Growers....... 312
Mennonites and Lancaster Town. 314
" and Ship Diseases... 314
" Petition Governor to Trust Thun 316
" Pledge Loyalty to Government of Penna.. 316
" in Lancaster in 1754. 317
" Invited to Settle in Massachusetts 319
" Primitive Churches... 323
" Boehm Secedes....... 324
" Virginia Despair 324
" and Indians.......... 326
" Oppose Slavery...... 327
" Clear Land.......... 335
" Befriend Indians..... 336
" Raise Hemp.......... 338
" and Agriculture..... 341
" and Silk Raising.... 348
" Poor Immigrants..... 349
" Clover Seed Producers 351
" and Revolutionary War 352
" New Confession of Faith 353
" and the Military..... 353
" and Window Taxes... 355
Mill, First, On Conestoga........ 194
" Creek Settlement 213
Mills, Mennonites' Right to Make. 224
Migration Into Cumberland Valley 271
" to Western Pennsylvania 272
Mittelberger Tells of Ocean Travel Horrors 305
Mills. German, Sold by Sheriff... 339
Miller, Peter, Dunker's Troubles.. 343
Military Laws and Local Germans 353
Morals of Anabaptists............ 39
Moravia, Taufers in.............. 52
Moravian Religious Printers...... 65

INDEX OF ITEMS. 363

Moravia, Restrain from 73
" Migration 71
" 70,000 Crushed Out of... 77
Morals. Code of.................. 90
" Slip of, Among Palatines. 248
" Occasional Slip of........ 248
Mortality in Sea Voyages.......... 266
Moravian and Lutheran Controversy 294
Munzer, Graybill and Manz as Mennonite Fathers, 1524.... 17
" Against Anabaptism 18
Muller as a Mennonite Father, 1529 34
" Hans, Labors and Troubles 34
Musical Instruments Not Allowed 108
Mylin as a Mennonite Father..... 49
" the Chronicler 97
Mylin's Gun Factory............. 212
Naturalization in Pennsylvania (Anabaptists)... 121
" Palatines 134
Navigation Laws and Palatines... 259
Naturalization of Germans, 135, 136, 137, 221, 223, 225, 232, 247, 249
Navigation Act Injuries.......... 259
Naturalization 265, 267, 268, 270, 280, 281
Navigation Acts and Mennonites.. 354
Netherland Anabaptist Growth.... 18
" Intercedes 88
" Defends Swiss Anabaptists 100
Neuberg Mandate 101
Neubern Settlement 136
New Berne Colony Destroyed..... 163
" Mennonites Formed........ 191
" York Palatines Come to Pennsylvania 218
" Holland Pioneers.......... 227
" Danville Original Church.... 323
Newspaper in Lancaster........... 330
Nimewegen, Reception of, Departition Down Rhine, 1710......... 154
Nickel Discovered in Lancaster Co. 248
Night Watch Among Germans..... 339
Non-Resistants, Troubles 3
" Persecutions of.. 7
" Growth in Bohemia 7
Northern Coast Anabaptists...... 55
Norwegians and Anabaptists..... 68
Non-Resistant Friends 98
Oaths, Taking of................. 80
Ocean Perils 133
Octoraro Settlements 218
" Mennonite Neighbors at. 223

Ocean Voyage Horrors............ 305
" Travel, Hardships of...... 310
" Travel, Horrors of Crowding and Disease......... 319
Ores Discovered at Conestoga..... 217
Papal Tithes Demanded.......... 15
Palatinate, Swiss Migration...... 60
" Persecutions in....... 60
" Religious Prominence. 84
Palatine Swiss Not in Accord.... 109
Palatinate Migration, 1761........ 113
" Poverty of Mennonites, in 1672 119
" Exodus to England in 1709 142
" Exodus of 1709.......... 142
Palatines, English Settling Among 194
" Declaration of Fidelity. 227
Palatinate Mennonites in 1731.... 237
Palatines Leave New York........ 218
" Condition in Palatinate.. 246
" Thrift of 253
" Decendents' Inventory.. 253
" Refuse to Pay Quit Rents 254
" and Navigation Acts.... 259
Palatinate, Condition in 1761..... 332
Paxton Murder, Germans Try to Stop 335
Palatines, Law to Protect Our Ship 339
Pennsylvania Names (Earliest Appearance) 2
Persecutions, New Swiss......... 84
Peters Dirk, Execution 1546...... 56
Peasant War, Anabaptist Accused of 100
Penn, Wm. and Anabaptists...... 120
Pequea Valley Settlement, Preparations for... 138, 147, 149, 150, 151
Penn's Conference With First Colony 162
Pequea Colony, Size of........... 163
" Colony, Additions to...... 192
" Additions 195
Pennsylvania Fearful of Mennonites 202
Penn's Friendship to Mennonites. 204
Pennsylvania's Government Fearful of Mennonites 205
Pequea Additions 211
Pennsylvania, Western Part Settled 272
" Government and the German Swiss 277, 278
" Maryland Line Dispute 296

INDEX OF ITEMS.

Philip II and Charles V 59
" (Cruel) and Frederick (Generous) 61
Philadelphia, Outlet to 216
Pirates Rob German Emigrants.. 284
Plauroch as a Mennonite Father, 1529 37
Plockhoy, Sole Survivor.......... 130
Political Contest of 1749......... 301
" Affairs and German Swiss 307
Politics and German Swiss....... 308
" and German Swiss....... 342
Poverty of Some German Immigrants 349
Political Career of Zimmerman Endorsed 350
Poems, Early Mennonite.......... 17
"Potter's Field" for Anabaptists.. 51
Poverty of Immigrants........... 247
" of German Swiss Emigrants 269
Poor German Immigrants........ 315
Printing and Books (by Anabaptists) 55
Prussian Margrave Banishes Anabaptists 62
" Anabaptists 62
Preacher, Anabaptist, First in America 123
Prussian Migration 152
Privateers Prey Upon German Emigrants 284
Quakers Friends of Mennonites... 271
Quarantine Against Ship Diseases 280
" , Against Ship Diseases 282
" of the German Swiss. 299
" and Contagious Diseases 303
Rack Used on Berne Anabaptists. 97
Reformed Church, Rise of........ 3
Religious Struggles, 13th Century 4
Reformed and Anabaptists....... 9
Reublin Aids Mennonite Father, 1523. 14
"Resistance" and "Non Resistance," 1541 52
"Reformed" vs. Anabaptists...... 72
Religious Rules and Code of 1688. 122
Redegelt on Susquehanna........ 134
Reformed and Mennonites Compromise Matters 135
Reist and Amman Mennonites.... 163
Reform Church Sympathizes With Mennonites 197
Redemptioners Among Palatines. 219
Reamstown Laid Out by Everhard Ream 220

Redemptioners, List of........... 260
" and Transportation Fares....... 269
Registration on German Emigrants 227
Repeating at Election of 1749..... 301
Religious Liberty in Penna....... 322
Redemptioners (Poor) 330
" German and Swiss 351
Revolutionary War Taxes and Germans 354
Rhine, Expedition Down That River 145
" Deportation of 56 Mennonites, 1710 154
" Expedition of 1710, List of Members 159
" Attempted Deportation Down, in 1711........... 170
" Five Vessels to Carry Refugees 177
" Down Rhine, 28500 Florins Passage Money Collected 178
" Valley, Mennonites in..... 237
Rittenhouse, Great Mennonite Preacher, Germantown 142
Ritter and The North Carolina Project 145
Ritter's Expedition With Mennonites 145
" Expedition 145
"River Corner" Church........... 323
Romish Church (Desertions)..... 2
Roman Church (Reformed Spirit) 3
Rote or Roth as Mennonite Father, 1532 42
Robbers Play Upon Mennonites... 233
Roads in Early Times............ 269
Russia, Anabaptists In.......... 46
Runkle, Ambassador at Berne.... 144
Sattler, Michael as a Mennonite Father, 1525 19
Sattler Aids Anabaptism......... 19
Salsburg and Martyrdom......... 29
Sacrament, Earliest Form of the Ministry 209
" of Baptism, Earliest Form of 209
Salunga and Chickies Settlement. 220
Sauer, Christopher, on Liberty in Penna. 322
Schaeffer as a Mennonite Father, 1528 30
Schneider as a Mennonite Father, 1528 31
Schwenkfelders' Origin......... 38, 44

INDEX OF ITEMS. 365

Schumacher, a Mennonite Father, 1538 50
Schneider a Mennonite Father, 1546 56
Scheffer's (Dr. Hoop) View of Immigration 142
Schnebli On Torture............. 196
Schlegel's Mill 194
Schlegel and His Mill............ 211
Seckler as a Mennonite Father, 1527 26
Seckler's Religious Principals.... 26
"Separation From World" Defined 57
Sea Voyages, Extreme Hardships. 243
" " 26 Weeks.......... 243
" " Death Rate in Transit 266
Servants Leave German Masters and Enter Army.......... 272, 273
Sea Travel, Horrors of.......... 300
Shumacher's Death 53
Sharr David to Zugg............. 96
Ship Records of German Emigration 227
Ships, Filthy Condition.......... 264
" Filthy and Contagious Diseases 275
" Horrors on Board......... 300
Ship Diseases and Germans...... 303
" Loading Law Regulating.... 304
" Diseases of Palatines....... 314
" Horrors, Crowding and Diseases 319
Shipping Regulations 321
Ship Travel Horrors............. 339
Simon's, Menno, Works.......... 59
Silk Production in Lancaster Co. 348
Skippack Colony (Telner)........ 123
" Settlement 132
Slavery and Anabaptists (Mennonites) 123
" Mennonites Oppose....... 327
Small Pox Infection............. 266
Snow Storm, Great, of 1741...... 275
Socinianism, Anabaptists Accused of 99
Spinning and Weaving Among Germans 347
Staff and Sword, Anabaptists..... 36
Strasburg Religious Convention.. 58
St. Saphorin's Friendship.... 145, 146
" " " 166
Strasburg Laid Out.............. 200
" Additions 212
Storm, Great, at Conestoga....... 251
Stiegel's Glass Factory........... 351
Susquehanna, Mennonite Lands On 125
Subdivision of Pequea Track..... 150

Susquehanna, Additional Settlements 200
" Valley Additions... 221
" Land Grants....... 226
Switzerland (Sixth Century)..... 2
" Migrations from Italy 3
Swiss Anabaptists Flee.......... 12
Swabia and the Mennonite Faith, 1528 33
"Sword" Mennonites. 1529........ 36
Swiss, All Combined Against Anabaptists 46
Swenkfeld's Death 63
Swiss Anabaptists Pray for Holland's Help 98
" Independence 99
" Anabaptist Relief Organized 103
" Exodus Into Palatinate, 1671 111
" Refugees (1672) List of... 118
" Refugees Tale of Misery... 119
" First Settlement 135
" Persecution 197
" Edict of 1711 and 1714..197, 198
Switzerland, Destitution of Mennonites 287
Swiss Mennonite Tenants........ 310
Switzerland and Lancaster County 340
Synod, First Mennonite, 1527..... 22
"Taufers," Rise of............... 14
" A Name of Reproach (1531) 39
" Migration Into Prussia 39
" A Contemptuous Term. 40
" On the Baltic.......... 42
Taylor's Survey 149
Taxation Without Representation Among Mennonites... 204
" of Mennonites 225
" Without Representation 270
" and Taxes Raised...... 329
Telner, Jacob, Comes to the Delaware 121
Telner's Skippack Colony........ 123
Telner and the Skippack Settlement 134
Thrift and Industry of Our Ancestors 265
Thomas, Governor, Friend of Mennonites 271
Tortures in Flanders and Zurich.. 66
Transportation Pleaded For...... 147
Trade Between Philadelphia and Lancaster ...'................. 269
Treason, Jacob Fries Tried for... 355
Venezuela (First Germans in America) 53
Venice and the Galleys.......... 112

INDEX OF ITEMS.

Virginia and Dunkers............ 309
" Mennonites Despair..... 324
" Mennonites, Holland Aids 325
" Brethren Helped by Holland 326
" Muller's Account........ 326
Waldenses, Origin of............ 3
Waldensean Translation 4
Waldensees, Origin of Mennonites 5
Wagner as a Mennonite Father, 1527 26
Wagner's Execution 26
War Weapons and Taufers....... 52
Walloons Help Anabaptists...... 104
Wagoning Between Philadelphia and Lancaster 269
Walnut Groves in Early Lancaster County 286
War, French and Indian.......... 327
Weidman as a Mennonite Father, 1529 36
Weidman's Death 50
"Weidertaufers," Origin of, 1559.. 61
Welfare, Michael, Preaches in Philadelphia 251
" Michael's Wanderings and Preachings 262
Western Pennsylvania, Mennonite Migration to 272
Weiser, Conrad's Great Labors... 285
" Conrad, Attempted to Burn His House 286
Weaving Among German-Swiss... 347
Wheatfield Battle............... 263
Wheat Crop, Great German....... 312
Winkler as a Mennonite Father, 1530 38

Wild Beast Ravages.............. 208
" Beast Depredations 235
Witchcraft Believed In Among Palatines 252
Wills and Legacies, Law Allowing 282
" German-Swiss Right to Make 328
Willow Street Church............ 323
"Window Tax" and the Mennonites 355
Worms Persecutes Anabaptists... 23
"Worldliness" Warned Against... 77
Wood Famine in Eastern Penna.. 331
Wyckliffe and Waldenseans....... 6
Zeller's Account of 1710 Expulsion 155, 158
Zimmerman (Henry) Arrives..... 130
" Emmanuel, A Great Leader 207
Zimmerman's (Emanuel) Political Career 320
Zimmerman Appointed Judge..... 329
" Emanuel, The German Leader........ 350
Zolothurn and Anabaptists....... 28
Zurich's Wickedness 10
Zurich and Mennonite Faith (1523) 13
Zurich's Friendliness 13
Zurich Proselytes Anabaptists.... 21
" Apologizes for Anabaptists' Torture 88, 89
Zurich's Decrees Against Anabaptists, 22, 23, 66, 84, 86, 92, 94, 95, 102
Zwingli and Romish Church...... 10
Zwinglians, Decrees Against, 1521 11
" and Anabaptists Condemned 11
Zwinglism and Officials.......... 14

"INDEX OF PERSONAL NAMES"

NOTE: It is probable that some names are omitted, by oversight, from this index.

Abel 243, 264	Andiere 344
Abell 317	Appel 245, 254, 263, 283, 302
Abercrombie.283, 303, 312, 313, 314, 318	Arisman 205
Abrahamissen 109	Arnold.....263, 264, 270, 275, 299, 310
Acker 243	313, 314, 318
Ackers 243	Arndt 249, 250, 303, 310
Ackerman 65, 310	Armstrong 285, 288
Adams....249, 250, 269, 267, 299, 302,	Arnott 299, 314
303, 312, 314	Arnatt 299
249, 269, 267, 299, 302, 303, 312, 314	Arnot 312, 313, 314, 318
Adr 172	Athleridge 348
Achersold 162, 173, 181, 184	Atkinson 217, 218, 226, 256
Achı 237	Ausbach 33
Aeschbach 190, 197	Ax 233
Aeschbacher	Aybe 210, 233
186, 187, 188, 190, 189, 239	Baer....84, 226, 228, 229, 233, 236, 238
Aeschman 127, 151, 160	247, 260, 285, 303
Aeschlimann	Basle............................ 4
127, 159, 171, 173, 184, 191, 210	Balthaser 25
Aister 269	Bausmans 76, 119, 260, 314
Aken 172	Baumgardner......79, 81, 95, 102, 103,
Alasco 55	104, 106, 119, 151, 159, 161, 170, 173,
Albert 242, 243, 263, 265, 267, 268, 303	184, 191, 195, 196, 197, 232, 209, 233,
Albrecht 61, 81, 253	242, 243, 260, 263
Albright....242, 245, 254, 283, 285, 303	Barell 5, 195, 196, 205, 243, 245
310, 312, 313	Bassler 243
Alexander 27	Bachman 92, 93, 119, 129, 192,238, 267
Allenberg 2	Barber 189
Allen 224, 267, 270, 275, 312	Balmer 220, 253
Allison 224, 227	Baldwin 210
Allenbach 238	Baltzli 129
Alleman 299	Bar 129, 193, 267
Althouse 184, 190	Baker 137, 144, 283, 285, 314
Alba 100	Bauman 92, 173, 193, 242
Aman 276	Bauer 177, 187, 189
Amman..81, 87, 128, 129, 163, 195, 237	Balli 181
Amos 218	Barber 185, 335
Amster 76	Bare 209
Ammon 172, 177	Barnett 226
Andrews 239, 243,255, 283	Bazillion 226
Andres 185	Baeschtold .... 237.
Anderson 223, 227	Bachtel 238
Andes 253	Bair 57, 243, 268
Anken 187, 188, 190, 191	Balzer 247
Annis 148	Ball 251
Annesley 273	Baughman 256
Antes 299, 317	Bassler 266, 268, 310, 317
Antonius 57	Basseler 268
Anthony 119	Ballendine 303
Anslo 68	Barnes 314
Ansbach 33	Barr 299, 303

INDEX OF PERSONAL NAMES.

Bauer 302, 310
Baker 144
Beisinger 331
Beatus 115
Bestmiller 47
Berve 41
Bender....67, 81, 82, 243, 268, 242, 264, 269, 283, 285, 302, 312
Beck....49, 266, 267, 270, 293, 297, 299, 302, 310, 312, 313
Beaver 243
Benli 190
Beiers 192
Bellas 201
Bellar 204
Berr 205, 246
Beisel 249
Bebber 211
Bennings 182
Bebber 133
Beer 134, 184
Benedict 167
Bear 170, 173
Beets 172, 183
Becker....184, 190, 263, 266, 265, 267, 268, 270, 275, 302, 310, 312, 313
Berger....159, 243, 249, 251, 270, 275, 285, 293, 294, 303, 310, 312, 318
Beissel 215, 233
Beyer 224, 249, 264
Berkley 226
Bennett 233
Berntheisel 243
Bechtold 243, 246
Bern 251
Beatty 256
Bersinger 268
Bell 275
Bechtol or Bichsel........ 293, 294
Benzel 269
Benners 302, 310
Bendets 310
Berch 269
Bernharts
    274, 285, 302, 310, 312, 313, 314
Benezet 315
Beyer 269, 270, 283, 299, 310, 313
Beiler 119
Bent 154
Beam 323, 324, 325
Bheme 233
Bitner 275, 119, 236
Biezler 275
Bixler 47, 79, 229
Bieris 127
Bieri 159, 171, 184
Bizalion 210, 211, 214

Binkley 131, 268, 238, 266, 260
Bieri 119, 159, 210, 233
Biniggeli 131, 188, 189
Birk 249, 251, 264, 265
Bigging 256
Bishop 263
Bintgens 69
Bittinger 327
Blum 268, 266
Blaurock 19, 27, 252
Blaker 212
Blanck 129
Blaser.... 159, 170, 172, 173, 181, 188
Blank 185
Blumm 171
Blumston 230, 259
Bloetscher 237
Blath 246
Bluckenmeyer 266
Blau 92
Bohemia 4
Bollinger 63, 72, 243
Born 76
Bogart 76, 102
Boyer 192, 205, 220
Bohm 233, 324, 325
Bogli 109, 185, 190
Bowman....192, 204, 205, 206, 209, 212, 229, 231, 233, 237, 238, 239, 247, 249, 253, 263, 264
Bodeur 181
Bohlen 184
Bohner 185
Bomberger 226
Bossart 232
Book 248
Boyd 255, 344
Bohn 297
Bomgardner 293, 294
Pond 299, 303, 315
Bonner 269
Beswell 303
Bowman 299, 303
Boutemps 92
Bollenbom 109
Boenes 109
Borchalder 118
Boyer 323
Boener 325
Bouquet 327
Broithausen 109
Bracher 127, 128
Brackbill....84, 147, 151, 153, 154, 155, 156, 157, 158, 159, 162, 167, 168, 169, 170, 171, 172, 173, 177, 192, 193, 269, 270, 327
Brandenburg 3

INDEX OF PERSONAL NAMES.

Braucht 5, 74, 97, 101, 109, 111
Brubacker 38, 151
Bruner 12, 254
Brigger 43
Bruker 48
Brons.57, 61, 62, 64, 74, 77, 78, 111, 121
Brubaker....85, 86, 191, 233, 246, 319
Probst 79, 161, 173, 197
Broithhunsen 109
Brenneman 118, 202, 323
Brantam 125
Brechbuhl 151, 188, 190, 191
Brinton 193
Broadpather 205
Brand 205, 233, 185, 237, 238, 243
Bretzighoffer 171
Brast 173
Brenzikoffer 173, 184
Bremen 193
Bruzer 190
Bryner 186, 190
Breller 226
Brackin 227
Bricker 236, 264, 243
Breckley 243
Brenner 243
Brock 249, 251, 264
Bretter 266, 268
Brady 303
Braghts 109, 300
Brant 303, 312
Brenner 314
Brobsts 79, 293, 294
Bricker 310
Broderick 319
Browning 303
Brown.283, 285, 299, 302, 303, 314, 318
Brosius 270
Brunner 283, 302
Brunnholtz 317
Breitinger 92
Bradford 335
Bub 38
Bullinger 19, 40, 41
Burkhalter.127, 228, 229, 237, 238, 243
Burkard 38, 249, 264, 267
Butzer 52, 53
Burkholder.....84, 101, 110, 118, 128,
 131, 132, 147, 153, 155, 179, 180, 206,
 224, 226, 236, 233, 249, 250, 287, 288,
 290, 293, 294, 295, 298, 299, 310, 312,
 313, 314, 323
Bundely.87, 149, 150, 152, 156, 157, 200
Burger 98, 99, 236, 293
Burkey....119, 147, 155, 162, 167, 168,
 175, 177, 179, 180, 181, 183, 190, 191,
 292, 293
Burrows 193
Bundeli 193
Bugholder 205
Bucher 188,191, 220, 243, 254
Buhler 186, 187, 190, 192, 238
Burd 221
Buchanan 224
Buckwalter 233, 266, 268
Burchdolph 239
Bushong 245, 265
Buth 246
Buszhaler 246
Butt 256
Buckley 256
Busch 260
Bull 263, 269
Buch 264
Buden 267
Bushong 268
Buner 317
Buckenmeyer 268
Bumgardner 283, 293, 294, 310
Burkhart 283, 293, 302, 310, 312
Buck 299
Buchman 303
Bucher 312
Burki 157, 159
Byler 66
Byghboom 109
Byerly 243
Campel 215
Carterer 212
Carpenter
 130, 192, 193, 204, 224, 233, 350
Cartlidge 194, 216, 210, 211, 217
Carr 221
Calvin 100
Cassel 5
Capito (Wilfong) 23, 25
Caspar 48, 218
Carter 210, 226,253, 263
Catton 213
Cameron 253
Cammel 218, 253
Cartho 221
Capp 243
Candle 265
Camile 268
Campbell 310, 312, 313
Cantom 310
Casper 270, 283
Carpenter 320, 342
Care 303
Carlstadt 89

INDEX OF PERSONAL NAMES.

Carnell	109
Calbert	109
Chenstsy	246
Christians	102, 104, 106, 243, 267, 303
Christopher	211, 233, 323
Charles	5, 11, 44
Christen	198
Churts	210, 233
Christ	232, 242, 250, 249, 263
Chartier	226
Christman	260
Cheeseman	299
Chilton	270
Chalkley	148
Christy	336
Chase	355
Civility	216
Cirkel	269
Cloud	200, 226, 227
Clark	218
Clists	243
Cliffer	256
Clinton	285
Clarke	319
Cline	317
Coffman	210, 233
Coningham	110, 139, 207, 208, 209, 239
Conrad	137
Cope	193, 205, 207, 218
Comb	210, 211
Conradt	220
Cooksin	218
Cohalan	222
Cooher	265
Cook	267
Coatman	275
Coatam	303, 312, 313, 318
Coob	269
Cook	270
Cookson	270, 297
Cooper	310
Coolan	314
Conrads	302, 310, 313, 319
Conradt	311
Coller	109
Croyden	210, 233
Cremer	172, 188, 189
Creamer	60, 176, 242, 243
Craighead	224
Cresswell	226
Cressman	232, 269
Cresap	257, 252
Cramer	270, 313, 314
Cranch	275
Crawford	314
Creagh	303
Crellius	282
Crawford	331
Cuyper	57
Cunningham	312, 317
Cusack	283
Cutts	268
Daemen	109
Dasbach	238
Dayrolle	138
Danzler	162
Daesher	24
Dawson	201
Davis	205, 210, 218, 284, 348
Danager	206
Daniel	224, 264
Davenport	227
Denmark	2
Denlingers	229
Denck	21, 23, 24, 25, 103, 16, 252
De Vreede	107, 114
Devour	221
Detwiller	135, 239, 247, 260
Dewees	132
Dellenbach	79
Detchar	240
Dettenbern	265, 268
Deis	266
Dellinger	303
Dellyn	276
Deer	303
Deeringer	269
DeGrove	303
Decker	312
Deinig	269
Deknatel	289, 298
Deshler	268
Detterman	269
Detweiler	303
Diter	237
Diehl	264, 267
Ditcher	219
Dinkleberg	229
Dickinson	195
Diffenderfer	143, 227, 229, 342
Dieboldswiler	48
Dirks	83, 176
Direckson	109
Dinzler	119
Dierstein	237, 238
Dietrick	242
Diller	266
Diggs	296, 297
Dietz	303
Dietrich	310, 313
Diffenderfer	143
Dobbs	225, 233
Dougherty	217, 333
Doom	108, 109

INDEX OF PERSONAL NAMES. 371

Dock 137
Donens 147
Doneder 210, 233
Donnager 211
Dohltan 129
Dock 220
Dorwart 267
Doebler 285
Dotterer 269
Doeck 109
Doemen 109
Dreier 26, 293
Druckmiller 145
Duster 98
Dumbach 229
Dummersmuth 132
Duchti 186
Dubach 188
Dustler 256
Dubbs 260
Dunlap 313
Duraell 284
Durell 285
DuLuc 145
Dyer 226
Dylander 268
Dyles 318
Ebersoles 310
Eberly 254, 310, 313
Eby....3, 49, 63, 110, 134, 139, 200, 205, 206, 210, 224
Ebersole....162, 173, 181, 184, 191, 229
Eberman 243, 247
Eberhard 299
Eberhart 283, 303, 312, 313, 254, 262, 263
Eckert....5, 247, 266, 283, 302, 310, 312
Eckman 303, 312
Edwards 214, 226, 270
Eder 72
Egli....81, 84, 85, 87, 104, 171, 191, 332
Einsberger 119
Eicher 186, 238
Einmann 188
Eigelberger 266, 268
Eigster 269
Eiselman 299
Elsi 79
Ellenberger 159, 160
Elsbeth 190
Ellmaker 268
Ellis 314
Emsler 81
Emmett 226
Empson 13, 221
Engle 160, 229, 263, 264, 267
Engerston 237

End 295
Enghert 269
Engles 285, 293, 314
Engler 119
Enders 119
Erisman........ 190, 193, 197, 209, 233
Eramus 62
Erb 260, 294, 303
Ernst 303
Eshleman......127, 159, 229, 232, 240, 241, 242, 249, 251, 303
Estauch 201
Eschbacher 238
Etshberger 268, 266
Everling 3, 113, 119, 120
Evans 224, 226, 229
Everson 109
Ewing 313, 318
Eyers 201, 202, 222
Falkner 205
Fahnestock 249
Fauck 25
Fautz 249, 251
Fallman 238, 239
Farricks 240
Fairchild 300
Falck 310
Farrick 25
Fahrm 151, 160, 187, 191
Falkney 348
Ferie 233
Fexersteins 220
Ferrell 48
Fenner 81
Ferree..110, 191, 205, 218, 226, 253, 260
Fegley 249, 251
Fehl 264, 266
Fearer 31
Fontainmansdorf 145
Fierre 193, 201, 353
Fierer 31
Fisher.....242, 243, 249, 250, 263, 264, 267, 269, 270, 283, 302, 310, 312, 313, 314
Fink 263, 268, 266, 270
Fillar 266
Flamming 119
Flumer 38
Flickinger 48, 171, 191
Floss 118
Flickiger 173, 184
Flaharty 242
Fletcher 130
Flicks 312
Forry 78, 80, 229, 253, 193, 219
Forney 117, 162
Foutz 192

INDEX OF PERSONAL NAMES.

Fortgens 177
Fogel 174
Forsterman 148
Foltz 299, 303, 310
Fox 267, 299, 300, 302, 310, 312
Frantz......201, 236, 238, 243, 256, 263
Franciscus
    150, 202, 204, 205, 206, 212, 224, 233
Frick 151, 191
Freytorren 199
Frixilly 192
Fries 172, 182, 195
Fridy 106
Frider 104
Froshour 43
Freidley 47
Frederick 62, 69, 205, 263
Fricks 84
Fredericks 119, 233
Frey......161, 188, 189, 190, 191, 197,
    229, 231, 238, 242, 243, 249, 251, 252,
    254, 266, 267, 269, 270, 274, 283, 299,
    303, 310, 314
Fritzer 264
Franklin 243, 262, 281
Frieman 242
Frank 243, 25, 302, 312
Friedt 246
Frame 21
Frutinger 171, 186
Frutiger 173
Frant 302
Frantz 270, 299, 303, 312
Freeh 269
Fritz 303, 310, 132
Freeh 269
Fritz 303, 310, 312
Froschauer 54
Friedley 79
Fricken 92
Fredericksen 154
Fries 355
Furst 38
Fuchs 51, 74, 238
Fuhrman 52
Funk....56, 119, 133, 147, 150, 152, 192,
    193, 198, 202, 204, 205, 208, 220, 221,
    229, 232, 233, 238, 239, 256, 264, 299,
    326, 348
Fullmers 264
Futhey 218
Furer 187
Furxer 189
Furney 297
Furst 38
Fugee 327
Gamerslaugh 109

Gattschalks 137
Gasser 173, 184, 187
Gaumann 173, 180, 183, 184, 191
Galbi 184
Gautschi 187, 190
Gardner....210, 218, 230, 260, 263, 310
Galt 218
Galbreti 227
Galli 190, 191
Garber
    47, 48, 54, 219, 220, 263, 283, 336
Gaul 81
Gatschell 224
Garret 220
Garlbseath 218
Gauman 237, 293, 294
Gable 243, 267, 264
Gabrill 38
Galbraith 270
Gamber 317
Garack 306
Gallete 269
Gauler 293
Gabito 89
Gevotli 132
Geishbuchler 132
Gerfer....76, 81, 126, 127, 159, 162, 163,
    170, 173, 179, 183, 185, 186, 187, 190,
    191, 238
Geibel 127
Geiger 129
German 185, 188
Gerwanni 190
Gehrhart 243, 267
Gerlach 243, 245
George 247
Geldbaugh 269
Geisberts 269
Gergory 273
Geiser 293
Gerber 48, 51, 76, 294
Gerhart 299, 312, 313, 314
Gerlach 310
Gerhmann 310
Genter 349
Gilleser 109
Gilles 109
Gillius 57
Gingrich 110
Gilbert 79
Gissler 184
Giseler 190
Gilberts 283, 310
Gierbach 109
Glaus 187
Gletler 237
Glerecki 238

INDEX OF PERSONAL NAMES. 373

Geller 238
Golthe 60
Gonertzs 83
Gochnauer 95, 151, 191, 243
Good...... 100, 209, 210, 229, 233, 237,
    238, 246, 267
Goyen 199
Gontchi 197
Godschalk 142
Gouman 171
Gordman 224
Gordon 230, 232, 233, 244, 261
Godfrey 256
Goodman 264, 267
Gotshall 269
Goervertz 83
Graff....49, 130, 205, 206, 220, 232, 238,
    256, 260, 268, 317, 336
Graffenreid 136, 137
Grasser 170
Grauser 6
Graybill
    17, 18, 19, 20, 38, 79, 103, 226, 229
Gross 220, 229, 237, 21
Graaf 49
Greisinger 49
Graf 185, 191
Gruner 65
Gran 237, 238
Griffith 227
Graeff 198, 210, 212, 227, 266
Grubb 224, 252
Grimpson 213
Griter 205
Grieb 159
Grimn 124, 179, 263
Grilden 201
Grasser 190
Gruner 180
Grunbacher 184
Groff 193, 213, 220, 229
Greider 200
Grey 247
Greir 260
Graffts 260, 262
Grove 263
Graenu 265
Greybill 17, 18, 34
Graubunden 20
Graybill 20, 293
Graeme 275, 299
Grassold 268
Greene 315
Grenhenbuhl 293
Greenawalt 270
Greiff 268
Groff 268, 285, 312
Grier 293
Grove 299, 314
Groeme 303
Grors 310
Grubb 269, 295
Gusper 48
Gut.104, 119, 151, 104, 106, 129, 152, 191
Guth 219
Gulden 193
Guildin 191, 194
Gutzler 238
Gutwohl 246
Guth 266
Gysler 127
Hafele 187, 190
Hauri 185, 191, 205
Hackbrett 161, 196, 197
Haer 83, 204
Haldeman 48, 53, 110, 184, 191
Hager 5, 302
Hain 192
Haller 43, 254,27, 180, 249, 264
Hammerlin 6
Harvey 202, 204
Hatzler 20, 24, 25
Hatz 48
Haslibach 48, 65
Hattauer 92, 94
Hauser 192, 252, 250
Hagen 98
Harnish 209, 233, 243
Hassler 218, 238
Hapegger 129
Habegger 173, 184
Hagy 193, 265, 268
Hafeli 197
Haiggy 204
Harman 204
Hayne 204
Hare 210, 233, 256, 323
Hampher 210
Haas 262, 312
Harlan 24
Hassert 226
Hahns 220
Haggeman 226, 333
Hartman....236, 243, 264, 266, 268, 285,
    299, 302, 312, 131, 314, 319
Hattel 238
Hamilton 247
Haith 256
Hobecker 263
Harrison 267
Hasel 65
Haberly 47
Hahn 299, 302, 312
Haines 286

INDEX OF PERSONAL NAMES.

Haldeman 48
Hall 270, 299
Halling 268
Hamp 318
Hamilton 284
Hamburgh 314
Harle 269
Hart 270, 283, 285
Harris 270
Hartline 269
Haslibach 48
Hassler 302
Hass 302
Hasselton 310
Hazlewood 310
Hanke 269
Hauser 302
Haer 83
Hallonius 92
Hagen 98
Hackman 333
Herr....2, 6, 7, 49, 84, 86, 100, 39, 148, 150, 192, 193, 202, 203, 204, 206, 207, 224, 228, 238, 245, 262, 212, 220, 256, 205, 301, 302, 303, 310, 313
Herman 48, 56, 193, 210, 233, 243
Henry 57, 238, 275
Hershey
  913, 202, 206, 226, 228, 256, 337
Heinberg 81
Hess....88, 93, 192, 224, 230, 232, 236, 238, 264, 267
Hendricks 94, 122, 201, 210, 213
Hertig 170, 173, 183
Heimann 173
Heiniger 184, 190
Hearsey 204
Hearse 205
Herchy 193
Hews 210
Henison 221
Henry 348
Hensel 229, 242, 340
Hellar
  239, 251, 264, 270, 283, 299, 312, 314
Hertzler 236, 302
Hersh 237, 238
Henrick 94, 245, 344
Hetrick 249, 251, 303
Hendrick 92, 154, 255, 271, 344
Hershel 260
Hergebrat 266
Heyer 266, 268
Heargelrat 268
Herger 269
Hersh 270, 303
Hertzog 275

Hermans
  283, 285, 297, 299, 303, 310, 312, 313
Hess 275, 302, 310, 312, 313
Hertig 293
Hensel 299, 308, 309, 310
Heller 302, 333
Heinzelmann 317
Hedia 89
Hinkle 224, 222, 269
Hinden 101
Hinnelberg 102, 104
Hickman 192, 226
Highstetter 205
Hilligart 226
Hickenbolten 226
Hiestand 229, 242, 246, 237
Hicht 237
Hildebrand 253
Higgenbottom 257, 263
Hickner 269
Hilligas 315
Hillengas 269
Hinnige 269
Hirsh 312
Hirschler 291
Hirt 296
Hitchock 277
Hitner 317
Hirsche 325
Hoberly 47
Hoffmeister 43
Hoffman....13, 35, 36, 37, 43, 52, 103, 187, 228, 229, 236, 243, 248, 252, 264, 265, 266, 267, 270, 275, 299, 302, 312, 313, 314
Hollinger
  14, 103, 263, 296, 299, 310, 313
Hock 43, 268
Hoffer 47, 76
Hove 71
Hochstetter 103, 206, 212
Honenck 193
Hollingsworth 211
Hostetter 201, 243, 256
Hodgen 200
Hodgson 264
Hoover 192, 230, 264, 265
Hoffman 189, 249
Hoffs 137
Hoffer 159, 229, 231, 243, 245, 47
Holtzer 171
Homnore 178, 182, 183
Hoober 205
Hource 205
Houser 210, 233, 310
Hoff 251
Howry 204, 212

INDEX OF PERSONAL NAMES. 375

Howard	218	
Honenger	224	
Hoorn	144, 226	
Hostler	229	
Hodel	237	
Hofstetter	237	
Hodel	238	
Hoffnagel	239	
Hollenbaik	239	
Hoak	243	
Hostetter	243, 274	
Honbley	245	
Hornberger	247	
Howell	263	
Hope	264	
Houston	264	
Horst	266	
Hoffmeier	25, 32	
Hollenbach	317	
Hogmans	310	
Honor	314	
Hope	269	
Hozendorf	89	
Hubner	269, 317	
Hull	238, 264	
Huber	47, 76, 95, 100, 152, 186, 191, 220, 229, 238, 254, 260, 275, 283, 285, 299, 302, 312, 313	
Hupmeier	22, 25, 28, 29, 103	
Hubmier	251, 252	
Huss	6	
Hunsecker	48, 135, 228	
Humberger	90	
Huetwold	120	
Hunsberger	35	
Husser	129	
Hunter	143, 218, 231	
Hugo	184	
Hughes	210	
Hufford	233	
Huberts	242	
Huppart	264	
Huebmeier	29, 88	
Hummel	303	
Hunter	319	
Hut	35	
Hyndman	303	
Huth	36	
Hunsicker	48	
Hughes	342	
Hyde	200	
Imhoff	294	
Immel	118, 119, 266, 268	
Ingold	293	
Iseman	249, 251, 302	
Isott	160	
Iseli	237	
Jansons	133	
Jansen	142	
Janthauser	159	
Jansz	172	
Jackson	109, 224	
Jacobs	264	
Jacob	293, 310, 348	
Jacoby	302, 310, 314	
Jackson	319	
Jager	269	
Jarger	269	
Jacobson	109	
Jefferson	312, 355	
Jenruy	48	
Jennie	186	
Jerome	6	
Jenner	181	
Jeggli	184, 191	
Johns	253	
Jonsen	80	
Joost	184	
Jones	211, 213, 230, 274	
Johnson	222, 348	
Kahlor	109	
Kalonford	16	
Kampen	80	
Kauffman	104, 106, 121, 123, 137, 162, 202, 204, 237, 238, 239, 243, 256, 263, 264, 283, 297, 299, 312, 319, 325	
Kasdorp	136, 142, 239	
Kaester	145	
Kaner	184	
Kautz	21, 22, 124, 250, 285, 313	
Kallen	185, 188	
Kampf	187	
Kaiggey	202	
Kalb	48	
Kapp	275	
Kasper	299	
Kast	314	
Kancmans	302	
Keister	132	
Kern	38, 303	
Keller	23, 68, 220, 254, 260, 266, 268, 283, 299, 302, 310, 313, 38	
Kemp	249, 251	
Kempis	62	
Kendig	102, 110, 149, 191, 192, 193, 202, 204, 206, 229, 237, 238, 239, 294	
Keelers	229	
Keener	229	
Kennett	211	
Keague	205	
Keith	202, 213, 208, 209, 222, 231	
Kesselberrys	137	
Kellar	237, 243, 217, 265	
Keplinger	237, 243	

INDEX OF PERSONAL NAMES.

Keagy	256	Kobel	238
Kendrick	256	Kolg	246
Kerr	260	Koffee	256
Keffer	266, 268	Kocks	274, 283
Kepler	269	Kolb	269
Keiper	275	Koppenheffer	268
Kemper	275	Koplin	269
Kessler	303	Kommer	294
Kenneway	313	Konard	311
Keppely	315	Kopp	109, 317
Keppele	317	Kohn	330
Keanke	317	Krayton	206
Keck	317	Krahenbuhl	48, 189, 191, 237
Khehr	266	Krutzen	185
Kissler	25	Kraehel	119
Killer	38	Krick	126
Kingelsbecker	119	Kraymbuhl	162, 186
Kieffer	119, 243, 245, 274, 303	Kropf	128
Kitzmiller	229, 230, 297	Kreybuhl	173
Kirkpatrick	224	Krenbuhl	186, 238
Killian	220	Krebs	187, 189, 190, 191
King 210, 224, 233, 270, 285, 310, 312, 313		Kreider	201, 238, 243, 260
Kilheffer	232	Kryter	212
Kindig	148, 205, 232	Kroff	185
Kilhaver	256	Kropfli	185, 189
Kipp	257	Krow	224
Kinzer	264, 266	Kraetzingen	238
Kiehl	303	Kresey	242, 243
Kirk	331	Kruntz	246
Klare	119	Kriemer	256
Kling	184, 243	Kraws	263
Klugh	256	Kramer	267, 302, 303, 310
Kleh	237	Krantz	303
Kline 239, 243, 254, 263, 264, 266, 267, 268, 269, 285, 299, 302, 312, 314		Kraus	269, 303
		Krafts	283
Klinehons	243	Krees	270
Klein	247, 269, 283, 313	Kreestman	269
Klaws	48	Kreider	283
Kmidlich	232	Kreybill	310
Knauss	269	Kristler	269
Knappenberger	269	Kulp	48
Knor	293	Kuene	119
Knopf	199	Kunstel	98
Knoubuler	171	Kursten	134
Knoll	172	Kuenbuhler	181
Knenbuhal	189	Kurtz	215, 285, 299, 302, 317
Knoppenheffer	266	Kuhns	212, 213, 251, 191, 249
Koch	64	Kuenzi	186, 89, 191, 238
Koster	122, 134	Kuoff	173
Kohler	28, 159, 184	Kupperschuised	185, 190
Kolb 129, 133, 136, 142, 171, 243, 245, 147		Kuntz	256
		Kunzler	266
Koffman	205	Kuller	294
Koner	190	Kulp	48
Kocherthal	137	Kuhl	317
Konig	186, 294, 302	Kuhn	73, 283, 301, 302, 309, 314, 322
		Kuysen	109

INDEX OF PERSONAL NAMES.

Law 226
Lang 185, 266
Lartscher 180
Laurens 154, 162
Lavall 130
Landis.....5, 49, 51, 74, 75, 76, 85, 92, 93, 94, 135, 151, 152, 191, 193, 202, 229, 231, 233, 238, 243, 246
Landuno 5
Lantz 43, 266, 299
Langhams 81
Lauhel 119
Lauenberger 162
Lauffer 187, 190, 191
Lauffen 191
Laman 205, 266
Lagerd 226
Lawrence 240, 267
Lambert 262, 303
Labar 269
Lackley 314
Landes 295, 296
Lanyz 303
Lawson 299
Latimore 349
Lescher 119
Lefever.110, 192, 193, 200, 201, 205, 218
Leiby 196
Lemmeker 61
Lehmann 173, 188, 193, 204
Lehner 187, 189
Lewis 226, 213
Leets 220
Leadus 230
Lee 219, 220, 251
Letort 213
Leeghti 210, 233
Leemann 129, 224
Lefever 139, 206
Lenti 170
Lentswyler 190, 197
Lein 192
Leman 193, 246
Leonard 195, 264, 239, 247, 314
Leaman....202, 210, 229, 233, 237, 242, 243, 263, 310
Lerow 210, 233
Lesher 220, 237, 252, 294, 299
Ley 266
Lemon 297
Leeman 268
Leinbach 283, 310
Lehman 283, 293, 303, 310
Leivening 294
Lederich 300
Lerch 293
Lenhart 302

Ley 268
Lichtenstein 28, 36, 37
Linki 43
Linschoten 71
Lichten 101
Lichty 118, 119, 293
Liebe 161
Line 233, 210, 212
Light 210, 233
Lierstein 237
Lintner 256, 226, 285, 312, 318
Lites 264
Lieberger 265, 268
Lickty 314
Liechty's 310
Lidick 317
Linkey 43
Linde 92
Limberger 109
Lloyd 205, 213
Loffer 5
Loher 65, 129
Logan..163, 210, 218, 223, 230, 256, 258
Lortsches 185, 188, 189
Long...190, 226, 243, 251, 263, 264, 268
Longnicker 210, 232, 237
Longhmane 210, 233
Love 226
Longnecker 228, 229, 233, 247
Lorenz 245
Lower 266
Luther........8, 62, 68, 111, 15, 35, 39
Luthi....48, 119, 128, 159, 161, 173, 188, 195, 197, 293
Ludwig 144, 268, 303, 313
Lundes 204, 205
Lusser 180
Lutzenfilick 184
Luichart 238
Lutz 251, 299, 302, 310
Luginbuhl 293
Lummsdaine 275
Ludwig 144
Lyonites 3
Lynch 225, 233
Mace 194
Madler 144
Mack 137, 212, 232
Maydock 125, 223
Mangold 97
Martin...85, 86, 227, 229, 238, 267, 274, 303, 310, 312, 318
Manz 17, 18, 20, 25, 103
Marpurg 4
Margrave 69
Marsh 230
Matti 119

INDEX OF PERSONAL NAMES.

Mackell	224
Mail	148
Maurik	172, 182
Maier	187
Maurer	191
Mayer	193, 220, 256
Marlow	194
Mathews	213
Mayley	220, 221
Mays	220
Magee	253
Marshall	254, 264
Matz	245
Mazer	2, 217
Manning	256
Macjnd	269
Magee	302
Mauss	317
Mann	299, 303
Manusmith	268
Marshe	314, 317
Mason	312, 314, 318
Mast	310
Markle	302
Marchant	269
Marsh	283, 284, 308
Marshall	303
Matthias	45
Marti	293
Marstaller	269
Marks	270
Mason	283, 285, 303, 310
Maurer	294
Mayhew	319
Mangeld	97
Marcus	109
Madler	144
Marsteller	342
Merchaiet	254, 260, 261
Megonder	43
Melchoir	38, 245, 263
Melanchlhon	21
Mettenbasle	38
Meyer	39, 233, 245, 246, 265
Media	44
Meisiher	48
Meulen	64
Meyli	85, 86, 98, 191
Meii	238
Meier	129, 186, 189, 190, 209, 110
Mellinger	129, 239
Meylin	193
Melkerman	202, 204
Meck	243
Metzgar	242, 310, 313, 314
Melbrin	1
Mentzer	245
Meister	253
Mehring	4
Meliss	54
Mercy	270
Meredith's	276
Metzler	285, 299, 310
Meylin	278
Meihuisen	292
Messier	297
Messner	302, 312
Meyer	302, 310, 312, 313
Melcher	38
Megander	43
Meylich	92
Millinus	3
Michel	6
Miller	34, 65, 66, 69, 70, 73, 74, 79, 81, 82, 84, 89, 91, 93, 94, 95, 96, 97, 99, 100, 103, 107, 117, 127, 128, 144, 148, 162, 169, 184, 185, 190, 192, 195, 196, 197, 198, 199, 200, 202, 204, 226, 229, 232, 236, 240, 243, 245, 246, 247, 249, 250, 251, 253, 254, 255, 256, 260, 263, 264, 265, 266, 267, 268, 330, 333, 342, 344
Minnich	236, 263
Middleton	212
Mittelberger	133, 305, 306, 310
Michelle	136, 138, 146
Milan	204
Milen	205
Mitchell	264, 277, 303, 337
Michel	6, 144
Misel	65
Michaels	285, 337
Mirry	269
Miley	148
Moritz	79
Morider	43
Mowrers	117
Moyer	83, 201, 202, 204, 205, 212
Mozart	125, 126
Montgomery	224
Moseri	171
Moser	159, 173, 188, 238, 269
Mowrer	195, 260
Morris	203, 217, 266, 303
Morgan	210, 218
Moor	218, 231, 251, 264, 266, 268
Morrison	221, 226
Moore	236, 249, 266, 267, 270, 285, 299, 313, 314, 318
Moseman	243, 249
Mosser	159, 264, 285, 299, 381
Montpelier	312, 314
Moss	294
Muchli	38

INDEX OF PERSONAL NAMES. 379

Munzer 17, 18, 23
Munster 61
Mumprecht 104, 106
Mueller 238, 310
Mutrich 159
Musser.....159, 192, 229, 243, 248, 250
Musgrove 192, 274
Mussleman......210, 233, 238, 266, 285
Musgraves 221, 222, 224, 226
Mumaw 243
Muller...3, 4, 5, 19, 20, 34, 37, 92, 151
Muchli 38
Muir.......303, 310, 312, 313, 314, 318
Muller's 287, 292, 293
Muntz 269
Muhlenberg 317
Muller 109
Mylin......49, 85, 94, 97, 101, 139, 150, 207, 208, 212, 220, 232, 250, 280, 274
Myers....38, 70, 81, 180, 229, 236, 238, 239, 242, 243, 247, 254, 260, 263, 264, 266, 270, 274, 283, 285, 293, 299
McNair 201
McNeal 217
McMaster 256
McNile 227
McAllister 250
McConnell 274
McMillan 300
McFilley 331
Natts 205
Nagle 264
Nauman 253
Nagley 53, 68
Newell 261
Neiff 209, 232, 233
Newcomer 129, 229, 239, 256, 293
Neff 92, 94, 205, 237, 250
Negeli 46, 68, 129
Nespler 38
Newhauser 94, 128, 186, 190
Newswanger 162, 293, 294, 310
Neukomet 173
Neuenschwender.....179, 184, 237, 327
Neukomm 184, 191, 237
Neicomer 205
Newcomat 210, 233
Neff 229, 266, 267
Negley 233
Neuivkomme 246
Nelson 256
Neaff 268
Neffs 283, 313
Nevin 318
Newlin 226
Nissleey 233
Nicholas 303
Nickolson 310
Noble 253
Noland 226
Norris 227
Noaker 266
Nohaker 268
Nornings 310
North 283
Nusbaum 51, 159
Nysti 238
Oachselhofer 72
Oberlin 54, 47
Oberhasli 38
Oberly....48, 171, 173, 184, 191, 310, 48
Oberholtzers......60, 61, 148, 229, 236, 238, 243, 256
Oberholtz 193
Odenbach 24
Ogi 185, 190
Oherhoften 128
Olfinger 54, 55
O'Neil 211
Orell 160
Oswold 29, 254
Oster 270
Ottinger 269
Otzerberger 195
Ouchterlony 313
Orenheim 118
Painter 269, 270, 267
Parish 312, 314
Passage 268
Park 218
Pare 206, 210
Pastor 57
Pastorius 130, 131, 134, 137
Pannebecker 133
Parli 173
Paxton 221
Patterson 226, 331
Palmers 26
Pattison 256
Paynter 264
Patton 264
Paulley 350
Peters......243, 251, 254, 264, 56, 102, 119, 187, 190, 191, 197, 247, 303, 310, 312, 351
Percy 251, 263, 267, 269
Penn.......120, 204, 207, 208, 223, 248, 257, 267, 300, 316, 337
Pech 52
Petri 190
Pennypacker
  66, 121, 142, 215, 239, 247, 300, 317
Peelman 233, 210, 243
Petersheims 60

INDEX OF PERSONAL NAMES.

Peinerz 317
Pfoutz 303
Pfauderin 72
Phlein 246
Pheffley 229, 238
Phiester Myer 48, 92, 93
Phillips 57, 264, 54, 57, 62
Pierce 200
Pickel 243, 247, 268
Pickle 266
Pipson 267
Pickeman 285
Pieffer 297, 299, 303
Pitcairn 314, 318
Pitmaier 36
Pleam 129
Plank 186
Ploetscher 237, 238
Plaettle 238
Plockhoy 130
Poll 73
Powell 212, 218
Povan 299
Pownall 317
Porter 339
Prenamon 205, 233
Pretter 201
Pratorius 16
Preneman 203, 205, 206, 210, 212
Prupacher 204, 206
Probs 170, 184
Pratt 256
Pupather 193, 202, 205, 210
Pyfer 144
Rappenstein 48
Ramseier 159, 177
Ranch 232
Rasy 237
Ranck 229
Rausch 262
Rabe 317
Randolph 303
Raeber 79
Reist 128, 129, 160, 172, 177, 178
Reublin 14, 58
Reich 79
Reher 79, 175, 179, 180, 181, 184
Reauformet 119
Reumschwenger 119
Reuscher 119
Reusommet 119
Reigshoerer 119
Reittenheisens 122
Reichert 266, 342
Reichen 176, 185
Reusser 186, 190, 267
Ream 213
Reiff 239, 247
Ressler 220
Reed ... 214, 249, 251, 253, 258, 260, 266
Reuger 213
Redelgeldt 211
Ream 210, 219, 220, 233, 267
Reese 109, 264, 265
Reichman 201
Ressor 233
Reinhart 245, 249, 270
Reidenbach 247
Reublin 252
Reisner 252
Reinwald 253
Reinholdt 253
Reuplin 21
Reason 283
Reinhart.s 297, 303, 310, 312, 313
Reese 275, 299
Reed 268
Reeb-Camp 269
Reissner 270
Ressler 269
Reith 285, 297, 299
Rerig 269
Reusser 119
Rockey 342
Rhode 264, 270
Ries 18, 109, 228
Rictisecker 47
Risser 119, 198, 310
Ricker 187
Richardson 224
Richard 201, 202, 243
Richman 198, 200, 224
Rife 226
Ritschard 186
Rittenhouse 142
Ritter 138, 145, 154, 160, 167, 177, 178, 180, 188, 229, 242, 243, 263
Ringer 152, 191
Richen .178, 180, 185, 187, 188, 190, 191
Richener 183
Richeuer 184
Risk 223
Ringsthacher 237
Richter 251, 253
Riegel 263
Ricksecher 38, 47
Ricks 299
Richer 303
Richey 314
Righter 269
Ring 92
Rine 342
Richards 355

INDEX OF PERSONAL NAMES. 381

Riss	355
Robel	119
Rouplin	13, 14, 20
Rothlisperger	79
Rossen	74, 129
Roades	226, 251, 265
Ross	224
Rodte	210
Roth	185, 187, 188, 189, 239, 242, 264, 267, 269, 285, 299, 303, 310, 312, 313
Rothenbubler	184
Rotenbuler	170
Rohrer	162, 173, 181, 184, 191, 238, 242, 243, 299, 310
Rothenbuhler	173
Robinson	192, 221
Royer	210, 233, 331
Rote	232, 233, 263
Rohrbach	238
Root	249, 251
Romler	266, 268
Roab	269
Roberts	276
Rohr	293
Root	283
Roop	299
Rohr	303
Rothmantel	36
Ross	318
Rorer	331
Rummel	256
Ruth	253, 263, 264
Rupp	47, 48, 132, 171, 191, 206, 220, 232, 255, 257
Rusbacher	38
Rusterholtz	85
Rubeli	162, 186, 190
Rupp	5, 93, 97, 100, 110, 119, 147, 149, 150, 154, 162, 172, 201, 238, 243
Rust	9
Rudolph	150, 193
Runckel	166, 170, 171, 172, 173, 174, 175, 176, 177, 178, 179, 180, 181, 188, 189
Rugen	172
Russer	173, 186
Rugsegger	173, 186, 191
Ruff	92, 186
Rubi	187, 191
Rubin	173, 189, 190
Rush	239
Rusher	249
Rutt	266, 268
Runsberger	268
Rupe	5
Ruplin	17
Rubel	317
Rudolf	314
Rupser	47
Rupp	47, 48, 270
Ruth	275
Russel	299, 303, 310, 312, 313, 314, 318
Ruschacher	38
Ruch	79
Ruttimyer	95
Rudisill	331
Ryland	308
Rynell	277
Salzman	48, 173
Salmunger	24
Sattler	19, 24, 15, 58, 159, 21, 22, 35
Saphorin	145, 164, 165, 166, 167, 177, 205
Savanaiolo	8
Saylor	125, 243
Sagimann	184
Salkeld	200
Sauck	226
Saches	231
Sauter	238, 256
Sauer	239
Sauder	239, 243, 249, 251
Saddler	159, 243
Salzman	48
Saylor	270
Sander	310
Savanarola	8
Salr	75
Sattler	159
Sauer	322
Schwenkfeld	38, 44, 63
Schwartz	38, 127, 229, 238, 239
Schneider	31, 38, 56, 128, 266
Schnebeli	67, 84, 87, 119, 151, 152, 161, 171, 196
Schlecta	11
Schwarzenberg	4
Schoener	29, 30
Schaeffer	30, 142, 147
Schmidt	38, 84, 104, 189, 229, 237, 238, 239
Schwartzentrub	184
Schellenberg	48, 254
Schwendimann	48
Schlechter	76
Scheider	184, 104, 170, 173, 220, 237, 238, 239
Schnebly	92, 104, 229, 233
Schappe	119
Schilling	189
Schlagel	192, 193, 194, 210, 263
Schangnua	179
Schallenberg	185, 187, 191
Schlapbach	185

INDEX OF PERSONAL NAMES.

Schlappach 186, 190
Schar 190
Schmied 185, 188, 189, 190
Schenk.....76, 160, 181, 201, 202, 204, 206, 210, 237
Scher 171, 245
Schin 172, 176
Schilt 173, 179, 181, 188
Schyn 183
Schallenberg 185
Scholls 137
Schurch 170, 173, 184, 191
Schonauer 173, 184
Schwarwalders 220
Schotts 220
Schnepach 237
Schaerer 238, 243, 264
Schrack 239
Schuymeyer 243
Schuyler 243
Schutbly 246
Schwab 254
Schell 266
Schearer 266, 267
Schumacher 50
Schellenberg 48
Schaeffer 270, 285, 302, 303
Schar 299
Schieds 302, 314
Schild 294
Schlough 309
Schonauer 294
Schipes 310
Schlatter 317
Schmedly 283
Schneyders 317
Schneider 38, 56
Schnegg 293
Schrack 317
Schwartz 303, 38
Schwarz 38
Schwendimann 48
Schmeid 159
Seckler 26
Seiler 26
Sewer 38
Seager 218
Sellinger 226
Seitz 229
Sellers 229
Seltzer 239
Seyler 242
Sekimmer 246
Seber 266
Seeshotlz 268
Seigenthaler 294
Seitz 303

Seix 318
Seiger 293
Shaubach 128
Shaernaker 47, 83
Shumaker.........48, 50, 302, 313, 315
Shindler 48
Shank....49, 128, 162, 220, 233, 76, 119, 192, 205, 210, 263, 264, 274
Shaar 96
Shultz......192, 210, 229, 233, 236, 242, 253, 262, 267
Shertz 193, 229
Shar 184
Shellenberger 184, 190, 238
Shirk 144, 229
Shenck 193, 233, 238
Shoope 210, 264, 265
Shultz 214
Sherricks 219
Shong 224
Shaffer
  229, 243, 249, 251, 264, 266, 267
Shwope 233
Shever 236
Sheetz 248
Shantz 263
Shenckel 239, 247
Shocks 243
Shuman 243, 302
Shaub 243, 283, 313
Shilling 243
Shissler 247
Sherman 251
Shubert 253
Shriver 263
Shober 263
Sharp 264
Shaver 266, 268
Shreiner 266, 268
Shrum 266
Shlong 268
Shell 268
Shaffner 310, 350
Shaeffer
  268, 270, 299, 310, 312, 313, 319
Shavely 299
Shawanese 283
Sherts 283
Sherman 303
Shock 303
Shocklier 268
Shoemakers 270, 283, 269, 299
Sholtze 317
Shoop 310
Shucmaker..60, 137, 185, 229, 247, 264
Shippen 337
Shultz 342

INDEX OF PERSONAL NAMES.

Simon....14, 21, 44, 45, 46, 55, 56, 57, 58, 59, 260, 8, 53, 61, 62, 100, 303
Simon (Menno).8, 21, 187, 252, 53, 54
Simler 19
Sittler 38, 252, 38
Singel 83
Sieinverts 183
Siegler 229
Siegrist 229
Sigman 243
Sickommel 246
Sickman 247
Siegenthaler 293
Singer 303, 269
Siegenthal 293
Slecker 47
Slabach 102, 104, 106
Slaremaker 210, 233
Slough 243, 266, 342
Sleydonius 89
Sluys 109
Smith.....137, 141, 150, 192, 195, 218, 226, 233, 236, 242, 243, 249, 251, 253, 254, 260, 262, 263, 264, 265, 267, 268, 269, 270, 275, 283, 285, 299, 310, 312, 313
Small 221
Smeltz 303
Snyder....48, 87, 92, 126, 184, 212, 229, 232, 242, 243, 251, 263, 264, 266, 267, 269, 270, 275, 283, 285, 297, 299, 302, 310, 312, 313, 314, 326
Snavely....119, 192, 210, 226, 249, 251, 302, 313
Snep 109
Sommer 184, 210, 198
Sowers 233, 285, 38
Soutter 285
Spattig 38
Sprogle 224
Spangler 243, 247, 263
Sprecher 243, 245, 312
Springer 263
Spurrier 303, 312, 314, 318
Snangler 303, 310
Sprenger 302
Sprunger 293
Spencer 303
Stayman 128
Stephen 38
Stoll 38
Stuck 185
Strassburg 4
Stehli 43, 47, 187, 189, 191
Stumpf 13, 265, 268
Steitz 266
Stettler 53, 162, 184, 266

Straten 71
Steyn 71
Studer 79
Stroedel 79
Stauffer....94, 119, 184, 191, 229, 237, 243, 256, 291, 299, 302, 303, 310, 312, 325
Stuss 98
Strom 119
Steiner........126, 162, 185, 253, 256
Stramm 171, 113, 183
Stutzman 189
Stoner 192, 256, 339, 348
Steele 194, 210, 254
Stehman 204, 206, 210
Strettle 193, 53
Stein 192, 266
Strahm 191
Stone 205, 206, 210, 339, 342
Steiner 159, 173, 188, 195, 256, 186, 190
Strine 144
Strict 184, 187, 190
Stucki 189
Stadler 187, 190
Stockli 186, 187, 190
Stutzwarm 185
Stolls 137
Stattler 197
Stultzen 197
Stein 264
Steff 205
Stoneman 210, 232
Staner 210, 348
Stay 210, 233
Starr 264
Sterman 226
Stewart 226, 230
Staner 233
Steiger 262, 302, 312
Steckley 237
Stoeger 239
Steinman 243, 249, 251, 256
Strauss 243, 264, 267
Straub 249, 251, 312, 313
Stedman 253, 263, 264, 275, 315
Stake 256
Stout 263, 264, 267
Sterling 264, 269
Stoltz 266
Stetler 268
Starr 271
Stamms 283
Steli 47
Stehle 43
Steitz 268
Steinmetz.......268, 285, 299, 303, 312

INDEX OF PERSONAL NAMES.

Stein......270, 285, 299, 303, 310, 312
Stiegler 293
Steigerwalt 302
Steele 303, 310, 312
Still 314
Steiner 293, 348
Stevenson 285
Stout 275, 299
Steutz 98
Stohley 342
Stewart 347
Stour 269
Steel 314
Stall 38
Streiker 299
Strohm 292
Strickler 310
Stecker 47
Stump 303
Stumpf 32
Staley 47
Stulzer 190
Studer 79
Stuss 98
Sturler 101
Stevens 109
Stanin 146
Stover 331
Sutzer 43
Sutter 48
Surer 190
Sultzheim 237
Subert 266
Susholtz 317
Suter 88
Sweitzer 47, 254
Swobia 2
Swinderin 62
Swisser 104
Swaor 205
Swustut 246
Swafort 252
Swartz........262, 267, 283, 293, 294
Swenk 267
Swenkfeld 63, 44
Switzer 303
Swope 307
Taylor.....149, 163, 194, 205, 217, 218, 230, 233, 249, 251
Tauber 247
Tainey 260, 262
Tannegg 293
Tanner 51
Tell 207
Tenant 255, 344
Teuscher 185, 189
Telner 121, 123, 134, 141, 412
Teme 172
Tersey 248
Tester 95
Thabor 18
Thoresly 192
Thomas.....62, 263, 264, 267, 271, 275, 285, 297, 303
Thouen 162, 185, 187, 189, 190
Thommen 186
Thome 258, 260
Thompson 263, 310
Timmer 26
Tiller 268
Tittenhoffer 266, 268
Tise 266, 268
Tiffin 299
Tieffenderfer 342
Tilghman 347
Tower 201, 202
Toup 205
Toren 138, 174
Torne 138
Townsend 147, 165, 166
Tran 318
Trombonrger 269
Trump 318
Trachsel 188
Trasser 48
Trussel 184, 170, 171, 173
Trulberger 193
Trout 249, 251
Tsibbald 186
Tschageler 187, 189
Tschdbold 189
Tschantz 192, 237, 278
Tshudy 151, 264, 303
Tuber 202, 204
Turner 187, 293
Tuscher 189
Twisk 50, 90
Ulait 36
Ulrich 48, 159, 47
Ulweiler 256
Ummel 119
Unrook 266, 268
Unter 47
Updegraff 83, 297, 122
Utt 43, 48
Utzenberger 79
Van Leer 226
Vanbibber 201, 137
Van Webber 191, 220
Van Suitern 142
Van Giente 119
Venerick 196, 205
Vet 27
Vergetter 48

INDEX OF PERSONAL NAMES. 385

Vergerter 48
Vittery 267
Vitery 270
Vlaming 64
Vogel 303
Vogt 48, 72
Vogel 242, 245, 263
Vollen Veiders 237
Von Ravenstein 120
Vorsterman 172, 178, 183
Von Aylva 178
Von Guten 187, 189
Vondel 68
Vollmer 75
Vrauken 156
Walti 47
Wallace 319
Ware 318
Wacker 270
Walther 317
Wadham 310
Wanners 310
Walburn 268, 283
Walters 270, 303, 310, 312, 313
Walker 303, 264
Waters 303
Wattenbach 49
Wanamaker 303, 242, 264
Warfel 303
Wagner.....26, 103, 172, 173, 181, 182,
  237, 243, 251, 253, 263, 264, 275, 283,
  285, 297, 299, 303, 310, 312, 313, 314,
  318
Wagsel 195
Waldo 3, 252
Walte 119
Wahley 126
Waldenseans 44
Walti 47
Wagman 98
Wattenbach 49
Warenbuer 116, 193
Warenburger 110, 193
Wachsel 198
Wattenwyl 210
Walters 213, 247, 264, 220
Warley 226
Wald 242
Wallace 264
Ware 264
Walburn 266
Waldhauer 266
Wechingen 109
Wertz 104, 106
Weinmann 184
Weitzel 263, 266, 40
Weiner 38

Weiler 47
Wesel 7, 62
Wenger....106, 107, 132, 162, 185, 187,
  190, 224, 264
Weninger 43, 48
Weiser 48
Wenenschwander 48
Weher
  87, 192, 243, 245, 253, 254, 263, 267
Weaver.....87, 104, 106, 205, 213, 219,
  229, 232, 233, 243, 264, 267
Wenger....119, 186, 189, 191, 231, 238
Weitrich 161
Welch 263
Wenrich 192
Weber 219, 264
Wendel 243
Welfare 251, 263
Weybrecht 266, 268
Welchans 267
Weidman.....36, 49, 128, 220, 254, 267
Webb 342
Whitlock 161, 348
Whitman 248, 251
Widower 192
Willading 174
Wissler.....127, 170, 173, 191, 184, 238
Willer 47
Witmer..49, 135, 237, 254, 256, 266, 268
Willink 169, 174, 182
Williner 187
Widner 198
Widwer 205
Wilmer 205
Wilkins 210, 230
Willis 220
Wister 221
Wiggins 225, 233
Wislor 233, 338
Wise 251, 254, 263, 264, 266
Winger 254
Wilson
  254, 264, 310, 269, 275, 283, 285, 298
Wiser 255
Wistler 256
Wickliffe 6
Willer 47
Widmer 294
Widmyer 303
Wilki 310
Wises 303, 310, 312
Wissner 303
Wistar 315
Winkler 38
Witmer..........49, 285, 293, 299, 303
Wilkinson 298
Wilhelon 269

INDEX OF PERSONAL NAMES.

Witman 269
Wise 283, 285, 299, 311
Wingert 109
Wolfgong 100
Wolf..218, 220, 229, 243, 263, 264, 267
Worley 200
Wooklegh 209
Woork 218
Wook 220
Woolslegh 233
Wormley 256
Wood 264
Wolpert 267
Wolfes 270, 283, 313
Wolfe 275, 299, 310
Wolf 299, 303, 312
Worrall 301
Workman 303
Woolman 327
Wright 226, 256, 271, 286, 342
Wurgler 190, 197
Wuthrich 197
Wyler 187
Wyckliffe 6
Wymann 173
Yawh 128
Yeager 303, 310
Yerkes 233
Yeager 253
Yenger 187
Yeagley 95
Yost 79, 195, 303
Yordea 192, 210, 233
Yorte 205
Young.....253, 265, 266, 268, 283, 285, 297, 299, 303, 310, 312, 313, 314

Yanghley 260, 262
Yobes 293
Yoder 38
Zahler..........156, 167, 187, 188, 190
Zalfanger 159
Zahn 170, 173
Zann 184
Zaug 101, 102, 104, 106
Zacharisas 269
Zerfoss 303
Zetz 238
Zehner 51
Zellers....147, 153, 155, 158, 159, 167, 168, 240
Zehnder 74, 179, 180
Zenricher 195
Zell 44, 89
Zehnyder 87, 88
Zink 48
Ziegler....133, 239, 256, 247, 263, 264, 243, 299, 302, 310, 314
Zimmerman....130, 132, 133, 201, 207, 208, 224, 229, 239, 243, 247, 253, 264, 267, 283, 297, 302, 310, 312, 313, 320, 329, 350
Zolner 293
Zolothurn 40
Zolfinger 129
Zorn 109
Zugg 48, 94, 95, 96, 229
Zurcher 188, 191
Zurich 21
Zwingle....8, 10, 14, 84, 100, 111, 151, 252, 16, 19, 20, 35, 40
Zwally 260, 303
Zyles 61

www.ingramcontent.com/pod-product-compliance
Lightning Source LLC
Chambersburg PA
CBHW051625230426
43669CB00013B/2185